# basic biology

# basic biology

## Richard A. Goldsby
UNIVERSITY OF MARYLAND

**Harper's College Press**

A DEPARTMENT OF **Harper & Row** PUBLISHERS, NEW YORK, HAGERSTOWN, SAN FRANCISCO, LONDON

**A Leogryph Book**

|  |  |
|---|---|
| Project Editor: | Susan Hajjar |
| Magazine Editor: | Daniel Liberatore |
| Design: | Jan V. White |
| Line Art: | Vantage Art |
| Rendered Drawings: | Howard S. Friedman |
| Production Manager: | Stevan A. Baron/Eileen Max |
| Production Editor: | Virginia Kudlak |
| Composition: | Helvetica Light, The Clarinda Company |

Library of Congress Catalog Card No.: 76-28651
ISBN: 0-06-042399-4

# contents

# PART I CELLULAR LEVEL

# PART II   CONTINUITY OF LIFE

**PART III   ORGANISMIC LEVEL**

Color Portfolio   Diversity

Magazine "Keeping Healthy"

Magazine "Animal Children"

Magazine   ''States of Mind''

preface

It is hardly necessary, in our day, to recommend biology as an exciting subject. So much is being discovered almost daily that the problem is to keep up with what is going on in this exploding, vitally important field. But it is not always easy to convey this excitement in a textbook—especially one designed, as this one is, for use in a less than full-year course. It has been our hope to convey it here.

Two tactics in particular have been employed to achieve this goal without sacrificing a rigorous presentation of principle and data. One is the inclusion of several "magazine" sections. These focus on a number of biological or biology-related topics of interest to many college students —backpacking, health, houseplants, transcendental meditation, and the like—and offer entertaining articles, test-yourself quizzes, amusing sidelights, and other features designed both to provide information and to excite further curiosity. Another tactic has been to draw on the help of many different professionals in various fields of biology, to insure that the text would contain up-to-date information and interpretation in every aspect of biological science. The expertise of experienced and effective classroom teachers has also been called into service, to make certain that the content would not only be accurate and current, but would also be presented in a manner accessible to the student. Finally, special attention has been paid to reading level; the text avoids elaborate vocabulary and needlessly complex structure that might confuse the students and discourage them from real interest in the subject.

# Organization

The text is divided into seven major parts; in general, the divisions correspond to topic areas of biology. The sequence is programmed so that the student moves from the level of the cell through the level of the organism to that of the group.

## Introduction

This introduces the student to some of the most fundamental processes of life, and raises the question of life's origin, presenting the various theories that have at different times been offered to explain it. The discovery of cells is described, and its importance for biological science made clear.

## Part I: Cellular level

This consists of three chapters. Beginning with a discussion of some basic biochemistry, the section moves on to consider the structure, functions, and various specializations of cells, and the dynamic processes by which they act.

## Part II: Continuity of life

This focuses on reproduction at the cellular level. The first of the three chapters deals with cell replication; it is followed by chapters on patterns of inheritance and molecular genetics.

## Part III: Organismic level

This acquaints the student with the structural and functional diversity of life forms. The four chapters cover viruses and unicellular life, fungi and plants, the lower invertebrates, and arthropods and chordates.

## Part IV: Life functions

This centers on physiological systems and their workings. The chapters deal with plant systems, animal systems in general, human anatomy, human physiology, neurobiology, and chemical coordination—the latter two primarily but not excusively in vertebrates.

## Part V: Development of organisms

This contains three chapters. The first is on plant development; the second on animal development; and the third is more specifically on human growth and development.

## Part VI: Evolution and survival

These chapters deal with mechanisms and interpretations of the evolutionary process. They present, respectively, the basic principles and processes of evolution; human evolution; and behavior in the context of evolution.

## Part VII: Aspects of the biosphere

This section treats the subject of ecology. It opens with a chapter on patterns in the ecosystem, including some of the principles of population ecology; then it goes on to look at the biotic community and the problems of resources and pollution in today's world.

## Additional features of the text

### Summaries

Each chapter concludes with a brief summary of the most important material, which serves as a useful study aid.

### Glossary

Near the back of the book there is a glossary of over 600 scientific terms introduced in the text. This reference aid helps students check their mastery of concepts as well as vocabulary.

### Bibliography

For each of the seven parts of the book, there is a substantial bibliography, which concentrates primarily on classic sources and those readily accessible to students. An additional section offers readings to those interested in pursuing the applications of biology to various areas of human affairs, such as medicine, nutrition, and exobiology.

### Taxonomy appendix

A brief appendix explains the reasons for biological classifications, and presents the respective merits of two-, three-, four-, and five-kingdom systems. Diagrams of several systems are included.

### Color portfolios

The book contains five thematically organized color portfolios, each accompanied by a short text. The themes are cell forms and functions, diversity of life, mechanisms of adaptation, human reproduction, and the major biomes.

### Study Guide

A separate *Study Guide* is available for the student's use. It provides an overview of the basic themes, important concepts, and fundamental questions of each chapter, and exercises and self-test questions by means of which the student can check his or her progress and reinforce what has been learned. The questions are designed to test not merely retention of facts but also mastery of concepts. A unique feature is a brief glossary of "stumblers" —words that are used in the text in a somewhat specialized sense, but that are not technical enough to be included in the main glossary.

### Instructor's Manual

This provides reviews and learning objectives for each section of the book, and suggests class activities and various outside resources available to the instructor —films, articles, books, and so on. Test questions, both essay and objective, are provided. For greater convenience, the *Manual* is cross-referenced to both the text and the *Study Guide*.

## Acknowledgments

In addition to those whose names appear on the title and copyright pages, a few collaborators in the project deserve special mention. Notable among them are Dr. Joseph Gennaro, who was indefatigably helpful in supplying photographs for the cellular-level chapters, even taking some of them "to order"; Dr. Barbara Panessa, who contributed photographs, criticism, and advice for many chapters; and Karen Reixach, whose knowledge and organizing skills were invaluable in regard to several chapters. Appreciation is due also to the many scholars who served as reviewers and consultants, and to all who contributed their abilities toward the process of turning a promising manuscript into a book which, we hope, fulfills that promise.

introduction: phenomenon of life

**b**iology is defined as the study of life. But what is life? The question teases the imagination, but the answer is not easy to spell out. We can recognize many things that we cannot define. Often we feel that we understand them as well. Asked to define poetry, the English man of letters Samuel Johnson replied, "Why, Sir, it is much easier to say what it is not. We all *know* what light is; but it is not easy to *tell* what it is." So it is with life. It is easy to recognize the extremes of living and nonliving things. Anyone will say without hesitation that a sparrow is alive. He will also say that a stone is not. Yet even here there is room for ambiguity. Many primitive peoples, for instance, view the earth itself as a living thing. When we look more closely at the natural world, the ambiguity only increases. The borderline between the living and the nonliving is not sharply defined. As a result, no single definition of life can satisfy all investigators. We must consider the possibility that life cannot be given a general, abstract definition.

But if we cannot define life, still we can study it from different viewpoints. We can hope to understand some of its typical qualities. To explore the characteristics of life in general, three approaches are available. The first can be called the **functional** approach. It is based on a simple idea: life is what life does. It is easy to list all the characteristic activities of life, or the behavior of living things. In fact, a few decades ago such lists were often used as the basis for defining life. But this was a purely physiological definition. The second approach is **genetic**. It is based on the premise that if we can learn how life began we will then understand what life is. Finally there is the **structural** approach. We can try to understand life by studying the physical and chemical organization of life. This way we can see how living things carry on their vital processes. Each of these approaches has its limitations. Together, however, they form the basic tools with which the biologist is able to explore the nature of life and the nature of all living things.

# The processes of life

In recent years, the exobiologists of the National Aeronautics and Space Administration have devoted much thought to the nature of life. They must consider ways of recognizing life if we should meet it elsewhere in the universe. Such forms of life may differ greatly from any we know on earth. Thus, scientists have tried to define life in the simplest terms possible. Their conclusion is that only two characteristics distinguish living things from nonliving things. These are the ability to **reproduce,** and the ability to produce and perpetuate **genetic variations** among offspring. Further on, we will see the importance of this latter ability. The former, though, immediately suggests other related abilities. For a life form to perpetuate itself, its individual members must survive at least long enough to reproduce. Survival requires interaction of two kinds between the life form and its environment: **metabolism** and **adaptation.** Thus there are four basic abilities of life forms. They are metabolism, adaptation, reproduction, and genetic variation.

## Metabolism

All living things carry out a large number of vital activities. For example, they build new molecules needed for growth, repair worn out parts, and reproduce. All of this requires a steady flow of materials from the environment. It also demands the ability to transform such materials into usable form. Together, these transformations and the activities they make possible are called metabolism.

In higher animals, for example, the lungs absorb oxygen and use it to "burn" high energy substances such as sugars. These substances are taken in (along with other foods that can be converted into sugars) through the digestive tract. The organism returns to the environment what it cannot use—nitrogen in the air, for example, and cellulose in plant food. It also returns the products of its metabolic processes—carbon dioxide ($CO_2$) from the lungs, uric acid from the kidneys, and so forth.

## Adaptation

The second characteristic of living things is adaptation. This is the ability to make useful responses to environmental stimuli. Both living and nonliving things can change in response to changes in their environment. Water freezes with falling temperature; carbon forms a diamond under great pressure; a crystal grows as the liquid about it slowly evaporates. But the changes living things display are of a different kind. They are not simple, automatic, or passive. Often they involve an intricate pattern of activity. For example, a tiny change in the length of the day causes some birds to fly thousands of miles. Hens respond to a similar change by eating less and laying fewer eggs. Sheep respond by growing heavier coats, and squirrels begin to collect and store food. In each case the creature is receiving a steady flow of information from its environment and is reacting to it in a complex way. Such responses to external conditions all have a single purpose. They assist the organism's chances for survival.

On a simpler level, we can say that living things adapt to external changes by trying to keep their internal conditions as nearly unchanged as possible. This tendency of living beings to maintain a constant internal environment despite changes in the outside environment is called **homeostasis.**

## Reproduction

Metabolism and adaptation are necessary processes. They ensure the survival of the individual. But individual survival is not enough. Since no living creatures that we know of are immortal, they must be able to reproduce themselves. In this way, they ensure that their species will be continued. Nature has evolved many reproductive mechanisms. They range from the fission of the amoeba to the complex sexual system of man. Some reproductive mechanisms

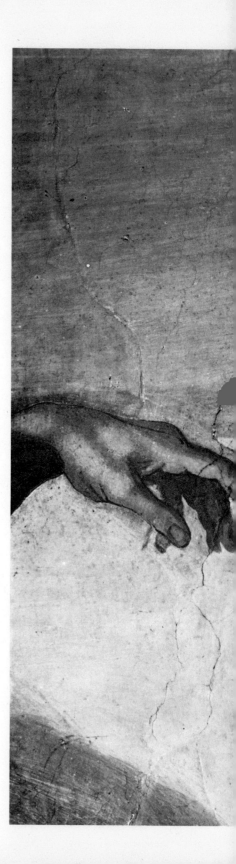

I-1
Adam receiving the spark
of life from Jehovah
(fresco on the Sistine
Chapel ceiling painted
by Michelangelo).

produce a single offspring with a high chance of survival. Others deliver thousands of young to a hostile environment and the mercy of chance. But all reproductive systems have two things in common. For one thing, they work. If they did not, the species using them would have died out long ago. Second, they all employ the same "genetic code." This is a chemical mechanism for creating offspring almost identical to their parents.

## Variation

The word "almost" in the last sentence, however, is very important. Exact reproduction is not enough to ensure the survival of the species. We can understand this if we realize that existence is always a struggle for survival. It is not just a matter of competing with another organism for food. The environment itself is a potential enemy. It is always changing in ways that may exceed the organism's ability to adapt—ways that may kill the organism. For instance, a late frost may kill thousands of seedlings before they have a chance to grow. A drought may kill thousands of plants before they have a chance to seed.

If all organisms of a species were identical, they would all have identical chances of surviving changes in their environment. Conditions fatal to one would be fatal to all. But in any population numerous small variations occur. Individuals are created with traits not identical to those of their parents. These variations add to the chances for survival of the species.

The presence of just a few individuals with unusual resistance to cold, for example, would enable a species to survive catastrophic frosts. If the climate grew steadily colder, as at the beginning of an ice age, this ability to resist cold would give its possessors a great advantage. They would be able to thrive while less fortunate individuals died. And since genetic variations are inherited, most offspring of the survivors, and eventually the whole population, would have the useful trait.

This process is known as **natural selection**. The best-adapted individuals of a species are the ones most likely to reproduce, and so they will contribute a larger share of the next generation. Eventually, those individuals with the valuable variation will supplant their rivals. In fact, the species itself will have changed. Thus individual **variation** and **selection** give the species the ability to adapt to long-term changes in the environment.

## The origin of life

We must view life now on earth as the sum total of many adaptive mechanisms. These have enabled life forms to survive and change with their changing environments. Thus we see that change is at the heart of life. Life is not static. Like gravitation and mass, it is a process. But how did this process begin? Did it have a beginning at all? The theory of **evolution** tries to trace the development of life on earth back to its beginning. The genetic approach leads to a search for life's origin. It theorizes that if we know how life began, we will understand it.

### Early theories

The creation myths that have come down to us usually involve the direct intervention of a divine being. God, or many gods, created life from nonliving matter—rocks, seas, the earth itself. The story of creation told in the Book of Genesis is a beautiful and familiar example. But theories of origin also developed along other lines.

*Spontaneous generation* Anaximander, a Greek philosopher who lived about 600 B.C., was probably the first to suggest a purely mechanical theory of creation. He spoke of animals arising from moisture, and of how men were originally born of fish. Later, Aristotle refined this idea into the theory of **spontaneous generation**. This theory claims that life arose from nonliving things. Spontaneous generation was accepted by most philosophers and religious authorities

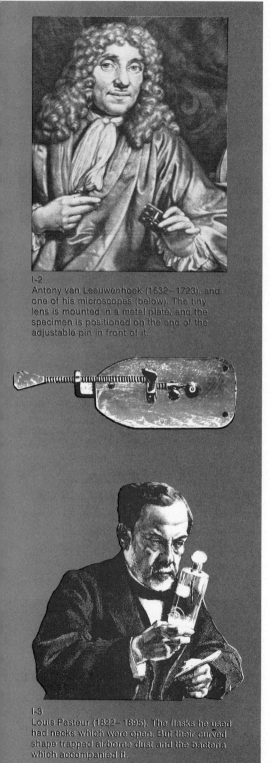

I-2
Antony van Leeuwenhoek (1632–1723), and one of his microscopes (below). The tiny lens is mounted in a metal plate, and the specimen is positioned on the end of the adjustable pin in front of it.

I-3
Louis Pasteur (1822–1895). The flasks he used had necks which were open. But their curved shape trapped airborne dust and the bacteria which accompanied it.

until the middle of the seventeenth century.

No scientific test of the theory was made until the year 1668. Then an Italian physician, Francisco Redi, began a series of simple experiments. They marked the beginning of the end for this idea which had survived for more than two thousand years. Redi placed pieces of raw meat in several jars. He covered the mouths of some with gauze, and left the others open. The decaying meat in the open jars was soon crawling with maggots. But the meat in the gauze-covered jars remained free of maggots, though it, too, decayed.

Redi had seen flies alight on the meat in the open jars. He had seen them alight also on the gauze of the closed jars, and had even watched them laying their eggs on the gauze. His conclusion seemed inescapable. Maggots, and the flies which develop from them, did not come from the meat itself. They came from eggs left on the meat by other flies. So it seemed that life came only from other life. But Redi hesitated to press his conclusions too far. There was still not enough experimental evidence to confirm his radical theory.

Then, in 1674, Anton van Leeuwenhoek made a discovery that further complicated the issue of spontaneous generation. Using lenses which he himself had ground, he assembled a microscope. Through it this Dutch amateur scientist was the first to observe microorganisms. Other investigators soon found these "animalcules" in a variety of habitats. Even a boiled and filtered broth became infested immediately. It seemed that the microbes were suddenly created from nothing—spontaneously. Leewenhoek's discovery provided the theory of spontaneous generation with a 200-year reprieve. But it was marked by almost continuous controversy.

The issue was finally settled in 1861 by the great French biologist Louis Pasteur. He placed a broth containing nutrients in swan-necked flasks. These permitted air to enter, but trapped particles of dust. He found that the broth could remain sterile indefinitely. But he also found that the same broth would soon develop microscopic life if the neck of the flask were broken. Thus Pasteur showed that the microorganisms did not arise from the broth itself. Instead, they or their spores were carried onto the broth by airborne dust.

*Panspermia* Now that spontaneous generation seemed to be dead, scientists sought other explanations. Few of them were willing to accept the theory that life began as a result of divine intervention. Some proposed that life had always existed. Therefore the origin of life could never be determined. Most scientists, however, felt that this was only evading the issue. By the late nineteenth century geologists and astronomers had learned a great deal about the earth. The fossil record went back very far, but only to a certain age. Before that, no remains of living things could be found. In fact, it appeared that the earth had once been molten. The evidence thus suggested that the earth had not always sustained life.

Still, perhaps life had always existed in other parts of the universe. Perhaps it had originally arrived on earth from elsewhere in the cosmos. This theory was known as **panspermia** or cosmozoa. It aroused considerable interest around 1900. A Swedish chemist, Svante Arrhenius, proposed that spore-like forms of life might be propelled from planet to planet by radiation pressure. He presumed that these spores were hardy enough to survive the hostile environment of space. On such an interstellar trip they would encounter vacuum, intense radiation, and extremes of temperature. Modern investigators, however, are extremely skeptical of this theory.

## The modern theory

Today scientists are interested in another theory of the origin of life. This theory is only half a century old, but its roots go back 2500 years. In a way, it revives spontaneous generation, but not as a continuing process that could produce life forms as they exist today. Instead, it suggests that a form of spontaneous generation might have occurred under the unusual conditions which existed on the earth four billion years ago.

*The Oparin–Haldane hypothesis* In 1924, a Russian biochemist, Alexander Oparin, published a new theory of the origin of life. It soon revolutionized the thinking of scientists. Oparin's original work was a brief monograph outlining his ideas. It was never translated from the Russian, and at first attracted no attention in the scientific community. Nor did the very similar ideas arrived at independently by the English biochemist, J. B. S. Haldane, which were published a few years later. But in 1936 Oparin wrote a fuller account of his new theory. This second book was translated into English two years later. Since that time, the ideas of Oparin and Haldane have had a tremendous impact on biological thought.

Oparin proposed that living things developed by a process of **chemical evolution**. Elements and simple compounds

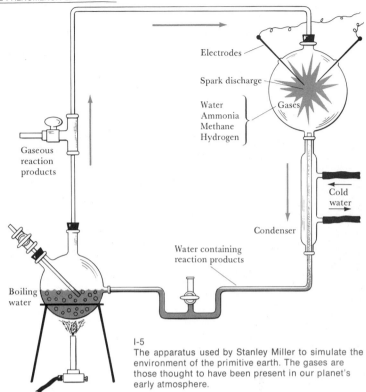

I-5
The apparatus used by Stanley Miller to simulate the environment of the primitive earth. The gases are those thought to have been present in our planet's early atmosphere.

were present in the atmosphere and seas of primitive earth. Eventually they formed larger molecules, and then even more complex combinations of molecules. Finally a chemical combination developed which could create others like itself. At this point life was born. The key point in Oparin's theory is that the entire process followed the laws of physical science. It did not require a special act of divine creation or a mysterious "vital force." In Oparin's view:

> There is no fundamental difference between a living organism and lifeless matter. . . . The complex combination of manifestations and properties characteristic of life must have arisen in the process of the evolution of matter.

*Miller's experiment* It was only in 1953 that Oparin's theory received experimental support. Stanley Miller, a graduate student working under the eminent chemist Harold Urey, performed an experiment which is now classic. In the laboratory he recreated the atmosphere of the early earth. He circu-

I-4
The comet Kohoutek. The molecules found in comets are like those that most scientists think were present on the earth before the origin of life.

lated a mixture of hydrogen, ammonia, methane, and water vapor past an electric spark discharge that simulated lightning. After a week, Miller analyzed the water that had accumulated in the condenser of the apparatus. He hoped to see if it contained organic molecules—that is, molecules of living matter. The result surpassed expectations. About two dozen different compounds had been created. They included urea, lactic acid, and four different amino acids. He also discovered a number of other substances important in the chemistry of living things. But the presence of amino acids was particularly significant. These are the building blocks which compose proteins—the basic molecules of life.

## The development of life

Haldane was probably right when he described the earth's primeval oceans as a "hot, dilute soup." But how did this soup give birth to a living organism? Perhaps we will never be able to answer this ultimate question with complete assurance. If we

I-6

Viking biology instrument. Contained in a package about a cubic foot in size, each of the three complete biological laboratories aboard the Viking spacecraft will be able to analyze Martian soil for signs of life.

I-7

Photo of Jupiter, taken by Pioneer 11. Finding life elsewhere in the universe may transform our understanding of the origin of life on earth. Scientists are trying to learn if the patches of reddish material on the planet are organic molecules.

discover life elsewhere in the universe, our understanding of the origin of life here on earth could be transformed. In the meantime, many parts of the story remain in the realm of reasonable guesswork.

*The primitive earth* Present knowledge of astronomy indicates that the earth is about 4.6 billion years old. The planets of our solar system probably condensed out of a large, diffuse cloud of dust and gas, left over from the newly formed sun. Most of the earth's original atmosphere was made up of hydrogen and helium. These gases formed the bulk of the primeval cloud. When the earth was formed, they escaped into space. In time, however, they were replaced by gases expelled from the hot interior of the earth. The early atmosphere must have contained very little free oxygen. This is a point of critical importance to the Oparin—Haldane theory. If any appreciable amount of free oxygen had been present, the organic compounds that formed the basis of life would have broken down rapidly into their inorganic components. In today's atmosphere they never could have been created at all.

The chemical processes suggested by Oparin and Haldane do not happen spontaneously. An outside source of energy is necessary. On the primitive earth many sources of energy were available. Without oxygen, the upper atmosphere did not contain ozone ($O_3$). Today a protective layer of ozone absorbs most of the sun's ultraviolet radiation. The surface of the primitive earth, however, was bathed in high energy ultraviolet light. Radioactive decay and volcanic eruptions must also have produced intense heat. Such localized heating would have speeded up the cycle of evaporation and condensation of water vapor. This, in turn, would result in torrential rains and violent electrical storms. The Miller experiment suggests that under these conditions, it must be considered almost a certainty that a wide range of organic compounds were formed in the earth's oceans.

*Chemical evolution* Once a variety of small organic molecules were present in quantity, they could combine into the larger molecules. These were the molecules necessary for life—sugars, lipids, proteins, and nucleic acids. Whatever mechanism was involved in the formation of these large molecules, the chief ally of the process must have been time—hundreds of millions of years.

The frontier between life and nonlife is vaguely defined. Some scientists think that the first thing to cross this frontier may have been a large organic molecule that somehow developed the ability to duplicate itself. The hereditary mechanism of this molecule would have passed on nothing but its own makeup. In time, such molecules might have evolved the capacity to build complex structures around themselves. This would have increased their chances of survival.

*Biological evolution* Whatever the precise sequence of events, one point seems certain. The key step on the road to life occurred when some chemical entity became able to reproduce itself. This probably happened between 3.5 and 4 billion years ago. Once these primitive life forms existed in large numbers, the struggle for survival began. That struggle has continued until today. A crucial element in this battle must have been competition for food. Early forms of life cannot have been able to manufacture their own food. They had to find it ready-made in their environment. Thus, the survival of the earliest living organisms can be accounted for only if we presume that the earth's primeval oceans contained a great variety of organic molecules.

But as the living population multiplied, the supply of key substances must have become depleted. Natural selection would then favor any organism that could make some of its own "food." We can thus imagine the evolution of new life forms. These were able to synthesize almost everything they needed for their metabolic processes from the simplest compounds in their environment. They would need, however, a source of energy to carry out the synthesis. At first the energy was derived from inorganic chemical reactions. But, in time, a far more efficient process evolved. This was **photosynthesis**, a way of tapping the sun's energy.

When the first photosynthesizing organisms began to flourish, they brought about a great change in the terrestrial environment. Photosynthesis produces free oxygen. When this oxygen was released into the atmosphere, the atmosphere was transformed. Once it had been made up of ammonia, methane, carbon dioxide, and water. The new atmosphere, however, was composed of nitrogen and oxygen, as it is today. A layer of ozone formed high up in the ionosphere, shielding the earth's surface from deadly ultraviolet radiation. Organisms no longer had to live in deep ocean waters. Now, protected from the lethal radiation, new life forms developed which could live in the shallower waters and later on land. Oxygen in the atmosphere allowed the evolution of an efficient method of respiration—the controlled chemical "burning" of organic molecules to release their energy. Previously, these molecules had been only partly broken down, by an inefficient process similar to fermentation. This new source of chemical energy was important to the development of modern cellular life forms. Of course, these changes happened slowly. The first photosynthetic organisms probably developed between 3.5 and 3 billion years ago. But the modern life forms made possible by free oxygen did not begin until about half a billion years ago.

## The cell

The drawback of the functional approach to understanding life is that it is very abstract. It focuses on what living things do, but not on how they do them. The genetic approach, too, is hypothetical. We can never be completely sure what happened; we only know what probably happened. A

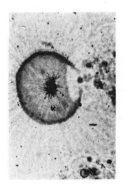

I-8
These fossil forms are thought to be the remains of primitive early cells, perhaps similar to the bacteria of today. They are about 2 billion years old.

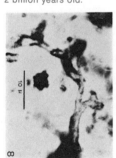

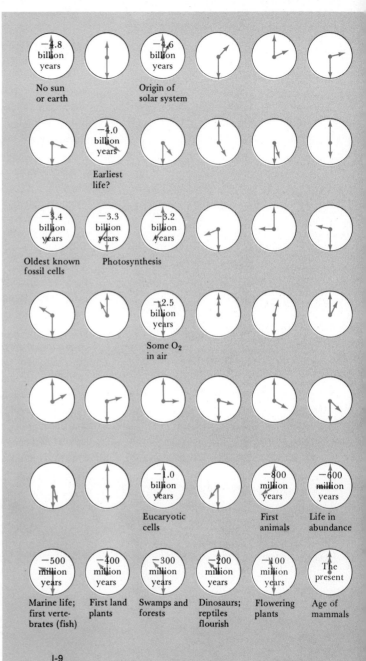

I-9
The history of the earth. In this figure the last 4.8 billion years are represented as a single 24-hour day. On this time scale, each half hour equals 100 million years. For the first few hundred million years, the earth must have been molten and sterile. The first living creatures could not, therefore, have appeared much earlier than 4 billion years ago. The most ancient known fossil remains are almost 3.5 billion years old. The first cells may have been similar in their metabolic processes to certain types of bacteria of today. Soon, these cells evolved the ability to perform some sort of photosynthesis.

third approach to the problem is the structural approach. It focuses on the patterns of organization evolved by living things to help them perform their life functions.

The basic pattern of organization is the cell. Except for viruses, which occupy an unclassified position on the border between the organic and the inorganic, all living things are made up of cells. **Cells** are the smallest entities that show all the properties of life, and perform all the processes characteristic of life. (In fact, the smallest living creatures consist of single cells.) They metabolize material from their environment, react to external stimuli, and grow. Most important, they reproduce themselves. A vital property of the cell is that it is bound by a membrane. Without this, a cell could not control its internal chemical environment. As a result, it could not perform its metabolic processes.

We might expect that as complex organisms evolved, larger cells would also develop. But the pattern of organization is strictly limited in terms of cell size. If a cell doubles in length, width, and height, its volume becomes eight times as great. Its need for food and energy increases by the same amount. To get these additional materials,

the cell must have a correspondingly greater surface area, the crucial membrane through which exchanges with the environment take place. But a cell which doubles in size has only increased its surface area four times. And that amount of surface would have to handle twice as much exchange activity as before.

Thus, instead of expanding in size, cells expanded through association. They grouped together first to form simple colonies. Much later, they formed organisms with complex physiological systems. These groupings gave cells some of the advantages that come with large size. These include greater stability and efficiency. By grouping together they could also specialize their functions. But most important of all, grouping together did not affect the limiting ratio of surface to volume for the individual cells.

## The discovery of cells

Cells were discovered as a direct result of the development of the microscope. In 1665 the English scientist Robert Hooke examined a thin slice of cork under a microscope. He described to the Royal Society the tiny, regular, rectangular structures he had observed. Hooke named these hollow structures "cells," because they resembled the small, bare chambers occupied by monks.

It took scientists more than 150 years to understand the full significance of Hooke's discovery. But by the early nineteenth century biologists had begun to realize that the cell was the universal unit of living things. This idea was stated as a formal scientific assumption by two German scientists. They were M. J. Schleiden, in 1838, for plants, and Theodor Schwann, the following year, for animals. In 1858, another German, Rudolf Virchow, added a crucial point to the emerging cell theory. He said that all cells originate from previously existing cells. Just a few years later, Pasteur's experiments provided impressive support for Virchow's theory.

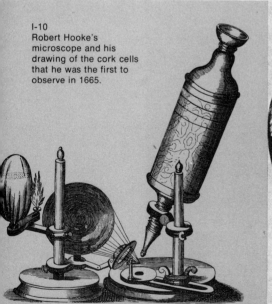

I-10
Robert Hooke's microscope and his drawing of the cork cells that he was the first to observe in 1665.

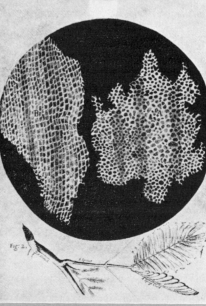

summary

We can easily classify most things as being either living or nonliving. But what do we use as the basis for such classification? Exobiologists at NASA have concluded that only two characteristics can be considered truly fundamental to life. One is the ability to reproduce. The other is the ability to produce and perpetuate genetic variations among offspring. This second characteristic is important because it enables a species to survive drastic environmental change by itself changing. Individuals with a trait that has survival value under changing conditions are more likely to live and reproduce. Those with the valuable trait will thus pass it on to their offspring. In time, the entire population will possess it. This process is called natural selection. It is the motive force behind the evolution of species.

To these basic functions we can add two corollary ones, metabolism and adaptation. Metabolism is the capacity of organisms to absorb and use materials from the environment. These materials provide energy, and serve as building blocks in the synthesis of molecules required for life processes. Adaptation is the ability of organisms to respond to environmental stimuli in ways that will help them to survive.

Another approach to understanding life is the study of its origins. Most cultures have evolved myths of divine creation. But the first attempt at a scientific explanation developed in ancient Greece. There the theory of spontaneous generation took shape as early as 600 B.C. It postulated the perpetual birth of living creatures from nonliving matter. This theory was challenged in the seventeenth century by the experiments of Francisco Redi. But it was once again revived with the discovery of microorganisms by Anton van Leeuwenhoek. Finally, in the early 1860s, Louis Pasteur convincingly refuted the notion that microbes could somehow arise through spontaneous generation.

It is of course not possible to rule out a divine, or even extra-terrestrial, origin of life. But scientists today are most interested in a theory of life first outlined in the 1920s by Alexander Oparin and J. B. S. Haldane. These biochemists proposed that life could have arisen through a process of chemical evolution. A key assumption of their theory was that the fundamental organic compounds used by living creatures formed from the gases of the earth's primitive atmosphere. Natural energy sources (such as lightning) could have triggered the synthesis. This hypothesis received experimental confirmation in 1953. It was then that Stanley Miller duplicated in his laboratory the conditions which prevailed on the primitive earth. He found that a great variety of organic molecules were indeed produced.

The details of the process of chemical evolution are still partly speculative. But it seems quite likely that all the large molecules characteristic of living things might have arisen through the natural chemical combination of simpler compounds. Eventually, a molecule or group of molecules was produced that could create others like itself. At that point, we can consider inorganic matter to have crossed the threshold of life.

The first living creatures were probably dependent on molecules already present in their environment. Then there came organisms which could make their own molecules. They eventually did this by photosynthesis, a process which uses light energy from the sun. In time, photosynthesis changed the composition of the atmosphere to its present makeup, free nitrogen and oxygen. A byproduct of this process was the creation of an ozone layer in the upper atmosphere. This shielded the earth's surface from the sun's deadly ultraviolet rays. It thus paved the way for life to emerge from the ocean depths. Free atmospheric oxygen led to the development of efficient mechanisms of respiration by which higher organisms today derive their energy.

Using a third approach to understanding life we can consider the structural organization of living things. Except for viruses, all living things are composed of cells. Cells are the smallest units that show all the properties, and carry out all the processes, of life. Cells are bound by membranes. They are thus able to regulate their internal chemical environment. To perform interchanges with the environment efficiently, a cell must have a rather high surface-to-volume ratio. Thus it cannot exceed a certain limiting size. As a result, larger organisms must consist of many individual cells.

1 **biological molecules**

n Alexander Oparin's view, shared by most modern scientists, there is no fundamental difference between living and nonliving matter. Biological evolution is, in a sense, merely an extension or continuation of chemical evolution. Though the transition from large, complex organic molecules to living entities remains shrouded in mystery, few scientists today doubt that it could have, and did, take place.

But a century and a half ago, scientists held a very different view of the nature of life. They still believed that living matter differed from nonliving matter in some mysterious and perhaps unknowable way. All biological organisms were thought to have an inexplainable "vital force" that was beyond the laws of physical science. In this view, then, the substances obtained from living tissues—organic substances—are fundamentally different from inorganic materials. For this reason it was believed that chemical analysis could not tell us anything significant about living creatures.

In 1828, however, a young chemist named Friedrich Wohler made a discovery. He found that he could convert ammonium cyanate to urea. (The former is an inorganic compound. Urea is formed by living creatures as the end product of breaking down proteins.) Wohler's equation was a simple one:

$$NH_4CNO \xrightarrow{\text{heat}} H_2N - \underset{\underset{O}{\|}}{C} - NH_2$$

It indicated that living matter might not be so unique after all. In fact, living matter seemed to be made up of ordinary compounds. Granting that these compounds were probably very complex, they nevertheless could be subjected to physical and chemical analysis.

Since the time of Wohler's discovery, we have learned an enormous amount about the chemical structure of living substances. Indeed, we now have definitive proof that Wohler's idea was correct. This proof has come from the laboratory, where many of the most intricate of biological compounds have been synthesized.

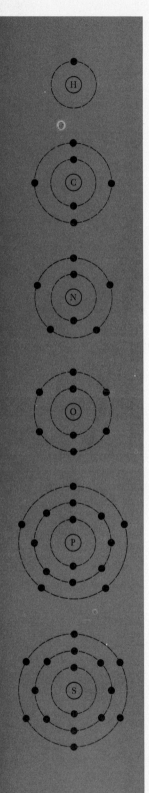

1-1
The atomic structures of hydrogen, carbon, oxygen, nitrogen, sulfur, and phosphorus. Each small circle represents an atomic nucleus, while the outer dashed circles represent electron orbitals or shells. Note that the innermost orbital can hold only two electrons, whereas the second and third can each accomodate eight.

# Basics of chemistry

We now know that a black kitten and a lump of coal are made of the same basic substances. And we know that these substances obey the same basic physical and chemical laws. The only thing that distinguishes living matter from all the rest of the material in the universe is its chemical structure.

## Elements, atoms, and molecules

The basic building blocks that make up all matter in the universe are called elements. An **element** is a substance that cannot be broken down into any other substance by ordinary chemical reactions. There are 92 naturally occurring elements, and a handful more that have been created artificially in the laboratory. Of the 92 natural elements, only 16 are found in all life forms. Some eight or nine more, such as boron and iodine, are present in limited distribution in living organisms.

The smallest unit of an element that still has all the properties of that element is called an **atom**. Atoms are indivisible by ordinary chemical reactions. Atoms of one element differ from atoms of a second element in mass, physical properties, and chemical reactivity.

Although the atom is the smallest unit of an element that still exhibits all its basic properties, it is not the smallest particle in nature. Each atom is composed of three fundamental particles: protons, neutrons, and electrons. The proton carries a positive electrical charge of +1. The electron has the opposite charge of −1. The neutron does not carry a charge. Protons and neutrons, roughly equal in mass, constitute most of the mass of an atom. The electron has a mass only 1/1830 that of the proton.

Protons and neutrons are located in the center, or nucleus, of the atom. The number of protons in the nucleus is called the **atomic number**. It is different for each element. Atomic number is designated by a subscript written in front of the chemical

symbol. A hydrogen atom, with one proton in its nucleus, is $_1H$. An oxygen atom, with 8 protons, is $_8O$. The number of neutrons in the nucleus, however, is not unique for each element. This number can vary without affecting the chemical identity of the element.

The electrons of an atom circle the nucleus, held near it by the attraction of opposing electrical charges. The electrons of each element orbit the nucleus in a certain configuration. The electron configuration can most easily be visualized as a series of concentric shells. Each shell represents a separate energy level. Energy levels increase as the distance of the shell from the nucleus increases.

Each shell can contain a certain number of electrons, and the tendency is for the inner shells to be completed before electrons fill the outer shells. It is the number of electrons in each shell that gives an element its characteristic properties. The number of electrons also determines how and with what each element will combine. The number used to indicate an element's combining power is called its **valence** number. An element's valence often is the same as the number of electrons in its outermost shell.

The most stable electron configuration is one in which the outermost shell is filled. But most atoms do not have full shells. The number of electrons in the outer shell is

H
H : N : H
or
H
|
H — N — H
Ammonia, $NH_3$
H : O : N :: O
or
HO — N = O
Nitrous acid, HONO
: N ::: N :
or
N ≡ N
Molecular nitrogen, $N_2$

1-2
Some representative compounds of nitrogen. Because it tends to share 3 electrons to complete its outer octet, nitrogen has three bonding possibilities: a triple bond, a double and single bond, or three single bonds. Each bond can be represented either as a pair of dots or a line.

determined by the amount of positive charge in its nucleus. This makes the atom electrically neutral, since the positive protons balance the negative electrons. Thus for most atoms there are two conflicting tendencies at work. The electron shells would be most stable if they were full. But they cannot be filled without destroying the electrical balance of the atom, thus producing an even greater instability. These opposing forces can be reconciled when two atoms join together in a chemical bond.

## Chemical bonding

When an atom gives up one or more valance electrons to another atom, an ionic bond is formed between them. The donor atom becomes chemically more stable through the loss of its "surplus" outer electron. The receiver atom becomes chemically more stable because it fills up its outer shell. This process also produces a **positive ion** (the donor) and a **negative ion** (the receiver). Therefore an electrostatic attraction exists between the two atoms. **Ionic bonds** are commonly found in inorganic molecules. Biologically the most important are salts, such as potassium chloride and sodium chloride (responsible for electrolyte balance). When ionic compounds dissolve in liquids, the component ions often separate.

Two atoms sharing one or more electrons form a **covalent bond**. Covalently bonded atoms draw together so closely that their outer shells overlap. As a result, each shell receives an additional electron to complete its outer shell. No net charge is created, since the atoms have neither lost nor gained electrons. Rather, they are held tightly together by their shared attraction for the same electron. Covalent bonds are generally stronger than ionic bonds.

Covalent bonds occur in all of the biologically important elements. Hydrogen, for example, is most often found covalently bonded together in pairs to form hydrogen gas ($H_2$). Atoms with higher valences, such as carbon, characteristically form covalent

Electrons needed to complete outer shell

1-3
To show the bonding potential of various atoms. Each electron in the outermost shell is represented by a dot. Carbon, the most versatile element, can share four electrons; it can thus form single, double, or triple bonds. Carbon plays a major structural role in virtually all the large molecules of life.

bonds with more than one other atom.

When two or more atoms bond together, they form a **molecule**. Many elements, especially gases, ordinarily exist in the form of two-atom molecules. The process through which molecules are formed or broken down is a **chemical reaction**. The generalized reaction is designated as:

$$A + B \rightarrow C + D$$

In this reaction, A and B are starting materials, or reactants, and C and D are the products of the reaction.

The common feature of all chemical reactions is that molecules contain **potential energy** which may be released in a chemical reaction. The natural tendency of reactions is to proceed to a state of lower energy. Just as the gravitational potential energy of a boulder atop a hill is stored by virtue of its position relative to the ground, so the potential energy of a molecule, which may be released in reaction, is stored in the form of the chemical bond. High energy is associated with instability. Thus there is a tendency to proceed downward toward a lower potential energy. When molecules with high energy react to form more stable compounds, energy is released as heat as the atoms form a new, more stable bond. Once a new bond is formed it contains a potential energy of its own, equal to the amount of energy needed to form that bond. In order to break the new bond, energy must be added.

*Acids and bases* Among the most important classes of compounds are the acids and bases. **Acids** can be defined most simply as substances that can contribute hydrogen ions (that is, hydrogen nuclei which have lent their single electrons to other atoms) to chemical reactions. A **base** is a substance that will accept hydrogen ions in a chemical reaction. The most common inorganic bases are those that contain hydroxyl ions ($OH^-$), which combine with the hydrogen ions ($H^+$) to form water ($H_2O$). This is called neutralization. In organic compounds, the $NH_2$ group (see Wohler's equation) also functions as a base.

## Solutions and solvents

A **solution** exists only when the molecules, atoms, or ions of one substance are completely scattered among the molecules, atoms, or ions of another. If the scattered particles are larger than molecules, the result may be a thorough mixture, but not a true solution. The substance present in the largest amount is called the **solvent**. The other substance (or substances) is called the **solute**. The most common solutions are those in which the solvent is a liquid, such as water or alcohol.

Ions in solution play a very important role in biochemistry. The concentration of certain ions in the bloodstream, for example, is critical to the survival of living organisms.

*The pH scale* In order to measure the acidity of a solution, the **pH scale** was devised. Water has a pH of 7, which is considered to be neutral. With increased acidity, the pH number becomes lower. If the pH rises above 7, the solution has more $OH^-$ ions than $H^+$, and is said to be basic. Thus, pH is a direct measurement of $H^+$.

## Biological matter

The most important biological elements are carbon, hydrogen, oxygen, nitrogen, sulfur, and phosphorus. These six account for over 97 percent of the atoms of the human body. (The relative abundance of calcium is due in part to its heavy concentration in human bones.)

Most elements of life, in addition to those already mentioned, are metals: calcium, sodium, magnesium, iron, manganese, cobalt, copper, and zinc. In organisms these metals occur primarily as positively charged ions. Chlorine is also abundant, as the negatively charged chloride ion, $Cl^-$. These ions play many different roles. They are important for the maintenance of fluid balance between the cell and its environment, the transport of substances into and out of cells, the conduction of nerve impulses, and the promotion of many vital chemical reactions.

Several of the so-called "trace" elements have an importance to living creatures much greater than their low concentrations might suggest. Iodine, for example, normally makes up no more than about 4 parts per million of a person's body weight. Yet iodine deficiency can produce serious illness, and a complete absence of iodine in the diet is fatal. That is why a tiny amount of this element is commonly added to ordinary table salt ("iodized salt"). Similarly, many plants seem to require a concentration of boron in their soils of about one part in ten billion. A slightly higher concentration will poison the plant, but a slightly lower concentration may cause deficiency disease.

The elemental makeup of living things does not mirror that of the world around them. For example, one of the most abundant elements in the earth's crust is silicon. Yet silicon is present only in trace amounts in living organisms. This suggests that the elements used by organisms must have certain properties which make them particularly suitable for their roles.

The most important of these properties is shared by all six of the common biological elements. They all readily form stable covalent bonds with other atoms. Hydrogen, as we have seen, shares its one electron to

| Composition of: | | Human body | | Seawater | Earth's crust |
|---|---|---|---|---|---|
| Symbol | Element | Percent of weight | Percent of number of atoms | Percent of number of atoms | Percent of number of atoms |
| O | Oxygen | 65 | 25.5 | 33 | 47 |
| H | Hydrogen | 10 | 63 | 66 | .22 |
| C | Carbon | 18 | 9.5 | — | .19 |
| N | Nitrogen | 3 | 1.4 | — | — |
| Ca | Calcium | 2 | .31 | .01 | 3.5 |
| P | Phosphorus | 1 | .22 | — | — |
| Cl | Chlorine | .17 | .03 | .33 | — |
| K | Potassium | .37 | .06 | .01 | 2.5 |
| S | Sulfur | .25 | .05 | .02 | — |
| Na | Sodium | .11 | .03 | .28 | 2.5 |
| Mg | Magnesium | .04 | .01 | .03 | 2.2 |
| Si | Silicon | trace | | trace | 28 |
| Al | Aluminum | — | — | trace | 7.9 |
| Fe | Iron | trace | | trace | 4.5 |
| Ti | Titanium | — | — | trace | .46 |

1-4
The chemical elements of life (after Friedan).

form a single bond. Oxygen and sulfur each tend to share two electrons. Nitrogen and phosphorus each tend to share three electrons.

Carbon has the greatest variety of bonding arrangements open to it. Since carbon can form so many kinds of stable bonds, it is a remarkably versatile element. Of particular importance to living things is the tendency of carbon atoms to link up with one another in long chains. Because of this, the number of carbon compounds possible is virtually limitless. The number of carbon compounds which actually exists is immense. As a result a major branch of chemistry, **organic chemistry**, is concerned entirely with the study of carbon compounds.

## The unique molecule: water

Of the chemical compounds which comprise living matter, water is by far the most abundant. Water makes up about 65 percent of the total body weight of a human being, and up to 95 percent of the weight of some jellyfish. In organisms, water serves as a lubricant and transport medium. Most of the chemical reactions of life occur in dilute water solution. Nutrients and waste products are carried into and out of cells

1-5
If we visualize the oxygen atom of a water molecule at the center of an imaginary tetrahedron, the hydrogen atoms will occupy two of the vertices. The molecule has a polar character—the hydrogen atoms assume a partial negative charge which is concentrated at the other two vertices.

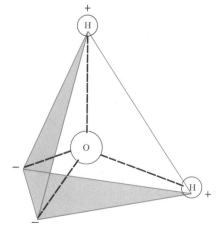

dissolved in water. Blood and lymph (the fluid that bathes the tissues) are mostly water. In fact, the composition of these fluids still reflects that of sea water, in which the first living things evolved.

Water is a covalent compound. But the electrons of the covalent bond are not equally shared—they are attracted more strongly by the oxygen atom. Thus the end of the water molecule with the oxygen atom has a partial negative charge. And the end with the hydrogen atoms has a slightly positive charge. Such a distribution of charge makes water a **polar** molecule. As such, it can dissolve a wide variety of other polar substances, and thus plays a central role in the maintenance of life. The water molecules are electrically attracted to ions or charged parts of larger molecules, and cluster around them. But nonpolar substances are forced out into a separate layer. This is because water molecules have more attraction for each other than for the nonpolar substances. Fats and oils, for example, will not dissolve in water.

The interaction between water molecules is the result of hydrogen bonding. A **hydrogen bond** is the attractive force between a hydrogen atom carrying a slight positive charge and another atom (such as oxygen) that bears a slight negative charge. Although it is not a strong force, the hydrogen bond has great importance in living organisms. For water molecules, the large number of such bonds confers many unique properties. It is because of hydrogen bonds, for example, that water is commonly a liquid rather than a gas.

The attraction between water molecules also makes it difficult to force them apart with heat. It takes a lot of heat to cause a small change in the temperature of water. You may have noticed how a lake will warm up much more slowly than the air on a summer day, and will similarly cool off more slowly at night.

This **high heat capacity** of water allows organisms to keep their internal temperatures relatively constant despite large temperature changes in their environment. This is very important, for most of the biochemical processes of living creatures can occur only within a relatively narrow temperature range. Warm-blooded creatures (such as mammals) must, in fact, maintain a nearly constant internal temperature.

Water also has a high **heat of vaporization**. When water evaporates it absorbs a large amount of heat. Therefore many organisms can keep cool, when the external temperature is high, by evaporation from their body surfaces.

Finally, when water freezes, it forms a solid (ice) that is less dense than water, and which therefore floats. Thus large bodies of water freeze from the top down. The layer of ice that forms on the surface is a good insulator. Often, it keeps the water below from freezing completely. This enables many aquatic creatures to survive cold winters that would otherwise prove fatal.

## The molecules of life

Most of the major constituents of living matter are **macromolecules**—large molecules made up of hundreds or even thousands of atoms. One of the most obvious functions of such molecules is to provide structural integrity and strength for living tissues. In general, macromolecules are **polymers**. Polymers are made up of many smaller molecular units—**monomers**—which become linked together in the process of **polymerization**. Cellulose, for example, consists of long chains of the simple sugar molecule glucose linked end to end. But the formation of a biological macromolecule often involves more complicated linkages. Many polymers, such as collagen, form cross-links between adjacent chains. The major chemical change involved in the tanning of leather is the breaking of these cross-links.

1-6
Hydrogen bonds are formed among water molecules by the mutual attraction between the positively charged hydrogen atoms and the unbonded electrons of the oxygen atoms. Such bonds account for many of water's unique properties. They also figure prominently in the structure of many larger molecules. (See The unique molecule: water)

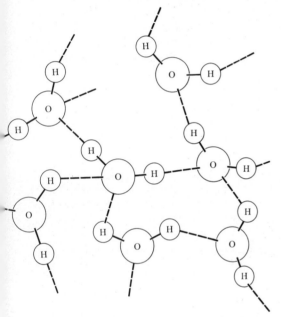

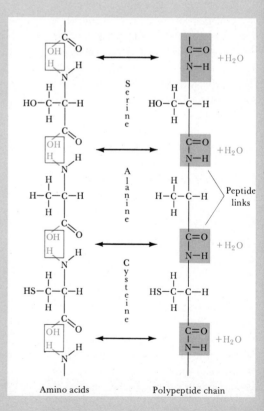

1-7
Proteins consist of amino acids linked together in long polypeptide chains. The amino acid group of one acid is joined to the carboxylic acid group of another, splitting out a water molecule and forming a peptide bond.

Most important, macromolecules can store information. The greater the variety of its monomeric units, the more information a molecule can encode. In living cells, for example, long chains of nucleic acids store and transmit genetic information. Each nucleic acid polymer has only four different kinds of monomer. That is, only a four-letter "alphabet" is available to spell out genetic messages. But each nucleic acid is immense. It carries up to several million of its four kinds of monomer arranged in different sequences, like letters in words of our written language. In effect, then, each molecule consists of millions of different words strung together.

## Proteins

Proteins are polymers of great structural variety and complexity. Because of this they are able to play many roles in living organisms. Enzymes are proteins which speed chemical reactions in living tissues. Many structural components, such as the collagen of connective tissue, are made of protein. So is hemoglobin, an iron-containing pigment that carries oxygen in the red blood cells of vertebrates. Proteins are involved in muscular contraction, in sensory perception, and in the transport of materials into and out of cells. They participate in many protective reactions, such as the secretion of toxic venoms, the clotting of blood, and the development of immunity to infectious agents.

Even considering only the role of proteins as enzymes, we can see how varied their structures must be. The number of known chemical reactions which occur in living cells is well up in the thousands. Each reaction is assisted by a different enzyme—a protein molecule with a unique structure. Moreover, an enzyme promoting a particular reaction in one organism may be quite different structurally from an enzyme promoting the same reaction in a different organism. In fact, the extent of such differences can provide a clue to the evolutionary relationship between two organisms.

The proteins of men and monkeys, for example, are much more similar than the proteins of men and horses.

This great structural variety is achieved through the use of a 20-letter "alphabet." Proteins are linear polymers of **amino acids,** and there are twenty different amino acids found in the structure of most common proteins.

The amino acids of a protein chain are linked together end to end in a **polypeptide chain**. These chains may contain only a few dozen amino acids, or as many as several thousands. Some proteins consist of a single polypeptide chain. Others contain two or more such chains wrapped about one another.

We might, then, imagine a protein as a long stretched-out molecule. Studies of proteins, however, indicate that this is not the shape that all proteins assume in cells. Instead, the chain is often wound around on itself in specific ways. Proteins are classi-

1-8
A three-dimensional model of the enzyme ribonuclease based largely on X-ray diffraction data.

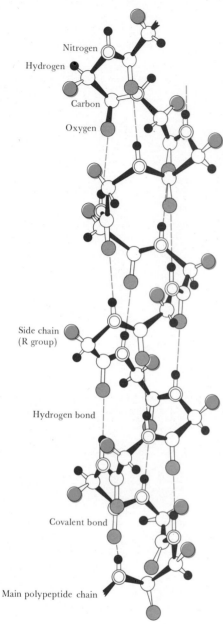

Nitrogen

Hydrogen

Carbon

Oxygen

Side chain
(R group)

Hydrogen bond

Covalent bond

Main polypeptide chain

1-9
The α helix, a common secondary structure in many proteins. The corkscrew shape is stabilized by hydrogen bonds connecting successive turns of the helix. Because of the spatial configuration of the amino acids, only the right-handed form of the helix can exist. Even in complexly folded proteins, relatively straight regions of the polypeptide chain often exhibit this structure.

fied in two groups based on the amount of folding of their polypeptide chains. The molecules of **fibrous proteins** remain extended and do not fold back on themselves. The long chains of fibrous proteins can be joined together in several ways to form sheets or strands of great strength. For this reason, such proteins play an important role as structural elements for many organisms. The proteins whose polypeptide chains are elaborately wound back upon themselves to form compact shapes are called **globular proteins**. These are generally somewhat soluble in water and water solutions. Most enzymes and blood proteins belong to this class, and so do certain hormones.

*The architecture of proteins* The simplest and most fundamental structure—the sequence of amino acids that make up the polypeptide chain—is known as the **primary structure**. Primary structure is purely one-dimensional. It does not specify how the protein chain is bent or folded in space. Nor does it indicate how the chain may be joined to itself or to other chains. These

three-dimensional aspects of protein structure are known as the **secondary**, **tertiary**, and **quaternary structures**.

The most common and most important secondary structure is the **alpha (α) helix**. In this arrangement, the protein chain assumes a form rather like that of a corkscrew or a spiral staircase. The structure is stabilized by hydrogen bonds between successive turns of the helix. This pattern is found in many fibrous proteins. Others exhibit a different secondary structure. Collagen, for example, is formed by three intertwined helical strands. In silk, the polypeptide chains line up in parallel rows that are cross-linked to form a sheet-like structure.

We have mentioned that the typical globular protein is folded back upon itself in a complex three-dimensional structure. These teritiary structures are held together by forces much more fragile than the ordinary chemical bonds that form the backbone of the chain itself. As a result, globular proteins are delicate molecules. At high temperatures, or in the presence of strong acids or bases, the weak forces that stabi-

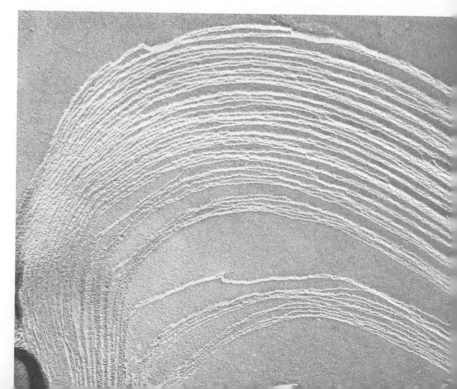

lize their unique three-dimensional structures are disrupted. This process is called **denaturation**. It causes great changes in the physical properties of the protein, and loss of its biological activity. The coagulation of egg white during cooking, for example, is caused by the denaturation of its chief protein.

Many important biological substances are associations of several polypeptide chains. The blood protein hemoglobin, for example, consists of four chains, each containing more than 140 amino acids. It also includes an atom of iron in its center. In order for oxygen transport to take place, the four chains must be twined together in a very precise way. Such associations constitute the quaternary structure of proteins.

### Nucleic acids

The sequence of amino acids in a protein chain determines its three-dimensional structure, and thus the biological role it can play. But what determines the amino acid sequence in the first place? To answer this question we shall need to know something about the structure of another class of macromolecules—the nucleic acids. There are two general types of nucleic acid: **deoxyribonucleic acid**, or DNA, and **ribonucleic acid**, or RNA. Both are informational molecules. The blueprints that specify the amino acid sequence of every biological protein are coded into their structures.

All the hereditary information that an organism possesses is preserved in the structure of its DNA. Only a small part of this information, however, will be expressed by any one cell. For a cell to use any part of its hereditary blueprint, a portion of the genetic information must be transferred from DNA to RNA. The RNA then moves out into the cell to guide the synthesis of specific proteins. (The question of how a particular cell "knows" what part of its total blueprint to express is one of the most intriguing in modern science.)

Just as proteins are linear polymers of amino acids, nucleic acids are linear polymers of **nucleotides**. A nucleotide consists of a **purine** or **pyrimidine** base, a phosphate group, and a sugar—**ribose** in RNA

**1-10**
Freeze-etch electron micrograph of myelin, a membranous coating on nerve fibers. Proteins are most numerous in those membranes involved in dynamic cellular activities. Myelin is low in protein and high in lipid, a chemical composition suited to this membrane's function as an insulator. Freeze-etching reveals the absence of globular proteins (note the smooth fracture face).

**1-11**
The nucleotides of DNA and RNA differ in only two of their constituents. Each nucleotide consists of a phosphate group, a sugar, and a base. The sugar in RNA is ribose; in DNA it is the very similar deoxyribose. The bases in DNA are adenine and guanine (purines), and cytosine and thymine (pyrimidines). In RNA uracil substitutes for the closely related thymine.

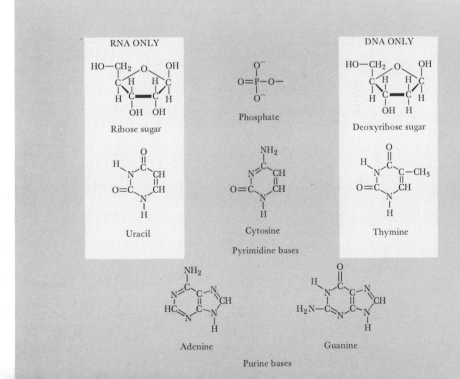

RNA ONLY

Ribose sugar

Phosphate

DNA ONLY

Deoxyribose sugar

Uracil

Cytosine

Thymine

Pyrimidine bases

Adenine

Guanine

Purine bases

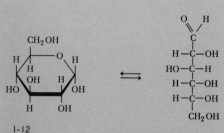

**1-12**
In solution, both the ring and the chain forms of simple sugars such as glucose exist in equilibrium. At any one time, a majority of the molecules are in the ring configuration.

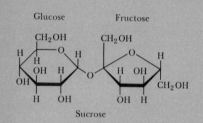

**1-13**
Two monosaccharides can combine to produce a double sugar or disaccharide, such as sucrose (ordinary table sugar), and a molecule of water. Certain digestive enzymes reverse this reaction, splitting disaccharides into monosaccharides.

and **2-deoxyribose** in DNA. However, as noted, proteins generally consist of twenty different amino aicds. But each molecule of nucleic acid consists of only four kinds of nucleotide. In the nucleotides of RNA there are four different bases: **adenine** (A), **guanine** (G), **cytosine** (C), and **uracil** (U). DNA is very similar. But instead of uracil, it contains a close structural relative, **thymine** (T). A and G are purines; C,U, and T are pyrimidines. The only known function of nucleic acids is the storage and transmission of information. But as we shall see in a later chapter, this function is vital to the continuity of life.

*ATP* The base adenine also occurs in the compound **adenosine triphosphate** (ATP). ATP is an energy-carrying molecule which participates in virtually all chemical transactions within the living cell. As we shall see in chapter 3, cells must oxidize the sugar glucose to obtain metabolic energy. The chemical energy released during this reaction is trapped in the bonds of ATP molecules and stored for use by the cell. Whenever there is an energy need, the cell can draw on its ATP supply.

## Carbohydrates

The proteins and nucleic acids of each species—and even, to some extent, each individual—are unique. The other two large classes of biomolecules, carbohydrates and lipids, seem to be quite similar in all known organisms. This is because their function is not to store information or regulate vital processes, but to supply energy and play a structural role. Carbohydrates and lipids are used chiefly as fuels.

Carbohydrates consist of carbon, hydrogen, and oxygen. The hydrogen and oxygen are always present in the 2:1 ratio found in water. Structurally, the grouping $H-C-OH$ recurs frequently in these compounds, accounting for this ratio. The smallest carbohydrate molecules are the simple sugars, or **monosaccharides**. Two simple sugars can be linked together to form a double sugar, or **disaccharide**. When many sugar molecules are joined together in a long polymer chain, the result is a **polysaccharide**.

*Simple sugars* Most simple sugar molecules contain either five or six carbon atoms. These sugars can exist in two dif-

**1-14**
Both cellulose (above) and starch (below) are polysaccharides—long chains of the simple sugar glucose. They differ in the arrangement of the bonds linking the individual sugars. The bonds in cellulose are extremely strong and resistant to chemical attack, making cellulose useful structurally to plants.

material for plants.

ferent forms—a ring structure and a straight chain structure. One of the simple sugars, glucose, plays a central role in the chemistry of the living cell. It is the main fuel that the cell "burns" to supply energy for its various vital functions. Other sugars are converted into it, as are some fats and proteins. Conversely, these substances can be synthesized from glucose.

*Double sugars*   Many common sugars, such as sucrose (table sugar) and lactose (milk sugar) are double sugars, or disaccharides. Sucrose is a combination of two different monosaccharides, glucose and fructose (fruit sugar). But some disaccharides are double sugars made from the same simple sugar. Maltose, for instance, a double sugar obtained from the digestion of starch, consists of two linked glucose molecules.

*Polysaccharides*   Long polymer chains of simple sugars are called polysaccharides. A single sugar can form such a chain in various ways, giving different polysaccharides. Those of greatest biological importance are starch, glycogen, and cellulose. All of these are polymers of glucose, but they differ in structure. Cellulose is a polysaccharide that contributes to the rigidity of the plant cell wall. It can perform this function because it is insoluble and not easily broken down to its component glucose. A number of animals, such as cows and rabbits, and some species of insects such as termites, harbor within their digestive tracts certain microorganisms that break down cellulose. This allows the hosts to digest plant foods with much greater efficiency.

## Lipids

There are several different kinds of lipid molecules, but all of them are relatively small, for lipids do not polymerize to form macromolecules. The various classes of lipids have only one other thing in common: they are all insoluble in water. This is be-

Glycerol   Fatty acids (stearic acid)        Triglyceride (fat)

**1-15**
A fat is formed by the combination of a molecule of an alcohol—generally glycerol—with three molecules of fatty acid. The reverse process—hydrolysis of a fat—takes place when fats are digested. Because they consist mostly of carbon and hydrogen, with little oxygen, fats can undergo a greater degree of oxidation than carbohydrates when metabolized in the body. They are thus a richer source of energy, ounce for ounce, than sugars or starches.

cause their structures contain a large proportion of nonpolar hydrocarbon—rings or chains of carbon atoms with only hydrogen attached. Lipids have no other common structural features. The most important types of lipids are the **fats**, the **phospholipids**, and the **steroids**.

*Fats*   The most abundant lipids are the neutral fats, or **triglycerides**. These are the chief constituents of adipose tissue (animal fat). This tissue serves several functions. Two of these are thermal insulation to keep the body warm and protective padding for vital organs. Fats can also be burned by organisms for energy. In fact, they are a richer source of energy, ounce for ounce, than carbohydrates. However, extracting that energy is more difficult. For this reason, most organisms rely primarily on sugar and starch for sources of energy.

Organisms form many different fatty acids, which, in turn, are components of fats. When a fatty acid has only single bonds in its hydrocarbon chain, we say that

Butyric acid
(saturated)

$CH_3(CH_2)_{24}COOH$

Cerotic acid
(saturated)

Oleic acid
(singly unsaturated)

Linoleic acid
(polyunsaturated)

**1-16**
A variety of fatty acids, with carbon chains of different lengths, are created by living organisms. Cerotic acid, for example, is found in beeswax, while butyric acid is a constituent of butter. Fatty acids containing only single bonds are termed saturated; those containing one or more double bonds are unsaturated.

it is **saturated**. That is, it has as many hydrogen atoms as the carbon chain can accomodate. One that contains a double bond is called an **unsaturated** fatty acid. That is, the carbon chain could accept more hydrogens if the double bond were replaced by a single bond. Fatty acids with more than one double bond are called **polyunsaturated**.

The physical properties of a fat are related to the degree of unsaturation of its fatty acid components. In general, the greater the degree of unsaturation, the more likely the substance is to be liquid at room temperature. Plant fats tend to be highly unsaturated. Hence, plant oils, such as corn oil, are usually liquid. The more saturated animal fats, such as butter, are solid.

*Phospholipids*  Another class of lipids, the phospholipids, are closely related to fats. In these compounds, the basic triglyceride structure is slightly modified. One of the fatty acid chains is replaced by a phosphate-containing group. This group is charged, and makes the part of the molecule to which it is attached highly polar. Thus phospholipids have a polar head, and a nonpolar tail (the two fatty acid chains). This property makes phospholipids especially important in biological membranes.

*Steroids*  Steroids are molecules made up of carbon atoms interlocked in a four-ring structure that resembles chicken wire. Various other groups of atoms may be attached to the basic ring framework at different points. Even very small differences in the makeup or location of these attached groups can make a vast difference in the biological activity of the steroid. For example, two steroids produced by the human body, progesterone and testosterone, are almost identical in structure. Yet one is a female sex hormone and the other a male sex hormone. Steroids have many important functions. Not only some hormones, but also some vitamins are steroids. In addition, steroids are known to play a large role in membrane structures.

1-17
The structure of a typical phospholipid. Because they have highly polar heads and nonpolar (hydrophobic) tails, phospholipids are well adapted to their role in cell membranes.

1-18
Very small chemical variations often distinguish steroids with widely different biological effects, such as progesterone, a female sex hormone, and testosterone, a male sex hormone. The steroid cholesterol is thought to play a role, not yet fully understood, in the development of coronary artery disease and heart attacks.

summary

An element is a substance that cannot be broken down into any other substance by ordinary chemical reactions. An atom is the smallest unit of an element which retains all the properties of that element. Atoms are composed of three fundamental particles. Protons and neutrons are located in the atom's nucleus. Electrons orbit the nucleus and can be visualized as a series of concentric shells. The number of protons in the nucleus is called the atomic number. The valence number of an atom indicates its capacity to combine with other atoms.

An ionic bond is formed when an atom gives up one or more valence electrons to another atom. When two atoms share one or more electrons a covalent bond exists. Ionic bonds are commonly found in inorganic molecules. Covalent bonds occur in all of the biologically important elements. Two or more atoms bonded together form a molecule. The formation or breakdown of molecules occurs through the process of chemical reaction, releasing energy.

The most important biological elements are carbon, hydrogen, oxygen, nitrogen, sulfur, and phosphorus. These readily form covalent bonds. Carbon can form an almost limitless number of compounds important to living things. Living material also contains the metals calcium, sodium, magnesium, iron, manganese, cobalt, copper, and zinc. These metals occur primarily as positively charged ions.

Water is the most abundant compound in living matter. It is a highly polar molecule and can dissolve a wide variety of other polar substances. Water molecules also form hydrogen bonds. Thus water can exist primarily as a liquid. It has a high heat capacity, and helps to maintain stable temperatures within an organism.

Most compounds in living matter are macromolecules, which provide strength to living tissue. These molecules are polymers, consisting of chains of smaller units called monomers. Many polymers form crosslinks between adjacent chains. A variety of monomers linked in different sequences enables macromolecules to store information.

Proteins are the most complex and varied of polymers. They can function as enzymes, which catalyze almost all chemical reactions occurring in life processes. They can also function as structural components, carriers in cellular transport, immunological agents, and in many other capacities. The structural variety of proteins is achieved through a 20-letter "alphabet" of amino acids, linked together in polypeptide chains. Proteins are classified according to the amount of folding of their polypeptide chains. The molecules of fibrous proteins remain extended and do not fold back upon themselves. Globular proteins are elaborately wound polypeptide chains.

Proteins display four levels of structural complexity. The primary structure is the sequence of amino acids in the chain. It is purely one-dimensional. Increasingly complex three-dimensional patterns are classified as the secondary, tertiary, and quaternary structure of proteins. These structures, especially globular proteins, are easily denatured by breaking of the bonds that maintain the three-dimensional pattern. This causes changes in biological activity.

DNA and RNA are nucleic acids, carrying information which specifies amino acid sequences. DNA stores genetic information and is expressed by transfer to RNA which guides protein synthesis. Nucleic acids are linear polymers of nucleotides—a purine or pyrimidine base, a sugar, and a phosphate group. The nucleotides make up a four-letter alphabet: for RNA, adenine, guanine, cytosine, and uracil; for DNA, uracil is replaced by thymine.

Carbohydrates consist of carbon atoms bonded to hydrogen and oxygen atoms which are in the 2:1 ratio found in water. They may be simple sugars (monosaccharides), double sugars (disaccharides), or many sugar molecules joined in a long polymer chain (polysaccharides).

Lipids include fats, phospholipids, and steroids. They are insoluble in water and do not polymerize to form macromolecules. Triglycerides are the most abundant lipids. They are the chief component of adipose tissue, which stores energy and provides insulation. Fatty acids are saturated when the carbon atoms contain only single bonds. They are unsaturated when the carbon atoms contain double bonds. Polyunsaturated fats contain more than one double bond. Phospholipids are modified triglycerides, containing a highly polar phosphate group. Steroids are lipids composed of four interlocked rings of carbon atoms. Their individual differences result from the different atomic groups attached to the rings. Steroids function as hormones and vitamins, and play a role in membrane structure.

# 2 cell forms and functions

the arrangement of the chemical components of a cell is one of nature's wonders. The cell is the lowest level of organization which can be called "living." But it would be difficult, if not impossible, to duplicate this organization in a laboratory. We might throw together a random mixture of proteins, nucleic acids, carbohydrates, lipids, and other organic compounds. But we still would not have a cell. It is the precise structure of a cell that enables it to engage in thousands of physical and chemical interactions. Through these the cell can grow, repair itself, reproduce, and thus sustain its individual life.

Cells could not survive if these interactions occurred randomly. For example, if a business is going to provide goods and make a profit, it must coordinate a variety of related functions. It must control the type of raw materials purchased. It must transform these materials into usable products. And it must sell and deliver the finished products to the consumer. Furthermore, different departments must be in close contact with each other. Otherwise there would be a wasteful overlapping of activities, and mistakes in production. Without control and coordination, the company would deteriorate and soon go bankrupt.

Cells too would degenerate and die if their various activities were not carefully balanced. They must get the right kind and quantity of inorganic and organic compounds, to build new cells and repair old ones. They must get energy, either from the sun or from organic molecules, and distribute it so that it furnishes power for various cell processes. And they must dispose of materials they cannot use, either by storing them or releasing them into the environment.

In some organisms all these processes happen within a single cell. In multicellular plants and animals, they are divided among various kinds of specialized cells. But whether cells function independently, as in unicellular (single-celled) organisms, or whether they work in groups, as in multicel-

| | | |
|---|---|---|
| 39.37 inches | = | 1 meter (m) |
| 1 centimeter (cm) | = | 1/100 meter ($10^{-2}$m) |
| 1 millimeter (mm) | = | 1/1000 meter ($10^{-3}$m) |
| *1 micron ($\mu$) | = | 1/1000 millimeter ($10^{-3}$mm) |
| | = | 1/1,000,000 meter ($10^{-6}$m) |
| *1 nanometer (nm) | = | 1/1000 micron |
| | = | 1/1,000,000,000 meter ($10^{-9}$m) |
| 1 Ångstrom (Å) | = | 1/10 nanometer |
| | = | 1/10,000,000,000 meter ($10^{-10}$m) |

*Micrometer ($\mu$m) and millimicron (m$\mu$) are equivalent terms for micron and nanometer, respectively, but are not generally preferred.

2-1
Equivalent
measurements.

2-2
Nucleated red blood cell
(irregularly shaped
structure in center of
each photo) in capillary
of frog, photographed by
four different techniques.
Actual size of the cell is
approximately 10$\mu$.

lular organisms, their activities are interrelated. Thus they require a consistently maintained level of cellular organization.

## Microscopy

Two basic instruments are used by biologists and other life scientists to study cells. They are the light microscope and the electron microscope. The **compound light microscope** consists of two or more lenses and uses light to illuminate the specimen. A concave mirror at the base of the instrument reflects light through the **condensing lens**. The condensing lens focuses the image on the **objective lens**, which is closest to the object. This, in turn, magnifies the image so that it can be observed through the **eyepiece**.

Light microscopy can be modified in several ways. One of these is the **phase contrast microscope**, used to study the dynamic processes of living cells. The human eye responds only to intensity, or color. It cannot perceive phase changes. That is, it cannot perceive that the velocity of light waves advances or is slowed down as the waves travel through a substance.

The phase contrast microscope translates phase changes into intensity changes perceptible by the eye.

Another modification of the standard light microscope is the **interference microscope**. It has enabled biologists to study cell division and life cycles of certain organisms. It operates on much the same principles as the phase contrast technique. But the interference microscope presents a clear view of the image, which in phase contrast may be surrounded by a halo. It also reveals gradual changes in the way different areas of a specimen bend the light waves passing through them. Phase contrast microscopy shows only those areas which present abrupt changes.

A third modification is the **darkfield microscope**. It produces dramatic differences in light intensity by illuminating a specimen obliquely (from the side). The structures of the specimen thus stand out against their background, which remains dark.

These and other modifications have rendered the light microscope one of the most important of biological tools. But its chief limitation is that many important cell

ORDINARY LIGHT MICROGRAPH

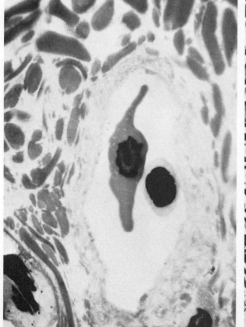

PHASE CONTRAST

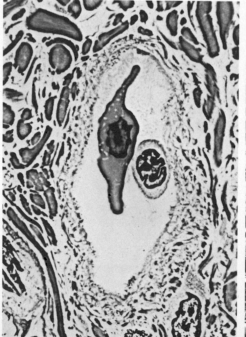

INTERFERENCE CONTRAST.

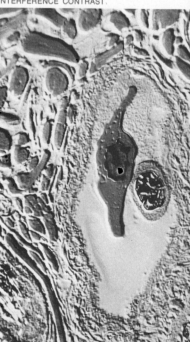

structures are below its limit of resolution. The **limit of resolution** is the smallest distance between two points at which they can be distinguished as separate and distinct. A microscope with a limit of resolution of 200 nm, then, would be able to distinguish two objects as distinct if they were 200 or more nanometers apart. This, in fact, is the ultimate limit of resolution of the modern light microscope. The light microscope can magnify objects as much as 2000 times. But it can never achieve the resolution needed to study the cell's inner structure. It depends upon light whose shortest wavelengths (400 nm) are too long to be scattered by macromolecules.

This limitation has been overcome by the **electron microscope**. It uses electrons for illumination, with wavelengths of as little as .005 nm. Basically, it consists of an electron gun which sends streams of electrons through a vacuum chamber. A magnetic lens focuses the electrons so that they strike the specimen properly and pass through it. The electrons then strike a photographic plate, producing an image which later can be enlarged. In passing through a specimen, electrons are scattered. Regions of the specimen with atoms of a high atomic number appear darker than regions with atoms of a lower atomic number. This is because the heavier atoms scatter more electrons away from the plate.

The most important feature of the electron microscope is that it provides useful magnification of 300,000 times (before photographic enlargement). Since its practical limit of resolution is 1nm, it has contributed to the detailed study of proteins and other macromolecules. But a major disadvantage of the electron microscope is that only superthin specimens can be used. Electrons cannot penetrate thicker substances.

The **scanning electron microscope (SEM)** has overcome this limitation. It focuses electrons into a narrow stream which travels over, or scans, the surface area of a specimen. The result is a three-dimensional image which is projected onto a TV screen. Areas of the specimen which reflect many electrons appear brighter than those areas which reflect few. The limit of resolution of the SEM is about 100 times less than the electron microscope. But its great advantage is the ability to scan specimens of any thickness.

## Cellular diversity

When we speak of "the precise structure characteristic of cells," we simply mean that the chemical components of each cell are arranged in a definite pattern. We are not suggesting that all cells show the same overall structure. In fact, no single cell necessarily exhibits every feature of cells in general.

### Size and spatial form

Cells exist in a broad range of sizes. Some can be viewed easily with the naked eye. Birds' eggs, for example, are really single cells that have been fattened by huge stores of nutrients. They may be several centimeters in diameter. The nerve cells of some large mammals are several meters in length. But these large sizes are not typical.

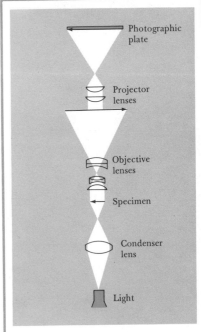

2-3
Schematic diagram of light microscope with photographic attachment.

2-4
Schematic diagram of electron microscope, showing electron beam.

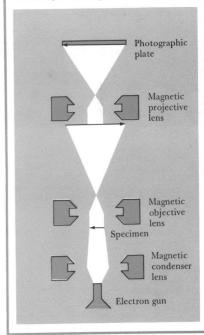

FIELD

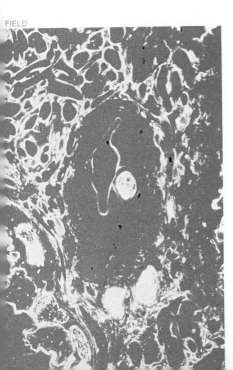

Cells which can be seen are usually visible as small specks. And most cells are too small to be viewed without a microscope.

On the level of microscopic cells alone, we find a variety of sizes. The cells lining the human mouth, for instance, are about $60\mu$ in diameter. But other body cells are only about one-tenth that size. The smallest animal cells are about $4\mu$ in diameter, but many bacterial cells are only about one-fourth that size. Probably the smallest cells are those of the microorganisms called **mycoplasmas**. These measure about $0.1\mu$ in diameter.

All cells are three-dimensional, but may vary in shape. They may be fat or flat. They may be disk-shaped, like many red blood cells. They may be ovoid, elongated, or many-sided. Or they may be thread-like, as with nerve and muscle cells. Cells may be regular or irregular in shape, or the shape-less masses found among white blood cells. Their shape may be constant, or periodically changing as in the case of amoebas.

Several factors influence the size and shape of a cell. These include the pressure of neighboring cells and the particular function of the cell. For example, the nerve cell transmits stimuli across long distances. It is therefore long and thin. On the other hand, red blood cells are small and compact. This enables them to carry oxygen through the smallest capillaries. Even the same type of cell may show more than one form. Granulocytes and lymphocytes are both white blood cells. But the former are large, and the latter are usually small and rounded.

### Structural features

The cells of every living thing are bounded by a thin, flexible membrane. This **plasma membrane** gives the cell shape and strength, and provides some protection. Most important, it regulates the passage of substances between the intracellular and extracellular environment—that is, between the environment within the cell and that which surrounds the cell. The plasma

2-5
Upper photo shows high resolution scanning electron microscope of Dr. Alec N. Broers. Below it is a scanning electron micrograph of red blood cells from a salamander. The thread-like material is fibrin.

2-6
Diagram of a bacterium. Procaryotes have protein complexes which are sites for many of the processes which are carried out in the organelles. These complexes sometimes involve infoldings of the plasma membrane. In the bacteria, the infoldings have different shapes and are called mesosomes.

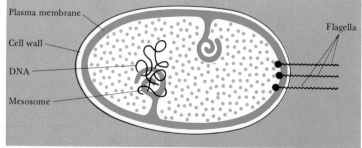

membrane is probably the only structural feature that belongs to all cells.

Cells may be divided into two general categories according to structural complexity. Mycoplasmas and bacterial cells have a relatively simple substructure. They are called **procaryotic** cells. The cells of all other organisms, both unicellular and multicellular, have a more complex substructure. These are called **eucaryotic** cells. Both types can carry out similar life-sustaining functions. In eucaryotic cells, these functions occur in membrane-bound compartments called **organelles**. Each organelle engages in specific activities. In a way, they are like the organs, such as the heart and lungs, of some multicellular life forms. In procaryotic cells, on the other hand, vital processes are more diffusely organized.

There is another important difference between the two types of cell. Eucaryotic cells have a membrane-bound **nucleus**. In fact, their name is based on this feature— eu: true + karyon: nucleus. A **nucleoid**, or **nuclear region**, is present in procaryotic cells. But there is no membrane to separate it from the rest of the cell contents.

Structural differentiation gives the eucaryotic cell greater flexibility in dealing with its environment. This is one reason that all higher organisms are made up of eucaryotic cells. But there are also many advantages to being procaryotic. For example, the small size of a bacterium gives it a high surface-to-volume ratio. This means that every part of the cell is close enough to the external environment to have easy access to needed materials. Furthermore, these materials can be exchanged between the inner cell area and the environment much more rapidly than in the larger, eucaryotic cell. The small volume of the bacterium also enables it to double in size sooner than the eucaryotic cell. And once it has done this, it can then divide. Before the larger cell can achieve even one division, it may be surrounded by the offspring of its initial bacterial competitor. These offspring can then bar access of the larger cell to nutrients.

# Eucaryotic cells

We may think of the eucaryotic cell as consisting of two major areas. One is the cytoplasm, in which the organelles are found. The other area is the nucleus. It is separated from the cytoplasm by its own pair of membranes. The **cytoplasm** is a complex, semifluid substance. Its primary components are proteins, lipids, sugars, and minerals. The cytoplasm helps to coordinate organelle functions. It is the medium through which materials are passed from one organelle to another, or to the extracellular environment. Parts of the chemical process undertaken by some of the organelles actually occur within the cytoplasm itself.

We should note that not all eucaryotic cells have all possible organelles. Nor does any single cell necessarily show every

2-7
Composite sketch of animal cell.

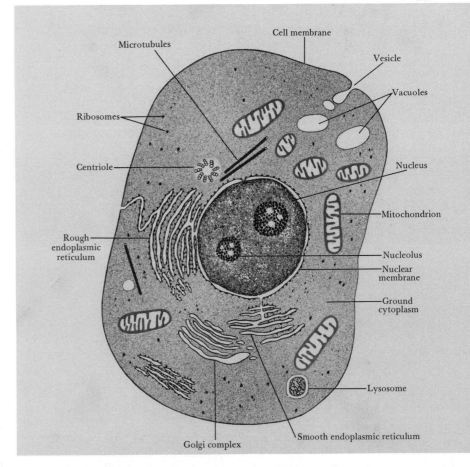

**2-8**
Electron micrograph of nucleus from chick embryo fibroblast prepared by freeze-fracture technique. The living tissue was frozen in liquid nitrogen and put into a vacuum. It was then fractured along the membrane face and its surfaces were shadowed with platinum and carbon. Bleach was used in order to dissolve the original membrane face away and a platinum–carbon replica (an exact casting of the nuclear surface) was then examined using electron microscopy.

characteristic of eucaryotic cells in general. There may be differences between eucaryotic cells of multicellular and unicellular organisms. There can be variations in substructure among eucaryotic cells of the same organism. And there are important contrasts between eucaryotic plant and animal cells. But each organelle retains basically the same structure and performs the same function no matter where it occurs.

## The nucleus

The major structure in all eucaryotic cells is the nucleus. It contains the genetic material DNA, or deoxyribonucleic acid. DNA determines the cell's potential action in all its vital processes. These include reproduction and differentiation. In reproduction, a cell divides and becomes two new cells. In differentiation, a cell changes from a generalized form to a specialized form, as it matures. In multicellular plants and animals, differentiation produces the highly specialized cells such as muscle or leaf cells. These enable organisms to make complex adaptations to changes in their environments. DNA also determines an organism's potential range of behavior. Other factors, such as the environment, determine what actions the organism will take within that range.

The nucleus is bounded by a membrane called the **nuclear envelope**. It also contains a granular **nucleoplasm**. Within the nucleoplasm are two main types of structure. These are the **chromosomes** and the **nucleolus**. The appearance of these structures varies during the cell's life cycle. Their number depends on the type of cell.

*Chromosomes*  DNA is carried by the chromosomes. During cell division, they appear as dense, thread-like structures when viewed under the light microscope. Their name means "colored bodies." It was given to them by early investigators, who found that chromosomes bind to certain dyes.

*The nucleolus*  Almost all cells possess one or more nucleoli, small spherical structures in the nucleus. The nucleolus is not enclosed by a membrane. It seems to be composed primarily of protein and nucleic acids. The nucleolus is the site for the manufacture of ribonucleic acid (RNA), a substance needed for protein synthesis.

## Ribosomes and the ER network

**Ribosomes** are tiny spherical structures within the cell. They are only about 20 nm in diameter. But they can synthesize all the enzymes and various other proteins used in digesting foods, building and repairing cells, and carrying out those processes

Mitochondrion    Nuclear Membrane    Nuclear Pores

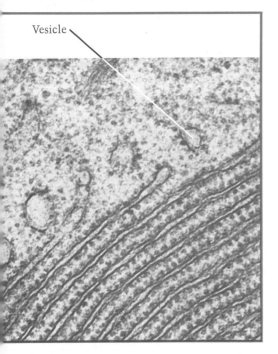

Vesicle

synthesize proteins, have a large amount of rough ER. During cell development and under some conditions of trauma, the amount of ER increases: first the rough ER and then the smooth. The smooth type may be formed when some of the ribosomes separate from rough ER.

The structure of the ER seems well suited to the making of organic materials. It also can store such materials until they can be transported through the cell. The rough ER, for example, forms long **tubules** and large flattened bags known as **cisternae**. These can store newly synthesized proteins.

Pancreas cells give a good illustration of synthesis, storage, and transfer of proteins by the ER network. Pancreas cells secrete important digestive enzymes for use outside the cells. The enzymes are synthesized in inactive form on the ribosomes dotting the surface of the rough ER. From there they move into the cisternae and ac-

**2-9**
Left, electron micrograph of the rough ER. The tubules may form cisternae or break off to form vesicles. The black dots are ribosomes.

**2-10**
The Golgi complex is the organelle involved in repackaging proteins received from the ER network. It is called a dictyosome when found in a plant cell. The dictyosomes in the micrograph below are seen producing pouches, or vesicles, some of which travel outward to the cell membrane with which they fuse, depositing their contents in the cell wall.

which make energy available to the cell.

Some ribosomes float unattached within the cytoplasm of eucaryotic cells. (This is often true of the small ribosomes found in bacterial cells.) Proteins secreted by the floating ribosomes are used within the cell. The proteins released outside the cell are made by ribosomes located on the **endoplasmic reticulum (ER)**.

The membranes of the endoplasmic reticulum form a series of enclosed spaces. They may or may not be connected with each other. The **rough endoplasmic reticulum** is so called because ribosomes are attached to its membranes. The membrane system without attached ribosomes is called the **smooth endoplasmic reticulum**. Both the smooth and rough ER appear to be sites of lipid synthesis. The rough ER is also a site of protein synthesis by virtue of its ribosomes.

The total amount of smooth and rough ER and their proportions vary from one cell type to another. They also vary during a single cell's lifetime. Some cell types, such as muscle cells, may have very little rough ER. Many others, particularly those which

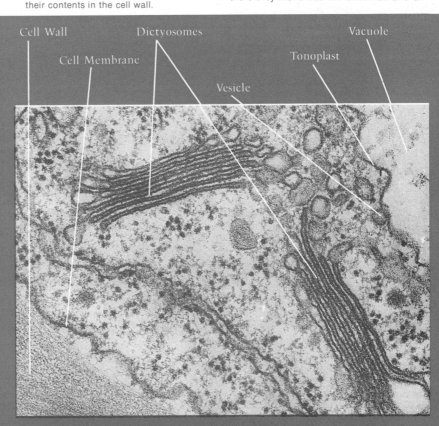

Cell Wall

Cell Membrane

Dictyosomes

Vesicle

Vacuole

Tonoplast

cumulate. They then migrate through the tubular system of the rough ER to the vicinity of another organelle, the **Golgi complex**. Extensions of the rough ER pinch off and form small pouches or **vesicles** in the Golgi complex. (The pouches hold the newly synthesized proteins.) New vesicles then develop, containing the enzymes in a concentrated form. They move to the cell surface, fuse with the plasma membrane, and empty their contents into the pancreatic duct. The duct transports the enzymes to the intestine. Once there, the enzymes become active in digestion.

## The Golgi complex

Electron microscopy confirms that the Golgi complex takes part in the synthetic and secretory activities of some cells. It does not appear to be a site of protein synthesis, but it may be involved in making nonprotein materials. Its main function is processing and repackaging materials which will be used in other parts of the cell or secreted extracellularly.

The Golgi complex usually consists of vesicles and a stack of several flattened cisternae. Each of these is curved to form a shallow cup. The number of cisternae per stack may vary, and so may the total number of stacks. Some rare cells have as many as 25,000 stacks.

## Lysosomes

Not all digestive enzymes packaged by the Golgi complex are secreted extracellularly. It is believed that some of the membranous sacs are distributed within the cell as **lysosomes**. These structures commonly occur in animal cells. Lysosomes contain enzymes used to digest complex substances *within* the cell. Importantly, they do this in isolation from the rest of the cytoplasm. The steps of the process appear simple. For example, some cells engulf food particles from the outside environment. They then enclose these particles in vesicles. Eventually, a lysosome merges with such a vesicle. Its enzymes begin to break down the

complex molecules which make up the particle into smaller molecules usable by the cell. These small molecules are then released into the cytoplasm, to provide nutrition or energy for other cell processes.

The membranes of the lysosomes are a vital means of control. If they ruptured, enzymes would be released into the cytoplasm. The result would be **autolysis**. That is, the cell would digest itself. Sometimes, the destructive action of these enzymes is supportive of life. If dying or damaged cells were left to disintegrate at their own pace, without the help of the enzymes, formation of new cells or cell parts would be delayed or prevented. So lysosomes prepare the way for the regeneration of life. By breaking down the contents of a dying cell, they provide the component molecules needed to build a new one.

## Peroxisomes and glyoxisomes

Some of the membranous sacs secreted by the Golgi complex are not involved in digestion. Instead, their enzymes assist in oxidation. In animals, these structures are about $0.5\mu$ in diameter. Because they contain enzymes called peroxidases, they are known as **peroxisomes**. In plants, the structures can be twice as large. Since they contain enzymes that are used to process a substance called glyoxylate, these structures are known as **glyoxisomes**. Glyoxylate is formed during the breakdown of lipids. Therefore glyoxisomes occur in large numbers in plant tissues that are rich in lipids.

## Mitochondria

As stated earlier, lysosomes help break down complex substances into simpler molecules. These simpler molecules can penetrate the membrane of another organelle, the **mitochondrion**. There they take part in the chemical reactions which make energy available to the cell.

Mitochondria are only about $0.5\mu$ to $2.0\mu$ long and $0.1\mu$ to $0.5\mu$ wide. Yet they contain all the enzymes and structural components

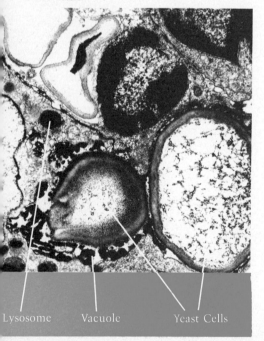

2-11
Electron micrograph of lysosomes in a white blood cell. A yeast cell has been encapsulated in a vacuole (a membrane-bound space in the cell) and is being digested by lysosomal enzymes (dark masses surrounding yeast cell). An intact lysosome is also visible.

Lysosome    Vacuole    Yeast Cells

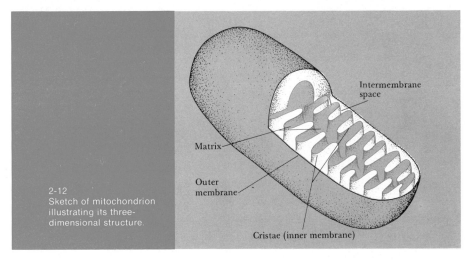

2-12
Sketch of mitochondrion illustrating its three-dimensional structure.

Intermembrane space

Matrix

Outer membrane

Cristae (inner membrane)

needed to break down organic molecules into simpler substances and store the energy released. The energy is stored in molecules of a substance called **ATP**. When a cell needs an instant source of energy, it can draw on the reserve of ATP molecules formed in the mitochondria.

Mitochondria vary in number among different types of cell. It seems that they tend to move to parts of a cell which need the most energy. For instance, there are many mitochondria in the parts of nerve cells that transmit electrical stimuli. They are also concentrated in the parts of muscle cells which are involved in contraction, and in the parts of secretory cells that produce protein or other substances. Large numbers of mitochondria are found in amoebas and other tiny organisms. They undoubtedly provide a convenient source of energy for the characteristic movement of these organisms.

The mitochondrial structure resembles a small bag. This encloses a second, much larger bag which has been neatly folded and pleated so that it will fit. The folds and pleats of the inner membrane are called **cristae**. The space between the inner and outer membranes is called the **intermembrane space**. The **matrix** is the liquid enclosed by the inner membrane. It contains granules and some of the enzymes used by the mitochondria to produce energy. The

matrix also contains DNA fibrils, which probably account for this organelle's limited degree of independence from the cell nucleus. Finally, it contains ribosomes smaller than those found in the cytoplasm.

Most studies show that the membranes are intricately adapted to the mitochondrion's chemical functions. Most of the enzymes which take part in the mitochondrion's chemical activity are woven into the inner membrane. This is not surprising, since the folds provide the large surface area needed for the sequential chemical reactions carried out within a mitochondrion. (If the groups of enzymes which catalyze these reactions were not adequately spaced from each other, the reactions could not occur in an orderly, step-by-step fashion.)

## Plastids

The term **plastids** refers to three specialized plant cell structures. These are **chloroplasts**, **leucoplasts**, and **chromoplasts**. They all develop from smaller, simpler structures called **proplastids**. Like mitochondria, proplastids have their own unique ribosomes as well as some of their own DNA. The DNA allows them to multiply independently of the cell nucleus.

Chloroplasts and mitochondria may be considered partners. The raw materials of each are the products of the other, as shown in the following chart:

|  | Chloroplast | Mitochondrion |
|---|---|---|
| Raw materials | Carbon dioxide<br>Water<br>Light energy | Simple organic molecules<br>Oxygen |
| Products | Simple organic molecules<br>Oxygen<br>Chemical energy | Carbon dioxide<br>Water<br>Chemical energy |

The chloroplast contains a characteristic green pigment, **chlorophyll**. This enables it to capture solar energy. The solar energy is then used to convert water and carbon dioxide into sugars, starches, and oxygen. This conversion process is known as **photosynthesis**. It is responsible for producing most of the chemical energy

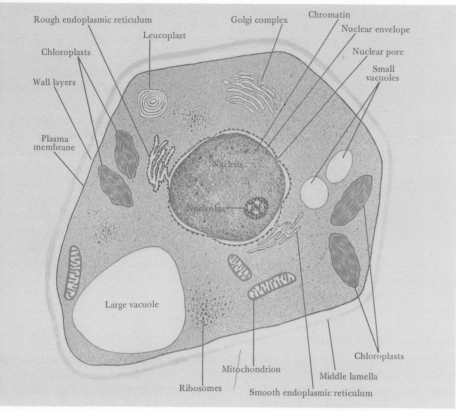

Rough endoplasmic reticulum

Leucoplast

Chloroplasts

Wall layers

Plasma membrane

Golgi complex

Chromatin

Nuclear envelope

Nuclear pore

Small vacuoles

Nucleus

Nucleolus

Large vacuole

Mitochondrion

Ribosomes

Smooth endoplasmic reticulum

Middle lamella

Chloroplasts

**2-13**
Composite sketch of plant cell. The middle lamella is a polysaccharide substance which virtually cements together adjacent cells. It is deposited by vesicles from the Golgi complex.

needed by plants and the animals which feed on them.

The ability of chlorophyll to trap solar energy is closely related to the internal structure of the chloroplast. The chloroplast is small and ovoid in shape. It is enclosed by two layers of membranes, which in turn bound the inner substance of the organelle. This substance is known as the **stroma**. It corresponds to the matrix of the mitochondrion, and contains ribosomes and many enzymes. The inner membrane is shaped into folds called **lamellae** or **thykaloids**, which jut into the stroma. The chlorophyll is contained in these membranous folds. The precise organization of the chlorophyll and membrane components makes possible the process of photosynthesis.

In some higher multicellular plants, the lamellae are arranged in stacks. The stacks vary from two or three to twenty or more lamellae, and are connected at intervals by a single lamella. These stacks are called

**grana**. They can be easily seen only under an electron microscope.

Photosynthesis does not occur in the chromoplasts, which contain only yellow, orange, or red pigments. These pigments give characteristic color to flowers, fruits, and roots, such as buttercups, tomatoes, and carrots. In some cases, chromoplasts develop from chloroplasts. This is possible because chloroplasts normally contain other pigments which are hidden by the green chlorophyll. When the amount of chlorophyll diminishes, the colors of the other pigments become dominant. The changing colors of ripening fruits and autumn foliage are examples of this process. Leucoplasts are colorless plastids which store nutrients such as starch, protein, or fat, depending on the cell in which they are found.

## Vacuoles

The **vacuole** is an organelle most commonly found in plant cells. Essentially, a vacuole is a space in the cell. In plants it is separated from the cytoplasm by a membrane called the **tonoplast**. The vacuole is filled with a watery solution known as **cell sap**.

The vacuole is a reservoir for water. It also holds deposits of other substances which, in solution with the water, make up the cell sap. These substances may include organic acids, some carbohydrates, inorganic salts, certain water-soluble pigments and proteins, and various gases. Some of them are stored permanently in the vacuole. Others are only held in temporary reserve. For example, cells may accumulate unusable quantities of salt from the soil. These can be stored in the vacuoles until they are needed. Vacuoles are also the source of the "juice" extracted from most herbaceous plants by crushing them.

In many protozoa and other single-celled organisms, the vacuoles may hold actual particles of food in reserve. Assisted by lysosomal enzymes, the organism can digest these particles over a period of time.

The waste materials left behind are then periodically eliminated from the cell by other vacuoles.

## Microtubules and microfilaments

The cytoplasm of both plant and animal cells contains structures called **microtubules**. These are long, hollow, and fairly rigid tubes, about 20 to 25 nm in diameter. They are made of a protein called **tubulin**. Each microtubule is made up of 10 to 14 protein subunits arranged in a circle.

Scientists believe that microtubules have a fundamental role in cell movement and support. This belief is based on their most common locations within the cell. The exact way in which they cause movement is not yet known, but researchers have made some interesting observations. For example, it has been found that all microtubules can bind to colchicine, a poisonous drug which is used in small doses to relieve gout. The mechanism by which microtubules facilitate movement is apparently "jammed" by colchicine. In cells treated with colchicine, all movements cease.

Many embryonic animal cells contain layers of **microfilaments** about 4 nm wide. These are arranged in bundles or sheets. It is believed that the filaments are contractile. They may be responsible for changes in cell shape during embryonic development. Little is known about their synthesis. However, it has been suggested that they are assembled from preexisting subunits in the cytoplasm.

## Centrioles

The **centriole** is an organelle that is commonly seen in animal cells, but not in most higher plants. The centriole is a hollow, cylindrical structure. Its wall consists of nine parallel sets of three microtubules. Centrioles apparently function in the process of cell division. Some centrioles also form a cylindrical structure called the **basal body**. This is located at the point where the appendages known as cilia and flagella are attached to the cell.

## Cilia and flagella

**Cilia** and **flagella** are hair-like structures which project from the plasma membranes of many animal, bacterial, and plant cells. Short, densely packed projections are referred to as cilia. Relatively long and sparsely packed ones are known as flagella.

For one-celled organisms living in watery environments, cilia or flagella serve a double purpose. They can provide an efficient way of moving about, the flagella acting as whip-like tails and the cilia as finely synchronized oars. Cilia also may create currents which bear floating particles of food to the hungry organism. In multicellular organisms, cilia and flagella play similar roles. In the human reproductive system, a single flagellum propels the male sperm cell. The rhythmic movement of cilia lining the cells of the female fallopian tubes assists the journey of the egg cell from the ovaries to the uterus. Cilia found in other passageways of various multicellular organisms similarly aid in the movement of certain particles. For example, cilia project from the cells lining the respiratory tract. There, they help to distribute protective mucus across the membranes and to expel foreign materials such as dust.

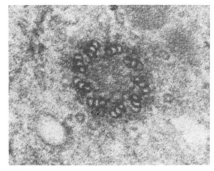

2-14
Electron micrograph of centriole from white blood cell showing nine parallel sets of triplet microtubules. Centrioles are about 0.7 to $0.3\mu$ in length and $0.2\mu$ in diameter. It is possible that the small and rather shapeless masses often visible near the surface of the centrioles contain the substances from which new centrioles are constructed.

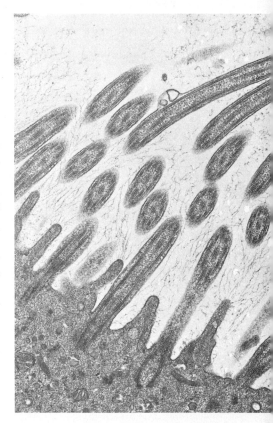

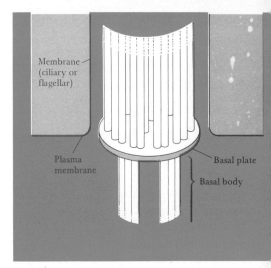

Membrane (ciliary or flagellar)

Plasma membrane

Basal plate

Basal body

2-15
Top, electron micrograph showing longitudinal section of cilia on surface of epithelial cell from turtle bladder. The diagram shows ciliary (and flagellar) structure longitudinally. The microtubules of mature cilia are not affected by colchicine, suggesting that their structure is somewhat different from that of ordinary microtubules.

With one exception, cilia and flagella show the same internal structure, no matter where they are found. Essentially, cilia and flagella are cylindrical extensions of the basal bodies. They are thus very similar in structure to centrioles. However, in contrast to centrioles, the walls of the cilia and flagella consist of nine doublets, rather than nine triplets, of microtubules. Another pair of microtubules also runs up the center of each cylinder. Hence, the structure of cilia and flagella is referred to as the "nine-plus-two" pattern. The membrane which sheathes each entire cylinder is probably an extension of the plasma membrane enclosing the cell.

The "nine-plus-two" pattern is not the only arrangement of microtubules which is capable of independent movement. The single exception mentioned above is the procaryotic flagellum. This exhibits a simpler structure than the flagella or cilia of other cells. Procaryotic flagella do not have microtubules. They are also made of a distinct kind of protein.

2-17
Intertwining cellulose fibrils run at different angles in each layer of the plant cell wall.

| Structural Feature | Eucaryotic Cells | Procaryotic Cells |
|---|---|---|
| Nucleus | Nuclear membrane | Lacks nuclear membrane |
| Chromosomes | Contain DNA only | Contain DNA and protein |
| Endoplasmic reticulum | Present | Absent |
| Golgi complex | Present | Absent |
| Plastids | Present. | Absent, but chlorophyll may be present. |
| Mitochondria | Present | Absent |
| Microtubules | Present | Absent |
| Flagella | 9 + 2 pattern | Simpler structure than 9 + 2 |
| Ribosomes | Present | Present |

2-16
Comparison of eucaryotic and procaryotic cells.

## Cell coatings

The plasma membrane of a cell is usually coated with a layer of organic materials. These provide some additional protection to the cell. In some cases, they hold together those cells which border on one another. These coatings may be found on both plant and animal cells. In plant cells they play an especially important role. When a plant cell dies, the outer coating, or **cell wall**, may still remain. It can provide strength for various parts of the plant, or serve as part of a transport system that permits water and other materials to travel through the plant.

## Cell membranes

Vital to all cells is the exchange of materials, both intracellularly and with the extracellular environment. For unicellular organisms living in oceans, lakes, and ponds, the extracellular environment consists of fresh or salt water. For the cells of multicellular plants, it consists of sap. And for the cells of multicellular animals, this environment is made up of blood and lymph. Whatever the external medium, cells must be able to extract a variety of materials from it, such as water, oxygen, and nutrients. They must have a means of expelling materials which are no longer needed. And they must have some way of controlling the rate of flow and the quantity of materials exchanged. As we noted earlier, individual cells and organelles are bounded by membranes. Therefore, it is logical to suspect that membranes and their properties will affect the passage of materials into and through the cell, as well as the expulsion of wastes from the cell. If cell membranes were as porous as cheesecloth, most substances would be able to pass through them unimpeded. That is, the membranes would be permeable to these substances, and would be incapable of regulating their passage. But cell membranes are not permeable to all substances. For this reason they play a remarkably versatile and vital role in cell survival. Membranes maintain the integrity of organelles by separating them from the cytoplasm. They serve as sites for many specific reactions in both procaryotic and eucaryotic cells. They maintain an orderly spatial arrangement of enzymes. (This assures that each step in chemical reactions regulated by the enzymes will occur in its proper sequence.) And membranes help to regulate the intracellular and extracellular exchange of materials. In short, membranes are protectors, organizers, and administrators.

## Membrane structure

The permeability characteristics of membranes once provided the only information by which scientists could make educated guesses about membrane structure. In the past few decades, new and improved techniques and equipment, such as the electron microscope, have permitted us to test early theories. They have refined our understanding of the role membranes play in biological systems.

2-18
Danielli – Davson model
of membrane structure.

In the 1930s, two scientists, J. F. Danielli and H. Davson, devised a model of the plasma membrane structure that has withstood the more sophisticated experiments of later decades remarkably well. The mod-

el is largely based on the properties of phospholipids, substances which were known components of membranes. According to the Danielli – Davson model the phospholipids in membranes are arranged in a double molecular layer called a **bilayer**. These two layers are parallel and back-to-back. On the basis of other measurements, the model was also built to show that both sides of the plasma membrane are covered with protein molecules. The Danielli – Davson model thus resembles a molecular sandwich. The two outer protein layers can be thought of as the bread and the back-to-back phospholipid layers as the filling.

*Fluid mosaic model*    Studies in the past several years have added a new dimension to this view of membranes. The idea which sparked these studies and experiments was that both lipids and proteins might be mobile, rather than rigidly fixed, components of the membrane structure. A recent theory which evolved from these studies is the **fluid mosaic model** proposed by S. J. Singer and G. L. Nicolson. According to this model, it is quite likely that all membranes possess a more or less continuous sheet of phospholipid bilayer. This functions as a selective barrier, permitting the passage of certain substances and hindering or preventing the passage of others.

But the bilayer is not completely covered with proteins as Danielli and Davson proposed. Large regions of the bilayer are exposed. It now seems more accurate to view membranes as phospholipid bilayers which are embroidered with patterns of protein, carbohydrates, and other lipids. These give the membrane its distinguishing features. It is also believed that some lipids are intimately involved in the functioning of certain proteins.

Studies of red blood cells indicate that the proteins of plasma membranes may occupy three different locations. This is partly due to the fluidity of the membrane structure. Some proteins are found in or on

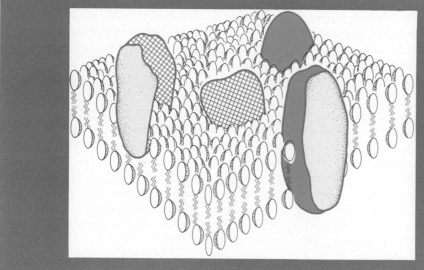

2-19
Fluid mosaic model. Globular proteins can be seen randomly distributed through a lipid matrix. (The zigzag lines are the hydrocarbon tails of the lipid molecules; and spheroid structures on the top and bottom layers are the polar heads.) These proteins are integral; that is, they cannot be easily dissociated from the membrane structure. The size and structure of the protein molecules apparently determines the extent to which integral proteins are embedded in the membrane.

the plasma membrane, and are exposed only at its outer surface. Others are located in or on the plasma membrane, but are exposed only at the inner surface. And some proteins which are exposed at both the inner and outer surface seem to penetrate the entire width of the membrane. According to the fluid mosaic model, the bilayer serves as a solvent for those proteins which are deeply embedded in its structure.

The mobility of membrane components seems to vary with different cell types and different types of membrane. The movement of lipid molecules seems affected by the proteins which extend across the bilayer from one surface to another. When the movement of lipids is unrestricted it seems to occur laterally through the bilayer, rather than up and down. The proteins themselves are restricted in their movement from one surface of the bilayer to the other. But they too can usually move laterally.

## Principles of transport

During investigations of membrane structure, scientists have noted the kinds of material which can enter cells. Most cell membranes are permeable to water, fats, simple sugars, and a few other small molecules. They are more or less impermeable to large molecules such as proteins. In general

membranes are also less permeable to ions (atoms or molecules carrying an electric charge) than to neutral particles.

There are five ways in which substances may enter and exit cells. Two of these—diffusion and osmosis—are physical processes governing the movement of all matter. The other three are specifically associated with living membranes. They are facilitated diffusion, active transport, and vesicular transport.

*Diffusion*  If a drop of ink is placed in a container of water, it will color the entire water sample. This familiar phenomenon is the result of molecular motion. Molecules of any substance are constantly engaged in random movement. They change direction when they collide with each other or with some physical barrier. Given enough time, this movement causes them to be distributed uniformly throughout the space in which they are enclosed.

The movement of molecules obeys the physical laws which govern the movement of all randomly moving particles. As long as molecular distribution is not uniform, the overall movement of molecules is from areas of high concentration to areas of lower concentration. The drop of ink, for example, does not maintain its concentrat-

2-20
The ink molecules diffuse from a region of high concentration to one of lower concentration

ed form when it is put into the water. Its molecules immediately move outward from the region in which they are most concentrated into areas occupied by the molecules of water—the region of lower concentration of ink molecules. Some ink molecules will collide with other molecules and be diverted back to the area of higher concentration. But the overall, or net, movement is away from this area. The net movement of particles caused by their random motion is called **diffusion**. When the ink molecules have diffused through the entire water sample and are distributed uniformly, they are still moving. But it is no longer noticeable, for as each ink molecule leaves an area, another replaces it.

*Osmosis*    Suppose we separated two solutions from each other by means of a selectively permeable membrane—a membrane through which molecules of certain substances can pass but other molecules cannot. In this experiment, we cover the open bottom of a long-necked thistle tube with a piece of cellophane. We then fill the oval portion of the thistle tube with molasses. This mixture has a very high concentration of sugar molecules and a very low concentration of water molecules. We place the thistle tube in a beaker of pure water, securing it with a fastening mechanism so that the cellophane-covered base of the thistle tube does not press against the glass base of the beaker.

In this instance, the cellophane cover will act as a selectively permeable membrane. Water molecules can pass through it, but not sugar molecules. What can we expect to happen? We know that the pure water has a higher concentration of water molecules than the molasses solution. Since water molecules can pass through the cellophane membrane, we can expect that there will be a net movement from the beaker to the thistle tube. The molasses solution has a higher concentration of sugar molecules than the pure water solution. But the selectivity of the cellophane membrane

prohibits the passage of sugar molecules from the thistle tube to the beaker.

The process by which water molecules diffuse through a selectively permeable membrane is called **osmosis**. From a chemical standpoint the diffusion of any solvent through a selectively permeable membrane could be called osmosis. However since water is the universal solvent in biological systems, the definition of osmosis offered above is more precise for our purposes.

In the simple osmosis experiment above, we noted a net movement of water molecules into the molasses solution. Because of this movement, the level of the solution rises and the level of pure water drops. But no matter how much water diffuses through the barrier, the molasses solution is always less concentrated in water molecules than pure water. This might seem to imply that the diffusion process goes on indefinitely. It does not. As the level of the molasses solution rises, its extra weight exerts increasingly greater pressure on the molecules in that side. This pressure tends to push water molecules back across the membrane into the pure water. When the rate of water molecules going in both directions—that is into the beaker containing pure water and into the molasses solution—is equal, we say that the total system is in equilibrium. The pressure which is exerted on the molasses solution at the point of equilibrium is called **osmotic pressure** (or sometimes **osmotic potential**).

The osmotic pressure (which is measured in pressure units) is not the same for all solutions. This would become clear if we conducted a series of osmosis experiments using varying concentrations of substances. We would find that the greater the total number of particles dissolved in a solution—that is, the higher the concentration of dissolved particles—the more molecules of water would pass into that solution from the pure water side before equilibrium was achieved. Obviously, with each increase in the amount of water passing into the solu-

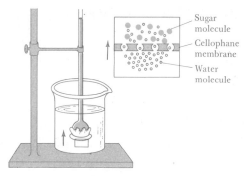

2-21
Water molecules are seen diffusing through a selectively permeable membrane.

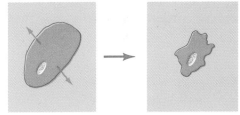

Hyperosmotic medium

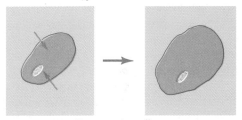

Hypoosmotic medium

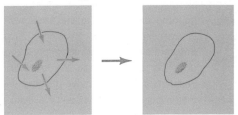

Isosmotic medium

2-22
The selective permeability of biological membranes helps to regulate the concentration of solutes within the cell and, consequently, the osmotic pressure of the intracellular fluid.

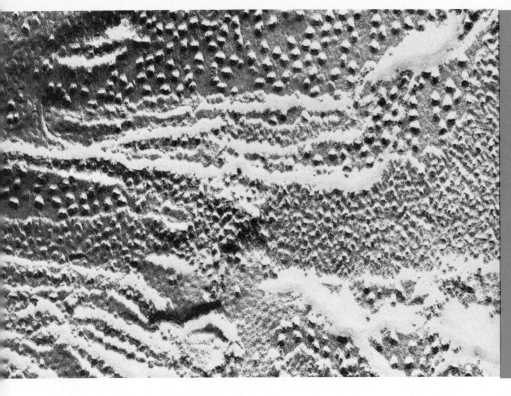

2-23
Freeze-etch of thylakoids (lamellae). The numerous globular integral proteins visible on the fracture face are probably involved in active transport and the processes by which energy is packaged in the chloroplast.

tion, there would be a corresponding increase in osmotic pressure. Such differences in the tendency of water to move into solutions—which we see can be measured as differences in osmotic pressure—play a significant role in biological systems and the activities of cells.

*Cell–water relations* If the surrounding medium has more dissolved particles than the cell itself, it is said to be **hyperosmotic**. That is, it has a higher osmotic pressure than the cell. Water therefore tends to move from the intracellular to the extracellular environment, and the cell shrinks. A **hypoosmotic** external environment has fewer dissolved particles than the cytoplasm. Thus it has a lower osmotic pressure than the intracellular environment. In such a medium, cells swell up, and may eventually burst, if the diffusion of water into them is not counteracted. If the extracellular environment has an osmotic pressure similar to that within the cell, it is called **isosmotic**. In

such a system, the two environments—internal and external—are in equilibrium. The cell may exchange only small amounts of water with its surrounding medium. It does not change in size or shape.

Some cells are specially equipped to deal with osmotically unfavorable environments. In plants, for example, the extracellular fluid is hypoosmotic relative to the cells. However, the cell wall is somewhat elastic. It exerts a counterpressure which prevents excess water from seeping into the plant cells and causing them to burst. Some simple animal organisms, such as the amoeba, live in fresh-water hypoosmotic environments. They are equipped with vacuoles which can contract periodically and expel excess water that has accumulated by osmosis.

## Cellular transport

**Passive diffusion** is the movement of materials from an area of high concentration to an area of lower concentration. It can take

place with either artificial or cell membranes serving as the selectively permeable barrier. But there are specific mechanisms of transport which are characteristic only of cells. Some of these mechanisms require energy and are related to functions of proteins in the membrane structure. Others involve the ingestion of bulk liquids or solids by the cell.

*Facilitated diffusion* When we measure the rate at which some water-soluble substances with small molecules pass through the plasma membrane into cells, we find it to be faster than we would expect from passive diffusion. This is because each molecule of the incoming substance initially combines with a "carrier" on the surface of the membrane. This carrier is called a **permease**. The carrier transports the molecule across the membrane, and then releases it to the interior of the cell.

This type of transport involves movement from an area of high concentration to

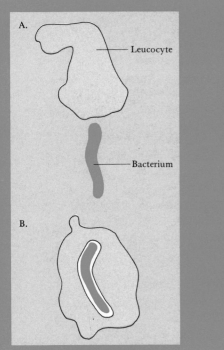

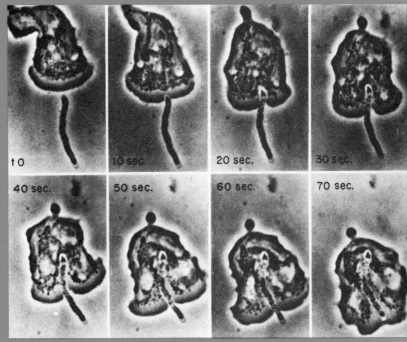

2-24
Right, sequential
phase contrast
micrographs that show
a type of human white
blood cell phagocytizing
a bacterium, Bacillus
megaterium. The
drawings (left) show the
white blood cell and
bacterium (A) prior to
phagocytosis and (B)
when the bacterium is
enclosed in a vacuole
within the blood cell.

A.
— Leucocyte

— Bacterium

B.

↑ 0       10 sec.       20 sec.       30 sec.

40 sec.       50 sec.       60 sec.       70 sec.

one of lower concentration. But since it also uses specific carrier molecules (probably protein) in the membrane, it is called **facilitated diffusion**. Instances of facilitated diffusion include the rapid uptake of sugars by red blood cells, muscle cells, and liver cells.

*Active transport*    Sometimes the carrier moves substances against a **concentration gradient**. That is, it moves them from a region of low concentration of a given substance to one of higher concentration. This process is called **active transport**. It is a permease activity that requires energy. Examples of active transport include the recovery of sugars by kidney tubule cells. Also included is the movement of newly synthesized sugars from the food-making cells into the food-transporting cells of higher plants.

Sources of chemical energy for active transport and some of the substances required for processing this energy have

been found in cell membranes. But the precise way in which chemical energy is harnessed to drive active transport is not yet fully understood. It remains one of the most active areas of research in membrane biology.

*Vesicular transport*    Along with passive diffusion and active transport, there are other processes by which cells obtain materials from their environment. Not all cell types use these methods of transport, and those which do usually employ the other mechanisms as well.

The process of ingesting large amounts of fluids is termed **pinocytosis**. Nutrient particles are usually available to cells in the form of a solution. The particles may be dissolved in the fresh- or salt-water environment of unicellular organisms, or in the sap or blood and lymph of multicellular organisms. In pinocytosis, the solution interacts with certain sites on the outer surface of the plasma membrane. The membrane folds inward at these sites to form vesicles which enclose small volumes of the solution. These vesicles then move into the interior of the cell.

Many cells can also take in large particles of solid matter. Some one-celled organisms use this method, called **phagocytosis,** to ingest food. For other cells such as the macrophages—a group of human white blood cells—phagocytosis provides a method of dealing with invading bacteria and dead tissue.

When a phagocytizing cell or unicellular organism, such as an amoeba, makes contact with a particle of food, it engulfs the particle in a **pseudopod.** This is a cytoplasmic extension of the cell. The pseudopod actually adheres to the particle as it moves over its surface. Eventually the pseudopod forms a food vacuole which is taken into the cell. The vacuole fuses with a lysosome, and the engulfed particle is digested by enzymes.

## Cell specialization

In our discussion of cell structure and membrane functions we have referred to organisms as "unicellular" or "multicellular." We noted that both types of organism must continuously carry on certain fundamental processes for survival. But the way in which they do this varies enormously as a consequence of specialization.

Organelles represent the lowest level of specialization. A eucaryotic one-celled organism is thus a more organized and specialized form of life than a procaryotic unicellular organism such as a bacterium. But it represents only an early stage in the evolutionary trend toward specialization. Such an organism functions as a biological "renaissance man" in that it performs all its life-sustaining activities by means of a single cell. The real "specialists" which have emerged from the long history of evolution are the interdependent cells of multicellular organisms.

Most of the organisms we are familiar with are multicellular. These organisms include the flowering plants and most of the animals. They are composed of specialized eucaryotic cells. Like their specialist counterparts in human society, these eucaryotic cells function cooperatively. Each type performs only a part of the range of activities necessary to the existence of the organism. But in order to do this, the eucaryotic cells have been "streamlined." Unlike the eucaryotic cells of a unicellular organism, each type of cell in a multicellular organism contains only the certain numbers, sizes, and kinds of organelle which will enable it to do its specific job. The inevitable result is that such cells cannot function independently. They must rely on each other to provide services which are vital to their individual existence. For example, the cells which generate chemical energy for the activities of the organism as a whole also provide energy to other specialized cells which cannot produce their own.

Interdependence is a feature of the entire multicellular organism. It is reflected in the specialized and cooperative functioning of tissues, organs, and systems. A **tissue** is a collection of specialized cells which are similar in structure and function. These cells are usually contained within a matrix which they themselves secrete. An **organ** is a combination of tissues which may vary in type but which work together as a functional unit. The next level of organization is the **system**. It is made up of groups of organs that perform related or interacting functions. The highest level, finally, is the **organism** itself. At this level, a number of systems work together in a mutually beneficial association.

Higher plant and animal organisms have had to adapt to their environment in different ways. This is revealed in the more elaborate structure of the higher animals. But the specialized structures and functions of both types of multicellular organism—plant and animal—are the result of cellular activity. To put it simply, cells are the basis of specialization.

**summary**

All cells are three-dimensional. They are bounded by a thin and flexible plasma membrane. Cells may vary in size, spatial form, and the complexity of their inner structure. Procaryotic cells have a nuclear region and a relatively simple substructure. Eucaryotic cells have a segregated nucleus and a comparatively complex substructure.

The two major compartments of a eucaryotic cell are the cytoplasm and the nucleus. The nucleus contains chromosomes. These carry the genetic material, DNA, which determines a cell's potential action in a variety of processes. Within the cytoplasm are structurally differentiated compartments called organelles.

Ribosomes are needed for the manufacture of proteins. In eucaryotic cells, some ribosomes float free in the cytoplasm. Many are bound to a system of membranes known as the endoplasmic reticulum (ER). The portion of the ER with ribosomes attached is called rough ER. It is a site of both protein and lipid synthesis. The portion lacking ribosomes is called smooth ER. It is a site of lipid synthesis.

The main function of the Golgi complex is to process and repackage various materials for use within and outside the cell. Membranous sacs, called lysosomes, contain enzymes used in the intracellular digestion of organic substances. They are believed to arise from the Golgi complex. This is also the source of other sac-like bodies, called peroxisomes in animals and glyoxisomes in plants. They contain enzymes involved in oxidation.

The mitochondrion is another organelle. It is involved in the oxidative generation of chemical energy from foodstuffs. Plastids are organelles found only in plants. The chloroplast captures solar energy and uses it in the process of photosynthesis. It contains the pigment chlorophyll. Chromoplasts contain other pigments which give color to flowers and fruits. Leucoplasts are colorless plastids used for storage of nutrients.

The vacuole is a space in the cell. In plants, it is separated from the cytoplasm by a membrane called the tonoplast. It is also filled with a solution called cell sap. It can serve as a water reservoir or a depository for organic and inorganic substances.

Microtubules function in cell movement and support. They are structural components of centrioles, cilia, and flagella. Cilia and flagella are hair-like structures which enable certain cells to move. Cilia may also help to move particles past the cells from which they project.

Cell membranes are selectively permeable barriers. They maintain the integrity of organelles and serve as sites for many chemical reactions. The membranes maintain an orderly spatial arrangement of enzymes. They also help to regulate the intracellular and extracellular exchange of materials.

Diffusion is the net movement of randomly moving particles from a region of high concentration to one of lower concentration. When water molecules diffuse through a selectively permeable membrane, the process is termed osmosis. Osmotic pressure is the pressure which must be exerted on molecules of a given solution to maintain a state of equilibrium with water (or with a solution having a lower concentration of dissolved particles).

In living systems the extracellular environment is termed hyperosmotic if it has a higher osmotic pressure than the intracellular environment. If it has a lower osmotic pressure relative to the cells, it is called hypoosmotic. It is isosmotic if it has an osmotic pressure similar to that of the intracellular medium.

Cell membranes are usually permeable to substances with small molecules, and relatively permeable to substances with large molecules. They are less permeable to ions than to neutral particles. According to the Danielli–Davson model, the plasma membrane is composed of a double molecular layer (bilayer) of phospholipids, flanked on either side by a layer of protein molecules. According to the fluid mosaic model, the bilayer is embroidered with varying patterns of proteins, carbohydrates, and other lipids. The lipids and proteins are mobile components of the membrane structure.

Diffusion which uses specific carrier molecules (permeases) on the membrane is called facilitated diffusion. When the carrier moves substances against a concentration gradient, this energy-requiring activity is called active transport. Pinocytosis is a transport process by which substances are ingested in the form of fluids. In phagocytosis, bulk quantities of solid foods are ingested.

Multicellular life forms function by using several types of specialized cells. Each type is modified to perform only certain of those activities which simpler organisms must perform with a single cell. The specialized cells must function interdependently, as do the tissues, organs, and organ systems which they comprise. Cells are the basis of plant and animal specialization.

the functional basis for multicellular forms of life is cell specialization. In the higher plants and animals, the coordination of specialized cells, tissues, and organs makes possible ways of adapting that are beyond the capacity of simpler organisms. Cartilage and bone are specialized tissues which contribute to the protection and support of higher forms of animal life. Cartilage forms the skeleton of all embryonic vertebrates. As with bone cells, cartilage cells are widely spaced within a secreted matrix of proteins and connective fibers. But unlike bone, cartilage lacks a formal channel for receiving body fluids. The cells must take in nutrients via fluids which diffuse through the matrix. Bone tissue, on the other hand, is penetrated by a network of blood vessels. These supply nutrients via channels, or canaliculi, in the matrix. The overall structure of bone consists of two primary elements. One is compact bone, which forms a firm mass penetrated by microscopic openings. The other element is spongy bone. It includes bone marrow and some harder substances. The formation of compact bone from spongy bone is a response to the need for greater structural support as an organism grows.

Secretion and excretion are functions important to organisms of varying complexity. Secretion may be viewed as the total range of activities related to the synthesis, packaging, and release of a number of chemical substances. For Venus's flytrap, the secretory process helps to provide a more efficient way of adapting to the environment. Being green, the plant is capable of photosynthesis. But, partly as a result of the enzymes it makes, the plant also can digest insects. The enzymes are synthesized and packaged in the appropriate organelles. They are then transported to cells in glands on the surface of the leaf. When the insect has been captured, the gland secretes its enzymes. The enzymes break down the insect into components that can be assimilated by the plant's cells.

Mechanisms such as secretion are used to adapt to the external environment. Systems have also developed for keeping a stable relationship between cells and the internal environment. Among vertebrates, the urinary system provides a method of controlling the salt and water content of the blood. It also provides a way to excrete the waste products from various cellular processes. One example is the nitrogen waste resulting from protein metabolism. The excretory organs of the urinary system are the paired kidneys. Within each there are over 1 million tiny units of structure called nephrons. Each nephron consists of a renal corpuscle and a renal tubule. Each corpuscle has a two-part structure, Bowman's capsule and the glomerulus. Bowman's capsule consists of two spherical walls separated by a cavity, Bowman's space. The glomerulus consists of a cluster of capillaries within the capsule. A filtrate of blood plasma passes from the glomerulus into Bowman's space. The filtrate then moves through various tubules and ducts of the urinary system. In the process, certain cells reabsorb water and nutrients from it. Other cells contribute additional waste products. The final product, urine, is excreted.

Vital activities on the organismic level are dependent on orderly and precise

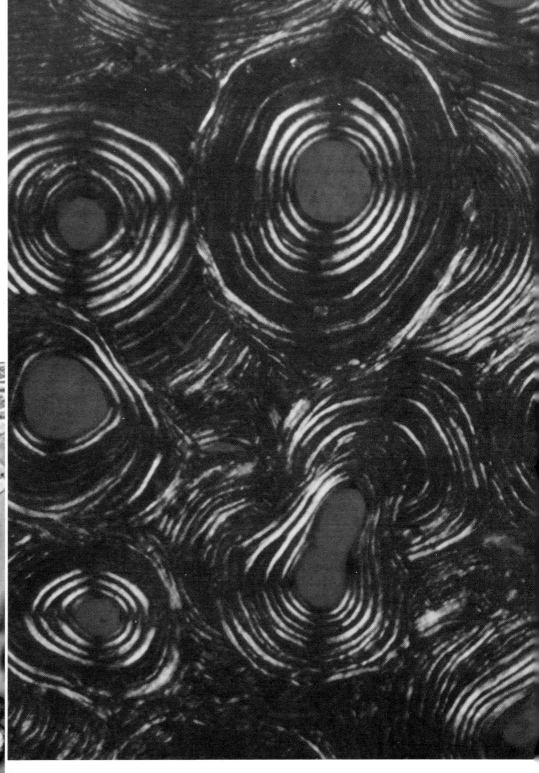

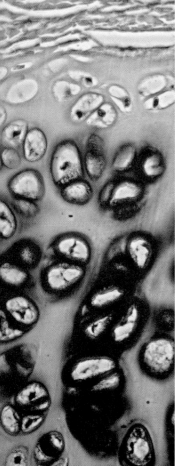

Left: Phase contrast image of hyaline cartilage. Growth
may occur through the formation of new cells at the
inner surface of the perichondrium (top of photo).
Above: Polarized light image of compact bone. Bone
remodeling involves the development of Haversian
systems (concentric layers of bone visible in the photo).

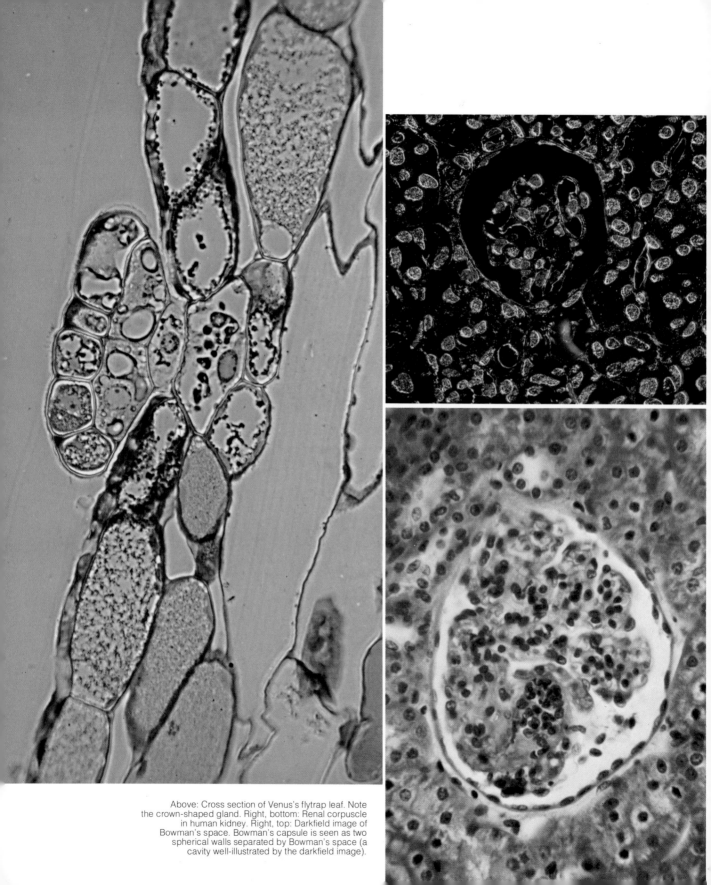

Above: Cross section of Venus's flytrap leaf. Note the crown-shaped gland. Right, bottom: Renal corpuscle in human kidney. Right, top: Darkfield image of Bowman's space. Bowman's capsule is seen as two spherical walls separated by Bowman's space (a cavity well-illustrated by the darkfield image).

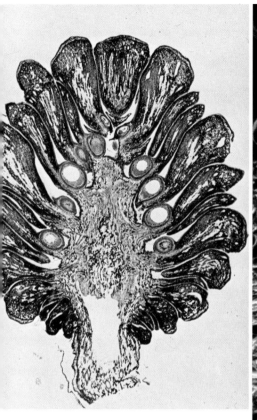

Above: Female pine cone showing ovules. The ovules are eventually transformed into seeds, which fall from the cones and take root in the soil.

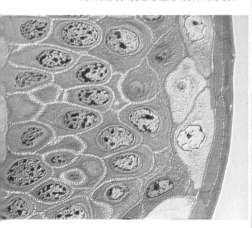

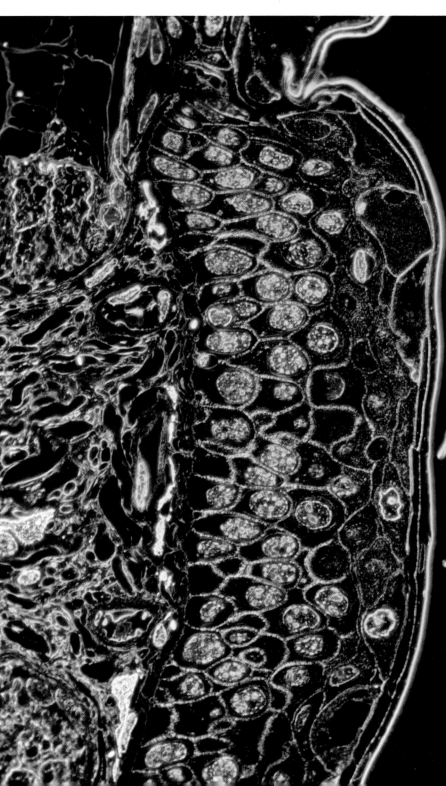

Above: Interference contrast image of epithelium. Right: Darkfield image of epithelium. On the extreme left of each photo is the germinative, or basal, layer of the stratified tissue; on the extreme right can be seen the flattened out epithelial cells of the surface tissue layers.

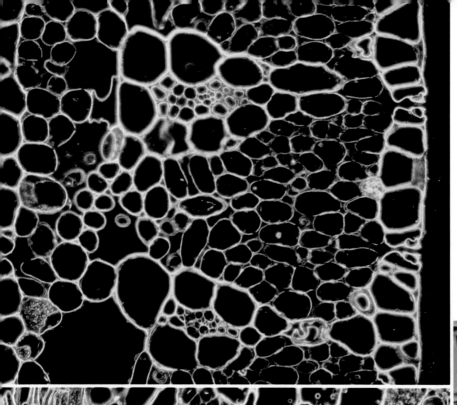
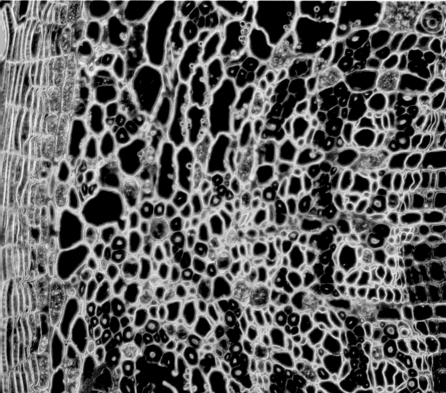
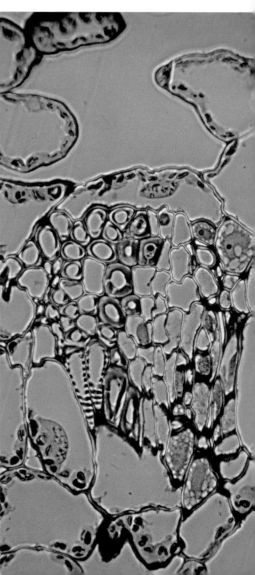

Top: Cross section of water hyacinth leaf.
Bottom: Cross section of root tissue taken from
*Tilia americana*, a lumber tree of tropical
North America. Right: Phase contrast image of
vascular bundle, a combination of special plant
cells that function in support and transport.

functioning on the cellular level. One such activity is reproduction. There must be mechanisms for reproducing similar, yet independently viable, members of a given type of organism. There must be mechanisms by which cells become specialized. And there must be mechanisms by which damaged or destroyed cells can be replaced throughout the lifetime of a single organism. An illustration of the first type of mechanism is reproduction in the pine tree. The process begins with the development of female and male cones. Pollen grains develop in the male cones. They are usually then carried via air currents to the female cone's egg cells. They enter by a tiny opening in the scales of the female cone. Eventually, the pollen grains release sperm and thus fertilize the eggs, a process that takes about a year. By the end of about the second year, the ovules have been transformed into seeds. These seeds—consisting of embryo, nutrient tissue, and a seed coat—fall from the cones and take root in the soil.

Regeneration and proliferation of a different sort—not of new organisms, but rather of the cells of existing tissue—is well illustrated by the epithelium. Epithelial cells line the inner and outer surfaces of the body of an animal organism. Skin, for example, is comprised of epithelial cells. So are the linings of the mouth, nostrils, and digestive tract. The epithelial tissue illustrated in this portfolio was taken from the skin of an amphibian. It is termed stratified epithelium because it consists of several layers. Surface cells which are sloughed off or destroyed are replaced by cell division in the bottom (basal) layer. The new cells are relatively undifferentiated at first. But they specialize into epithelial cells as they move toward the surface.
The photos of root and leaf tissue suggest the multiple cell functions which contribute to the survival of the total higher plant organism. The roots serve as "anchors" and supportive structures. They also provide a primary means of absorbing water and mineral salts from the soil. Sometimes they are even used to store food. Leaves, on the other hand, are most importantly the sites for food manufacture through the process of photosynthesis. They also regulate the entry and release of water vapor and other gases. This exchange of gases occurs through tiny openings, or stomata, which are usually most numerous on the undersurface of the leaf. (Water lilies, however, float on the surfaces of ponds. Therefore stomata are found only on the upper sides of their leaves.) In the leaf and petiole (the thin stalk that attaches leaf to stem) are found vascular bundles. These are associations of different types of specialized plant cells. They transport water and salts taken up through the roots and stem. They also conduct food (carbohydrates) photosynthesized in the surrounding cells to other parts of the plant. Growth for both the synthetic (leaves) and absorbing (root) parts of the plant organism occurs by means of meristematic tissue. This tissue consists of cells which are simple and undifferentiated. They are among the few types of plant cell which are capable of division. As they divide and reproduce themselves, the resultant new cells can develop into any of the specialized cells required by the plant.

3 cell dynamics

fundamental law of physical science states that molecules and atoms in all systems tend toward a condition of greater disorder in which the energy available for work (**free energy**) continually decreases as randomness (**entropy**) steadily increases. This bears sobering implications for the ultimate fate of the universe. To put it simply, the entire universe is slowly winding down. It is approaching a final equilibrium position of minimum order and maximum entropy, in which there is no free energy and thus no power of action or motion.

When we consider this inexorable process, the existence of life seems paradoxical. After all, new living matter is being created all the time, and at all levels it reflects a high degree of organization. Molecules are intricately patterned to form the various parts of the cell. Each cell part is precisely structured to serve its particular function. And higher organisms are able to function because of the hierarchical arrangement of cells, tissues, organs, and organ systems.

But the paradox is only apparent. Biological systems follow the same physical laws which govern nonliving systems. Cells can maintain order, and hence life, only because they can continually extract energy from the environment, using it to perform a variety of tasks. One of these is the synthesis of new molecules for cell growth and repair. Others include active transport of molecules and ions against a concentration gradient and restriction of materials within the cell against the tendency of molecules to become randomly distributed; mechanical work such as contraction of muscle cells and the motion of cilia and flagella; and electrical work, as in the transmission of nerve impulses.

By continually accomplishing these and other tasks, cells maintain a highly ordered and stable system. But the physical laws still apply. There is an overall increase in entropy, since order is created inside the cell only at the cost of increasing disorder in the universe as a whole. Moreover, if cells could not obtain and use energy, they, too, would follow the natural tendency of systems to become increasingly randomized. Eventually, their structural and functional order would be destroyed.

## Energy transformations

The form of energy which cells can use is the potential energy stored in chemical bonds. But the ultimate *source* of energy for nearly all organisms is the sun. Green plants, algae, some protozoa, and several types of bacteria are able to capture radiant energy. They use it to synthesize carbohydrates and other complex molecules, all of which store large amounts of chemical energy. Organisms that can convert the energy of sunlight into the energy of chemical bonds are called **autotrophs**, from the Greek words *autos* (self) and *trophe* (food). Autotrophs are responsible for more than half the biological production of organic compounds. It is from these compounds that nearly all other organisms obtain their energy. These other organisms are called **heterotrophs**, from the Greek *hetero* (other). They are ultimately dependent for their nutrition on the autotrophic organisms.

Potential energy cannot be used by an organism until it has been liberated as free energy. This can be done in either of two general ways. It depends on the type of organism involved and the availability of oxygen. **Aerobic** organisms can use molecular oxygen ($O_2$) to degrade organic molecules to the inorganic molecules $CO_2$ (carbon dioxide) and $H_2O$ (water). Organisms which lack oxygen, or which are **anaerobic** and so unable to use oxygen, can achieve only a partial breakdown of organic substances. Despite the difference in overall effect, the two methods share several features. In both, complex organic molecules are broken down to simpler substances with a lower energy content. The release of energy results from oxidation reactions in which a substance loses electrons and

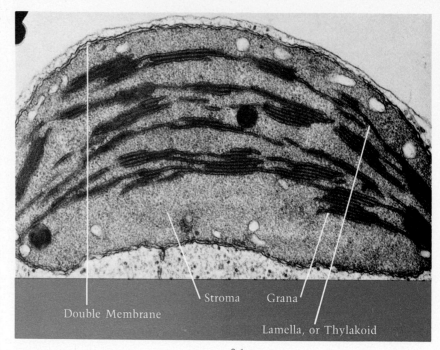

Double Membrane    Stroma    Grana    Lamella, or Thylakoid

3-1
Many autotrophs have chloroplasts which enable them to trap radiant energy for use in photosynthesis. Shown is an electron micrograph of a chloroplast from *Nicotiana tabacum*. The interior of the thylakoids is called the thylakoid space. The double membrane region where the layered thylakoids join is the partition.

usually hydrogen atoms. And the oxidation reactions are made to occur at low temperatures and proceed in an orderly and controlled manner, with each step catalyzed by a different enzyme.

As we noted, the free energy released in oxidation reactions is used in a number of cellular activities. In biosynthesis, the energy is once again changed into the potential energy of chemical bonds. For example, with an input of energy, polysaccharides, proteins, and fats can be built from simple sugars, amino acids, and fatty acids. In the other energy-consuming processes described earlier, such as muscle contraction and transmission of nerve impulses, chemical energy is converted into a variety of other forms.

In these energy transactions, it is important that energy-yielding, or **exergonic**, processes are linked with energy-requiring, or **endergonic**, reactions. If an organism had to carry out the complex steps required for breakdown of organic materials wherever energy was needed, then all the enzymes which catalyze each of the chemical reactions would have to be present throughout each cell. Obviously this would be a cumbersome and inefficient system. It would also make it difficult to keep the various synthetic and degradative reactions separate. Organisms have therefore evolved an ingenious way to compartmentalize reactions and still have a ready supply of energy for all their cell needs.

## Putting energy on tap

In all cells, one substance plays the middleman in energy exchanges. It is adenosine triphosphate, or **ATP**. ATP is formed by the process of **phosphorylation**. In general terms, the process involves adding an inorganic phosphate group to a given molecule. To form ATP, the phosphate group is added to the two-phosphate tail of adenosine diphosphate, or **ADP**, a compound very similar in structure to ATP. The bond of this third phosphate group stores a considerable amount of energy. Thus the conversion of ADP to ATP is an energy-consuming process. This same energy is released when ATP undergoes **hydrolysis**, a process by which the bond of the third phosphate group is broken and ADP is regenerated.

3-2
Adenosine diphosphate and triphosphate. Note the special bonds on the last two phosphate groups of the tail. The darker lines of the ribose ring imply a three-dimensional structure.

The convertibility of ADP and ATP provides a compact and convenient way of handling energy exchanges. Exergonic reactions can be used to synthesize ATP. Endergonic reactions can derive energy by breaking down ATP. There are three major processes for ATP production. Each of these is based on the methods for obtaining energy described earlier.

Autotrophs can phosphorylate ADP using the radiant energy of the sun. This method of producing ATP is called **photophosphorylation**. It occurs during the process of photosynthesis. Some of the ATP molecules are used for immediate energy needs, and some are stored. Many are used to synthesize the carbohydrates on which heterotrophs depend. In the absence of light, autotrophs themselves derive energy from carbohydrates. The way in which this energy is commonly released and repackaged comprises the second method of ATP production. We noted earlier that in aerobic cells, organic substances such as carbohydrates can be completely broken down in a series of oxidation reactions. When the energy for these reactions is used in the phosphorylation of ATP, the process is called **oxidative phosphorylation. Fermentation** is a similar process, but it proceeds in the absence of oxygen. Since the anaerobic breakdown of organic compounds can never be complete, fermentation produces fewer molecules of ATP. For example, the complete breakdown of a single molecule of glucose to $CO_2$ and water releases 686 kilocalories of free energy. But when the same amount of glucose is converted to ethyl alcohol by the fermentation process which occurs in yeast, only 40 kilocalories are released.

All these methods of producing ATP supply cells with discrete and portable units of chemical potential energy. These units can be placed "on tap" for any of the energy-consuming processes occurring in different areas of the cell. For example, oxidative phosophorylation occurs in the mitochondria. The degradative oxidation reactions are thus localized, and cannot interfere with other biochemical pathways. But the ATP produced in this organelle can be sent to any other part of the cell on demand.

It is no wonder that ATP is often called the "energy currency" of the cell. Like money, it is the single medium of exchange which relates diverse goods and services. But it is of a rather small denomination. For example, the complete oxidation of one glucose molecule yields about 100 times as much energy as the hydrolysis of an ATP phosphate bond. The conversion of the energy of a glucose molecule into the new chemical bond energy of ATP molecules is thus roughly equivalent to changing a dollar bill into pennies. The efficiency of this conversion is also limited. The cell receives only about 40 pennies of ATP for each dollar of glucose.

# Control of metabolism

Before we enter a more detailed discussion of the reactions involved in ATP production, we must examine the mechanisms which control metabolism. Metabolism is the sum of all chemical reactions which occur in living tissue. One obvious way that cells prevent different reaction pathways from conflicting with each other is by localizing them in various cellular compartments. For example, the oxidation of fatty acids occurs in the mitochondria, but the synthesis of fatty acids takes place in the soluble part of the cytoplasm. Enzymes are also a vital way of controlling reactions. At the molecular level, in eucaryotic and procaryotic cells, enzymes regulate virtually all metabolic processes.

Enzymes help to control the rate at which raw materials enter a reaction pathway and at which end products are synthesized. They ensure that oxidation occurs in a series of discrete steps so that small units of energy can be released and captured in the form of ATP. They also serve to lower the level of energy needed to activate oxidation reactions which do not occur spontaneously. Moreover, they enable reactions to occur under conditions which a chemist would consider very mild—atmospheric pressure, neutral pH, and a temperature of 37°C.

## Enzymes

Like inorganic catalysts, **enzymes** enhance the rate of reactions without themselves being changed in the process. They cannot trigger reactions which do not already have a tendency to occur. (Reactions which tend to occur are those which release free energy.) What enzymes do is simply speed up the reaction.

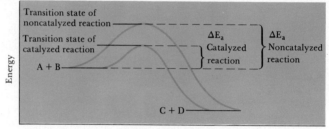

Progress of reaction

3-3
Effect of a catalyst on $\Delta E_a$ (energy of activation) required for the reaction $A + B \rightarrow C + D$. The catalyzed path has a lower energy of activation than that of the uncatalyzed path, so that proportionately more molecules possess the energy required for reaction.

For reactants to form the activated transition state needed for them to chemically change into the products of the reaction, they must collide productively. That is, their molecules must collide with sufficient force and in the proper orientation. Heating a mixture speeds up the reaction by increasing molecular motion. This increases the frequency of collisions between reactant molecules and, in turn, the number of productive collisions. But heating accelerates all other possible side reactions, and also raises the temperature to a level that living organisms cannot tolerate.

An enzyme increases the frequency of productive collisions. It binds the reactants close to one another in an orientation favorable to very particular interactions. Thus it increases the reaction rate by lowering the level of energy needed to start these reactions. That is, it lowers the **energy of activation**. Inorganic catalysts also lower the energy of activation. But they would not be suitable for living systems. Enzymes are much more efficient, both in terms of rate enhancements and because they can function under mild conditions. They are also

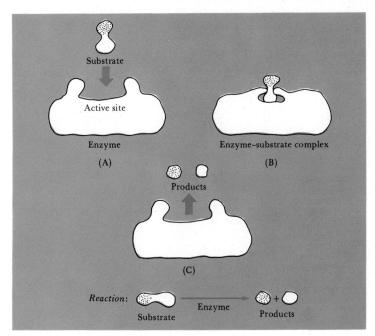

3-4
Enzyme specificity. Current findings suggest that enzyme specificity is accomplished through "induced fit": the enzyme is a flexible framework with active sites which move around to fit colliding substrate molecules, as in the illustrated sequence A, B, and C.

ed to catalysis. This active site is usually part of the more extensive **binding region**, the part of the enzyme that recognizes its **substrate**—that is, the particular substance with which the enzyme is reactive.

The tidy correspondence between enzymes and substrates is not an accident. Enzymes have evolved in conjunction with the substances with which they are reactive. Through a long and complicated procedure much like trial and error, enzymes have become efficient and highly specialized tools of cellular chemistry. The evolutionary necessity for this precision is obvious. An inactive enzyme, or an inefficient one, or one that acted on the wrong substance, could disrupt any number of the intricately interlocking metabolic processes on which life depends.

## Vitamins, coenzymes, and hormones

Enzymes themselves are regulated by a variety of other agents, including other enzymes. For example, potentially destructive digestive enzymes are synthesized in an inactive form. They cannot function until after they have been altered by another enzyme molecule. Control is also exercised by **inhibitors**. These substances, many of which are proteins, tend to reduce the activity of a particular enzyme. In the pancreas, where many of the digestive enzymes are made, inhibitors are always present. Thus any prematurely activated enzymes can be neutralized before they destroy vital tissue.

**Vitamins** are substances of varied chemical structure which are required in the diet, usually in small amounts. Those that are important to the functioning of enzymes are the water-soluble vitamins: niacin, riboflavin, thiamine, pyridoxine (vitamin $B_6$), ascorbic acid (vitamin C), pantothenic acid, biotin, folic acid, and vitamin $B_{12}$.

In the body, these vitamins are altered and converted into **coenzymes**, small nonprotein molecules that act in conjunction with enzymes. An example is the vitamin

highly specific. Unlike inorganic catalysts, most enzymes will catalyze just one, or a very few reactions. They do not trigger unwanted side reactions. Moreover, they can control reaction rates to keep different metabolic pathways balanced and in tune with the needs of the organism. For example, when an organism is well nourished, it can afford to break down some of its foodstuffs and store their energy in the form of ATP. All the steps involved in these breakdown, storage, and mobilization pathways are controlled by enzymes.

The ability of enzymes to act in highly specific ways is a direct consequence of their structure. All enzymes are globular proteins, large and complicated molecules composed of a number of amino acid chains. These chains are elaborately coiled and folded, giving each enzyme molecule a distinctive architecture. The actual work of catalysis takes place in a region of this structure called the **active site**. It usually consists of a few amino acid units, which construct an environment particularly suit-

| Vitamin | Coenzyme form | Participatory reactions |
|---------|---------------|-------------------------|
| "B₁" (Thiamine) | thiamine pyrophosphate | loss of $CO_2$ in oxidative pathways—oxidation of pyruvic acid to acetyl-CoA |
| "B₂" (Riboflavin) | FMN—flavin mononucleotide, FAD—flavin adenine dinucleotide | oxidation-reduction reactions, in carbohydrate, fat and protein metabolism as electron carriers |
| Niacin (Nicotinic acid) (Nicotinamide) | NAD—nicotinamide adenine dinucleotide, NADP—nicotinamide adenine dinucleotide phosphate | oxidation-reduction reactions |
| "B₆" (Pyridoxal) (Pyridoxine) (Pyridoxamine) | pyridoxal phosphate | transamination and decarboxylation of amino acids; fatty acid metabolism |
| "B₁₂" (Cyanocobalamine) | cobamide coenzyme | isomerizations, particular oxidation-reduction reactions |
| Pantothenic acid | coenzyme A | activation of carboxylic acids, in fatty acid metabolism |
| Folic acid | tetrahydrofolic acid | transfer of single carbon units, biosynthesis of serine and glycine |
| Biotin | biotin | $CO_2$ fixation |
| "C" (Ascorbic acid) | ascorbic acid | hydroxylations (addition of OH groups) |

3-5
Vitamins and coenzymes (common and chemical names). After vitamins are consumed, they are furhter modified, often by the addition of other chemical groups, to produce the coenzyme form which acts in metabolism.

niacin, or nicotinamine, which is converted into a coenzyme called nicotinamide adenine dinucleotide, or **NAD**. Structurally it resembles ATP. It also occurs in a phosphorylated form, abbreviated **NADP**. In oxidation reactions, either NAD or NADP will readily accept electrons and a hydrogen atom. The resulting NADH or NDAPH will donate electrons and a hydrogen atom just as readily. We shall see later that the capacity of both NAD and NADP to accept and donate electrons serves an important function in cellular processes.

**Hormones** are chemical messengers which regulate metabolism in multicellular organisms. They are secreted by particular glands or organs and transported to other sites in the organism. There they may regulate the activities of only certain cells or of a large and diverse population of cells. Hormonal effects are often much less restricted

or specific than those of a given enzyme, and they have several modes of action. Some hormones direct the growth or differentiation of tissue by stimulating the production of certain proteins. Others maintain the balance between two competing chemical processes.

In addition to these "natural" and essential regulatory molecules, many other substances can influence enzyme activity. In most cases their action is detrimental. Examples of this are heavy metals such as lead and mercury, which are toxic to organisms. They react with certain chemical groups in protein molecules to alter the three-dimensional conformation of the protein. As a result, the catalytic activity of enzymes is lost. But sometimes the harm done to one type of organism by an enzyme inhibitor serves a beneficial function for another type. Penicillin, for example, is a useful drug for many organisms, since it blocks an enzyme needed for construction of bacterial cell walls. The penicillin resembles the substrate of the enzyme and binds at the active site. Unlike a true substrate, however, it remains permanently bound, thus inactivating the enzyme molecule. Synthesis of the cell wall halts, and the bacterium dies. But animals harboring the bacteria are normally unharmed. Their cells have only membranes, not cell walls.

A final mechanism of enzymatic regulation is **feedback control**. In cells, the synthesis of a particular end product is achieved by means of a series of chemical reactions. Each reaction is controlled by an enzyme and results in an intermediate product. When the cell contains enough of the end product, the synthesis of the first intermediate product is slowed or stopped. This feedback control is the result of a specific interaction between the end product and the enzyme controlling synthesis of the first intermediate product.

## Photosynthesis

Photosynthesis is an **oxidation–reduction reaction**. This term refers to processes in which electrons are transferred from one substance to another. The substance that loses electrons (electron donor) is said to be oxidized or to undergo an oxidation. The substance that gains electrons (electron acceptor) is reduced and undergoes a reduction.

In photosynthesis, electrons are extracted from water, which is thereby oxidized, and donated to carbon dioxide, which is thereby reduced. Since the process takes place in an aqueous medium, hydrogen ions can be drawn from water at any time and combined with the transported electrons to form hydrogen atoms. Thus the net effect of the reaction is to transfer hydrogen atoms from water (leaving free oxygen) to carbon dioxide (producing carbohydrate).

This simple scheme can account for what flows into and out of the plant during

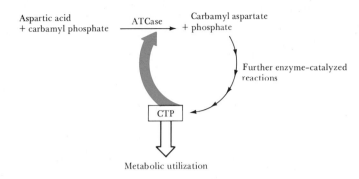

3-6

Feedback control in pyrimidine synthesis. The pyrimidine CTP (cytidine triphosphate) is formed through a series of enzymatic reactions acting on the result of an initial reaction between aspartic acid and carbamyl phosphate, which is catalyzed by the enzyme ATCase (aspartate transcarbamylase). As the reactions proceed, and a critical concentration of CTP is built up, it slows its own formation by inhibiting ATCase. When CTP concentration is sufficiently lowered by metabolic utilization, inhibition ceases, and synthesis is renewed. (The reaction as shown occurs specifically in the bacterium *Escherichia coli*.)

3-7

The structure of chlorophyll *a*, the principal form of chlorophyll found in higher plants. It consists of a magnesium atom within a porphyrin-like ring with various side chains. The porphyrin ring structure is also found in hemoglobin and in cytochromes, with an atom of iron substituted for magnesium within the ring.

photosynthesis. However, it hardly describes what goes on inside the leaves and other pigmented parts of the plant. Water does not give up electrons directly to carbon dioxide. In fact, the oxidation of water and the reduction of carbon dioxide need not proceed simultaneously. Neither reaction can continue for very long without the other, but they are distinct and can be made to take place independently. The processes associated with the oxidation of water can occur only when the plant is illuminated. They are therefore called **light reactions**. The reduction of carbon dioxide can occur in the absence of light, and is the ultimate result of the **dark reactions**.

## The light reactions

The substances in plants that absorb light are called **pigments**. The most important pigments are the chlorophylls. Various forms of these are found in some bacteria and in all photosynthetic plants, including algae and flowering plants. The role of chlorophyll in photosynthesis derives from its capacity to absorb light energy.

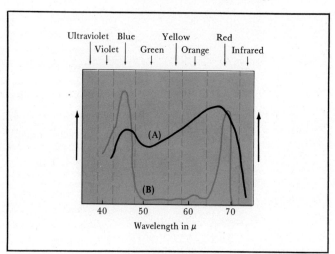

3-8
(A) The action spectrum shows relative amounts of photosynthetic activity occurring at various wavelengths of light. The highest amount of activity is found in blue and red light. (B) The absorption spectrum of chlorophyll *a* shows the relative amount of light absorbed at each wavelength. Blue and red light, the two colors with the highest photosynthetic activity, are the most highly absorbed.

Light consists of **photons**, or **quanta**, which are discrete units of energy. The energy is correlated with the wavelength of the light, and therefore with its color. The more energetic quanta correspond to the shorter wavelengths (violet and blue light), and those of lesser energy to the longer wavelengths (red light).

The absorption of light by a plant pigment can be measured at each of various wavelenths. When a complete set of measurements is made for all the wavelengths of visible light, the result is called the **absorption spectrum** of the pigment. The principal form of chlorophyll in higher plants has an absorption spectrum charac-

terized by strong peaks at both the long and the very short wavelengths. In other words, it absorbs blue and violet light and red light. However, it does not absorb the intermediate wavelengths very efficiently. These wavelengths pass through or are reflected. Since they comprise mainly the greens and yellows, most plants are green in color.

When a chlorophyll molecule absorbs light, one of its electrons becomes "excited." That is, its energy is increased. This energy is passed on from one chlorophyll molecule to another until it is finally captured by a specific chlorophyll molecule in a position to use the energy to do chemical work. (All of this must happen in about a billionth of a second, or the excitation energy will be reradiated and lost to the plant.) Two processes are triggered by this absorption of light. The first is **cyclic photophosphorylation**, which may be a surviving remnant of what was once the only system of photosynthesis. The other, **noncyclic photophosphorylation**, is probably a later evolutionary development. It is somewhat more efficient, and probably accounts for most of the energy stored by a plant.

*Cyclic photophosphorylation*  In this process, the specific chlorophyll molecule mentioned above temporarily loses its excited electron. The electron is handed off to a series of carrier molecules, including several kinds of protein molecules called **cytochromes**. During each transfer from one carrier to another, some of the energy of excitation is lost. When the electron is at last restored to the chlorophyll molecule, it has returned to its initial, energy-poor state.

In transfers between carriers, however, some of the energy dissipated by the electron is used to convert a molecule of ADP to ATP. Work is therefore done in the course of the cycle, and some portion of the light energy absorbed is stored in a chemical bond.

*Noncyclic photophosphorylation*  Cyclic photophosphorylation uses a functional

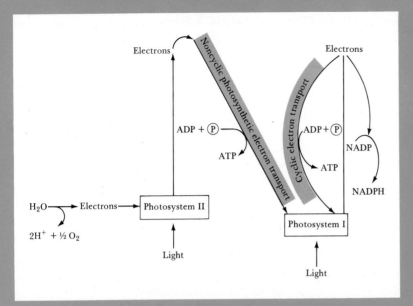

**3-9**

The light reactions. Photosystem I, with chlorophyll *a* as the primary pigment, can be either cyclic, returning the original excited electron pair to chlorophyll and forming ATP and ADP and ⓟ (inorganic phosphate) in the process; or noncyclic, with NADP gaining the electrons. Photosystem II involves equal amounts of chlorophyll *a* and *b*. The excited electron pair passes to chlorophyll *a* in Photosystem I. Photosystem II regains electrons by oxidizing water to $O_2$.

**3-10**

Dark reactions. Each complete turn of the Calvin cycle begins with the addition of $CO_2$ to ribulose diphosphate (RuDP). (The diagram follows the cycle of one of the 3 RuDPs). A six-carbon intermediate substance is formed, which immediately splits into two molecules of PGA. Each PGA then reacts with the products of the light reactions (ATP and NADPH) to form a molecule of PGAL. The PGAL can then combine to form carbohydrates for the organism's consumption, or be converted back into RuDP molecules with the help of ATP

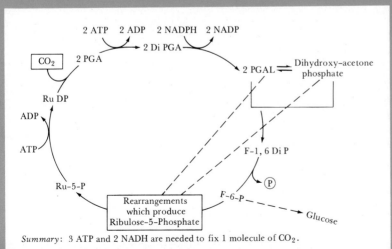

*Summary:* 3 ATP and 2 NADH are needed to fix 1 molecule of $CO_2$.

unit of molecules and pigments known as **photosystem I**. The noncyclic process uses additional molecules and pigments (of a different absorption spectrum) known as **photosystem II**. In the noncyclic process, light is absorbed by the chlorophyll in photosystem II. It is passed down a sequence of carrier molecules similar to that in cyclic photophosphorylation. Also, as in the cyclic process, ATP is generated from ADP. But instead of being restored to the original chlorophyll molecule in photosystem II, the electron is passed to the chlorophyll in photosystem I. (Photosystem II regains electrons by oxidizing water to $O_2$.)

To complete the process of noncyclic photophosphorylation, another quantum of light must be absorbed by the pigments in photosystem I. This causes another excited electron to be transmitted from the chlorophyll along a chain of carrier molecules, and generates more ATP. But instead of returning to the chlorophyll, the electron ultimately reaches the coenzyme known as NADP. When NADP receives two such electrons, it joins them with a hydrogen ion taken from the aqueous environment to form NADPH.

The formation of ATP and NADPH completes the light reactions of noncyclic photophosphorylation. The net effect of the process is the transfer of electrons (and hydrogen atoms) from water to NADPH. But their route through the photosynthetic apparatus is exceedingly complex.

## The dark reactions

The remaining process in photosynthesis is conversion of carbon dioxide into carbohydrate. It does not require light. The complicated series of reactions which make up the process was discovered by Melvin Calvin and his colleagues. Calvin and his co-workers found that $CO_2$ initially joins to a sugar compound. The resulting substance then immediately splits into two molecules of an acid abbreviated **PGA**.

PGA reacts with the products of the light reactions. It is phosphorylated by ATP and reduced by NADPH to yield **PGAL**, a molecule with many uses in the cell. PGAL can be broken down again to $CO_2$, yielding up its energy. It can also be employed to regenerate the sugar compound needed to continue incorporation of carbon dioxide. Most important, PGAL can be combined in multiple units to form glucose, starch, cellulose, and other carbohydrates. These serve the long-term energy needs of the cell, and are important to the structural integrity of most plants.

## Anaerobic ATP production

For most autotrophic organisms, and ultimately the heterotrophs as well, photosynthesis provides all the organic substances needed to sustain life. But to benefit from this, the cells of both types of organism must be able to degrade these substances chemically in such a way that their energy can be released and captured in a usable form.

Glycolysis and fermentation are two processes which partially break down complex organic molecules to liberate some of their free energy. Both processes involve sequential chemical reactions, each of which is catalyzed by a specific enzyme. Both result in the formation of ATP, the ultimate energy-exchange medium. And neither process depends upon the presence of oxygen.

### Glycolysis

Carbohydrates, such as glucose, are relatively stable under cellular conditions, and will not break down at any appreciable rate. However, in the process of **glycolysis**, carbohydrates are activated and can be made to undergo energy-releasing reactions. The activation is accomplished by phosphorylation. An enzyme catalyzes a transfer of the terminal phosphate group of an ATP molecule to one end of the glucose six-carbon chain. In the next step, the phosphorylated glucose undergoes a structural change to become a different six-carbon sugar phosphate—fructose phosphate. Subsequently, a second ATP molecule contributes a phosphate group to the other end of the glucose chain. The resulting fructose diphosphate is then split into 2 molecules of PGAL. Each of these molecules contains a single phosphate group.

So far in this sequence, each reaction has occurred in the presence of an appropriate enzyme. The glucose molecule has been split into 2 smaller molecules, but as yet no energy has been released. In fact, 2 molecules of ATP have been consumed. But in the subsequent steps, the investment of energy is more than recovered.

Each PGAL molecule is oxidized by the coenzyme NAD, which is thereby reduced to NADH. During this reaction, another phosphate group is added to each PGAL molecule, so that they now have 2 phosphate groups apiece. (Since the energy released in the oxidation reaction is used to drive this phosphorylation, no more ATP is used.) The resulting molecules then undergo a sequence of enzymatic reactions during which each of their phosphate groups is transferred to a molecule of ADP. The net result is the formation of 4 ATP molecules, while each PGAL molecule is converted into another type of compound, **pyruvic acid**.

There is little difference between the amount of energy stored in the glucose molecule and the amount stored in the pyruvic acid molecules. But it is obvious that more ATP has been gained than lost. Two ATP molecules are used in initial priming reactions, but 4 ATP molecules are ultimately produced. This represents a net gain of 2 ATP molecules for each glucose molecule consumed. The remaining energy derived from the conversion process is either stored in the 2 NADH or released as heat.

### Fermentation

Glycolysis can proceed in the presence or absence of oxygen. We have noted that if no oxygen is present, NAD may be used as the

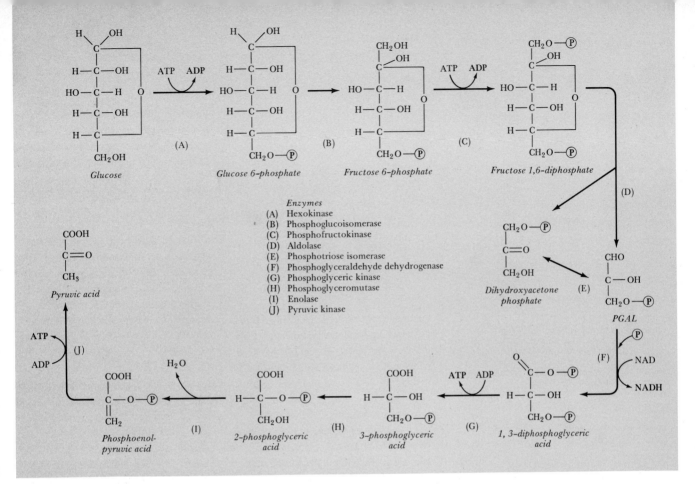

**3-11**

Glycolysis. (A) Glucose is phosphorylated, forming glucose-6-phosphate. (B) The atoms of this molecule are rearranged to form fructose-6-phosphate. (C) Through another phosphorylation, the molecule is converted to fructose 1.6-diphosphate. (D) It is then split into PGAL and another three-carbon sugar. (E) The latter sugar is also usually converted to PGAL. (F) Each PGAL is transformed by the addition of inorganic phosphate and by the reduction of NAD to NADH to form 1,3-diphosphoglyceric acid. (G) ADP picks up a phosphate to form ATP. (H) The resulting 3-phosphoglyceric acid is rearranged to form 2-phosphoglyceric acid. (I) $H_2O$ is given off, forming phosphoenol-pyruvic acid. (J) Another ATP is formed, giving rise to pyruvic acid.

oxidizing agent (electron acceptor). Moreover, in the absence of oxygen the products of glycolysis (pyruvic acid and NADH) react with each other. Pyruvic acid or its products are reduced by NADH to either lactic acid or ethyl alchol. The NADH itself is oxidized, thereby regenerating the NAD coenzyme needed for glycolysis. When this occurs, the entire pathway from glucose to end products—lactic acid or ethyl alcohol—is called **fermentation**.

The reduction of pyruvic acid to lactic acid occurs in some microorganisms and in certain cells of multicellular animals. For example, the contractile activity of muscle tissue requires considerable quantities of energy. This energy is derived from ATP molecules, which in turn are produced by

oxidation of glucose. Normally, the oxidizing agent is oxygen, which is supplied by the action of the heart and lungs. However, during periods of sustained muscular activity the muscle cells need more oxygen than they can get. When this happens, the muscle cells must produce ATP by the fermentation of glucose (the source of which is glycogen contained in muscles). The anaerobic breakdown of glucose to pyruvic acid is followed by the reduction of pyruvic acid to lactic acid. A feeling of soreness and fatigue in overworked muscles is partially the result of an accumulation of lactic acid.

Alcoholic fermentation may occur in plant cells and many microorganisms. In this process, the biochemical pathway for

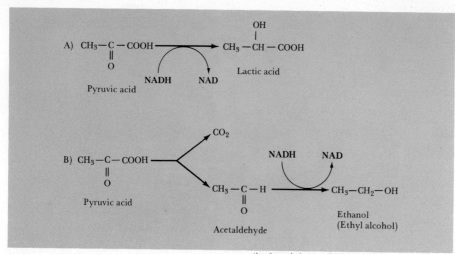

A) $CH_3-\underset{\underset{O}{\|}}{C}-COOH \longrightarrow CH_3-\underset{\underset{OH}{|}}{CH}-COOH$

Pyruvic acid     **NADH**    **NAD**     Lactic acid

B) $CH_3-\underset{\underset{O}{\|}}{C}-COOH \longrightarrow$   $CO_2$

$CH_3-\underset{\underset{O}{\|}}{C}-H \longrightarrow CH_3-CH_2-OH$

Pyruvic acid    **NADH**    **NAD**

Acetaldehyde     Ethanol (Ethyl alcohol)

**3-12**
Anaerobic regeneration of electron acceptor. (A) Lactic acid is produced in higher animal cells from pyruvic acid via reduction by NADH. (B) In yeast cells, pyruvic acid initially forms $CO_2$ and acetaldehyde. The acetaldehyde, through its reduction by NADH, forms ethanol (ethyl alcohol).

**3-13**
Electron micrograph of mitochondrion from bat pancreas. Variations in the number and structural complexity of cristae appear to be related to the energy demands of a given cell. For example, if the energy needs are great, there will be a correspondingly greater number of cristae. These serve to augment the surface area of the internal membrane and thus multiply the functional capacity of the mitochondrion. (See Oxidative phosphorylation)

the breakdown of glucose to pyruvic acid is the same as in muscle fermentation. It also results in the same net gain of 2 ATP molecules. But the ultimate fate of pyruvic acid is different. NAD is regenerated by a process that culminates in the production of $CO_2$ and a molecule of ethyl alcohol. When yeast is deprived of enough oxygen, it carries out this latter kind of fermentation. This process is effectively utilized in the production of both alcoholic beverages and baked goods. In the wine industry, ethyl alcohol is the important product. The rising of dough, on the other hand, depends on the gaseous carbon dioxide resulting from the fermentative process.

## Aerobic ATP production

Anaerobic glycolysis and fermentation are essentially inefficient processes. Their end products—pyruvic acid, lactic acid, or ethyl alcohol—contain only slightly less energy than the starting material. In other words, only a small amount of the stored energy of the starting material is liberated as free energy.

Far more efficient is the process by which organic substances are broken down completely to inorganic molecules. This process requires the presence of molecular oxygen. Known as **cellular respiration**, it is the most important method of ATP production in animals and most microorganisms.

### Oxidative phosphorylation

Both fermentation and respiration make use of the products of glycolysis—pyruvic acid and NADH. In fermentation, pyruvic acid is reduced by NADH. But in respiration, the ultimate electron acceptor for NADH is oxygen. However, NADH does not directly interact with oxygen. Instead, there is an **electron transport chain** made up of several carriers (mostly cytochromes) which transport electrons from NADH to $O_2$. In this way, the energy of the oxidation reaction can be trapped in the phosphorylation of ADP to form ATP. Because this phosphorylation is fueled by the oxidation of NADH, this part of the respiratory process is termed **oxidative phosphorylation**.

As in photophosphorylation, the electron transport system of respiration is organelle-bound. The preliminaries to the process—the reactions of glycolysis—take place in the cytoplasm. But oxidative phosphorylation itself is confined to the mitochondria.

This compartmentalization of reactions has an important effect on the overall ATP yield. When NADH is *inside* the mitochondria, every pair of electrons it passes along the carriers to $O_2$ goes through all the ATP-forming steps of the electron transport chain. The result is that 3 ATPs are formed. But the NADH resulting from glycolysis is

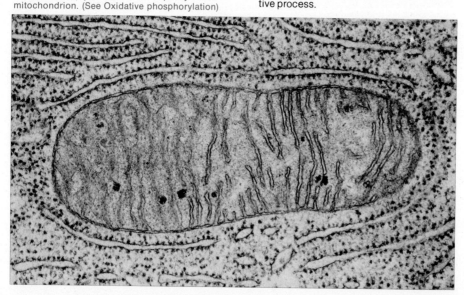

located in the cytoplasm. It must therefore transfer its electrons to certain carriers which are able to pass through the mitochondrial membrane. Some energy is lost during this transfer, and consequently the electrons enter the electron transport chain at a point *after* the first ATP-forming step. The net effect is that each of the two NADH molecules formed during glycolysis yields only 2 ATPs. Under aerobic conditions, then, 6 ATP molecules are formed in the process of degrading glucose to pyruvic acid. Of these, 2 result from glycolysis itself, and 4 from oxidative phosphorylation.

## The citric acid cycle

When oxygen is present, the pyruvic acid product of glycolysis is broken down all the way to $CO_2$ and $H_2O$. This releases the bulk of the 686 kilocalories stored in the original glucose molecule. A sizable fraction of it is used in ATP production. The entire sequence of reactions involved in breaking down pyruvic acid takes place in the mitochondria. It is a cyclical process, beginning and ending with citric acid. For this reason, it is often called the **citric acid cycle**. It is also termed the **Krebs cycle** after Sir Hans Krebs, the English biochemist who first discovered this important biochemical pathway.

Before entering the cycle, the 2 molecules of pyruvic acid resulting from glycolysis are converted into 2 new molecules called **acetyl-CoA**. In this process (which occurs in the mitochondria) electrons are released. This allows 6 more ATPs to be formed via oxidative phosphorylation. Each acetyl-CoA molecule then joins with a four-carbon compound to form citric acid. The oxidative reactions of the cycle now begin. By the end of two turns of the cycle, the two acetyl-CoA molecules are completely oxidized to carbon dioxide and water. With each turn of the cycle the four-carbon compound is regenerated, enabling it to combine with new molecules of acetyl-CoA.

During the oxidative reactions, 3 NAD are reduced to 3 NADH for each acetyl-CoA

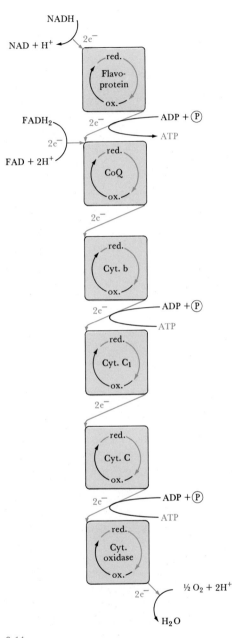

**3-14**
Oxidative phosphorylation. Initially, NADH is oxidized by a flavoprotein. A pair of electrons pass "downhill," reducing acceptors—coenzyme Q and various cytochromes—with the released energy at transference used at three specific sites to form ATP. An additional electron donor active in this process is $FADH_2$. Since it has less reducing power than NADH, the first acceptor it can reduce is coenzyme Q. The first ATP production site is thus skipped, and only 2 ATPs are formed.

traveling the cycle. As noted, the oxidation reactions occur within the mitochondria. Thus the 6 NADH that are formed lead to the production of 18 ATPs via oxidative phosphorylation. (You will recall that every pair of electrons donated by NADH *inside* the mitochondria yields 3 ATPs.) Also, 1 FAD is reduced to $FADH_2$ for each acetyl-CoA traveling the cycle. (FAD is an abbreviation for one of the coenzyme forms of riboflavin.) However, the 2 $FADH_2$ that are formed yield only 4 ATPs. This is because the electrons which they donate enter the chain after the first ATP-forming step.

Within the citric acid cycle itself another 2 ATPs are formed. This happens during one of the oxidation reactions.

## Energy yield

The energy products of cellular respiration can now be summarized and totaled. In the first part of the process, glucose is broken down to pyruvic acid. This yields 2 ATPs and 2 NADH. The oxidation of NADH via the oxidative phosphorylation chain produces 4 more ATP molecules. The breakdown of 2 molecules of pyruvic acid to 2 molecules of acetyl-CoA in the mitochondria produces an additional 6 ATPs. Finally, in the breakdown of 2 acetyl-CoA, 24 molecules of ATP are formed. (Of these, 22 result from oxidative phosphorylation). Thus a net sum of 36 molecules of ATP are formed for every molecule of glucose degraded to carbon dioxide and water.

The free energy released in the conversion of a molecule of ATP to ADP is about 7.3 kilocalories. So in the aerobic breakdown of a molecule of glucose, approximately 262.8 kilocalories are conserved in the form of chemical energy. Since about 686 kilocalories of energy are stored in a molecule of glucose, the overall efficiency of cellular respiration is about 38 percent.

The production of energy from carbohydrates is not the only service provided by the biochemical pathways of cellular respiration. Some of the intermediate products of the process can be drawn off and used in

3-15

Citric acid cycle. Strictly speaking, pyruvic acid is not part of the cycle. It is first converted to acetyl-CoA. During this process, it is changed from a three-carbon structure to a two-carbon acetyl group. Coenzyme A is bound to the acetyl group; $CO_2$ is released; and NAD converts to NADH.

Acetyl-CoA enters the cycle by combining with oxaloacetic acid. The coenzyme A group is released and citric acid is formed. Citric acid is converted to isocitric acid. During the conversion of isocitric acid to $\alpha$-ketoglutaric acid, $CO_2$ is formed, and NAD forms NADH. The next step is the formation of succinyl-CoA. During the reaction, which involves NAD and CoA as cofactors, $CO_2$ and NADH are formed.

The very next reaction involves the addition of guanosine diphosphate (GDP) and inorganic phosphate. Succinic acid, GTP, and ATP are formed; CoA is released. In the next reaction two hydrogen atoms are removed from succinic acid, FAD accepts them to form $FADH_2$, and fumaric acid is formed. $H_2O$ is then added to fumaric acid to form malic acid. The cycle is completed when malic acid is oxidized to form oxaloacetic acid, with NAD converted to NADH in the process.

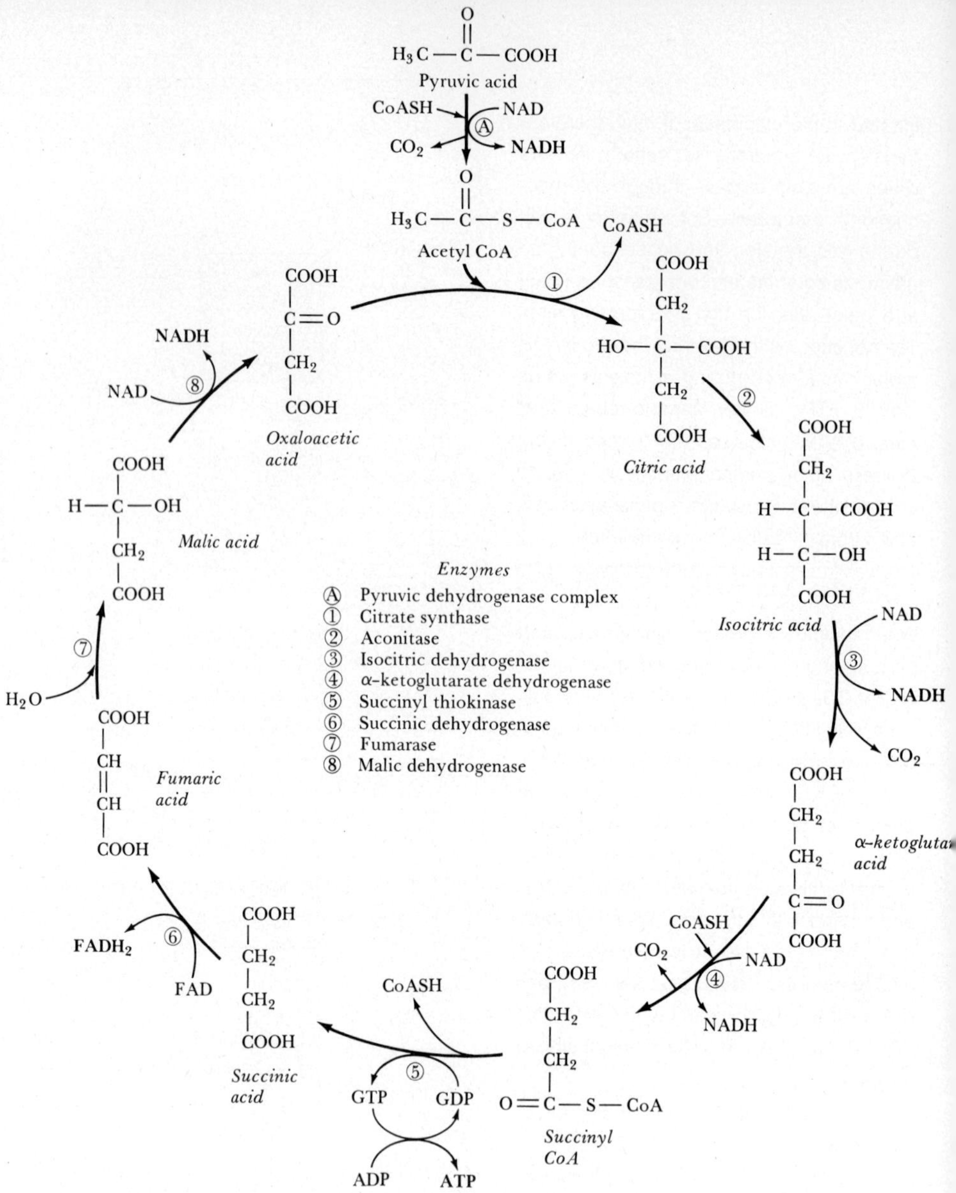

**Enzymes**

| | |
|---|---|
| A | Pyruvic dehydrogenase complex |
| 1 | Citrate synthase |
| 2 | Aconitase |
| 3 | Isocitric dehydrogenase |
| 4 | $\alpha$-ketoglutarate dehydrogenase |
| 5 | Succinyl thiokinase |
| 6 | Succinic dehydrogenase |
| 7 | Fumarase |
| 8 | Malic dehydrogenase |

Pyruvic acid — Acetyl CoA — Oxaloacetic acid — Citric acid — Isocitric acid — $\alpha$-ketoglutaric acid — Succinyl CoA — Succinic acid — Fumaric acid — Malic acid

the manufacture, of various other cellular materials. These include fatty acids and some amino acids. The process of cellular respiration also couples the metabolism of carbohydrates with the breakdown of other types of organic compound.

PGAL, for example, is an intermediate product of both the metabolism of glucose and the metabolism of glycerol, which is a component of fats. Once the PGAL has been formed in the process of fat metabolism, it can enter the biochemical pathway of glycolysis at the same point at which PGAL is formed in glucose metabolism. Then it undergoes the remaining series of reactions which characterize glycolysis. Proteins also enter the degradative pathway at a different point. But, like fats and carbohydrates, they meet their ultimate fate in the citric acid cycle. In other words, organisms which rely on noncarbohydrate substances for energy production do not need unique metabolic mechanisms. Their breakdown products can be channeled into the biochemical pathways already available for carbohydrate metabolism.

summary

Living cells must continually extract energy from the environment in order to perform a variety of tasks and maintain a highly ordered state. Autotrophs use radiant energy in synthesizing organic molecules. These molecules store chemical potential energy useful to both autotrophs and heterotrophs. Chemical potential energy is liberated as free energy by means of oxidation-reduction reactions. Aerobic organisms use molecular oxygen to break down organic molecules completely. They are inherently more efficient at extracting the energy of foodstuffs than anaerobic organisms, which cannot use oxygen and so can effect only a partial breakdown.

Exergonic processes are those which release free energy. Endergonic processes consume free energy, either by converting it into new chemical potential energy (biosynthesis) or into other forms of energy (such as muscle contraction). The two types of process are linked by ATP. Exergonic reactions can be used to synthesize ATP molecules. Endergonic reactions can derive energy by breaking down ATP. In the former reactions, ADP is phosphorylated to form ATP. In the latter reaction, ATP undergoes hydrolysis. Three methods of ATP production are photophosphorylation, oxidative phosphorylation, and fermentation. The chemical reactions involved in ATP production are localized in specific subcellular compartments or regions. But ATP units can be dispatched to any other part of the cell to serve immediate energy demands.

Enzymes catalyze and regulate virtually all intracellular chemical processes. Enzymes are proteins which enhance the rate of a chemical reaction, without themselves being altered in the process. They lower the energy of activation—that is, the energy needed to start the reaction. They are highly specific, and their reaction rates are regulated to correspond to the needs of the organism. Specificity is a consequence of structure. An enzyme has an active site which recognizes its substrate, the specific substance with which the enzyme reacts.

Enzymes may be regulated by other substances, including other enzymes. Inhibitors tend to reduce the activity of certain enzymes. Coenzymes, altered forms of vitamins, act in conjunction with enzymes in certain chemical reactions. Hormones, chemical substances outside the cell, regulate metabolism in multicellular organisms. In feedback control, the end product of a series of reactions inhibits the activity of the enzyme needed in the first reaction of the series.

Photophosphorylation occurs during photosynthesis. It is an oxidation–reduction process in which electrons (and their hydrogen atoms) are transferred from water (leaving free oxygen) to carbon dioxide (producing carbohydrate). The light reactions produce NADPH and ATP. These are used in the dark reactions to reduce $CO_2$ to carbohydrate and other organic compounds.

Two processes which release free energy through partial breakdown of organic molecules are glycolysis and fermentation. Both are anaerobic processes which use the coenzyme NAD as the oxidizing agent. In glycolysis, each glucose molecule is degraded to pyruvic acid. This results in a net gain of ATP. Fermentation results in the same net gain of ATP molecules. But pyruvic acid is further reduced to lactic acid or ethyl alcohol. Also, NAD is regenerated.

Because it occurs in the presence of molecular oxygen, cellular respiration results in the complete breakdown of organic substances to $CO_2$ and water. The anaerobic processes produce only 2 molecules of ATP for every molecule of glucose. But cellular respiration, utilizing oxidative phosphorylation and the citric acid cycle, produces 36 molecules of ATP. All of the reactions involved in oxidative phosphorylation and the citric acid cycle occur within the mitochondria. Glycolysis occurs in the cytoplasm. The breakdown products of noncarbohydrate substances, such as fats and proteins, can be channeled into the glycolytic and respiratory pathways.

**4 cell replication**

*mnis cellula e cellula*—all cells arise from other cells. This postulate was first advanced by Virchow in 1858. It became the keystone of the evolving cell theory, and soon was dramatically proved by Pasteur's experiments of the early 1860s. As we saw in our introduction, the ability to reproduce is central to the best definition of life we can devise. All cells reproduce by division, two daughter cells forming from the division of a single parent cell. But even the simplest living cell is an intricately organized entity. It constantly performs hundreds of complex chemical transactions. So the division of a cell to form two identical daughter cells cannot be as simple a process as, for instance, splitting a crystal into two identical smaller crystals.

All the activity of the cell—everything it is and does—is controlled by one set of master plans. In eucaryotic cells, these plans are located within the nucleus. This has been demonstrated by numerous experiments. For instance, if we remove the nucleus from a unicellular animal, the creature may survive for a week or more. For a while it may even seem to function normally. Presumably enzymes are still present in the cell, produced in accordance with previous directions from the nucleus and still maintaining the processes of life. But after a few days the organism starts to lose its ability to perform such vital activities as feeding and locomotion. Eventually, it dies. Interestingly, this process of decay is reversible. If a new nucleus is implanted soon enough, the animal may resume its normal pattern of activity as if nothing had happened.

Other experiments have shown that even the structure of the cell is dictated by the nucleus. This was shown quite dramatically in a series of classic experiments by Joachim Hammerling. Hammerling worked with two different types of *Acetabularia*, an unusually large unicellular alga, measuring 1 to 2 inches in height. The cells of *Acetabularia* have a characteristic crown atop a long spindly stalk. The stalk is supported by

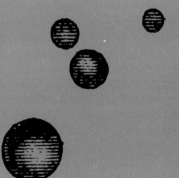

**4-1**
Found in warm marine waters is the one-celled alga, *Acetabularia mediterranea*. The cap-like structures float near the surface of the water, catching the light and enabling the plant to carry on photosynthesis.

a root-like base which contains the cell nucleus. The crown structure of *Acetabularia mediterranea* is umbrella-like. *A. crenulata* is divided into petals. These algae are able to regenerate their crowns if their stalks break. Hammerling succeeded in grafting pieces of stalk from one species onto severed bases of the other species. He thus produced two types of crownless hybrid. Each had the base and nucleus of one species, and the stalk of the other.

Hammerling found that the crowns which these hybrids regenerated did not match the stalks from which they grew. Instead, they reflected the character of the nucleus in the base. *Crenulata* nuclei produced *crenulata* crowns, and *mediterranea* nuclei produced *mediterranea* crowns, regardless of the nature of the stalk.

Successful reproduction, then, must depend on some mechanism which distributes the nuclear master plans in such a way that each new organism receives all of the vital information. Only in this way can genetic continuity be maintained from generation to generation. The essence of cell division is an intricate and orderly sequence of events that ensures the proper distribution of hereditary material to the daughter cells.

## Mitotic cell division

The process which produces two identical daughter cells by division of a single parent cell is called **mitotic cell division**. Almost all single-celled eucaryotic organisms reproduce asexually through mitotic division. Within multicellular animals and plants, this same process is necessary for growth and regeneration. Embryos develop from a single fertilized egg cell by mitotic division. And when tissue cells in the mature organism die or are damaged by injury, they are replaced by the mitotic division of other cells.

### Mitosis

Mitotic division comprises two processes. **Cytokinesis** is the splitting of the cell's cy-

toplasm, which takes place during the last stages of mitotic division. It is as a result of cytokinesis that the cell as a whole actually divides. The heart of mitotic division, however, is **mitosis** — the creation of two new identical nuclei for these daughter cells, each bearing the same genetic information as the parent. The bearers of this information within the nucleus are the chromosomes. Before the start of mitosis, the chromosomes are replicated by the cell so that a full set is available for each of the daughter nuclei. Thus mitosis is a series of steps by which pairs of identical chromosomes are sorted, separated, and distributed to the new nuclei.

*The chromosomes*   Except during mitosis, the chromosomes are not visible as separate structures under the light microscope. But with the aid of certain stains, the observer can see a dense tangle of thin dark threads called **chromatin**. This gives the nucleus a mottled, granular appearance. The thread-like chromosomes are composed largely of DNA — the long molecule that contains the genetic information of the cell in the form of a chemical code.

At the start of mitosis, the chromatin fibers begin to condense, coiling and recoiling themselves like the cord of a telephone receiver. In the early phases of mitosis the chromosomes are still long and thin, but have shortened enough to be visible as a number of separate strands. As mitosis proceeds, the individual chromosomes become even shorter and more compact. Under high magnification we can now see that each chromosome consists of two strands, held together by a small structure called the **centromere**. The centromere has a precise location on each chromosome. It is sometimes near the center, but often closer to one end. The two strands are called **chromatids**. They are identical, the result of the replication process that took place before mitosis began. These chromatids must be separated to form the chromosomes of the new nuclei.

For descriptive convenience, mitosis has been subdivided into a number of phases. Each is characterized by particular events that occur within the nucleus as the process runs its course. The phases were first named by Walther Flemming, who studied mitosis in detail during the late nineteenth century. The principal phases of mitosis are called **prophase**, **metaphase**, **anaphase**, and **telophase**. We should remember, however, that the entire process is continuous. There are no sharply distinct boundaries between phases.

*Prophase* The first stage of mitosis begins when the chromosomes appear under the microscope as clearly visible strands. The chromosomes become progressively shorter through the prophase and reach their maximum contraction in the metaphase. Meanwhile other changes occur within the cell. In the cells of animals and lower plants the two **centrioles** move toward opposite ends of the nucleus. There they will serve as poles, from which masses of microtubule fibers radiate in all directions. Some of these fibers merge with others from the opposite pole. They form a structure called the **spindle**, which surrounds the chromosomes. During late prophase the nucleolus (or nucleoli) usually disappears. Prophase ends as the nuclear membrane also breaks down, and the chromosomes are no longer partitioned off from the cytoplasm.

*Metaphase* In metaphase the chromosomes move to the central region of the cell. During this stage, chromosomal fibers from each pole of the spindle become attached to the centromeres. At the end of metaphase the centromeres divide, and the chromatids become separate daughter chromosomes.

*Anaphase* During anaphase one set of the new daughter chromosomes migrates toward each pole of the spindle. The chromosomes are moved toward the poles as the chromosomal fibers shorten. If a chro-

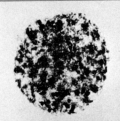
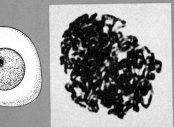

Interphase
The cell in this phase is undergoing no division process at all.

Early prophase
The chromosomes are visible as discrete strands in the nucleus.

Middle prophase
Formation of the spindle begins and the nuclear membrane fades.

Metaphase
Chromosomes align in the equatorial plane; spindle fibers attach to centromeres.

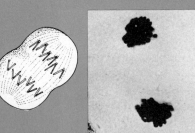

Anaphase
New daughter chromosomes migrate toward each pole of the spindle.

Telophase
At opposite spindle poles, chromosomes uncoil and nuclear membranes form.

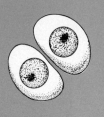
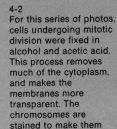

Daughter cells
Each has the same number of chromosomes as the parent cell.

4-2
For this series of photos, cells undergoing mitotic division were fixed in alcohol and acetic acid. This process removes much of the cytoplasm, and makes the membranes more transparent. The chromosomes are stained to make them more distinct.

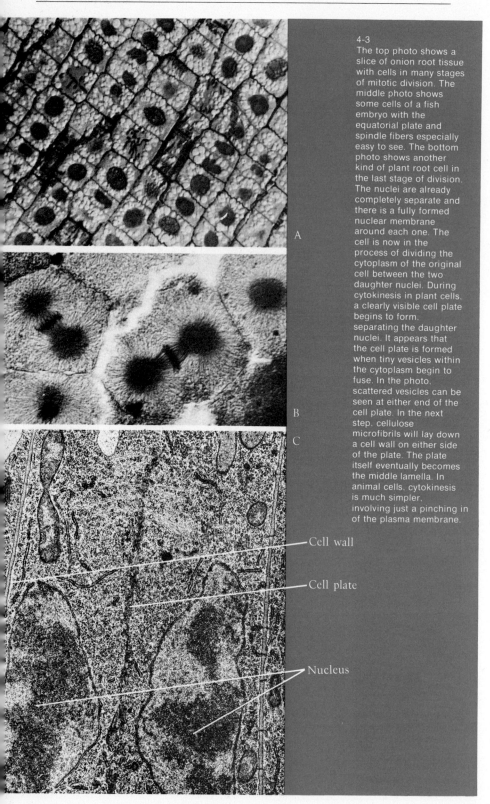

**4-3**
The top photo shows a slice of onion root tissue with cells in many stages of mitotic division. The middle photo shows some cells of a fish embryo with the equatorial plate and spindle fibers especially easy to see. The bottom photo shows another kind of plant root cell in the last stage of division. The nuclei are already completely separate and there is a fully formed nuclear membrane around each one. The cell is now in the process of dividing the cytoplasm of the original cell between the two daughter nuclei. During cytokinesis in plant cells, a clearly visible cell plate begins to form, separating the daughter nuclei. It appears that the cell plate is formed when tiny vesicles within the cytoplasm begin to fuse. In the photo, scattered vesicles can be seen at either end of the cell plate. In the next step, cellulose microfibrils will lay down a cell wall on either side of the plate. The plate itself eventually becomes the middle lamella. In animal cells, cytokinesis is much simpler, involving just a pinching in of the plasma membrane.

A

B

C

Cell wall

Cell plate

Nucleus

mosome breaks, the portion without a centromere cannot move toward a pole and is lost.

*Telophase* The next phase begins with the arrival of the daughter chromosomes at the opposite poles of the spindle. At this point the new nuclei begin to take form. The processes which occur are the reverse of the changes occurring at prophase. The chromosomes become uncoiled, new nuclear membranes form, and the nucleoli reappear. The centrioles are duplicated, and the fibers of the mitotic apparatus disappear. Telophase and anaphase are the longest stages of the mitotic sequence. Together they comprise about 80 percent of the process.

*Cytokinesis* Division of the cytoplasm may begin during anaphase or telophase. It is completed with telophase. In animal cells the plasma membrane pinches inward until it completely divides the cytoplasm. The walls of plant cells are too rigid to undergo cytokinesis by the pinching method. Instead, they form a barrier called a **cell plate**. The cell plate begins in the center of the cell, halfway between the two newly formed nuclei. It extends outward until its edges fuse with the cell wall, dividing the cell in two.

## The cell cycle

The process of mitosis occurs within a larger framework known as the **cell cycle**. A cell newly formed by mitotic division grows, prepares for division, and divides in its turn. Most cells grow to nearly twice their initial size before dividing again. The offspring are thus the same size as was the parent cell when it divided. The length of this cycle varies considerably from organism to organism and tissue to tissue. It may also be affected by external conditions such as temperature. There are unicellular eucaryotes that double their numbers every few hours. Typical procaryotes require even less time for their cycles. Some bacteria, for instance, will divide every 20 minutes under

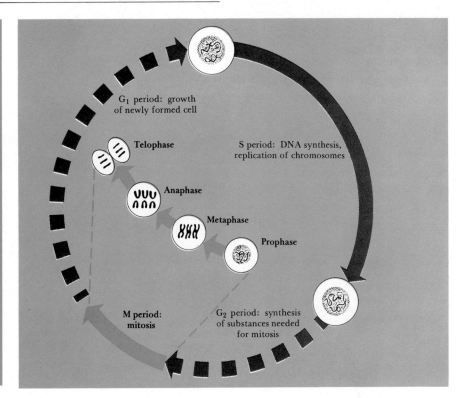

4-4
The diagram shows the cell cycle. The first stage of the four-part cycle that all eucaryotic cells undergo is called the $G_1$ (first growth) period. During this time, the daughter cells grow to full size. The S (for synthesis) period follows, a time of DNA and chromosomal protein synthesis. During the $G_2$ period, specific molecules needed for cell division are synthesized. The cell next enters the M period, the phase of mitotic division.

$G_1$ period: growth of newly formed cell

Telophase

S period: DNA synthesis, replication of chromosomes

Anaphase

Metaphase

Prophase

M period: mitosis

$G_2$ period: synthesis of substances needed for mitosis

favorable conditions. At the other extreme, the cells of certain plants divide only about once a week. Multicellular organisms even have some specialized cells that function throughout the organism's lifetime without ever reproducing at all. The cells of the human central nervous system, for example, never divide after reaching maturity. But most cells do divide. The cycle length for average cells ranges from 10 to 24 hours.

*Interphase*  The period during which the cell is not actually dividing is called **interphase**. It is typically much longer than the period of division itself, which averages only an hour or two and so accounts for no more than 5 or 10 percent of the cell cycle. Interphase is sometimes described as a "resting" state. This is hardly an apt term, however. During interphase the cell is not only carrying on all its normal metabolic functions, but is also growing and preparing for its eventual division.

The interphase period can be divided into three stages. Immediately after the "birth" of a new cell by division there is a period of growth designated $G_1$. Next comes a phase during which the cell's chromosomes are duplicated. This process cannot be seen with the microscope, but we can trace its progress by chemical means. During this period, called **S**, growth continues. Molecules for the new chromosomes are also synthesized. DNA molecules are synthesized within the nucleus and protein molecules within the cytoplasm. There follows another period, $G_2$, which is generally shorter. During this phase the cell does not usually become larger, since it has already reached full size. But at this time it synthesizes certain molecules required for the reproductive process. On completion of the $G_2$ stage, the process of mitotic division, **M**, commences, resulting in the production of two daughter cells. Then the cycle begins again.

The duration of the different phases of the cell cycle varies considerably with different kinds of cell. The M period is the shortest, while $G_1$ and S are the longest.

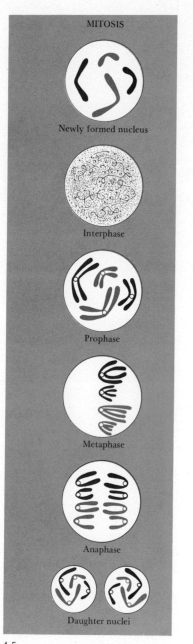

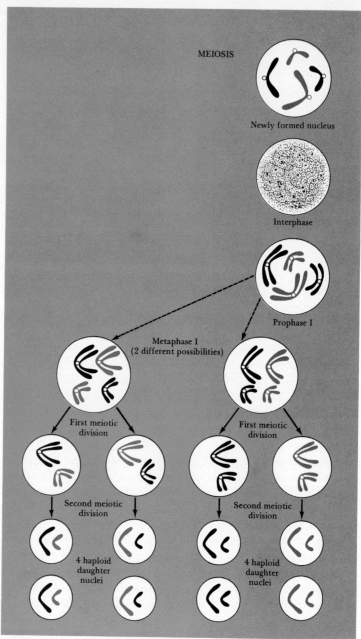

4-5
Diagrams summarizing the processes of mitosis and meiosis.

The latter have a typical duration of 6 to 8 hours each—30 to 40 percent of the cycle. The $G_2$ cycle usually accounts for only about 15 or 20 percent of the total.

Certain tissues of multicellular organisms maintain a reserve of cells arrested in the $G_2$ phase. Since these cells have already duplicated their chromosomes, they are ready to divide quickly in case of injury to the organism. Thus fresh cells can be produced on very short notice to replace or repair damaged tissues. The generative cells of some fungal spores and in the pollen of many plants also have protracted $G_2$ periods. These reproductive cells hold off division until they are in a suitable environment for the organism's development.

$G_1$ is the most variable, the most important, and the least understood of the three interphase periods. During $G_1$ the future course of the cell is determined by mechanisms about which little is yet known. Cells of multicellular organisms that undergo differentiation do so during the $G_1$ period. Cells that will not divide again remain in $G_1$ for their entire lives. Those cells with unusually long cycles (except for those frozen in the $G_2$ "holding pattern") spend most of the extra time in $G_1$. Division itself, though it follows the $G_2$ period, is in effect initiated during $G_1$, since the chemical signal that instructs the cell to begin duplicating its chromosomes is given at some point in the $G_1$ phase. Once that process is begun and the cell enters the S phase, there is no turning back; the cell must divide. We see, then, that a fuller understanding of the timing and control mechanisms of $G_1$ cells might shed light on many important areas of biological research, including embryonic development, cell differentiation, aging, and cancer.

# Meiotic cell division

Although organisms exhibit a wide variety of reproductive patterns, they all can be divided into two basic categories: **sexual** and **asexual**. In asexual reproduction a single organism gives rise to offspring with characteristics essentially identical to those of the parent. Asexual reproduction generally involves only mitotic cell division. But mitotic division is not the only kind that cells can undergo. For the sexual reproduction of organisms, another kind of division is necessary: **meiotic cell division**.

Meiotic cell division results in the production of specialized cells known as **gametes**. In animals, the female gametes are called **egg cells (ova)**. The male gametes are called **sperm cells (spermatozoa)**. A new individual of the species is conceived when a male gamete fuses with a female gamete. This fusion creates a single cell known as the **zygote**, or fertilized egg. The zygote divides mitotically, forming first the embryo and eventually the mature organism. Meiotic division is the essential mechanism in **gametogenesis**, the formation of the gametes. The chromosomal transactions that characterize meiotic cell division are termed **meiosis**.

## The function of meiosis

Most of the cells of an organism are **diploid**. That is, they contain pairs of similar chromosomes, known as **homologous pairs**. One member of each pair was inherited from the mother, one from the father. Each species has a characteristic number of chromosomes. Human cells, for example, have a diploid number of 46—23 pairs of chromosomes. The cells of the fruit fly, so often used for genetic studies, contain 8 chromosomes (4 pairs). Those of a lily have 24, a cat 38, and a goldfish 94. This number is perpetuated in all the cells of the organism by mitotic division. During the S period each cell doubles its chromosomes, and during mitosis each daughter cell is provided with a complete diploid set.

If the gametes, too, were formed by mitotic division, the zygote would receive two full diploid sets of chromosomes at fertilization. Since all the cells of the mature organ-

4-6
Chromosomes of a human male, photographed during metaphase, when they are most visible. They can then be grouped in 23 pairs on the basis of similarities in form and function. Each pair has a characteristic size and structure, so it is easy to spot abnormalities. (Carolina Biological Supply Company)

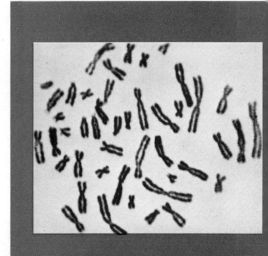

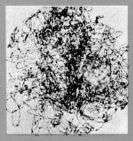

Early prophase I
The chromosomes are not yet short and thick enough to be seen individually.

Middle prophase I
With additional coiling, the chromosomes are visible.

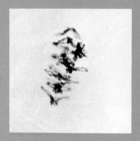

Metaphase I
Paired homologous chromosomes line up side by side at the equatorial plate.

Anaphase I
The paired chromosomes separate, each moving toward a different pole.

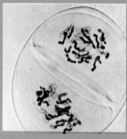

Prophase II (Above)
After a brief pause, division begins again. The chromosomes coil once again in preparation for the next division (right).

Metaphase II
The new equatorial plane is at right angles to the first one.

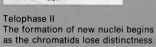

Telophase II
The formation of new nuclei begins as the chromatids lose distinctness.

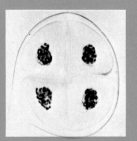

Daughter cells
Four haploid cells are formed by meiosis of one diploid cell.

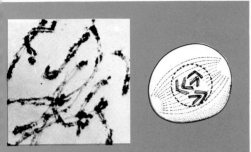

**Late prophase I**
The four chromatids of each tetrad lie side by side, with some crossing over.

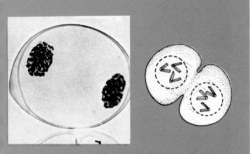

**Telophase I**
As the dyads reach the poles, new nuclei form.

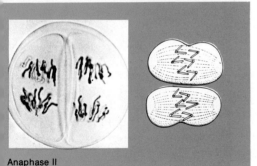

**Anaphase II**
The parted sister chromatids begin to migrate to opposite poles.

**4-7**
Although many of the stages of meiosis closely parallel those of mitosis, there is a key difference. In mitosis, the daughter cells are diploid, with two of each kind of chromosome; in meiosis, they are haploid, with one chromosome of each kind.

ism are formed by mitotic division of the zygote, the cells of a human baby formed by such a union would have 92 chromosomes. Its offspring would, in turn, have 184. In other words, the chromosome number would double and redouble with every successive generation. But this does not happen. The reason is that gametes are formed not by mitotic but by meiotic division.

The essence of meiosis is that it produces gametes that are haploid—they have only half the number of chromosomes found in the other cells of the parent organism. Haploid cells contain only one representative of each type of chromosome, instead of a pair. Because meiosis halves the number of chromosomes, it is sometimes called reductive division. When two haploid gametes unite, the resulting zygote has a full diploid set of chromosomes, two of each kind. Thus the chromosome number remains constant from generation to generation.

### The meiotic process

Many of the events of meiotic division parallel closely those of mitosis. The appearance and disappearance of the spindle, nuclear membrane, and nucleolus, for example, are similar in both processes. For this reason we use the same terminology—prophase, metaphase, anaphase, and telophase—to describe the stages of meiotic division. But meiosis differs importantly from mitosis in its characteristic movement and distribution of the chromosomes. Like mitosis, meiosis is preceded by the duplication of the chromosomes. This duplication, however, is followed by two successive cell divisions rather than the single division of mitosis. The result is four daughter cells sharing only two sets of chromosomes. Thus each daughter cell is haploid. It possesses only half the normal complement of chromosomes found in other cells of the organism.

In each diploid cell, half the chromosomes are replications of those originally donated by one parent and half are replications of those donated by the other. Each chromosome, then, has a homologue—a mate which resembles it in terms of size, shape, and type of genetic information. During the first meiotic division the linked chromatids—identical copies of each other—do not separate as in mitosis. They remain joined by the centromeres. But the homologous chromosomes pair off and then separate, one member of each pair going to each daughter cell. Since these chromosomes are not identical, the two daughter cells receive different genetic material. The second meiotic division is very similar to ordinary mitosis. Each chromosome of the daughter cells still consists of two linked chromatids. These now separate, producing four haploid daughter cells.

*Prophase I* A number of events occur during this protracted and important stage. Prophase begins when the chromosomes become visible as separate strands. At this point the twin chromatids cannot yet be seen. As the chromosomes become shorter and thicker, homologous chromosomes start to pair off. Eventually they are lying parallel to each other along their entire length. This pairing process is known as **synapsis**. In time individual chromatids become visible and the homologous pair appears as a **tetrad** of four chromatids.

While the four chromatids of each tetrad are lying side by side, an important process known as **crossing over** may take place. Occasional breaks may occur in the chromatids. Often these breaks are patched up. That is, the broken pieces rejoin to form the original chromatid again. But if breaks occur at the same point in nonsister chromatids lying side by side in a tetrad, the broken segments may be exchanged before the break is mended. The reconstituted chromosomes will then contain genes which were originally part of nonsister chromatids. A recombination of genetic material has thus occurred. The two chromatids which exchange segments are known as

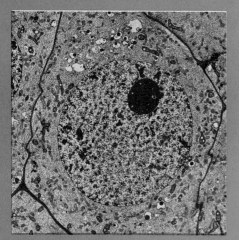

**4-8**
The photo above shows a lily microsporocyte in early prophase. The chromosomes are not yet visible in the nucleus and the nucleolus is still very distinct. But the outline of the nuclear membrane is beginning to blur.

**4-9**
During prophase, the chromosomes of each tetrad begin to separate, but points of contact, or chiasmata, remain. They are the visible results of crossing over, a process which leads to greatly increased variability in sexually reproduced offspring.

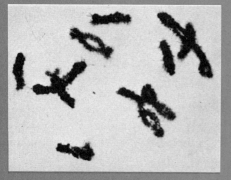

crossover types. The other two, each with its original sequence of genes, are noncrossover or parental types.

As the chromosomes of each tetrad separate during the subsequent stages of the prophase, points of contact between them known as **chiasmata** can be seen with the light microscope. Crossing over has not been observed directly, but chiasmata are believed to be visible results of crossing over. Most of the tetrads in plant and animal cells have at least one chiasma, and longer tetrads often display several. The chiasmata link the four chromatids of each tetrad. But as the chromatids drift farther apart, these points of contact move toward the ends of the chromatid arms. During this stage the nucleolus disappears and the nuclear membrane starts to break down. A spindle forms, and spindle fibers become attached to the centromeres.

*Metaphase I* The chromosomes align themselves in the equatorial plane of the cell. By this we mean that paired homologous chromosomes line up side by side, with one member of the pair closer to one pole and the second nearer the other pole. In mitosis, each chromosome is connected to both poles. But in meiosis each chromosome is attached only to the pole nearest it. Thus homologous chromosomes are connected to opposite poles.

*Anaphase I* The paired chromosomes now separate. Each moves toward the pole to which it is attached. The centromeres do not divide, and each chromosome (now termed a **dyad**) still consists of two linked chromatids. Because of crossing over, however, these sister chromatids may no longer carry identical hereditary information.

*Telophase I* When the dyads reach opposite poles, two new nuclei begin to form. New nuclear membranes appear, and the chromosomes uncoil. During this stage cytokinesis usually occurs, resulting in the

formation of two daughter cells. A brief pause in the meiotic process may follow. However, the chromosomes are still double-stranded. Thus they are ready to divide again, and the second meiotic division soon begins.

*Second meiotic division* The second division closely parallels mitosis. During Prophase II the chromosomes condense once more, the spindle forms, and the nuclear membrane disappears. In Metaphase II the chromosomes line up at the cell's equatorial plane. Each is attached by spindle fibers to both poles. The centromeres are duplicated and separate from each other. And the sister chromatids are now finally parted. In Anaphase II they migrate to opposite poles, and in Telophase II the nuclei reform. Each nucleus now contains a haploid set of chromosomes. Cytokinesis usually occurs during this phase. Four haploid daughter cells are thus formed from the meiotic division of a single diploid cell.

## Life cycles

Since asexual reproduction involves only simple cell division, it can occur quickly and efficiently. Sexual reproduction is a much chancier affair. Two cells from different organisms must find one another and fuse before further cell division can occur. Despite this element of risk, a large majority of the species on earth reproduce sexually. Why should sexual reproduction predominate when individuals can proliferate so much faster asexually? The overwhelming success of sexually reproducing species is due to their greater adaptive ability.

Each offspring of the sexual process possesses characteristics of two individuals thrown together by chance. Chromosomes are shuffled in meiosis, and further recombination of hereditary material is produced by crossing over. This ensures that the new organism will possess a true mixture of its parents' genes. Man, for example, has 46 chromosomes and can produce over 8 million combinations of chromosomes in his gametes. Any of these may combine with one of a like number of possible gametes of the opposite sex. A single mating, then, could produce any of over 70 trillion genetically different offspring. And this figure does not even take into account the results of crossing over.

By contrast, asexually reproducing organisms are essentially identical to their single parent. Thus there is more variety among offspring in sexually reproducing species. The more variety there is in a species, the more likely it is that individuals of that species are able to live in different conditions. If the environment changes—as environments often do—some members of the species will probably be able to survive the change. Such a species may be better able to withstand environmental fluctuations. Over the long haul, then, the asexually reproducing species are less able to adapt. They are more likely to become extinct despite their reproductive capacity. A high reproductive capacity is meaningless if the organism does not live to reproductive maturity.

## Asexual reproduction

Organisms display various modes of asexual reproduction, depending on their complexity. Unicellular organisms—both procaryotes and eucaryotes—reproduce asexually by simple cell division, called **fission**. Since procaryotes do not have a discrete nucleus, they cannot undergo mitosis. However, they do replicate their single chromosome when they divide. The metabolic activities of the procaryotic cell seem to remain constant throughout all phases of its life cycle. Bacteria continue their growth even while dividing. They usually divide transversely. Such single-celled eucaryotes as protozoans also reproduce by fission. Those which propel themselves by cilia generally divide transversely, while those with flagella usually divide longitudinally.

Some organisms, both unicellular and multicellular, reproduce by an asexual

4-10
Bacteria reproduce asexually by fission. The scanning EM below shows a staphylococcus bacterium dividing. The dark area in each new half is not a nucleus but a single chromosome. The bottom photo shows a common bacterium, *E. coli,* as it undergoes fission. The white areas visible in the cell are the scattered nucleic acids; the dark dots are the ribosomes. Metabolism of the bacterial cell remains unchanged all during the process of fission.

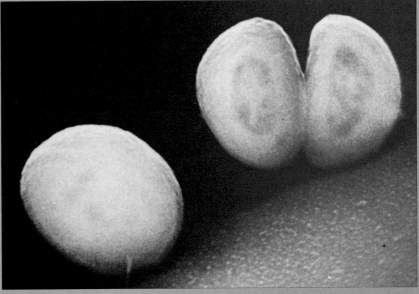

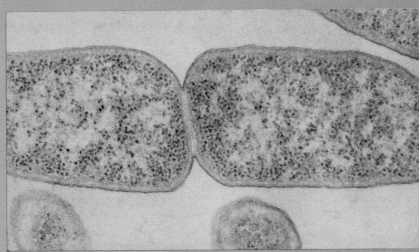

method called **budding**. In this process a new organism begins to grow as an offshoot of the parent organism. When it grows to full size, it can either remain attached to its parent or detach itself entirely. The unicellular fungus, yeast, commonly reproduces by budding, as does the multicellular hydra.

Many plants and fungi reproduce asexually by **sporulation**. That is, they form spores, single cells which can produce multicellular organisms without fertilization. Spores can usually remain viable for long periods of time, until the environmental conditions become suitable to the development of the organism. Because of their size and structure, spores are generally more mobile than the rooted organisms that form them. Plants and fungi are able to produce very many of these resistant and mobile cells. They can thus spread their species far and wide. If the spores find conditions suitable, they can colonize new areas.

Plants may also reproduce asexually by **vegetative propagation**. This is what happens when stem cuttings of plants such as begonias and ivy develop into new complete plants by sprouting roots. In other plants different organs, such as potato tubers, crocus corms (underground stems), and strawberry plant runners have this capacity to form new individuals.

Some animals, notably certain types of insect, can reproduce asexually by the process of **parthenogenesis**. This is the development of a multicellular organism from an unfertilized egg. The worker ants and bees form in this way. These organisms are haploid, so in this process the gamete is essentially serving as a spore. Parthenogenesis can occur naturally, as it does in insect societies, or in response to chemicals or electric shock.

*Conjugation* Some unicellular organisms, even the procaryotic bacteria, display sex-like behavior called **conjugation**. During conjugation two unicells of different strains (but the same species) snuggle up to each other. Where their surfaces touch, they make a fairly fragile connection. However, this connection may last long enough for them to exchange genetic material. Conjugation has some likeness to sexual reproduction, since it involves mating between two individuals of different strains and a mixing of their genes. But it is not basically a reproductive process. The two conjugating cells do not fuse to form a single reproductive cell. After conjugation they separate, and later reproduce independently by fission. But their daughter cells may in fact have genes from both conjugating individuals. Conjugation, therefore, allows unicells to bring together genetic information from two individuals in one individual. In short, these simple organisms can display sexual behavior, but they reproduce asexually.

## Sexual reproduction

True sexual reproduction involves the fertilization of an egg cell, produced by a female organism, by a male gamete, produced by a male organism of the same species. In multicellular organisms sexual reproduction is essentially the same at the cellular level. A haploid sperm cell fuses with a haploid egg cell to form a diploid zygote. But the overall pattern of sexual reproduction in animals is very different from the pattern displayed by plants and fungi. This difference lies mostly in the way sexual reproduction fits into the life cycles of these organisms. The **life cycle** of an organism is the sequence of events from the time it is conceived until it reproduces in like manner. So the life cycle of a sexually reproducing organism covers its life history from the moment of fertilization until its own gametes fuse with those of the opposite sex. Meiosis must occur at some point in this life cycle, since fertilized eggs are diploid and gametes are haploid. In animals, meiosis occurs during gamete formation (gametogenesis). Special cells of the diploid multicellular individual undergo meiotic cell division to form sperm or egg cells. The only

**4-11**
Another kind of asexual reproduction occurs in the multicellular hydra. Small buds form on the parent hydra; as soon as a bud has developed a mouth and a set of tentacles, it breaks away and begins to lead an independent existence.

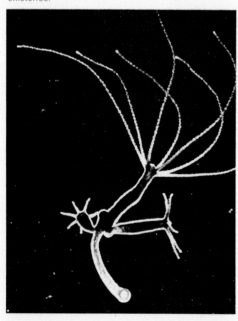

haploid phase in the animal life cycle is the gamete. But in plants and fungi, meiosis usually *precedes* gamete formation. Their gametes are generally formed by mitotic cell division of a multicellular haploid individual.

*In animals*   The cells of most multicellular higher animals are diploid. Haploid cells occur only in the gamete-forming organs. In the male the sperm are produced in the **testis**. The egg-producing organ of the female is the **ovary**. These organs have special cells which undergo meiotic cell division to produce gametes.

The testis is a bag-like organ. It contains a great many long, coiled tubes called **seminiferous tubules**. These tubules all empty into a larger collecting tube called the **epididymis**. In microscopic cross-section we see that these tubules comprise concentric rings of different types of cell. The innermost layer of cells, called **primary spermatocytes**, undergo meiosis. Each spermatocyte forms four equal-sized **spermatids**. These spermatids become sperm as they develop flagella and lose most of their cytoplasm. The sperm then travel through tubules until they reach the epididymis. There they are stored for later release. New primary spermatocytes can be formed when **spermatogonia** (primitive germ cells) divide. Once it has begun, **spermatogenesis** (formation of sperm) can continue throughout the male organism's lifetime.

In the female ovaries, each egg-producing cell is called the **primary oocyte**. The oocyte is encased by a sphere of cells called a **follicle**. In the first meiotic division, the oocyte divides to form two unequal-sized cells. The larger cell is called the **secondary oocyte**. The smaller is the **first polar body**. In the second meiotic division, the secondary oocyte also divides unequally to form the larger **ootid** and the smaller **secondary polar body**. The first polar body may also divide again to produce two more secondary polar bodies. Meiosis of the pri-

**4-12**
Spermatogenesis is the meiotic divisions of a diploid primary spermatocyte to produce four haploid sperm. Each division forms two different combinations of chromosomes. The total number of possible combinations is $2^{23}$, or 8,388,608. Since a single ejaculation of semen contains almost a quarter of a billion sperm cells, the chances are good that the female will receive at least one sperm cell of each possible combination. Thus even offspring of the same parents can be expected to vary greatly. This variability is thought to give a real evolutionary advantage to the species, permitting adaptation to new environments.

**4-13**
Within each seminiferous tubule, the cells are arranged in concentric circles. The primary spermatocytes (one of which is shown here in a stage of first meiotic division) are located in the outer circle. Next, is a double layer of secondary spermatocytes, which will divide again to form spermatids. The innermost layer, the cells with very small nuclei, are the mature sperm.

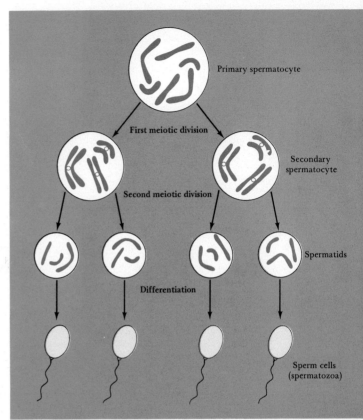

Primary spermatocyte

First meiotic division

Secondary spermatocyte

Second meiotic division

Spermatids

Differentiation

Sperm cells (spermatozoa)

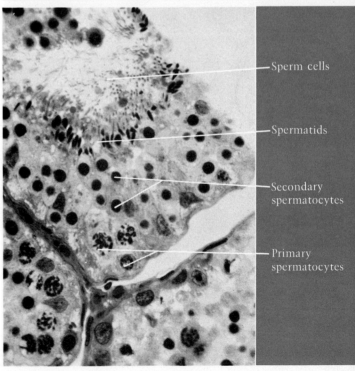

Sperm cells

Spermatids

Secondary spermatocytes

Primary spermatocytes

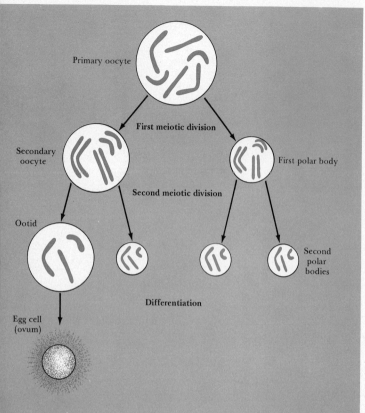

Primary oocyte

**First meiotic division**

Secondary oocyte

First polar body

**Second meiotic division**

Ootid

Second polar bodies

**Differentiation**

Egg cell (ovum)

4-14
The first meiotic division of the primary oocyte produces one large cell, the secondary oocyte, and one smaller cell, the polar body. In the next stage of oogenesis, the first polar body divides again to form two more. The secondary oocyte divides to form one more polar body and the much larger ootid. The ootid then undergoes differentiation to form a mature ovum, or egg cell, while the polar bodies disintegrate. At birth, the human female's two ovaries contain about 400,000 primary oocytes. All of these remain in the first prophase of meiosis until hormones stimulate the resumption of meiosis at puberty.

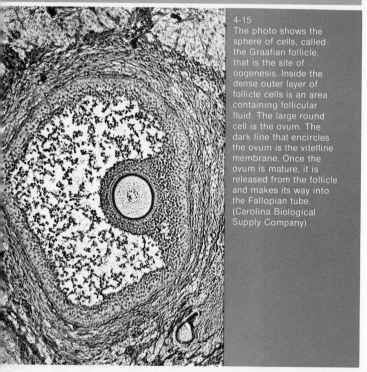

4-15
The photo shows the sphere of cells, called the Graafian follicle, that is the site of oogenesis. Inside the dense outer layer of follicle cells is an area containing follicular fluid. The large round cell is the ovum. The dark line that encircles the ovum is the vitelline membrane. Once the ovum is mature, it is released from the follicle and makes its way into the Fallopian tube. (Carolina Biological Supply Company)

mary oocyte can produce four haploid cells, but only the ootid can develop into a mature egg (ovum). This cell has hoarded most of the cytoplasm of the dividing primary oocyte. Since the fertilizing sperm has no cytoplasm to contribute, the ovum provides most of the cytoplasm and initial nutrients for the embryo which develops from the fertilized egg. The primary oocytes are not replenished after the egg matures. So the female can produce eggs only as long as her original supply of primary oocytes lasts.

*In plants*  Several different patterns of sexual reproduction occur in the life cycles of plants and fungi. Many plant life cycles differ from those of animals because plants often display two multicellular forms, one diploid and the other haploid. We shall discuss the general features of such a plant life cycle. But we must remember that it does not apply to some plants, and applies to others only with modifications.

In general, the diploid plant undergoes meiotic cell division to produce haploid reproductive cells. But these cells are spores and not gametes, because they give rise to a multicellular haploid individual without fertilization. In this segment of the life cycle the reproduction is asexual. However, when the haploid individual matures it develops male and female organs. These organs produce gametes. Since this individual is haploid, gametogenesis occurs by mitotic rather than meiotic cell division. The cycle is completed when the gametes fuse to form a diploid zygote. This zygote then develops into the diploid plant. The diploid plant which produces the spores is called the **sporophyte**. Similarly, the haploid plant which produces the gametes is the **gametophyte**.

Thus the life cycle of a plant often includes two multicellular generations—the haploid gametophyte and the diploid sporophyte. This mode of reproduction is called **alternation of generations**. In this way plants enjoy the advantages of both asexual and sexual reproduction.

summary

All organisms arise from previously existing organisms, and all cells arise from previously existing cells. In mitotic division, cells reproduce by dividing to form a pair of daughter cells. The heart of the process is mitosis. Mitosis is the division of the cell nucleus in such a way that each new cell inherits a full set of chromosomes identical to those of the parent cell. This is crucial for the maintenance of genetic continuity.

Mitosis is divided for convenience into four stages—prophase, metaphase, anaphase, and telophase. Before mitosis, the chromosomes cannot be seen as discrete structures. But when mitosis begins, the chromosomes condense, coiling and recoiling into shorter, thicker shapes. Since the genetic material has already been replicated prior to mitosis, each chromosome consists of two identical strands called chromatids. During mitosis these separate and become the new chromosomes of the daughter cells. The division of the cell's cytoplasm to form two new cells is called cytokinesis.

Mitosis typically takes 60 to 90 minutes. The time between mitotic divisions is known as interphase. It varies greatly from one type of cell to another. The interphase period is subdivided into three stages: $G_1$, a period of growth; S, during which DNA is made and the chromosomes are replicated; and a shorter $G_2$ period, during which substances necessary for mitosis are synthesized.

Mitotic division is essential for the growth, development, and regeneration of tissues in multicellular organisms. Most single-celled eucaryotes also use this mechanism to reproduce. (Procaryotes cannot undergo mitosis. But they replicate their single chromosome and divide to reproduce.) Organisms that reproduce sexually make use of another kind of cell division, meiosis. Its function is the production of special cells called gametes. A male gamete fuses with a female gamete to form a zygote. (It is the zygote which grows into the mature organism.) If the gametes were formed by mitosis, each would have a full set of chromosomes. That is, they would be diploid. As a result, the number of chromosomes would double with each generation. But, through meiosis, each gamete has only half the normal number of chromosomes. Each has a single chromosome of each type characteristic of the organism. Such cells are called haploid. Meiosis is thus a mechanism for reducing the number of chromosomes from diploid to haploid.

Prior to the start of meiosis, the chromosomes are replicated. Two nuclear divisions follow, rather than the single division of mitosis. During the first division, chromosomes of the same type (homologous pairs) are brought together. One member of each pair is distributed to each daughter cell. During the second meiotic division, the sister chromatids separate to form new nuclei. These chromatids may no longer be identical, because of the exchange of segments of nonsister chromatids. This process is called crossing over. It often occurs when homologous chromosomes pair up during the first meiotic division.

Chromosomes are shuffled at random in meiosis. Additional recombination of genetic material is produced by crossing over. Thus the offspring of sexually reproducing creatures have a true mixture of their parents' genes. A human, for example, can produce over 8 million genetically different gametes. Such variety increases the ability of a species to adapt to environmental change, and thus enhances its ability to survive. (This is probably why most creatures on earth now reproduce sexually.) Offspring from asexual reproduction, on the other hand, are essentially identical to their parents.

There is great diversity in reproductive techniques and life cycles. This is true of both sexually and asexually reproducing organisms. Some plants alternate haploid and diploid generations. They may also use purely asexual reproductive techniques. These include sporulation and vegetative propagation. Various animals also reproduce asexually. Some methods used are fission, budding, and parthenogenesis.

5 patterns of inheritance

O f all the billions of people on earth, no two look exactly alike. Facial characteristics, hair, eye, and skin color, hair texture, and body build make us distinct from one another. In addition to the many combinations of differentiating characteristics that are visible, there are many more that are invisible. These include blood chemistry, mental and physical aptitudes, susceptibility to certain diseases, and other traits which contribute to our individuality.

But there is also a sameness among human beings. What is the mechanism responsible for this "similarity with differences," and how is it transmitted from one generation to another?

People have known for centuries that traits are passed down from parents to offspring. They have also understood that animals and plants could be changed—"improved"—through selective breeding. Fossil remains of wheat and corn ears indicate that early agriculturalists were able to develop plants with a food yield dramatically greater than that of their wild relatives. Until recently, though, people were unaware of the principles by which these changes were brought about.

Past observers noted that offspring seem to be a blend of traits passed on to them from their parents and other ancestors. They proposed the idea that sexual union brings about a mixture of bloods (or other fluids), thus determining the traits of the offspring. This idea lingers on in the language of the layman who speaks of "blood lines," "bad blood," or "mixed blood." But scientists have now rejected the concept of fluid inheritance.

We now know that the same basic unit responsible for the identifying characteristics of our species is also responsible for our individual differences. This basic unit of heredity is the **gene** (from the Greek word for birth). **Genetics** is the science which studies the structure and behavior of the gene. It was born late in the nineteenth century, when Gregor Mendel, an Augustinian monk and amateur horticulturist, performed a few simple experiments with ordinary garden peas.

# Mendelian principles

Mendel was educated in mathematics and the sciences at the University of Vienna. Perhaps it was this training that made him approach the problem of heredity in an entirely new way. Mendel was the first person to study heredity in an exact and strictly controlled manner. Beginning in the 1840s, Mendel crossbred pea plants with different characteristics. He then counted the number of offspring displaying each characteristic. By determining the ratio of offspring with each characteristic, Mendel found evidence of a consistent pattern. This enabled him to propose an explanation for the transmission of traits from one generation to the next. Unfortunately, his mathematical analysis of these experiments was passed over or not understood by his contemporaries. As a result, his contribution lay dormant until 1900. In that year three separate investigators independently came to similar conclusions and rediscovered Mendel's published paper. Nowadays Gregor Mendel is generally considered to be the father of modern genetics.

## Principle of segregation

Mendel chose to work with the garden pea *(Pisum sativum)* because its floral structure was well suited to breeding experiments. Normally, fertilization occurs before the flower opens. To prevent the pea plant from fertilizing itself, Mendel had only to open the flower bud and remove the anthers, which bear the male gametes. He could then dust the stigma, or female sexual structure, with pollen from a pea plant of a different strain.

Mendel worked with seven pairs of distinct traits which were constant from one generation to the next. The plants he used varied in height, flower color, the position of the flower on the stem, pod form and color, and seed form and color. Using one strain

as the male (pollen) parent and a second as the female (seed) parent, he produced hybrids. Mendel found that when any two strains were crossed, it made no difference which strain contributed the male gametes and which the female gametes. The same type of hybrid resulted in both instances. This showed that male and female plants contributed equally to the offspring.

Mendel's experiment with the color of unripe seed pods is an example of his first series of experiments. He used a pure yellow-podded strain and a pure green-podded strain as parental types, producing hybrids by artificial cross-fertilization. All plants of the hybrid generation, called the first filial ($F_1$) generation, had green seed pods. But when these reproduced by self-pollination to form the second filial ($F_2$) generation, some plants in the new generation showed yellow seed pods and some showed green seed pods. It was clear that while none of the $F_1$ plants had yellow seed pods, they somehow harbored the hereditary trait. So Mendel referred to green as the **dominant** trait of this pair of traits. Yellow was called the **recessive** trait, because it did not appear in the hybrid generation, but reappeared in some offspring of the hybrids. Of the 580 $F_2$ plants, 428 had green pods and 152 had yellow ones. This represented a ratio of 2.82 green to 1 yellow. Mendel obtained similar results from corresponding experiments with the other six pairs of characteristics. In this series of experiments, the $F_2$ generation always had about three times as many dominant types as it had recessive types.

Mendel based his explanation of this inheritance pattern on a few simple assumptions. Although they appeared to be identical, the green-podded plants of the $F_1$ generation must have differed in some invisible way from the pure-bred green-podded plant of the parental generation. The parent plants had produced only green-podded offspring when permitted to self-pollinate. (Mendel did not take anyone's word for this. He checked it himself by allowing the plants to self-pollinate over two generations.) But the $F_1$ plants produced both green-podded and yellow-podded plants upon self-pollination. While the visible characteristics (phenotype) of their seed pods were identical, these plants differed in their genetic makeup (genotype) for this character.

Mendel proposed that each trait of an individual is determined by two particles, or genes. One gene originates from the male gamete, or pollen, and the other is contributed by the female gamete, or ovum. He saw that for each character there may be different genes (alleles) which cause different expressions of that character. So an individual might have two identical genes for a character (homozygous condition) or two different genes for that character (heterozygous condition). In the latter case, one allele may be dominant, so that a heterozygous individual will display the characteristics dictated by the dominant gene, (Today genes are represented by letter symbols. A capital letter represents the dominant gene and the corresponding lower-case letter represents its recessive allele.)

Mendel concluded from the above experiment that the pure-breeding parental strains were each homozygous. The green pods of one parent were due to the dominant genotype (GG). The yellow seed pods of the other strain were due to the homozygous recessive genotype (gg). Mendel proposed that, through the gametes, each parental type contributes one allele to the hybrid. Since the pure-breeding parents have only one kind of allele each, the green-podded parent can produce only gametes carrying the G gene. The yellow-podded parent can produce only gametes carrying the g gene. The hybrid offspring, therefore, have a heterozygous genotype (Gg). An individual heterozygous for a single set of alleles is a monohybrid. A mating of monohybrid parents is a monohybrid cross.

But what about the $F_2$ generation? To understand why Mendel obtained the par-

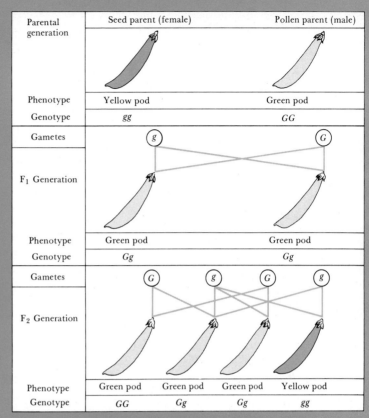

5-1
First- and second-generation color distribution and genotypes in crossing of homozygous green- and yellow-podded peas.

ticular results he did, we must first recall how the plants' gametes were formed during the process of meiosis. Each monohybrid of the $F_1$ generation received one gene for pod color from each of its pure-bred parents. Each cell of the $F_1$ plants contained one gene for green pods and a homologous gene for yellow pods. The genes for green pods were dominant, so the $F_1$ generation were phenotypically green-podded. When meiosis took place in the $F_1$ plants, the genes for green pods and the genes for yellow pods were segregated into separate nuclei. Thus half of the female gametes carried an allele for yellow pods and the other half carried an allele for green pods. Likewise, half of the male gametes were of each type.

If male and female nuclei were to combine at random in self-pollination, the progeny would have a ratio of 1 GG : 2 Gg : 1 gg. So the expected genotypic and phenotypic ratio in the $F_2$ progeny is three dominant (green pods) to one recessive (yellow pods). The genotypes and phenotypes of the $F_2$ generation can be shown schematically by a diagram known as a Punnett square. This square is named after Robert Punnett, the English biologist who devised it. The square shows the possible combinations of the two alleles contributed by each parent. Each segment represents a zygote in which one of these combinations occurs. The whole thus displays the expected genotypic ratio. Note that although the genotype of each gamete is different, the pheno-

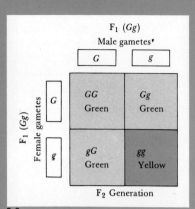

F₁ (Gg)

Male gametes'

| | G | g |
|---|---|---|
| **G** | GG<br>Green | Gg<br>Green |
| **g** | gG<br>Green | gg<br>Yellow |

F₁ (Gg) Female gametes

F₂ Generation

5-2
Punnett square representing the pea-pod findings. (See Principles of segregation)

type can be the same. So the two heterozygotes, like the dominant homozygote, will be green because they contain the dominant allele *(G)* for that trait. Only the zygote without the dominant allele *(gg)* will be yellow.

It is important to remember that the genotypic ratio of the F₂ generation is arrived at through the law of probability. It may not always correspond with the results of actual crosses. If a coin is flipped, the probability that it will land on heads is equal to the probability that it will land on tails. The ratio of heads to tails is therefore 1:1. But actual tosses may deviate from this ratio. It is possible (though improbable) for a coin to land on heads 20 times in 20 flips. But the more flips, the closer the ratio of heads to tails will approach 1:1.

In the same way, the Punnett square shows only the statistical probability that the zygotes produced by the two individuals will display particular phenotypes and genotypes. So if the two pea plants depicted in the diagram were bred, it is only probable—not certain—that they would produce zygotes with characteristics in the ratio shown—that is, three green-podded and one yellow-podded. But if a large number of monohybrid pea plants were bred—say 4,000—we could accurately predict that about 3,000 of the progeny would bear green pods and 1,000 would bear yellow pods.

## Independent assortment

Mendel's next step was to study the **dihybrid cross.** He wished to determine how one set of alleles is inherited in relation to another set. Therefore, he made crosses between parental pea strains which differed from each other in two characters— seed shape and seed color. He crossed a pure strain having round yellow *(RRYY)* seeds with another pure strain having wrinkled green seeds *(rryy).* All of the F₁ seeds were round and yellow—the two dominant traits. This indicated that inheritance of neither trait had any effect on the other. Of the

possible F₁ genotypes, one-fourth were heterozygous for two traits, or **dihybrid** *(RrYy).* Self-pollination of the dihybrids produced 556 F₂ seeds of the following types:

| Seed Phenotype | Number | Approximate Proportion |
|---|---|---|
| round yellow | 315 | 9/16 |
| wrinkled yellow | 101 | 3/16 |
| round green | 108 | 3/16 |
| wrinkled green | 32 | 1/16 |

As we can see, some F₂ seeds were formed which were unlike either parents or grandparents (wrinkled yellow peas and round green peas). This indicated that the genes for the two characters segregated independently of each other. The phenotype frequencies observed are approximately those we would expect if we assume segregation of alleles during both egg and pollen formation of the dihybrid plants, and random fertilization during self-pollination. Mendel concluded that genes of one allelic pair pass into gametes independently of genes from other allelic pairs. This is known as the **principle of independent assortment.**

According to this principle, in a dihybrid a gene for yellow seed should occur in the same gamete with the gene for wrinkled seed as often as it occurs with the gene for round seed. In the same way, the gene for green seed is as likely to occur with the gene for wrinkled as with its allele for round. So all four combinations of these genes should occur in gametes with equal frequency. Each should represent one-quarter of the total number of eggs or pollen. If male and female gametes combine at random, then the frequencies of genotypes and phenotypes can be predicted for the offspring, or dihybrid cross. The predicted phenotypic proportions are 9/16 round yellow: 3/16 wrinkled yellow: 3/16 round green: 1/16 wrinkled green—or 9:3:3:1— very close to the observed results. Mendel's thoroughness is shown by his tests which determined that the nine genotypes of this

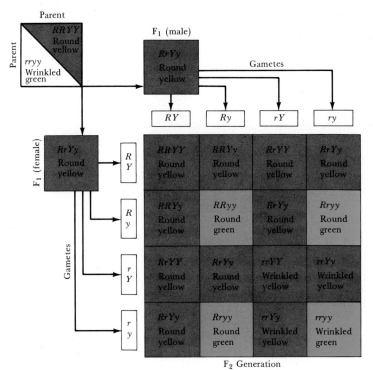

**5-3**
The dihybrid cross—phenotypic and genotypic distribution in F₂ generation (See Principle of independent assortment)

F₂ generation were present in the proportions of 1/16 *RRYY* : 2/16 *RRYy* : 1/16 *RRyy* : 2/16 *RrYY* : 4/16 *RrYy* : 2/16 *Rryy* : 1/16 *rrYY* : 2/16 *rrYy* : 1/16 *rryy*. These proportions match the ratios which would be predicted by the Punnett square. Mendel further substantiated his results with matings of other dihybrids, as well as trihybrids.

The number of possible combinations grows rapidly as more pairs of alleles are added. Try the following exercise to determine the traits of the individuals which result when three traits are crossed. Draw a Punnett square with 64 boxes and indicate the male and female gametes with the following letters: *RYZ, RYz, RyZ, Ryz, rYZ, rYz, ryZ, ryz*. The result would be 27 different genotypes and 8 different phenotypes. When we consider that each human carries not just three but an estimated 10,000 pairs of genes, we can easily see why no two individuals—except monozygotic twins (siblings which form from a single zygote)—are exactly alike.

## Test cross

Heterozygous dominant offspring show the same phenotype as their homozygous dominant siblings. So geneticists—and others interested in pedigrees, such as breeders—have devised a way to determine the genotypes of these individuals. This is done by making a **test cross** of the phenotypically dominant individual with one or more homozygous recessive mates. If a recessive offspring appears among the progeny, the dominant individual must carry the recessive allele. If the offspring are all of the dominant phenotype, the dominant parent is probably homozygous. For example, among Siamese cat breeders, albinism (a recessive phenotype) is considered undesirable. Test crosses of normal Siamese cats to albinos may be used by breeders to determine which Siamese carry the gene of albinism. Production of any albino young would show that the Siamese parent carries an albino gene. The heterozygous Siamese could then be excluded from further breeding to eliminate the undesirable gene.

## Gene inheritance

Even in Mendel's day there was evidence that the precision of cell division is vital to heredity. Since the gametes alone bridge the generation gap in sexual reproduction, they must carry the genes. It is now known that genes are located on chromosomes in the nucleus of the cell. Each gene has its specific place (**locus**) on a specific chromosome. Since genes are carried by chromosomes, and chromosomes have regular patterns of movement during mitotic and meiotic cell division, Mendel's principles of segregation and independent assortment based on these patterns do indeed provide a description of the transmission of genes on different chromosomes. But genes display differing degrees of control over their traits. So other patterns of inheritance are observed, which do not always seem to parallel the universal patterns of gene movements. To understand how these do in fact fit the pattern, we must consider other factors such as gene potency, gene interaction, and gene location.

## Intermediate inheritance

Many traits are determined by pairs of alleles in which neither allele achieves full phenotypic expression, and neither is entirely obscured. Instead, there is a blending or combination of effects. This results in a heterozygous offspring which is different from either of its homozygous parents. For example, when purebred red-flowered snapdragons *(RR)* are crossed with white-flowered ones *(R'R')*, a pink-flowered hybrid is produced. When these $F_1$ plants are allowed to self-pollinate, the result is an $F_2$ generation composed of 1/4 red *(RR)*, 2/4 pink *(RR')*, and 1/4 white *(R'R')* types. Since each genotype is represented by a distinct phenotype, the phenotypic ratio is identical to the genotypic ratio.

## Multiple alleles

Some traits are governed by a gene for which there are more than two alleles. Any individual carries only two genes (either identical or specified alternate characteristics) for the trait. But other individuals in the population may carry completely different alleles. So a population of interbreeding individuals may have patterns of inheritance which are determined by three or more alleles for a given trait. When multiple alleles exist within a population, there is a greater variety of possible genotypes and phenotypes for individuals.

A good illustration of multiple alleles is provided by the ABO system, one of dozens of systems used in classifying blood types. The letters "A" and "B" refer to **antigens**. Antigens are molecules (commonly protein) often found on the surface of various cells. When a foreign cell enters the human body, its antigens trigger the production of special proteins called **antibodies**. This is called an **immune response**. The antibodies inactivate the antigens for which they

were specifically produced. In consequence, the foreign cells on which the antigens are located are forced to clump together. This phenomenon is known as **agglutination**.

Agglutination was a common hazard in early blood transfusions, before the existence of several blood types was known. It is now understood that humans have antigens on the surface of their red blood cells. They also have specific antibodies floating in their bloodstream. A person is known as A type if he has A antigens on his red blood cells and his bloodstream contains antibodies against the B antigens. He is B type if he has B antigens and antibodies against A antigens. He is AB type if he has both kinds of antigen, but lacks antibodies against either A or B antigens. Or he is O type if he has neither A nor B antigens on his red blood cells, but has antibodies against both types of antigen. A person with O-type blood is a "universal donor." That is, he can give blood to persons of any blood type. This is because his blood will not react with antibodies against the A or B antigens. An individual with AB-type blood is a "universal receiver." Since AB blood lacks antibodies against either the A or B antigen, he can receive a blood transfusion of any of the four types without experiencing an immune response.

Human blood types of the ABO series are determined by three alleles. The dominant gene $I^A$ causes the synthesis of antigen A. Similarly, antigen B is synthesized

5-4
The ABO system. (See Multiple alleles)

| Blood Type | Antigen/Antibody Relationship | | Donor to | Recipient from |
|---|---|---|---|---|
| A | Red cells: A antigens | | A, AB | O, A |
| | Plasma: Antibodies against B | | | |
| B | Red cells: B antigens | | B, AB | O, B |
| | Plasma: Antibodies against A | | | |
| AB | Red cells: A and B antigens | | AB | O, A, B, AB |
| | Plasma: No antibodies | | | |
| O | Red cells: No antigens | | O, A, B, AB | O |
| | Plasma: Antibodies against A and B | | | |

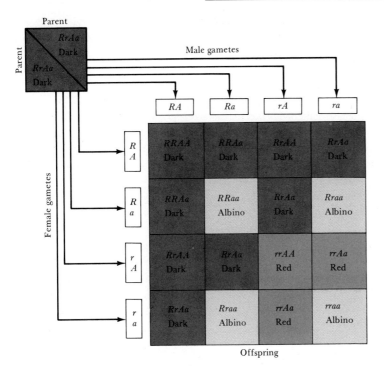

Parent

*RrAa* Dark

*RrAa* Dark

Male gametes

| | *RA* | *Ra* | *rA* | *ra* |
|---|---|---|---|---|
| *R* *A* | *RRAA* Dark | *RRAa* Dark | *RrAA* Dark | *RrAa* Dark |
| *R* *a* | *RRAa* Dark | *RRaa* Albino | *RrAa* Dark | *Rraa* Albino |
| *r* *A* | *RrAA* Dark | *RrAa* Dark | *rrAA* Red | *rrAa* Red |
| *r* *a* | *RrAa* Dark | *Rraa* Albino | *rrAa* Red | *rraa* Albino |

Female gametes

Offspring

5-5
Epistatic effect of albino gene on hair color. (See Epistasis)

5-6
Not an ermine, but an albino ferret, a domesticated relative of the generally dark-colored mink and weasel. Ferrets are used in Europe and Asia to drive rats and other animals from their burrows, so they can be killed.

when the dominant gene $I^B$ is present. The recessive allele, $i$, does not cause any synthesis. An individual who is homozygous for the recessive gene *(ii)* has O-type blood. Since $I^A$ is dominant to $i$, A-type blood may be due to the genotypes $I^A I^A$ or $I^A i$. B-type blood results from genotypes $I^B I^B$ or $I^B i$. AB type results from genotype $I^A I^B$. Since $I^A$ and $I^B$ are dominant to $i$, but neither is dominant to the other, they are considered **codominant**. Thus three alleles for this locus produce four different phenotypes. A combination of parents with $I^A i$ and $I^B i$ genotypes can produce all of the four ABO phenotypes. Other combinations cannot produce certain phenotypes. Consequently, blood types may be used to clarify cases of disputed parentage. They cannot prove that a child belongs to a specific pair of parents, but in many cases they can show whether or not such a relationship is possible.

## Gene interaction

Many phenotypes result from the interaction of two or more sets of alleles. These sets of alleles are located at different chromoso-mal sites. They affect the same character, but in different ways. The alleles present at one site may affect the expression of the alleles at the other site. The phenotypic ratios observed may therefore differ from those expected for noninteracting gene pairs.

*Epistasis*　Some gene pairs completely mask the expression of genes at a different chromosomal locus. This interaction is known as **epistasis**. Examples occur in pigment characteristics, such as hair color in humans. Red hair is due to a homozygous recessive genotype *rr*. Most other hair color depends on the presence of a dominant allele *R*. The various shadings of nonred hair are controlled by other factors, and will not be discussed here. But the important point is that hair color also depends on the production of melanin, a dark pigment found in hair, skin, and eyes. Melanin production is controlled by the dominant gene *A*, whose chromosomal locus is entirely distinct from those genes which determine hair color. Certain individuals are homozygous for the recessive gene *a*, which prevents melanin formation. These individuals develop into albinos. They exhibit white hair, very pale skin, and pink iris of the eye. Since melanin pigment is necessary for the expression of either red or dark hair, an individual unable to form melanin will be albino regardless of the genes he carries for hair color.

*Polygenic inheritance*　A phenotype may be determined by the cumulative, quantitative effects of a group of several sets of alleles that have similar or related expression. None of the alleles is dominant, so none by itself controls expression of the unit. The result is quantitative inheritance, with gradations from one extreme to another. Size, eye color, and skin pigmentation are **polygenically** determined traits.

Consider skin color as an example. Presence or absence of melanin is determined by the *A–a* set of alleles. But the

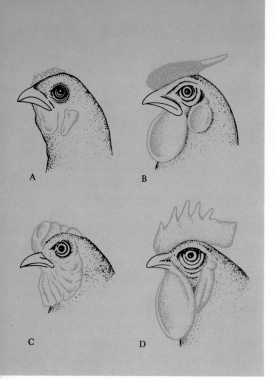

5-7
Comb types produced by genetic collaboration:
(A) pea; (B) rose; (C) walnut; (D) single.
(See Collaboration)

amount of melanin pigment in human skin appears to be a matter of polygenic inheritance. If only two sets of alleles are involved, then black skin color results from four contributing genes, which we may call *BBCC*. White skin would be due to four noncontributing genes *(bbcc)*. The mulatto phenotype, *BbCc*, is intermediate in color between black and white. Of the various possible mating combinations, children of mulatto parents show the greatest variety of pigmentation. They may show any of five different depths of skin color:

| | |
|---|---|
| *BBCC* | black |
| *BbCC* or *BBCc* | dark |
| *BbCc, BBcc* or *bbCC* | mulatto |
| *Bbcc* or *bbCc* | light |
| *bbcc* | white |

Observations of families of this type, and of the color variations in mixed populations such as those of Jamaica and Bermuda, show that an even greater number of classes can easily be distinguished. So geneticists generally believe that not two but at least four pairs of alleles determine the amount of melanin in the skin.

*Collaboration*    Another phenomenon involves the interaction of gene pairs to influence the same character. This is known as **collaboration**. As the name suggests, the genes involved act together to produce phenotypes that neither pair could produce on its own. For instance, two sets of alleles govern the form of the comb in chickens. The dominant *R* allele produces a rose comb, while the recessive *r* allele produces a single comb. The other pair of alleles, *P* and *p*, produce a pea comb and a single comb respectively. But the interaction of the *P* and *R* genes results in a walnut comb, which neither pair of genes can produce by itself.

## Linkage

So far, we have examined dihybrid crosses whose inheritance patterns show phenotyp-

ic ratios with even-numbered denominators (eights, sixteenths, and so on). This is to be expected when the different sets of alleles are assorted independently. But genes responsible for many characteristics are located on the same chromosome. They cannot assort independently of one another. In other words, these genes are linked. They transmit their effects as a unit. Such genes are sometimes called a linkage group, and may show phenotypic ratios with odd-numbered denominators. The phenomenon of linkage was discovered early in this century by the American geneticist Thomas Hunt Morgan. He and his students at Columbia University made extensive studies using the fruit fly, *Drosophila melanogaster*.

The wild-type, or normal, *Drosophila* have red eyes and long wings. Other strains, however, have purple eyes and/or vestigial wings. In one experiment, matings between purple-eyed, long-winged males and red-eyed, vestigial-winged females produced only wild-type flies in the $F_1$ generation. This showed that purple eye and vestigial wing are recessive to their respective wild-type alleles. But a mating between a wild-type $F_1$ male and a purple-eyed, vestigial-winged female did not produce equal numbers of four phenotypes, as we would expect with independent assortment. Instead, it produced 50 percent purple-eyed, long-winged flies and 50 percent red-eyed, vestigial-winged flies. Similar results were obtained each time the experiment was repeated. In a sample this large, the lack of red-eyed, long-winged flies and purple-eyed, vestigial-winged flies is strong evidence that the two sets of alleles are not assorted at random. Therefore they are probably linked.

## Crossing-over

In another experiment, Morgan crossed a wild-type $F_1$ female from the above experiment with a purple-eyed, vestigial-winged male. He obtained the following results:

purple-eyed, long-winged          44%

| | |
|---|---|
| red-eyed, vestigial-winged | 44% |
| red-eyed, long-winged | 6% |
| purple-eyed, vestigial-winged | 6% |

If these genes were assorted at random, the frequency of each of the four types should be about the same. The predominance of the two parental types, however, supports the belief that the genes are linked. But what about the 12 percent which are unlike the parents? Note that the two new combinations are about equal in frequency. Have the genes perhaps switched places in these individuals and formed new linkage groups? Morgan suggests that they have. He claimed that recombinations of linked genes result from breakage of the parental linkage groups, followed by genetic exchange and fusion to form new linkage groups. This could occur through the phenomenon of crossing-over, which we discussed in the previous chapter. In fact, the concept of crossing-over was originally based solely upon statistical data of the type observed in the above experiment.

## Chromosomal mapping

The discovery that chromosomes can exchange genes by crossing-over gave Morgan and his associates a key to understanding chromosomal structure. Morgan assumed that crossing-over occurs at random, breakages and recombinations taking place with equal frequency at any given point along the length of the chromosome. He reasoned further that the genes most likely to cross over are those closest together on the chromosome. This assumption is very much like saying that, in a class of elementary school students who must sit in alphabetical order, a child named Anderson is more likely to become friends with a child named Arbuthnot than with one named Zimmerman. If we could observe such a class during free play, without being told their last names, we might be able to guess which pairs of children had names whose first letters came close together in the alphabet, merely by noting which of them played together most frequently. Similarly, by noting the relative frequency with which certain traits appeared together in fruit flies whose phenotypes showed evidence of crossing-over, Morgan was able to estimate the relative closeness of linked genes to one another on the chromosome. He used this data to draw a map of the chromosomes under study, showing the positions of the genes governing each trait as well as the amount of space between them.

# Sex and genetics

Aside from the formation of new linkage groups by crossing-over, the most important method of genetic recombination is sexual reproduction. This form of reproduction enables the offspring to inherit an almost infinite number of variations on the parental traits. Sex itself is determined by genes. Since the sex gene is carried on a chromosome with other genes, it also forms part of a linkage group, giving rise to what are known as sex-linked and sex-influenced traits.

## Sex determination

In life forms where individuals are of one sex or the other, sex is determined by a single pair of chromosomes that are quite dif-

5-8
Sex determination: XX-XY type.

ferent physically from each other. These are known as the **sex chromosomes**. The other chromosomes are called **autosomes**.

*Drosophila* possesses two types of sex chromosome, called X and Y, as well as three pairs of autosomes. The X chromosome is straight. The Y chromosome is J-shaped. Females have three pairs of autosomes plus two X chromosomes. Males have three pairs of autosomes plus one X and one Y chromosome. Such a distribution is known as XX–XY sex determination. The male fruit fly produces equal numbers of two types of sperm. One has an X chromosome, the other has a Y chromosome, and both possess the three autosomes. Therefore, the male is the **heterogametic** sex. The female, as the **homogametic** sex, produces only one type of egg. Female offspring result from fertilization by X-bearing sperm, males from fertilization by Y-bearing sperm. Occasionally abnormal sperm occur, possessing only a set of autosomes and no X or Y chromosome. These can also fertilize eggs to produce males, though such males are sterile. Studies have been made of other abnormal chromosome complements in *Drosophila*. These show that while genes for femaleness are carried on the X chromosome, genes for maleness are located on the autosomes. The Y chromosome turns out to be genetically inactive.

Sex determination in the human species is also an XX–XY type, with the male as the heterogametic sex. But it differs from the situation in *Drosophilia* in that the large X and small Y chromosomes are the primary sex determiners. The 22 pairs of autosomes have little effect on sex characteristics. Moreover, masculine effects are produced by the Y chromosome even if extra X chromosomes are present.

Does this mean that maleness in humans is "stronger" than femaleness? Studies of somatic cells (cells not involved in sexual reproduction) suggest another explanation. Sexual differences are evident in the somatic cells of humans. Cells from the lining of the cheek in females show a deeply staining chromatin body, known as a Barr body. Normal males, and females with only one X chromosome, lack these bodies. But those with extra chromosomes have them. Since the number of Barr bodies is one less than the number of X chromosomes for any given individual, it has been found that Barr bodies are inactive X chromosomes. This means that males and females, both normal and abnormal, have only one functional X chromosome in each cell. The functional balance of X chromosomes to autosomes would then be the same in both sexes. Thus it would be easy to understand how a single Y chromosome determines maleness even though as many as four X chromosomes may be present.

Several plant species, like humans, have the XX–XY type of sex determination. In contrast, birds, butterflies, moths, and some fish have the XY–XX type of determination. In these organisms, the female is heterogametic and the male is homogametic.

## Sex linkage

Genes located on the sex chromosomes are **sex-linked**, even though they may have no effect upon the sexual phenotype. In *Drosophila* and in humans, most sex-linked genes are found on X chromosomes and are called X-linked genes. Y chromosomes seem to carry few genes, and these do not seem to be paired with those on the X chromosomes.

The normal male has one X chromosome, received from its mother, and one Y chromosome, received from the father. These facts have two important consequences for heredity. First, the male inherits all of its sex-linked traits from the mother. Second, since the male has only one X chromosome, it has only one gene for each of the X-linked sets of alleles. So in the male, each X-linked gene is expressed, whether it is dominant or recessive. In the female, which has two homologous sex chromosomes, the usual dominance relationships are effective. Therefore the pattern of inheritance for X-linked genes may differ from one sex to the other.

One of the first X-linked genes was discovered in *Drosophila* by Morgan. A unique white-eyed male fly appeared in a culture of red-eyed flies. It was mated to a female red-eyed fly, and all of the $F_1$ flies were red-eyed. Matings between $F_1$ flies produced 3,470 red-eyed flies and 782 white-eyed flies. But the white eye reappeared in the $F_2$ generation. This showed that the white-eye trait was the result of a stable genetic change, or **mutation**. The red-eye gene had mutated to a white-eye gene. Data from the crosses indicated that white eye is recessive to red eye.

But two bits of data did not fit the classical pattern. For one thing, the ratio of red-eyed to white-eyed flies was considerably higher than 3 to 1. And all 782 white-eyed flies were male. Furthermore, of the red-eyed flies, 2,159 were female and 1,011 were male, instead of half and half. **Backcross mating** between the original white-eyed male and his $F_1$ daughters produced 132 red-eyed males, 129 red-eyed females, 86 white-eyed males and 88 white-eyed females—thus demonstrating that females could have white eyes.

Morgan suggested that the gene for white eye is located on the X chromosome and is recessive to its allele for red eye. The original male carried the mutated white-eye gene on his single X chromosome and demonstrated the recessive phenotype. His X chromosome was passed to his daughters. But since they also had an X chromosome with the dominant red-eye gene from their mothers, they showed the dominant phenotype. The parent male's Y chromosome carried no gene for eye color. But his male offspring were red-eyed, since they too received the X-linked red-eye gene from their mother. The heterozygous $F_1$ females passed the white-eye gene on one X chromosome to approximately half of their male offspring, and the red-eye gene on the other X chromosome to the other half. All of the $F_2$ females were red-eyed because each re-

ceived an X chromosome with the dominant red eye regardless of which gene she received from her mother. In the backcrosses between $F_1$ females and their male parent, both parents must have carried an X chromosome with the white-eye gene, in order to produce the homozygous recessive female offspring.

There are nearly sixty known abnormal conditions governed by X-linked genes in humans. Among these are colorblindness, hemophilia, some sexual abnormalities, muscular dystrophy, and the production of certain blood antigens. Heterozygous female carriers of X-linked recessive genes do not show the recessive phenotype. But they will usually pass the recessive allele to about half their sons, who will show the recessive phenotype. However, the sons cannot transmit X-linked genes to *their* sons, since they do not give them an X chromosome. X-linked genes are transmitted from the maternal grandfather or grandmother to the grandson through the mother. So an X-

5-9
Inheritance of sex-linked characteristics: X-linked white-eye gene in *Drosophila*.

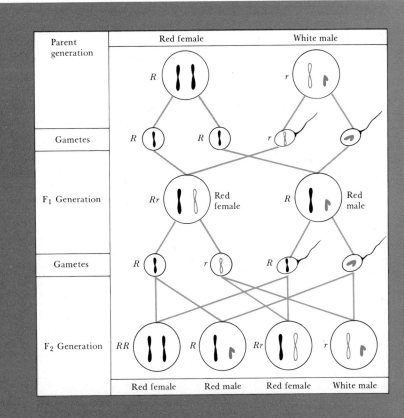

linked recessive trait may skip a generation before it reappears in the offspring.

More men than women show X-linked recessive traits. This is because the dominant allele in women is usually present on one X chromosome or the other. For example, colorblindness in humans is as much as 20 times more frequent in men as it is in women. However, the daughter of a heterozygous female and a recessive male could receive the recessive trait from both parents. She would then show the recessive phenotype.

One of the few genes carried on the human Y chromosome is one for hairy ears, a phenomenon observed in the population of India. This Y-linked gene is passed from father to son. It does not appear among females.

### Sex-influenced traits

Baldness is a human trait which occurs commonly among men. It appears in women only infrequently. However, the fact that it appears at all among women is an indication that the gene must not be Y-linked. Since the trait is transmitted from father to son, it cannot possibly be X-linked. So baldness genes must be transmitted by autosomes. The trait seems to be dominant in the male and recessive in the female. It is termed a **sex-influenced** trait. The level of male sex hormones (androgens) is the main factor which causes baldness to develop in those who carry baldness genes. A high level of androgens permits baldness to occur in most men heterozygous or homozygous for the baldness gene. Hetero-

zygous women, and eunuchs of any genotype, normally do not become bald. Eunuchs who carry the baldness gene may become bald if treated with androgens. Women who are homozygous for the trait rarely have a high enough level of androgens to cause them to become bald.

**Sex-limited** genes affect the phenotype of only one sex. Among cattle, both sexes carry genes for milk production, but they are expressed only in females. Genetically determined abnormalities of sexual organs are sex-limited because the organs are found only in one sex.

## Chromosomal abnormalities

Each species or individual has a **karyotype** — a set of chromosomes characteristic of its somatic, or body, cells. The human karyotype includes 46 chromosomes, which can be divided into seven groups according to size. Human females typically have 22 pairs of autosomes plus a pair of X chromosomes. Males have the 22 pairs of autosomes plus one X and one Y chromosome. The distinctive size and shape of the Y chromosome readily distinguishes the male karyotype from that of the female. Each type of autosome can be distinguished from the others by differences in size, position of centromere, and other factors. So chromosome loss or visible changes in structure can be ascribed accurately to a specific chromosome. A number of phenotypic abnormalities have been correlated with unusual karyotypes.

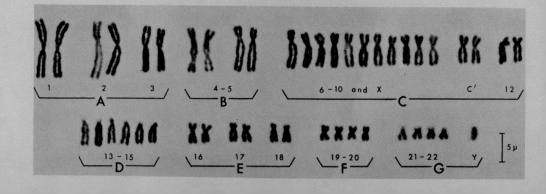

5-10
Karyotype of human male. A ''scrambled'' chromosome picture such as that in chapter 4 is cut apart, and the chromosomes are identified and grouped on the basis of size and shape. (Courtesy of Carolina Biological Supply Company). See Chromosomal abnormalities.

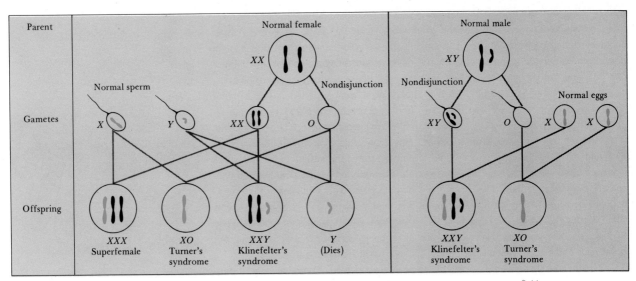

5-11
Possible abnormal sex
chromosome constitu-
tions resulting from
nondisjunction during
formation of one parent's
gametes. (See Abnormal
chromosome number)

## Abnormal chromosome number

Variation in the number of chromosomes often produces abnormal individuals. Such variation may be the result of a mishap during meiosis, or it may happen when a single egg is fertilized by two sperm cells. In humans, the chromosomes of the somatic cells are normally diploid. The nucleus of each cell contains two haploid sets of chromosomes, each numbering 23. An individual with three or more haploid sets of chromosomes is called a **polyploid**. In humans, polyploidy is lethal. Triploid karyotypes (with three haploid sets) are frequent among spontaneously aborted human fetuses. Tetraploids (with four sets) also occur. However, polyploidy is not lethal in all species. Plant polyploids are viable. Often they are larger than the diploid forms of the same species.

Since multicellular organisms usually arise from mitotic divisions of a single cell, all their body cells should have identical karyotypes. But occasionally something goes wrong during mitosis, and the chromosomes are not distributed equally or wholly. Individuals having cells with different karyotypes are called **mosaic**. Mosaic humans, with both polyploid and diploid

cells, have a better chance than polyploids of surviving to birth or beyond. However, they generally have multiple defects. An exception to this occurs in the liver. Many liver cells are polyploid in otherwise normal diploid individuals.

Among live-born humans, most abnormal karyotypes are **aneuploid**. That is, one or more chromosomes are represented more frequently than the others. Of these, **monosomics** (missing one chromosome) and **trisomics** (with one extra chromosome) occur most frequently.

About half the abnormal human karyotypes involve unusual sex chromosome constitutions. Klinefelter's syndrome is shown by males with an extra X chromosome—the XXY karyotype. The symptoms include sterility, enlarged breasts, and possibly severe mental deficiency. A female who lacks an X chromosome—the XO condition—has Turner's syndrome. She is short, lacks secondary sexual characteristics, and may be mentally retarded. Some human XXX females are normal and fertile, but others are infertile and mentally defective. Males of the XYY type are taller than average, and may be more aggressive than normal males.

Individuals with three sex chromosomes

usually occur as the result of nondisjunction—the failure of paired chromosomes to separate during meiosis. When this happens, both daughter chromosomes go into one cell and the other daughter cell receives none. Thus an egg cell may have two X chromosomes and be fertilized by a Y-bearing sperm to produce an XXY individual, or by an X-bearing sperm to produce an XXX female. Note that abnormal phenotypes are often associated with these karyotypes, even though they differ from the normal karyotype by only a single chromosome. The normal karyotype appears to be so delicately balanced that gain or loss of a single sex chromosome results in abnormality.

Extra autosomes also occur in humans. Down's syndrome, or mongolism, is due to the presence of an extra chromosome 21, one of the smallest. The syndrome is characterized by severe mental deficiency and the presence of slanting eye folds, as well as other traits. It is most common among children born to older women. This suggests that nondisjunction becomes more likely as the sex cells age. A high mortality rate accompanies Down's syndrome, though modern medicine can often prolong the lives of its victims.

## Chromosomal aberrations

Karyotypes may also be abnormal because of alterations in the chromosomes themselves, rather than because of an abnormal number of them. Such alterations are called **chromosomal aberrations**. They result from breakage of chromosomal material at some point during meiosis. Crossing-over is an example of such breakage. But this is not harmful if the breaks occur in the same spot on both chromosomes, so that the new chromosomes formed by the crossing-over have the normal number of genes for the proper traits. However, when part of a chromosome gets lost, or out of place, or accidentally attaches itself to another whole chromosome, there is likely to be trouble.

For example, not all individuals with

Down's syndrome appear to have an extra chromosome 21. Some have the normal number of 46 chromosomes. But in such cases, examination shows that one chromosome, usually number 14, is abnormally long. What has happened is that a major portion of chromosome 21 has become attached to the nonhomologous chromosome. This type of chromosomal aberration is called **translocation**. An individual with a translocated number 21 plus two ordinary chromosomes 21 is *functionally* trisomic in this chromosome and develops Down's syndrome. A variety of other translocations have been described for humans. Often they have no noticeable effect.

A second type of chromosomal aberration is the absence, or **deletion**, of part of the chromosome. Deletions of the Y chromosome are known, but they do not have a serious effect. This is probably because the Y chromosome carries little genetically active material to begin with. **Duplication** is just the reverse of deletion. In this aberration a part of the chromosome is repeated as a result of unequal crossing-over between two nonsister chromatids. Small deletions can be lethal, but small duplications are less likely to be so.

**Inversion** is a type of chromosomal recombination in which part of the chromosome becomes looped, causing a reversal in gene sequence. This relocation may affect the ways in which the genes are expressed. Both duplication and inversion are difficult to identify in human chromosomes.

Changes of karyotype may occur spontaneously without apparent cause. However, a variety of agents are known to induce them. For instance, the drug colchicine, which is used to arrest chromosome movement during cell reproduction, may cause a doubling of the chromosome number. Certain chemicals and viruses can cause cells to have either more or less than the normal number of chromosomes, sometimes leading to cancerous growth. Chromosome breakage can be caused by radiation (such as X-rays), chemicals, or viruses.

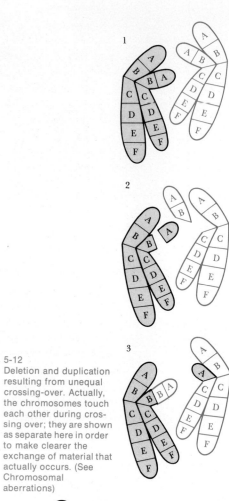

5-12
Deletion and duplication resulting from unequal crossing-over. Actually, the chromosomes touch each other during crossing over; they are shown as separate here in order to make clearer the exchange of material that actually occurs. (See Chromosomal aberrations)

# summary

Gregor Mendel was the first to develop the concept of particles (genes) that determined the patterns of heredity. Using pure strains of yellow and green garden peas, he demonstrated that both male and female parents contributed equally to the offspring. He determined that green was the dominant trait and yellow the recessive. While phenotypes were identical for some offspring, genotypes were shown shown to vary with the individual plant. Mendel assumed that each characteristic is controlled by a pair of genes (alleles) — one from the male gamete, the other from the female. A characteristic determined by two identical genes is homozygous. When determined by two different genes, it is heterozygous. Heterozygous characteristics are usually dominant. The resulting individual is a monohybrid. A mating between two monohybrids is a monohybrid cross, the gene for each characteristic being segregated into separate gametes in each parent. Mendel proposed a principle of segregation which states that the genes of allelic pairs segregate at gametogenesis and reassociate at random during fertilization.

Mendel also did experiments with dihybrid crossing, involving pairs of characteristics. He concluded that genes from allelic pairs for one characteristic passed into gametes independently of genes from other pairs. This is the principle of independent assortment. The statistical possibilities of combinations of characteristics become almost unlimited in humans, who have about 10,000 pairs of genes.

Many traits are determined by genes that show no dominance. For example, red and white flowers produce pink offspring. Also, different pairs of alleles may affect the same trait. This yields a greater variety of genotypes and phenotypes. Codominance can occur when two alleles are dominant to a third, but not to each other. Genes for human blood are an example.

Several sets of genes often interact to produce phenotypes with variations in characteristics, because each affects the characteristic differently. Epistasis occurs whenever there is a gene present that completely masks a characteristic. For instance, the gene for albinism completely masks any gene for hair color. Polygenetic traits result from the cumulative effects of a group of nondominant contributing genes. This results in a quantitative gradation of the characteristic, such as is found in skin color. Collaborative interaction of gene pairs leads to phenotypes that neither pair could produce alone.

Genes for many characteristics are located on the same chromosome. They cannot assort independently and so are considered to be linked. Sex determination is achieved by sex chromosomes. Other chromosomes are called autosomes. The male is heterogametic since it carries chromosomes for each sex. The female is homogametic, carrying female chromosomes only. Genes located on the sex chromosomes are responsible for sex-linked characteristics. Since Y (male) chromosomes carry few genes, all sex-linked characteristics are transmitted to the male through his mother. Colorblindness and hemophilia are examples of sex-linked characteristics that occur almost exclusively in the male. Some traits are sex-influenced. The genes governing the trait are transmitted by autosomes, and the characteristic is dominant in one sex and recessive in the other. Baldness is an example.

Each species has a chromosome number — karyotype — that is characteristic to it. The human karyotype is 46. Male karyotypes can be distinguished from female by the size and shape of the Y chromosome. Autosomes often show distinctive characteristics. Abnormalities in chromosome number will often produce abnormalities in the individual. These variations may occur during meiosis. Extra sets of chromosomes are called polyploid. In humans this condition is lethal. However, many polyploid plants show no ill effects. When the cells of an individual have different karyotypes — a mosaic — multiple defects often result. In humans, most abnormal karyotypes are a result of alterations in sex chromosome numbers. Examples are males with extra X chromosomes, females lacking an X chromosome, XXX females, and XYY males. Karyotypes are so delicately balanced that a change by one chromosome can lead to a defect. Mongolism is the result of an extra chromosome 21. Aberrations or breaks in the chromosomes themselves will lead to abnormal karyotypes.

# Going Places

Take a one-day walk in the wild. You may never want to return!
Ever Tried Squirrel Stew? Or Boiled Pokeweed?
Weather for woodsmen.
6 Quick things to do in an emergency.
How long could you last in the wild? Take a survival test and see.
Choosing packs, boots, sleeping bags.

# Planning a One-Day Hike

The outdoors is a powerful magnet. Each year, millions of Americans shoulder packs and don hiking boots and parkas to spend a day, a weekend, or weeks exploring the backcountry on foot. These hardy backpackers respond to the lure of the wild for many reasons. Some like the thrill of discovery and adventure. Some jump at the chance to escape the tensions of civilized life and get in touch with nature. Others do it just to get in shape.

The mere mention of the subject of backpacking to the uninitiated but interested individual immediately releases a flood of questions. Where should you go? What equipment do you need? How far should you walk? What should you do when you get there? How dangerous is it? One of the best ways to answer these basic questions is to plan a one-day excursion for one to three people.

## WHERE TO GO

Let's consider the first question: "Where to go?" No matter where you live, the list of possible places is surprisingly long. Every large city has its islands of greenery and interesting areas. In New York City, for example, Central Park in Manhattan and Prospect Park in Brooklyn provide hundreds of acres within which an eight or ten mile hike can easily be planned. Fairmount Park in Philadelphia is another good possibility, as is Rock Creek Park in Washington, D.C., and Golden Gate Park in San Francisco.

Those who live in the suburbs have even better resources at their disposal because these people are usually surrounded by acres of greenery and woodlands. It is also possible to travel by auto or public transportation to a state park or other green area set aside specifically for picnicking, boating, and other outdoor activities. Such areas usually have special trails that are well-maintained and marked so you need not even carry a map. In places without such facilities, however, it is always a good idea to get a map of the area and study it before pushing off.

Then there is the most challenging National Trails system which includes trails of two major kinds. First are the National Recreation Trails which have been designed for short hikes or for bike or horseback riding. There are some 250 miles of these located near large urban areas; they vary in length from a quarter of a mile to 30 miles. Examples include the Fontenelle Forest Trail (3.9 miles) in Nebraska, the Greer Island Nature.Trail (3 miles) in Fort Worth, Texas, and the Fred Cleator Interpretive Trail (1.3 miles) in Washington State.

The second part of the National Trails system, the National Scenic Trail, is a 22,000-mile system intended for adventurous souls who wish to take more challenging hikes. The most famous and best maintained of these trails is the Appalachian Trail which entends from Springer Mountain in Georgia to Mount Katahdin in Maine. There are numerous lean-tos and shelters along its 2,000-mile length. For Westerners, there is the 2,300-mile Pacific Crest Trail which begins in Southern California and stretches clear up through the Northern Cascade Mountains at the Canadian border, and the Rocky Mountain Route which runs 3,000 miles along the Continental Divide from Mexico to Canada.

Much of the 450 million acres of federally owned public land—from Arizona to Alaska—is managed by the Bureau of Land Management. Most of this land, which is rough backcountry, lies in the West and Northwest and contains campgrounds. Information about these lands is found in the U.S. Department of Agriculture's publication, *Access to Public Domain Lands*. Then, of course, there are some 154 national forests with 165,000 miles of trails, 33 national parks with 12,000 miles of trails, and 320 national wildlife refuges—all with campsites. Maps and information on any of these facilities can be obtained from hiking and outdoor groups such as the Sierra Club, the Wilderness Society, or American Youth Hostels. (Incidentally, these organizations also organize hikes of varying lengths for backpackers with all degrees of experience. They are well planned and led by skilled backpackers. It might be a good idea to give one of them a call to see what they offer.) State and Federal agencies and campground operators are other good bets as information sources. Finally, there are two excellent hiking books which contain the names and addresses of many organizations dedicated to the outdoors. These are *The Hiker's Bible* by Robert Elman and *America's Backpacking Book* by Raymond Bridge.

*I am what might be called a compulsive walker. Any free weekend I am liable to pick up a road map, choose a large, blank area that intrigues me, drive to the edge of it, park my car, walk in with a pack on my back, and find out what's there. Once, on something suspiciously like impulse, I spent a summer walking from one end of California to the other — Mexico to Oregon. In six months I walked well over a thousand miles, through deserts and mountains. And I have never for a moment regretted it.*

Colin Fletcher, The Man Who Walked Through Time

## WHAT TO TAKE

Calvin Larsen/Photo Researchers, Inc.

Once you've chosen your destination, the next step is to determine what equipment you'll need. Most experienced hikers make a checklist of things to take. On Robert Elman's list, for example, are boots, backpack, sleeping bag, and parka. In addition to these, for a half-day or one-day hike, you should pack these basic essentials:

Pocket knife with versatile blades
Waterproof matches with waterproof container
Candle or fire starter
Flashlight
Map and compass
Canteen—aluminum or plastic (one-quart capacity)
Water purification tablets (halozone)
Thirst quenchers (lemon, lime, raisins)
Energy food for snacking (candy, fruit, nuts, cheese, or the so-called "birdseed"—a mixture of dried cereal, nuts, seeds, raisins, and other goodies which is eaten by the handful)
Lunch (chicken or turkey legs and wings; lunchmeat sandwiches; thermos of coffee, fruit juice, or soup)
Soap and/or premoistened towelettes
Kleenex and a few paper towels

For emergency repairs, you might take along a sewing kit, some lengths of nylon cord, and a kit for repairing rubber items. (A tear in the knee of your pants, or a broken bootlace can be an awful nuisance, even on a short walk.) For first aid, tanning lotion to prevent sunburn, and vaseline or balm to guard against chapping are essential. Insect repellent, bandages, antiseptic, and aspirin can also help relieve minor aches or pains. For larger hikes, of course, a more complete first-aid kit should be packed. Information about this and other long-distance hiking equipment can be obtained by consulting one of the books already recommended.

A pair of field glasses or binoculars can also add to the enjoyment of your day in the wild. Use them for focusing in on plants, animals, and other objects that catch your fancy. Similarly, a camera with a protective lens cap and several rolls of film will permit you to capture sights that interest you. And last but not least, packing a field guide to the flora and fauna of the area is an excellent idea. It will help you identify trees, flowers, animals, and birds that you don't get much opportunity to meet and enjoy if you're a city-dweller.

## SOME BACKPACKING BASICS

Keith Gunnar/Photo Researchers, Inc

Since a hiker's clothing is the only protection he or she has against the elements, the choice of clothing—from hat to pack to pants to boots—is of utmost importance. Let's start with the basics: underwear. A cotton T-shirt absorbs perspiration in summer and serves as added insulation in winter. (Women may want to wear a lightweight bra under it.) Warm weather underpants should be of light cotton and loose fitting. In very cold weather, "long johns," either of pure cotton or cotton plus synthetic are called for.

The next layer is a bit more important. The shirt should have long sleeves to prevent scratches from protruding tree limbs and branches and to protect your skin against sunburn. It should also have two or more pockets for carrying maps, snacks, and doodads. In summer, a light cotton shirt will do fine, whereas cold weather calls for flannel, corduroy, or some similar fabric. In winter, it's also a good idea to take along a quilted thermal vest that can be worn over the shirt for extra insulation. For cool summer evenings, a light windbreaker is recommended.

Since trousers with cuffs tend to snag the underbrush—and can cause you to tumble—cuffs should not be worn. The same goes for bell-bottoms; these drag along the ground and catch roots and other exposed objects. Make sure your pants have belt loops for a nice strong belt. You'll be thankful for this rarely appreciated article when you're looking for a place to hang your knife or canteen. Tightfitting denim jeans, comfortable and fashionable as they are in the city, are taboo in the wild. They impede free walking by binding and bunching; and there's nothing more irritating than a pair of wet jeans chafing the skin with each step. Besides, jeans are thermodynamically unsound. Denim is one of the world's worst insulators: it lets in the cold air in winter and attracts and traps heat in summer.

Having tossed aside your favorite kind of trousers, what on earth is left to wear? Anything tough and loose-fitting, such as chino, poplin, or drill. Also, the pants should have at least four pockets—you'd be surprised at all the things that will end up in them.

## 24 HOURS ON THE TRAIL

Serious backpackers probably have different ideas about how a typical day is spent on the trail, but Colin Fletcher, one of the most experienced hikers, gives the following breakdown:

|  | Hours | Minutes |
| --- | --- | --- |
| Walking, including ten-minute breaks every hour | 7 |  |
| Extension of half the ten-minute halts to twenty minutes because of sights, sounds, smells, ruminations and inertia |  | 30 |
| Dallying for photography and general admiration of the scene—about 4 minutes every hour |  | 30 |
| Photography, once a day, of a difficult and utterly irresistible object | 1 |  |
| Conversations with mountain men, desert rats, or bighorn sheep | 1 |  |
| Cooking and eating four meals | 3 | 30 |
| Camp chores |  | 30 |
| Usual business of wilderness traveler: contemplation of nature and/or navel |  | 30 |
| Time quite unaccountable for |  | 30 |
| Sleep, including catnaps | 8 | 59 |
| Reading, fishing, elevated thinking, unmentionable items, and general sloth |  | 1 |
|  | Total | 24 |

## HOW TO WALK

Alexander Lowry/Photo Researchers, Inc.

From the beginning, we are taught to walk incorrectly. Everyone from schoolteachers to gym instructors to army sergeants tell us to walk with the toes pointed outward at a slight angle. But this is wrong because it strains the arch and cuts the length of the stride. According to Elman in *The Hiker's Bible*, the three parts of the human foot most important to walkers are the heel, the ball under the big toe, and the ball under the small toe. A 175-pound man who walks ten miles over level terrain will put about 1,540 tons of pressure on these three parts of the feet by the end of his trip. Ouch! That's why it's so important to learn how to hike correctly from the start.

The first step, says Elman, is to point your feet in a straight line. Keep the weight of your body balanced over your feet at all times. When you start out, swing your right leg forward. As you do so, your knee should be relaxed and your toes pointing straight ahead. Now bring your right foot down—it should land about 24 to 27 inches ahead of your left foot. The heel should touch ground slightly before the toe does. As you move your left leg in the same manner, your right foot should begin to push up, using the toes as a lever.

The most important part of hiking is maintaining a pace, or rhythmic stride, that uses your leg muscles most efficiently. Your stride should be easy and natural. The same goes for your arm swing. But don't swing your hips and shoulders—these are the pivots that carry the weight of your body and pack. Moving these joints may set you off balance. You should walk erect with your eyes on the trail ahead of you. The only time you should lean your body backward or forward is when you are going up or down a steep hill. Don't walk too fast or too jerkily—this makes the muscles function inefficiently, and it makes you tired, causing you to stop for frequent rest breaks. As you find your stride, you should be able to walk about two miles an hour while lugging a 30-pound pack.

As you move along the trail, use your eyes as efficiently as you use the rest of your body. Sidestep obstacles such as fallen trees, large rocks, and such. Don't step over or climb over obstacles. Each time you do this, you waste energy because you are needlessly lifting your body and your pack. Although walking over, rather than around, a fallen tree may seem the easiest thing to do at the time, remember that all these extra steps-up accumulate—at the end of the day they can add up to a lot of unnecessary climbing and energy consumption.

The only time you should interrupt your pace is when you're going up or down a hill. When climbing a hill, use the "lockstep," or rest step as it is sometimes called: straighten your trailing or downhill leg, locking the knee, and rest on it for a few seconds. Repeat this with each step you take. By using this step, you're putting all your weight on your leg bones instead of your muscles, thus saving strength. You can also use the same step when descending a steep hill only in reverse, of course. Incidentally, it's also a good idea to use some sort of wooden staff for steep grades. A staff allows you to propel yourself forward when ascending a hill, and to brake yourself on the way down.

Your rest breaks should be brief and frequent, rather than long and less frequent, because a long rest causes the muscles to stiffen, making it difficult to get back into action. So it's a good idea to rest for five minutes every half-hour. Of course the frequency and duration of these breaks depends on the terrain. And don't be too rigid about your schedule. If something along the way catches your interest, stop and admire it. After all, that's what hiking is all about.

## GET IN SHAPE

Rodelinde Albrecht

Before setting out on your walk, you should remember three cardinal rules:

1. Never backpack alone—go with at least two companions. If you get hurt and can't move, someone can go for help.
2. Let someone know where you're going, when you're going, and when you're coming back.
3. You should be in reasonably good shape. If you have a heart conditior asthma, or some other potentially disabling disease, you should consult your physician before undertaking a long hike. But don't let these ailments discourage you; in 90 percent of cases, a hike would cause no damage; in fact, it would probably be beneficial.

If you're too flabby from easy city living and lack of exercise, you'll be no match for the challenges of nature. You might want to consider taking long walks throughout your city or around your college campus for one or two weekends before your hike. Without a pack, and taking time out for lunch and rest breaks, you can probably walk about 20 miles in one day. With a pack, you'll be carrying 20 to 25 pounds more. Similarly, jogging or walking up stairs instead of taking the elevator are good conditioners. But above all, don't strain yourself. Remember, backpacking is a pleasure. The more you do it and the better shape you're in, the more you'll enjoy it.

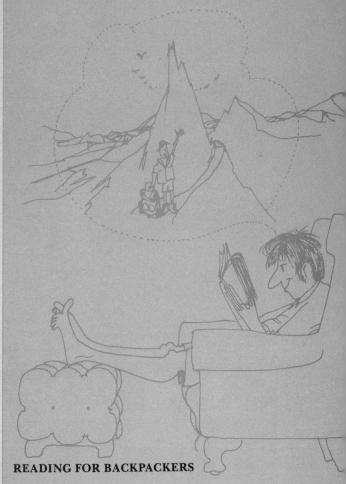

## READING FOR BACKPACKERS

*The Hiker's Bible* by Robert Elman. Garden City, N.Y.: Doubleday, 1973, 152 pp. ($2.50), illustrated. An excellent primer on the nuts and bolts of hiking with good selections telling where to get more information on hiking organizations, campsite locations, sources for equipment, and bibliography.

*America's Backpacking Book* by Raymond Bridge. New York: Charles Scribner's Sons, 1973, 417 pp. ($14.95), illustrated. A bit overpriced, but by and large a good primer with much detail on different kinds of outdoor activities. Also includes equipment appendix and an outdoorsmen's bibliography.

*The New Complete Walker* by Colin Fletcher. New York: Knopf, 1974, 470 pp. ($8.95), illustrated. A classic. A wise, witty, warm compendium on hiking by the man who walked through the Grand Canyon.

*The Last Whole Earth Catalog* (and earlier editions). $5.00. A joy to browse through, especially the "Nomadics" section. Fresh bright, objective information about backpacking.

*Wilderness Cookery* by Bradford Angier. Harrisburg, Pa.: Stackpole Books, 1970, 256 pp. ($1.95 in paper), illustrated. All you need to know about outdoor cookery by a master of the art. Includes recipes, information on equipment, tips on identifying wild edible plants.

*Backpacker Magazine.* A quarterly with offices at 28 W. 44th Street, New York City 10036. $2.50 a copy, $7.50 a year by subscription. A highly recommended magazine, edited and written by pros who cover all aspects of backpacking.

*Stalking the Good Life* by Euell Gibbons. New York: David McKay, Inc., 1966, 248 pp. ($5.95), illustrated. How to find, identify, and prepare wild edible plants. Gibbons's name is a household word among all who love the outdoors. Any book by him comes with the highest recommendation.

*The Survival Book* by Paul Nesbitt, Alonzo Pond, and William Allen. New York: Funk and Wagnalls, 1959, 338 pp. (1.95), illustrated. The bible of survival books. Don't go on your hike without this one written by three pros—two of whom ran survival schools for the U.S. government.

# Weather for Woodsmen

Any experienced outdoorsman knows that you don't need all the jargon and expensive paraphernalia of modern television meteorologists to predict the weather. With a pair of sharp eyes and ears, a bit of common sense, and a little practice, you can make an accurate forecast—perhaps even more accurate than the professional.

Since the best indicators of weather are the clouds, it's a good idea to learn as much as possible about them. One good source is the booklet, *Clouds,* available for under a dollar from the Superintendent of Documents, U.S. Government Printing Office, Washington, D.C.

Like everything else in nature, clouds follow certain patterns which you can learn to detect in a short time. For starters, clouds that look like mackerel scales mean a rainstorm in summer and a snowstorm in winter. As the old rhyme puts it,

Mackerel scales and mares' tails
Make tall ships carry low sails.

A mare's tail is a wispy cirrus cloud, part of which resembles a horse's tail.

The speed at which clouds form tells you a lot about the weather too. Rain right after the gathering of heavy clouds means a short storm. If the rain does not come for some time after the clouds have formed, look for a long storm.

The strength and direction of the wind is a good tip-off. A shifting wind, for example, carries a hint. If the sky is cloudy and the wind suddenly shifts from northwest to northeast, or from southeast to southwest, head for cover because a squall is on the way. If the day is clear and calm, and the smoke from your campfire rises straight up, you can expect the weather to remain stable for at least the next 12 hours.

The color of the sky can be just as revealing. Most of us are familiar with the old saw,

Red sky at morning, sailor take warning.
Red sky at night, sailor's delight.

By and large this is true. If the eastern sky glows with a dazzling red sunrise, there's a good chance for rain or snow within 18 to 24 hours. But if the sun sets in a bright red ball, you can bet on fair weather for the next day. If the horizon is tinged with a pale lavender during sunrise or sunset, chances are good for nice weather. An amber colored horizon means wind but no rain, whereas a light yellow color signals the approach of rain.

If you see a halo around the sun or moon, prepare for rain or snow. Rainbows also help give you clues about upcoming weather. A rainbow in the morning, for example, presages foul weather, whereas a rainbow at night (that is, a moon rainbow) means fair weather for the following day. The formation of dew in the morning indicates nice weather for the day, but dew at night foretells rain or snow.

The coming of a thunderstorm is difficult to predict, but it generally moves from west to east. If you're ever caught in a thunderstorm, you can avoid being struck by lightning by following this simple rule: stay away from open spaces and prominent objects. More specifically you should avoid:
1. Canoes or small boats in open water;
2. Open prairies (it's safe to lie down here);
3. Solitary trees or a single patch of trees;
4. Open fireplaces;
5. Telephone poles or wire fences;
6. Isolated lean-tos, or any other small building in the open.

Finally, animals and insects tip you off about upcoming weather changes. Low-flying insects—and the birds that prey on them—mean rain or snow is on the way, whereas birds or insects flying high means fair weather. Coyotes howling about nine in the morning are telling you to head for cover. Elk and deer vacate high ground when they sense a storm brewing. The approach of bad weather also seems to make these animals browse more than usual.

Photo credit: W. J. Schoonmaker/National Audubon Society/Photo Researchers, Inc.

Do you know what poisonous plants, animals, and insects look like? And what to do if affected or bitten by one? Here's your chance to test yourself by identifying the following potential troublemakers.

Can you identify these troublemakers?

## WILL "YANKEE DOODLE" DO?

Suppose you are out for a leisurely hike in one of the National parks and suddenly meet a grizzly bear? What should you do? Run? Wrestle the beast to the ground—all 1700 pounds of him— and finish him off with your scout knife? Or should you roll over and play dead? The best course of action, believe it or not, is to sing, whistle, or make any other loud, continuous noise.

While you're singing, start backing away from the animal—very s-l-o-w-l-y and c-a-r-e-f-u-l-l-y. Don't spin on your heel and take off because sudden movements will frighten the monster. If he doesn't like your singing and decides to attack, hit the ground, stay on your stomach, and put your hands over your head and face. Bears seem to prefer biting the neck, shoulders, and buttocks. Don't squirm or resist and the beast may lose interest. Remember, he's not attacking you because he's hungry, but because he sees you as an invader of his turf.

The best advice of all, of course, is to avoid a bear if you spot one. Keep at least 100 yards of space between you and him. Don't rush toward him to snap his picture—this will only frighten him and you will lose your camera, or worse. Finally, report all attacks by bears to the police, park rangers, or other authority.

## IF YOU GET LOST

Sooner or later, nearly everyone loses his way in the woods. When the inevitable happens, don't lose your head. Sit back, rest, and think. First, you must decide whether to stay where you are or try to find your way out. The Forest Service advises that you remain where you are under the following circumstances:

1. If you are injured or exhausted;
2. If the terrain is hilly or difficult to traverse;
3. If the weather is bad or darkness is approaching;
4. If you can find shelter;
5. If you think a search party may be looking for you.

You should try to get back to camp or civilization if:

1. Your strength allows you to travel;
2. The weather is good and there is sufficient daylight;
3. You are fairly certain that you can find the way.

# THE GREAT WILDERNESS SURVIVAL TEST

If you were stranded in the wilds, how long could you survive? Match wits with nature by answering true or false to the following statements.

1. Clothes should not be washed often in the wilds because dirt serves as an excellent insulator.     T/F

2. The best first aid treatment for frostbite is to rub the frozen area vigorously, preferably with ice or snow.     T/F

3. The best shelter for a person lost without a tent in a snowy area is one made of snow.     T/F

4. If you are stranded in the desert with a dangerously low water supply, you can get potable water by placing cool stones on a tarpaulin overnight to gather enough dew for a drink.     T/F

5. If you are lost in the desert and are out of water, you should drink your own urine.     T/F

6. In the jungle, a bitter, sour, or unpleasant-tasting plant should be spat out immediately because it is probably poisonous.     T/F

7. Generally, anything eaten by other mammals is okay for humans too.     T/F

8. A net and a small smudge fire will protect you against malaria-carrying mosquitos.     T/F

9. One of the best places to pitch your camp in the jungle is close to water.     T/F

10. Two ways to fend off a shark are to kick it and to slap the surface of the water to scare it off.     T/F

11. It's all right to drink seawater, provided it is taken in small amounts over a period of time.     T/F

12. You are settling in for the night in your cozy tent by curling up next to your warm, glowing stove. Suddenly, you feel a slight pressure on your temples, almost as if from the elastic band of a cap. You should get out of the tent quickly because you are being poisoned by carbon monoxide.     T/F

13. The best first aid treatment for sunstroke is a stimulant such as coffee, tea, or alcohol.     T/F

14. The best treatment for heat exhaustion is to keep the victim warm by wrapping him in a blanket and applying heated rocks or a hot water bottle.     T/F

15. Jumping up and down in cold weather is a good way to help keep warm.     T/F

16. You are trekking through a jungle and are suddenly attacked by a swarm of flies. Your best defense is to head for water or thick bushes.     T/F

17. If someone in your party breaks a bone, you should try to fix it by easing it back in place.     T/F

18. If someone receives a head injury, get him up and walking as soon as possible. This will get the blood circulating and prevent any possible brain damage.     T/F

19. If your water supply is low, you can alleviate thirst by eating lots of high-protein foods such as eggs and cheese.     T/F

20. You can start a fire in an emergency by using the lens of a camera.     T/F

## EMERGENCY!

The experienced backpacker Raymond Bridge has proposed these six general principles to be followed in an emergency.

1. Examine the injured thoroughly to find out what is wrong.
2. Get help, or send someone else for it, if possible and if necessary.
3. Give first aid to the injured.*
4. Move the injured person to a sheltered spot, especially if the weather is bad.
5. Talk to the victim. Calm him and comfort him; this is as important as taking care of injuries.
6. Write down all information, including what happened, what you found, what you did, and when each occurred. The sequence may be important to a doctor. Don't rely on memory!

* For more specific information on administering first aid, see *Mountaineering Medicine* by Fred T. Darvill, a pocket-size medical guide available from Backpacker Books, Bellows Falls, Vt. 15101, for under $2.00.

# The Outdoor Gourmet

The outdoors gives you a hearty appetite. The smell of bacon, bread, or coffee cooking over a crackling fire can make even the most blistered backpacker agreeable. Small wonder, then, that mealtimes, especially the evening repasts, are looked forward to by hikers with great relish. When you go on a long trip, you'll undoubtedly pack complete meals that have been freeze-dried and sealed in packages which make them virtually spoil-proof. These foods include well-balanced main dishes of every possible type—from frontier stew (a hearty mixture of ground beef, beans, corn, peppers, and seasoned gravy) to chicken á la king, ham and scrambled eggs, omelettes, pork chops, dehydrated fruit cocktail, even a Mexican taco dinner. To help you plan nutritious meals there's an excellent, inexpensive book available from the Sierra Club: *Foods for Knapsackers* by Hans Bunelle.

If you're really adventurous and hunger for a taste of pioneer life, why not try to catch and prepare some wild game or fish for your entree? Possum, squirrel, woodchuck, beaver, muskrat, coon, rabbit, even crow and porcupine, can make scrumptious meals when properly prepared. For example, the noted outdoor culinary artist, Bradford Angier, gives this recipe for squirrel stew.

*After catching and skinning a squirrel, cut up the meat into bite-size chunks. Brown the meat in a pan, using about three tablespoons of margarine or butter. Pour in three cups of water, season with one teaspoon of salt and ½ teaspoon of chopped onion, ½ cup of chopped celery, and ½ cup of sliced carrots. Thicken this with a paste you have made by blending three tablespoons of flour with ½ cup of water, and cook for about one hour. Bon appétit!*

Another woodsmen's staple is freshly caught fish. Angier's recipe for fried trout goes like this.

*Dip the cleaned fish first into a pan of evaporated milk, then into some beaten eggs. Roll in cracker or bread crumbs. Heat up about ½ inch of cooking fat in a thick frying pan. Cook lightly, turning the fish only once. When you can flake the trout with a fork, it's ready.*

Still hungry? How about some dessert? Angier's recipe for open strawberry pie is mouthwatering.

*First, make the 9-inch pie shell by sifting a cup of flour with ½ teaspoon of salt. Mix in ½ cup of shortening (if you just happen to have any lying around, rendered bear grease is best). Add about 3 teaspoons of water and knead. Roll out this dough, then spread it into the 9-inch greased pie pan. Bake in a hot oven for about 15 minutes. Next, make a thick syrup by simmering 1 cup of crushed wild strawberries, ½ cup of sugar, and 2 tablespoons of cornstarch. Put the strawberries into the pie shell, then pour the hot steaming syrup over them. Allow to cool, then dig in. You can use the same recipe for other wild fruits as well—raspberries, thimbleberries, and blackberries will all make delicious open pies.*

For more woodsmen's recipes, see Bradford Angier's *Wilderness Cookery*, available in an inexpensive paperback edition.

Morton Beebe Asscs./Photo Researchers, Inc.

## WILD PLANTS YOU CAN EAT

There are hundreds of edible wild plants that are nutritious and delicious when properly prepared. If you've never tasted any of these delectable goodies, you're in for a pleasant surprise! Herewith is a brief description of some edible wild plants likely to be found throughout the United States.

For further reading: *Stalking the Good Life* by Euell Gibbons (or any of his other books). *Feasting Free on Wild Edibles* by Bradford Angier.

### FOOD ENERGY

How much food energy does a hiker need for one week in the wilds? Colin Fletcher estimates the energy value of selected foods in his seven-day supply as follows.

| Lbs. | Oz. | | Energy Value (Calories) |
|---|---|---|---|
| 2 | 0 | Dry cereal mixture (Fini or Familia) | 3200 |
| 0 | 12 | 3 Pkg. dehydrated fruit (@4 oz.) | 1200 |
| 0 | 9 | 6 Energy bars | 1200 |
| 0 | 4 | Beef jerky | 410 |
| 1 | 4 | 8 Pkg. dried soup (average) | 2400 |
| 0 | 1 | 1 Pkg. instant gravy powder | 100 |
| 1 | 5 | 7 Meat food product bars | 3590 |
| 1 | 4 | 5 Pkg. dehydrated beans (@4 oz.) | 1930 |
| 0 | 8 | 2 Pkg. dehydrated potatoes (@4 oz.) | 800 |
| 0 | 4 | 1 Pkg. dehydrated mixed vegetables (4 oz.) | 400 |
| 0 | 1 | Herbs and spices | 0 |
| 1 | 6 | Powdered nonfat milk | 2230 |
| 1 | 8 | Granulated sugar | 2620 |
| 0 | 8 | 1 Bar semisweet chocolate | 1150 |
| 1 | 5 | 3½ Bars Kendal Mint Cake candy (@6 oz.) | 2290 |
| 1 | 0 | Dry raisins | 1310 |
| 0 | 3 | 30 Tea bags | 0 |
| 0 | 6 | 2 Pkg. fruit drink mix | 600 |
| 0 | 4 | Margarine | 820 |
| 0 | 3 | Salt | 0 |
| 0 | 1 | Salt tablets (about 40) (30 percent dextrose) | 30 |
| 0 | 3 | Emergency ration: 1 meat bar | 510 |

| | | | |
|---|---|---|---|
| Total for one week | | | 26,790 |
| Average daily total | | | 3,830 |

*Amaranth*. A cousin of the beet, this plant has green leaves which are somewhat tasteless by themselves, but terrific if mixed with some more hardy plant such as wild mustard. Amaranths are relatively high in protein, iron, and vitamin A.

*Lamb's quarter* (also known as goosefoot or smooth pigweed). Related to beets and amaranths, this weed is really wild spinach, but is more nutritious than its civilized relative. It thrives all over the country and is rich in protein, and vitamins A and C.

*Wild mustard*. This plant, which is one of the best health foods, is rich in Vitamins A, $B_1$, $B_2$, and C. Only the lyre-shaped leaves on the lower half of the plant are edible. Pick in early spring when the blossoms are yellow, boil for 30 minutes, and season.

*Dandelion*. Millions of dollars worth of herbicides are spent every year to get rid of this common lawn weed. It is related to lettuce and endive, but it is richer than these in protein, iron, and vitamins A and C. Gather in early spring, cut off the outside and top leaves, and use the young leaves as a salad ingredient.

*Pokeweed*. The tender *young* leaves of this weed are second in use only to dandelion greens. The plant grows to a height of six or eight feet and is very rich in protein, iron, vitamins A and C, and other nutrients. Boil for about ten minutes, drain, add seasoning and butter, simmer for a half-hour, then serve with hollandaise sauce. The seeds, roots, and older leaves of this plant are poisonous—so don't eat them.

There are three basic pieces of equipment you should have—pack, sleeping bag, and boots. Because more people are taking an interest in the outdoors, many backpacking stores will allow you to rent these items. It makes sense to rent your equipment for the first few hikes. That way, you can determine whether you love the sport enough to invest more money in it. Renting also gives you a chance to try out different brands of gear.

## The Pack

There are many kinds of pack, and any salesman in a reputable sporting goods store can help you decide what's best for you. The best approach is to pick a pack that looks functional, load it up with 20 pounds of gear, and try it out in the store.

The simplest pack is the frameless rucksack, which is simply a sack carried on the back or hips by two straps. This type of pack is fine for short trips which do not require equipment.

As you begin to get more experienced, you'll choose one of the packs with a frame contoured to follow the curves of your back. These models include a waistband that lets you carry the weight of the pack with your hips, instead of with your back and neck muscles.

Packs come in many different sizes and differ in details, but here are some things you should be looking for: First, get the smallest bag possible. Buying a bag designed to carry enough supplies for a three-month hike is silly when the most you're planning to spend is a week.

Most hikers choose a nylon bag that is about 15 inches wide by 30 inches high. Make sure the bag is securely attached to the frame; a loose pack will rub and wear out with only moderate use. The seams should be reinforced, especially at points of strain. Zippers should work easily, without snagging, and should be of nylon. The frame

# Equipment Guide

Photos courtesy of Backpacking Magazine

should be of lightweight metal such as aluminum. It should have at least two wide nylon backbands, plus a wide, padded waistband. The shoulder straps should also be nylon, well padded, and securely attached.

## Sleeping Bag

The sleeping bag used by most experienced hikers is a form-fitting mummy bag insulated with goose down. Because it is an excellent conserver of body heat, this type of bag is warm enough for nearly all environments.

The bag's cover should be nylon. The zipper should run the full length of the bag so it can be opened on a hot night. The hood of the bag should offer good protection for your head and neck, while leaving an opening large enough for breathing.

Since the down in the bag has a tendency to shift as a result of your body movements, one of the most important features of a bag's construction is the way this problem is solved. The best method is the one that isolates the down into small compartments of tubes, thus holding it in place. The most efficient tubes are those that are horizontal (that is, their length lies across the bag) or shaped like chevrons. One way to check the insulating efficiency of a mummy bag is to test what is known as its "loft"—the amount of air that can be trapped by the insulating system. On a flat surface, unroll the bag and shake it out. If all of the cells seem to be full of air—which you can test by lightly prodding with your fingertips—then you've got a well-insulated bag.

## Boots

Sturdy hiking boots are mandatory if you plan to do any serious hiking. Boots should be of whole grain leather, with five- to eight-inch tops for good ankle support. The soles should be cleated and made of sturdy material such as Vibram. Above all, the boots should be light, weighing about 3 pounds.

Before buying your boots, try them on and wear them at home for a couple of hours. The boots should be about one size larger than your normal shoe size because your feet tend to swell after hours on the trail. After you have laced up, push your foot forward toward the front of the boot. If your toes touch the front get a bigger pair. If you get a boot that is too snug, your toes will suffer when they are jammed against the boot as you scurry downhill.

Keep boots away from extreme heat. Let them dry naturally, not near a stove or open fire. Grease or wax them every so often to keep the leather soft.

## Troublemakers Quiz Answers

*1. Poison ivy.      2. Poison oak.* If you touch either of these plants, vigorously scrub affected area with strong soap, then apply alcohol. Try not to scratch!

*3. Rocky Mountain Wood Tick.* If tick has burrowed into skin, don't brush off. Give it a good dose of alcohol, grease, or oil. When it drops out, step on it. See a doctor quick.

*4. Diamondback rattlesnake.* Immediately tie off area about 3 to 6 inches above the wound (between wound and heart). Tie loosely and loosen every minute in ten. Use sharp sterile blade to cut ¼-inch incision across the two fang wounds. Suck out venom with suction cup or mouth. Don't swallow! Keep area cool with ice or cold water and get victim to a doctor fast. (Remember, speed is essential in dealing with poisonous bites. Don't wait till disaster strikes—memorize the instructions in your snakebite kit *before* leaving home!)

*5. Wasp.* Remove stinger if present, and suck out poison. Apply ice pack, mud, or antiseptic.

*6. Black widow spider.* Same treatment as snakebite.

# ANSWERS TO SURVIVAL TEST

1. *False.* Dirt clogs the pores of clothing, decreasing insulation.
2. *False.* This is an old wives' tale. Rubbing can tear the skin; the application of ice or snow makes matters worse.
3. *True.* As the Eskimos have learned, snow is a good insulator.
4. *True.* A sitting stone does gather dew.
5. *False.* Urine, blood, gasoline, and salt water only increase dehydration because the kidneys must work harder to eliminate the wastes in these liquids.
6. *False.* Lemons and grapefruits are bitter and unpleasant tasting, but most nutritious.
7. *True.* There are a few exceptions, but by and large this statement is correct.
8. *True.*
9. *False.* Water draws mosquitos and animals.
10. *True.* It's even better to keep absolutely still if possible.
11. *False.* Another old wives' tale. Seawater should never be drunk unless you can desalinize it.
12. *True.* Never sleep with a lighted stove in an enclosed space.
13. *False.* Stimulants only worsen the situation. Give the victim cool water, get him to a cool place, and apply cold water packs. Then get him to a physician.
14. *True.* Oddly enough, these steps should be taken. Rubbing vigorously to help circulation and getting the victim to sip a stimulant also helps.
15. *False.* This only wastes energy. Instead, use isometric exercises to bend and unbend your muscles—this generates internal heat.
16. *True.* Flies and other insects won't follow you into the water or the bushes.
17. *False.* This is more dangerous than doing nothing at all. Elevate the limb if you can, and try to splint it.
18. *False.* Keep the victim quiet and lying down.
19. *False.* Proteins require lots of water for digestion. Instead, eat fruits, sweets, or plants.
20. *True.* Remove the back of the camera, hold the shutter open, and focus the sun's rays through the lens onto the tinder.

**How did you do?**

0 to 8 questions right: You'd die in no time. Better read *The Survival Book* by Nesbitt *et al*.

8 to 13 right: Okay. You might last till help comes in the spring.

14 to 20 right: Excellent. You must be a pro.

# Protect your wilderness

It is ironic that those who take up backpacking to escape the pollution of the city are contributing to the pollution of the wilderness. As the interest in backpacking among Americans increases, so does the possibility of damage to the land. According to *Audubon Magazine*, for example, there were about six million backpackers in this country in 1973, three times as many as in 1970. Many of these hikers tend to concentrate in certain popular areas which feature campsites, good water sources, and attractive scenery. *Audubon* estimates that there are two people for every mile of backcountry trail; in some areas, such as the White Mountains of New Hampshire, there are twenty-four hikers for every mile, particularly during the summer.

Understandably, this sudden interest in the wilderness has taken its toll in damage to the land. Some of the more common violations are litter, the erosion of numerous trails, the destruction of plants, water pollution as a result of emptying wastes into streams and rivers, and the collapse of some fragile ecosystems.

What can you, as a backpacker, do to alleviate this problem? Experts have devised a number of principles which should be followed. These include:

1. Pack out what you pack in. This is the cardinal rule among experienced backpackers. Don't bury trash because animals will only dig it up again.

2. Bury human wastes—don't empty them into streams. Some streams in several national parks are already polluted as a result of this thoughtless practice. Don't bathe or wash utensils in streams. Carry the water at least 150 feet away from the stream, and don't use detergents.

3. Eliminate soil erosion by camping only in places marked as campsites. Too many people camping in nondesignated campsites leads to flattening of the soil; this causes water runoff and eventually erosion. For the same reason, you should hike only on designated trails.

4. For obvious reasons, don't use boughs or branches cut from trees or shrubbery to sleep on.

5. Don't backpack in large groups. Limit group size to no more than 10 persons because too many people using a stretch of land contribute heavily to erosion, pollution, and other sins against the environment.

6. Don't dig a drainage ditch around your tent because this scars the land and causes erosion. If you have the right kind of tent, a drainage ditch shouldn't be necessary.

7. Don't build campfires. A campfire means raping trees and other green things for fuel. Besides, the ashes from campfires increase the acid content of the soil, a situation that can kill certain plants. If you must cook on the trail, use a portable gasoline stove or, better yet, eat foods that you can prepare without a fire.

molecular genetics

In the late seventeenth century, the microscope was still a newly invented instrument. At this time certain naturalists decided that semen would be a fascinating subject for microscopic study. It was known that semen carried the seed that somehow gave rise to a new individual. Perhaps the microscope would offer some clue to this mysterious process. Their curiosity was richly rewarded. There, within each individual sperm cell, was a tiny being. This homunculus (Latin for "little man") needed only the shelter of the womb to grow into a human infant. Here at last was direct visual evidence of the means which assured the continuity of life!

Of course, there were no homunculi, as later observers discovered to their disappointment. The investigators who claimed to have seen them had merely let wishful thinking interfere with scrupulous observation. (Leeuwenhoek, an uncommonly meticulous observer, had been the first to discover spermatozoa. But he had never reported seeing any miniature creature inside them.) The mystery of heredity could not be solved so easily. Whatever carried the genetic information from generation to generation was not easily visible. In fact, we shall see that the bearer of that information turned out to be a handful of molecules in each cell, weighing perhaps $10^{-15}$ g.

The entire subject remained obscure until 1900. Then Mendel's work was rediscovered, giving rise to the science of genetics. By the end of the first decade of this century, it was established that phenotypes are determined primarily by genes carried on chromosomes. Genes were thought of as indivisible units linked together to form a chromosome, much like beads on a string. It was known that chromosomes (and presumably genes) were chemically composed of nucleoprotein, a combination of nucleic acid and protein. But the secrets of gene structure and replication, and the nature of their relationship to phenotypic traits, remained mysterious for many years. The unraveling of these mysteries represents the greatest contribution to biology in this century.

Research has centered around the molecular structure and workings of genes and related molecules. The experimental material has been mainly viruses and bacteria such as the intestinal bacillus *Escherichia coli*. These organisms are small and relatively simple. Moreover, they reproduce very rapidly, sometimes producing two or three generations in an hour. So viruses and procaryotic cells make excellent subjects for experiments in molecular genetics. Eucaryotic forms, on the other hand, have much more complex genetic systems. Their generation times may be years in length. But the genetic material and its basic functions are the same in cells of all organisms. Discovery of this fact was itself one of the major achievements of modern biology. Eucaryotes differ from procaryotes in the organization of the genetic material and the way its functions are regulated.

## The chemistry of genes

A substance must have three important qualities in order to succeed as a gene:

1. Its structure must encode information that can be translated into a functional molecule. That is, genes must have subunits arranged in meaningful sequences which direct the formation of molecules—enzymes, structural proteins, and others—needed to maintain a cell.

2. It must be able to reproduce itself precisely, passing the information on unaltered to both daughter cells at the time of cell division.

3. It must be chemically stable in order to preserve the genetic information. But it must also be able to mutate as genes are known to do.

Chromosomes of eucaryotic cells are composed largely of protein and deoxyribonucleic acid (DNA). This nucleoprotein is often called **chromatin** because it is deeply colored by certain common staining techniques. We know today that DNA is the genetic component of chromatin. It determines the structure of proteins and other complex cellular molecules. But the theory that protein might be the genetic material was once very popular. About twenty different amino acids occur in proteins, and there are dozens of them in each protein molecule. So it would seem that proteins have a great potential for encoding information in the form of particular amino acid combinations and sequences. It was also thought that DNA could not possibly have the internal structural variety to carry the wealth of heredity information. After all, each DNA molecule contains only four different bases.

With this view of the two components of chromatin, it is not hard to see why most biologists once believed that protein was the genetic material. But there was also some contrary evidence. Chromosomal proteins do not have a uniform composition in all cells of an organism. But DNA appears to be the same for all types of cell in an individual. And the amount of DNA per cell is remarkably constant for each species (except in the gametes, which have only half the amount found in somatic cells), whereas chromosomal protein content varies greatly. As a result, the question remained unresolved for many years.

### Identifying the genetic material

In 1928 Fredrick Griffith discovered the transformation of bacteria from one genetic type to another. He worked with pneumococcus bacteria, which cause pneumonia in man. Mice also become diseased and die after injection with a culture of these bacteria. In pneumococcus, each cell is surrounded by a polysaccharide capsule. This capsule defends the bacteria against the immune reactions of the host organism. But occasionally pneumococcus undergoes mutation. This results in a bacterium without the capsule. The capsule-less form cannot protect itself against the host organism's antibodies and is therefore nonpatho-

6-1
Griffith's transformation experiment. Live type R bacteria and dead type S bacteria, each harmless by itself, proved lethal when injected together. Some agent in the dead type S cells transformed the normally harmless type R cells into virulent type S organisms. (See Identifying the genetic material)

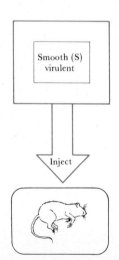

Smooth (S) virulent

Inject

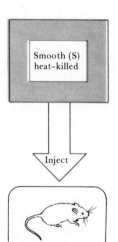

Smooth (S) heat-killed

Inject

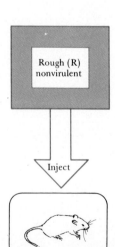

Rough (R) nonvirulent

Inject

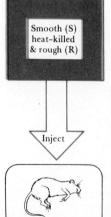

Smooth (S) heat-killed & rough (R)

Inject

genic. That is, it does not cause disease. When cultured on agar plates, the pathogenic types form smooth (S) colonies. Nonpathogenic types form rough (R) colonies.

Griffith found that live type S bacteria caused fatal infections in mice. But neither heat-killed type S nor live type R had any significant effect. Strangely, though, the injection of dead S and live R cells together proved lethal. Moreover, live pneumococci of the S type were found in the dead mice. Controls showed that neither the heat-killed type S nor the live type R alone could give rise to live type S organisms. So Griffith concluded that genetic material from the heat-killed bacteria was incorporated into the live R cells, causing them to be transformed into the pathogenic S bacteria.

Since transformed bacteria gave rise to more bacteria of the same type, the transformation *had* to be a genetic change. But the transforming substance was not identified until 1944. In that year O. T. Avery, C. M. MacLeod, and M. McCarty made a discovery that startled the scientific world. Working with the same pneumococcus bacteria that Griffith had used, they managed to extract pure DNA from the pathogenic variety.

They introduced the DNA into a culture of nonpathogenic pneumococcus and found that it caused the capsule-less bacteria to regain their capsule-forming ability. Their offspring also formed capsules. This proved that the change had been a genetic one. No protein had been involved, so DNA must have been responsible for transferring the genetic information. DNA, then, must be the genetic material after all!

A parallel line of investigation was pursued in 1952 by Alfred D. Hershey and Martha Chase. They worked with a type of virus which infects the bacterium *Escherichia coli*. Viruses which destroy bacteria are called bacteriophage or simply **phage**. Like many other viruses, this *E. coli* phage has a core of DNA encapsulated by a relatively complex protein structure. Prior to infection, the tail of the phage becomes attached to specific sites on the bacterial cell wall. Within a few minutes after attachment, the bacterium ruptures. It releases hundreds of phage identical to the original one. Evidently phage genetic material has entered the bacterial cell and used its metabolic machinery to produce the new phage particles. So identifying the compo-

6-2
By taking over the metabolic machinery of the bacteria they attack, bacteriophage can create hundreds of new viruses. Hershey and Chase labeled the protein of bacteriophage with radioactive sulfur and their DNA with radioactive phosphorus. It was the latter that was found to enter the bacteria when the phage attacked, thus proving DNA to be the genetic material.

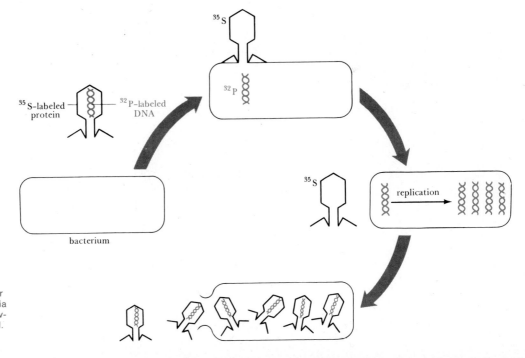

nent of the virus which enters the bacterium would be equivalent to identifying its genetic material.

Hershey and Chase used radioactive isotopes to label and trace viral DNA and protein during the cycle of replication. A **radioactive isotope** is an atom which has more than the usual number of neutrons in its nucleus. The nucleus is therefore unstable and tends to break down, giving off radioactive emissions in the process. It is for this reason that radioactive isotopes can be used to "label" certain substances and trace their progress through the course of a chemical reaction.

A radioactive isotope of phosphorus ($^{32}$P) was used to label DNA, but not protein because most proteins do not contain phosphorus. A radioactive isotope of sulfur ($^{35}$S) was incorporated into proteins, but not into DNA, which lacks sulfur. Viruses thus radioactively labeled were used to infect bacteria which had no radioactively labeled molecules. Sufficient time was allowed for attachment of the viruses and transfer of their genetic material. Then the bacterial culture was agitated in a blender. This sep-

arated the bacteria from the phage components which remained attached to the outside of their cell walls. Analysis of the extracellular phage material showed that $^{35}$S was present, but very little $^{32}$P. Just the reverse was found when the bacteria themselves were analyzed. Hardly any $^{35}$S was present, indicating that little or no protein had entered the cell. But most of the $^{32}$P was inside. Apparently DNA alone had transmitted the genetic information—the same conclusion reached by Avery and his colleagues.

## The structure of DNA

The confirmation that DNA comprised the genetic material led to renewed interest in its physical and chemical makeup. Investigation showed that it was a large, complex molecule containing many nucleotides. Erwin Chargaff found that the four types of nucleotide characteristic of DNA are not always present in equal amounts. However, he noted an important relationship. Of the four bases, adenine and thymine occur in equal amounts, and cytosine always occurs in the same quantity as guanine.

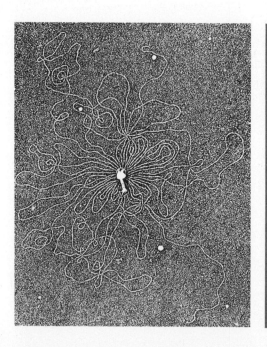

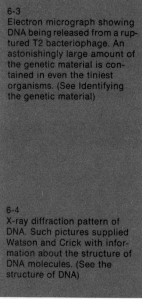

6-3
Electron micrograph showing DNA being released from a ruptured T2 bacteriophage. An astonishingly large amount of the genetic material is contained in even the tiniest organisms. (See Identifying the genetic material)

6-4
X-ray diffraction pattern of DNA. Such pictures supplied Watson and Crick with information about the structure of DNA molecules. (See the structure of DNA)

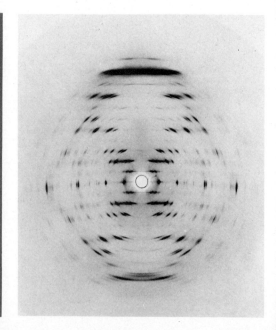

Other researchers pursued various lines of attack. During the early 1950s Maurice Wilkins, Rosalind Franklin, and their co-workers at King's College in London used X-ray diffraction techniques to study the physical structure of DNA preparations. The diffraction patterns of DNA showed it to be composed of regularly repeated subunits. The dimensions of the molecule could also be determined from the patterns. For instance, the distance between nucleotides was found to be .34 nm, while the diameter was 2 nm.

In 1953 a young American biochemist named James Watson had a research fellowship at the prestigious Cavendish Laboratory of Cambridge University. Here he met Francis Crick, an English physical chemist. The two soon became interested in a leading unsolved problem in biochemistry—the structure of DNA. They knew that Linus Pauling, the noted structural chemist, was working on this problem, and were determined to beat him to the solution. As it turned out, their talents matched their self-confidence. Watson and Crick also had one advantage over Pauling and other researchers in the field. They had available to them not only Chargaff's results, but also the X-ray findings from Wilkins' lab, which had not yet been published. Most important among these findings were experimental data and observations compiled by Rosalind Franklin. This data not only supported much of the theoretical work of Watson and Crick. It also helped guide their thinking about certain aspects of DNA structure. Without this guidance, their quest for a final solution might well have taken longer.

Watson and Crick collected balls, rods, and other hardware from the University machine shop. Working with these, they built models of the DNA molecule that would fit all the known data. Many possible structures were thus explored. Finally they concluded that DNA is composed of two polynucleotide chains. These chains are cross-linked and wrapped around each other to form a **double helix**. We can liken this structure to a spiral staircase. The sugar–phosphate chains form the edges of the steps. The steps themselves are the bases, projecting perpendicularly to the axis of the molecule into the space between the chains. Watson and Crick calculated that the length of a complete turn of the helix was 3.4 nm. So there are ten pairs of nucleotides for each complete turn.

Watson and Crick further suggested that these bases are arranged in complementary pairs, the bases on one strand being linked to those on the other strand by hydrogen bonds. The hydrogen bonds join-

6-5
The chemical structure of DNA. The two strands of the molecule are linked by hydrogen bonds between complementary base pairs adenine and thymine, cytosine and guanine.

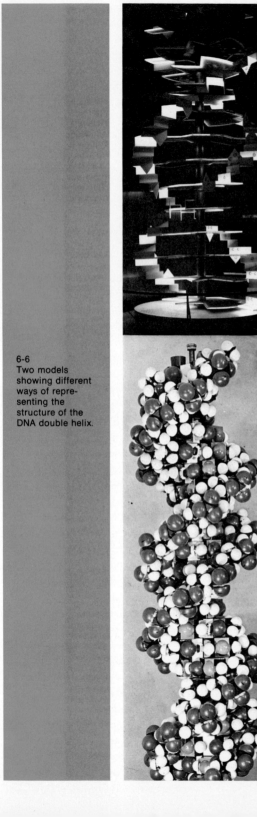

6-6
Two models showing different ways of representing the structure of the DNA double helix.

ing the base pairs are relatively weak. But their large number keeps the two strands firmly together. DNA is thus a very stable molecule. However, it was found that the size and structure of the individual bases limited the possibilities for such pairing. Adenine on one chain could pair only with thymine on the other. Similarly, cytosine would link up only with guanine.

The actual genetic information is encoded in the sequence of the base pairs. The bases make up a four-letter genetic "alphabet." These letters can form "words" which convey instructions to the cell. Four letters may seem like a very small number compared with the 26 letters of our English alphabet. However, this limitation makes little difference. After all, Morse code has only two "letters"—the dot and the dash. But it can be used to express virtually anything that can be conveyed in conventional language. In fact, we can see that the genetic information is, in effect, doubly encoded. Because of the complementary base pairing, each of the two strands of the DNA molecule contains the same message, just as a photographic negative bears the same image as a positive print made from it, or a mold the same pattern as the statue cast from it.

DNA molecules are enormous, as we might expect from the large amount of genetic information they must carry. For example, the DNA of the bacterium *E. coli* consists of several million base pairs. Its molecular weight is nearly 3 billion, and it is about 1 mm long when fully stretched out. It has been estimated that each human cell contains about 5 feet of DNA.

## Replication of DNA

The elaboration of the DNA model was one of the most important scientific feats of this century. For the first time, the structure of a biomolecule could be directly related to its function. For hereditary information to be conserved, the genetic material must be able to self-replicate when cells divide. A possible mechanism for replication is immediately suggested by the two complementary strands of the Watson–Crick model of DNA.

If the hydrogen bonds between the base pairs were broken, the strands could unwind and separate. Each single strand, freed from its partner, would have the structure necessary to direct the synthesis of a new **complementary** strand, identical to the one it had just parted from. For raw material it would use the pool of free nucleotides within the cell. Where the original DNA molecule had contained an A–T pair, for example, the A on one strand would link up with a new T, while the old T would acquire a new A as its partner. Similarly, G and C would each form new pairs with their complements. The eventual result would be two DNA molecules, each identical to the original. In other words, DNA provides the template—the model or pattern—for its own replication.

Watson and Crick proposed this hypothesis for DNA replication shortly after their first paper on DNA structure was published. It is called the **semiconservative** model because it proposes that each new DNA molecule contains one strand of the original molecule and one strand that has been newly formed. But two other possibilities also had to be considered. The first was that once the two new strands were synthesized, they might separate from the old strands that were their templates. They would then form a complete new molecule by coiling around each other. This would leave the old strands free to reassociate as well. The result would be one molecule composed of two newly synthesized strands and another composed of two old strands. This was known as the **conservative** model. It was *also* possible, though, that during replication both old and new strands might break into short pieces which reassociate more or less at random. This would result in a mixture of old and new material in the two newly synthesized DNA molecules. This was termed the **dispersive** model.

Only experimental evidence could decide among the three models suggested. In 1958 Matthew Meselson and Franklin Stahl carried out experiments which helped resolve the question. They cultured *E. coli* in a medium in which the only available nitrogen isotope was the heavy isotope $^{15}N$. After many generations in the culture medium, the bacterial nitrogenous compounds, including nucleotides and DNA, contained only $^{15}N$. The bacteria were then removed from this medium. After washing, they were placed in a new medium which contained $^{14}N$ as the only nitrogen isotope. Samples were taken from this culture at regular intervals. The nitrogen composition of their DNA was analyzed by measuring its density. This was done by a technique called **density gradient centrifugation**. DNA is placed in a tube of salt solution. The tube is spun at very high speed in a machine called a **centrifuge**. A centrifugal force of more than 100,000 times the force of gravity is exerted on the salt molecules. This causes them to move toward the bottom of the tube, so that the density of the salt solution increases progressively from the top of the tube to the bottom. The DNA molecules also move down the tube. When they reach a level where the density of the solution matches their own density, they remain there. Thus DNA molecules of differing density will form horizontal bands at different levels of the tube.

What might the investigators expect to find after a single generation of bacteria— that is, after one cell division with its accompanying DNA replication? If the DNA replicated in conservative fashion, there would be two bands of DNA in the tube— molecules consisting of two old (heavy) strands and molecules consisting of two new (light) strands. But if the DNA replicated according to the semiconservative model, there would be only a single band of intermediate density, since each newly replicated DNA molecule would contain one old (heavy) strand and one new (light) strand. This, in fact, was the situation observed. After one generation of bacterial

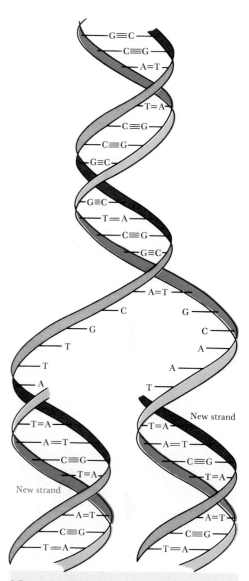

6-7
The Watson–Crick model for the replication of DNA. When the two strands separate, each serves as the template for the synthesis of a new complementary strand.

growth only one type of DNA was present, but it was less dense than the original $^{15}$N-DNA. After the second generation, two types of DNA were present. One was "light" with only $^{14}$N. The density of the other was intermediate between $^{14}$N-DNA and $^{15}$N-DNA, and had the same density as the DNA present at the end of the first generation. Evidently the latter DNA molecules were a hybrid type, containing equal amounts of $^{14}$N and $^{15}$N. In the third and later generations, the amount of hybrid DNA remained constant. But the light DNA increased with each generation.

All these observations support the semiconservative hypothesis of DNA replication. According to the hypothesis, replication of DNA in the first bacterial generation involves the separation of the two strands of $^{15}$N-DNA. Each acts as a template for synthesis of a complementary strand composed of $^{14}$N nucleotides. The template and its complement form the hybrid DNA. For the second round of duplication, half of the templates are the $^{15}$N type and half are the $^{14}$N type, both combine with $^{14}$N nucleotides. So half of the newly formed DNA is light DNA containing only $^{14}$N. The other half is the hybrid type. Only one type of hybrid DNA exists at the end of the first generation, rather than a graded variety of types from light to dense. This indicates that the individual strands maintain their integrity rather than being broken and reshuffled at random. Confirmation is found in the occurrence of two distinct types of DNA molecule at the end of the second generation, clearly showing that only two types of strand existed in the molecules of the previous generation. So the dispersive hypothesis can be safely ruled out. The complete absence of very dense $^{15}$N-DNA excludes the possibili-

6-8
The experiment by Meselson and Stahl that confirmed the Watson – Crick hypothesis of the semiconservative replication of DNA. (See Replication of DNA)

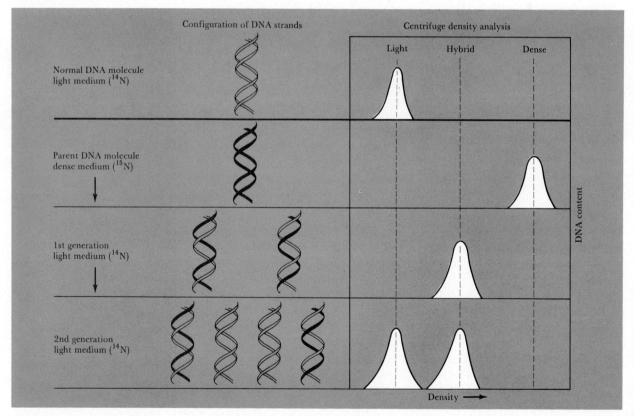

ty that the original molecules are preserved from one generation to the next. Thus, the conservative hypothesis is eliminated.

In 1957, Taylor, Woods, and Hughes obtained evidence for the semiconservative replication of DNA in the chromosomes of eucaryotic cells. They labeled the DNA in chromosomes of the broad bean, *Vicia faba,* with radioisotopes. Then they followed the distribution of the radioactive DNA during subsequent cell divisions. The dividing root tip cells were killed and flattened upon glass microscope slides at various times after the DNA labeling. The slides were coated with photographic film in the dark and then were stored and developed in the dark. Since the film was never exposed to light, the only radiation which could darken the film must be the radioactive material incorporated into the DNA of the cells. When the film was examined under the microscope, blackened grains were visible over the labeled chromosomes. Distribution of the labeled DNA could be detected after the first, second, and later divisions by observing the distribution of these black dots. The results showed that the replication process appears to be semiconservative, just as in the bacteria studied by Meselson and Stahl.

## Control of DNA synthesis

How is DNA replication controlled? This is an important unsolved problem, since we know that in most cells DNA replication occurs during only a small part of their life cycle. If we knew more about the regulation of DNA synthesis, we might learn how to deal with situations where this control breaks down and cells proliferate, as in cancer. It appears that control is exercised primarily at the time when DNA replication is initiated. Biochemically we still know little about initiation. We do know that it starts at a fixed point, or a few fixed points, on the chromosome. This information comes partly from genetic studies and partly from biochemical experiments. But the most direct

evidence comes from visualization of replicating DNA molecules, either by Taylor's technique discussed above, using radioactively labeled DNA, or by electron microscopy.

The accompanying figure shows an electron micrograph of replicating DNA from the egg of a fruit fly. The process is under way simultaneously at four regions of the chromosome (the colored loops or "eyes" on the map). DNA within the eyes has already been replicated. The remainder of the DNA has yet to be replicated. Further analysis of these structures shows that replication is proceeding in both directions at once. Thus replication originates halfway between the corners of the eyes. Each eye represents a "growing point" where parental DNA strands are unwinding and new DNA chains are being elongated at the same time. It has been very difficult to analyze chromosomal DNA replication in multicellular organisms, however, because of the very high molecular weight of cellular DNA and the structural complexity of the chromosome.

6-9
Replication is proceeding simultaneously at several locations along the molecule (colored segments). See text above this figure.

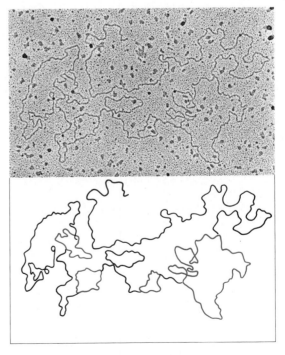

# Genes in action

The discovery of how DNA encodes and replicates genetic information is extremely important. But it does not tell the whole story of how organisms develop and reproduce. Just as a building cannot be created from blueprints alone, so a cell needs more than information in order to function, grow, and reproduce itself. How is the phenotype derived from the information carried by the genes? According to current scientific opinion, each gene determines the structure of a specific protein—often an enzyme—which contributes to the phenotype. We can better understand the effect of a functional enzyme if we look at what happens when the enzyme fails to operate properly. If an enzyme is not functioning, the substrate upon which it normally acts will accumulate. Therefore the end product of its reaction will not be formed.

But enzymes do not function independently of each other. As we noted in chapter 3, groups of enzymes are arranged in functional sequences called metabolic pathways. In these pathways the end product of one enzyme becomes the substrate of the next. The ability to synthesize a particular molecule often depends upon the successful completion of a number of discrete steps in its biosynthetic pathway. When one enzyme in a pathway is defective, the pathway is blocked there. So all the remaining molecules in the pathway cannot be formed. If such a metabolic block prevents formation of a required compound, the organism must be artificially supplied with the compound, or die.

## Genes and enzymes

As early as 1909, Archibald Garrod showed that certain enzyme defects in humans are inherited. He then suggested that genes are responsible for enzyme synthesis. But at that time the science of molecular genetics did not exist. Even biochemistry was not sufficiently advanced for Garrod's work to be followed up. In more recent years, though, it has been shown that many enzyme deficiencies display the kind of inheritance pattern that is usually caused by a single gene difference. Unfortunately, it is not practical to study enzyme inheritance in humans because the human generational cycle takes such a long time. For this reason, much of our present knowledge in this area comes from nutritional studies of certain microorganisms whose brief life cycles make them convenient experimental material.

About thirty years after Garrod's report, George Beadle and E. L. Tatum tested the hypothesis that genes control the formation of enzymatic proteins. They worked with the red bread mold, *Neurospora crassa,* which has a simple structure and a 10-day life cycle. *Neurospora* also has several other advantages as a biochemical "guinea pig." During most of its life cycle, it is composed of haploid cells. Since each cell has only one gene from each set of alleles, that gene will express itself. No dominant allele will mask its effect. In other words, in this relatively simple genetic system, the effect of an individual gene can be detected without interference from the effects of its alleles.

*Neurospora* is eucaryotic and has a sexual cycle similar to those of higher plants and animals. Molds of opposite sexual types fuse, producing a diploid cell which may be likened to the zygote produced by fusion of human egg and sperm. In *Neurospora,* each diploid nucleus immediately undergoes two meiotic divisions. These divisions yield four haploid nuclei, in an ordered row on a spore sac. The four haploid nuclei then divide mitotically to produce the eight haploid nuclei of the sexual spores. After a sexual spore germinates, the new mold may produce many genetically identical asexual spores. Each of these may be tested for a different genetic trait.

Perhaps most important to biochemical study is that normal *Neurospora* can grow on a minimal medium. This is a medium which consists of inorganic compounds, a

**6-10**
The normal *Neurospora* mold was first used to test the one gene/one enzyme hypothesis. Normal *Neurospora* can grow on a minimal medium. (See Genes and enzymes)

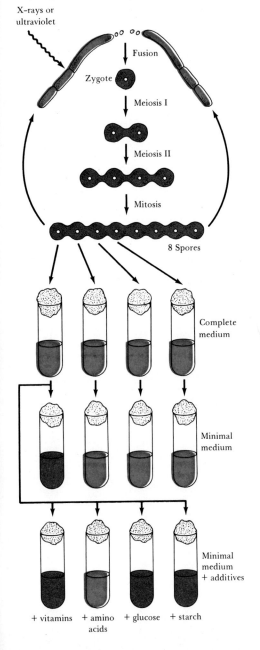

X-rays or ultraviolet

Fusion

Zygote

Meiosis I

Meiosis II

Mitosis

8 Spores

Complete medium

Minimal medium

Minimal medium + additives

+ vitamins    + amino acids    + glucose    + starch

vitamin (biotin), and a sugar. Out of these few substances, it can synthesize all of the vitamins (except biotin) and all the 20 amino acids which it needs to live. (Interestingly, simple organisms like *Neurospora* can often accomplish such marvels of chemical synthesis while advanced organisms such as humans lack this ability. Humans must eat a "balanced diet" to provide themselves with the many substances they cannot manufacture.)

Since *Neurospora* requires so few organic compounds in its diet, it must have enzymes and metabolic pathways to synthesize almost all of its needed biochemicals. It is relatively easy to detect metabolic deficiencies in such an organism. Spores are cultured first on a complete medium, consisting of the minimal medium plus a supplement of amino acids, vitamins, and other nutrients. Then a portion of the culture is transferred to minimal medium. If it does not grow on minimal medium, it is assumed to have one or more enzyme deficiencies which block one or more metabolic pathways.

Further tests of the culture will show where the deficiency lies. Portions of the original culture are transferred to tubes of minimal medium supplemented by amino acids, vitamins, or other substances. If the mold grows only on the medium containing amino acids, we can conclude that the mold is deficient in one or more amino acids. Next, the culture is transferred to tubes of minimal media each supplemented by a single amino acid to determine which pathway is not working. Biochemical analysis or additional nutritional studies will show which enzyme is deficient.

To test the hypothesis that each gene controls the formation of an enzyme, Beadle and Tatum needed mutant strains of *Neurospora*. Spontaneous mutations do not occur frequently. But the experimenters took advantage of the fact that X-rays greatly increase the frequency of mutations. Asexual spores were X-rayed and allowed to pass into the sexual phase of the life cycle.

These sexual spores were grown individually on a complete medium. Then, a portion of each mold was transferred to a tube of minimal medium. Each mold that did not grow on minimal medium was tested further to determine which other nutrients were required for its growth. If one did not grow on minimal medium but grew when the B vitamin—niacin—was added, the conclusion was that it had lost the ability to produce niacin.

Beadle himself used the analogy of an automobile plant to explain this method of research. Ordinarily, if we examine the cars built in a particular plant, we cannot tell which worker installed which part. But if workers who each made some regular and characteristic mistake could be introduced into the assembly line, we could then tell from the finished product who was responsible for each part. Similarly, by breeding defects into *Neurospora*'s genes, Beadle found a way to demonstrate the connection between the genes and the enzymes which they produced.

The deficient mold was then crossed with the wild (normal) type, producing hybrid sexual spores. Of the eight spores produced in each spore sac, four could survive on minimal medium. The other four required a supplemental source of niacin. The fact that the niacin-synthesizing deficiency showed up in the hybrid generation confirmed that the defect was hereditary.

Since half of the spores from each spore sac produced molds like one parent, and half produced molds like the other parent, only one pair of genes could be involved — one for niacin production and one which prevented niacin production. If two or more pairs of independently assorting genes had been required to prevent niacin formation, one-fourth or fewer of the sexual spores would be expected to produce molds unable to synthesize niacin. Further experiments of this type repeatedly showed the one gene/one enzyme relationship in *Neurospora* and other organisms.

The studies of Garrod and others uncovered various examples of enzyme deficiencies in humans. One of these, alkaptonuria, is a relatively mild condition. It is caused by an enzyme deficiency which prevents the conversion of alkapton (an organic acid) to carbon dioxide and water. Accumulated alkapton is excreted. The urine of affected individuals darkens as it comes in contact with air, because alkapton combines with oxygen to form a dark oxidation product. Garrod demonstrated that alkaptonuria is inherited as a simple recessive trait.

Phenylketonuria (PKU) is another inherited metabolic disorder of humans. In this condition the conversion of phenylalanine to tyrosine is blocked by an inherited enzyme deficiency. The phenylalanine is converted only as far as phenylpyruvic acid. Accumulated phenylpyruvic acid poisons nerve cells before it is excreted in the urine, and may result in mental deficiency. This can be prevented by restricting the amount of phenylalanine in the diet of affected persons. It is now usual to test newborn infants for this defect, so that measures may be taken before damage is done.

Alkaptonuria and phenylketonuria are both hereditary metabolic disorders which are characterized by accumulation of an intermediate metabolic product preceding the metabolic block. Albinism, on the other hand, is caused by a metabolic block which precedes the formation of melanin. So in this case, the distinguishing characteristic is the absence of a substance—melanin. All three of these conditions, along with others, are associated with different parts of the same biochemical pathway.

*One gene/one polypeptide*   Evidence was piling up to support the one gene/one enzyme hypothesis. But at the same time, seemingly contradictory examples also turned up. In some cases, it looked as though several genes were necessary to produce a single enzyme. Further study showed that certain enzymes and other proteins—hemoglobin, for example—are com-posed of two or more polypeptide chains, each determined by a single gene. When this was recognized, the one gene/one enzyme theory had to be restated as: one gene/one polypeptide. But in other instances, a single gene seemed to have multiple effects. How could this be possible if each gene produces only a single polypeptide?

To answer this question we can use the example of sickle-cell anemia. This is an inherited condition, chiefly affecting people of African descent, in which the red blood cells are deficient in their ability to transport oxygen to the tissues. Scientists have clearly established that it is due to a single set of alleles. But homozygotes show a variety of effects, including clumped red cells; rapid destruction of red cells; damage to the circulatory system, brain, lungs, and kidneys; weakness; rheumatism; and other impairments. Research shows that the ultimate cause of all these effects is an amino acid substitution in one polypeptide chain of the hemoglobin molecule. Sickle-cell hemoglobin is known as hemoglobin S. It causes the red cells containing it to assume distorted shapes (often sickle-shaped), to clump together, and to be destroyed more rapidly. The latter two effects cause blockage of blood vessels and failure of the blood supply, leading to the damage of other organs. Thus a single gene change can cause many phenotypic changes by producing a single polypeptide change.

## Protein synthesis

Exactly how do the genes control the formation of polypeptide chains? We know that proteins are synthesized in small structures called ribosomes. The chemical intermediate that passes the chromosomal directions to the ribosome is ribonucleic acid (RNA). There are three types of RNA present in cells. Each plays a different role in protein synthesis.

*Transcription*   The first step in this process is **transcription**. This is the formation

**6-11**
An electron micrograph showing molecules of RNA being transcribed from DNA. The long strands are protein-coated DNA; the feathery shorter filaments are growing molecules of RNA, as many as 100 of which are being formed at the same time from each gene. Transcription starts at the end of a gene, and the RNA fibers become longer as the process continues. Between the genes there are regions of DNA which appear to be genetically inactive. (See Transcription)

of a molecule of **messenger RNA (mRNA)** using one strand of the chromosomal DNA as a template. As in DNA replication, free nucleotides form complementary base pairs on the template DNA strand. The exception is that uracil rather than thymine pairs with adenine. An enzyme, RNA polymerase, then catalyzes the process by which the nucleotides form a molecule of RNA. The single strand of mRNA contains in its nucleotide sequence all the genetic information of the DNA template. Once formed, it separates from the DNA and passes into the cytoplasm. There the strand of mRNA will ultimately serve as the template for the synthesis of protein molecules.

From this description, we can see that transcription is somewhat similar to replication. However, only one strand (the "sense" strand) of the DNA in any gene is transcribed, whereas during replication both strands of the DNA molecule are duplicated. Moreover, replication duplicates the entire chromosome. Transcription, on the

other hand, has definite starting and ending points. These points correspond to the ends of genes or sequences of genes. In this view, a gene can be regarded as a region of the DNA molecule which contains the instruction for the synthesis of one polypeptide chain. Often several genes are transcribed as a unit. This produces a long mRNA molecule which can serve as a template for forming several protein chains.

Along with nucleotide sequences which ultimately specify amino acid sequences, DNA must contain sequences for control and punctuation. For punctuation, RNA polymerase must somehow be told to bind to DNA and start transcribing at a point corresponding to the beginning of a gene. And it must be told to stop when it has reached the end of that gene or of that jointly transcribed group of genes. If several genes are transcribed as a unit, the mRNA sequence must contain additional punctuation. It must specify the nucleotide sequence corresponding to the end of one protein and the beginning of the next. This information must also be built into the original DNA nucleotide sequence.

*The genetic code*    Information is handed on from one DNA molecule to two new ones during replication. The same information is passed along from DNA to mRNA during transcription. Finally, it is translated into still another form—a sequence of amino acids—when a polypeptide chain is synthesized. Before we describe this final process, we must look at the nature of the chemical code which transmits the information. Deciphering this **genetic code** was one of the great achievements of biology in recent decades. But even before the code was broken by laboratory experiments, scientists had deduced one of its important features. It had to be a triplet code, with a sequence of three bases on the molecule of DNA or RNA to represent each amino acid. The molecules of nucleic acid contain only four different units. These are the nucleotides of adenine, guanine, cytosine, and either thymine (in DNA) or uracil (in RNA). If each one represented a single amino acid, only four amino acids could be specified. If sequences of two bases were the "code words," there would be 16 such pairs possible. This is still not enough to code for the twenty amino acids commonly found in proteins. But a triplet code, with words consisting of three adjacent bases, could represent as many as 64 different amino acids.

A variety of experiments have proved this theory correct. Since there are 64 possible nucleotide triplets, or **codons**, to represent only 20 amino acids, the code is quite redundant. Most of the amino acids can be represented by more than one codon. For example, arginine can be "written" in six different ways. The nucleotide sequences CGC, CGU, CGA, CGG, AGA, and AGG in a molecule of RNA can each direct the placement of an arginine residue in a polypeptide chain. The complete code was spelled out through a number of ingenious experiments in the 1960s. It is given in the accompanying table.

Only 61 of the 64 possible codons "make sense"—that is, specify an amino acid. The other three—UAG, UAA, and UGA—are "nonsense" codons, since they do not direct the addition of any amino acid to a polypeptide chain. Apparently they are used for punctuation of the genetic message, to show the "period" that indicates the end of a chain. (Alternatively, we could translate them as "stop.") The triplet AUG is used to start a new polypeptide chain. However, AUG can also represent methionine in the middle of a chain. It is not known how these two meanings are distinguished in protein synthesis.

It is interesting to note that viruses, bacteria, plants, and animals all appear to use the same genetic code. That is, the nucleotide triplet which codes for a given amino acid codes for that amino acid in all forms of life. For example, the codon GGG dictates bonding of glycine in the cytoplasm of any cell. This common code undoubtedly will have increasingly important medical implications in the years to come.

*Translation* The synthesis of an amino acid chain from information coded in a molecule of mRNA is called **translation**. This process takes place on the ribosomes. The complex structure of the ribosome includes binding sites to which the mRNA becomes attached. The long molecule of mRNA, carrying the coded message of the cell's DNA, seems to move along or through the ribosome much as magnetic tape moves between the heads of a tape recorder. Such tape carries a coded message magnetically imprinted upon its molecules, that can be translated into a sequence of sounds. In the same way, the mRNA carries a chemical message encoded in the sequence of its nucleotides. This message can be translated into a series of amino acids in a polypeptide chain. The ribosome, like the playback machinery of a tape recorder, helps accomplish the translation.

We now know how this takes place in broad outline, though many details are not fullly understood. Two other kinds of RNA take part in the process: **transfer RNA (t-RNA)** and **ribosomal RNA (rRNA)**. The precise role of rRNA is not yet clear. However,

| | | SECOND LETTER | | | | |
|---|---|---|---|---|---|---|
| | | U | C | A | G | THIRD LETTER |
| **U** | | UUU } phe<br>UUC<br>UUA } leu<br>UUG | UCU }<br>UCC } ser<br>UCA<br>UCG | UAU } tyr<br>UAC<br>UAA Stop<br>UAG Stop | UGU } cyc<br>UGC<br>UGA Stop<br>UGG trp | U<br>C<br>A<br>G |
| **C** | | CUU }<br>CUC } leu<br>CUA<br>CUG | CCU }<br>CCC } pro<br>CCA<br>CCG | CAU } his<br>CAC<br>CAA } gln<br>CAG | CGU }<br>CGC } arg<br>CGA<br>CGG | U<br>C<br>A<br>G |
| **A** | | AUU }<br>AUC } ile<br>AUA<br>AUG met | ACU }<br>ACC } thr<br>ACA<br>ACG | AAU } asn<br>AAC<br>AAA } lys<br>AAG | AGU } ser<br>AGC<br>AGA } arg<br>AGG | U<br>C<br>A<br>G |
| **G** | | GUU }<br>GUC } val<br>GUA<br>GUG | GCU }<br>GCC } ala<br>GCA<br>GCG | GAU } asp<br>GAC<br>GAA } glu<br>GAG | GGU }<br>GGC } gly<br>GGA<br>GGG | U<br>C<br>A<br>G |

FIRST LETTER

6-12
The genetic code.

it is important to the structure of the ribosome, and thus to protein synthesis. We know much more about the participation of tRNA, which has a twofold function. Transfer RNA molecules carry free amino acids in the cytoplasm to the ribosomes. There they link together, directed by the coded instructions of mRNA, to form a polypeptide chain. Most important, though, the tRNA molecules decipher the coded message and carry out its instructions. In effect, tRNA molecules "read" the mRNA codons, translating their message into a particular sequence of amino acids.

Unlike mRNA and rRNA, molecules of tRNA are relatively small—about 75 or 80 nucleotides in length. They resemble the other species of RNA in that they consist of a single strand, but that strand is folded and looped to form a complex structure. It includes several regions where complementary bases are paired by hydrogen bonding, as in the double-stranded molecules of DNA. There are many different classes of tRNA molecules. Each is specific for one of the 20 amino acids that appear in proteins. For example, certain molecules of tRNA can transport only the amino acid alanine. Others can carry only glycine, still others leucine, and so forth. Each molecule of tRNA picks up a single amino acid molecule of the appropriate type. It carries that molecule to a special binding site on a ribosome where the translation of a strand of mRNA is in progress.

The matching of mRNA codons with tRNA **anticodons** determines the precise sequence in which the amino acids are added to the polypeptide chain. These are sequences of three bases, located at a particular point in the structure of each tRNA molecule. The codons and anticodons must contain complementary bases in order to pair up in this way. Others will not fit together properly. Suppose, for instance, that a section of an mRNA molecule with the base sequence CAU occupies the binding site of the ribosome. The only tRNA molecule that can match up with this codon is

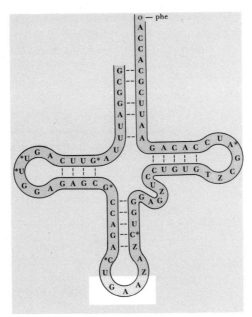

6-13
The structure of the tRNA molecule that carries the amino acid phenylalanine, isolated from yeast cells. The Xs designate nucleotides other than the common A, G, T, and C; nucleotides marked with asterisks are modified forms. The three nucleotides in the white box constitute the anticodon, which pairs with the mRNA codon during assembly of the polypeptide chain. Many different kinds of tRNA have been found to have similar "clover leaf" forms.

one bearing the anticodon GUA. CAU is one of two codons which specify the amino acid histidine. And the molecule of tRNA that carries the anticodon GUA is always one that transports histidine. So we can think of the tRNA molecule as a kind of link or adapter between the nucleotide "language" of mRNA and the amino acid "language" of proteins. For each mRNA codon there is a matching tRNA molecule bearing the specified amino acid.

As the molecule of mRNA moves along the ribosome, each codon in turn matches up with the appropriate tRNA molecule. The amino acids that they carry are thus properly positioned to join with the growing polypeptide chain. Each successive amino acid is held in place just long enough to form a peptide bond with the one preceding it. When this happens, the molecule of tRNA is released from both the amino acid it has been carrying and the codon bases with which it has paired off. It is now free to acquire and transport another amino acid molecule. Thus amino acids are added to the polypeptide chain one by one until it is completed. The completed chain is released and the mRNA may join with another ribosome to repeat the cycle. In fact, an

mRNA molecule may join with several ribosomes at the same time, each ribosome producing a polypeptide. The combination of mRNA and several ribosomes is called a **polyribosome** or **polysome**.

## Gene mutations

Fortunately for the continuity of life, DNA is a very stable substance. Its genetic message usually passes unaltered from generation to generation. But spontaneous changes in genes do occasionally occur. These are called mutations. Such gene mutations may produce a significant change in the phenotype of the organism which possesses them. And since the genetic material itself has altered, the change will be inheritable.

Not all genes are equally stable. Some mutate 100 or even 1,000 times more frequently than others. But the average frequency is very low. For a typical human gene it is about $4 \times 10^{-5}$. This means that among a hundred thousand gametes, we can expect to have only four in which a specific gene has mutated to one of its alleles. In any set of alleles, the gene which occurs most frequently is considered the normal or wild-type allele. The others are

**6-14**

The mechanism of protein synthesis. At top, a strand of mRNA is transcribed from a region of a DNA molecule. At bottom, the mRNA becomes attached to a ribosome. Amino acids are brought to the ribosome by molecules of tRNA, each of which contains an anticodon corresponding to the particular amino acid it carries. The anticodons link up with the appropriate codons on the mRNA strand. The amino acids are thus brought together in proper sequence and held long enough to be joined together, forming a polypeptide chain.

considered mutant alleles. Reverse mutations from the mutant type to the wild-type gene occur, but less frequently than the forward mutations. As noted in the discussion of *Neurospora*, the frequency of mutations can be increased artificially. Exposure to X-rays, ultraviolet radiation, and a variety of chemicals all tend to induce mutation. But like spontaneous mutations, induced mutations occur at random. It is not possible to predict which genes will be affected, or how they will change.

At the molecular level, mutations represent changes in the sequence of DNA nucleotides. These changes include addition, deletion, inversion, or substitution of nucleotides along the DNA molecule. If the codon transcribed from the mutant gene

happens to specify the same amino acid as the codon transcribed from the normal gene, the changes may produce no phenotypic effects. But when a nucleotide alteration causes a different polypeptide to be formed, there is the possibility of a difference in the phenotype of the organism.

Addition or deletion of a single nucleotide may have very serious effects upon a gene. The loss or gain of even one nucleotide means that the mRNA transcribed from that particular gene will have a completely different sequence of codons from the point of change onward. If this affects an important portion of the polypeptide produced, it will not perform its normal function. And if the mutation causes a terminating codon (UAA or UAG) to be transcribed

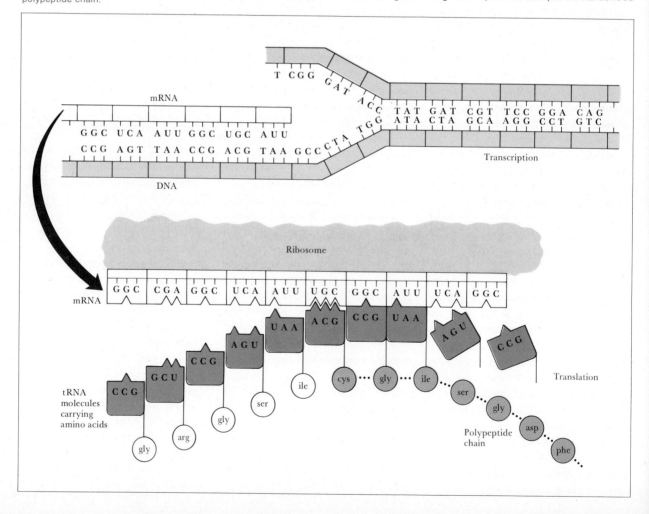

in the first part of the mRNA molecule, no polypeptide may form at all. Many mutant genes are recessive in nature. This is because they lead to a failure of polypeptide formation, rather than to the production of abnormal proteins.

Sometimes gene mutations do not result in alterations in the phenotype because of normal repair processes that go on in the cell nucleus. Remember that during RNA transcription only one strand of the DNA molecule plays an active role. The other is a reserve strand, used only to guide in repair and replication. In many cases, the cell can spontaneously correct changes or omissions in the code, thus nullifying the effects of mutation. This has been shown in the laboratory, where bacteria exposed to ultraviolet light have displayed ability to repair the damage caused to their DNA by radiation. Just how the repair process is regulated is not fully understood. But it is thought that one or more specialized enzymes act as "testers" of the DNA strands. Upon finding errors in the code, they remove that section and cause an accurate one to be replicated in its place.

*The cistron*   In the light of our present knowledge of molecular genetics, we must now reconsider the classical definition of the gene. When the concept of the gene was first introduced early in this century, it was thought that the gene was in every sense the basic hereditary unit. In other words, it was the smallest unit of genetic recombination, the smallest unit of function (that is, the smallest unit that contributes to the organism's phenotype), and the smallest unit that could be affected by mutation. But we now realize that there is a hierarchy of genetic units. The smallest is the individual nucleotide in the DNA or RNA chain. We have seen that the individual nucleotides can be recombined in any sequence, and that there are mutations which affect only single nucleotides. So the nucleotide must be considered the basic unit of mutation and recombination.

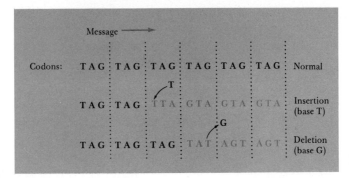

6-15
The addition or deletion of a single nucleotide at any location in the DNA molecule may change the entire message from that point onward, creating a mutant gene. (See Gene mutations)

The next largest unit is the codon, three nucleotides that dictate the placement of a particular amino acid in a protein. Finally, there is the region of the DNA molecule—several hundred to several thousands of nucleotides in length—that determines the structure of an entire polypeptide chain. This is the genetic functional unit which we have thus far referred to as the gene. But to avoid confusion with the older, less clearly defined use of the term "gene," molecular geneticists often use the term **cistron** instead.

## Regulation of gene activity

We have seen that phenotypic differences can be due to allelic differences, or to interaction between sets of alleles which determine protein structure. Such genes are called **structural genes** because they de-termine the structure of proteins which make up the cell and carry out its functions. Recent evidence shows that some phenotypes are affected by genes and other molecules which promote or inhibit the action of the structural genes. In some organisms, gene regulation systems seem to work like switches that turn genes on or off. Such mechanisms are obviously necessary to account for the enormous differences between cells. In multicelled organisms, for example, each cell contains the same genetic information. But one cell somehow "knows" that it should function as a muscle cell, another as a blood cell, still another as a nerve cell. The study of gene regulation is still at a rather tentative stage, although great progress has been made in recent years. Like other aspects of molecular genetics, gene regulation is better understood

6-16
The language of molecular genetics. (See The cistron)

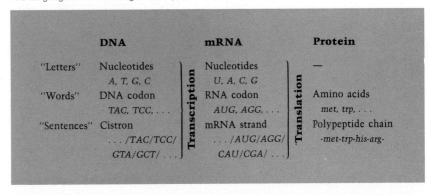

in bacteria than in eucaryotic organisms. Control of lactose metabolism in *E. coli* has been studied more than any other genetic regulatory system.

The metabolism of *E. coli* is well adapted for glucose utilization. It usually has an adequate supply of glucose both in culture and its native habitat of the human intestines. But this bacterium can also use lactose as an energy source. *E. coli* cultured without lactose is inhibited from producing enzymes for lactose metabolism. When such inhibited cells are transferred to a lactose medium, they are stimulated to produce the enzymes needed for lactose metabolism. They produce an enzyme which splits lactose into glucose and galactose, and another that increases cell permeability to lactose. This group of enzymes is inhibited after the transfer from lactose me-

dium to lactose-free medium. It seems that lactose acts as a signal to start production of the enzymes that metabolize it. Absence of lactose, on the other hand, inhibits these enzymes. But how does this occur?

Certain *E. coli* mutants can produce the lactose-metabolizing enzymes whether lactose is present or not. Ingenious experiments have been performed involving the conjugation of normal and mutant bacteria. These experiments show that normal bacteria produce a chemical **repressor** which inhibits synthesis of lactose-metabolizing enzymes. The repressor substance has been identified as a protein. It is produced by a **regulator gene**. The mutant strains cannot produce an effective repressor protein because of a mutation in the regulator gene.

Current theory has an explanation for this type of gene regulation. Repressor protein is synthesized by the action of a regulator gene. This repressor may combine with an **operator site**, a segment of DNA adjacent to one or more structural genes, to prevent transcription of the structural genes. The unit composed of an operator site and the structural genes associated with it is called an **operon**. The operator site and structural genes which produce lactose-metabolizing enzymes are known as the **lac operon**. Lactose combines with the repressor of the lac operon to prevent it from attaching to the operator site. So in normal *E. coli* the lac operon can be transcribed only if lactose is present.

We have seen how genes may be repressed. Certain factors also act to initiate transcription. The cyclic form of adenosine monophosphate (cAMP) plays an important part in transcription of the lac operon. After combining with its receptor protein, cAMP activates the so-called **promoter site**. This site is the point on the DNA chain at which RNA polymerase can attach. Once attached, RNA polymerase will begin to transcribe mRNA from the lac operon unless it is blocked by the lac repressor at the operator site.

**6-17**
A diagram of the Jacob–Monod model of the operon. Accumulation of a substrate A serves to deactivate the repressor, thus allowing the operator to turn on the structural genes. These genes direct the synthesis of enzymes needed for the series of reactions that transform A into a product, C. Accumulation of C activates the repressor, enabling it to bind to the operator site; the operator then cannot turn on the structural genes, and the synthesis of enzymes stops. Biologists are studying the applicability of this bacterial model to eucaryotic systems.

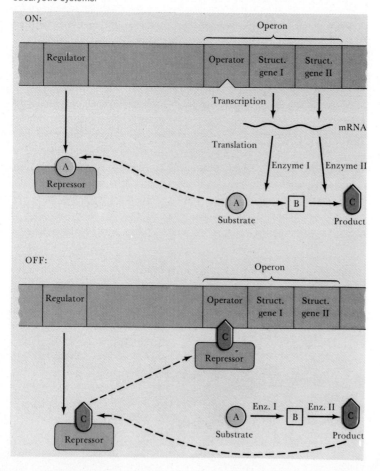

**summary**

A gene must encode information that can be translated into a functional molecule, must be able to reproduce itself precisely in order to pass on information during cell division, and must be chemically stable but able to mutate. It was once believed that protein, composed of many different amino acids, was the genetic material, rather than DNA, composed of only four bases (adenine, guanine, cytosine, and thymine). In 1944 O. T. Avery and his colleagues proved that DNA is responsible for the transmission of genetic information.

Investigation showed that DNA is a large complex molecule containing many nucleotides. But its structure was a mystery until Watson and Crick hypothesized the double helix—a DNA molecule composed of two polynucleotide chains, cross-linked and wrapped around each other. They also suggested that the bases are arranged in complementary pairs, with the bases on one strand linked to those on the other strand by hydrogen bonds. The actual genetic information is encoded in the sequence of the base pairs.

To conserve hereditary information, the genetic material must have the capacity for self-replication when cells divide. The two complementary strands of the Watson–Crick DNA model suggest a possible mechanism for replication. If the hydrogen bonds between the base pairs were broken, each strand—unwound and separated from its partner—would have the structure necessary to direct the synthesis of a new complementary strand, identical to the one it had just parted from. It would use as raw material the pool of free nucleotides within the cell. That is, DNA provides the template, or model, for its own replication.

If DNA is the genetic material, then how is a phenotype derived from information carried by the genes? It is thought that each gene determines the structure of a specific protein—often an enzyme—which contributes to the phenotype. In 1909, Archibald Garrod suggested that genes are responsible for enzyme synthesis. Later biologists have demonstrated that many defective enzymes show an inheritance pattern characteristic of a single gene difference. This substantiates the one gene/one enzyme hypothesis. Further study has shown that certain enzymes and other proteins (such as hemoglobin) are composed of two or more polypeptide chains, each determined by a single gene. So the one gene/one enzyme theory was replaced by the one gene/one polypeptide theory.

Protein synthesis begins with transcription. This is the formation of a molecule of messenger RNA (mRNA), containing all the genetic information of the DNA template. This information is encoded in nucleotide triplets called codons, which consist of combinations of the four bases with each triplet representing a different amino acid. The synthesis of an amino acid chain from information coded in a molecule of mRNA, called translation, takes place on the ribosomes. Transfer RNA molecules (tRNA) carry free amino acids in the cytoplasm to the ribosomes. There they are linked together, according to the coded instructions of mRNA, to form a polypeptide chain. Amino acids are added to the chain in sequence by the matching of mRNA codons with complementary anticodons containing tRNA.

Each successive amino acid is held in place just long enough to form a peptide bond with the one preceding it. When this happens, the tRNA molecule can acquire and transport other amino acids, adding them to the polypeptide chain one by one until it is completed. The completed chain is released, and the mRNA may join with another ribosome to repeat the cycle.

DNA is very stable. The genetic message it carries usually passes on unaltered from generation to generation. But spontaneous changes in genes, called mutations, sometimes occur. Gene mutations may produce a significant and inheritable change in the phenotype of the organisms possessing them. Mutation can be induced by exposure to radiation or chemicals. But induced mutation, like sponaneous mutation, occurs at random. It is impossible to predict which genes will be affected or how they will change. The change may affect the phenotypic characteristics of an organism if the nucleotide alteration causes formation of a different polypeptide.

There is a hierarchy of genetic units. The basic unit of mutation and recombination is the individual nucleotide in the DNA or RNA chain. Next largest is the codon, the nucleotide triplet that dictates the placement of a particular amino acid in a protein. Finally, there is the region of the DNA molecule which determines the structure of the entire polypeptide chain. This is the genetic functional unit which molecular geneticists call the cistron.

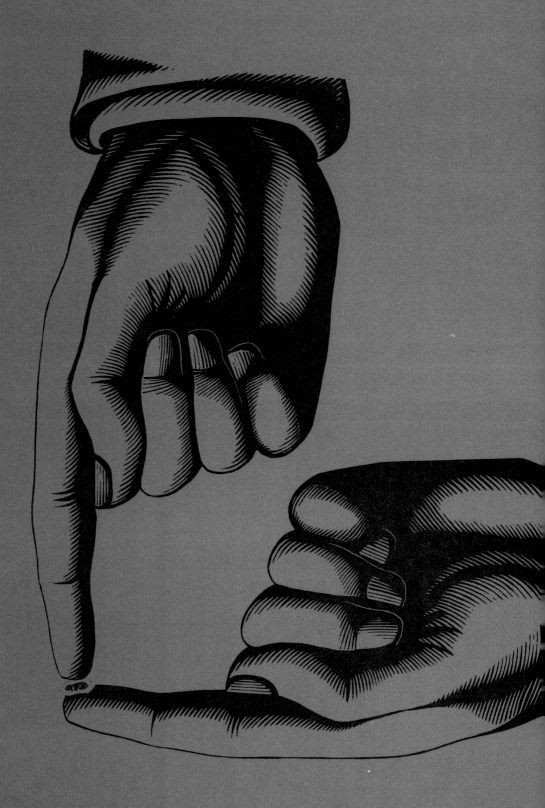

**7 viruses and unicellular life**

ince the time of Aristotle, investigators of the natural world have divided living things into two broad categories, plants and animals. As with all systems of classification, the distinction is arbitrary. But for a long time it did seem to be reasonable and empirically justifiable. Animals obviously moved about as they gathered and ingested food, and it was clear enough that most plants were green and rooted. As more was learned about living things and their diverse forms and modes of existence, finer distinctions among organisms became possible. Attempts were made to group similar kinds of organisms in a way that indicated some degree of relationship among them. But these divisions and subgroupings retained the traditional two-kingdom approach. Indeed, this approach was formalized in 1735 when Carl Linnaeus classified all known organisms as either plants or animals.

The two-kingdom system of classification, however, is inadequate in the light of our present knowledge. This is partly because many organisms do not fit neatly into either category. For example, fungi neither make their own food like plants, nor ingest food like animals. Moreover, early classification systems implied only present relationships. And these relationships were based on varying degrees of similarity in morphology—that is, the form and structure of organisms. Until Darwin's book on evolution was published in 1859, no thought of phylogeny—the chronological and genetic relationships of different kinds of organisms—was expressed or implied.

At this time, one classification system seems most logical and conceptually rigorous in recognizing the broad diversity of organisms and their evolutionary relationships. This is the five-kingdom system formulated by Whittaker. In this text we will follow the Whittaker system, at least in its broadest outline.

Throughout this chapter we will also observe a classification pertinent to microbiology, one of the disciplines within the

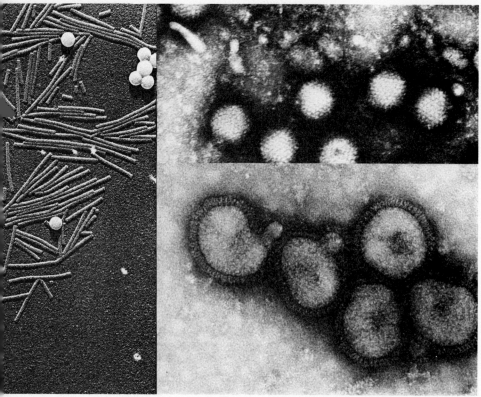

7-1
Virions. Left, rod-shaped virions of tobacco mosaic virus, produced in cells of tobacco leaves. Right: top, virions of human influenza virus; bottom, virions of human adenovirus, which may produce upper respiratory disease or conjunctivitis.

field of biological science. Microbes, or microorganisms, are generally defined as those organisms which cannot be clearly seen with the unaided eye. They have traditionally been the subject for study by microbiologists. Microorganisms include bacteria (Monera) and eucaryotic unicellular algae and protozoa (Protista). They also include viruses. Technically speaking, these latter particles may not be "organisms" at all. But they are within the realm of the microbiologist's concern on the basis of their size, their importance to the study of biological processes, and their function as agents of disease.

## Viruses

In chemical terms, viruses are simply nucleic acids produced by living cells. The viral nucleic acid is wrapped in coats of protein (or protein and lipid) as units, or virions, and then released from the cell. A virion, or its nucleic acid alone, can enter another cell of the same type as the one in which it was made. There it induces the newly infected cell to produce more of that same type of virus. If the production of virions interferes with the cell's metabolic activities, or if the release of newly synthesized virions disrupts the cell surface, infection may destroy the cell.

It is hard to detect the presence of a virus unless it causes characteristic changes in infected cells. In fact, viruses were discovered as agents of disease. Virus diseases of humans include several of the "childhood" diseases of Western civilization, such as measles, mumps, and chicken pox. Viruses are the cause of such nuisances as "fever blisters" and warts. They are also responsible for a number of much more serious conditions—poliomyelitis, smallpox, infectious hepatitis, and influenza. Two other serious viral diseases are transmitted by the bite of insects (yellow fever) and mammals (rabies). The class of diseases known as "colds" also has a viral origin. Finally, there is the possibility that some cancers and certain chronic diseases of the nervous system (perhaps including multiple sclerosis) will one day be attributed to virus infections.

## Bacteriophages

The study of virus-infected cells has yielded a wealth of information about control of cell metabolism. This is partly because cause and effect are easier to recognize in a system undergoing change than in a system in a steady state. The paramount role of nucleic acids as directive molecules becomes clear when we see that entrance of viral nucleic acid into a cell is followed by a major shift in synthetic processes.

The most exhaustively studied viruses are those produced by bacteria, the so-called **bacteriophages** (from *phagos:* one that eats). In fact, many of the fundamentals of virus infection and its consequences were first learned in studies of bacteriophage-bacterium systems. Two of the most thoroughly characterized of these systems

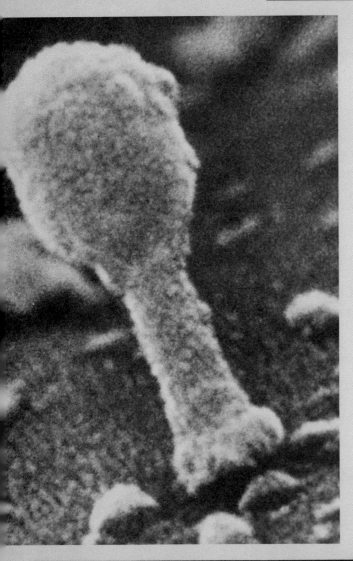

7-2
One of the first pictures of T4 coliphage (a virus which grows only on *E. coli*) to be taken with a scanning electron microscope that uses high-energy scattered electrons to produce a surface image with extremely high resolution. A coating of gold (seen as globules on the surface) makes the phage electrically conductive and enables it to scatter electrons. (Actual size of virus: approx. 200 nm.)

7-3
Lysis of an *E. coli* bacterium by T4 coliphage.

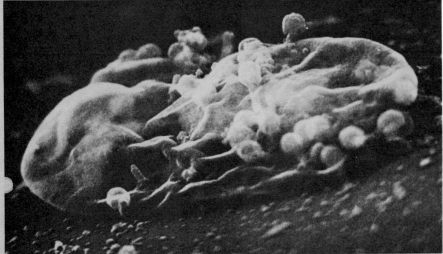

are those of virulent and temperate bacteriophages.

A **virulent bacteriophage** typically kills every cell it infects. The virion attaches its tail to the surface of the bacterium. It releases its DNA through its tail into the cell cytoplasm. Viral nucleic acid then directs the metabolic machinery of the cell. Cellular growth stops as a result, and virus components are manufactured. Units of newly synthesized nucleic acid are assembled into virions. Eventually, the bacterial cell disintegrates, releasing the mature virions.

In a **temperate bacteriophage** system some infected cells remain alive. When a bacterium is infected by a temperate phage, viral nucleic acid is integrated into the host's genetic material. The viral nucleic acid is then replicated along with the host cell's DNA. Thus successive generations of the bacterium receive viral as well as bacterial nucleic acid. In this stable association with the bacterial DNA, which may last indefinitely, the viral nucleic acid is known as a **provirus**.

Under normal conditions, the most obvious effect the provirus has on the phenotype of the bacterial cell is to render it incapable of productive infection. That is, the bacterium is immune to infection by another phage of the same kind which results in the synthesis of new virions. But under certain conditions, the bacterial cell can be induced to manufacture virions of the original infecting phage. In other words, the stable association with the bacterial DNA alters, and the temperate phage begins to function as though it were a virulent phage. Its nucleic acid takes over, and new temperate virions are produced and then released.

*Eucaryotic systems* Basically similar to the bacteriophage–bacterium system is the virus–eucaryotic system. One of the major differences is the alternative of sites within a eucaryotic system where viruses can be produced. These sites include the nucleus, cytoplasm, and chloroplast. In animal cells, the nuclear or plasma mem-

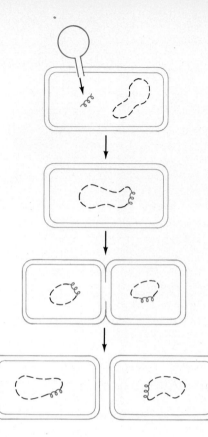

7-4
Temperate bacteriophage system. Black
dashes: bacterial chromosome; colored coil:
viral DNA. Only one cell division is shown, but
the viral DNA may be transmitted through an
indefinite number of such divisions.

7-5
Specific transduction. Dashed black line:
bacterial DNA not involved in the transduction.
Solid black line: gene for galactose (six-
carbon sugar) fermentation. Plus sign: ability
to ferment. Minus sign: inability to ferment.
Coiled colored line: DNA of lambda prophage.
(A) production of transducing particles. (B)
production of a transductant.

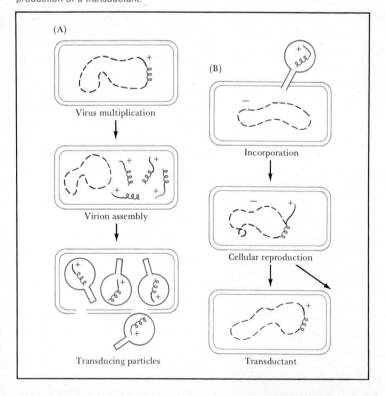

(A)

Virus multiplication

Virion assembly

Transducing particles

(B)

Incorporation

Cellular reproduction

Transductant

brane may contribute to the outer wrapping
of the virion. The virion may be taken into
the cell by phagocytosis. Or the virus may
be transferred from cell to cell without being released into the extracellular environment. Also, the entire infection cycle is
slower in most eucaryotic cells than in bacterial cells.

## Transduction

Time may prove that the principal role of
some viruses is not even related to the origin and development of disease. For example, a lengthy study of bacteriophage systems has revealed a viral function that
could be especially valuable for organisms
in which sexuality is rare or absent. This
phenomenon is known as **transduction**. It
makes possible the exchange of genetic
information within bacterial populations. It
also allows new combinations of genetic
characters within the species independently of mutations and sexuality.

The genetic information is transmitted
by temperate bacteriophages. One way in
which this transmission occurs is called
**specific transduction**. When a provirus
becomes active (in the manner of a virulent
phage) it leaves the bacterial DNA. Occasionally, it carries with it a piece of the host
cell's genetic material. When the viral nucleic acid is copied and assembled into
new virions, the piece of the host cell's
genetic material is copied also. The new
virions, carrying the excess information, are
called **transducing particles**.

When a transducing particle infects another bacterium, it can carry into that cell's
nucleus the information from the original
bacterial cell. The previous and present
host bacteria may differ with respect to the
nature of the transduced information. That
is, they may possess different alleles of the
transduced gene. If this is the case, the
second cell may experience a heritable
phenotype change. It is then a **transductant**, and its offspring will display the
transduced phenotype.

# Monera

Bacteria are interesting and important organisms for study, apart from their interactions with viruses. For many decades, bacteria and the blue-green algae have been treated as the two members of the procaryotic kingdom Monera. But a growing number of microbiologists now believe that blue-green algae are themselves bacteria. As such, they have endured almost as long as there has been organic material on earth.

Bacteria are typically rod-shaped organisms (*bacter* means rod). But some cells may be tapered, spheroid, curved, or coiled. Bacteria are usually found as single-celled organisms. There are in fact some truly multicellular forms. But in most cases, the multicellular organisms are composed of only one kind of bacterial cell. That is, they are undifferentiated. **Trichomes** are multicellular bacteria which consist of chains of cells. **Mycelia** grow into long, branching tubes with or without internal walls or partitions. **Budding colonies** are cells linked together by a network of cytoplasmic strands that grow out from the cells.

## Bacterial diversity

The longevity of bacteria results partly from their diverse modes of nutrition. There is no known naturally occurring organic substance that cannot be metabolized by some kind of bacterium. Some bacteria can even live in a completely inorganic environment.

Many bacteria are aerobic **chemoheterotrophs**. These organisms obtain energy for their life processes from the respiration of organic compounds. They can use all the compounds that animals and protozoa use as sources of carbon (needed for growth) and energy. But they also can utilize many other sources which more specialized organisms cannot metabolize. These other nutrients include hydrocarbon gases, organo-metal compounds, cellulose, agar, pectin, woody substances, rubber, leather,

and even hair, horn, and nails (which are all made of the same kind of protein).

Unlike animals and most protozoa and fungi, many types of chemoheterotrophic bacteria do not need atmospheric $O_2$. Instead, they may use nitrates, sulfates, or organic compounds. These anaerobic organisms include the denitrifiers, the only known source of atmospheric $N_2$ whose activities since the beginning of life on earth have provided a principal component of our modern atmosphere. Also included are the fermentative bacteria.

The **chemoautotrophs** are also widespread in nature, but not nearly as diverse as the chemoheterotrophic bacteria. Chemoautotrophic organisms are unlike any kind of plant, animal, or eucaryotic microorganism. They can grow in the dark in a completely inorganic environment. They are typically aerobes that respire $H_2$ or reduced inorganic compounds (such as ammonia) and sulfides to obtain energy for metabolism.

**Photoheterotrophic** bacteria use organic compounds as the source of electrons for photosynthesis. Consequently, they do not produce $O_2$ as a by-product. On the contrary, they can grow only under anaerobic conditions.

**Photoautotrophy** is a fourth mode of nutrition. Some bacteria in this category use reduced inorganic sulfur compounds or $H_2$ as their source of electrons for photosynthesis. Others—the blue-green bacteria—use water as the source of electrons, and so release $O_2$ as a by-product. It is this latter type of photosynthesis that the eucaryotic algae inherited. They, in turn, passed the method on to the plants.

Many bacteria fall into more than one of the categories described above. That is, they are able to live under more than one set of environmental conditions. For example, the blue-greens can shift the proportions of their photosynthetic pigments so that they absorb whatever usable wavelength of light is available.

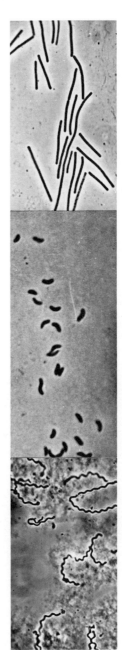

7-6
Top: *Bacillus macroides* rods. (From J. F. Bennett and E. Canale-Parola, 1965. Arch. f. Mikrobiol. 52:197. By permission of Springer-Verlag, Berlin, Heidelberg, New York.) Center: *Desulfovibrio* cells. These semispiral forms are known as vibrios, or comma bacteria. (From L. L. Campbell, M. A. Kasprzycki and J. R. Postgate, 1966. J. Bact. 92:1122. By permission of the American Society for Microbiology.) Bottom: *Arthrospira* cells. (Courtesy of R. A. Lewin.)

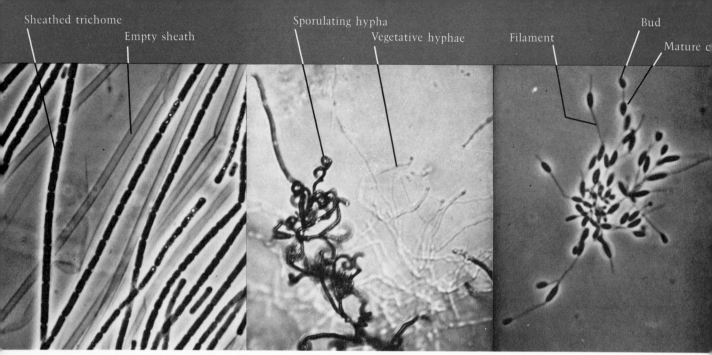

Sheathed trichome     Empty sheath     Sporulating hypha     Vegetative hyphae     Filament     Bud     Mature c

**7-7**
Multicellular forms. Left: *Sphaerotilus natans:*
sheathed trichomes and empty sheaths. Center:
*Streptomyces fradiae:* vegetative mycelium and
sporulating branches. Right: *Rhodomicrobium*
microcolony.

**7-8**
A dividing cell of *Pseudomonas fluorescens*, a
highly versatile pseudomonad (a type of bacterium) that produces fluorescent pigments. All
pseudomonads are capable of growth as
aerobic chemoheterotrophs, but many are
capable of alternative physiologic modes.
(See Bacterial diversity)

**7-9**
Encystment is a complicated process in the "fruiting"
myxobacteria. It is preceded by aggregation of vegetative cells in a common mass of slime. Each cell may
then become modified into a cyst as the slime hardens
around the group, enclosing and protecting the
dormant cells. A mass of slime containing dormant
myxobacteria is called a fruiting body, and is illustrated by the *Chondromyces apiculatus* shown below.
The dormant cells are within the pointed bodies of
the apical cluster. (See Reproduction and dormancy)

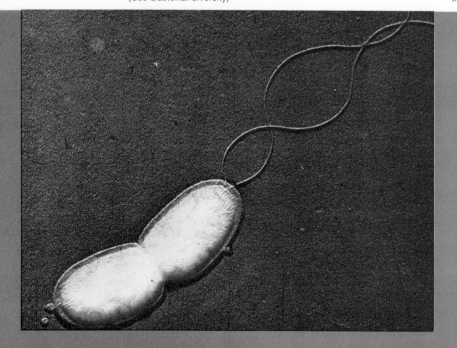

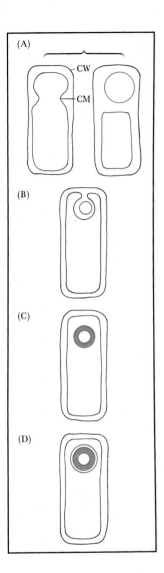

(A)

CW

CM

(B)

(C)

(D)

7-10
Endospore formation is the outstanding characteristic of the aerobic chemoheterotrophs called bacilli. (A) Separation of spore and vegetative cytoplasm within the cell wall (CW) by constriction of the cell membrane (CM). (B) Engulfment of spore by vegetative cytoplasm. (C) Development of spore cortex. (D) Development of spore wall.

7-11
*Euglena.* (See The algae)

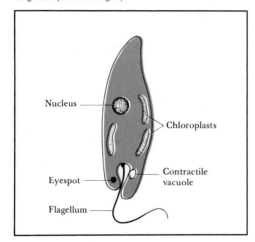

Nucleus

Chloroplasts

Eyespot

Contractile vacuole

Flagellum

vation and penetration by chemicals. Dry bacterial endospores can survive an hour or more at 180°C. This remarkable capacity is the basis of standards for heat disinfection and sterilization in hospitals, laboratories, space flights, and food processing.

## Protista

The organisms of the kingdom Protista evolved from the simple Monera. (The kingdom Protista was given its name before its evolutionary past was recognized— *protistos* means "first of all.") This group includes organisms which are eucaryotic and mostly unicellular. Some are regarded as plant-like (algae) and others as animal-like (protozoa). But the distinctions between them remain a matter of controversy between botanists and zoologists. From the Protista evolved the three higher kingdoms. Each is characterized by its most prevalent mode of nutrition—the plant kingdom by photosynthesis, the animal kingdom by ingestion, and the fungi by absorption.

### Reproduction and dormancy

Binary fission is the usual method of bacterial reproduction. But it is not the only method. For example, budding occurs in scattered groups. Some types of bacterium also can produce cells specialized for a condition of nongrowth (dormancy) through the process of sporulation. One such cell is a **cyst**. It is modified by a thickening of its cell wall and often a piling up of reserve foods. Another dormant cell is the **endospore**. Its multilayered coating makes the endospore highly resistant to heat inacti-

### The algae

The plant-like part of the kingdom Protista can be separated into five major divisions, or phyla. These vary from one another in gross structure, but share certain properties on the cellular level which imply a single line of evolutionary descent. We will focus on members of only three of the phyla.

The euglenoid algae (phylum Euglenophyta) frustrate attempts at strict classification. Nearly all members are flagellates. Some lack photosynthetic pigments and are solely heterotrophic. This suggests a common ancestry with flagellate protozoans (zooflagellates). Others have chloroplasts and so, like plants, can use photosynthesis as a source of carbon and energy.

The euglenoids lack a typical cell wall. They are unicellular, and reproduce asexually by longitudinal cell division. A flagellum protrudes from a cavity at the anterior end of the cell. Its helical movement, like that of a constantly turning corkscrew, pulls the animal through its freshwater environment. *Euglena,* one of the motile algae, also has a specialized structure near the cavity which contains carotenoid pigments. This structure is called the **stigma** or "eyespot." It probably influences the organism's movement in response to differences in the direction and intensity of light.

The diatoms (phylum Chrysophyta) are important because they form much of the phytoplankton (the photosynthetic portion of the plankton) floating like a dilute soup in the surface layers of all the seas and oceans. Along with members of the phylum Pyrrophyta (especially the dinoflagellates, which we will discuss shortly), they create most of the food material available to animal life in the oceans. At the same time, they contribute to the world oxygen supply by fixing carbon dioxide and releasing oxygen.

Diatoms extract silica from the sea water, where it occurs in very dilute solution. They deposit this silica in their cell walls. Silica does not decompose. So when the diatom dies, the silica skeleton remains and sinks to the ocean floor. Over thousands of years, vast deposits of silica accumulate. With changes in the earth's crust, some of these deposits have been elevated above sea level where they form beds of diatomaceous earth, sometimes over 1,000 feet thick. This is mined for use in industry, particularly as an abrasive, insulating, and filtration agent. The individual surface markings in each diatom skeleton can still be seen in the deposits of diatomaceous earth.

Diatoms are found in a variety of geometric forms. Some, for example, are spindle-shaped, and others have a disc-like appearance. Diatoms usually exist singly. But sometimes, after cell division, the new cells stick together to form a colony. Two overlapping halves of silica enclose the cytoplasm of each diatom, which contains one or more chloroplasts and one nucleus. The cells also contain oils. These provide the buoyancy which keeps them near the surface of the ocean where they can receive light for photosynthesis. The silica cell walls often have many pores which facilitate contact with the environment.

Some species of the phylum Pyrrophyta can reproduce sexually through the fusion of haploid gametes. But most reproduce by simple cell division or by means of **zoospores** (spores that have flagella). The class of pyrrophytes called dinoflagellates have two flagella and a characteristic groove running the length of the cell wall. Most species in this phylum have a characteristic brownish color because of a carotenoid pigment contained in their plastids. There are also colorless dinoflagellates which lack pigment. These feed on particulate organic matter or ingest solid particles of food, nutritional modes usually associated with animals. Still another group contains red pigment. This group is probably the most familiar, since it includes the poisonous variety of pyrrophytes. These organisms form the "red tides" responsible for the death of countless fish.

## Protozoans

Protozoans are small (0.1 – 2mm long) free-living or parasitic single-celled protists. Their organelles perform the essential body functions characteristically performed by whole organ systems in multicellular animals. Protozoans often have a mouth aperture or other means of engulfing food particles such as bacteria, algal cells, and animal microorganisms. They may also have contractile vacuoles that maintain water balance, vacuoles for storage and digestion of food, and, in two cases, cilia or flagella. All free-living protozoans respond to light, temperature, and other physiochemical stimuli. Protozoans reproduce asexually by fission, or sexually by conjugation or fusion.

Foraminiferans (phylum Sarcodina) live almost exclusively in the sea. They secrete a shell, containing silica and calcium carbonate, which partially covers the body. Foraminiferans are of considerable importance in geological history, since many limestones were formed by their shells. For example, the pyramids of Gizeh, Egypt, were made of limestone blocks produced by *Numulites,* a Mesozoic foraminiferan. The Sphinx was carved from a residual limestone mass of the same origin. Fusulinids, fossil foraminiferans from the Paleozoic, measured as large as ten to twelve centimeters. They produced limestones found all over the world.

The Ciliophora are multinucleated organisms that usually have large portions of their surface area covered with cilia. They are among the most complicated and beautifully coordinated of all animal-like protists. Ciliophora are common in both freshwater and marine environments. Since they are known to feed on bacteria in polluted rivers and lakes, they are used in sewage treatment plants.

Many species of ciliophora, such as *Paramecium,* use their cilia as a propulsion system. In these organisms the mouth aperture funnels suspended food particles into

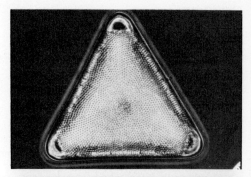
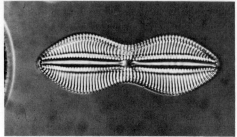

7-12
Diatoms. Top: *Triceratium formosum.* Bottom: *Diploneis crabo.* (See The algae)

7-13
A dinoflagellate, *Ceratium Hirondella.* (See The algae)

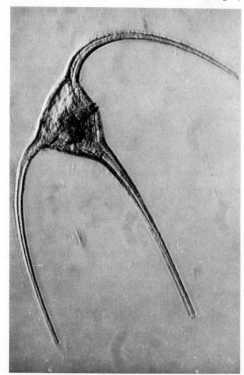

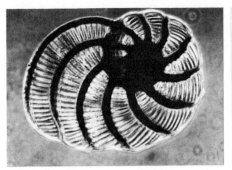

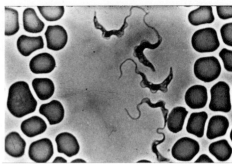

7-14
Left: a foraminiferan, *Peneroplis pertusus*. (See The algae) Center: Conjugation among paramecia is initiated by joining along their oral grooves. (See Protozoans) Right: *Trypanosoma gambiense*, a protozoan parasite that causes African sleeping sickness, is transmitted by the tsetse fly. Death is the usual result in untreated cases.

7-15
A species of Ciliophora, *Vorticella microstoma*. These bell-shaped protozoans are sessile— incapable of movement. They are attached to stems which enable them to contract as, for example, when in danger. Shown are two cells, one contracted, the other extended.

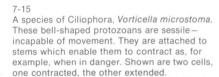
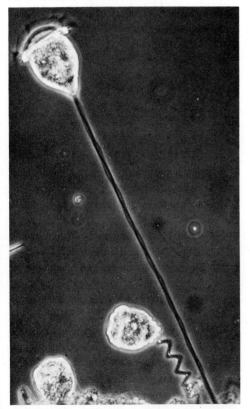

vacuoles as the animal moves through its watery habitat. The **pellicle**, an inner area of the organism's membranous surface coating, contains thousands of bottle-shaped organelles called **trichocysts**. When the animal is disturbed by a predator or by unfavorable environmental conditions, the trichocysts discharge a sticky, toxic substance resembling a thin thread. This also seems to be used as an "anchor" while the animal feeds.

Paramecia usually reproduce by transverse fission. However, they sometimes reproduce sexually by the process of conjugation. It appears that sexual reproduction causes rejuvenation in some unknown way. Paramecia lines will die out after several hundred generations in the laboratory if they are not allowed to conjugate occasionally. In nature, paramecia often switch to sexual reproduction when the environment becomes less hospitable—that is, high in $CO_2$ and low in food. It is believed that the exchange of genetic materials through conjugation may allow genes to reactivate in a new cell environment, restoring the active metabolic state.

One of the most important protozoans to humans is *Plasmodium vivax* (phylum Sporozoa). This is the malarial parasite which lives in the *Anopheles* mosquito. The parasites, which are incapable of self-movement, gain entry to the human bloodstream in the saliva of the mosquito. Once there, they pass into the red blood cells where they reproduce. Eventually the red blood cells burst, releasing toxin and allowing the parasites to enter other cells where they continue to reproduce. Apparently the fever and chills that occur at regular intervals in a person with malaria are caused by the periodic release of toxin from millions of bursting cells.

## Pathogens and hosts

Along with viruses and many bacteria, we have noted that certain protozoa are also agents of disease. That is, they are **pathogens**. A major branch of microbiology deals with the control of such harmful microorganisms and the prevention and treatment of the diseases they cause. As a result of research and experimentation, we now follow certain sanitary practices which help us to control microbes in our environment. These include the sterilization of foods, purification of water supplies, and treatment of sewage. And we now have available vaccines and antibiotics which cure us of infection after it has occurred.

But our bodies are not toally helpless without these practices and medicines. As potential "hosts" we have a variety of ways to defend ourselves against microbial infection and subsequent disease. Some of these defenses are shared with nonhuman organisms.

Many potential hosts are covered by relatively impermeable tissues. If this covering is penetrated, the tissues can respond by forming shells or building additional walls around the invaded region. Also, cells can "recognize" whether another

**7-16** Antibodies and their modes of action against microbial cells.

| | |
|---|---|
| *lysins* | cause disintegration of the microbial cell. |
| *opsonins* | increase susceptibility to phagocytosis and digestibility within phagocytes; |
| *neutralizers* | somehow eliminate the ability of the invading microbe to multiply and/or elicit disease symptoms; antitoxins are neutralizing antibodies; |
| *agglutinins* | cause microbial cells to clump, decreasing their mobility and increasing the likelihood that they will be phagocytized; |
| *precipitins* | cause soluble products of the microbes to become insoluble (i.e., to precipitate) |

cell is of the same organism or is alien. If the cell is indeed alien, the organism may respond by phagocytotically attacking it. In humans and many other vertebrates some specialized cells can respond to alien cells by synthesizing special proteins called antibodies. The molecules of the foreign cells that cause the antibody response are called antigens. Often they occur on the surface of foreign cells. But they also may be molecules that are enclosed and then released after the cell enters the body.

## Immunity

When infection occurs due to a bacterial or viral agent, the human body mounts a defense by employing an immune mechanism. Actually, there are two such mechanisms. In the first, the foreign material is met and engulfed by free-moving white blood cells called **macrophages**. By some unknown mechanism, additional macrophage cells are produced which specifically recognize this particular kind of foreign material. These cells remain in the system and will mount a more accelerated attack if infection recurs. This process is called **cell-mediated immunity.**

In an alternative response to foreign materials, white blood cells called **lymphocytes** are converted to **plasma cells.** The plasma cells can synthesize antibody molecules and release them into the bloodstream. Each antibody molecule is believed to possess combining sites which complement the structure of specific antigens. This enables an antibody to "lock" with the ap-

propriate antigens and thus inactivate them. If the antigens are located on the surface of foreign cells—rather than floating separately in the bloodstream—these cells will be forced to clump together as a result of the antigen–antibody combination. This phenomenon, noted in chapter 5, is called agglutination.

Potential pathogens have their own variety of resources and characteristics that allow them to overcome host defenses. They can digest and penetrate protective coverings—such as the mucous membranes of mammals and the external skeletons of insects—as well as newly formed barriers. They can resist chemical attack by soluble antimicrobial substances and the digestive enzymes of phagocytes. They cannot protect themselves against antibodies formed specifically in response to their presence in the body. But they can overcome antibody protection by multiplying or producing toxins more rapidly than antibodies can be formed. And they may grow within host cells, where antibodies cannot reach them.

The interaction between host and pathogen is complicated. The ultimate victor may be determined by the heredity, diet, general health, age, sex, or history of infection by the host. It also may be determined by the number of pathogens present before host response begins, the route by which the pathogen enters the body, or even the weather at the time of the meeting between the potential host and the potential pathogen.

**7-17**
Inactivation of antigens. Different kinds of lymphocytes may be able to identify specific types of antigens and pass on information concerning the configurations of these antigens to the plasma cells. These cells would then be able to produce antibodies with an active site complementary to the inducing antigen.

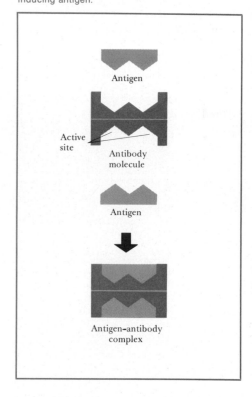

summary

Viruses are responsible for a wide variety of plant, animal, and human diseases. Basically, they are nucleic acids produced by living cells. The viral nucleic acid is wrapped in a coat of protein to form a virion. As such, it can enter a cell of the same type in which it was made, and cause it to produce more of the virus. Those viruses which invade bacteria are called bacteriophages. Infection by a virulent bacteriophage results in the production of new virions and the disintegration of the host cell. Infection by a temperate bacteriophage does not usually cause the death of the bacterium. The viral nucleic acid is simply replicated along with the host cell's DNA. Temperate bacteriophages are also involved in transduction. They transmit genetic information from one bacterium to another. This allows new combinations of genetic characters within the species, independently of mutation and sexuality.

Bacteria (kingdom Monera) are typically unicellular and rod-shaped. Multicellular bacteria include trichomes, mycelia, and budding colonies. Bacteria exhibit many diverse modes of nutrition and metabolism. Several species can survive under a number of extreme environmental conditions. Some bacteria exhibit budding or sporulation, but most reproduce by binary fission. A few kinds of bacteria produce cysts or endospores, cells specialized for nongrowth (dormancy). A cyst is a cell modified by a thickening of its wall and a stockpile of reserve foods. An endospore has a special wall which renders the spore highly resistant to heat and chemical penetration.

The kingdom Protista comprises the eucaryotic, mostly unicellular, organisms from which plants, animals, and fungi all evolved. The plant-like algae consist of five phyla. They vary from one another in gross structure, but share certain properties on the cellular level. Some euglenoid algae are heterotrophic; others can perform photosynthesis. *Euglena,* one of the flagellated algae, has an eyespot which is sensitive to differences in the direction and intensity of light. The diatoms form much of the photosynthetic part of the plankton in seas and oceans. They serve as food for animal life in oceans, and contribute to the world oxygen supply. The dinoflagellates include poisonous organisms which form the "red tides" and which are responsible for the death of numerous fish.

The animal-like protists are called protozoans. They are small free-living or parasitic unicellular organisms. Protozoans often have an orifice or other means of engulfing food. Contractile vacuoles help maintain water balance. Other vacuoles are used to store and digest food. All free-living protozoans respond to light, temperature, and other physiochemical stimuli. Reproduction occurs asexually by fission or sexually by conjugation or fusion. Some protozoans are motile, as in the case of *paramecium.* Others are incapable of self-movement. An example of the latter is *Plasmodium vivax,* the malarial parasite which lives in the intestine and salivary glands of the *Anopheles* mosquito.

Viruses, many bacteria, and certain protozoans are pathogens, or agents of disease. Potential hosts have various mechanisms for defending themselves against these agents. In some cases, the defense is a protective coat of tissues. Some animal organisms have specialized cells which can "recognize" and respond to alien cells by phagocytically attacking them. In cell-mediated immunity, infectious agents are engulfed by special white blood cells, the macrophages. New macrophages are then produced and remain in the system. They are thus available to the organism should infection recur. In an alternative response to microbes, antigen molecules on the surface of foreign cells trigger the production of plasma cells. These plasma cells, in turn, produce antibodies and release them into the bloodstream. The antibodies combine with and inactivate the antigens. This results in the clumping, or agglutination, of the foreign cells.

**a**typical lichen appears to be a single organism, rather like a moss in its general appearance. Actually it is an association of two very different organisms—a matrix of fungal filaments through which a large number of algal cells are scattered. The fungi in a lichen are the beneficiaries of a remarkably intimate and efficient partnership. They are supplied with carbohydrates and vitamins synthesized by the algal cells that they shelter. In return, the fungus absorbs water vapor directly from the air for use by the algae in photosynthesis. The fungi also shade the algae from excessively strong light.

Both sedentary and mobile lifestyles involve complex adaptations. This is especially true in terms of food-gathering and reproductive behavior. Coral animals, for example, possess an immobile skeleton of calcium carbonate. They must therefore wait passively for food to come within reach of their tentacles. If the environment proves inhospitable, they cannot seek out a better one. This limited mobility also influences reproduction. Coral animals reproduce in two ways. Members of colonial species form buds, which remain attached to the parent polyp. The older polyps eventually die as new buds develop over and around them. But their skeletons remain to form the reefs and stony structures commonly called coral. Coral polyps also reproduce sexually. They produce a larval form that has cilia and can therefore move about. The larva may swim for weeks before establishing itself on a suitable solid surface and developing into an adult polyp. In this way, the corals can spread their species and colonize new areas.

The five-armed form of the sea star (or starfish) makes it appear radially symmetrical. This is a trait possessed by the animal organisms known as coelenterates, which include the jellyfish and the coral animals. In reality, however, the starfish possesses bilateral symmetry. This is a feature of the echinoderms, organisms more advanced than the coelenterates. Sea stars have hundreds of tube feet on each of their arms. These feet are tipped with structures that function as tiny suction cups. The sea star can therefore cling powerfully to surfaces or creep along them. It can also pull apart the shells of the various mollusks (such as clams) on which it feeds.

*Daphnia*, the water flea, belongs to the animal group known as crustaceans. Its legs have many fine hairs which strain food particles—even as small as bacteria—from the water. The water flea's swimming pattern is governed by a very clever mechanism. Green algae are a staple of *Daphnia*'s diet. A high concentration of them in the water absorbs much blue light. Thus the light reaching the swimming *Daphnia* is mostly reddish. In response, the water flea limits its activity to a series of vertical bobbing motions. This keeps it in the vicinity of the rich food supply. Blue light in the water indicates fewer algae. *Daphnia* consequently swims horizontally over a wider range in search of a more promising food supply.

Both the bullhead and the alligator are adapted to foraging for food at the boundary of two mediums. The bullhead, like most catfish, is a bottom feeder.

Above: Slowly decaying caribou antler covered by several types of lichen. Left: Mushrooms, Rocky Mountains. Most fungi are saprophytic, digesting the dead organic matter on which they grow. Other species are parasites of living animals or plants. But in lichen, fungi and algal cells function in a mutually beneficial way.

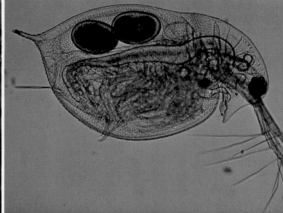

Above: *Daphnia*, a water flea. Enclosed within a casing, the legs of this crustacean are useless for locomotion; but they are equipped with many fine hairs, which form an efficient strainer for water-borne food particles.

Above: Sea star and tube corals. Coral animals must wait for food to come within reach of their tentacles. Sea stars have hundreds of small tube feet, tipped with suckers, on each of their arms. They can thus pull apart the shells of clams and other mollusks on which they feed. Right: Long-horned grasshopper.

Top: Cattle egret. Birds such as this one may feed by plucking insect parasites directly from the hides of cattle that are grazing. Above: Brown bullhead, a catfish which feeds along the bottoms of lakes and streams. Right: Alligator, a reptile which forages for food at the boundary of two mediums.

Swift and graceful in the water, the sea lion (right, bottom) is one of the most awkward creatures on land. The Dall ram (right, top) and the squirrel monkey (above) are among the most agile. The mountain sheep forage for food along the slopes of Alaska and Canada. Squirrel monkeys travel along treetop "pathways."

Its body is somewhat flattened. Its head is equipped with long barbels ("whiskers"). The barbels have many sensory receptors, both chemical (smell and taste) and mechanical (touch). They enable the fish to locate edible morsels on the muddy, murky bottoms of lakes and streams. Though an air-breather, the alligator spends much of its time in the water. Its favorite hunting strategy is to lie submerged just below the surface. Barely noticeable, it waits in ambush for its prey (fish, birds, and small mammals). The alligator's principal sense organs are its eyes, ears, and nostrils. These are located high on the alligator's head. Thus they protrude above the surface of the water. All three can be sealed by membranous coverings for protection when the animal dives. Birds seem still more mobile and versatile. Various species are adapted to land, air, or water—and sometimes to all three. The order to which the egret belongs includes herons, flamingos, storks, and ibises. Many of these birds are fishers. But the cattle egret finds its food on dry land. Its principal food supply consists of insects stirred up by herds of grazing animals. It may also pluck insect parasites directly from the hides of cattle.

Mammals too have made themselves at home on land, in water, and even (in the case of bats) in the air. Like the alligator, the sea lion is equipped with membranes for its eyes and nose which make possible long stays underwater. The sea lion is warm-blooded, like all mammals. It can maintain its normal body temperature in the cold ocean waters because it has a lot of insulation (fat) and a high rate of metabolism. In fact, its rate of metabolism is double that of comparable land animals. On land, where the sea lions rest and breed, getting rid of excess metabolic heat can be a serious problem. One means of solving the problem is to stay wet. This allows for cooling by evaporation. Another means of coping with the problem is to sleep. A sleeping sea lion has been found to produce about 25 percent less metabolic heat.

Flippers enable the sea lion to move rapidly and efficiently through the water. But they also make the sea lion one of the slowest and clumsiest of creatures when living on land. The Dall sheep and the squirrel monkey, on the other hand, are among the most agile of land-living animals. Despite their bulk, the mountain sheep are astonishingly surefooted as they forage for grass along steep mountain slopes. The squirrel monkeys are also remarkable in their ability to travel along the tops of trees. Squirrel monkeys are highly social animals, traveling in groups that may number in the hundreds. Generally they follow a particular individual who leads the troop in single file. The young monkeys cling to the back of one of their parents.

**fungi and plants**

**8**

hen we think of plants, we usually mean the most familiar ones — trees, grass, shrubs, garden flowers, grain and vegetable crops, and even roadside weeds. But not all plants are like these, possessing roots, stems, leaves, flowers, and hard-coated seeds. Plants with these characteristics are late arrivals on the evolutionary scene. They were preceded, over hundreds of millions of years, by simpler forms. Like animals, plants began in the warm surface waters of the primitive oceans as fragile single-celled organisms. The complex structures which allowed them to spread to less favorable environments were evolved very slowly. Eventually, they invaded land, the least favorable environment of all. In this chapter, we shall examine some representatives and groupings, both living and extinct, of that long history.

It is hard to overemphasize the importance of plants. They provide the basic food supply on which all other organisms depend, either directly or indirectly. They provide for the continual renewal of the earth's oxygen. Their buried remains are transformed into coal and oil for energy. In addition, plants furnish an enormous number of substances necessary to our daily life, from chemicals for medicine to fiber for clothing, lumber for building, and rubber for shoe soles and tires. Finally, plants form the overwhelming bulk of the diet for the many human societies which are vegetarian through religious conviction or economic necessity.

Another group, the fungi, are closely associated with plants. At one time they were classed as plants, largely because fungi resemble plants more than they resemble animals. Nevertheless, the fungi differ from plants in significant respects. Perhaps the most obvious difference is that fungi do not contain chlorophyll. This renders them unable to produce their own food by photosynthesis. Therefore, the tendency today is to regard fungi as members of a separate kingdom, neither plant nor animal, with their own particular tasks to perform in the earth's ecosystems. We shall consider them here in a general way before turning to a more detailed study of plants.

## Fungi

Fungi depend upon living or dead organic material for their food supply. In the kingdom of fungi we find both **saprophytes**, living off dead plant and animal remains, and **parasites**, which subsist on living plants and animals.

The word "fungus" tends to remind us of disease and decay. Indeed, many organisms are killed by fungal infections. But fungi display an amazing variety of useful qualities in addition to the harmful ones. They act as garbage disposers, breaking down dead vegetation and recycling the nutrients they absorb. True, many varieties of mushroom are poisonous to humans. But others, such as truffles, are excellent food.

Among the blue-green molds, some cause food to spoil, but others are used to ripen cheeses such as Roquefort. Still other molds are important for the manufacture of life-saving antibiotics such as penicillin.

The various kinds of yeast perform such functions as assisting in the fermentation of wine and beer and causing bread to rise.

One form of yeast, *Torula,* can be grown on almost any organic waste and doubles its bulk in less than an hour. *Torula* is an important source of protein and is often added to other food products. In years to come it may prove a valuable supplement to the earth's diminishing food supply.

Fungi can be divided into two groups: the **slime molds** and the **true fungi**. Slime molds, or *Myxomycophyta,* probably represent a very primitive and ancient form of life. They seem to be an evolutionary dead end, since they gave rise to no higher forms. Slime molds are found in moist woodland areas. They live on rotting logs or other organic matter. In their vegetative state, they consist of a mass of living matter, without cell walls, spreading out amoeba-like over the substance on which they are living. The body of true fungi, or *Eumycophyta,* is composed of a **mycelium**—a mass of interwoven, thread-like hyphae. By means of these, the fungi spread over the surface of, and penetrate, the material they grow on.

Fungi reproduce by minute **spores** which are commonly airborne. But the reproductive structures which produce the spores differ among the members of the phyla. This gives rise to various class divisions. Most fungi produce at least two types of spore in their life cycle, and some produce up to five types.

About 200,000 species of fungus are estimated to exist, although only about 50,000 have been described. New species are being discovered at the rate of about three a day. They have been found in the frozen polar regions as well as in the more suitable habitats of the tropics.

## Lichens

Fungi normally exist on organic substrates, living or dead. Unicellular algae, as we saw earlier, are normally found in water or in moist situations. Yet, when the two get together in a mutual or symbiotic relationship, they can live on dry rocks, ground, and trees, in a wide variety of improbable situa-

8-1
Sporangia of the slime mold *Physarum.* Even at this, the most structured stage of its life cycle, the slime mold appears rather amorphous and unformed. (Carolina Biological Supply Company)

**8-2**
A true fungi, the edible morel *(Morchella)* is highly prized by gourmets.

**8-3**
Included among the true fungi are basidiomycetes, a group including mushrooms, puffballs, rusts, and smuts. Shown, from the top, are the deadly *Amanita;* the edible *Agaricus campestris; Polydorus,* a bracket fungus; and *Clavaria,* the coral fungus.

tions. This symbiotic form is a **lichen**. The algae photosynthesize, providing carbohydrate nutrients for the fungus. The sponge-like fungus, in turn, anchors the lichen and absorbs water from the environment.

The fungus reproduces independently of the alga. But because the fungal species can live only symbiotically, the spores it produces can grow only if they come into contact with the correct species of alga. Since the possibility of this contact is fairly small, lichens can also reproduce vegetatively. Tiny portions, consisting of a few cells of alga and fungus, break off and are carried by the wind to a new growing place.

Lichens are important for two principal reasons. First, masses of lichens, such as reindeer "moss" *(Cladonia),* cover great areas of the northern arctic and subarctic regions. Here they serve as pasturage for reindeer and other herbivores. Second, lichens are important as the first colonizers of newly exposed rock surface. They begin the process of decomposing the rock. Eventually this produces the soil needed by other plants.

## Plant classification

People have probably been naming and classifying plants ever since they first distinguished food from nonfood plants. But a modern phylogenetic classification, by plant characteristics and sequence of evolutionary development, was not devised until the time of Darwin in the mid-nineteenth century. In such a classification, each succeeding group possesses a more complicated vegetative structure and a more protected embryonic development. One important trend which bears some explanation is in the reproductive cycles of various groups.

### Alternation of generations

In chapter 4 we discussed alternation of generations in the life cycle of a plant. Throughout the plant kingdom the importance of each generation varies widely. We

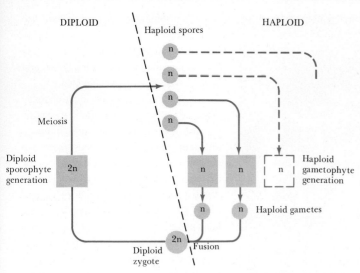

DIPLOID  HAPLOID

Haploid spores

Meiosis

Diploid
sporophyte
generation

Haploid
gametophyte
generation

Haploid gametes

Diploid
zygote  Fusion

**8-4**
Alternation of genera-
tions, typical in plants.
The relative importance
of haploid and diploid
stages varies; in lower
plants the haploid is
usually dominant, in
higher plants the diploid.

see this in terms of both its size and its life span. For some plants one of the two forms is insignificant in size. We therefore commonly know the plant only by its major form. For many plants one of the forms is so reduced in size and complexity (perhaps to only a few cells) that it never leaves the protection of the other generation.

The relative importance of each generation provides a rough guide to evolutionary relationships among the various plant groups. Two lines of evolution developed in the plant kingdom. In one the gametophyte dominates. In the other the sporophyte is dominant. The flowering plants are in the line with the dominant sporophyte. That is, the gametophyte generation consists of just a few mitotic divisions of haploid cells confined within the sporophyte flowers. The bryophytes (mosses and liverworts), less advanced in terms of evolution, are in the line with the dominant gametophyte. And still lower on the evolutionary scale, among the algal groups, either generation may predominate, or both may exist equally.

In some algae one generation is so predominant that the other is confined to a single cell. Some algae have only a single-celled diploid phase, as the zygote undergoes meiotic rather than mitotic cell division. This is the reverse of the animal life cycle, in which the haploid phase is the

unicellular one. (Some algae, however, display this latter type of life cycle as well.) The algae are believed to be most directly related to the original plant ancestors. Thus it seems likely that the two evolutionary lines of the higher plants developed from different algal lines. The evolutionary line leading to the flowering plants was the most successful.

## Algae

The algae are the organisms which turn water green, exist as blanket weed in ponds and sluggish rivers, make up some of the fresh-water pondweeds, and comprise all the seaweeds. While most are aquatic, others will live wherever moisture is found, even on tree trunks. Algae have an extreme range in size, from microscopic single cells to giant seaweeds as much as a hundred feet in length. Their structure is fairly simple, though it varies immensely within the group.

The vegetative structure of algae is highly diverse. The cells may be separate or joined into colonies or filaments. Some algae have many nuclei without being di-

**8-5**
*Volvox,* a colonial green algae. Each of the regularly arranged dots on the large sphere is a cell of the colony; the dark spheres are daughter colonies developing within the parent.

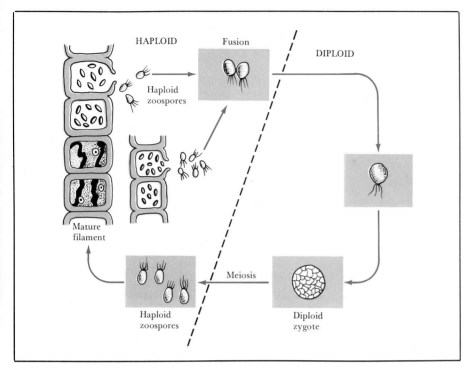

**8-6**
Life cycle of *Ulothrix* (a filamentous green algae) showing sexual reproduction. The newly liberated zoospores (flagellated spores) may also germinate asexually to form new haploid plants, bypassing the diploid stage.

**8-7**
*Euthora,* a red algae (phylum Rhodophyta).

vided into many cells. Such **coenocytic** algae vary in shape from spherical to filamentous. Still others consist of masses of cells or filaments which combine to make up a larger **thallus,** or total plant body. Some tissue differentiation occurs here, forming simple organs such as the stalk (stipe) and blade. Algae contain no rigidifying tissue nor mechanisms to restrict water loss. Nevertheless, stalks of seaweed can be extremely tough, capable of withstanding the forces of water currents and waves.

Reproduction among algae may be either asexual or sexual. Asexual reproduction usually occurs when conditions are favorable for growth. Sexual reproduction results from the fusion of two haploid gametes. The two sexes may be produced on the same (**homothallic**) or on different (**heterothallic**) plants. Sexual reproduction is frequently initiated by the advent of unfavorable conditions. It results in the production of a resting zygote which can survive until favorable conditions return.

Algae are classified on the basis of the photosynthetic pigments in their cells. While they all contain chlorophyll, other pigments are sometimes present in sufficient quantity to produce colors other than green. (These pigments are sensitive to wavelengths other than red, which chlorophyll responds to. Since water screens out the reds first, these pigments enable plants to colonize deeper waters by capturing light energy and passing it on to the chlorophyll.) Fortunately, vegetative and reproductive features fall into groupings consistent with pigment content. Color thus becomes a useful feature of classification.

The individual groups probably separated long ago and followed their own evolutionary trends. Green algae, or Chlorophyta, probably gave rise to the higher plants, since their modern forms share a number of important characteristics: chlorophylls *a* and *b* plus carotenoids are the photosynthetic pigments; cell walls are composed of cellulose; and food is stored in the form of starch.

# Bryophyta

The liverworts and mosses (Bryophyta) form the simplest group of plants that have made the transition from water to land. Mosses are generally found covering the ground in moist, shaded areas where the soil may be too shallow for larger plants. Mosses typically form short, green, upright stems with tiny leaves. They seldom reach more than an inch or so in height. Liverworts have a horizontal branching thallus and are found in very moist places. Neither mosses nor liverworts have conductive tissue, or a thick cuticle on the surface to prevent water loss.

In addition to having a more complex vegetative structure than that of green algae, the bryophytes have a more complex reproductive structure. They contain multicellular sex organs: **antheridia**, which produce **antherozoids** (sperm cells), and **archegonia**, which produce egg cells. After fertilization, the developing embryo is retained in the archegonium, and nourished by the parent plant.

Alternation of generations occurs in many, but not all, algae. But the primitive land plants all display a clear-cut alternation of haploid (gametophytic) and diploid (sporophytic) generations. The two generations are quite dissimilar in form. In the bryophytes, the gametophyte is the dominant plant; the sporophyte remains attached to the gametophyte and is largely parasitic on it. This contrasts with higher evolutionary forms, in which the gametophyte becomes greatly reduced and simplified, and is parasitic on the sporophyte.

It seems unlikely that such a dramatic switch in generation dominance would occur by evolution. Bryophytes may have developed by modification of the haploid generation of a green alga. Vascular plants may have arisen from the diploid generation of a different line of green algae. Thus the bryophytes are an isolated primitive group, an indication of the possible nature of the first land colonizers.

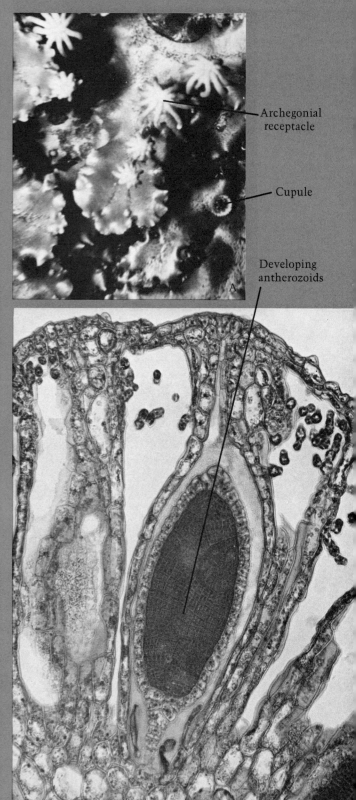

8-8
Liverwort structures: Top, thallus of *Marchantia*, showing multibranched structures known as archegonial receptacles (on which it carries its sex organs) and cupules (cup-like structures on the upper surface of the thallus which contain balls of vegetative cells termed gemmae). Bottom, cross section of antheridium. (See Bryophyta)

Archegonial receptacle

Cupule

Developing antherozoids

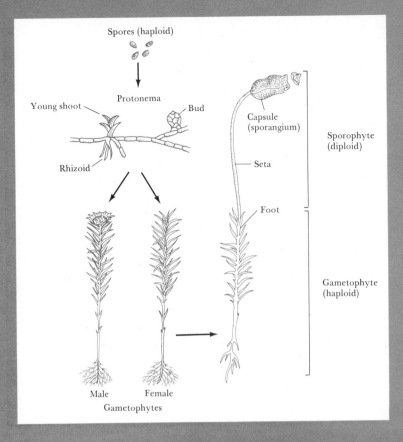

Spores (haploid)

Young shoot

Protonema

Bud

Rhizoid

Capsule
(sporangium)

Sporophyte
(diploid)

Seta

Foot

Gametophyte
(haploid)

Male      Female
Gametophytes

8-9
Stages in moss life cycle.
A spore germinates into
an alga-like multicel-
lular branching filament
called a protonema (often
seen on the soil in
greenhouse flowerpots).
The foot absorbs
nutrients from the game-
tophyte. The seta is the
stalk on top of which is
the capsule containing
the spores. (See
Bryophyta)

8-10
Bed of *Polytrichum* moss,
showing leafy gameto-
phytes below, and the
setae (stalks) and
capsules containing the
sporophytes above.

# The transition to land

None of the plants we have considered so far possesses the type of tissue needed to conduct water and photosynthetic products through the plant. Nor have even the land plants developed strong roots, or supportive tissue in the stem that will allow them to grow to any great height in the open air, where they no longer have the buoyancy once imparted by the surrounding water. Finally, they are still heavily dependent on a moist environment for reproduction. Sperm cells must move through water to reach and fertilize the ova. Even under ideal conditions many of them never arrive. In addition, the gametophyte is the dominant generation among the bryophytes, and the germinating embryo is poorly protected against drying.

Now we shall consider plants which have solved these problems to a great extent, and so are more fully suited to land life. It is such plants that can become great trees, or adapt to the arid climate of deserts. All of them are distinguished by possessing **vascular tissue**—a tissue specialized for transporting water and nutrients inside the plant. They also are distinguished by the fact that the sporophyte, not the gametophyte, is the dominant generation. As we shall see, this provides greater protection for the embryo in its early stages. Within these general characteristics, we can further distinguish between those plants which bear seeds and those which reproduce by means of spores. Like the bryophytes, both spore-bearing and seed-bearing vascular plants probably originated in the green algae. The spore-bearers are the more ancient, and were probably more or less contemporary with the earliest terrestrial animals. But primitive seed plants followed shortly, about when the Appalachians were being born. Only later, when insects became abundant to pollinate them, did the majority of flowering plants put in their appearance.

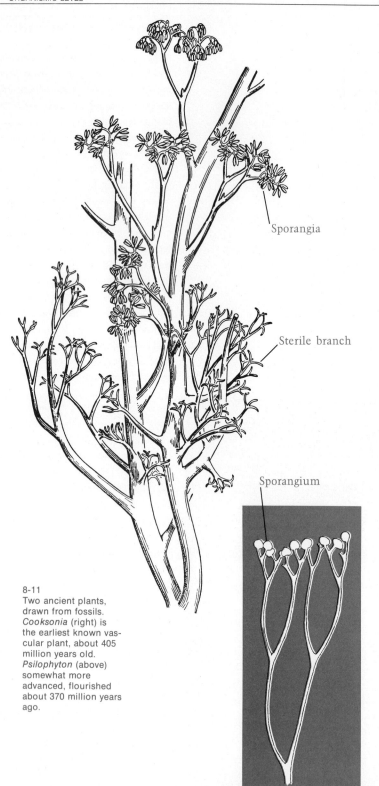

Sporangia

Sterile branch

Sporangium

**8-11**
Two ancient plants,
drawn from fossils.
*Cooksonia* (right) is
the earliest known vas-
cular plant, about 405
million years old.
*Psilophyton* (above)
somewhat more
advanced, flourished
about 370 million years
ago.

## Vascular spore-bearers

Seedless vascular plants formed the bulk of
earth's flora from 400 to 250 million years
ago, but few living representatives of most
groups remain. One group, however, has
survived in much greater abundance and
variety. These are the *Pterophyta,* or ferns,
which are commonly found in shady woodland all over the world. In the tropics and in
New Zealand some ferns reach the size of
trees. One species, the bracken fern, is so
abundant and vigorous in its growth that it
is classified as a serious weed in the British
Isles, where it is a stubborn invader of pas-
tureland.

Ferns grow mainly in moist, shady environments. They are perennial, and in the
temperate zones they survive from year to
year by means of fleshy-rooted underground stems called **rhizomes**. They have
large leaves, sometimes reaching a length
of several feet. Each spring a new crop of
leaves unfolds from the apex of the rhizome,
dying at the end of the growing season. The
leaf is, therefore, the prominent organ of the
plant.

Fern leaves vary from simple to highly
divided structures. **Sporangia**, or reproductive structures, develop either on a special
spike, on modified leaves, or directly on the

8-12
Left, tree ferns (Pterophyta),
remnants of prehistoric vegetation,
still thrive in the tropics. (See
Vascular spore-bearers)

8-13
Fern sorus, with sporangia clustered under protecting indusium. Drawing shows how annulus
of sporangium pops open when dry to release spores. (See Vascular spore-bearers)

Sporangia    Indusium

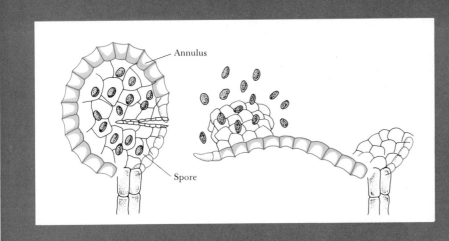

Annulus

Spore

lower side of the vegetative leaves. In *Dryopteris*, the shield fern, the stalked sporangia are grouped in sori (clusters of sporangia) on the lower side of the leaf. Each group of sporangia may be covered with a small flap of protective tissue, called an **indusium**. The sporangia are lens-shaped. Around part of the edge is a line of cells with thickened inner and lateral walls, forming a ring or **annulus**. The cells within the sporangia form spores by meiotic division. When the spores are ripe, the indusium shrivels. This allows the cells of the annulus to dry out. The tension developed inside the cells by loss of water causes the unthickened outer walls to buckle inward, while the thickened walls remain rigid. As a result, the annulus tries to invert its shape. At one end of the annulus, unthickened cells suddenly give way under the tension. The annulus springs backward, ripping the sporangium open. With further drying the annulus springs back even further, scattering the spores.

## The gametophytic generation

All the seedless vascular plants produce haploid spores. These spores germinate into a separate gametophytic plant which looks nothing like the parent sporophytic plant. The gametophyte is usually minute. It varies from a small green independent plant to one which, though independent, carries on no photosynthesis and relies solely on the food reserve in the spore.

With the club "moss," *Selaginella,* there is a marked reduction in the independence of the gametophyte, though in other respects it is more primitive than the ferns. More important, we find the development of two types of spore: large **megaspores**, which develop in **megasporangia**, and smaller **microspores** formed in **microsporangia**. The possession of two different spore types is called **heterospory**. The microspores develop into male gametophytes and the megaspores into female gametophytes. The gametophytes are greatly reduced in size. They do not manu-

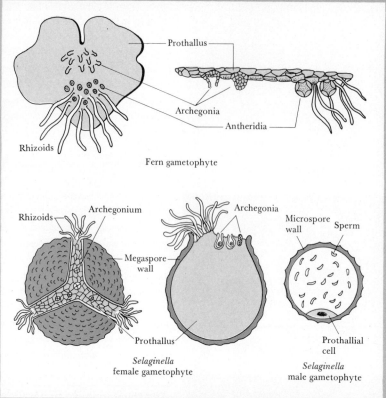

8-14
Gametophyte generation of fern and *Selaginella*. In *Selaginella*, the female gametophyte is enclosed within the megaspore wall, a development foreshadowing the evolution of true seeds. In the fern, spores germinate to form a green filament. This then develops into a heart-shaped prothallus with antheridia and archegonia on its lower side.

8-15
Young fern sporphyte developing from fertilized archegonium on prothallus. (See The gametophyte generation)

facture their own food, but rely solely on food reserves laid down in the spore during development on the sporophytic plant.

The development of heterospory and the reduction in the size and complexity of the gametophytes show the kinds of evolutionary trend which probably led to the development of the reproductive system in seed plants. The seed plant pollen is the successor to the microspore. The ovule represents the remnants of the female gametophyte retained on the sporophyte. Further structural developments lead to the formation of other tissues around the zygote, producing a seed.

## Seed plants

The seed-bearing plants first appeared during the late Devonian or early Carboniferous period. Their rapid spread shows the adaptive superiority of this new reproductive arrangement they had evolved. The advantage of seeds lies in the protection they offer to the young embryo. The gametophyte is no longer an independent plant, on its own in a risky environment. Now it is completely enclosed within the tissues of the dominant sporophyte. Thus fertilization and early development take place in a more protected environment. Then, when the embryo has begun to form, it is provided with a food supply and enclosed in a hard coat, resistant to drying. Here it can rest and wait until conditions are favorable for its growth as an independent plant.

The seed plants can be divided into two main groups, those that bear naked seeds, the **gymnosperms**, and those which bear the seeds within fruits. Since the latter also have flowers, they are known as the flowering plants, or **angiosperms**.

### Gymnosperms

With the coming of the gymnosperms, plants no longer needed water to carry the male gamete to the female. The male gametophyte is now reduced to a pollen grain which can be released into the air and dis-

8-16
Cycad *(Zamia),* showing crown of leaves and large central cone. In some species, this cone may be as much as a foot long. (See Gymnosperms)

tributed by the wind. We can see the success of this change in the abundance of coniferous forests that cover our high mountain slopes and cold northern flatlands. A number of groups now completely or nearly extinct possessed similar features. Among these were the seed "ferns," of which no living species remain. Also included were the Ginkgoae. These are now represented by only one species, the ginkgo or maidenhair tree, with its odorous fruits and unusual bilobed, fan-shaped leaves.

Almost all the gymnosperms are woody trees. The most familiar are the coniferous trees, such as spruce and pine. A less well-known group are the palm-like **cycads.** These are a small tropical group of slow-growing, long-lived, cone-bearing plants. The conifers are a varied and extensive group. They are commercially important as sources of timber and wood pulp for the manufacture of paper. Most conifers are evergreen (larch is an exception) and are woody trees, bearing slim or needle-like leaves.

## Reproduction in conifers

Conifers are characterized by the production of cones, which bear the reproductive organs. Male cones, or **microstrobili,** and female cones, or **megastrobili,** are found on

8-17
Pine branch with young female cones (dark) at the tip, and male cones (light) below them. (See Reproduction in conifers)

the same tree. The small male cones are produced in clusters at the beginning of the growing season and may frequently be yellow or red in color. They can easily pass unnoticed, but at the time of pollination, clouds of pollen can sometimes be seen drifting from branches with male cones whenever the branch shakes in the wind. "Pine cones" as we commonly know them are the mature female cones. These tend to grow high on the trees, where there is more chance for good seed dispersal. At maturity they are woody and range in length from about an inch to nearly two feet, depending on the species. But at the time of pollination the female cone is small and oval, about one-quarter inch long. In pines it takes two full years for the cone to reach maturity. The seeds are shed in the spring two years after pollination. Some conifers, however, need only one season for cone development.

The microstrobilus consists of a main axis bearing **microsporophylls,** the "leaves" of the cone. Each of these has two microsporangia on its lower surface. Within the microsporangia, microspores are produced by meiosis, and these become the pollen grains. Each pollen grain is a male gametophyte. It consists of a generative cell, a tube cell, and two prothallial cells (which, in time, degenerate). Two air bladders also develop in the pollen wall. They later help to distribute pollen via air currents.

The megastrobili also have a central axis bearing **megasporophylls,** each of which carries two ovules on the upper surface. The **ovule** consists of a multicellular female gametophyte surrounded by a tissue called the **nucellus,** which is equivalent to the megasporangium. This, in turn, is surrounded by a new tissue layer of sporophytic tissue, the **integument.** A channel called the **micropyle** reaches from the outer edge of the integument down to the nucellus. The pollen travels down this channel to reach and fertilize the female gametophyte. The micropyle secretes a small drop of sticky fluid, which catches wind-blown pol-

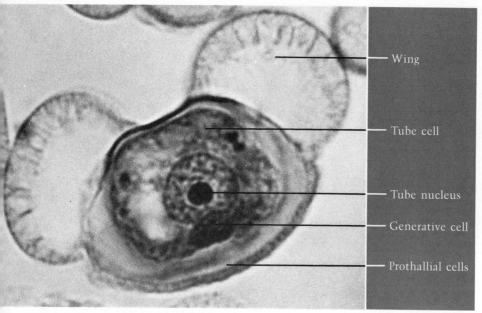

8-18
Pine pollen grain. (See Reproduction in conifers)

One of the sperm nuclei fuses with the egg nucleus to form the zygote. After multiple cell divisions, the zygote gives rise to a **proembryo**. The cells of the proembryo nearest the archegonial neck now elongate and push the immature embryo into the tissues of the female gametophyte. Here the embryo develops, nourished by the food reserves of the gametophyte. The cells of the integument harden, forming the **testa**, or seed coat. By the following spring the seed is mature. Each seed has a wing, formed from an extension of the seed coat, to help in dispersal. The seeds loosen, fall, and are scattered. Eventually they germinate, using up the food stored in the female gametophyte. At last they take root, to become independent seedling plants.

## Angiosperms

Flowering plants, or angiosperms, exist in almost endless variety. The first main division is into two subclasses. They are named for the number of **cotyledons**, or food storage organs, possessed by the embryo plant. **Dicotyledons**, familiarly known as dicots, have two storage organs. **Monocotyledons**, also known as monocots, have one. There are, however, other important differences between the two groups. Monocotyledons typically have long, thin leaves with parallel veins, and scattered bundles of vascular tissue. Their floral parts (sepals, petals, and sex organs) are arranged in threes. Dicotyledons, on the other hand, have leaves of various shapes with a vein network and a continuous cylinder of vascular tissue in the stem. Their flower parts are mostly arranged in fours or fives. Monocot leaves are usually attached directly to the stem. Dicot leaves usually have short stalks called **petioles**. The dicots include both herbs and trees. Monocots are mainly herbaceous, though a few, such as the palms, succeed in reaching tree dimensions.

len grains. The pollen germinates, forming a **pollen tube** which grows into the nucellus. Meanwhile the ovules and the whole megastrobilus grow in size. Two or three archegonia are then formed at the micropyle end of the female gametophyte.

This period before fertilization takes about 13 months. The pollen tube then resumes its growth, and the generative cell divides to produce two nonmotile sperm. The pollen tube grows through the neck of the archegonium and releases its contents.

8-19
Pine ovule. (See Reproduction in conifers)

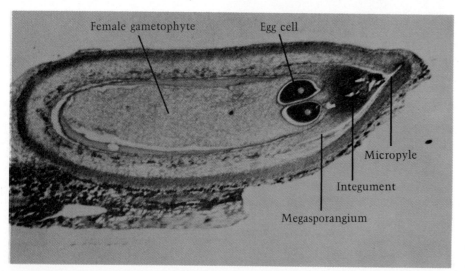

Further classification into families, of which there are approximately 300, is based almost exclusively on floral structure.

8-20
Mangroves are among the most salt-tolerant of all angiosperms. This one is thriving in shallow water on an ocean reef, where most trees would quickly die. Note the prop roots, typical of this tree. (See Flowering plant morphology)

## Flowering plant morphology

We have already referred many times to the principal vegetative organs of plants. Their basic structure is similar in all vascular plants. We will describe them here as they appear in their most developed form, before we go on to the reproductive organs which now, in the flowering plants, occur for the first time. A flowering plant is made up of **roots** and **shoots**, the latter consisting of stems and leaves. **Flowers** are the reproductive organs. But, unlike the other organs, they are not present throughout the life of the plant. Each of these organs may be modified to various degrees, to perform special functions or to enable the plant to survive in unusual habitats.

*Stems*    The stem is typically an upright aerial structure, though it may be prostrate. It is highly strengthened to support the leaves and withstand the forces of wind, rain, and snow. The stem also transports materials between the root and the leaves. Much of its supporting tissue is in the form of conducting channels.

The shape of any plant is the result of the pattern of branching of the stem. This pattern is largely caused by the position and relative growth of the different buds.

Such factors are genetically controlled, so that each species has a typical shape. However, environmental factors will also affect the growth of a plant. For instance, its shape will vary according to whether it is solitary or in a community.

A typical stem has a bud at the tip and leaves at regularly spaced points or **nodes** below the bud, with the oldest leaves farthest from the bud. Stem branches arise from **lateral** or **axillary buds** which originate just above the **axil** of each leaf—that is, the point where it meets the stem. Woody plants (trees and shrubs) can produce additional conducting and supportive tissue within the stem, so that the stem increases in size and strength. Some plants, however, reach a considerable height above the ground without having to invest in much supportive tissue. These are the vines which climb over other plants, using them for support. They can, of course, be successful only where taller woody species also exist. Vines may either be woody (such as grape vines) or herbaceous (as runner beans).

The stem may have other functions in addition to support and transport. One of these is spreading the plant. Thus, herbaceous plants may have horizontal stems either above ground or below (rhizomes). Lateral buds grow upward from these stems, forming new plants at intervals. Rhizomes are sometimes used by the plant for food storage. Another place for food storage is in the **stem tuber**, the swollen tip of the underground stem (such as a potato). **Holdfasts**, such as those of Virginia creeper, are a form of stem modification used for gripping rocks, walls, and similar supports. Still another modification is the thorn.

*Leaves*    The leaves are the photosynthetic organs of the plant. They are borne on the stems, usually attached by a leaf stalk, or petiole. (In some plants, such as grasses, the leaves do not appear to be attached to a stem. In these plants the stem is hidden in sheathing leaf bases.)

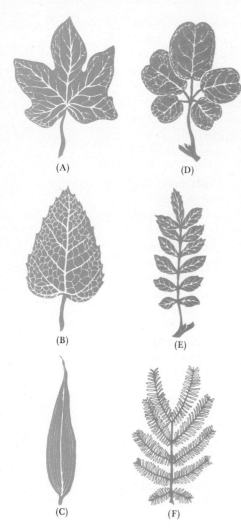

8-21
Angiosperm leaf types. (A) ivy, (B) grape, and (C) bamboo, are simple leaves; (D) *Akebia,* (E) Brazilian pepper, and (F) *Acacia,* each composed of many leaflets joined to the plant stem by a single petiole, are compound. *Acacia,* which branches into several sprigs, is double compound. Note parallel veins in the bamboo leaf.

Leaves may be modified in several ways. They may become succulent for water storage in desert plants, or swollen into bulbs to provide food storage. They may be reduced to form tendrils or spines. A plant also may have more than one type of leaf. For example, leaf shape may vary as the plant ages, going from juvenile to adult, as in English ivy. Shape also may vary in aquatic plants, whose submerged leaves are minutely divided and very different from the floating or aerial leaves.

*Roots*   The roots anchor the plant to the soil and take up water and nutrients. They may form a many-branched or **fibrous** system, or a single enlarged vertical **tap root** with smaller lateral branches. Either of these may be swollen to serve as food storage for the plant, as in the case of the carrot. Both fibrous and tap root systems arise from the root tissues of the embryo in the seed. But roots can also grow directly from stem tissue, in which case they are called **adventitious**. This is quite common and is easily seen in creeping stems such as strawberry, or in the rooting of stem cuttings. Adventitious roots are found above as well as below ground. Orchids may have aerial roots to absorb water, while ivy uses them to cling to tree trunks and buildings. Occasionally roots may grow into the ground from points on the stem well above ground level. These are **prop roots**, which serve to buttress the stem, as in corn, or provide multiple anchorage points, as in mangroves.

## Reproduction in flowering plants

In the gymnosperms, the greatly reduced female gametophyte is retained on the sporophyte. Sperm cells reach the archegonium by means of a pollen tube. In the angiosperms we see even further reduction and simplification of the gametophytic generations. In addition, the ovules are completely surrounded by the tissues of the **ovary**, which can be considered as a highly modified megasporophyll (called a **carpel**).

This tissue is folded over and sealed around the ovules. When the seeds ripen, the ovary forms the **fruit**. The reproductive organs are grouped into the flower, from which the angiosperms take their common name. The angiosperm reproductive system represents a very successful adaptation. Of the 350,000 known plant species, 250,000 are angiosperms.

Angiosperm seeds give rise to an adult vegetative, sporophytic plant. Then, at a certain time, the stem apex ceases to form leaves. Instead, it forms the tissues of the flower, which include the reproductive organs. The male sex organs, or **stamens**, consist of four fused microsporangia (the **anther**) carried on a stalk or **filament**, which is equivalent to the microsporophyll. Inside the anther the cells undergo meiosis to form the microspores from which the pollen develops. When the pollen is shed it contains two nuclei, the **tube nucleus** and the **generative nucleus**—all that remains of the male gametophyte. On or before germination, the generative nucleus will divide into two sperm nuclei. The pollen wall is often highly sculptured in a manner characteristic of the species. In fact, pollen is so distinctive that when it is found preserved in bogs, changes in the types of pollen can be used to tell what changes have occurred in the vegetation in the surrounding area.

The female sex organ consists of the ovule, carried in the space formed by the enclosing ovary. On the upper side the ovary is extended to form a column of tissue, or **style**. At the tip of the style is the **stigma**, a surface for the reception and germination of pollen. The ovule is further reduced from that in the gymnosperms. But the basic setups are the same. A cell (the megasporangium) near the apex of the nucellus undergoes meiosis, producing four megaspores. Three of these abort. The remaining megaspore divides mitotically into 8 nuclei to produce a structure called the **embryo sac**, which constitutes the female gametophyte. Three of the nuclei migrate to the lower end of the sac, forming a

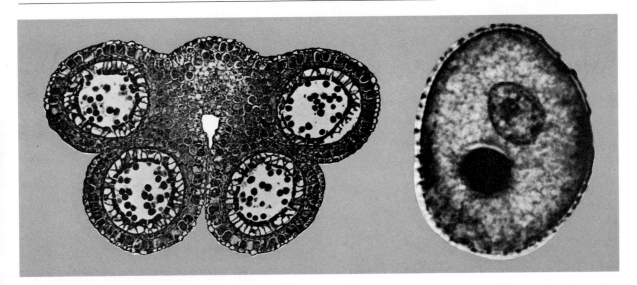

group called the **antipodal cells**. These probably represent the vegetative part of the gametophyte. Their function is to absorb food from the nucellus. Two nuclei (the **polar nuclei**) move to the center of the sac, where they are suspended at the center of a vacuole. The remaining three nuclei move to the micropyle end of the sac. One of them becomes the egg nucleus. The three nuclei together constitute the archegonium. Compared with the female gametophyte of most gymnosperms, that of the angiosperms has little differentiation and only a brief exis-

tence, during which it is completely supported by the sporophytic plant.

In most insect-pollinated plants, the reproductive organs are surrounded by **petals** and **sepals**. The sepals are structures protectively folded over the developing flower parts in the bud. The petals serve to attract insects after it opens. When the flowers open, the microsporangia of the anthers split open and release the pollen, which in insect-pollinated plants is usually slightly sticky.

Insects visit plants to collect either pol-

**8-22**
Left, cross section of anther of *Lillium*, showing clearly the four fused microsporangia. Right, enlargement of one pollen grain. (See Reproduction in flowering plants)

**8-23**
Ovule and embryo of *Lillium*, deep inside the tissues of the parent sporophyte plant. The function of the synergids, cells in the mature embryo sac, is not known. (See Reproduction in flowering plants)

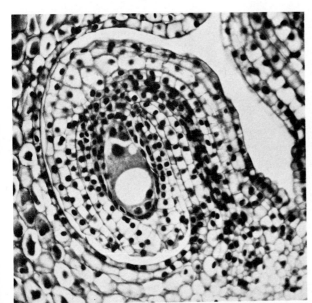

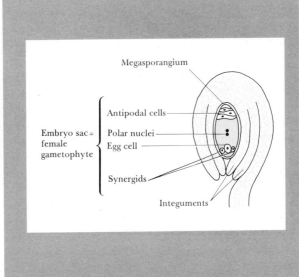

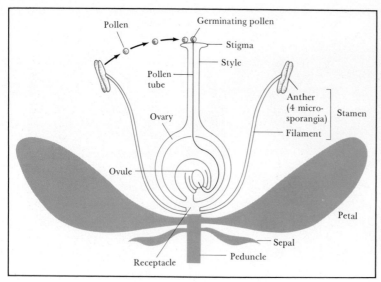

8-24
Parts of typical floral structure, with path of the growing pollen tube, preparatory to fertilization.

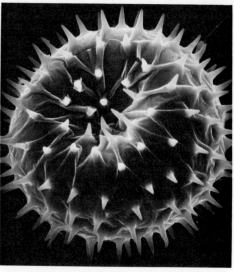

8-25
Scanning electron micrograph of an angiosperm pollen grain, making evident one reason why pollen tends to stick to visiting bees.

len or nectar as food. The nectar is usually in a **nectary** at the base of the petals, so that the insect must rub against the anther and stigma in order to reach it. Some of the pollen sticks to the body of the insect and is transferred to the stigma of the next flower.

Once the pollen has reached the stigma, it germinates. It produces enzymes which dissolve some of the cells of the stigma, providing nutrition for the growing pollen tube. The pollen tube grows down the style to the female gameotphyte. There the tip bursts open, discharging its nuclei into the cytoplasm of the female gametophyte. One sperm nucleus fuses with the egg nucleus. The other migrates to the two polar nuclei, and all three fuse to form a triploid nucleus. The triploid nucleus then divides and develops cell walls to form a special nutritive tissue called the **endosperm**. We see, therefore, that fertilization in angiosperms is different from all other types in that it is a **double fertilization**.

Pollination and fertilization cause enlargement of the tissues of the ovary to form the fruit. Ovule enlargement also follows fertilization, while the zygote divides and develops into an embryo plant. In some species the endosperm remains as the tissue which nourishes the seedling during germination. In others, the cotyledons become the food storage organs. They absorb food from the endosperm as the embryo develops within the seed so that by maturity the endosperm has disappeared. As development of the embryo nears completion, the tissues of the ovule dry out and the integuments harden, forming the seed coat.

During seed maturation the tissues of the ovary undergo distinctive changes. They either enlarge slightly and dry out, or enlarge even more and become fleshy. Drying out is usually a prelude to a splitting of the ovary wall, sometimes explosively, scattering the seeds for distribution by the wind. The fleshy fruits are designed to attract animals. When the fruit is eaten, the protected seeds pass through the digestive system and are distributed with the feces. Nuts form a special category. They are dry fruits usually containing only one seed. These fruits do not split open, as occurs with other types of fruit. Rather, they are distributed as a unit.

8-26
Date palms *(Phoenix),* among the few monocotyledons which reach tree size. (See Angiosperms)

**summary**

Fungi differ from plants in that they lack chlorophyll. Therefore they need organic material for food. Saprophytic fungi live off dead plant and animal remains. Parasitic fungi feed on living organisms. The two main groups of fungi are the slime molds and the true fungi. Certain fungi live in a symbiotic relationship with unicellular algae. The combination is called a lichen, and can live where neither fungi nor algae can live alone.

Among plant groups today, the algae are the most primitive. The most advanced are the flowering plants. Each group has a more complicated vegetative structure and a better-protected embryonic development than the group below. There is also a difference in generation dominance. In the algae either generation may be dominant, or both may be equal. In the bryophytes, the gametophyte is dominant. In the angiosperms and gymnosperms, the sporophyte is dominant, and the gametophyte is insignificant.

Algae are relatively simple organisms. They are classified on the basis of their photosynthetic pigments. Green algae, commonly found in fresh water, are probably the evolutionary ancestors of the higher plants.

The simplest plants to have made the transition to land are the liverworts and mosses, or Bryophyta. They are more complex than algae. However, they do not have the vascular tissue needed to conduct water and photosynthetic products through the plant. Nor are they able to reproduce without a relatively moist environment. They are therefore only partially suited for life on land. Plants with vascular tissue and a dominant sporophyte have solved these problems.

The ferns are the principal living members of the earliest group of vascular plants. These plants reproduce by spores rather than seeds. Heterospory—the production of male and female spores—first appears among the vascular spore-bearing plants. The gametophyte is still a separate, independent plant, but it is much smaller and less complex than the sporophyte. These two developments suggest the evolutionary trend which eventually resulted in the seed plants.

In seed-bearing plants, the sporophyte encloses and protects the gametophyte. This offers a more protected environment for fertilization and early development of the embryo. Then the embryo is provided with a food supply and enclosed in a hard coat to create the seed. Seed plants are divided into gymnosperms, which bear naked seeds, and angiosperms, which produce flowers and bear seeds enclosed within fruits.

The gymnosperms include mostly cycads and conifers. They were the first plants in which the male gamete could reach and fertilize the female without having to swim through water. Male pollen is carried by the wind to female ovules. The male sperm are released inside the ovule to fertilize the egg cell.

The angiosperms are classified as either monocotyledons or dicotyledons, depending on whether the seed contains one or two food-storage organs. Other differences also characterize the two groups. In the angiosperms, the embryo is even more protected than in the gymnosperms. Also, there are more means of dispersing pollen to ensure fertilization.

The reproductive organs of the angiosperms are the male stamens and the female ovules, both found in the flowers. The ovules are surrounded by the tissues of the ovary, which will later form the fruit. In most insect-pollinated plants, the ovary forms a style, topped by a stigma. When insects visit the plant, pollen from the stamens sticks to their bodies and is transferred to the stigma of the next flower they visit. The pollen germinates on the stigma, and a pollen tube grows down through the style to the female gametophyte. There the sperm nuclei are discharged. Fertilization is double, resulting in the formation of both a zygote and a special nutritive tissue, the endosperm. The ovule then enlarges, while the zygote divides and develops into an embryo plant. When the embryo is sufficiently mature, the tissues of the ovule dry out, forming the hard seed coat. The embryo and its food supply—contained either in the endosperm or in the cotyledons—can wait for long periods inside this protecting coat, until conditions are right for the germination of a new plant.

# keeping healthy

*Medical authorities estimate that some 16,000 American physicians practicing today are incompetent Moreover, 1 in 5 elective operations is unnecessary.*

# Does your doctor know what he's doing?

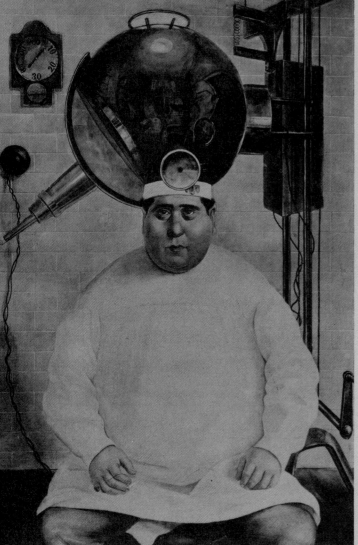

Otto Dix
Oil and tempera on wood
Collection, The Museum of Modern Art, New York
Gift of Philip Johnson

A man was admitted to a prominent New York City hospital for the replacement of a heart valve. After the operation, he was taken off the heart-lung machine. Suddenly, his blood pressure dropped and his circulation failed. Within minutes, he was dead. An autopsy revealed the cause of death to be a stupendous blunder on the part of the surgeon—he had put the artificial valve in backward, preventing blood from flowing through the patient's heart.

Was this tragedy a fluke, a one-in-a-million mistake? Apparently not. A series of revealing articles published in the *New York Times* indicates that such errors occur with shocking frequency. In 1975, for example, some 18 million Americans underwent surgery. Of these, 250,000 died on the operating table or shortly afterward. The *Times* is quick to point out that many of these patients were so far gone that they would have died if surgery had not been attempted. For others, however, it was the surgery itself that killed.

What are some of the things that can go wrong during or immediately after a surgical procedure? The risks are many. They include pneumonia, infection, blood clots, shock, hemorrhage, and the detrimental effects of the anaesthetic on the nervous, excretory, and respiratory systems. Not to be forgotten, of course, is the possibility of surgical error, as in the unfortunate heart-patient above.

According to the *Times*, one study showed that some 1,493 patients over a two-year period experienced complications following surgery. Nearly one-half of the 1,451 nonfatal complications could have been prevented. And one-third of the deaths were unnecessary. Indeed, slightly more than three-fourths of these preventable complications resulted from errors on the part of the surgeon, and one-half were due to faulty surgical techniques. And fully 11,900 deaths that occurred last year from surgery could have been avoided because no operation was called for in the first place.

The *Times* cites studies which indicate that about one in five optional operations in the United States is not necessary. (Optional operations comprise about 80 percent of all surgical procedures performed in this country.) In some of the more common operations, such as tonsillectomies and hysterectomies, roughly one-third to two-thirds of the procedures are avoidable. The operations are performed because the patient insists upon it, or because the doctor misjudges the seriousness of the

*"Nearly 12,000 surgery-related deaths last year could have been avoided because the operations were not needed."*

case, or because he wishes to hedge against a possible legal action.

How many incompetent doctors are practicing in the United States today? At least 5 percent of the nation's 320,000 physicians—roughly 16,000—are thought to be incompetent. This estimate was produced by the Federation of State Medical Boards (FSMB), the body which grants and revokes medical licenses in this country. The doctors, who see about 7.5 million patients a year, are so incompetent that the FSMB believes they should have their licenses revoked, be required to get additional education, or practice only when supervised by competent physicians.

## Drugs a problem, too

Added to the danger of dying at the hands of a bumbling physician is the risk of dying or becoming seriously ill from the drugs a doctor prescribes. Each year, some 30,000 people in the United States die from taking drugs prescribed for them by their physicians. And possibly another 300,000 are incapacitated by side effects such as loss of hearing or vision, kidney damage, or mental depression.

Part of the problem is the enormous number of pharmaceuticals on the modern marketplace. An estimated 1,200 different drugs are available to physicians, a number too large for even the most conscientious doctor to keep track of. Yet, under law, any physician can dispense any drug to any of his patients, regardless of how long he has been practicing or how up-to-date his knowledge is. At times, the only guidelines he has about the drug's action are in the advertisement he reads in his medical journal, or in the sales talk he gets from the pharmaceutical company's salesman.

## Incompetents are protected

In most professions, incompetents are weeded out by their colleagues, by government regulatory agencies, or by the public whom they serve. This is not so within the medical profession. Over the last 13 years, for example, state licensing agencies have revoked an average of only 66 medical licenses a year. The reasons for this are easy to determine. For one thing, the medical profession has drawn around itself a shield of silence which insulates members from outside scrutiny. In short, doctors are loathe to report an errant colleague. And so, apparently, are hospitals. In some cases, for example, when a hospital regulatory board discovers incompetency, it merely asks the offending physician for his resignation. Typically, he then moves to another state, applies for privileges at a hospital there, and is usually accepted because the hospital which he left does not mention his shortcomings when asked to do so. Finally, officials have difficulty getting patients to complain or testify in court against their doctors.

Lately, more and more medical incompetence is coming to light as a result of two factors. First, the federal government is being asked to play an increasingly greater role in the nation's health care programs. Then, too, there is the growing activism of various consumer groups who press for better craftsmanship, fair prices, and improved safety in the goods and services they pay for. Perhaps the medical profession, too, will begin policing its members. Then Americans can benefit more fully from the services of the best-trained doctors in the world.

## How to choose a good doctor

How does one go about finding a qualified physician? Among the suggestions offered by the *New York Times* are the following:

1. Consult the American Medical Directory, available in most libraries, to learn a physician's professional credentials. This publication will tell you how long he's been practicing, what his specialty is, and whether he is a member of any of the various specialty colleges. Another way to find a good MD is to call a nearby medical school and ask for the names of the school's professors who see patients. Finally, you can choose a doctor who has privileges at a hospital that is affiliated with a medical school. These doctors receive superior up-to-date training.

2. Select a physician while you are healthy, not during an emergency when you haven't the time to evaluate his capabilities. Your first visit to a doctor should be for a routine checkup, not for the removal of your gall bladder.

3. Choose a doctor who engages in family or general practice, rather than a specialist who is interested in only one aspect of the body.

4. If possible, select a doctor who belongs to a medical group. Such physicians usually pool their knowledge and probably have screened one another for competence before allowing a newcomer to join.

5. If you have no regular doctor and an emergency strikes, go to the emergency room or the outpatient clinic of a teaching hospital. Don't pick a name out of the phone book or rely on the advice of friends.

Myron Wood/Photo Researchers

## Medicine cabinet checklist

Do you have a well-stocked medicine chest? The following list, suggested by the American Pharmaceutical Association, has been compiled by the editors of *Science Digest*:

1. Analgesic. Aspirin, Tylanol or something similar for headache, and minor aches and pains.
2. Anti-diarrheal medicine. A product containing kaolin and pectin, for temporary attacks.
3. Antacid. Liquids, powder or tablets for temporary stomach upsets.
4. Eye drops or eye wash. To take care of minor irritations.
5. Laxative. Some mild product, such as milk of magnesia.
6. Petroleum jelly. For chapped skin, lips or blisters.
7. Rubbing alcohol. For pulled muscles, bruises, or to sponge-bathe someone who has a temperature.
8. Spirits of ammonia (smelling salts). For reviving one who has fainted.
9. Miscellaneous. Cotton, bandages, swab sticks, tweezers, scissors, and a thermometer.

The APA estimates that the cost of all the items on the list should be about $20.

"Tests showed that some illnesses can be picked out with a good percentage of accuracy by personality alone."

Jan Lukas/Photo Researchers

*Your emotions may make you prone to asthma, backache, arthritis, cancer, and a host of other ailments.*

# Does your personality make you sick?

For centuries, men have intuitively known that a connection exists between human personality and the susceptibility to certain diseases. The father of modern medicine, Hippocrates, pointed out the link between temperament and disease. Later physicians observed that individuals of certain physical and mental makeup were prone to particular illnesses. Thus, long, lean people were more apt to contract tuberculosis than were chubbier, robust types (who had a higher incidence of cerebral hemorrhages).

In recent years, this tacit knowledge has been put to the test and found to be remarkably accurate. In their book, *Psychosomatics*, for example, Howard and Martha Lewis report on the recent personality studies of several researchers, including psychiatrist Floyd O. Ring of the University of Nebraska College of Medicine. Ring wanted to determine if an individual personality pattern could be proven to stand out for a given disease. To test this hypothesis, he asked his colleagues to refer to him some 400 patients who were victims of any of these diseases: asthma, backache, coronary occlusion, degenerative arthritis, diabetes, dysmenorrhea, glaucoma, hypertension, migraine, neurodermatitis, peptic ulcer, rheumatoid arthritis, and ulcerative colitis.

### The experiment

Ring's plan was to determine the personality patterns of each of the patients by interviewing them for 15 to 25 minutes apiece. With this information in hand, he would then try to determine the ailment of each patient. Elaborate means were taken to eliminate all clues to the patients' illnesses. Each was instructed, for example, to keep mum about his symptoms, diet, medical situation, or anything else that might tip off the psychiatrist about his physical condition. Moreover, each patient's body was completely covered during the interview so the therapist could get no hints. Finally, during the interviews, at least two other psychiatrists served as referees. If a patient let slip the slightest hint about his condition, or even if he accidentally let the psychiatrist see his hand or any other part of his body, he was rejected by the referees.

The results? Ring found that "persons with some illnesses can be picked out . . . with a good percentage of accuracy by personality . . . alone." For example, Ring detected all of the hyperthyroid cases solely on the basis of his knowledge of the patient's personality. Eighty-three percent of the peptic ulcer and rheumatoid arthritis cases were detected, as were 71 percent of those with coronary occlusions. Between 60 and 67 percent of those suffering from asthma, diabetes, hypertension, and ulcerative colitis were uncovered without knowledge of the patients' symptoms.

As a result of this study, Ring has classified personality types into three broad categories. The first, the "excessive reactor," is likely to be very apprehensive and physically and verbally active. He is quick to say what is on his mind and quick to express his feelings of fear or anger. Nearly all the individuals in this category suffered from coronary occlusion, degenerative arthritis, and peptic ulcers.

Just the opposite is the "deficient reactor." He holds back his words and actions as well as his fear and anger. In fact, he is not even aware that he is expressing these feelings. Most of these patients were prone to neurodermatitis, rheumatoid arthritis, and ulcerative colitis.

Finally, there are the "restrained reactors," who are aware of their emotions but fail to act on or express them. Diseases characteristic of this group include asthma, diabetes, hypertension, hyperthyroidism, and migraine.

## Personality affects other diseases

More recent studies, reported in the journal *Science News*, also support the belief that there is a definite link between personality and such ailments as cancer and heart disease. Caroline Thomas, a researcher from Johns Hopkins University, gathered information on 1,337 medical students for the years 1946 to 1964. Data for each student included the results of physical examinations, psychological tests, and family history. Thomas followed up on each student with yearly questionnaires. Through 1974, the subjects reported 43 cases of cancer, 14 heart attacks, 38 cases of mental problems, and 16 suicides.

Thomas interpreted this data in the light of the students' dossiers, and developed a number of interesting conclusions. For one thing, she found that quiet, non-aggressive, emotionally-neutral individuals tended to have higher incidences of cancer than those with other personality profiles. Many cancer victims were loners who had no close ties with their parents. Some 30 percent of the cancer cases, for example, stated that their fathers were not understanding or warm.

Thomas also found a correlation between personality and heart attacks. Thus, the 14 heart cases were prone to anxiety, nervous tension, and depression. They also had difficulty sleeping, had low energy levels, and did not do as well in school as their colleagues.

What do these studies prove? Nothing definite as yet. But, as *Science News* concludes, "Although the complexities of the mind-body connection are far from being explained, it is long-range prospective studies . . . that will eventually help untie this particular Gordian knot."

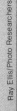

Ray Ellis/Photo Researchers

## Weather can cause illness

Ever since the time of the Greeks, scientists have suspected a connection between weather and human health. Now, that suspicion has been confirmed by a Texas meteorologist. According to *Science Digest*, Professor Dennis M. Driscoll of Texas A & M University examined 114 studies conducted by other researchers between 1930 and 1960. He found an extraordinarily high positive correlation (83 percent, to be exact) between weather and health. In his own study, he analyzed weather conditions and mortality in ten large cities throughout the United States. He found that high humidity, coupled with temperatures above 90 degrees, exerts a strain on the cardiovascular system. Driscoll says that deaths increase with rising temperatures just before the approach of weather fronts. Similarly, the death rate declines after the fronts have passed.

Mental health also seems to be affected to some extent by weather conditions. Dr. James T. Garvey of the University of Minnesota found that psychiatric hospital admissions shoot up about 25 percent between February and April. A second but less drastic increase occurs in November and December. Finally, says Garvey, more women than men seem to be affected during these periods.

# What's so healthy about "health foods"?

F. B. Grunzweig/Photo Researchers

**What's the difference between "health," "natural," and "organic" foods?**

In practical terms, there's very little. "Health" foods are those which supposedly enrich health by supplying many vitamins, minerals, and other nutrients. "Natural" foods, prepared with little or no processing, contain no additives or preservatives. "Organic" foods, grown without pesticides, use natural rather than commercial fertilizers.

**Why are health foods so expensive?**

There are several reasons for this. First, there isn't much competition among health food stores, so they can charge whatever the traffic will bear. Then, too, their small volume and small distribution force them to charge more just to break even. Finally, growing food without commercial fertilizers is a costly business. For example, the cost of the nitrogen in commercial fertilizer is a mere 7½ to 15 cents a pound. The same amount of nitrogen from garbage composts costs the organic farmer about $12 a pound, or $5 a pound if he uses cow manure.

**Are health foods actually more nutritious than supermarket foods?**

Apparently not. Tests conducted at the United States Plant, Soil, and Nutrition Laboratory at Cornell University showed that plants grown in organic fertilizer were no different nutritionally from those grown with chemical fertilizers. Indeed, Harvard nutritionist Jean Mayer points out: "While organic foods tend to escape chemical pollution, biologically speaking they tend to become the most contaminated of all. Organic fertilizers of animal or human origin are obviously the most likely to contain gastrointestinal parasites."

**But aren't all those chemicals in fertilizers and pesticides harmful to us?**

Most scientists think not. The United States Food and Drug Administration is constantly monitoring the agricultural chemicals in our foods. A couple of times a year, their scientists visit some 18 regions around the country, buy about two weeks' supply of food, cook it, and analyze it. They are looking for traces of some 50 pesticides, attempting to discover if the chemicals in the food exceed the international amounts for "acceptable daily intake" (ADI). The scientists find that the worst offender is DDT, which generally runs about one-twentieth of the ADI. Doses of other pesticides are quite miniscule—having levels of about one-two hundredths of the ADI.

**Granted. But don't these small amounts accumulate in our bodies?**

Not according to the FDA. Volunteers have consumed DDT and a number of other pesticides in tests conducted by the FDA. The tests showed that the chemicals are, for the most part, excreted by the body. Tiny amounts may end up in fatty tissues, but these chemicals are not dangerous. And the liver destroys others. The proof of all this, of course, is the fact that both government and independent medical authorities have discovered no significant number of illnesses from pesticides. Finally, Dr. Leo Lutwak of Cornell University has this to say about celery (one of the plants which absorbs the largest quantity of pesticides): "If you ate only celery for 75 years, you might . . . accumulate enough stores of insecticide in your tissues to do some damage."

**With all this controversy, what can the average consumer do to eat wisely and economically?**

One good piece of advice is to avoid fads—health food diets, vegetarian diets, and macrobiotic diets—unless you are being advised by a physician or nutritionist. Most medical authorities agree that the great majority of Americans should reduce their intake of fatty foods (which have been linked to heart disease); salt (which is one of the villains behind high blood pressure); and sweets (which can lead to excess weight gain and tooth decay). Generally, you should eat a balanced diet, making sure that you get the right proportion of proteins, fats, and carbohydrates. Your doctor can guide you on this. For more information on the subject of nutrition, read *Panic in the Pantry*, by Drs. Elizabeth Whelan and Frederick Stare, two acknowledged experts.

The barely legible label on a can of frozen orange beverage informs the diligent shopper that the ingredients include:

citric acid, tri-potassium phosphate, sodium carboxymethylcellulose, potassium citrate, ascorbic acid, tricalcium phosphate, natural and artificial flavors, magnesium oxide, artificial colors, copper gluconal, niacin, pantothenic acid, palmitate, thiamine hydrochloride, folic acid, and riboflavin.

What are the chemicals on this forbidding list? What nutritional value do they give the food? A few are vitamins, but the majority are additives, nonnutritive substances added in small quantities during the manufacturing process to improve flavor, appearance, texture, or storage characteristics. Each American annually consumes some three to five pounds of these emulsifiers, stabilizers, preservatives, flavoring agents, and colorings. Today, more than 2,500 artificial substances are added to foods from pablum to peanut butter. Some accumulate in the body for days, months, even years. Some may interact synergistically to produce effects that are only now being studied. The questions uppermost in the minds of many concerned individuals are: how safe are the chemicals and how necessary are they?

*Many additives are essential*

There is no doubt that a large number of additives are both necessary and safe. Many have been in common use for centuries: salt, pepper, baking soda, vinegar, and numerous spices all help to preserve food or to perk up its flavor. Moreover, as microbiologist Michael Jacobson points out in his book *Eater's Digest*, additives have made available a greater variety of foods, especially convenience foods such as frozen TV dinners, instant cake mixes, and powdered juices and soups.

# Is our food being poisoned?

Many additives that have received the government seal of approval have yet to be tested. Some of these could be dangerous.

And additives have many benefits. In bread, for example, emulsifiers retard staleness, lengthening shelf life, and preservatives prevent the growth of molds. Antioxidants, such as the ethylenediamine tetraacetic acid (EDTA) added to mayonnaise and other oily foods, prevent rancidity. Stabilizers, such as carrageenan, keep in solution the solid parts of liquid foods such as evaporated milk. In addition, a host of other chemicals improve certain properties of food. Antibiotics attack spoilage organisms in fish and poultry, humec-

with other chemicals naturally present in bread to produce a poison which causes convulsions. Similarly, coumarin, in use for 75 years as a vanilla flavoring, was found to damage the livers of dogs. And there is evidence that certain artificial colorings and flavorings in some foods may be linked to the incidence in children of hyperkinesis, a disorder which renders its victim inordinately active and unable to concentrate. Other chemicals, such as monosodium glutamate (MSG) and butylated hydroxytoluene (BHT), are dangerous if taken

moved "Red No. 2," a common dye used in foods, cosmetics and drugs, from its list of color additives. Large doses of the chemical have been shown to cause cancerous tumors and infertility in laboratory rats. The ban comes some 20 years after scientists and consumer advocates began agitating for the restriction or removal of the dye from the marketplace.

*Stronger controls needed*

Who decides what chemicals are fit for consumption and how are these tested? In the United States, the safety of an additive is determined by the Food and Drug Administration (FDA), which requires manufacturers to prove that a new chemical is not dangerous to health. The FDA maintains a list of some 687 chemicals "generally recognized as safe" (GRAS), but many of these have not been tested, thoroughly or otherwise, because they have been in use for a good many years. The reliability of this list is therefore questionable. In 1969, for example, two artificial sweeteners which appeared on the GRAS list—cyclamate and saccharin—burst into the news as possibly dangerous to human health. Cyclamate was found to induce bladder cancer in rats; the possible carcinogenic role of saccharin, still on the market, is currently undergoing scientific scrutiny.

How can such mistakes be prevented in the future? A number of solutions have been proposed. The best of these seem to include immediate testing of all chemicals on the GRAS list, periodic inspection of all additives to take advantage of newly developed analytical techniques, and limiting the introduction of new additives unless they offer definite benefits over existing chemicals which perform the same function.

## Hotdog headaches

Eating a hotdog or two has been known to cause stomach aches, but can it also cause headaches? Apparently yes, says *Science Digest*. A team of researchers at the University of California has discovered that the villain behind the headaches is sodium nitrate, a chemical added to hotdogs—as well as to bacon, ham, and salami—to give them an appetiz-

ing pink color. Another additive, the flavor enhancer known as monosodium glutamate, is also responsible for headaches, along with stomachaches and burning sensations in the fingertips. This group of symptoms is known as the "Chinese restaurant syndrome," so called because monosodium glutamate is a staple of Chinese cuisine.

tants absorb moisture in confections to help assure freshness; anti-caking agents prevent salt and baking soda from lumping.

However, some additives, such as colorings, have no nutritional or practical value; they are designed solely to improve food appearance and so increase sales. And there are many chemicals that have definitely been proven detrimental, even after long use. Agene, for example, was used for some 25 years as a bleach in white flour before the discovery that it reacts

in amounts above certain levels. In addition, there are synthetics whose effects are either unknown or questionable, but which continue to appear in foods on supermarket shelves. Among these are sodium nitrite and sodium nitrate (preservatives which give meats their red color), propyl gallate (a preservative used in cereals and instant potatoes), and butylated hydroxyanisole, or BHA (a preservative used in shortening and other foods).

Most recently, the Food and Drug Administration re-

*"Some additives are undeniably necessary and safe. But there are others whose effects are either unknown or questionable."*

# What do you know about your eyes?

## 1. If you have 20/20 vision, your eyes are perfect.

Not necessarily. When an eye specialist says that you have 20/20 vision, he is merely making a statistical statement. It means that you can see as clearly at 20 feet as the average person can. Thus, if you can see objects at 20 feet that a normal individual can see at 40 or 80 feet, then you would have 20/40 or 20/80 vision, respectively.

## 2. Your eyesight will worsen if you don't wear your glasses.

This is an old wives' tale. Your eyes will get worse with time, but not because you don't wear your glasses. Since wearing glasses does not change the organic structure of the eyes, not wearing glasses cannot affect the eyes. But you can fall victim to a host of side effects if you don't use your glasses. You can get eyestrain, for example. This is often accompanied by headaches, itching burning eyes, nervousness, difficulty in concentration, and possibly even dizziness and nausea. In effect, if you don't wear your specs, you are making your eyes work harder than they normally would, and these symptoms are their way of complaining. So wear your glasses.

## 3. Wearing glasses can cure bad vision.

Your glasses can help relieve the symptoms of many eye deficiencies, but they can't cure any of them. Glasses merely change the image transmitted by the eye to the brain; they have no effect at all on the eye itself.

## 4. Reading in poor light can damage your eyes.

Reading, or doing any fine detail work under poor lighting can give you eyestrain, or a pain in the neck—but it can't actually ruin your eyes. You can avoid eyestrain by making sure you have sufficient light, and by adjusting your light source so that it eliminates glares and shadows.

## 5. A person who is color-blind cannot perceive colors.

While such a condition is possible, it is rare. The great majority of color-blind people have difficulty distinguishing either red or green. This condition, then, is more properly called "red-green color blindness."

## 6. Staring directly into the sun can ruin your eyes.

Theoretically, this is true. The ultraviolet and infrared rays emitted by the sun can damage your eyes, particularly the retina and the lens. In practice, however, this type of eye damage is virtually impossible because your eyes will not tolerate your looking into the sun for any length of time. They will automatically close before any serious damage can be done. Generally, you can protect your eyes from the strong light of the summer sun by wearing good sunglasses; that is, glasses that have been ground by an optician to eliminate aberrations and scratches.

## 7. Some people never have to wear glasses.

This statement is true for some young people. But as the years roll on and age takes its toll, sooner or later all of us have to wear glasses. Thus, when a person reaches 40 or so, a condition known as presbyopia, in which the lens loses its elasticity, begins to set in. By age 50, practically everyone has this condition and must correct it by wearing eyeglasses.

## 8. Since they can see distances, farsighted people have better vision than nearsighted people.

Not really, because the farsighted individual cannot see things at close range. The nearsighted person, by contrast, can clearly make out objects that are near at hand, but has difficulty seeing things in the distance.

## 9. An individual with a blind spot should not be permitted to drive a car or perform other tasks which would jeopardize the safety of others.

If this statement were true, there would be no cars on the road because we all have blind spots. A blind spot is located in a tiny part of each eye, at the point where the optic nerve connects to the retina. This nerve transmits images to the brain, but cannot form them. The blind spot does not hamper eyesight because we have stereo vision: one eye will see an object, or part of an object, that is temporarily hidden by the blind spot of the other eye.

## Employment opportunities

There are many high-paying, meaningful jobs for qualified life scientists. Here is a sampling adapted from the journal *Science*:

*Aquatic ecologist.* Position available for an aquatic ecologist specializing in quantitative population or community ecology with interest in food chain dynamics and community structure. Duties will include teaching and the designing and coordination of field research.

*Biomathematician.* Position open for Biomathematician, Ph.D. Duties include collection and analysis of patient data from medical records, and research laboratories, advice on design and analysis of research, including therapeutic trials and epidemiology studies. Salary depends upon qualifications. Recent graduate preferred.

*Microbiology.* Two positions available. (1) Professor of Microbiology ($28,000 to $30,000). M.D., with experience in teaching and research in medical microbiology and immunology. Must have international recognition in immunology research. (2) Associate Professor of Microbiology ($24,000 to $26,000). M.D. or Ph.D. with experience teaching and research in microbiology and cellular immunology. Both positions require teaching of microbiology and immunology to medical, dental, and graduate students, supervision of graduate student research, and independent research activities.

*Microscopy technician.* Five years experience in perfusion, embedding, fixing tissue for electron microscopy; use of ultramicrotome; darkroom experience with EM materials; histochemistry and fluorescent histochemistry; knowledge of scientific English and German helpful. Major West Coast institution.

*Toxicologist.* Require Ph.D. with at least three years experience. Pesticide and drug metabolism, enzyme induction and developmental toxicology. Salary range $18,000 to $21,000 a year.

## "Rock" singing can be dangerous to your health

For some time, scientists have known that rock and roll music can damage hearing. Now, a speech pathologist says it can also harm the vocal cords. According to *Science Digest*, Dr. Eugene Batza of the Cleveland Clinic says many rock singers are abusing their vocal cords by singing loudly for long periods of time. Many also try to jack up their decibel output by working themselves into an emotional frenzy, a situation that does the rest of the body no good. Batza thinks that some 75 percent of professional rock vocalists are probably damaging their hearing as well as their voices.

He first noticed this condition when he routinely examined a five-man group of well-known rock stars who sing in a modified rock style. All five had traumatic laryngitis, nodules, and warty growths on their vocal cords. "The enormous popularity of these musicians," says Batza, "makes exhausting demands on them. Some groups perform almost every evening, and for some, there are recording sessions, frequent rehearsals, and considerable arduous travel from engagement to engagement."

The condition can be treated by correcting singing techniques, by giving the voice a rest, and, in some cases, by surgery. But few professional rockers will submit to these measures, largely because they feel the treatment will change their vocal styles for the worse.

# Bio-briefs

*Eye color and pain sensitivity.* Blue or green eyes may add to a person's attractiveness. They also make him easier to hurt. Anyway, that's what ophthalmologist Michel Millidot says. Millidot, who teaches at the University of Wales Institute of Science and Technology, discovered that individuals with light-colored eyes are more sensitive to pain than those with dark eyes. According to *Science News*, Millidot conducted an experiment involving 112 Caucasians and 44 nonwhites. He found that the corneas of blue-eyed people are twice as sensitive as those of brown-eyed people. Similarly, hazel eyes and green eyes are a bit more sensitive than brown eyes. What's more, the corneas of brown-eyed nonwhites are only half as sensitive as the corneas of brown-eyed whites, and only one-fourth as sensitive as those of blue-eyed whites. Millidot thinks that corneal sensitivity may be related to the overall sensitivity of the body. If this is so, he says, it may indicate why "acupuncture may be more acceptable in China than in countries inhabited by blue-eyed people."

*Do we have too many teeth?* Humans may have as many as 12 teeth more than they actually need, says a British dentist. Dr. R.V. Tait states that our early ancestors may have needed all of their 32 teeth to chop and grind their fibrous vegetable foods, but our soft diet no longer requires so much oral clutter. Tait believes that some of our teeth do not get enough work to do, so he proposes paring them down to 25 or even 20 by extracting 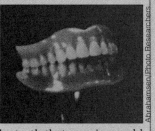 some during childhood. Since the teeth that remain would get more of a workout, they would be healthier and need less professional attention. The new spacing would also facilitate self-cleaning. Tait would extract the first baby back teeth and the second baby molars to remove some of the clutter. Now, if someone could do something about all of this unnecessary hair we've got growing all over our bodies . . .

*Finger-lickin' good.* All of that fried chicken you've been devouring may help you live longer. That's the latest word on nutrition from Dr. Harold Horowitz, professor of biophysics and biochemistry at Yale University. Dr. Horowitz came to this conclusion after studying the famous Hammond report of 1963, which linked cigarette smoking in men with cancer. The report, which surveyed more than 422,000 men, also obtained information on eating and sleeping habits. According to the Yale researcher, the death rate for men who never ate fried foods was 72 percent higher than those who ate fried foods 15 times or more a week. Indeed, says Horowitz, "the death rate decreases as the amount of fried food eaten increases." And one of the nation's top nutritionists, George Mann of Vanderbilt University Medical School, supports Horowitz. Abstaining from fried foods, he says, is "just part of the popular folklore about diet and health." But Horowitz cautions that "more study of the effects of fried foods is needed" before any firm conclusions can be drawn.

*Achoo!* Catching a cold may be harder than you think. According to the *New York Times*, a study conducted at the University of Wisconsin indicates that catching a cold takes many hours of togetherness between recipient and the donor who has a severe cold. Some 24 married couples took part in the study, during which one partner from each of the couples was infected with a common cold virus. The couple spent a good deal of time together—more than 17 hours a day. In barely 40 percent of the cases was the cold virus actually transmitted from one spouse to another. This result raises the possibility that some simple means may be discovered to make transmission of the cold even more difficult. "It may be possible," the report concludes, "for some mechanical or antiseptic device to break the chain of transmission."

**t**he world of living things is divided into producers, consumers, and recyclers. We have already seen how members of the plant kingdom produce energy-containing substances from sunlight, air, and water. We have examined the way fungi and bacteria break down organic material. The animal kingdom contains the consumers which feed on protists, plants, or other animals. Their way of life is specialized primarily for ingestion, although some invertebrates are parasitic and specialize in absorption.

Animals cannot process a constant flow of energy from the sun as plants do. They must seek out prepackaged units of energy. Thus they need special systems to sense their surroundings and to reach their food. Even if they are immobile, filtering their food from currents of water, all but the simplest animals have at least rudimentary skeletons, muscles, sensors, and nerves.

Once the food is obtained, it is usually in a form the animal cannot use. It must therefore be broken down and processed, with harmful by-products being neutralized and safely eliminated. This requires specialized systems for digestion, circulation, excretion, and gas exchange. Furthermore, the food comes in intermittently and in variable amounts. So the animal needs some way of sensing the variations in its internal environment and coordinating all these systems. As we climb the evolutionary ladder, we find that animals become less passively reliant on the environment and gain greater control over their own internal environment.

This does not mean that the higher animals are more successful. Instead, they have adapted to new habitats that remain closed to other animals. There are about 25 or 30 animal phyla, and most of these are composed of aquatic organisms. A few of the most important are discussed in this chapter. Only two phyla, the arthropods and the chordates, evolved really satisfactory strategies for escaping their watery environment to become successful terrestrial animals. They will be discussed in the following chapter.

# Phylum Porifera

The Porifera (from the Latin meaning "pore-bearers") or sponges are an evolutionary blind alley. This is true of most species which become highly specialized. Sponges appeared about 550 million years ago, and current forms are much like many ancient fossil specimens. Not until the middle of the nineteenth century were sponges identified as animals. Before the discovery that they feed by ingestion, they were lumped with lower plants.

Sponges are ecologically more important in marine environments than in fresh water. They are common only in the shallow ocean waters. Sponges feed on plankton, and are seldom eaten by other animals. They are characterized by a division of labor among individual specialized cells. Outer and inner layers contain **epidermal** (outer skin) **cells** and cells specialized for different roles such as feeding, food transfer, and building of skeletal material. But since there is no coordination of cells into tissues, sponges show a very simple kind of organization.

There are about 5,000 species of sponge. There is no typical shape, but many sponges are vase-like. The skeletal structure which supports the body is composed of spicules, rod- or star-like fragments imbedded among the cells. The outer layer is made up of epidermal cells and specialized **pore cells**. The latter have a pore through the center of the cell, leading to the inner body cavity of the sponge. The inner layer or lining of the body cavity consists of "collared" **choanocyte** cells. These are similar to some algal forms but have no chloroplasts. The choanocytes have flagella that extend into the cavity. Their motion produces a water current that enters through the pore cells and leaves by a large opening, the **osculum**. As water passes the choanocytes, food particles are filtered out and engulfed by these cells. A sponge may filter 23 quarts of water a day.

Sponges have several means of reproduction. Most sponges produce both male and female germ cells. After fertilization, a free-swimming larva is formed. Eventually the larva attaches itself to a permanent resting place, and goes through a series of changes, ending as an adult sponge. Sponges are also capable of asexual reproduction, either by packaging special cells with a hard protective coating or by regeneration. They can regenerate a whole organism from even a single cell.

# Phylum Coelenterata

The phylum Coelenterata (sometimes called Cnidaria) includes jellyfish, coral, sea anemones, and hydra. These organisms have a more precise and complex structure than sponges since they possess tissues. But they do not have all the basic tissue layers and organ systems of higher

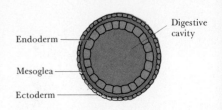

COELENTERATE

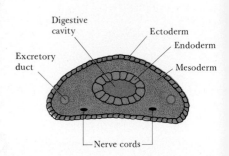

PLATYHELMINTHES

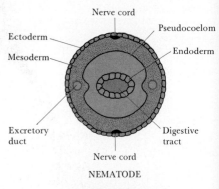

NEMATODE

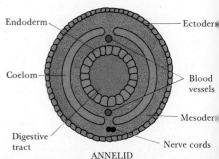

ANNELID

9-1
A colony of sponges (left), showing the oscula through which water is ejected.

9-2
Typical body structure in four phyla of lower invertebrates, showing increasing complexity.

animals. The phylum takes its name from the central gastrovascular cavity, or **coelenteron**. All coelenterates are **radially symmetrical**. That is, they have a body form which is the same in every direction from a central axis. The body consists of an outer layer of skin cells and an inner layer of digestive cells surrounding a central sac. An unstructured gelatinous area (**mesoglea**) lies between the two tissue layers. This is the "jelly" of jellyfish. The mouth is the only body opening. It is surrounded by tentacles which collect food. The tentacles have cells known as **cnidoblasts** which either paralyze prey on contact or entangle it in a "lasso"-like extension. The food particle is then transferred to the mouth and digested in the coelenteron. Undigested particles are expelled through the mouth.

Respiration and excretion occur by diffusion, since no cell is far from the surface. There is no circulatory system, and food is circulated to the cells as an incidental effect of normal movement.

Coelenterates are the lowest animals to possess true nerve cells. These form an irregular net beneath the epidermis throughout the animal's body. Nerve connections in most species are not polarized. That is, impulses set up in one part of the body move equally in all directions. There is no head or central concentration of cells, as in higher organisms, to receive messages or send out instructions for response.

Hydras, common fresh-water coelenterates, reproduce asexually by budding. But when the carbon dioxide concentration of the water becomes very high, particularly in autumn, the hydra forms ovaries and testes. Eventually these produce fertilized eggs surrounded by protective coats. The eggs survive freezing and drying weather to start the population again in the spring.

Many coelenterates have two stages. One is a **sessile** (sedentary, or attached to a base) **polyp** or hydra-like stage. The other is a feeding jellyfish or **medusa** stage. This differs from the alternation of generations in plants, in that both stages are diploid.

9-3
Right, jellyfish (phylum Coelenterata).

9-4
Life cycle of *Obelia,* a coelenterate usually seen as a plant-like growth on rocks and wharves. Each "plant" is a linked colony of polyps. Some of the polyps are specialized for reproduction. They produce buds which develop into medusae, break loose, and become free-swimming. Male and female medusae shed their gametes into the water, fertilization occurs, and ciliated larvae (planulae) are produced.

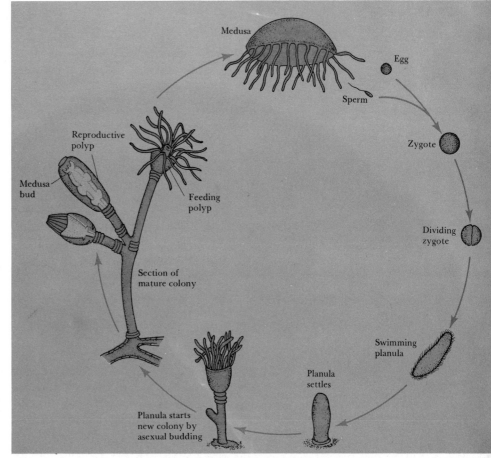

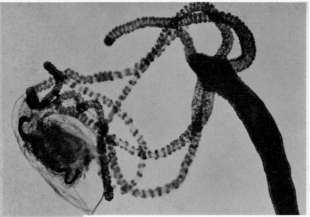

**9-5**
Right, hydra (phylum Coelenterata) eating a waterflea. The tentacles of the hydra contain a poison which is released upon contact and paralyzes the victim within a few seconds. The outline and the eye of the prey can be seen through the transparent and greatly enlarged belly of the hydra (below) after the prey has been ingested.

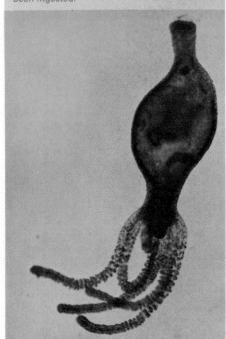

## Phylum Platyhelminthes

The flatworms (*platy:* "flat"; *helminth:* "worm") represent another advance up the evolutionary ladder. Their bodies develop from three basic cell layers, while the lower phyla have only two. The new **mesoderm** ("middle-skin") layer allows more complex internal development. Flatworms also show true **bilateral symmetry**. That is, they have a left and a right side which are mirror images of one another.

Bilateral symmetry makes possible the establishment of a definite front end. Flatworms move about, and they must be able to determine where it is desirable or safe to go. For this, it is most efficient to concentrate the sensory apparatus at one end, and then see to it that this end travels in front. Such a concentration provides the beginning of a head.

Two classes of Platyhelminthes are completely parasitic, and therefore somewhat specialized. It is easier to see the general flatworm body plan in the free-living flatworms of the class Turbellaria. Most turbellarians are marine, but a few live in fresh water. They are usually ciliated for free movement. Like the coelenterates, they have a single gastrovascular cavity. This is sometimes extensively branched, and is connected to the outside by a single opening. The mesoderm gives rise to many-layered tissues and organ systems, including excretory and reproductive organs. Clearly formed muscles run lengthwise, circularly, and from top to bottom (dorsoventrally) giving the animal a wide range of possible movements.

Along with a nerve net like that of the coelenterates, the turbellarians also have a simple form of central nervous system. In the fresh-water planarians, one of the best-known groups, this system includes a two-lobed mass of cells loosely called a brain, "eyespots" (pigment-containing structures which are sensitive to changes in light), and taste receptors in the so-called "ears." There is no respiratory system. Respiration occurs by diffusion through the body surface. Probably for this reason, flatworms must remain flat, so that no cells are very far from the external source of oxygen.

Flatworms are a major medical problem, because so many of them are harmful parasites. Millions of humans are parasitized by flukes and tapeworms. The blood fluke, *Schistosoma,* causes the disease called

**9-6**
Two segments in the long body of a tapeworm (phylum Platyhelminthes). The dark masses are eggs: a good demonstration of why tapeworms are difficult to eradicate.

schistosomiasis. In Egypt today more than one-third of the population suffers from this disease.

The evolutionary relationships between the flatworms, the coelenterates, and other animals are still uncertain. The Platyhelminthes are not "descended from" the coelenterates, but the two groups are believed to have a common ancestor. Many biologists believe that it may have resembled the free-swimming larval stage of modern coelenterates. Such a flattened, ciliated form—known as a **planula**—could have evolved both into the coelenterates and into a forerunner of the flatworms and other bilaterally symmetrical animals. However, this is only one of the several theories about the relationship.

## Phylum Nematoda

The nematodes, cylindrical white worms, are sometimes considered a class of another phylum, Aschelminthes. They are a very successful group. About 13,000 species have been identified. These organisms include both free-living forms and a wide variety of plant and animal parasites. Many nematodes constitute a serious problem for growers, and others are among the most debilitating human parasites. More than two-thirds of the readers of this book currently are hosts to nematodes.

The nematode, or roundworm, is essentially a tube within a tube. This is the first phylum to have evolved a **complete digestive system**. It has a mouth at one end and an anus at the other for the exit of indigestible materials. This one-way flow reduces the loss of good food with undigestible materials, as happens in animals with gastrovascular cavities.

This body plan also includes a cavity between the gut and the outer body wall. Here the muscles, reproductive system, and other organs are housed. In the flatworms, this area is packed with mesoderm. Flatworms are therefore classed as **acoelomate**—lacking a coelom or body cavity.

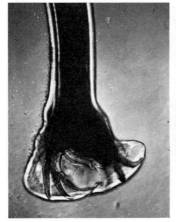

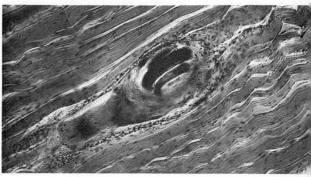

9-7
Hookworm (left). Note the hook-like structures at the sucker end which attach the hookworm to the tissues of its host. The trichina worm (above) is encysted in a muscle. When larvae are released, they encyst elsewhere in the body. They may cause terrible muscular pains, weakness, fever, anemia, swelling, and sometimes, death. (See Phylum Nematoda)

The fluid-filled cavity of the roundworm is called a **pseudocoelom**, since it is not formed entirely out of the mesoderm. The next phylum, the Annelida, and all others following it, have a true **coelom**, a cavity in the mesoderm itself.

The development of a coelom was an important evolutionary step. It provided room for organs to enlarge and become more elaborate. For instance, the gut could elongate and coil within the body cavity, gaining more surface area for digestion and absorption. This was just one of a number of developments that enabled animals to become larger and more active. Eventually, it allowed them to adapt to terrestrial habitats.

## Phylum Annelida

Annelids are the most complex of the worms, and can attain the largest size. About 9,000 species are known, including the common earthworm. The long, cylindrical body is divided into segments. Internally, the segments are separated by a thin partition, or **septum**. If an earthworm is cut in half by a predator, the head can survive and regenerate a new "tail" because the septae maintain the integrity of each part of the body.

The intestine runs from the anterior ("head") segment to the posterior segment, passing through the septae. There is also a circulatory system which runs throughout

9-8
Earthworms copulating. (See Phylum Annelida)

**9-9**
A single meal of blood may suffice a leech (phylum Annelida) for several months. The animal can expand to several times its normal size in order to store the food.

the body. The reproductive system extends through several segments. Otherwise each segment is like a semi-self-contained drum. It has its own excretory organs, longitudinal and circular muscles, and external appendages. Because the organs of respiration, excretion, and circulation are more highly organized, annelids can be larger, thicker-bodied, and more active than animals in the lower phyla.

Most annelids reproduce sexually, and two of the three classes are primarily **hermaphroditic.** That is, each individual has both male and female organs. However, in many species copulation is still necessary, as the hermaphrodite individual cannot fertilize its own eggs.

The annelids are very important in the soil of marine, fresh-water, and terrestrial habitats. The oligochaetes (or bristle-worms), including the earthworm, are found mainly in fresh water and on land. Leeches (class Hirudinea) are common in fresh water, and the polychaete worms are mostly restricted to the oceans. Most polychaetes and oligochaetes feed on decaying organic matter. Leeches tend to be parasites. They attach themselves to the outside of vertebrate hosts, but a few feed on snails and other invertebrates.

## Phylum Mollusca

The mollusks (from the Latin *mollis,* or "soft") are a successful phylum or more than 110,000 species. They include six classes, but only three are major. These are the gastropods, bivalves, and cephalopods. Mollusks have successfully colonized many habitats, and are dominant organisms in many marine environments. Here we find oysters, clams, snails, octopuses, slugs, and squids.

The basic mollusk body plan is a ventral muscular **foot,** topped by a dorsal **visceral mass,** which is surrounded by a thin tissue called the **mantle.** Glands in the mantle secrete a shell. Mollusks are bilaterally symmetrical animals and true coelomates.

**9-10**
Snails (above) and a slug (below). The tentacles usually serve for vision as well as for touch. In some species, the eyes are at the tips of the upper tentacles, which can be rolled back for protection. In others they are at the base of the tentacles. Also worthy of note is the textured surface of the snail. The slug, a shell-less relative of the snail, is very vulnerable to drying, and must stay in a moist and protected environment. (See Phylum Mollusca)

They possess all the basic organ systems of the segmented worms, but lack their segmentation and their duplication of organs. There is one pair of excretory organs, one heart, and one pair of reproductive organs. The digestive system is a single tube, which may be coiled. In most classes it includes a toothy **radula,** which is used like a rasp to chip off pieces of plants or animal bodies or shells. Bivalves, however, feed by filtering plankton through their gills, and therefore lack a radula. The circulatory system is open. That is, blood flows out of vessels into sizable cavities and eventually back to the heart through the veins. Paired "kidneys" remove metabolic wastes and discharge them near the anus. The nervous system consists of several ganglia ("local brains") and two pairs of nerve cords. Most mollusks are slow-working animals lacking quick reflexes.

The class Gastropoda is the largest and most varied group of mollusks. It includes snails, slugs, and whelks. The bodies of these relatively primitive mollusks undergo a 180-degree twist during development. Though some snails are filter feeders, most have radulae which they use to scrape food from the rocks, or to tear and eat tissues of other invertebrates. Land-dwelling snails have simple lungs rather than gills, and are well developed for life on land.

Clams, oysters, and mussels (class Pelecypoda) possess a two-part hinged shell, hence their common name of bivalves. They have neither head nor radula. Well-developed gills collect food and also perform respiratory functions. Cilia on the gills bring in plankton-containing water through a siphon, at the rate of two to three quarts per hour for a medium-sized clam. Food particles are carried to the mouth, while water passes through the gills and out another siphon. In clams the foot is the organ of locomotion, operating through the combined effect of foot muscles and blood pressure.

Squid, octopuses, and cuttlefish (class Cephalopoda) are quite unlike the bivalves and other mollusks. The most obvious difference is that they lack an external shell. They range in size from half-inch octopuses to giant squid which can be over 60 feet long. Cephalopods are quick-moving and intelligent; some can learn better than the lower classes of invertebrates. The foot, divided into a number of tentacles, encircles the head (the name Cephalopoda means "head-footed"). They have become adapted to swimming, and almost all are carnivores. Such fast-moving animals need sensors that can detect events at a distance.

9-11
Squid (left). Cuttlefish (below). Note the human-like eye, a feature characteristic of cephalopods. (See Phylum Mollusca)

The brain is large, and the eye of an octopus is actually better designed than the vertebrate eye. It looks so much like the vertebrate eye that one is surprised to find that it is formed in the embryo in quite a different way. This is a good example of **convergent evolution**, an adaptation which is so useful that two or more species reach it by different paths.

## Phylum Echinodermata

Echinoderms (Latin for "spiny-skin") are among the most familiar animals of the sea. They include starfish, brittle stars, sea urchins, sea cucumbers, and crinoids. Echinoderms are exclusively marine, and are predominantly bottom-dwellers. They are almost the only major animal phylum to have no parasitic species. During early development they show bilateral symmetry, but this is replaced by radial symmetry in adults. Echinoderms are easy to recognize because all the members possess five-sided (or a multiple of five) radial symmetry. They also have a unique water vascular system and an internal skeleton of bony plates, or **ossicles**, covered by a tough skin.

The common starfish (class Asteroidea) is a good representative of the phylum. It has a central disc from which radiate from five to 20 or more arms. The mouth is located in the center of the underside of the disc **(oral surface)**. On the dorsal surface is a

button-shaped structure called the **madreporite**. Through this, sea water passes into the **water vascular system**. This system is an extraordinary bit of biological engineering. Its active organs are hundreds of muscular tube feet on the oral side of each starfish arm. These are connected to a canal which joins a ring in the central disc. The ring is connected to the madreporite, so sea water can move in and out of the system. By regulating water pressure on the tube foot, and secreting a sticky substance at the tip of the foot, the starfish can hold on to surfaces. By a coordinated movement of thousands of tube feet (a process not yet thoroughly understood), it can move slowly over the ocean floor. It can also grasp prey with its tube feet and even pull open clam shells. In the latter case, it turns its stomach inside out, pushing it out through its own mouth and in between the opened valves of the shell. There it secretes enzymes to digest the soft parts of its prey.

Another important function of the tube

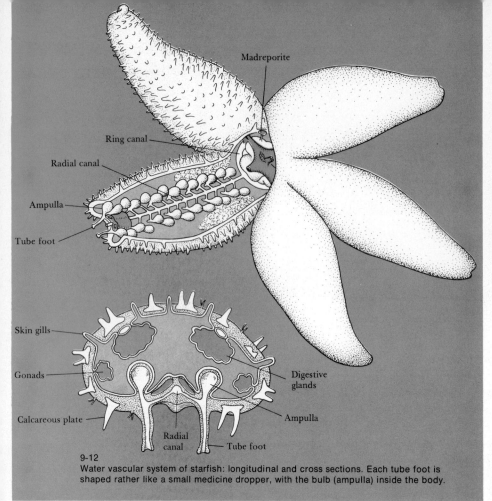

Madreporite

Ring canal

Radial canal

Ampulla

Tube foot

Skin gills

Gonads

Digestive glands

Calcareous plate

Radial canal

Ampulla

Tube foot

9-12

Water vascular system of starfish: longitudinal and cross sections. Each tube foot is shaped rather like a small medicine dropper, with the bulb (ampulla) inside the body.

9-13

Two dissimilar echinoderms. Top: sand dollars (live adult; empty shell; live juvenile). Bottom: starfish opening a clam.

9-14

Top: sea urchin, an echinoderm with ossicles closely fitted together to form an armor case. Bottom: sea cucumber, an armless echinoderm with a muscular body wall.

feet is respiration. Experiments show that nearly 60 percent of respiration in echinoderms occurs in the tube feet. The rest takes place in small finger-like projections, the **skin gills**, which extend through spaces in the bony plates. Perhaps because respiration is thus well taken care of, the starfish has a rather poorly developed circulatory system.

All starfish have amazing regenerative ability. From as little as a single detached arm and a tiny portion of the disc, an individual can grow an entire new body. Starfish can be significant predators in a community. Currently the purple starfish is so common in the South Pacific that it is destroying large areas of atolls by feeding on the atoll-forming corals.

Unlikely as it seems, the echinoderms are the phylum most closely related to our own, the chordates. Primitive members of both phyla are quite similar in their early embryonic stages. The mesodermal layer is formed in the same way, and the primitive forms share a particular type of larva. There is also another significant similarity. On the mollusk–annelid–arthropod side of the evolutionary tree, the embryo forms the mouth before the anus. This branch is therefore named **Protostomia**, from the Greek for "first mouth." In echinoderms and chordates, the first opening in the embryo becomes the anus. The mouth is formed later, from a second opening. These phyla are called **Deuterostomia**, "second mouth."

The echinoderm–chordate line apparently shares a common ancestor far back in time. Since then, it has taken a different evolutionary path than the line leading to the mollusks and arthropods. In the next chapter we will discuss the highest branches of the two lines—arthropods and chordates.

**summary**

The animal kingdom consists of multicellular organisms that feed on protists, plants, or other animals. Their way of life is specialized primarily for ingestion. Animals need special systems to sense their surroundings and to reach their food. All but the simplest have at least rudimentary skeletons, muscles, sensors, and nerves. They also have specialized systems for digestion, circulation, excretion, and gas exchange. As we proceed up the evolutionary ladder, we find that animals rely less passively on the external environment. They also gain a greater degree of control over their own internal environment.

Among the simplest forms of animal life are the Porifera, or sponges. In sponges, there are two main layers. These contain cells specialized for such roles as feeding, food transport, and building of skeletal material. These cells, however, are not coordinated into tissues as in higher organisms. Specialized cells called choanocytes create a water current from which the sponge filters out and engulfs food particles. Sponges can reproduce either sexually or asexually, and can regenerate a whole organism from a small fragment or even a single cell.

More complex in structure than the sponges are the members of the phylum Coelenterata — including jellyfish, coral, sea anemones, and hydra. Members of this phylum are the lowest animals to possess true nerve cells. But they have no central concentration or "brain." The phylum takes its name from the central gastrovascular cavity, or coelenteron.

The Platyhelminthes, or flatworms, represent another advance up the evolutionary ladder, showing bilateral symmetry. That is, they have a left and right side which are mirror images of each other. Their body structure is more complex than that of the coelenterates, and their sensory apparatus is concentrated at the front end of their bodies. Flukes and tapeworms are parasitic flatworms which can be extremely harmful to humans.

Nematoda, or roundworms, are cylindrical white worms which include a number of parasites. This phylum is the first to have evolved a complete digestive system with a mouth at one end and an anus at the other. It also possesses a pseudocoelom.

The phylum Annelida, including leeches, bristleworms, and the common earthworm, is characterized by a long cylindrical body divided into segments. The segments are separated by a thin partition, or septum, and each contains its own excretory organs, muscles, and external appendages. There is a true coelom. Because their organs are more highly organized, annelids can be larger and more active than animals in the lower phyla. Most annelids reproduce sexually. Many are hermaphroditic. Members of this phylum are very important in the soil of marine, fresh-water, and terrestrial habitats.

Mollusca, the mollusks, are dominant organisms in many marine environments. This phylum includes six classes, most notably the bivalves (clams, oysters, and mussels), gastropods (snails, slugs, and whelks), and cephalopods (squid, octopuses, and cuttlefish). The basic mollusk body plan is a ventral muscular foot, topped by a dorsal visceral mass surrounded by a thin tissue called the mantle. Mollusks are bilaterally symmetrical. They possess all the basic organ systems of the segmented worms but lack their segmentation and duplication of organs. Most classes have a toothy radula which is used to chip off pieces of food. Bivalves have neither head nor radula, possessing instead a two-part hinged shell and well-developed gills. Cephalopods are quick-moving carnivores with large brains and well-developed eyes.

The phylum Echinodermata includes starfish, sea urchins, and sea cucumbers. They are carnivorous marine animals and are predominantly bottom-dwellers. This is almost the only major animal phylum lacking a parasitic species. Echinoderms display five-sided radial symmetry, a unique water vascular system, and an internal skeleton of bony plates, or ossicles, covered by a tough skin. They are the phylum most closely related to our own, the chordates. Primitive members of both phyla are similar in their early embryonic stages. Each forms its middle, or mesodermal, layer of cells in the same way and shares a particular type of larva. Among mollusks, annelids, and arthropods, the first opening in the embryo develops into the mouth. In the echinoderms and chordates, the same opening becomes the anus. The mouth is formed later from a second opening. This strongly suggests that man shares a common ancestor with the starfish and the sea cucumber.

# Animal Children

The birth of a foal
Animal babies and parents
How to feed wild orphan animal babies
Test your knowledge about baby animals

Keystone Pictures, Inc.

New York Zoological Society Photo

New York Zoological Society Photo

# Animal quiz

1. The best way to lift an injured baby animal is to hold its legs (or wings if it is a bird) with one hand and muzzle the mouth with the other hand.  T/F

2. Most pets (not birds) should be bathed at least once a week.  T/F

3. Baby monkeys make excellent pets.  T/F

4. Generally, the best food for infant squirrels is peanuts.  T/F

5. One good way to stop diarrhea in a baby bird is to feed it one or two drops of blackberry brandy.  T/F

6. The crow is generally acknowledged to be the smartest bird in North America.  T/F

7. It is easier to train a baby tiger born in captivity than it is to train a wild one.  T/F

8. Newborn baby giraffes have been known to be six feet tall.  T/F

9. An injured baby animal should be prevented from licking its wound because the saliva may cause an infection.  T/F

10. After its birth, a baby snake typically never sees its mother again.  T/F

11. Baby birds must be fed once an hour.  T/F

12. Rats and other rodents should be kept in wooden cages rather than metal ones.  T/F

USDA-Soil Conservation Service

# The birth of a foal

The long months of pregnancy over, a mare struggles to give birth, then turns her head to sniff curiously at the newborn foal, establishing the identification that will enable her hereafter to recognize it as her own. Ten minutes after birth, the foal is struggling to its feet; then, guided by its mother's nudging muzzle, it approaches its first attempt at nursing.

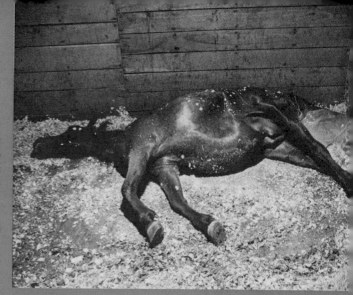

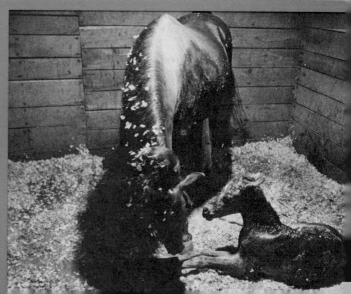

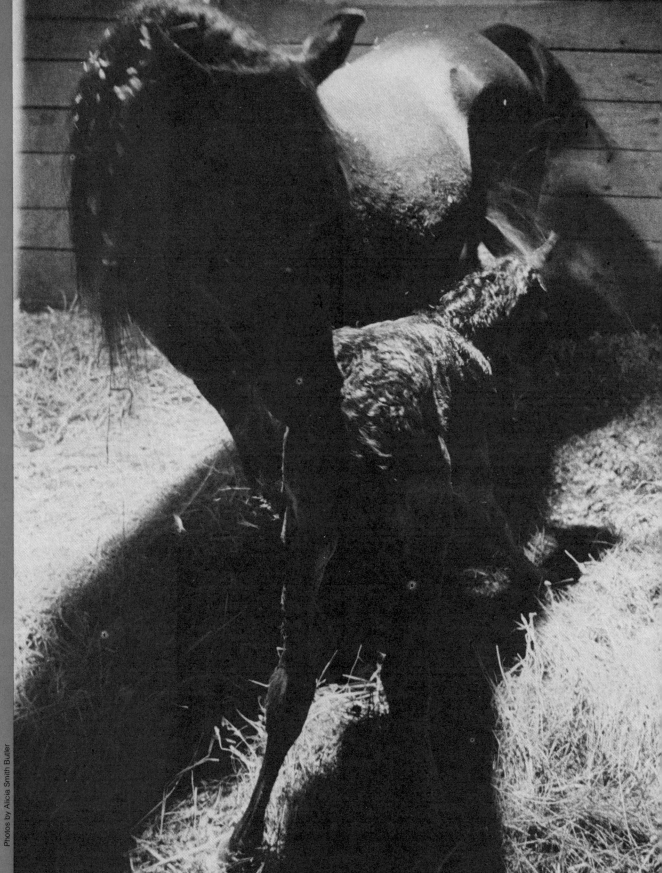

# What do you feed a wild orphan animal?

Suppose you were to come across a baby rabbit lost in the woods and decide to adopt it. Would you know how to give it the loving attention it needs to survive?

The first thing you must do when you get it home is to calm it down and make sure that it is warm enough. A nice thick towel and a cardboard shoe box will work wonders in soothing its jittery nerves and warming its trembling body. First, place a heating pad or hot water bottle under the box. Into the box put the towel, then the baby. Next to the box, you might also place a ticking clock to hold the animal's interest.

After warming the orphan up, the next step is to feed it. Not surprisingly, most baby mammals, including mice, rabbits, squirrels, and such, thrive on the same basic food as human babies—warm milk. But the milk must be diluted with water—two parts milk to one part water—because it is much too rich for small stomachs. This mixture should be heated in a saucepan till it gets warm, but not hot. The way you get the food from the saucepan to the mouth depends upon the animal. Here are some suggestions:

*For tiny animals such as mice.* Dip a Q-tip cotton swab into the warm milk-water mixture and gently ease it between the infant's lips. If the lips don't want to open, just swab them with the Q-tip. After a while, a tiny, pink investigatory tongue will appear and lick the lips. Swab the lips again. After tasting the milk the second time, the mouse will open its mouth wide to allow the swab to enter. A baby mouse needs only about two or three drops of milk because it has an extremely small stomach.

*For larger animals such as squirrels, rabbits, and chipmunks.* Use a medicine dropper to feed these animals. If the baby does not take the dropper at first, smear milk on its lips as with the baby mouse. Above all, don't force-feed the baby—let it discover the good taste of the milk on its own.

*For big animals such as baby foxes and raccoons.* A plastic squeeze bottle, similar to that used to hold ketchup and mustard, will do nicely. Insert the tip into the animal's mouth and keep the milk supply flowing by applying a steady gentle pressure on the bottle.

How much and how often do you feed a baby animal? That depends on the animal. Generally, the baby will refuse food when it is full. Most infants will eat only a small amount of food at one time, but at frequent intervals. Feeding the orphan small quantities every two hours should keep it content.

After the baby has been weaned, it will need solid food. You can get this in pet stores, most of which stock foods for a large variety of animals. Pelleted foods, for example, are available for rabbits, hamsters, and even elephants. You can determine what's best for your pet by experimenting—see what the animal likes by feeding it a variety of nourishing foods.

Meanwhile, here are some general dietary guidelines to get you started. Rodents and rabbits like sunflower seeds, lettuce, carrots, and apples. Because their teeth are constantly growing, these animals also require some hard foods such as nuts or bits of bone. Gnawing on these foods keeps the teeth worn down. Otherwise, the teeth would grow to such an enormous size that the animal would be unable to eat anything at all.

Animals such as raccoons and woodchucks love fruits and vegetables, as well as small pieces of meat or fish. Foxes and wildcats thrive on a similar diet: they enjoy berries, grapes, vegetables, grasshoppers, and crickets. Naturally, you should have lots of cool drinking water available for your growing orphan, making sure to change the supply every day.

For more information on the care and feeding of wild animals of all ages, there's a delightful book on the subject—*May I Keep This Clam, Mother? It Followed Me Home*, by Ronald Rood.

New York Zoological Society Photo

## Answers to quiz

1. *False. Use one hand to lift the animal by the nape of the neck, while you support its body from beneath with the other hand.*
2. *True. But most pet-care experts recommend bathing once every three days. Birds should be given enough water to bathe themselves.*
3. *False. Monkeys of any age should not be kept as pets—they're too destructive and may bite or scratch without warning.*
4. *False. Peanuts, not found in the squirrel's natural habitat, are not good for the animals.*
5. *True.*
6. *True. The crow learns quickly and is quite clever.*
7. *False. Oddly enough, the reverse is true.*
8. *True.*
9. *False. The animal's saliva helps keep the wound clean.*
10. *True.*
11. *False. Feeding baby birds small amounts two times an hour will help keep them content.*
12. *False. They can use their sharp teeth to gnaw their way out of wooden and cardboard cages.*

# Book Review

*Patty Cake* by Elizabeth Moody. New York: Quadrangle, 1974. 85 pages, illustrated. $2.95 (paperback).

This charming little picture book relates the story of a baby female gorilla named Patty Cake, and her parents, Kongo and Lulu. Patty Cake has been the star of New York's Central Park Zoo ever since her birth there a few years ago. She has attracted thousands of visitors to the zoo, partly because goril-las are rarely born in captivity, partly because of her efferves-cent personality. She is a born show-off, constantly surprising onlookers and keepers alike with her zany antics, many of which are shown in the book's excellent photographs.

One day, a near-tragedy oc-curred. Kongo, the baby's father, was in a separate cage next to that holding Lulu and Patty Cake. When the father playfully reached through the bars to touch his daughter, Lulu suddenly jerked Patty Cake away from him. As she did so, the baby's arm struck the bars, breaking the bone of her upper right arm.

Patty Cake was rushed to a nearby hospital where a pedia-trician worked frantically to mend the break. Her own doc-tor, who had attended her since birth, sat up all night with her, comforting her and feeding her chicken and pears. At the zoo, her parents were desolate: " . . . The parents seemed sad-dened by the loss of the lively little Patty Cake. They clung to each other, stroking each other's arms, hugging and run-ning their hands across each other's face. Lulu had a small cut above her eye and Kongo kept peering at it, touching it with his finger and licking it sol-icitously."

Upon her release from the hospital, Patty Cake was fed and looked after by human parents in another zoo because doctors feared her real parents might try to rip the cast and bandages from the baby's arm. You can read the rest of this de-lightful story for yourself. Need-less to say, it has a happy end-ing.

**10 arthropods and chordates**

**a**t the top of the two evolutionary branches of animals are the arthropods and the chordates. If asked to choose which phylum was more successful, the average person would pick the chordates without hesitation. Not only do humans belong to this group, but so do many of the species we rely on for food, pets, and labor. A trip to the zoo confirms this impression. We laugh at the antics of monkeys and seals, admire the brightly colored birds and tropical fish, watch the pacing of the great cats, and, of course, feed peanuts to the elephants. In each of these cases, the focus of our interest has been a chordate.

If we judge by numbers, however, the story is quite different. Some 800,000 species of arthropod have been identified, and perhaps another several million remain to be described. About 80 percent of all species belong to the phylum Arthropoda. They live in almost every conceivable habitat and do so in large numbers. In a sense we are living in the Age of Arthropods.

The arthropods have been around for a long time—about 600 million years. Their most obvious characteristic is a segmented body structure. They share this trait with the polychaete annelid worms (marine relatives of the earthworm), and the two groups are thought to have evolved from the same stock.

The evolutionary ancestry of the chordates is a good deal less certain. As we saw earlier, our closest nonchordate relatives are probably the echinoderms. The ancestral echinoderms were sessile (attached, or sedentary), like the sea lilies of today. One modern chordate-related phylum, the hemichordates, contains some very simple sessile forms, the pterobranchs, which may also be very old. The two groups are similar enough to have derived from a common ancestor.

In the chordate classes we can follow the gradual adaptation from water to land—from the fish through the water-based amphibians and the land-based reptiles to the two main offshoots of the reptiles: birds and mammals.

# Phylum Arthropoda

All arthropods are bilaterally symmetrical, with a body of three distinct regions—**head**, **thorax**, and **abdomen**. They have external jointed appendages that specialize as sensory, feeding, and locomotory limbs. The development of these appendages is most pronounced in the region of the head, which has specialized mouth parts, antennae, and the like.

The name arthropod comes from the Latin for "jointed foot." The appendages of the arthropods are moved by a much more elaborate muscle structure than the circular and longitudinal muscles of the worms and mollusks. This allows greater freedom of movement. The muscles are attached to a hard body covering, or **exoskeleton**, made of a hard polysaccharide called chitin.

Because of this hard external covering, an arthropod can grow only by shedding, or molting, the old skeleton periodically. Before molting, it secretes a new exoskeleton underneath the old. The new skeleton is soft, but essentially complete before the old one is molted. It contains folds which allow expansion. When the arthropod is ready to molt, it expands by taking in large amounts of either water or air. This expansion breaks the old exoskeleton, which is then molted, and fills out the new skeleton, which hardens within a short time.

Although the arthropods are segmented, many of the segments are fused. There are no internal septae dividing the segments. Nor are there serially arranged paired organs, such as annelids have. In possessing an exoskeleton, and lacking serial paired organs, the arthropods are like the mollusks. However, the mollusk shell is made not of chitin but of calcium carbonate. Mollusks may have antennae or tentacles, but they lack the appendages of the arthropods. Therefore, the two phyla are probably only distant relations. Annelids, on the other hand, are segmented. The polychaete annelids have rudimentary external limbs called the **parapodia**. This suggests that the arthropods probably evolved from annelid-like ancestors. The mollusks may have stemmed from an unsegmented worm similar to a flatworm.

As the most diverse group of animals, arthropods probably evolved from two different origins. The crustaceans and extinct trilobites form one distinct evolutionary line. Spiders, mites, centipedes, and insects form another.

## Trilobites

The Trilobita were a dominant group during the Cambrian period some 600 million years ago. (See the geologic chart which follows chapter 20.) They became extinct about 220 million years ago. Fossils of over 3,900 species have been found. Most were one to three inches long and were probably scavengers or filter feeders. Their very simple segmented body plan suggests that trilobites were the most primitive arthropods.

## Crustaceans

The Crustacea are a mostly aquatic class. They possess paired **mandibles** and **maxillae** (specialized mouth parts), eyes which are usually compound, and two pairs of antennae. The Crustacea include important human food animals such as crab, shrimp, crayfish, and lobster. Others, such as fairy shrimp, water fleas, and copepods, are even more important as food for many non-human species, including fish.

The rather unspecialized appendages of early arthropods have specialized in the crustaceans for marked division of labor. The variability and adaptability of appendages have helped the crustaceans, and arthropods in general, become successful at many "professions."

## Arachnids

The Arachnida are arthropods which invaded the land and became successful terrestrial animals. They include spiders, scorpions, mites, and ticks. The body is divided into two main regions, the cephalothorax

10-1
Fossil trilobite.

10-2
Land crab (class Crustacea). Note the broad carapace (protective casing) and the specialization of the first pair of legs into pincers.

10-3
Acorn barnacles (class Crustacea), named perhaps for their shape, are here attached to the outer shell of a crab. Note the calcareous covering of the barnacles, and the feathery organs in the center of their bodies which are modifications of leg structures.

**10-4**
Fat-tailed scorpion. The arrangement and function of the scorpion's legs represent an adaptive advantage to its predatory life style. The second pair of legs, large and equipped with pincers, is a feeling and grasping apparatus. The first pair is used to tear the prey apart, and the last four pairs are principally walking appendages. (See Arachnids)

**10-6**
Silverfish (right). This insect is named for the silvery-looking scales with which it is covered and its rapid movement. It is a well-known household pest which causes damage to fabrics and books.

**10-5**
Generalized body plan of an insect.

and the abdomen. The cephalothorax possesses six pairs of appendages, including four pairs of walking legs (not three as in insects). The arachnids lack antennae and have simple rather than compound eyes. Instead of jaws (or mandibles) they have **chelicerae**, appendages that are either pincers or fang-like claws. Most arachnids are carnivorous.

## Centipedes and millipedes

The general body plan of the centipedes and millipedes is a head and a long flexible trunk of many segments, each bearing legs. The centipedes have one pair of legs per segment. They are found in moist locations, such as under bark of decaying limbs or

under rocks. Centipedes are carnivorous, feeding mostly on insects, worms, and slugs. Millipedes, or "thousand-leggers," have two pairs of legs per segment, and are much slower runners than the centipedes. This is no great handicap, since they are primarily herbivorous. The many legs help the millipede exert great force, so it can push its way through humus, leaves, and loose soil. The maxillae are joined to form a heavy lower lip, good for crushing vegetation.

## Insects

Among the invertebrates, only the arthropods have been successful at living on land. Two advantages have allowed them to adapt to many different habitats and life styles. These are the light and flexible exoskeleton, which provides support and protection against drying out, and the jointed appendages.

Class Insecta contains more different kinds of animal than all other animal groups together. Almost a million species are known, and several million may remain to be identified. It is estimated that there are more than a billion billion insects on this planet.

Insects (from Latin *insectum,* "cut into") have bodies which are "cut into" three parts—head, thorax, and abdomen. They are distinguished from other arthropods in a number of ways. They have three pairs of legs and usually have two pairs of wings on the thorax. The head bears one pair of antennae and a pair of compound eyes. Insects are usually relatively small.

Insects were the first animals to fly, and they have fully exploited this ability. Wings permit an animal to cover a greater area in search of food. Thus, what might be a sparse habitat for an earthbound animal may provide a rich source of food for one which can fly from one place to another. Offspring can easily migrate elsewhere, thus reducing the stress on local resources. The ability to fly, in conjunction with mate-attracting scents, allows a species to sur-

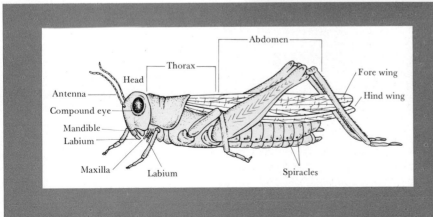

Abdomen

Thorax

Head

Fore wing

Hind wing

Antenna

Compound eye

Mandible

Labium

Maxilla

Labium

Spiracles

10-7
Assorted beetles, insects with the largest number of species. Top: Tiger beetle, adapted to predation by its ability to move rapidly and readiness to use its wings when necessary. Middle: Oil beetle. Note the armorlike covering, an excellent protective device. The body fluids of oil beetles contain a substance, called canthacidin, which used to be an important ingredient in love potions. Bottom: Stag beetle. Sometimes as large as the rest of the body, the mandibles, or jaws, of a stag beetle are well suited to procuring and chewing food.

vive at low densities. This permits specialization for dependence on rare food sources, by enabling males to locate and mate with widely dispersed females.

Many orders of insects develop by **incomplete metamorphosis**. There are three stages—egg, nymph, and adult—and the nymphs take on the adult characteristics gradually. But some have **complete metamorphosis** with four stages—egg, larvae, pupa, adult—and the adults are radically different from the immature stages. The larvae are specialized to be feeding and growing machines. Adults specialize in the manufacture of new individuals and in dispersal. Larvae and adults frequently feed on different food sources. For example, the caterpillar eats leaves, whereas the butterfly feeds on nectar. Thus, in the latter method of development, the species is more fully exploiting its habitat.

Increased specialization among insects has enabled several groups to be quite successful. The true flies (Diptera) include 87,000 species; bees, ants, and wasps (Hymenoptera), 115,000 species; butterflies and moths (Lepidoptera), 140,000 species; and beetles (Coleoptera), 280,000 species. On the other hand, the total number of vertebrate species from *all* classes is just over 50,000. The famous scientist J. B. S. Haldane was asked what he could conclude about the nature of the Creator from a study of His creation. Haldane is supposed to have answered, "An inordinate fondness for beetles."

## Phylum Chordata

The other major arm of the evolutionary tree is topped by the phylum Chordata (from Latin *chorda*, "cord"). All chordates at some period of their lives have three characteristics: a **notochord**, a dorsal hollow **nerve cord**, and paired **gill slits**. The notochord is a cartilage-like rod. It is flexible but firm, so that muscles attached to it have something to pull on. This allows the animal to make strong wavelike swimming motions, not possible for flabby organisms such as worms. When longitudinal muscles contract, the notochord prevents the body from being shortened, so it undulates instead. This notochord (or its replacement—the backbone of the vertebrates) sometimes extends behind the body as a tail. Few species outside the chordates have a tail.

The nerve cord is dorsal, above the notochord, instead of ventral as in the invertebrates. The gill slits are remnants of the life style of the earliest chordates, who were probably filter feeders. The slits permitted water to pass out of the digestive system as food particles were retained. They also functioned in breathing. In lung-breathing vertebrates, including man, gill slits appear in the embryo. But they do not develop very far and never become functional.

### Invertebrate chordates

"Chordate" is often used as if it were synonymous with "vertebrate." But there are chordates which never develop a bony structure. Some show chordate characteristics mainly during the larval stage, losing them as adults. These represent an early evolutionary stage in development toward the vertebrates.

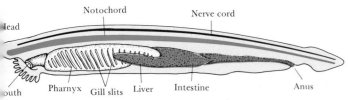

10 8
*Amphioxus*, an invertebrate chordate, showing the well-developed notochord, the distinctive characteristic of chordate animals.

*Amphioxus* is one of the most studied invertebrate chordates. It possesses a permanent notochord and nerve cord. There is no brain, and *Amphioxus* looks like a flattened, headless fish. Food and water enter the mouth and pass to more than 100 pairs of gill slits. The water continues on through the slits and out, while food particles are passed to the digestive tract by the cilia of the gill slits. There is some segmentation, in the form of V-shaped muscle blocks, and also excretory organs located near the dor-

sal end of each gill slit. Though specialized in many ways, *Amphioxus* suggests in other general ways what the ancestors of vertebrates may have been like.

### Vertebrates

The subphylum Vertebrata is made up of man and other mammals, birds, reptiles, amphibians, and four classes of fish. In addition to general chordate characteristics, vertebrates possess an internal skeleton of cartilage or bone. This reinforces or, more often, replaces the notochord. Most vertebrates have a **backbone** made up of a series of **vertebrae**. In these a notochord is visible only in early embryonic stages.

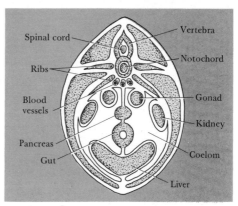

10-9
Generalized body plan of vertebrates.

Vertebrates are bilaterally symmetrical. As a group they are highly active. Their bodies are cigar-shaped, with two pairs of appendages. They have highly developed paired eyes, and paired ears which first evolved for balance and later became adapted for hearing.

We may never know the exact evolutionary origin of the chordates and vertebrates. We can make reasonable trees which fit in with the available evidence, but there are few chances of uncovering a fossil record of soft-bodied ancestors. Therefore our trees are based on detailed knowledge of developmental, anatomical, and physiological relationships, as well as on fossils when available.

*Fish*   The jawless fish (class **Agnatha**, from Latin for "no jaw") are the earliest fish found in the fossil record. For 100 million years they were a highly successful group. Today, however, only a few species exist—the cyclostomes ("circle-mouths"), which include lampreys and hagfish. These have long, eel-like bodies with cartilaginous skeletons. The skin is smooth and scaleless, and there are no jaws or paired fins. They attach themselves to an animal by their circular sucking disc, rasp away the skin with horny teeth, and feed on the victim's blood and other tissues. The cyclostomes are the only parasitic vertebrates.

Class **Placodermi** might be considered an early "experimental model" of jawed fish. Members of this class were active for more than 200 million years. By developing paired appendages and jaws, they were able to leave the bottom and become active predators. The paired appendages increased swimming stability by preventing them from rolling when they were no longer touching the bottom. Their jaws and teeth permitted adaptive radiation into a whole series of predatory niches previously occupied by giant arthropods and some mollusks. Eventually the placoderms became extinct (in the Permian period). But by then they had given rise to the sharks and bony

fishes which are successful classes today.

Sharks, rays, and skates are predominantly marine animals, unlike the earlier classes which were mostly fresh-water fish. This group (class **Chondrichthyes**) lacks bone; the skeleton is formed of cartilage. The leathery skin has no scales, but may have sharp, tooth-like protuberances.

All these cartilaginous fish (also called **elasmobranchs**) have paired fins and hinged jaws. They differ from other fish in that fertilization is internal. The eggs are laid in egg capsules, or the young may even be born alive. The sharks have a partly deserved reputation as voracious predators. Demonstrating the advantage of jaws, they can bite large chunks out of their prey. However, the largest shark, the 40-foot-long basking shark, is a harmless plankton feeder.

When we say "fish," most of us mean the bony fish (class **Osteichthyes**, from Latin *osteon,* "bone," Greek *ichthys,* "fish"). Over 20,000 species are known, and as the depths of the ocean are explored another 20,000 may be discovered. Bony fish fossils are known from the Devonian period, some 400 million years ago. These fish are among the most successful vertebrates to this day.

They also appear to have set the pattern

10-10
Below: Lamprey (class Agnatha). Note the round, sucking apparatus of the mouth which attaches the lamprey to the stone, and the seven separate gill openings on the side of its body, a relatively primitive feature. Right: Shark (class Chrondrichthyes)

of bone structure for all vertebrates. All the bony plates and bones of the early bony fish can be traced in the bone patterns of higher vertebrates. Most of the bones of the human skull can be directly compared with corresponding bones in the skulls of ancient bony fish. Although higher forms may lose bones, new ones are seldom added.

**10-11**
Lungfish, a subclass of the bony fish. The pectoral and pelvic fins of the lungfish, only one of which is visible in the picture, have been adapted into slender filaments which function as sensory apparatus to investigate the environment.

Like the cartilaginous group, the bony fish evolved from the early placoderms. Their gills are covered by a protective flap called the **operculum**, and the gill slits have merged into a single opening. Connective tissue in the skin gives rise to overlapping bony scales. Most bony fish have air bladders, which evolved from a primitive lung. This once served for supplementary respiration but now operates as a swim bladder. By carefully controlling the gas pressure in the bladder, the fish can adjust its buoyancy. Thus it can remain at a chosen depth without constantly fighting tendencies to float or sink.

A few bony fish do retain the primitive lung. These fish also have lobed or fleshy fins. They are believed to resemble the stock from which the amphibians evolved. Fleshy appendages permitted the ancient fish to pull themselves out of water onto the shore, and probably from one pond or stream to another. The air bladder enabled them to obtain oxygen during the overland trip. The Devonian period, when the am-

phibians first appeared, was a time of seasonal droughts. When water or food became scarce, fish that could migrate outcompeted those that could not.

Both the lungs and lobe-fins were structures which aided the ancient animals in their original habitats. The fact that these features also preadapted them to evolve into more land-suited animals is an evolutionary bonus. But it does not explain their occurrence.

*Amphibians and reptiles* By about 440 million years ago, plants had invaded the land. Except for a few arthropods, the land was still empty of animal life. Thus it offered a marvelous opportunity to organisms which could adapt to it. The opportunity was taken up by the amphibians (class **Amphibia**, from Greek *amphi*, "both," *bios*, "life"). Amphibians live both on land and in the water. Frogs, toads, salamanders, and newts are the remaining members of this once numerous class.

Fossils of early amphibians show that they were quite fish-like, with long bodies and tails. To the bodily characteristics of their fish ancestors, the amphibians added better-developed appendages. Their more efficient legs helped them to survive seasonal droughts. They could leave drying foodless ponds and take up residence in deeper ponds elsewhere. The amphibians became so successful that the Carboniferous period (some 350 million years ago) has been called the Age of Amphibians.

**10-12**
Bear Mountain spotted salamander (class Amphibia). The bold pattern of spots on the body of this salamander is characteristic of many species.

The success ticket was five-fingered arms and legs, the pattern still found in higher vertebrates today.

Modern amphibians are highly specialized. This is especially true of the frogs and toads, since their tails have been lost, their backs shortened, and their legs greatly modified for jumping. But the amphibians suffer from some built-in disadvantages. In most cases their legs are attached to the sides of the body, not the underside. Consequently, they must spend a good deal of energy simply to hold their bodies up off the ground. In addition, the amphibians are tied to water. Even if part of their lives is spent on land, most species must lay their eggs in ponds or puddles, so that the developing embryos will not dry out.

The reptiles (class **Reptilia**) are more fully adapted to land. Ancient reptiles showed a fantastic diversity. They included fish-like, porpoise-like, and bird-like reptiles, dinosaurs, and numerous reptiles similar to those living today. This great diversity is no more, but for 200 million years the reptiles were the dominant form of life.

Perhaps the single most important advance of the reptiles was developing shelled eggs. We usually think of eggs with shells as coming from birds. But the reptiles pioneered them, and thus were preadapted to live on land. In a shelled egg, the embryo develops within a private aquatic environment (the amniotic fluid) which is contained by the amniotic membrane. Attached to the abdominal region of the embryo is the yolk sac, with its food supply, and another sac which stores excretory wastes. The egg is covered with a shell which is tough but permeable to air.

The reptile egg is laid on land. This seems odd at first, since we know that primitive reptiles were water-dwellers. But two advantages have been suggested. First, land eggs would be less likely to be eaten, since there was relatively little animal life on land which might feed on them. Moreover, fossil evidence shows that seasonal droughts were characteristic of the Carbon-

10-13
Iguanas. The only marine iguanas in existence are found on the Galapagos Islands. The helmet-like head covering and the large size of these iguanas are characteristics typical of tropical reptiles. Also worthy of note are the well-developed limbs, advantageous in the time-consuming search for food.

iferous period. Eggs which contained their own water, and therefore could be laid on land, were not as susceptible to drying out as those which had to be laid in water.

Since reptile eggs form shells before the eggs are laid, the eggs must be fertilized internally. Reptiles developed a male copulatory organ, the penis, which made this possible. It also allowed fertilization to take place on land.

Reptilian bodies are covered with hard, dry, horny scales which protect against mechanical damage and drying. Their respiratory and circulatory systems are more advanced than those of amphibians. Reptiles have well-developed lungs and a circulatory system which keeps oxygenated and unoxygenated blood fairly well separated. Air is moved in and out of the lungs by a bellows-like action of the rib cage, an improvement over the gulp-and-swallow technique of amphibians. In limb structure, though, the reptiles have not improved much on the amphibians. They have not yet gotten their legs directly under the body.

Since reptiles are cold-blooded, they are most common in the tropics and subtropics. Here they use the environment to keep their body temperatures close to peak operating levels. By placing their bodies perpendicular to the sun's rays, they can absorb the maximum heat energy available. By lying parallel to the sun's rays, they can reduce the amount of absorption. To escape excess heat, they may seek shade, crevices, or burrows. Reptiles use these behavioral means of temperature regulation with wonderful precision. Their blood and bodies are seldom truly cold. Those in temperate climates are unable to absorb enough heat during the winter, so they hibernate.

*Birds*　Anything with feathers is a bird and belongs to the class **Aves**. Birds are descended from reptiles and are so much like them that they have been called "glorified reptiles" and "hot lizards."

Birds have a high metabolic rate, which keeps their body temperature constant. In many species this is several degrees hotter than human body temperature. To maintain this, they need a large flow of oxygen, rapid air uptake, efficient circulation, and good insulation. In addition to lungs, birds have air sacs distributed throughout the body and inside the larger bones. These sacs may add ten times the lung volume to the respiratory volume. Oxygenated and unoxygenated blood are kept completely separated in the circulation. The thick coat of feathers traps air and retains body heat.

Birds are quite successful vertebrates. Although there are only about 8,600 species, it is estimated that there are more than 10 billion land birds on the various continents and unknown billions of sea birds on the oceans. Birds have radiated into numerous habitats and lifestyles. Great variations in structure of beaks and feet allow a great variety of foods to be eaten by various bird species. Some, such as crows and gulls, eat almost anything. Others, such as the hummingbird, are specialized for a very limited diet.

Many birds have eyes larger than their brains. This emphasis on vision is hardly surprising, in view of the amount of information about obstacles, food, landing sites, and possible predators which a bird in flight must process swiftly. Muscular coordination is also well developed.

*Mammals*　We members of class **Mammalia** are currently a very successful class of animals. Although our class contains only about 4,300 species, its members live on all the continents, in the seas, and in the air. They are active all year round. And many species contain huge populations.

All mammals have mammary (milk-producing) glands, sweat glands, and hair. Their teeth are differentiated into incisors for cutting, canines for gripping and stabbing, and molars for grinding. They are warm-blooded, and the hair and sweat glands are closely involved in keeping the body temperature constant. Like birds, mammals have a heart which keeps oxygenated and nonoxygenated blood separate. A muscular sheet, the diaphragm, supplements the bellows-like action of the rib cage and thus improves efficiency of breathing. The mammalian brain is far larger than that of reptiles or birds. This is particularly true of the cerebral hemispheres. Originally these were devoted to the sense of smell, but then turned over to learning, training, and eventually thought in some hominid primates.

Amphibians and those reptiles with legs walk in a slow waddle. Many of the ancient "ruling reptiles" speeded their travel by running on their hind legs, using the heavy tail to counterbalance the trunk. Mammals solved the speed problem by evolving

10-14
Male tree swallow feeding its young. The forked tail, typical of swallows, makes for easy maneuverability in flight.

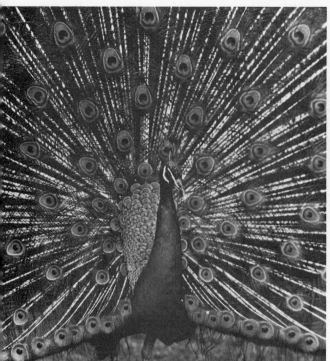

**10-15**
Left: Peacock. The dramatic sight of a peacock "in display" makes it apparent why feathers have been used by humans as objects of decoration since ancient times. At the tip of each feather in the peacock's train, there is an irridescent, colored eye. After raising the tail and bringing it forward, the cock struts about, quivers, and emits rather loud screams. Above: Opossum (order Marsupialia). An opossum may give birth to as many as twenty-five young at once. Only half the young survive their journey to the mother's pouch, where they attach themselves firmly to a nipple and undergo further development. After about a month in the pouch, the young spend an additional eight weeks clinging to the back of the mother, as shown here.

**10-16**
Beaver (Rodentia). To counteract the obvious ill effects of gnawing on trees, the teeth of beavers grow continuously throughout their life. Furry flaps surrounding the mouth close over the teeth when they are not in use.

limbs that were directly under the body and swung from front to rear. The knee joint was turned forward and the elbow to the rear. Thus most of their energy could be used for motion, rather than expended just to keep the body from collapsing the limbs.

Early in the evolution of mammals, one line branched off. It is now represented by the primitive egg-laying order **Monotremata** whose two species, the platypus and the spiny anteater, are found solely in Australia.

A second group of mammals is composed of the marsupials (order **Marsupialia**). These pouched mammals live principally in Australia, although the opossum is found in North America and several other marsupials in South America. The young are born at an extremely early stage (only eight days after conception for the opossum). They crawl into the mother's abdominal pouch, attach themselves to nipples, and thus continue to be nourished from the mother's body.

The third and major group are the **placental mammals**. They have outcompeted the marsupials in South America and pre-

sumably would have done likewise in Australia if they had had the chance. They have the advantage of a placenta, an organ which permits developing young to remain longer within the mother's body. Nourishment, oxygen uptake, and waste removal are carried on through the placenta, while complex brain and body structures develop in the protected uterine environment.

The **Insectivora** (shrews and moles) are most like the mouse-sized, insect-eating

ancestors of the placental mammals. From this insectivore stock evolved the 15 orders of placentals living today.

A large group of mammals are called **ungulates** (from Latin *ungula,* "hoof"). They belong to several orders and are mostly herbivorous. Ungulates include horses, pigs, cattle, deer, and many others. Their teeth have evolved from the sharp, pointed teeth of the insectivore to the enlarged, flattened grinding surface needed for use on abrasive materials such as grass. Their limbs have developed for fast running, and claws have turned into hooves.

Increase the size of the primitive placental stock and modify the teeth, and you have the **Carnivora**. These include cats, dogs, bears, seals, walruses, and others. Their teeth are specialized for ripping and tearing. There are no hooves. The carnivore must be speedy, but cannot give up claws as the ungulates did.

The greatest number of species and individuals are found in the **Rodentia**, the gnawing mammals. In some ways they are the most successful mammals, and have adapted to a wide variety of habitats. In the front of the rodent's mouth are four chisel-like gnawing teeth, separated by a wide gap from the grinding teeth behind. Unlike most teeth, these front teeth grow continually. The rodent can regularly gnaw through very hard natural materials—such as the alder trees cut by beavers for lodging and food—without wearing its teeth down to the gums. Squirrels, rats, mice, porcupines, and guinea pigs are common rodents. Rabbits and hares, however, belong to another order, **Lagomorpha**.

The **Proboscidea** are represented today only by elephants, although other mammals with a trunk—mammoths and mastodons—were once known before the recent ice ages.

The whales and porpoises belong to the order **Cetacea**. These mammals have so adapted to marine life that they are helpless if stranded on a beach. They breathe air, but are streamlined like fish, and their tail fins

0-17
Monkeys have been regarded as cute, nosy, mischievous, quarrelsome, and even sacred. Right: a squirrel monkey trails its long, heavy tail from a branch. Left, top: a spider monkey investigates a find. Left, middle: a capuchin, once the typical organ grinder's monkey, stares uncertainly at an intruder. Left, bottom: a lion-tailed macaque, with baboon-like muzzle, tufted tail, and splendid ruff, goes about its business in the trees. To most North Americans, monkeys are creatures to be enjoyed in zoos. In their native habitats, especially if they travel in large troops, their social proclivities can make them an ear-splitting nuisance, and their curiosity may transform them into habitual pilferers.

are horizontal rather than vertical like the tails of fish. Their bodies are heavily insulated by fat to protect against heat loss in the aquatic environment. Cetaceans have special adaptations for deep diving. Some whales have been found deeper than any atomic submarine is yet able to go.

**Primates** are basically tree-dwellers, and only a few species live on the ground. Living in trees called for feet with long toes and fingers that could grasp the branches. Swinging and leaping from branch to branch required good three-dimensional vision. So primate eyes moved forward in the skull, allowing greater overlap of the fields of view.

The most primitive living primates are the **Prosimii**. They include the lemurs, small animals that resemble monkeys because their hands have flattened nails and they have a monkey-like tail. Their faces are still elongated, however, more like that of a wolf. Tarsiers, another prosimian group, have a more flattened face, well-developed eyes, and well-developed visual areas in the brain. Some fossils of tarsiers and lemurs are difficult to distinguish. Evidently they are closely related.

Monkeys, apes, and man belong to the suborder **Anthropoidea**. The many species of **monkeys** are divided into Old World and New World groups. Only the New World monkeys possess a prehensile (grasping) tail. The Old World monkeys are anatomically closer to man. It is from an Old World ancestry that the great apes and man evolved. Monkeys are the most successful primates after man. They usually walk on four feet, but often sit upright. This frees their hands for manipulating food and other objects. Good eyesight, agility, curiosity, and the ability to handle objects contribute

10-18
Lowland gorilla. The sprinkling of gray hairs among the black signifies that this is an adult male. In captivity, the gorilla has been found to possess powers of memory, insight, and anticipation that accompany successful problem-solving. It may be as intelligent as its more frequently studied relative, the chimpanzee.

to the monkeys' success.

There are four types of **Pongidae** or great apes: gibbons, orangutans, chimpanzees, and gorillas. On the ground they all walk semi-erect at least some of the time In the trees they are brachiators (swinging from branch to branch by their arms), and they have a much wider range of limb movement than the monkeys. Their long fingers are specialized for grasping, making the orangutan, and especially the gibbon, champion brachiators.

The chimpanzees and gorillas have always fascinated people most. They spend much time on the ground and walk relatively upright. They possess larger brains and more intelligence than other primates, and suggest to us some of the characteristics our joint distant primate ancestors must have had. The pygmy chimpanzees of central Africa, in particular, have recently been recognized as perhaps our closest living relatives. Chimpanzees make and use tools in captivity and in the wild. They are bright and can reason. Recent experiments have even succeeded in teaching them simple sign language. Because they are our nearest relatives, chimpanzees are currently being closely studied. It is hoped that through better understanding of these fascinating primates we may gain some clues to the evolution of our own abilities and behaviors.

## summary

The arthropods are numerous and have adapted to a wide range of environments because of their external jointed appendages. These are variously specialized to serve as sensory, feeding, and locomotory limbs. The body of the arthropod is covered by an exoskeleton and is divided into three distinct regions—head, thorax, and abdomen. The segmented bodies and external limbs suggest an evolutionary link between arthropods and the annelids.

Insects are the most varied and successful of all arthropods. They differ from other arthropods—crustaceans, arachnids, centipedes, millipedes, and the extinct trilobites—in several ways. They have three pairs of legs, a head bearing a pair of compound eyes, and usually two pairs of wings on the thorax. Wings allow an insect to migrate far in search of food and mates, reducing the stress on local resources. The exoskeleton gives support and protection from drying out.

Members of the phylum Chordata are characterized at some stage of their development by a notochord (a flexible but firm rod to which muscles are attached), a hollow nerve cord, and paired gill slits. The gill slits appear even in the embryo of lung-breathing vertebrates, but never become functional.

Vertebrates have an internal skeleton of cartilage or bone that reinforces or replaces the notochord. They are bilaterally symmetrical, and have paired eyes and ears.

The jawless fish are the earliest fish found in the fossil record. They were followed by the placoderms, which developed hinged jaws and paired fins. From these evolved the cartilaginous fish (sharks, rays, and skates) and the bony fish of today. One branch of the bony fish, with paired lobe-fin appendages and lungs, seems to have been the stock from which the amphibians evolved.

Amphibians were among the first animals to adapt to life on the land. Retaining the lungs, strong skeletons, and lobe-fins of their fish ancestors, early amphibians evolved legs which allowed them to travel from one pond to another during seasonal droughts. The more fully adapted reptiles evolved the ability to lay hard-shelled eggs on the land. They also developed means to fertilize the eggs before laying, away from water.

Birds, members of the class Aves, are direct descendants of the reptiles. They have a high metabolic rate, a constant body temperature, an efficient circulatory system, and a thick coat of feathers to provide insulation and retain body heat. Air sacs distributed throughout their bodies add ten times the lung volume to their respiratory capacity. Great variation in beak structure, foot structure, and feeding habits has allowed birds to adapt to a wide variety of habitats.

Although mammals represent relatively few species, they have successfully spread to many different environments. They are warm-blooded, and have milk-producing glands, sweat glands, and hair. Mammalian groups include the egg-laying monotremes, the pouched marsupials, and the placental mammals, which develop their embryos within a protected uterine environment.

Primates are the mammalian order of which man is a member. Basically tree-dwellers, primates evolved feet with long, grasping digits, and good three-dimensional vision in order to swing from tree to tree. The most primitive living primates are the prosimians. Monkeys, apes, and man belong to the suborder Anthropoidea. Good eyesight, agility, curiosity, and the ability to handle objects contributed to the monkeys' success. Chimpanzees and gorillas are even more closely related to man. They have larger brains, more intelligence, and a more upright posture than other nonhuman primates.

reproduction, the process of creating one's own likeness, is something that characterizes every living thing, and invests it with wonder. Every one of these new likenesses begins as a tiny cell—from the single-celled, independently functioning amoeba to the highly specialized human fetus, an extraordinarily complex organization of interdependent cells. In handing on the gift of life from one generation to the next, no species can afford to be careless. Survival depends upon the ability of the newborn to sustain life, to grow to maturity, and, once again, to reproduce itself. In the higher forms of life, the young need time to develop specialized systems. The developing embryos must be nurtured until birth, then housed, fed, and cared for, until they are mature enough to survive on their own. Especially for the human fetus, birth is only a stage in the long, chance-beset journey from conception to maturity.

The meeting of the egg with the sperm is the first achievement. Once inside the ovum, the sperm loses its tail. Its chromosomes unite with those of the egg cell to form a single fertilized cell. At that instant the child's sex, together with other inherited characteristics that go far toward shaping its future, are determined. Following union, the cell begins to divide. A little over a single day after fertilization there is no longer a single cell, but two cells. At the end of two days there are four. Quickly the process begins to speed up. Within a few hours the new organism is multi-celled and spherical. All the while, tiny cilia steadily draw the cell complex down the Fallopian tube, propelling it toward the uterus. There, the cell complex will continue to develop, supported and protected, for nine months until the hour of birth.

Once in the uterus, the embryo absorbs nourishment, and implants itself firmly in its new home. Before 18 days have passed, it begins to form specialized blood and heart cells. By the third week the embryonic heart is beating. At this point the yolk sac is still very large. It is producing the nearly 100 germ cells which will move to the embryo and begin to specialize into ovaries or testes. These cells thus ensure future reproduction before the embryo is even one-eighth of an inch long. At the end of the first month the cells have begun to lay the foundation for brain, spinal cord, nerves, and sense organs. Early kidney and lung structures appear. They will be modified or discarded later. The cells also develop according to their function—digestive, muscular, vascular, and skeletal.

During the second month, the embryo becomes a fetus. It is only one-third of an inch long. But it is also 10,000 times larger than the egg from which it developed. Dark pigment appears in the area of the eyes, and the jaws start to form. The face can now be distinguished from that of a fish or chick embryo. By 6 weeks another truly human feature develops—hand plates. These paddle-like appendages will become, by 13 weeks, perfect tiny hands. By the third month the separate systems are integrated enough to allow the fetus to move. That is, it can respond to stimuli by way of messages sent by its own brain. By the end of this month, the fetus is a functioning organism. However, it is not yet an independent one. Its development still depends totally

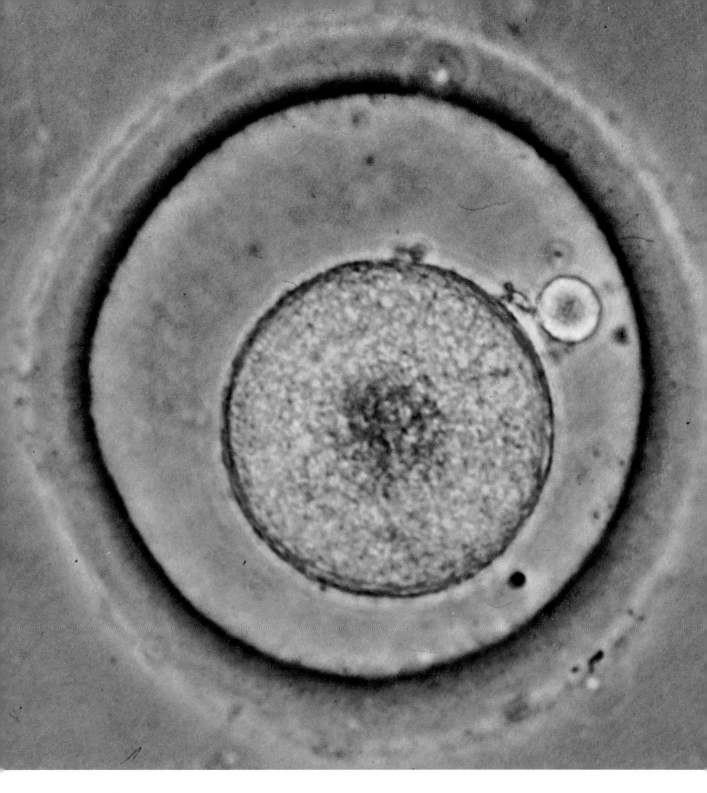

The human ovum. Although the mature female ovum contains one set of chromosomes, it cannot realize its life-giving potential without the other chromosomes contained in the nucleus of the sperm head. The odds against the sperm reaching and penetrating the ovum are enormous.

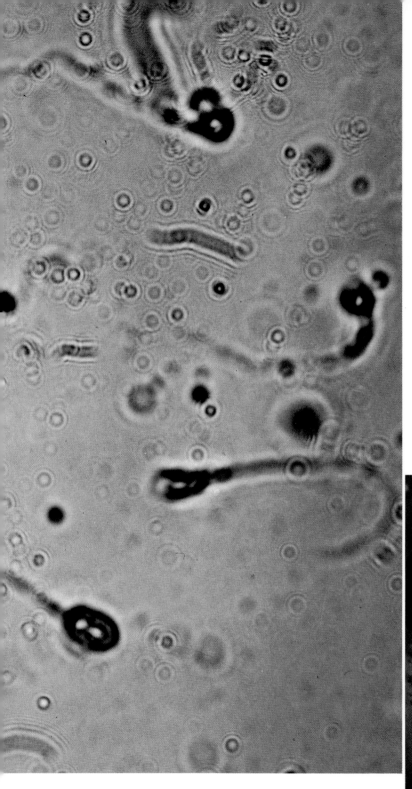

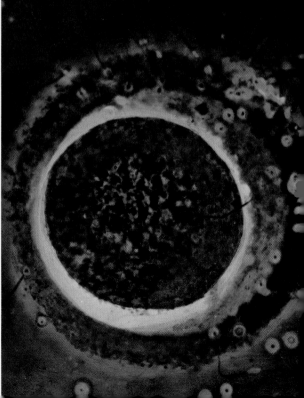

Above: Human sperm. Out of millions of sperm, only a few dozen ever reach the outer layer of the ovum. Those that succeed cling tightly to the zona pellucida surrounding the egg. Of these, only one will penetrate to the nucleus. Right: Single sperm penetrates the zona pellucida.

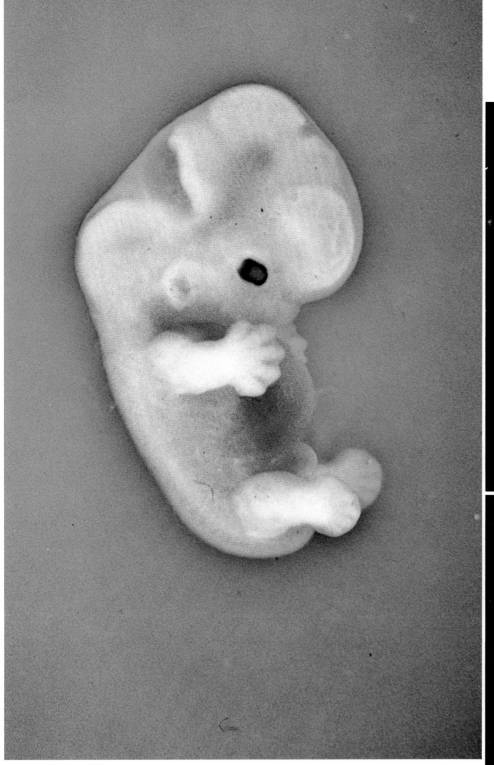
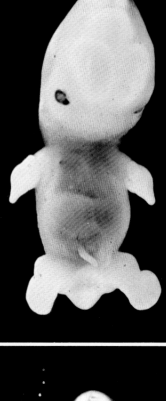
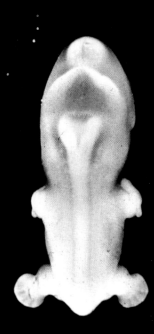

At the end of the first month the cells have all begun to organize, a process which continues well past birth. Left: Human fetus at 38 days, side view. Right: Human fetus at 40 days, with brain and spinal cord already visible. Front view (top) and back view (bottom).

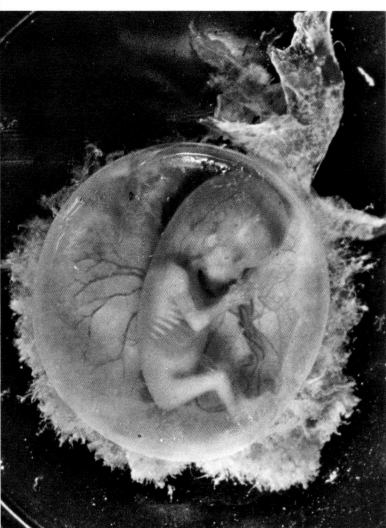

During the second month, the embryo begins to look human. Left, bottom: Human fetus at 5 weeks. Left, top: Human fetus at 7 weeks in amniotic sac surrounded by placenta. Above: Human fetus at 2 months. Opposite: Fetus at 14 weeks in amniotic sac attached to placenta by umbilical cord.

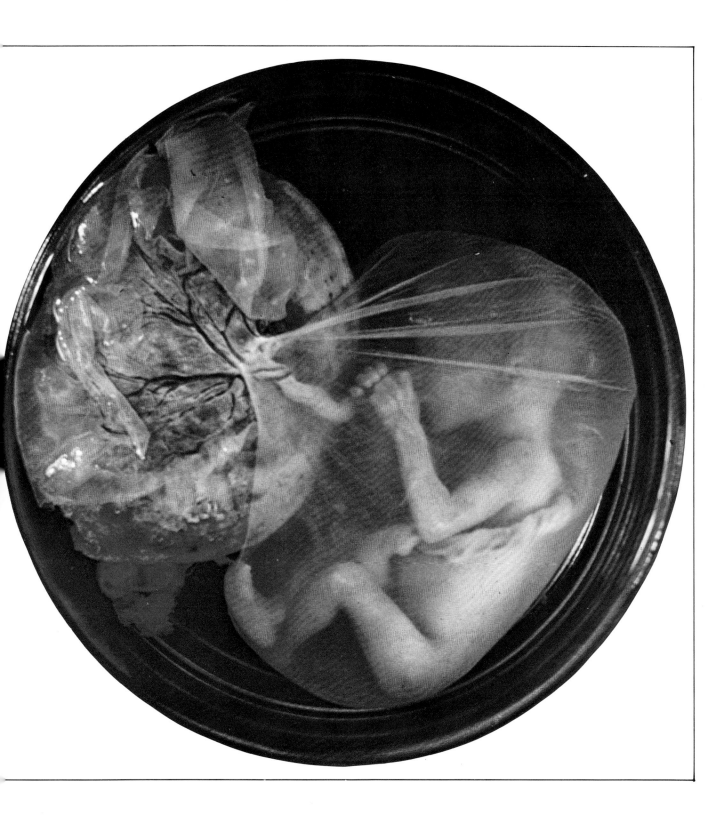

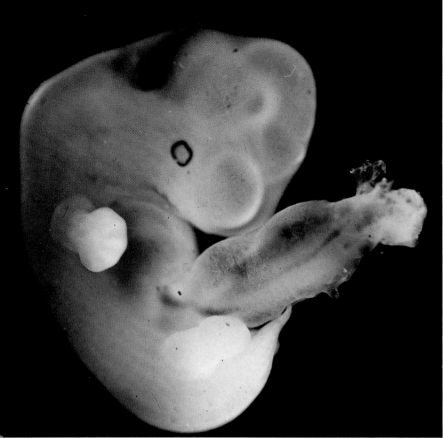

Development of the human hand. Above: At 4 weeks the hand and arm emerge from the the side of the embryo. Right: At 5 weeks the hand plates have formed.

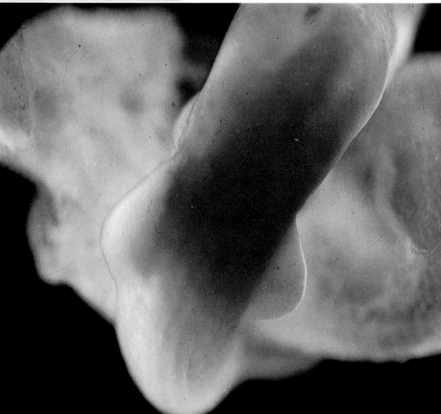

Above: At 18 weeks the fingers have developed with
rudimentary fingernails. Right: At 20 weeks the hand
can grasp, the thumb opposing the 4 fingers.

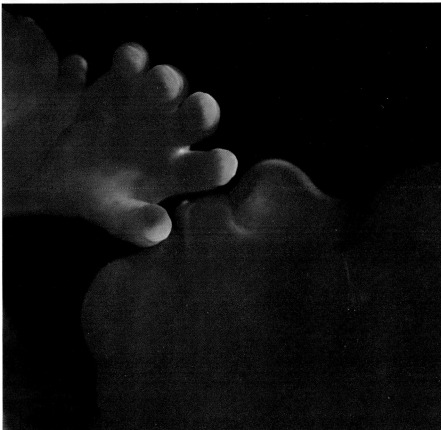

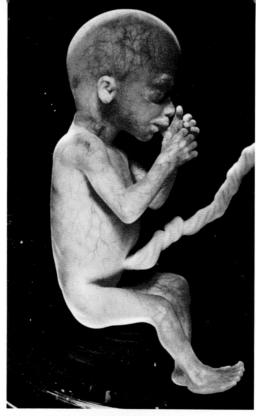

Left: Human fetus at 17 weeks, sucking its thumb.
Below: The newborn child. The nurturing process does not end with the severing of the umbilical cord. When the baby sucks the mother's breast, it eventually causes the release of a special hormone. This hormone, and another released at delivery, stimulate milk production.

upon nutrients received from its mother. These nutrients come by way of the placenta, the umbilical cord, and the tiny blood vessels of the fetus itself. During the fourth month the fetus doubles its size. The limbs now begin to catch up with the large head. Bones must replace cartilage in the skeleton. In fact, 222 bones are needed so that the fetus can remain vertical in the uterus. By the end of the second trimester the fetus has completed the development of its life systems. But it still could not survive outside the uterus without artificial support. The finishing touches are made in the last three months, and the chances of survival get better every day the fetus remains in the uterus. Vital stores of nutrients must still be absorbed. These include calcium for the skeleton, iron for the red blood cells, and protein for continued growth. The brain will localize control centers for speech, and for various sensory functions. These include vision, smell, and hearing. A system for controlling body temperature also develops. This is essential if the fetus is ever to live outside an incubator. Finally, in the ninth month, the fetus receives an additional aid to independent survival: antibodies against disease.

After so much preparation, the final adventure—birth—is at hand. Helped by the contractions of the uterus, the fetus normally turns itself upside down, and enters the world head first. It finally presents itself as a separate individual. When the baby is put to the mother's breast, it will often begin to suck vigorously. This sends impulses to the mother's brain center, which in turn signals the pituitary gland to release oxytocin. This hormone, and another released by the pituitary at birth, stimulate one more support system for the infant—the production of milk from the mother's breasts.

11 plant systems

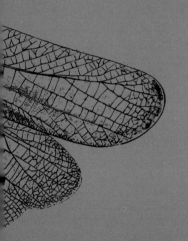

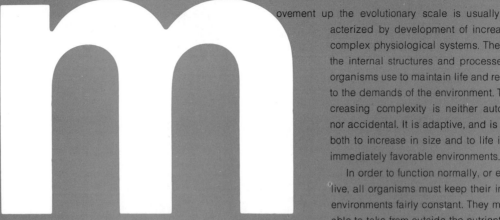

**m**ovement up the evolutionary scale is usually characterized by development of increasingly complex physiological systems. These are the internal structures and processes that organisms use to maintain life and respond to the demands of the environment. The increasing complexity is neither automatic nor accidental. It is adaptive, and is linked both to increase in size and to life in less immediately favorable environments.

In order to function normally, or even to live, all organisms must keep their internal environments fairly constant. They must be able to take from outside the nutrients, respiratory gases, and water they need. At the same time, they must wall out or dispose of harmful or unneeded substances. The external environment may be saltier, drier, hotter, wetter, or colder than the necessary internal environment. In such a case, the organism must be able to compensate. And the farther away a cell's position is from outside sources of supply, the more highly developed the system must be that brings substances to the cell.

By examining the specialized systems of higher plants, we can see the problems they must deal with in maintaining their life functions. While all living organisms are made up of cells, plant cells are different from animal cells in several important ways. These differences are strongly related to the ways in which a plant functions.

The first major difference between plant and animal cells is the rigid cell wall that surrounds the protoplast or living part of the plant cell. This cell wall serves several functions. It limits the size of the protoplast, provides rigidity to the cell, and acts as a channel for transport.

Another unique feature of plant cells is the presence of a vacuole or space in the middle of the cell. This vacuole is filled with a watery solution called cell sap. Many cell characteristics are determined by the transport of materials, particularly water, into and out of the vacuole.

A third significant difference is that dead cells play an important part in the activities of the plant. Dead cells leave behind their cell walls, which then function to strengthen the plant. They also aid in conducting water.

A final cellular difference is the presence of chloroplasts. Chloroplasts are found mostly in the cells of green leaves. There they carry out the essential process of photosynthesis.

Plants must be able to regulate moisture loss, so that they do not become dehydrated. They must be rigid enough to grow upward toward sunlight. And they must obtain nourishment from the soil. Every part of the plant — its stem, its root, and its leaves — reveals the specialized mechanisms that have enabled it to adapt and survive.

## Internal structure of plants

Each of the three main organs of the plant has a principal set of functions. Stems must lift the leaves up into the atmosphere where air and light are more available. They must also supply the leaves with water and distribute carbohydrates manufactured by the leaves. Roots anchor the plant in the soil and absorb nutrients. Leaves handle the function of photosynthesis. In addition, each of these organs may store food at certain times. With these points in mind, we will examine the features that enable each structure to carry out its role.

### The stem

The structural adaptations of the plant stem are related principally to the organ's chief functions — support and transport. Of the two, transport requires the more elborate equipment. The transport, or vascular, system is made up of two types of tissue. These are called the xylem and the phloem.

The **xylem** carries water and minerals from the ground through all parts of the plant. Because it consists of long, thick-walled cells, it also provides support for the plant. Almost all plant cells have a thin, rigid **primary wall** made of cellulose. Some cells, including many of those found in the

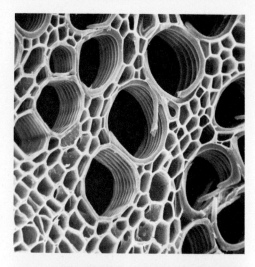

11-1
Scanning electron micrographs of xylem of *Ricinus*. Top: Transverse section. Bottom: Longitudinal section.

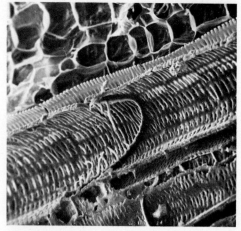

11-2
Conducting cells. (A) Tracheids. Perforated end walls permit water transport into overlapping cells. (B) Vessel elements. The lateral walls acquire secondary layers, but end walls progressively disintegrate. (C) Sieve cell. The mature cell retains a layer of cytoplasm, but its nucleus disintegrates. Its center contains a mass of fibrous protein material known as slime. No major changes occur in the organelles or cytoplasm of companion cells. Also, their nuclei are retained. (See The stem)

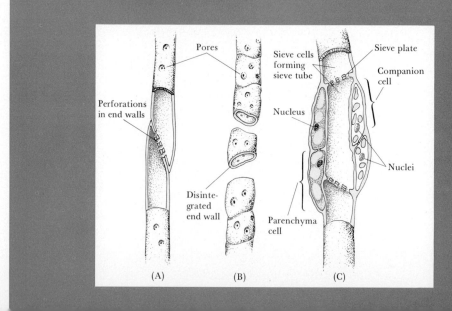

xylem, possess another thickening, the **secondary wall**. This is deposited on the inner side of the primary wall, and is thus the innermost wall layer. In addition to cellulose, this secondary wall may contain lignin, a complex organic substance which increases the rigidity of the layer. Wood is the mature xylem portion of tree trunks. It is hard and resistant to wear partly because its cells contain lignin in the secondary walls. The **middle lamella** coats the outer side of the primary wall. It serves to cement together adjacent cells.

Flowering plants have two types of conducting cell in the xylem—the **tracheids** and the **vessel elements**. Both types die at maturity. Their secondary walls remain, to function primarily as passageways for materials flowing through the plant. The tracheids are long cells arranged in an overlapping pattern. They exchange water through tiny holes in their cell walls. Vessel elements are arranged end to end. Their end walls are either lacking or partially disintegrated at maturity, so these cells form tubes or vessels through which water and other materials can flow.

The walls of tracheids and vessel elements provide support as a secondary function. But the thick-walled fibers also found in the xylem are primarily for support. These fibers are one of the two types of **sclerenchyma** cell found in plant tissue.

The only living cells in the xylem are the **parenchyma**, which are basic, unmodified cells. In young stems these help provide rigidity by pressing against each other. They may also act as padding, and they often store water and other materials.

In contrast to xylem, **phloem** tissue generally transports materials from their point of synthesis in the leaves to other parts of the plant. These materials include sugars and other organic molecules. The conducting cells of the phloem are the **sieve cells**. Sieve cells have perforated end walls called **sieve plates**, and are interconnected to form a **sieve tube**. Sieve cells remain alive at maturity, but lose their nucleus and

other cellular materials. They are connected by strands of cytoplasm to adjoining **companion cells**. Companion cells do not conduct materials. It is thought that they affect the maintenance of the sieve-tube cells. Phloem also contains parenchyma and sclerenchyma cells that function much as they do in the xylem.

*Dicotyledonous stems*  If we take a cross-section from the stem of a young herbaceous (nonwoody) dicotyledon and view it under a microscope, the **vascular bundles** stand out. They form a distinct ring about halfway between the center of the stem and the exterior. Each vascular bundle has large, moderately thick-walled, angular xylem cells toward the inside. Toward the outside are small, thin-walled angular phloem cells. Sclerenchyma fibers are scattered throughout. The xylem and the phloem are separated by the **vascular cambium**, a layer of small cells which appear brick-shaped in cross-section.

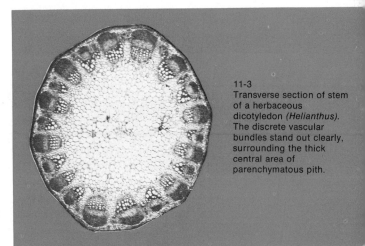

11-3
Transverse section of stem of a herbaceous dicotyledon *(Helianthus)*. The discrete vascular bundles stand out clearly, surrounding the thick central area of parenchymatous pith.

The remainder of the stem is composed largely of parenchyma cells. Those outside the vascular bundles form the **cortex**; those inside, the **pith**. Small parenchyma cells are also mingled with the xylem and phloem. The outermost layer of the stem is the protective **epidermis**. Epidermal cells have a thick outside wall that helps keep the plant from drying out. In addition, they

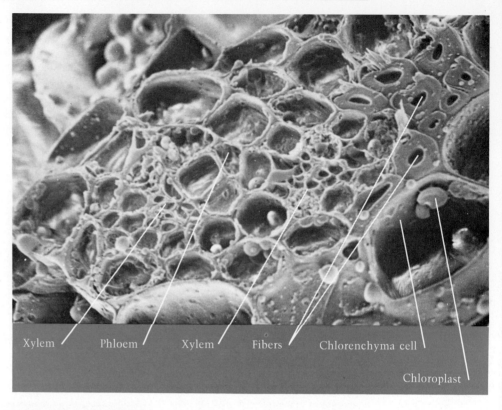

Xylem   Phloem   Xylem   Fibers   Chlorenchyma cell

Chloroplast

11-4
In the leaf and petiole (the thin stalk which attaches leaf to stem) fibers sometimes occur in association with the xylem and phloem to form vascular bundles. These provide support and a means of transporting water and nutrients. Parenchymal cells which contain chloroplasts are not considered part of the vascular bundle. (See Dicotyledonous stems)

manufacture a waxy substance called cutin. This combines with cellulose to form a protective surface known as the **cuticle**. Additional rigidity is provided by long, thick-walled **collenchyma** cells, which are found just inside the epidermis.

A cross-section of a mature, nonherbaceous dicotyledonous stem, such as a tree trunk, shows some significant differences between woody and nonwoody stems. The pith is still the same size as in the young stem, but it now occupies a far smaller proportion of the total diameter. Around the pith is a thick cylinder of **wood**, covered by a thin layer of **bark**. The wood is composed of old xylem cells, plus fibers and parenchyma. It serves principally for support. At its outer edge, just inside the cambium, is a ring of xylem still active in water transport. Outside the cambium is the bark. This contains an inner ring of phloem. Outside the phloem, the cortex and epidermis have been replaced by a surface layer of cork cells, which are continually produced by a

cork cambium. Pores called **lenticels** allow the cells under the new cork layers to respire. As the cork cells mature, their walls become impregnated with a waxy substance called suberin, forming the protective layers of the stem.

Why these changes? Obviously, the tree trunk must be strong enough to support a far greater weight of leaves and branches than the young stem. Furthermore, it must also be able to carry water and nutrients for all these leaves, and for a huge root system as well. It could not possibly do all this with the few vascular bundles of the young stem.

The process which creates the additional transportation and support tissue is called **secondary thickening**. The vascular cambium becomes a complete cylinder and starts dividing, producing new xylem cells on the inside and new phloem cells on the outside. These new tissues are known as **secondary xylem** and **phloem**. Secondary thickening continues throughout the life of the plant. Since the old xylem (but not

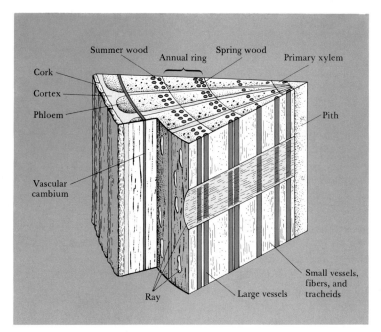

11-5
Segment of a woody dicotyledonous stem *(Quercus)*. Note the difference in size between the old xylem elements of spring and summer wood, resulting in visible annual rings. The rays are parenchymatous channels formed by the cambium. They facilitate the transverse passage of water and nutrients across the stem.

11-6
Top: transverse section of a monocotyledonous stem *(Zea)*. Bottom: Enlargement of one vascular bundle. Note orientation of bundles.

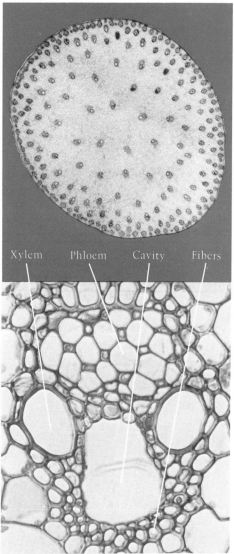

the old phloem) remains, the layers build up, and the trunk slowly grows stronger and thicker.

The cambium does not produce new cells at the same rate all year round. It is most active in the spring and slows down as the season progresses, ceasing completely in the winter. The size of the xylem elements also varies: those produced in the spring are often the largest. This difference in size produces concentric cylinders of xylem which form the **annual rings** seen on a cut tree trunk or stump. The number of rings tells us the age of a tree. Their thickness indicates variations in growing conditions.

The outer annual rings of the tree are called the **sapwood**. They are responsible for water transport. The older xylem, or **heartwood**, near the center has usually ceased to function in transport. Compounds such as tannin are deposited in the heartwood. They block the tubes and preserve the wood, so that it serves to add strength to the tree structure. We do not find annual rings in the phloem. The old phloem disintegrates as new phloem is formed each year.

*Monocotyledonous stems*   Most trees are dicotyledons. This is because monocotyledons in general lack a cambium, and thus cannot develop secondary thickening. All of their xylem and phloem is primary. That is, it was formed when the stem first developed and will never be increased or replaced. In the stems of herbaceous monocotyledons, such as corn, we find the same distinct vascular bundles as in young dicotyledons. But instead of being located in a ring, the bundles are scattered throughout the central region of the stem. Each bundle has an area of xylem on the side toward the center of the stem, and an area of phloem toward the outside. On each side is a large, mature, thick-walled xylem vessel, and between the two is a cavity. In the young stem, the cavity contained early-maturing protoxylem elements, which were later lost.

### The root

The main function of plant roots is to absorb water and nutrients and transport them to the stem. The root system must also be strong enough to anchor the plant in the soil, and adaptable enough to grow around obstructions. The pattern of the tissues in the fully formed root differs from that of the stem.

*Dicotyledonous roots*   In the root of a dicotyledon, the vascular tissue is located in the center of the root. There are no separate vascular bundles as in the stem. The primary xylem is at the center, and appears star-shaped in cross-section. Between the points of the star is the primary phloem, separated from the xylem by a layer of cambium. Outside the vascular tissue are some parenchyma cells which form the **pericycle**. These, in turn, are enclosed by a single-layered cylinder of cells called the **endodermis**. Each endodermal cell joins with other endodermal cells on four sides. These sides are banded by a waterproof structure called the **Casparian strip**. All tissues enclosed by the endodermis comprise the **stele**, or central core of the root. Outside the stele is the cortex, made up of parenchyma cells, and then a single-celled layer of epidermis.

The youngest parts of the root are specialized mainly for absorption. **Root hairs** grow out from the epidermis, near the tip of the root. These greatly increase the surface area of the root, aiding in water and mineral uptake. Root hairs are continually replaced as the root grows through the soil.

As roots grow older, their role shifts from absorption to transport of materials. They also begin to contribute more support to the plant. Secondary thickening increases the proportion of xylem in the root. This xylem functions in both water transport and support, as it does in the stem. The cambium cells, between the primary xylem and the phloem, begin to divide. They produce secondary xylem on the inside and secondary phloem on the outside. More xylem is made in the arcs of the star than at the points. The star shape is gradually lost, and the stele becomes a rod of central xylem surrounded by a cylinder of phloem. Outside the stele, cork is formed as it is in the stem, providing a protective covering for the mature roots.

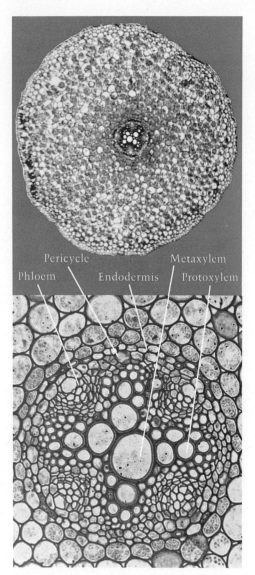

**11-7**
Transverse section of a young dicotyledonous root *(Ranunculus)*, with enlargement of central stele.

Pericycle  Phloem  Endodermis  Metaxylem  Protoxylem

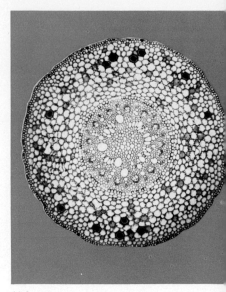

**11-8**
Transverse section of a monocotyledonous root *(Smilax)*.

*Monocotyledonous roots*   As was true of stems, the root of a monocotyledon has a different overall structure from that of a dicotyledon. The xylem and phloem are separate bundles. They alternate to form a ring just under the endodermis, so that a pith is present.

## The leaf

The functional tissues of the leaf are designed for maximum efficiency in producing carbohydrates. The xylem and phloem branch out, forming a network of veins. These veins collect the sugar produced by photosynthesis and distribute water to all parts of the leaf. Leaves are broad and thin to receive maximum light. Pores in their outer surfaces allow the exchange of gases during photosynthesis. The leaf is often shaped for a minimum of resistance to wind which might cause tearing.

*Dicotyledonous leaves*   The two surfaces of a dicotyledonous leaf differ somewhat in function. The upper surface re-

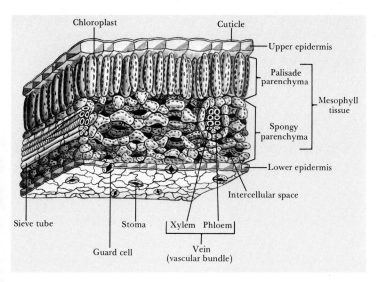

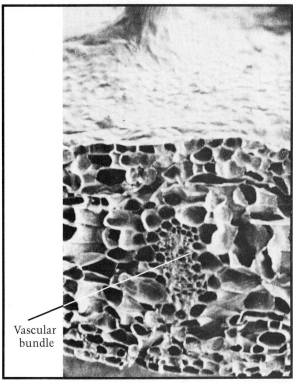

Vascular bundle

**11-9**
Cross section of leaf. The veins and layers of parenchyma cells (nearly all of which contain chloroplasts) comprise the mesophyll tissue. Large leaf veins (vascular bundles) may contain tracheids, sieve cells, vessel elements, and collenchyma cells (supportive cells which are elongated and thick-walled). Carbon dioxide entering through the stomata is accessible to the cells through interconnecting intercellular spaces.

ceives sunlight, and the lower carbon dioxide. The upper surface is protected by an epidermis covered with a waxy cuticle, which helps to decrease water loss. Below the upper epidermis are one or more layers of cylindrical cells, called the **palisade mesophyll**. These are specialized parenchyma cells, rich in chloroplasts for efficient photosynthesis.

Below this is the **spongy mesophyll**. The cells of this layer connect loosely with each other, leaving a large volume of air space between them. The resulting appearance is rather like that of a coarsely textured sponge. Finally, on the underside of the leaf, we find the lower epidermis. Like the upper, it is protected by a cuticle. It is also penetrated by the **stomata**, or pores. Each stoma is flanked by two specialized epidermal cells known as **guard cells**.

The most important function of the guard cells is to open and close the stomata. The guard cells' inner walls—on the side toward the stoma—are thicker than the outer ones.

Under certain circumstances, water moves into the guard cells from neighboring epidermal cells. This causes the guard cells to swell. Their thin outer walls puff out, pulling the thick inner walls apart and opening the stoma.

The stomata are the only openings in the virtually impermeable cuticle of the leaf. They are therefore vital in regulating the in-and-out flow of various gases. They permit the entry of carbon dioxide, essential to photosynthesis. They also allow the release of oxygen, which is a by-product of photosynthesis. To do this, however, the stomata must remain open during the day. As a result, large amounts of water vapor are also released through these openings. If the water loss becomes critical, the guard cells "wilt." This causes their inner walls to slacken, thus closing the stomata.

*Monocotyledonous leaves* The leaves of monocotyledons do not display such a clear two-level organization as dicotyle-

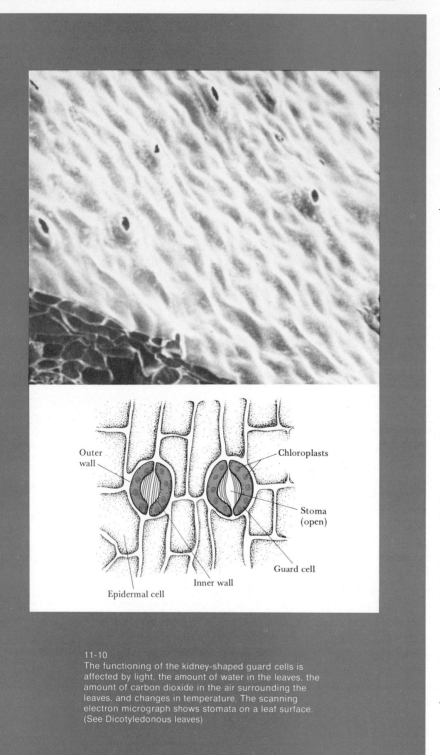

**11-10**
The functioning of the kidney-shaped guard cells is affected by light, the amount of water in the leaves, the amount of carbon dioxide in the air surrounding the leaves, and changes in temperature. The scanning electron micrograph shows stomata on a leaf surface. (See Dicotyledonous leaves)

Labels in figure:
Outer wall
Chloroplasts
Stoma (open)
Guard cell
Inner wall
Epidermal cell

donous leaves. In a monocotyledonous leaf the major veins run nearly parallel from the base to the tip of the leaf. They do not form a branching pattern.

# Water movement

The principal pathway of water movement in the plant is the xylem. Water is absorbed by the root hairs. It enters the xylem, and is then drawn up through the stem to all parts of the plant.

## Available water: the soil

Soil is essentially made up of tiny rock fragments produced from the underlying bedrock by weathering. The particles are classified according to size, sand being the coarsest and clay the finest. The soil also contains dead organic matter, water, dissolved salts, and living organisms. Only the salts and water are essential for plant nutrition. The other components provide anchorage, control nutrient balance, and enable oxygen to reach the roots.

Not all the water that reaches the soil is absorbed by it, and not all that is absorbed is available to the plant. The bulk of water that plants use is called **capillary water**. This is held in the spaces between soil particles by the forces of surface tension. The strength of the surface tension varies with the size of the soil particles. Sandy soil retains little water, but what it does retain is available to plants. Pure clay soil holds a great deal of water but does not release it as readily. The best soil type for supplying water to plants is a mixture of particles of all sizes. This mixture is called a **loam**, and contains a moderate amount of readily available water. Additional organic matter is also valuable, since it helps to loosen and aerate the soil.

## Cell – water relations

As in all organisms, the entrance of water into a plant and distribution of water through the plant is partly handled by diffusion across cell membranes. While diffusion is regulated by osmotic pressure and concentration gradient, an additional system operates in plant cells. This is **turgor pressure** or **pressure potential**. Turgor pressure builds up when water enters the vacuole and causes pressure against the fairly rigid cell wall. Diffusion of water through the membrane stops when the turgor pressure balances the tendency of water to diffuse into the cell. The cell is then **turgid**, imparting considerable rigidity to the surrounding tissue. This causes the stiffness of herbaceous stems, leaves, and flower stalks when there is adequate moisture. A loss of moisture—as on a hot afternoon in a dry field—causes a drop in turgor pressure, and eventually the plant wilts.

Turgor pressure alters the **water potential** of the cell. Water potential is the measurement of a cell's tendency to take up water under given conditions. It is determined by the combination of turgor pressure and osmotic potential. Normally, the osmotic potential of the cell sap inside the vacuole is always negative in relation to the water outside the cell. Therefore the cell "wants" to keep on taking in water. But

when the positive, "outward-pushing" turgor pressure inside the cell is high enough, it balances this negative osmotic potential, and no more water can diffuse in. We say that such a cell no longer has a negative water potential. A partly turgid cell has a slightly negative water potential. A cell that is not at all turgid has a very negative water potential.

Water diffuses along a **water potential gradient.** This gradient is the difference in water potential inside and outside the cell, or between cells. The water potential gradient determines water movement into the root from the soil, between adjacent cells in the plant, and from the plant into the air.

## Water uptake: the roots

When water is absorbed by the root hairs, it diffuses through the outer root tissue to the xylem, following a water potential gradient. During most of the journey, it may move either through the cell walls or through the living cells. But between the cortex and the

**11-11**
A good device for measuring the water potential of a shoot, and the negative pressure in a stem, is the pressure bomb. When a shoot is cut, tension in the xylem is released, and the surrounding cells can take up water. This causes the water to recede into the xylem from the cut end. The shoot is placed in the bomb, and pressure is applied by nitrogen gas to squeeze the cells back to their former size. The pressure at which the xylem sap is forced back to the cut surface equals the tension previously existing in the xylem. It thus gives a measurement of the water potential of the shoot. (See Cell-water relations and Water movement: the xylem)

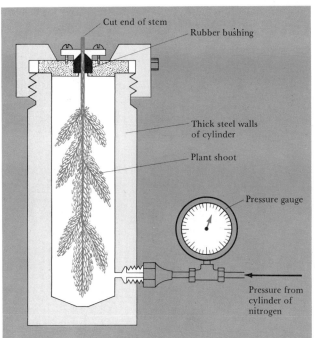

**11-12**
Water movement along a water potential gradient between pure water and a cell, and between two cells. The water potential (WP) of each cell is the sum of the osmotic potential (OP) of its cell sap and the cell wall pressure (P), which increases as the cell becomes more turgid.

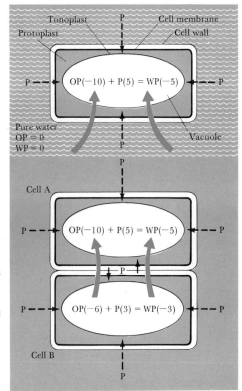

stele of the root, the water encounters the endodermis. The waterproof Casparian strip of the endodermal cells makes all their side walls impermeable to water. Here, therefore, the water can travel only through the living cell. Thus the root as a whole makes up an osmotic system. The soil solution and the cortex form the outside of the system, the xylem and other tissues of the stele form the inside, and the endodermis acts as the membrane. The xylem of the root has a negative water potential. So water diffuses into the plant through the endodermis just as it would into a cell.

## Water loss: the leaves

As water enters the plant through the roots, it also escapes from the leaves, largely through the stomata. The stomata are open during much of the day to permit photosynthesis to occur. As a result, water vapor diffuses out. The loss of water vapor from the leaf is called **transpiration**.

The rate of transpiration is affected by a number of factors. Air, like cells, has a water potential, so a gradient is set up between the air and the interior of the leaf. Anything that alters the relative humidity of the surrounding air will influence the steepness of this water potential gradient. The gradient will also be affected by the **water status** of the leaf—that is, by whether the plant is receiving abundant water from moist soil or insufficient water from dry soil. Wind also plays a part. It can increase transpiration by blowing saturated air away from the leaf, thus increasing the water potential gradient.

During the day, plants continually lose water through transpiration. This prevents the plant cells from becoming fully turgid, even under the optimum conditions of a warm, sunny day with adequate moisture in the soil. But at night, transpiration slows down, allowing water movement into the plant to exceed loss. When this happens, the cells slowly swell until they are turgid. Then water uptake stops.

Transpiration may pose a danger to the

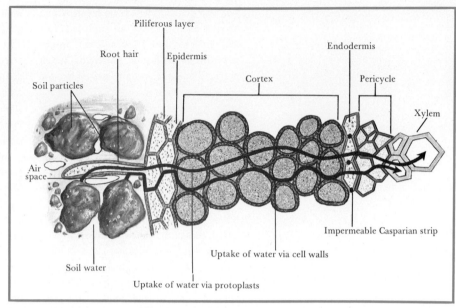

11-13
Water movement through the root, from soil to xylem, with enlargement of endodermal cell showing Casparian strip. It is this strip which forces water to cross through the cell at this point. It thus creates the osmotic system of the root as a whole. The piliferous layer is the outermost layer of the epidermis. It gives rise to the root hairs. (See Water uptake: the roots)

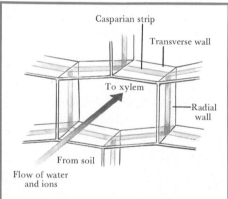

plant's survival, for when the soil is dry, the loss of water from the leaves exceeds uptake by the roots. When this happens, the protoplast shrinks and turgor pressure decreases until it reaches zero. In this situation, the plant will wilt. If the protoplast shrinks further, it will separate from the cell wall. This condition is known as **plasmolysis**. At this point the plant becomes permanently wilted. It is unlikely to recover, even if it is given water.

If severe water shortage occurs, the plant can reduce water loss somewhat by closing the stomata, even in the daytime. This cannot prevent permanent wilting under extreme conditions. However, it helps the plant to deal with transitional periods, such as the hours of late afternoon. Transient wilting, which commonly occurs late in the day, is remedied in the evening when the relative humidity increases. The stomata then close, reducing transpiration. Water uptake continues, now in excess of water loss, and the water deficit disappears.

## Water movement: the xylem

Once the water enters the xylem tissue of the root, the xylem distributes it upward to the stem and leaves. The water flows as a

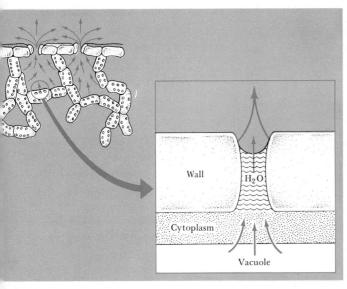

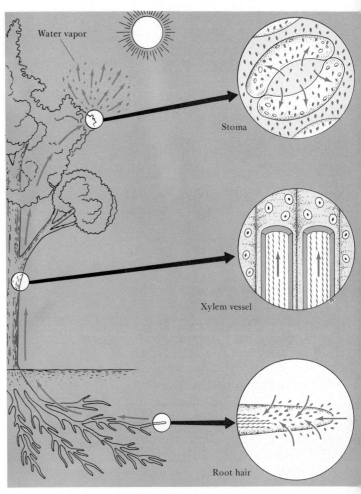

**11-14**
Diffusion of water vapor from the substomatal cavity (an air chamber below the stomata, within the spongy mesophyll) into the drier air outside lowers the relative humidity of the cavity. It causes water to evaporate into it from the microcapillaries of the surrounding cell walls. Because the stomata are spaced as they are on the leaf surface, the escaping water vapor can disperse quickly, keeping the rate of transpiration high. (See Water loss: the leaves)

continuous rising column through pipes made up of a chain of open-ended xylem vessel cells. Some water moves out laterally to supply the surrounding tissues at each stage. The rest reaches the leaves for use as needed, or for final diffusion out of the plant by transpiration.

But what is the power which drives this rising flow? For a long time plant physiologists were puzzled by this question. A mechanical suction pump can lift water only to a height of 10 meters—the extent to which the column of water is supported by the single atmosphere of air pressure exerted on the liquid around the intake pipe. Yet water flows upward through dead xylem pipes to the tops of trees which may reach 100 meters in height. To lift water to this height requires either a pressure of at least 10 bars at the base or a corresponding tension (negative pressure) at the top. We now know that the water in the xylem is in fact under tension, created by negative water potentials in excess of −10 bars at the top of the trees. The cause of these negative water potentials is the very negative water potential of the atmosphere, which can reach −1,000 bars.

So this is the driving force which sucks the water all the way up to the top of the tree (and into the air) from the soil solution. Wa-

ter vapor in the cavities of the spongy mesophyll, just below the stomata, is close to saturation. Therefore it diffuses through the stomata into the atmosphere. This water is replaced from the nearby cell walls. The water taken from the cell walls is replaced, in turn, by more water, drawn from more distant cells. The same process continues on back to the xylem in the leaf, and thence down to the root, where it causes water uptake from the soil. Thus the water is pulled all the way up through the plant by the evaporating power of the atmosphere. This force is called **transpiration pull**.

When this idea was originally proposed, it was objected that a column of water under such extreme tension would pull apart. However, it was possible to show that water

**11-15**
The path of transpiration pull in a typical tree. (See Water movement: the xylem)

11-16
An aphid feeding on a plant stem inserts its stylet deep into the phloem to extract the sweet liquid. If the stylet is cut, and the aphid removed, phloem sap will continue to exude through the stylet. This demonstrates that the contents of the phloem are indeed under pressure. (See Solute translocation)

Stylet

Phloem

molecules cling to one another, and to the walls of the xylem, with cohesive forces well in excess of the tensions in the xylem.

## Solute translocation

Sugar is produced by photosynthesis in the leaves. While water travels up the plant through the xylem, the sugar travels to all other parts of the plant through the phloem. We can demonstrate this by making a shallow cut all around a living stem, severing the phloem. The leaves will remain healthy, but the stem above the cut will swell from the accumulation of sugars and the roots will die. The phloem may transport amino acids, hormones, and minerals, as well as sugars.

Movement in the phloem is "from source to sink"—from the leaves or food storage organs to the various points in the plant where sugars are used. To understand this movement, we must first recall the structure of the phloem sieve tubes. These tubes consist of thin-walled, elongated cells, with perforated end walls called sieve plates. The cell membranes divide the sieve tubes into a series of osmotic chambers. The sugars move through these chambers in a bulk flow process called **mass flow**. Sugar is taken into the phloem in the leaf by an active process. This increases the tendency of water to move into the phloem in the leaf by an active process. This increases the tendency of water to move into the phloem cells. Water is drawn in from the surrounding leaf cells, creating pressure and pushing the sweet sap on down the phloem. At the other end, sugar is actively removed and water diffuses out.

Mass flow is an osmotically driven process. If phloem cells are killed or their metabolism is stopped, sugar is not transported. Some scientists argue that phloem transport shows the use of more energy than is needed just to maintain the membranes required for osmosis. But it seems clear that some active mechanism, in addition to active uptake in the leaves, must also contribute to phloem transport. The nature of this active process is not yet understood.

# Nutrition

Although it is generally known that plants photosynthesize and that crops need fertilizer, we know much less about what nutrients are actually required by the plant, and about how the plant distributes and uses them.

## Nutrient requirements and the soil

An early scientist working on plant nutrition found that a willow tree in a pot grew from 2 to 100 kilograms, while the soil lost only 30 grams. He considered this 30-gram loss to be within the limits of experimental error, and concluded that the water consumed by the plant provided everything the plant needed for nutrition. However, he was wrong. A plant grown in distilled water, without soil, will soon sicken and die.

Unlike animals, plants can manufacture all of the organic nutrients they require. But they must be supplied with the inorganic materials from which to do so. For most of these materials the ordinary source of supply is the soil. We saw earlier that certain elements, particularly carbon, hydrogen, oxygen, nitrogen, and phosphorous, make up the structure of the organic molecules which are the building blocks of life—proteins, nucleic acids, carbohydrates, and lipids. Of these elements, plants can normally obtain nitrogen and phosphorus only from the soil. Plants require other elements in smaller quantities. Among these are sulfur, which is essential for proteins; magnesium for chlorophyll; and calcium, to form the midpart of the cell wall. Another major element is potassium. Its function is not entirely clear, although it may be important in maintaining the osmotic balance of cells. These elements, with nitrogen and phosphorus, are commonly known as **macronutrients**.

Still other elements, the **micronutrients**, are needed only in minute amounts. Even so, the lack of these nutrients can be cata-

11-17 Principal minerals utilized by plants.

| Element | Taken up as | Typical percent of plant dry weight | Function |
|---|---|---|---|
| **Macronutrients** | | | |
| Nitrogen | $NO_3^-$ | 2.5 | Constituent of amino acids, proteins, nucleic acids, chlorophyll, hormones. |
| Phosphorus | $H_2PO_4^-$ | 0.3 | Important as constituent of proteins, nucleic acids, phospholipids; also in energy metabolism: ATP and coenzymes. |
| Potassium | $K^+$ | 1.5 | Role uncertain. Maintains osmotic balance of cells, e.g., guard cells of stomata; needed for protein synthesis and action of some enzymes. |
| Calcium | $Ca^{++}$ | 0.5 | Constituent of cell walls; constituent as calcium pectate of the middle lamella. |
| Magnesium | $Mg^{++}$ | 0.3 | Constituent of chlorophyll; involved in numerous enzymatic reactions; stabilizes ribosomes. |
| Sulfur | $SO_4^{--}$ | 0.2 | Constituent of proteins and coenzyme-A. |
| **Micronutrients** | | | |
| Iron | $Fe^{++(+)}$ | 0.05 | Needed in energy transfer molecules in respiration and photosynthesis; also chlorophyll synthesis. |
| Chlorine | $Cl^-$ | 0.2 | Needed for photosynthesis. |
| Copper | $Cu^{++}$ | 0.001 | Constituent and activator of various enzymes. |
| Manganese | $Mn^{++}$ | 0.05 | Constituent and activator of enzymes involved in photosynthesis, respiration, nitrogen metabolism. |
| Zinc | $Zn^{++}$ | 0.03 | Constituent and activator of various enzymes; needed for synthesis of auxin (a hormone) and protein. |
| Molybdenum | $MoO_4^{--}$ | 0.0001 | Involved in nitrogen metabolism and fixation. |
| Boron | $BO_3^-$ | 0.05 | Uncertain; possibly active in translocation of sugar, and in absorption and utilization of calcium. |

strophic for the plant. For example, iron is needed for the energy transfer molecules involved in respiration and photosynthesis. Copper, manganese, and zinc activate certain enzyme systems needed to carry out vital metabolic reactions. Absence or shortage of any nutrient element causes characteristic deficiency diseases.

Under certain conditions, plants can be grown in a solution of distilled water to which these mineral nutrients have been added. Does this mean that soil and organic matter are not really needed for healthy plant growth? Strictly speaking, they are not. But in a natural situation, they both play valuable roles. The soil particles support the plant and enable the roots to obtain air and water. Organic matter helps to hold water, and also contains the whole range of plant nutrients. When plants are grown in solution the roots cannot respire unless the solution is continually aerated. And while

necessary plant nutrients can be supplied by fertilizer, modern pure fertilizers do not ordinarily contain the micronutrients. Under natural conditions, these are provided by the remains of other plants and animals.

## Nutrient uptake

Minerals are absorbed from the soil not only by diffusion but by active processes at the cell membranes. In fact, most of the negatively charged ions important in plant nutrition, such as nitrate ($NO_3^-$) and phosphate ($H_2PO_4^-$) are actively taken up by the cells. In some cases a positively charged nonnutrient ion, such as $Na^+$, passively enters the cell in excessive amounts. That ion is then actively pumped out of the cell.

Once nutrients are absorbed into the root hair, they travel approximately the same path as water, and are carried to all parts of the plant. Active transport may be involved in getting them into and out of the

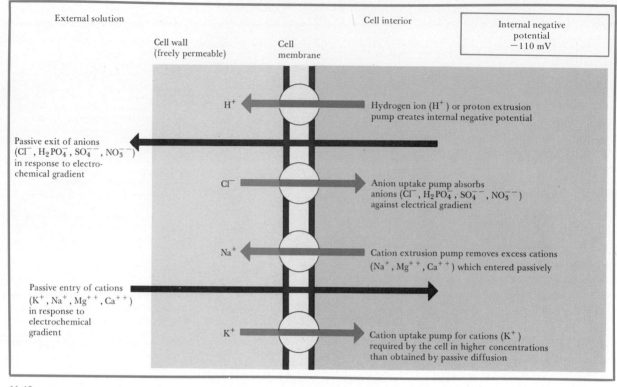

External solution

Cell interior

Cell wall
(freely permeable)

Cell
membrane

Internal negative
potential
−110 mV

$H^+$

Hydrogen ion ($H^+$) or proton extrusion
pump creates internal negative potential

Passive exit of anions
($Cl^-$, $H_2PO_4^-$, $SO_4^{--}$, $NO_3^{--}$)
in response to electro-
chemical gradient

$Cl^-$

Anion uptake pump absorbs
anions ($Cl^-$, $H_2PO_4^-$, $SO_4^{--}$, $NO_3^-$)
against electrical gradient

$Na^+$

Cation extrusion pump removes excess cations
($Na^+$, $Mg^{++}$, $Ca^{++}$) which entered passively

Passive entry of cations
($K^+$, $Na^+$, $Mg^{++}$, $Ca^{++}$)
in response to
electrochemical
gradient

$K^+$

Cation uptake pump for cations ($K^+$)
required by the cell in higher concentrations
than obtained by passive diffusion

11-18
Some of the active and
passive processes
involved in maintaining
proper ionic
concentration in the
cells. Active pumping of
some ions through the
cell membrane creates a
favorable electro-
chemical potential
gradient for the passive
diffusion of others, both
into and out of the cell.
(See Nutrient uptake)

xylem, both in the root and when they reach
the leaves. Throughout the plant, the ions
are then synthesized into various compounds, or used in the control of cellular
metabolism.

### Nitrogen metabolism

While nitrogen is abundant in the atmosphere in gaseous form, plants cannot use
it in this state. The nitrogen they use is taken
up from the soil as ionic compounds. Several processes provide these materials to the
plant.

One process is the addition of nitrogen
compounds to the soil from the atmosphere.
Nitrate is the most important of these compounds. It is formed when lightning or ultraviolet light binds together nitrogen and
oxygen in the air. Living organisms also
convert atmospheric nitrogen into organic
compounds, through a process called nitrogen fixation. This is accomplished by
bacteria living free in the soil or in plant
roots, particularly roots of members of the

pea family (Leguminosae). Free-living bacteria reduce atmospheric nitrogen to ammonia. The ammonia is then incorporated
into organic compounds or excreted into
the soil or water. The root-dwelling bacteria
invade the root hairs of the host plant and
penetrate into the cortex. There they cause
the cells to multiply, forming a small knob
or root nodule. The bacteria draw carbohydrates from the plant for their food supply,
and meanwhile fix nitrogen, much of which
they release into the plant as amino acids.
Still other bacteria recycle organic matter in
the soil, producing nitrogen compounds
that plants can use.

Nitrogen is usually taken up from the
soil as nitrate. The nitrate is immediately
reduced to nitrite and then to ammonium.
This ammonium is toxic and cannot be allowed to accumulate in the plant. Therefore
it is quickly transformed into glutamic acid,
a simple amino acid, and in this form is
transported through the plant. Other amino
acids are made in the cells where they are

needed, using the nitrogen contained in the glutamic acid.

## Photosynthesis

Like all the other processes we have studied, photosynthesis depends on the availability in the environment of certain necessary materials. In this case the determinants are carbon dioxide in the atmosphere and the light striking the leaf.

*Carbon dioxide supply*    Plant leaves are so efficient at removing carbon dioxide from the atmosphere that in summer, when many leaves are present, an insufficient supply may result in lowered photosynthetic rates. On the other hand, a high carbon dioxide concentration can increase the rate of photosynthesis. This effect is utilized in the management of some greenhouse crops, such as tomatoes, in Europe. The carbon dioxide content of the greenhouse air is artificially increased to raise the level of photosynthesis, particularly in northern Europe where sunlight is not very strong.

*Light intensity*    Just as higher carbon dioxide levels can increase photosynthesis, so can higher light intensity. Without any light, photosynthesis will not occur and carbon dioxide will be produced through respiration. At low light intensity, respiration may still exceed photosynthesis. But as light intensity increases, photosynthesis increases also. Eventually a **compensation point** is reached, at which photosynthesis equals respiration. If light intensity continues to increase, photosynthesis will then exceed respiration, until it reaches a point at which the plant is saturated with light energy. After this, further increase in light intensity will not increase photosynthesis.

In a field, at the light intensity which will saturate a single leaf, many of the lower leaves in a crop do not receive sufficient light. Only a small fraction of the light striking the upper leaves can filter through them to those below. The second layer of leaves usually receives about 10 percent of the light striking the top layer, and the third layer only 1 percent. Therefore, the best light intensity for a crop is far above that required for a single isolated leaf.

The arrangement and angle of the leaves help to determine how much light will pass to the leaf layers below. The more upright the leaves of a crop, the more sunlight can reach the lower layers, the more efficiently the plants can utilize full sun-

11-19
Nodules formed by sumbiotic nitrogen-fixing bacteria on soybeam roots. Farmers plant beans to encourage such bacteria and increase the nitrogen content of the soil. (See Nitrogen metabolism)

light, and the greater the leaf area that can be supported on a given area of ground. In agriculture these concepts are an important influence on choice of crops, planting time, and development of new crop varieties. Crops can be grown most efficiently if they have their maximum leaf area in midsummer, when the sun is high in the sky and light intensities are greatest.

# Respiration

Unlike higher animals, plants have not developed an elaborate system for taking in certain gases and releasing others into the atmosphere. Still, they do have to supply oxygen to their cells, in order to fuel the processes of cellular respiration. They can do so because the entire surface of the plant is porous enough to admit a considerable amount of oxygen. Roots can absorb oxygen by diffusion. In daylight the leaves produce oxygen by photosynthesis and it can also diffuse through the stomata. Even the lenticels in the bark of the stem lead to intercellular spaces through which gases can easily pass. In fact, the entire plant is filled with interconnected, intercellular air spaces for gaseous exchange.

## Photorespiration

It has recently been shown that some plants respire more in the light than in the dark. This is actually not true respiration, which involves glycolysis and the Krebs cycle. Instead, it is a direct breakdown of photosynthetic products, with the release of carbon dioxide. Thus **photorespiration**, as it is called, is a wasteful process. Lack of photorespiration may account for the increased dry matter production of some plants as compared to others. For instance, soybeans photorespire but corn does not. Corn is thus a more efficient producer. Plant breeders are now trying to develop varieties of photorespiring plants which will photorespire less, in order to increase their net photosynthesis. This may eventually prove to be an important means of increasing crop yields.

## Lower plants

We have seen that lower and higher plants are distinguished by their methods of reproduction. They differ also in the degree to which their nonreproductive tissues are specialized. At the simplest end of the scale are the marine plants; at the most complex, the vascular plants. Our discussion of plant systems has focused thus far on the vascular plants. However, we should also consider briefly the more limited — and limiting — systems of their less specialized relatives.

### Marine plants

For the most part, marine photosynthetic organisms have avoided the need for tissue specialization. Since they live in the ocean where all life began, their external environment has a temperature and chemical composition much like what they need internally. Their generally thin or narrow body shapes keep all cells in close contact with that environment. Thus nutrition, respiration, and elimination of wastes can be carried on almost entirely at the cellular level. The root-like holdfast, the stem-like stipe, and the leaf-like blade of some larger algae are specialized only for functions related to their shape. They do not possess xylem, phloem, or other differentiated tissue of true roots, stems, and leaves. But even here, body size has contributed to a beginning of specialization. Kelp, the largest of the seaweeds, possesses a simple apparatus. It is rather like the sieve cells of phloem, which speed transport of the products of photosynthesis down from the sunlit surface to the darker regions far below.

Fresh-water plants, interestingly, are mostly vascular — angiosperms which have left the land and readapted to aquatic life. Thus they are to be considered as higher, not lower plants.

### Bryophytes

For plants to invade the land successfully, more specialization was needed. The bryo-

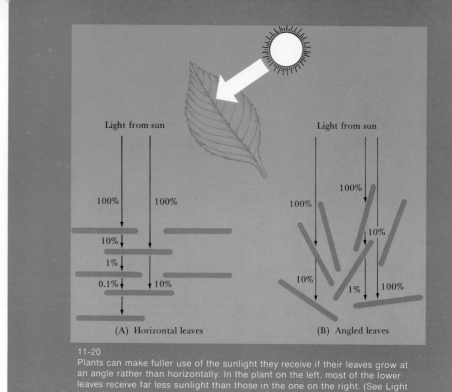

11-20
Plants can make fuller use of the sunlight they receive if their leaves grow at an angle rather than horizontally. In the plant on the left, most of the lower leaves receive far less sunlight than those in the one on the right. (See Light intensity)

phytes achieved this specialization only in part. For this reason, most of them are concentrated in relatively moist and protected environments. Like the algae, they have no vascular tissue. They continue to absorb water and mineral nutrients through exposed thin surfaces, which render them vulnerable to drying. However, some mosses do have a protective waxy cuticle, and take up water principally from the soil, through root-like rhizoids. Other bryophytes, the thallose liverworts, have thick, blade-like bodies, which probably help to conserve moisture and which are divided into specialized layers for photosynthesis and food storage. It is clear that such plants have begun to adapt to the specific demands of life on land. But it is only a beginning.

## Fungi

The fungi differ from plants and animals partly in that even the largest of them manage with very simple physiological structures. They are heterotrophic, requiring organic nutrients as animals do. But they take

in these nutrients by absorption rather than ingestion. That is, fungi secrete digestive enzymes onto the substrate on which they grow, dissolving it into liquid form. The dissolved nutrients are then absorbed through the thin wall. Once inside the cell, nutrients are distributed by **cytoplasmic streaming** — the steady circulating movement of the cytoplasm. This simple means of transport appears to suffice even in long hyphae.

As with the unspecialized marine plants, however, this simplicity imposes limitations. Most fungi are either quite small (as, for example, bread mold) or else are restricted to protected environments — below ground level or within the tissues of the host. Only in this way can they remain moist and keep the greatest possible surface area in contact with the nourishing substrate. Furthermore, each type can grow only on those substrates which its particular enzymes can digest. In some cases this allows a very limited range of habitat. We may note that the slime molds, which move about during a part of their life cycle, are adapted to a somewhat more varied diet than many of their sessile relatives.

**summary**

Higher plants have three main vegetative structures — stem, root, and leaf. Their anatomy depends upon whether the plant is a monocot or a dicot. Monocot stems have vascular bundles scattered throughout. The stems of dicots have vascular bundles in a ring, and may develop secondary thickening. Monocot roots have xylem and phloem as separate bundles alternating in a ring. Dicots have primary xylem at the center of the root in the shape of a star, with primary phloem between the points of the star. These two vascular tissues are separated by a layer of cambium. Monocot leaves have parallel veins and a less distinct two-level structure than dicots. The upper surface of a dicot leaf takes in sunshine. The lower surface takes in carbon dioxide. The vascular tissue is in the form of branching veins.

In both monocots and dicots the xylem contains two types of conducting cells: the tracheids (long, overlapping cells with pores in their cell walls) and the vessel elements (cells set end-to-end with end walls at least partially gone to form tubes). Xylem also contains thick-walled supporting fibers, the sclerenchyma cells. The only living cells in the xylem are the parenchyma, which are often used for storage.

The conducting cells in the phloem are the sieve cells. They have perforated end walls and are connected to companion cells by cytoplasmic strands. Unlike the sieve cells, these companion cells have nuclei. Parenchyma and sclerenchyma are also found in the phloem.

Most water used by plants is called capillary water. It is held in the pores between soil particles. The entry of water into a plant and its distribution through the plant is partially a process of diffusion across cell membranes. Along with osmotic pressure and concentration gradient, turgor pressure regulates diffusion in plant cells. Water entering a cell vacuole builds up turgor pressure until it balances the tendency of water to diffuse into the cell. The cell can then take in no more water.

The loss of water from a leaf is called transpiration.

If water loss through transpiration persistently exceeds uptake, the protoplast will shrink and separate from the cell wall. The resulting fatal condition is called plasmolysis. The evaporating power of the atmosphere is called transpiration pull. This power is responsible for bringing water from the roots into the upper regions of a plant.

Sugar, on the other hand, is distributed downward from the leaves to the rest of the plant through the phloem. Sugars are moved through sieve cells in an osmotically driven process called mass flow.

Plants must be supplied with the inorganic elements from which they manufacture organic elements. Some inorganic elements are needed in large quantities (macronutrients), and others in small quantities (micronutrients).

Photosynthesis can be increased by greater intensity of light and higher concentrations of carbon dioxide. Upper leaves transmit only a small fraction of the light which strikes them to the leaves below. Thus, leaf arrangement and angle are important in determining how much light reaches lower leaves. Respiration depends upon oxygen, which is in abundant supply in the porous interior of the plant. Photorespiration involves the direct breakdown of photosynthetic products, with a release of carbon dioxide.

In contrast to the higher land plants, marine plants have generally avoided the need for tissue specialization. They possess thin bodies which keep all cells in close contact with the environment. These plants can therefore carry on the processes of nutrition, respiration, and elimination almost entirely at the cellular level. The bryophytes began to specialize for survival on the land by developing the means to take up water from the soil and to conserve body moisture. Fungi have managed to survive with exceedingly simple physiological structures, depending upon absorption rather than ingestion for nourishment. Most fungi have remained small in order to minimize water loss and maximize contact surface with the nourishing substrate.

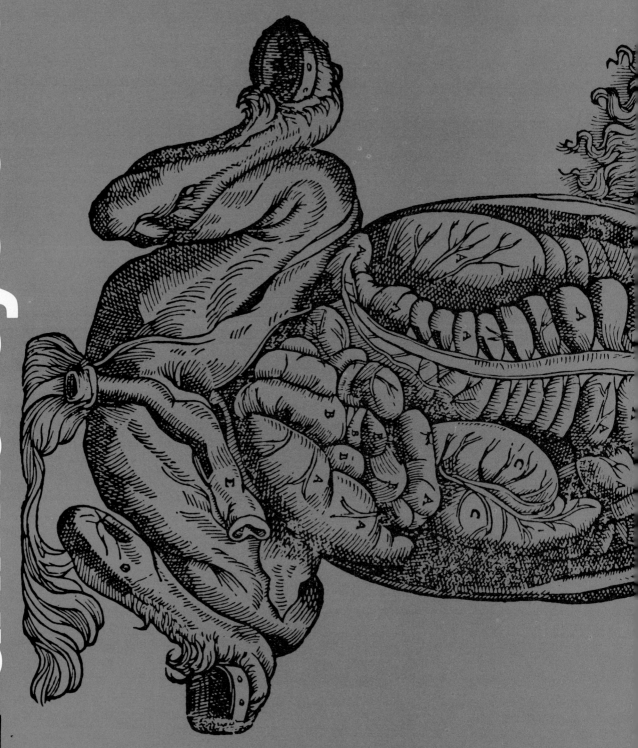

12 animal systems

**a** distinctive and important characteristic of animals is that they can move. Both land plants and fungi stay in one place once they start to grow. Even free-floating aquatic plants cannot voluntarily move elsewhere if their water dries up or becomes polluted. So if the immediate environment varies beyond their range of tolerance, individual plants die. Species survival must then depend on hard-coated seeds and spores which can lie dormant for years or centuries until conditions improve. But, in general, animals can move—to seek their food, to escape predators, and to find their mates. This has a good deal to do, both as cause and as effect, with the way in which their physiological systems have developed.

Animals share with plants the basic needs of all living organisms. Like plants, they require a supply of materials for synthesizing vital substances and for energy production. They must be able to process these materials, distribute them, and remove waste products. Finally, they need regulatory mechanisms to direct and control these life functions.

In single-celled organisms, all of these conditions are met within the cell or in its immediate environment. Materials pass directly through the cell membrane, or are converted externally by special secretions from the cell, and then absorbed. Transport and waste removal present no great problems because distances are so small. Regulation can be accomplished by mechanisms within the cell itself.

But multicelled animals have greater problems. These are due both to their size and to the varying specializations of their cells. Some of the individual cells of such animals cannot carry out these processes. Others are able to, but they are often so far removed from the necessary raw materials that these cells would starve, suffocate, or be poisoned by their own wastes if there were no system of supply and distribution. Simple diffusion is no longer sufficient.

The physiological systems of animals are shaped both by these basic needs and by the environment, or range of environments, in which the animal must live. In a sense, the most successful animals are the most flexible ones—those whose systems allow them to function in the widest range of environments. Such flexibility requires a complex internal structure—much more complex than anything we have seen in even the highest plants. In this chapter, we shall see how animals have developed from the very simple systems of the lowest forms to the highly sensitive and precise systems of the most advanced.

## Modes of nutrition

An animal's diet and means of obtaining it are closely related to its habitat and body structure. For example, all truly sessile animals are aquatic. Since they must depend on their environment to bring food to them, water is best for the purpose. Many such animals—clams, for instance—are **filter feeders**. They sieve water through gills or some other apparatus, extracting small food particles and letting the water flow on by. Others, such as the coelenterates, have a circular body plan and a set of tentacles which allow them to sweep food from a more or less extended area into the central mouth.

But neither of these feeding devices is unique to sessile animals. Some of the largest whales, for example, are filter feeders. Squid and octopuses, too, combine the radially symmetrical coelenterate body plan with swift, agile swimming. Similarly, other structural patterns and feeding systems repeat themselves at various phylogenetic levels. They are thus shown to be adaptively valuable in a wide range of situations. Aphids, for example, are **fluid feeders**. They insert their sensitive stylets into plant stems to suck out the juices. Mosquitoes are also fluid feeders, but so are vampire bats, which are not insects but mammals.

Another group which could also be considered fluid feeders borrow their technique from the fungi, secreting digestive

12-1
Sea anemone (a coelenterate) devouring a fish. The fish failed to recognize the bright-colored circle of tentacles for the deadly weapons they really are. (See Modes of nutrition)

enzymes outside their bodies to dissolve solid food before sucking it in. We have already seen this method in the starfish. Some insects also use it, notably the giant water bug, which can thus kill and devour animals as large as a small frog.

It is usual to classify most vertebrates not so much by their mode of feeding (which is generally by jaws and teeth in any case), as by their type of food. Thus we speak of plant-eating **herbivores**, meat-eating **carnivores**, and **omnivores** which eat both meat and plants.

## Digestive systems

No matter what the food is or how it is gotten, the process of digesting it is basically the same. Digestive enzymes must break it down into its component molecules so that it can be absorbed into the tissues of the eater. Furthermore, if the food particles are large, they must first be broken down mechanically, so that the enzymes have adequate surface area on which to work. In some small-particle eaters, digestion is almost entirely intracellular. In the majority of animals, however, some or most of it occurs in a special digestive cavity.

Some animals bypass the whole problem of digestion. They are parasites, such as tapeworms, that spend their lives in the blood or digestive tract of their hosts. Bathed continually in a nourishing bath of predigested food, they simply assimilate and use it, leaving the host to do all the work.

*Intracellular systems*   The sponge has about the simplest digestive system possible for a multicellular organism. The many pores or channels which penetrate the sponge's body on all sides lead to a central main channel or cavity. These channels are lined with flagellated cells. The flagella beat steadily, moving a current of sea water in through the pores, along the main channel, and out by another opening. As tiny particles of food are swept within reach by the current, they are seized by the flagella

12-2
Giant water bug with prey. It is suspended just below the surface by a bubble of air under its wing covers. The water bug grasps its prey with its long legs. Then it injects fast-acting digestive enzymes through its stylet. This dissolves most of the victim's body tissues into liquid food.

and ingested, phagocytically or pinocytically, by the cells. Digestion takes place intracellularly. Lysosomes fuse with the food vacuoles, and their enzymes digest the particles in the usual way. Thus in one sense the sponge's digestive system is really only a food-procurement system. The individual cells work together only to create the currents that bring the food within reach.

*The gastrovascular cavity*   A digestive system like that of the sponge has certain disadvantages. The principal one is that it can utilize only very small particles of food. If digestive enzymes were released into the interior cavity, to break down large particles for phagocytosis, they would be carried away by the moving water currents before they could perform their task. But if some other way of capturing food made this continual flow unnecessary, an animal might have an interior cavity with only one opening—perhaps even an opening that could be closed at will. Enzymes could then be retained in the cavity and used to break down large pieces of food. This is the arrangement that has developed in the coelenterates or cnidarians. Such a single-opening digestive cavity is known as a **gastrovascular cavity**.

The fresh-water hydra provides a good example of how this system works. The hydra uses its circle of long, flexible tentacles, armed with stinging cnidoblasts, to seize

12-3
Digestive system of hydra. The gastrovascular cavity extends throughout the body. It even extends into the tentacles. Thus it serves for food transport as well as digestion. (See The gastrovascular cavity)

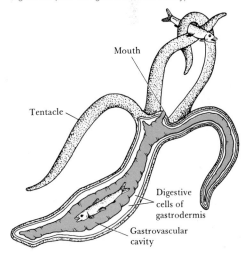

Mouth

Tentacle

Digestive cells of gastrodermis

Gastrovascular cavity

and immobilize tiny fish and other such prey. This food is then taken into the gastrovascular cavity through a mouth located in the midst of the tentacles. The cells of the cavity lining secrete enzymes to break down this relatively large bit of food. Eventually it is reduced to fragments small enough to be engulfed by phagocytosis. As with the sponge, the rest of digestion is completed within the cells.

The appearance of specialized enzyme-secreting cells is a significant development. Extracellular digestion by enzymes — or, to give it a more convenient name, **enzymatic digestion** — will continue to be important in all the more highly developed digestive systems.

Many flatworms also possess gastrovascular cavities. That of the planarians is a good example. Food is taken in through a muscular **pharynx** which can shoot out from the body to seize prey. This leads to the cavity, where some enzymatic digestion takes place. Digestion is then completed intracellularly, as in the coelenterates. But the planarian system is more advanced than the hydra's in one important way — it is extensively branched. Thus it has a greater surface area for food absorption into the body tissues. This characteristic will become increasingly important in more complex animals. Ultimately it will allow the digestive system to occupy only a small part of an organism's body instead of almost the entire interior space, as is true of coelenterates and flatworms.

***The complete digestive system*** Even the best of gastrovascular cavities has a major disadvantage — it permits no specialization of function. Since undigestible matter must be expelled through the same opening which takes in food, all the activities of digestion are mixed up together in a single open cavity. Enzymes must be secreted into the entire cavity, and the whole interior surface must be equipped for absorption. It would be much more efficient if the food could be moved in one direction

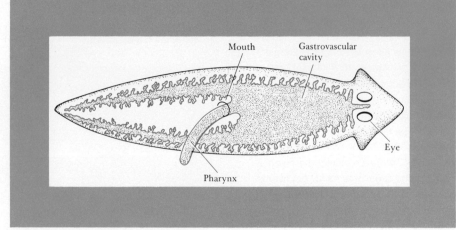

along a tubular digestive system. A section at the beginning could break up the food mechanically — perhaps by some sort of muscular action — into particles small enough for the enzymes to work on most effectively. Then, in a second region, the enzymes could take over and reduce the particles to proper size for absorption by the cells. Finally, any undigestible matter could be passed on to be processed as necessary in another section, and expelled. But for such a system two openings are needed — one to take in the food and another to release the wastes. Such a complete digestive system appears in the annelid phylum. It must have proved satisfactory, since it is essentially the characteristic digestive apparatus of all the higher animals, including ourselves.

12-4
Planarian digestive system. Note the extensive branching of the gastrovascular cavity. It increases the surface area for absorption. (See The gastrovascular cavity)

12-5
Complete digestive system, as found in the common earthworm.

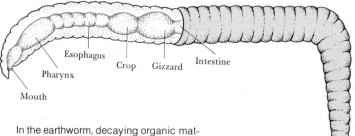

In the earthworm, decaying organic matter is sucked into the mouth by a muscular pharynx. It passes back through the **esophagus** to the **crop**, which is simply a storage chamber. Next the food goes to the thick-walled, muscular **gizzard**, where it is churned around and ground up. Tiny bits of gravel or sand have usually been taken in with the food, and they help with the grinding. At the same time, the earthworm's tissues secrete water into the cavity, making the food quite liquid by the time it leaves the gizzard and enters the **intestine**. Here the enzymes go to work. Starting with well-pulverized, well-moistened particles to act on, the enzymes break them down more completely. Hydras and planarians must finish up digestion intracellularly. But in the earthworm it is virtually completed in the digestive cavity. The absorptive cells of the intestinal lining receive the food as simple compounds, ready for use.

The posterior part of the intestine has its own specialization. Much of the water which was added to the food for digestion must now be reabsorbed. If it is lost, the earthworm will become dehydrated. The water is reabsorbed by the last part of the intestine, and the wastes are finally eliminated through the **anus**.

*Variations in digestive systems*    Within this basic pattern, we can find a number of variations in the type and placement of digestive organs. Often these have adaptive value. For example, the jaws and teeth of vertebrates are partly food-procurement organs, since they allow the animal to seize prey or tear off grass or leaves. But they may also serve to break up the food somewhat before sending it on to the storage organ. Consequently, the animal may be able to eat pieces of food too large to pass comfortably through its esophagus. On the other hand, birds swallow their food whole and break it up afterward. Clearly, a flying animal would be badly inconvenienced by having to carry a heavy set of jaws and teeth in its head, far in front of its wings.

The presence of a storage organ such as the crop makes **discontinuous feeding** possible. This has definite survival value. If an animal could not eat any faster than it could digest the food, it would have to eat virtually all the time. A crop or stomach can store excess food and release it gradually

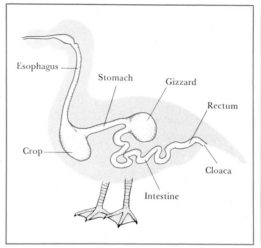

Esophagus — Stomach — Gizzard — Rectum — Crop — Cloaca — Intestine

12-6
Digestive system of a bird. Humans begin breaking up food even before swallowing. But birds store it first in the crop. Gradually, the food is passed on through the narrow stomach. It then enters the powerful, tough-walled gizzard. (See Variations in digestive systems)

for digestion. This leaves the animal free to do other things at least part of the time. Birds, for instance, can fill their crops with seeds, worms, or other food, and then get off the ground, where they are most vulnerable to their enemies. They can then return to the relative safety of the trees. There they can mate, build nests, or do something else while the food digests. Many of them also use the crop as a carrying bag to take food to their young.

Other adaptations are closely related to the type of food eaten. Ruminant herbivores, such as cattle, sheep, and deer, have four "stomachs" to handle cellulose digestion. The largest of the four stomachs—the **rumen**—contains colonies of bacteria which effectively digest cellulose, making it available as food. (This means of digesting cellulose, however, is not exclusive to the ruminants. Similar bacteria also inhabit the far simpler gut of such wood-eating insects as termites.) The small intestines of most herbivores are also longer than those of carnivores. This allows materials to remain in the digestive tract for a longer time, compensating for the interference of cellulose with digestion of plant cells. By contrast, carnivores can get along with a fairly short small intestine. Omnivores, such as men and bears, have small intestines of medium length.

# Gas exchange and respiration

An animal may be surrounded by food, but if deprived of oxygen it will die just the same. Oxygen is needed for cellular respiration and metabolism, so that energy may be released and cellular structures may be built and kept in repair. Without these activities, life cannot go on. So animals need a system for getting oxygen from the environment to the cells, and also for removing the carbon dioxide wastes left over from metabolism. That is, they require a system of organismic respiration. The term for this is **gas exchange.**

All animals need oxygen. Fundamentally, there are only two places they can find it—in the air, and in the water. But differences in size, body structure, habitat, way of life, and level of metabolic activity make for considerable variation in the way oxygen is obtained. The key factor that determines the type of gas exchange system a species develops seems to be the source of the oxygen—whether it comes from air or water. Air contains about 20 times as much oxygen as even the most air-saturated water. On the other hand, gas exchange must occur by diffusion of the gas across the moist membrane, and in air the membrane tends to dry out. So we see that while less energy is needed to obtain adequate oxygen from air, the exchange membrane must be more elaborately protected. Neither source is perfect.

The oxygen needs of organisms also vary widely. Relative to its body weight, a mussel needs only about one-tenth as much oxygen as a resting human. A fish needs from half to twice as much, a resting butterfly about three times as much, and a resting mouse over twelve times as much. The mussel, then, can get along with a relatively simple and inefficient gas exchange system. But the mouse must be able to take full advantage of every molecule of oxygen that comes its way.

## Variations in systems

There are four main aspects which differ in gas exchange systems according to differing requirements. These include how extensive the gas exchange membrane is, how exposed it is, how efficiently the system extracts oxygen and releases carbon dioxide, and what mechanisms are provided for bringing the air or water to the membrane surface.

*Integumentary systems*    Distinct organismic gas exchange mechanisms appear higher in the evolutionary scale than digestive systems. Sponges, coelenterates, and flatworms all get along without them. Since their body tissues are only a few cells thick, oxygen and carbon dioxide can diffuse directly between the surrounding water and the cells, all over the body surface. More elaborate arrangements are not needed.

Even the earthworm "breathes" by diffusion through the skin, but with a difference. Instead of diffusing directly into the body tissues, oxygen is diffused into the blood, which then carries it through the body. This is a revolutionary development. The earthworm's body is small, but still a good deal thicker than that of any hydra or planarian. Direct diffusion between cells and the environment could not possibly be fast enough to supply its needs. Without some sort of internal gas transport system, the earthworm could never have developed at all.

This tie between gas exchange and blood transport is found in nearly all the higher animals, except the insects. We shall see that the structure of many circulatory systems is designed first and foremost for the rapid transport of respiratory gases. Without this, large animals would probably have been an impossibility.

A number of higher animals also utilize skin or **integumentary respiration** for all or part of their gas exchange needs. Frogs and eels breathe partly through skin and mouth membranes, as well as through lungs or gills. Some salamanders get along entirely by integumentary respiration. As we might expect, the skin of such animals has a very rich blood supply.

But integumentary respiration has one serious disadvantage. When the body surface itself must act as the gas exchange membrane, it has to be kept moist at all times. This is usually done by immersion in water or by mucous secretions, which use up body water. So it is not surprising that animals began, at a fairly early stage, to evolve less troublesome ways of supplying their gas exchange needs.

*Gills* The first step toward efficiency was that a certain part of the body surface became specialized for gas exchange, with a particularly rich blood supply. This allowed other areas to be protected. The second stage was an increase in the area of the specialized surface, usually by means of folds and ridges. Finally, ways were evolved to protect the gas exchange surface without cutting off its water supply.

We can see the first stage in the marine worm *Tubifex*, a relative of the earthworm. *Tubifex*'s posterior end is so richly supplied with blood that it is usually bright red. The worm lives in a protected burrow. Only its scarlet rear end protrudes, gently waving. This simple system meets its needs so well that it thrives even in polluted, low-oxygen water.

The second stage is displayed by *Nereis,* another marine annelid. Thin, flap-like **parapodia**, well supplied with blood vessels, extend from the sides of each body segment. These provide a very large area for gas exchange—much larger than the general body surface itself could provide. (However, *Nereis* continues to use the body surface for gas exchange also.)

The sea star displays a variation on this system. It possesses tiny, finger-like **skin gills** scattered over most of the body surface. Like most of its fellow echinoderms, the sea star manages to do things differently. Its skin gills are linked to the coelomic

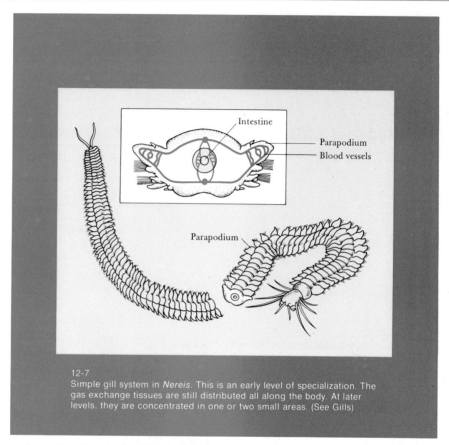

12-7
Simple gill system in *Nereis*. This is an early level of specialization. The gas exchange tissues are still distributed all along the body. At later levels, they are concentrated in one or two small areas. (See Gills)

cavity rather than to the blood system. Since the coelomic fluid lacks the oxygen-carrying pigments of blood, it would seem to be less well equipped for gas transport. But as we may recall, echinoderms handle much of the respiratory function through their water vascular system.

Fish and most other highly developed aquatic animals possess **gills** which are minutely subdivided, highly efficient, and well protected. In bony fishes, for example, the gills are supported on arches within a bony chamber. Each gill consists of a large number of feathery filaments. These are subdivided into secondary folds or lamellae, creating an enormous total surface area. Water flows constantly in one direction across the gills. It enters from the fish's mouth through the pharynx, and exits through the gill slits behind the gills. Some fish have a special pumping mechanism

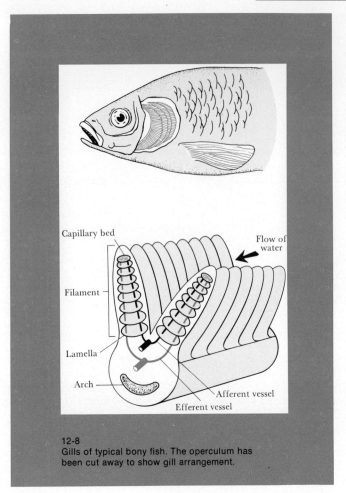

**12-8**
Gills of typical bony fish. The operculum has been cut away to show gill arrangement.

Capillary bed

Flow of water

Filament

Lamella

Arch

Afferent vessel
Efferent vessel

their oxygen from air, the first thing they had to do was deal with this problem of drying. Arthropods and vertebrates solved it in two rather different ways.

Insects, the largest group of terrestrial arthropods, developed a system of **tracheae**. These are ducts which originate at the body surface and carry air directly to the tissues, without any special link to the blood. Air enters the tracheae through **spiracles**, rows or openings along each side of the insect's body. From here the tracheae penetrate inward, branching repeatedly. They end in minute tracheoles less than a single micron in diameter. The tracheoles are in direct contact with virtually all the body cells. So oxygen and carbon dioxide can diffuse directly between them, just as in the simpler aquatic invertebrates.

Fundamentally, it is the concentration gradient of oxygen and carbon dioxide that moves air in and out of the tracheae. This is necessarily a rather slow process. Thus it makes the tracheal system unsuited for transporting respiratory gases over long distances, although contractions of body muscles help to speed the movement somewhat. This is undoubtedly one reason why insects, as a group, have remained so small.

But tracheal breathers have dealt effectively with the moisture problem. The spiracles can be opened and closed, and this appears to be partly a means of minimizing water loss. The air in the tracheae can be saturated with body water to keep the membranes moist, and the spiracles can be opened only as necessary to permit exchange of gases with the drier outside air.

*Lungs*  The other principal gas exchange system among air-breathing animals is, of course, the **lung**. Like the gills of fishes, lungs are minutely subdivided membranes. They are richly supplied with blood vessels, which present an extensive surface for oxygen and carbon dioxide diffusion. But instead of protruding outward from the body like gills, the lungs are buried deep inside.

to maintain water flow. Others, including sharks, tuna, and mackerel, lack this mechanism. They must therefore swim constantly to keep their gills supplied with oxygenated water.

Mollusks, such as clams, oysters, and squid, and aquatic arthropods, such as crabs and shrimp, also utilize gills of varying efficiency, providing them with the needed water flow in a variety of ways.

*Tracheal systems*  Gills are highly satisfactory gas exchange organs for aquatic animals. On land, however, they are of no use at all, since they are too exposed. A steady stream of air across their delicate surfaces would dry them out fatally in moments. When animals began trying to get

Before the air can reach them it travels through a long passageway where it is moistened. In warm-blooded animals the air is also warmed to prevent it from damaging the respiratory membranes. And unlike tracheal systems, lung systems have active pumping mechanisms to draw air into the breathing passages and force it out again. Lungs can thus supply the oxygen needs of animals as large as elephants and whales—and once supplied those of the great dinosaurs.

It is interesting to note that lungs probably began not among land animals but among certain early fish. These fish lived in stagnant water or in shallow lakes and streams that tended to dry up during periods of drought. For them, an alternate means of obtaining oxygen was a necessity.

Ventilation, or breathing, in lung-breathers is **tidal**—that is, air flows in and out. With most gill-breathers, the air flows in one direction only. Certain air-breathers use a **positive pressure** system of ventilation. Frogs, for instance, lower the floor of the mouth to draw air in. Then, with the nostrils closed, they raise the floor, creating a pressure gradient which forces air into the lungs. Lungfishes do much the same with the bubbles of air they gulp on trips to the water's surface.

Mammals, including humans, use a **negative pressure** system. Muscle contractions expand the chest cavity. This causes air pressure in the lungs to drop below that of the outside atmosphere, and air flows in. When the muscles relax, the chest cavity shrinks, raising the air pressure, and air flows out.

The degree of subdivision in lung membranes, and therefore the amount of absorptive surface, varies considerably. Fish lungs are basically simple sacs. Frog lungs are more elaborate, but do not yet function involuntarily, as ours do. Reptiles have still better-developed lungs, particularly the land reptiles which do not have the moist skin needed for integumentary respiration.

12-9
Tracheal respiratory system of a typical insect. The tracheae subdivide, like blood capillaries. They form a myriad of tiny tubules. These supply all the tissues and internal organs.

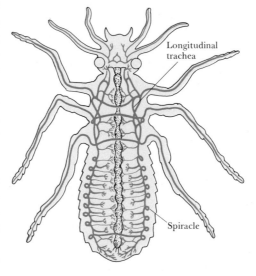

Longitudinal trachea

Spiracle

In the warm-blooded birds and mammals, with their high oxygen needs, lung systems reach their fullest development.

## Internal transport

Getting substances from one place to another in the body is the job of the transport system. Nutrients and respiratory gases must be delivered to the cellular "work sites" where they are needed, and waste products must be removed. Messages must be communicated by means of specialized chemicals or hormones, and defenses must be mobilized to repel invading organisms.

Simple animals such as sponges, most coelenterates, and flatworms, have no internal transport system for the same reason that they have no respiratory system. They do not need one because their cells are all in close or immediate contact with the environment. Jellyfish, though, have the problem of getting nutrients through the thick layer of jelly-like, noncellular mesoglea which separates their outer tissue layer from the inner layer around the gastrovascular cavity. Accordingly, they have developed a rather interesting arrangement to handle the problem. Jellyfish possess a number of wandering amoeboid cells These pick up food particles from the cells of the cavity lining, carrying them through the mesoglea to the outer body wall. This could be considered a primitive transport system, but at best it is sure to be slow and unreliable.

### Circulatory systems

All but the simplest animals have developed a means of transport known as a **circulatory system**. Some sort of fluid, or blood, follows a more or less circular path through a series of channels or cavities. The fluid returns again and again to the same spot, picking up and dropping off materials as it goes.

True circulatory systems appear about the same time that complete digestive systems do. Perhaps this is because when absorption of nutrients was assigned to a single part of the digestive system instead of the entire cavity, there had to be some way to distribute the nutrients around the body. But in most animals, the further development of the transport system has been closely linked with the respiratory rather than the digestive system. Oxygen, apparently, is even more vital than food.

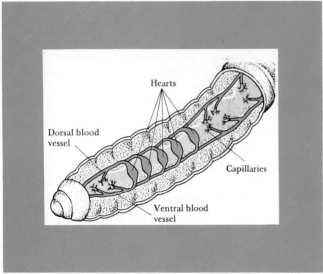

12-10
Closed circulatory system of the earthworm. The five pairs of hearts are little more than slightly specialized blood vessels. They are very different from the complex, chambered hearts of the higher vertebrates.

*Closed circulatory systems* The earthworm possesses the principal elements of a typical circulatory system. Blood is pumped by several pairs of enlarged chambers, or hearts, into a main vessel on the ventral or lower side of the body. The hearts are located near the anterior or head end of the animal, and the blood flows toward the posterior end. As it goes, it branches off into various smaller vessels and even smaller capillaries that carry it to all the tissues and organs of the body. It exchanges substances with the surrounding tissues through the thin capillary walls. Afterwards the blood collects again from the capillaries into branch vessels, and then into another large main vessel, this time on the upper or dorsal side. Finally it flows forward to the hearts.

Heart, main vessels, branch vessels, capillaries—our own human circulatory systems are made up of the same compo-

nents. Furthermore, even though the earthworm has no specialized respiratory system, it uses its blood as we do—to transport respiratory gases. Many of its capillaries run close to the surface of the body. When oxygen diffuses through the skin from outside, it is taken up by the blood in these capillaries. In our own bodies, oxygen diffusion from the lungs to the blood works in essentially the same way.

Most blood contains specialized **respiratory pigments**. These are metal-containing protein molecules. They can pick up and carry rather large amounts of oxygen—much more than could be dissolved in the liquid plasma alone. The respiratory pigment in earthworms and vertebrates is **hemoglobin**, which contains iron. Some organisms use other iron-containing pigments, while still others have pigments containing copper, vanadium, or other metals. In most lower animals these pigments are simply dissolved in the plasma. In many higher animals, though, they are enclosed in cells such as the red blood cells of humans. These animals require so much pigment to supply their high oxygen needs that if it were simply dissolved in the plasma it would make the blood too thick to flow through the capillaries.

The circulatory system of the earthworm is a **closed system**. That is, the blood stays in defined, relatively narrow vessels and channels, and is kept moving by pressure from the pulsing heart or hearts. Closed systems are found in some other invertebrates and in all vertebrates. A great many invertebrates, though, have developed an alternative type of system.

*Open circulatory systems* Some annelids, most mollusks, and all arthropods have an **open circulatory system**. In such a system the blood does not remain in special vessels, but flows out into large spaces called sinuses or **hemocoels**. These spaces occupy most of the coelom, the main body cavity. Here the blood bathes the organs and the surrounding tissues. It is

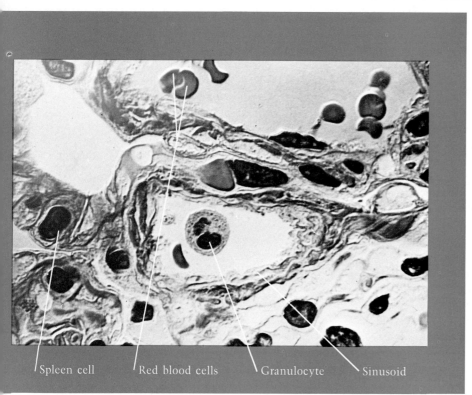

Spleen cell    Red blood cells    Granulocyte    Sinusoid

12-11
Monkey spleen. Shown are blood cells in the sinusoids. These are thin-walled structures. In some organs, they substitute for capillaries. Notice how red blood cells are deformed by each other as they circulate. The white blood cell is termed a granulocyte. This is because of its granular cytoplasm. It is also termed a polymorphonuclear leucocyte. This is because of its irregularly-shaped nucleus. (See Closed circulatory systems)

12-12
Open circulatory system of an insect. The dorsal heart vessel serves to keep the blood circulating more or less consistently in one direction. But there are no branching vessels or capillaries like those in closed systems.

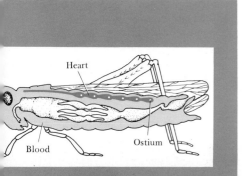

Heart

Blood

Ostium

finally returned, usually through pores called **ostia**, to the posterior end of the main blood vessel, which serves as the heart.

At first glance, such a system seems to be thoroughly inefficient. If the blood simply washes about in large open spaces, how can it be circulated fast enough to transport sufficient oxygen, or for that matter anything else, to the tissues? What assurance is there it will ever be circulated, rather than simply lying there in stagnant pools till the animal dies?

To begin with, gas transport is not a particularly important function of the blood in many of these animals. Some of them — especially insects — do not even have respiratory pigments. It will be recalled that insects breathe by means of tracheae. These carry oxygen directly into the depths of the body, without using blood vessels at all. Other substances, such as nutrients, can usually afford to travel more slowly. More-over, while the heart may not provide

enough pressure to move the blood quickly, the body can. The contractions of body muscles in ordinary movement stir the blood around. They may, in fact, cause it to circulate quite rapidly.

Still, the open system does seem to have certain disadvantages. It certainly would not serve for very large organisms, and one may wonder why it ever developed. Surely the animals which have it would do just as well or better with a closed system?

In one important respect they would not. Notice that open circulatory systems are found only in nonvertebrates, which have no stiffening interior skeleton. Especially in the arthropods and annelids, the circulatory system actually serves to some extent as a sort of skeleton. This is known as a **hydro-static skeleton** — one based on liquid pressure. By using muscle contractions to increase blood pressure in the body cavity, an annelid such as the leech can firm up its soft body. Its other muscles have something to pull against, just as vertebrates' muscles pull on jointed bones to produce body movement. Arthropods use blood in a similar way. They pump it to particular sections of the body to help raise the antennae, move the legs, or open crumpled new wings after emergence from a pupal case.

## Osmoregulation and excretion

Life began in the water, and in a sense all life still is in the water. To live and function, even a terrestrial animal needs body fluids — not only blood, but fluids around all the cells and in them. These fluids are not pure water. They contain molecules of various organic and inorganic substances. Some of these substances are more or less permanent parts of the fluid, while others are transported from one place to another. The presence of these dissolved substances creates a certain osmotic pressure. As noted, when osmotic pressures differ on two sides of a membrane, due to differing concentrations of solutes, water tends to diffuse through the membrane from the region of lower to the region of higher concentration. This equalizes the pressure. Depending on the permeability of the membrane, solutes may or may not pass through in the opposite direction. This rather simple chemical fact is the basis of one of the main problems animals must solve in dealing with their environment. The water–solute balance that is proper to a given animal's tissues—that is, the balance it needs for homeostasis—may not be the same as that of the environment. Yet the animal must interact with the environment. Therefore it must have membranes—gills, lungs, digestive tract, capillary walls—that permit diffusion between the environment and its body tissues. If it cannot find a way to do this without upsetting its balance of water and solutes, the animal will die. The process of maintaining this balance is usually known as **osmoregulation**.

## Problems of osmoregulation

Since living organisms began in the sea, we might expect that marine dwellers of today would have no serious osmoregulatory problems. But in fact things are not quite that simple.

Marine invertebrates do have a solute concentration like that of sea water. In other words, they are isosmotic to their environment. But the environment itself can be unstable, especially in tidal marshes and estuaries where the saltiness of the water varies with the changing tides. An invertebrate in such a situation can do one of two things. It can shut out the environment at unfavorable times, or it can adjust itself to the change. Bivalve mollusks generally do the first, closing their shells and "clamming up" when the water becomes too dilute. They can function anaerobically for a time, until the salt content of the water improves. The prawn *Palaemonetes varians* takes the other course. It changes the osmotic composition of its body fluids to match that of the water. Such animals are known as **osmoconformers**.

Osmoconformity is suited only to fairly simple animals, and to an environment that changes within fairly narrow limits. Of greater adaptive value is the ability to osmoregulate, and thus maintain a stable internal osmotic composition despite outside changes. Some early invertebrates developed the ability to do this. Such invertebrates gave rise to animals that could survive in fresh water and, ultimately, on land.

Fresh-water fish and invertebrates are descendants of osmoregulatory marine invertebrates that moved up rivers from the estuaries. These species gradually evolved to a lower osmotic concentration, but they were never able to get down to the level of fresh water. Hence these animals are hyperosmotic to (more concentrated than) their environment. Without some protection, they would tend constantly to absorb water till their cells swelled and burst, while the solutes in their bodies would leak steadily away.

Marine fish, the descendants of fresh-water animals that returned to the sea, face the opposite problem. While their ancestors had been developing a lower solute concentration, the sea had been getting saltier. So marine fish are hypoosmotic to (less concentrated than) the present marine environment. Their cells would naturally tend to lose water and take up salts from the surrounding ocean. Like a traveler lost in a desert, they would soon become dehydrated and die.

Terrestrial animals face the same danger as marine fish, but for a different reason. The drier air outside the body constantly tends to evaporate water through any unprotected body surface. The cells are thus dehydrated, and the concentration of solutes in the remaining fluids is raised above the level at which the animal can function. To complicate the problem, when the organism tries to dispose of these excess solutes and other body wastes, it must nearly always sacrifice some water to do so, principally in urine and feces.

Marine reptiles, birds, and mammals are

essentially terrestrial forms that, for one reason or another, have returned to the sea. Like the marine fish, they have found it saltier than when their ancestors left. So they, too, must deal with the problems of a too-concentrated environment.

The basic protections of all these species are similar. They must make as much of the body surface as possible impermeable to water. They must develop organs for excreting any unwanted water or solutes which do get in. And they must adopt helpful feeding habits. Thus, fresh-water fish rarely drink, and have scales to prevent water uptake through the skin. They can excrete a urine more dilute than their body fluids. This allows them to retain needed solutes while getting rid of excess water that inevitably does seep in, particularly through the gills.

Marine fish, in contrast, drink constantly. This gives them the water they need to replace what leaks away into the sea, but it also brings in extra salt. Since they cannot get rid of this salt by forming a urine more concentrated than their body fluids, they excrete the salt through their gills, by a special active transport mechanism across the membranes. Marine birds and reptiles use a similar technique, employing a special salt gland.

Both terrestrial and aquatic mammals have developed the extremely useful ability to form a concentrated urine. This enables them to dispose of a considerable quantity of excess salt as needed, with minimum loss of water. But the concentrating system has its limits, so marine animals limit their salt intake by rarely drinking. Instead, they obtain their water from the body fluids of the fish or other animals that they eat—animals which, like themselves, are hypoosmotic to the ocean environment. Terrestrial animals, including man, usually have no problem of involuntary salt intake. But they do require regular access to fresh water, to replace what they lose through excretion and evaporation. Thus development of the ability to conserve body water by excreting a con-

12-13
Giant petrel (above) and sea turtle (below). Both animals eliminate excess salt through special glands in the head. That of the petrel drains through the prominent nostrils atop its heavy bill. (See Problems of osmoregulation)

12-14
A sea otter relaxes comfortably on the ocean's swell. This is a playful and intelligent mammal. It lives almost wholly at sea. The sea otter dines on low-salt fish and juicy mollusks. This keeps its salt intake to a level its kidneys can handle.

centrated urine was an important step in adaptation to terrestrial life.

## Ionic regulation

Animals must not only maintain a proper total balance of water and solutes. They must also have solutes of the right kinds, in the right proportions. Many inorganic substances are used in regulating body functions. The presence of too much or too little of them can cause serious trouble. Because these substances are usually found in the body in ionic, or electrically charged, form, their control is known as **ionic regulation.** All animals require ionic regulation, even those that are isosmotic with their environment and therefore do not need to osmoregulate.

## Nitrogen excretion

Finally, all animals must get rid of nitrogen compounds, which are formed as waste products of protein metabolism. A buildup of these compounds in the body would upset osmotic balance and have other undesirable effects.

When amino acids are broken down, the nitrogen in the amino group unites with hydrogen to form **ammonia.** This substance is highly toxic and cannot be permitted to

accumulate in the body. Most aquatic invertebrates simply excrete it immediately into the surrounding water. Vertebrates, though, usually convert it into nontoxic **urea,** which can be retained for a time, and then excrete it in the urine. This is an advantage particularly for the vertebrates that can form a concentrated urine, since it causes less drain on the body's water supply. Continual excretion of ammonia, on the other hand, would entail continual water loss. Birds, insects, and most reptiles cut water loss still further by excreting solid, crystalline **uric acid.** It is important to these egg-layers that uric acid is insoluble in water. Therefore it cannot build up in the fluids of the egg. If it did accumulate, it would poison the developing embryo, as urea or ammonia would do.

One group of marine fish, the sharks and other elasmobranchs, have found a practical use for urea. They retain large amounts of it in their body fluids and use it for osmoregulation. Like the marine bony fish, they need an inorganic solute balance much lower than that of sea water. But the large quantities of organic urea in their fluids create an overall osmotic balance equal to that of sea water, which neatly eliminates most osmoregulatory problems.

## Excretory systems

In the simplest animals, excretion of unwanted substances can take place by diffusion across the general body surface, just as can respiration and even feeding. But we find the beginnings of special excretory systems at a very early stage. These usually consist of some sort of tubular structure, into which body fluids are filtered. Ions, glucose, and other substances needed in the body are then selectively reabsorbed, and the remaining water and solutes pass out. We shall examine a few of the principal excretory systems here.

Planaria and other flatworms have perhaps the simplest tubular excretory system. Two or more long tubules run the length of the body. Many short branches feed into them, each one ending in a tiny bulb-like structure. Tissue fluid filters into these bulbs, where clusters of moving cilia create a current that washes it along the branches into the main tubules and out through one of a number of excretory pores. The constant beating of the cilia suggests a multitude of tiny flames. Therefore, this excretory structure is usually called a **flame-cell system.**

It is probable that flame-cell systems are concerned mainly with salt and water balance, particularly in view of the large amounts of water taken in along with food particles from the gastrovascular cavity. Most nitrogenous wastes are probably excreted in other ways.

Earthworms and other annelids have more advanced excretory organs called **nephridia.** These have taken the flame-cell system and improved on it. They begin with an open, bulb-like funnel, the **nephrostome.** Body fluids enter this, and pass through a long, coiled tubule surrounded by a net of capillaries. Eventually a very dilute urine emerges into a bladder. (It is really only an enlarged section of the tubule.) Since annelids have a segmental body plan, each nephridial bladder has its own opening to the outside, called a **nephridiopore.**

The excretory organs of insects are a set of flexible tubular sacs (anywhere from 2 to more than 100), attached to the intestinal tract. These are called **Malpighian tubules.** Their closed ends extend into the hemocoel, where they are bathed in the insect's blood. Body fluids are filtered from the blood into the tubules. The urine that is formed does not pass to a specific urinary bladder but rather into the rectum, where it meets the waste products of digestion. The rectum has an enormous capacity to reabsorb water. Once the urine has been converted to uric acid and precipitated out of solution, nearly all the water that was in it and in the food wastes is taken back into the body tissues. In many insects, the final excretion is very nearly dry.

## Temperature regulation

Homeostasis requires more than a proper balance of substances in the body fluids. It also requires a proper temperature. Normally, the cells in an animal's body must be kept at a temperature between 10° and 40° C (50° to 104° F). A few degrees higher or lower, and they will die.

Animals receive heat in two ways—from the environment, and from their own bodies. The environmental source, ultimately, is sunlight. The internal source is the energy-producing reactions going on in the cells. If the environment does not produce enough heat, the animal must be able to retain some of its internally produced, or metabol-

The length of the tubule and its close association with the capillaries are key improvements. They significantly increase the animal's ability to reabsorb salts and water, and thus to regulate the composition of its urine and its own osmotic and ionic balance. There is more time for reabsorption because the tubule is longer. And blood flowing through the capillaries can pick up the reabsorbed substances and carry them quickly away. If these substances had to remain in the tissue fluid immediately surrounding the tubules, they would soon build up to such a high osmotic pressure as to make continued reabsorption impractical.

In animals with closed circulatory systems, the development of the excretory system continues along the basic lines of the nephridium. Refinements are gradually added, eventually culminating in the ability to form both concentrated and dilute urine. This allows the organism to maintain a stable internal fluid environment despite a wide range of variation in the environment outside. Animals with open circulatory systems, however, have taken another path.

12-15
While still in the egg, these baby black racers produced nitrogenous waste. It would have poisoned them if it had remained in solution in the egg fluids. But it was processed into insoluble uric acid. All that was left behind in the empty shell were a few hard crystals. (See Nigrogen excretion)

12-16
Flame-cell excretory system of a planarian.

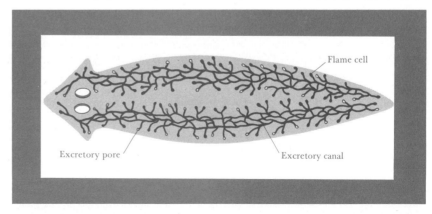

Flame cell

Excretory pore          Excretory canal

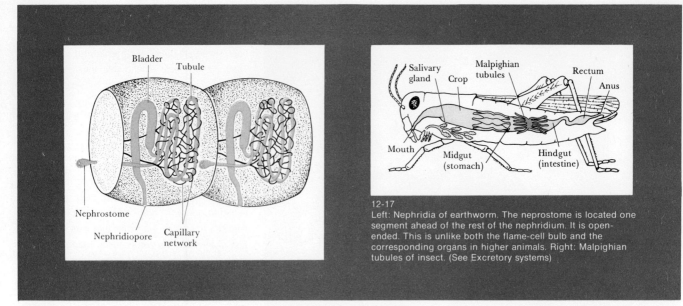

12-17
Left: Nephridia of earthworm. The neprostome is located one segment ahead of the rest of the nephridium. It is open-ended. This is unlike both the flame-cell bulb and the corresponding organs in higher animals. Right: Malpighian tubules of insect. (See Excretory systems)

ic, heat, to make up the difference. Likewise, if the environment produces too much heat, the animal must have a way to block it out or get rid of it. Animals that have internal means of doing this are called **homeothermic**, or "warm-blooded." Those that do not are called **poikilothermic**, or "cold-blooded." Most of the world's animals are poikilotherms—arthropods, fish, amphibians, reptiles, and all the lower phyla. Only birds and mammals are homeotherms.

Poikilothermy works well for aquatic animals, since water temperatures, especially in the ocean, usually stay within the 10°–40° C range. Thus the animal can simply let its body follow the temperature of its environment. But land temperatures vary much more widely—from far below freezing in the Arctic and Antarctic, to the burning heat of deserts. Land-based poikilotherms such as reptiles usually compensate by adopting special heat-regulating behavior. A desert snake or lizard may sun itself to absorb heat in the morning, crawl into a dark, cool burrow at midday, sun itself again in the evening, and go hunting after dark for its food. By such means it keeps its temperature quite constant.

But such behavioral means of regulating temperature take up a great deal of time.

Moreover, they do not generally work for very cold climates—there are virtually no reptiles in the Arctic. But the homeotherm, by basing its regulation on metabolic heat, is much less dependent on the environment. It can live where the poikilotherm cannot, and can be active at hunting, playing, or mating while the poikilotherm is busy finding enough sunlight to keep warm.

Birds and mammals retain body heat in a number of ways. One way is to insulate the body surface so that heat does not escape. This is the purpose of fur, feathers, and the layer of fat often found under the skin. Another way is to keep the heat from reaching the surface. For this, the small blood vessels near the skin can be closed off, forcing the blood to stay deeper inside. The surface and the extremities—fingers, toes, ears, and so on—may become very cold or may even freeze, but the essential organs inside are kept warm. Some animals have developed ingenious variations on this. For example, in the feet of the emperor penguin, which are exposed naked to Antarctic winds and ice, tiny blood vessels from the arteries form a network around the veins. Heat from the outflowing arterial blood is transferred directly to the returning venous blood, and saved. Without the net-

work, it would be lost on the slow journey through surface capillaries.

But the key advantage enjoyed by homeotherms is that they can speed up their metabolism when the environment grows colder. Various signals from nerves and hormones stimulate a higher level of energy-producing reactions in the cells. In this way, the homeotherms actually produce more body heat as the outside temperature drops. In contrast, the poikilotherms produce less. Their metabolism slows down.

When it comes to disposing of excess heat, homeotherms may simply let it radiate off from the body surface. Heavily furred animals sometimes have an area of naked skin which is useful for this. Seals, which are so well insulated that they have trouble keeping cool when on land, often wave their naked flippers to lose heat. Another method of heat loss is evaporation, by sweating or panting. Animals that cannot sweat or pant may lick themselves. An elephant may even spray its body with saliva to cool off. And the camel, which lives in the desert and cannot spare water for cooling purposes, simply stores heat. It allows its body temperature to rise several degrees during the day, and radiates the excess heat off during the night.

# summary

All animals must be able to obtain and process nutrients, absorb oxygen, transport nutrients and gases to the cells where they will be used, and remove wastes. Animals procure their food by a variety of means, but certain patterns tend to recur. Filter feeders sift food particles from flowing water, and fluid feeders extract fluids from other organisms. Vertebrates are usually classed according to what, rather than how, they eat. They can be herbivores, carnivores, or omnivores.

The simplest digestive system in a multicellular animal is that of the sponges. Food particles are merely carried to the cells and there digested intracellularly. Development of a gastrovascular cavity, with a single opening, allows ingestion of larger pieces of food. But it allows no specialization of function. Ingestion and waste disposal occur through the same opening. In a complete digestive system, food enters through one opening and wastes are excreted through another. Mechanical breakdown, enzymatic digestion, and absorption occur in different specialized areas. Some parasites bypass the whole problem of digestion by assimilating predigested nutrients from their hosts.

Animals also need a system of gas exchange, to take in oxygen and remove carbon dioxide wastes. The smallest animals, and some larger ones, rely wholly or in part on integumentary respiration, exchanging gases directly through the body surface. In fish, water flows constantly in one direction across the gills, entering through the mouth and exiting through the gill slits behind the gills. But gills are useless on land because they would suffer from the drying effect of air. In their place, insects evolved tracheae, ducts which carry air from spiracles on the body surface directly to the tissues. Air-breathing vertebrates developed lungs— membranes which, like gills, are subdivided to present an extensive surface for gas diffusion. Lung systems are most fully developed in birds and mammals. They employ tidal ventilation, in which air moves in and out of the lungs.

In all but the simplest animals, internal transport is by means of a circulatory system. All vertebrates and some invertebrates have closed circulatory systems. In these the blood stays in relatively narrow vessels and is moved by pressure from a pulsing heart. Many invertebrates have an open circulatory system, in which blood flows into large spaces called hemocoels, bathing the organs and tissues until it is finally returned to the short system of blood vessels which includes the heart.

Animal body fluids must contain a proper balance of organic and inorganic substances. This balance is rarely the same as that of substances in the surrounding environment. Animals must be able to maintain proper internal balance without cutting themselves off from the environment. Some animals are osmoconformers. They can change the composition of their body fluids as the surrounding waters change. But most are osmoregulators. They maintain a relatively stable internal osmotic composition despite changes in the environment. There are a variety of mechanisms for this. Mammals can conserve body water and dispose of excess salts by excreting a concentrated urine. Many birds and reptiles have special salt excretion glands instead.

Ionic regulation maintains the proper concentration of each inorganic substance. It is essential to all animals, along with the excretion of nitrogenous wastes.

In the simplest animals excretion of wastes occurs by diffusion across general body surfaces. Larger organisms need a special excretory system. It usually involves a tubular structure for filtering fluids. Needed substances are reabsorbed and retained, while excess water and solutes are eliminated. Excretory systems range from the planarian flame-cell system through the nephridia of the annelids to the longer, more sophisticated systems of higher animals. Among animals with closed circulatory systems, there is a gradual tendency toward a longer tubule more closely associated with the capillaries. This allows more time and area for reabsorption, and blood flowing through the capillaries can quickly distribute the reabsorbed substances.

Insects have open circulatory systems. They therefore have a different type of excretory system, called Malpighian tubules. These flexible sacs extend into the hemocoel and are bathed by the insect's blood. Body fluids filter into the tubules and pass into the rectum. There they are mixed with food wastes and almost all the water in them is reabsorbed before excretion.

Most animals need a body temperature between 10° and 40° C to function properly. Poikilotherms depend almost wholly on the environment for this. Homeotherms can regulate metabolic heat, so they can live in a wider range of environments. They can retain body heat in cold weather, and even speed up their metabolism to produce more. They can also get rid of heat in hot weather, often by some form of evaporation.

13 human anatomy

# h

ave you ever imagined what it would be like to have no bones? A human being without a skeletal structure would be quite helpless, to say the least. To begin with, he or she could not stand up, but would have to sprawl rather shapelessly on the ground. He could not move very well, because his muscles would have nothing rigid to pull on. His brain would be unprotected against bumps and other injuries. Since he would have no jaws or teeth, eating would present problems, too. However, he would probably never have a chance to suffer from all these problems. Lacking ribs to help keep his lungs open and working, he would have suffocated at birth.

It is obvious, then, that the skeleton is distinctly vital to vertebrate life. Basically, this collection of bones and joints serves three functions. It supports the body. It protects delicate and essential internal organs. And it provides a system of levers which enables the individual to move.

The power to operate these levers is supplied by the muscles. Muscles are tissues which, like the skeleton, also function in support and protection. For a person to stand upright, for instance, whole sets of muscles must work precisely, pulling against one another to balance the body against gravity. And without the help of the large muscle sheets surrounding the abdomen, the intestines could not be kept in place nor protected from injury.

Both bone and muscle have certain other functions as well. In particular, bones contain the marrow which manufactures many of the components of blood. Bone also provides a reserve supply of calcium and other important minerals which the rest of the body can draw upon. Muscles, because their cells do a great deal of work, produce much of the heat that is needed to maintain body temperature. Also, there are many muscles—the visceral muscles—that have nothing to do with the skeleton. They are entirely concerned with the functioning of the internal organs, of which they are a part. Most of our discussion of the visceral

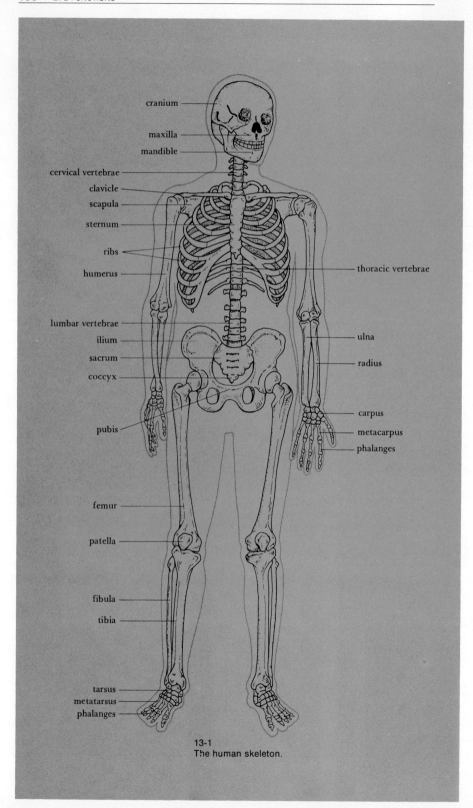

cranium

maxilla

mandible

cervical vertebrae

clavicle

scapula

sternum

ribs

humerus

lumbar vertebrae

ilium

sacrum

coccyx

pubis

femur

patella

fibula

tibia

tarsus

metatarsus

phalanges

thoracic vertebrae

ulna

radius

carpus

metacarpus

phalanges

13-1
The human skeleton.

muscles, along with their respective organs, will come in the next chapter. Here we shall be concerned mainly with the others—the so-called skeletal muscles—and the bones with which they work.

## The skeleton

The principal elements in the skeleton are **bones** and **cartilage**. As the diagram shows, bones come in a wide variety of shapes and sizes. They may be long, flat, round, or thoroughly irregular. And the size and shape of each is precisely adapted to the work it is called on to do.

### Bone structure

The architecture of our bones allows for maximum strength with minimum weight. Consider one of the long bones—the humerus of the upper arm. It is shaped rather like a dumbbell, with a long thin shaft and bulging ends. A tough fibrous membrane covers most of the surface. Running down the center of the shaft is a long cavity, filled with yellow fatty marrow. (The bone of the shaft is heavy and compact. But as a hollow structure it is much lighter than solid bone and yet retains much of the same strength.) The bulging ends of the humerus are rather large. One reason is that a large surface area at the joints (where the bones come together) spreads the weight and lessens the strain. However, a large knob of compact bone would be impossibly heavy. So the ends are made of spongy bone—that is, bone which consists of thin plates with many spaces between (giving it a "spongy" look).

Bone may look like an inert, lifeless substance, but it is very much a living system. The spaces in the spongy bone, for example, contain red marrow which is active in forming some types of blood cell. Penetrating the marrow are tiny blood vessels which run all through the bone. Under a microscope, a cross-section of living bone reveals a complex, carefully organized structure. It consists of many sets of concentric circles, crowded together, with a small channel at the center of each set. These sets are known as **Haversian systems**. The circles are plates, or **lamellae**, of nonliving protein fibers and mineral salts. They are secreted by living bone cells, which are visible as tiny dark spots embedded between the lamellae. Innumerable fine lines, running across the lamellae, connect the cells. These lines are actually extensions of the cells, and enable nutrients and other substances to pass between them. A blood vessel in the central channel, or **Haversian canal**, brings in needed substances from outside and removes wastes.

## Cartilage

When a child is born, it has a complete skeleton, in the sense that all the parts are present. But the skeleton is not made of bone. Rather, much of it is formed of another substance, called cartilage. True bone gradually replaces the cartilage, by a process called **ossification**, during childhood and adolescence. During this period of replacement, the bones can grow. Once the last of the cartilage has disappeared, though, their size is fixed. The age at which this happens varies for different bones, but is usually in the late teens or early twenties. However, some cartilage is never replaced by bone—for instance, that of the spinal discs, outer ear, and the central partition (septum) of the nose. In these areas, a layer of dense tissue, the **perichondrium**, covers the outer surface of the cartilage. Growth may continue through the formation of new cells at the inner surface of the perichondrium. Cartilage also continues to have other important uses in the body, even after the bones have completely hardened. It is particularly valuable in the joints, as we shall see.

Cartilage, like bone, is composed of scattered cells embedded in a noncellular substance, or matrix, that they have secreted. But whereas bone matrix is rigid, that of cartilage is more like a plastic or a stiff gelatin. Also, there are no blood vessels in car-

13-2
Anterior surface and partial cross section of a long bone (femur).

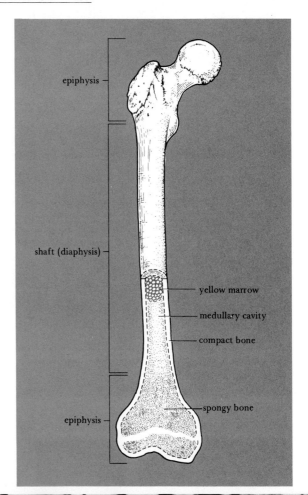

epiphysis

shaft (diaphysis)

epiphysis

yellow marrow

medullary cavity

compact bone

spongy bone

13-3
Cross section of compact bone showing Haversian system. The dark area in the center of the concentric circles (lamellae) is the Haversian canal. The smaller dark spaces dotting the lamellae are the lacunae in which are embedded the bone cells. The fine lines radiating from the lacunae to the Haversian canal are termed canaliculi. They provide "paths" by which nutrients can reach the bone cells.

tilage, so oxygen and nutrients must diffuse through the matrix to reach the cells.

The most common type of cartilage is **hyaline** cartilage. It is smooth and milky-looking, and is the kind that bones are composed of before ossification. **Fibrous** and **elastic** cartilage are specialized for tasks that require bending and stretching, or that involve much wear and tear. These types are strengthened by quantities of strong fibers, interwoven throughout the matrix.

## Joints

Where bones meet each other, we have **joints**. The structure of a joint must do three things. It must hold the bones firmly together, and it must allow enough—but not too much—movement for the functions of that part of the body. Finally, it must do both with a minimum of stress and strain on the bones. Some joints have to withstand considerable weight, as, for instance, the knee and the joints between the vertebrae of the spine. Others, such as the shoulder, must allow free movement in several directions. Each joint is therefore specially constructed for its particular job, and no two are precisely alike.

Joints fall into half a dozen types, but all can be classified as either **synarthroses** or **diarthroses**. The former are joints that permit little or no movement. The latter allow relatively free movement. For example, the joints between the vertebrae are synarthroses. Here the bones are tightly bound together by bands of strong, elastic, fibrous tissue known as **ligaments** (from the Latin word meaning "to tie"). Between the bones are discs of fibrous cartilage. These discs are slightly elastic, and serve to cushion the vertebrae against the weight of the body. Without them, we would be badly shaken up every time we took a step. Because the ligaments hold the bones tightly against the cartilage, each joint of the spine can move only a very little. But when all the small movements work together, the whole spine is fairly flexible.

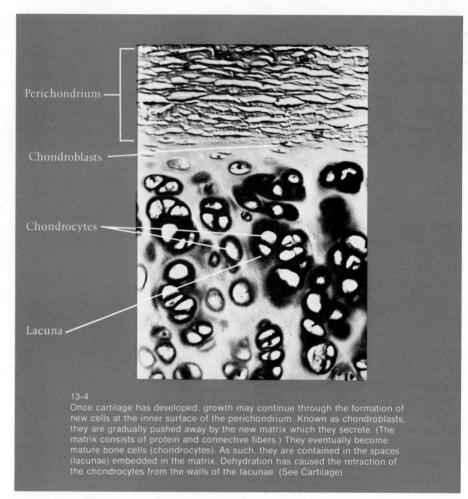

Perichondrium

Chondroblasts

Chondrocytes

Lacuna

13-4
Once cartilage has developed, growth may continue through the formation of new cells at the inner surface of the perichondrium. Known as chondroblasts, they are gradually pushed away by the new matrix which they secrete. (The matrix consists of protein and connective fibers.) They eventually become mature bone cells (chondrocytes). As such, they are contained in the spaces (lacunae) embedded in the matrix. Dehydration has caused the retraction of the chondrocytes from the walls of the lacunae. (See Cartilage)

13-5
Schematic diagram of longitudinal section of typical diarthrotic joint. (See Joints)

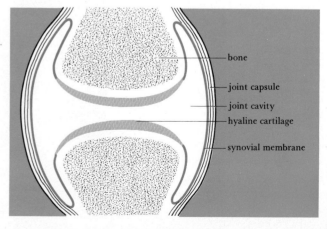

bone

joint capsule

joint cavity

hyaline cartilage

synovial membrane

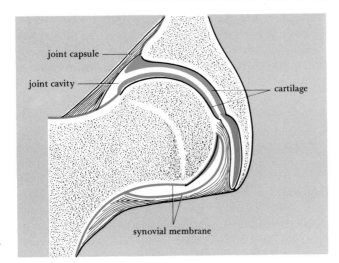

**13-6**
Schematic diagram of hip joint (ball-and-socket). The upper bone is the pelvic. The lower bone is the femur. (See Joints)

**13-7**
Cross section of vertebrae showing discs of fibrous cartilage. The nucleus pulposus is a soft, elastic substance in the center of each disc. A slipped, or ruptured, disc is a condition in which the nucleus pulposus presses on spinal nerve roots or on the cord itself. It may be caused by falling or by carrying or lifting heavy objects in such a way that the nucleus pulposus is pushed into the spinal canal. (See Joints)

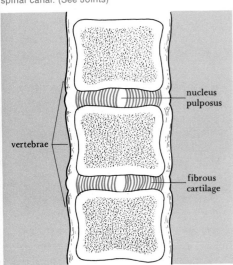

Diarthrotic joints, such as knees, elbows, and fingers, likewise need some sort of cushion between the bones. They also need good lubrication between the moving surfaces. A solid pad of cartilage will not do here, for it restricts movement too much. So a liquid is used instead. The end of each bone is covered with a thin layer of hyaline cartilage, which is very smooth and almost friction-free. The whole joint area is enclosed in a fibrous capsule, lined with a thin **synovial membrane**. This secretes a **synovial fluid** that fills the capsule and lubricates the joint. Ligaments bind the whole together, as in synarthrotic joints.

Many diarthrotic joints are of the type known as **hinge joints**. That is, they bend essentially in one direction only, like a door opening and closing. Fingers, knees, and elbows are all of this type. Shoulders and hips are **ball-and-socket joints**. In these, the long bone ends in a head that is actually quite ball-shaped. This ball fits into a socket in the hip or shoulder bone, and is held in place by numerous strong ligaments. The shape of these joints allows a wide range of movement. However, if the ligaments are stretched or weakened, the ball can sometimes slip out of the socket. This is especially true in the shoulder, where the socket is fairly shallow. The result is a painful dislocation.

In still other parts of the body, several types of joint may work together. This is true in the wrists and ankles, where many bones join in a variety of ways to permit movement in several directions.

## Muscles

However well designed the joints may be, they would be useless without muscles to move them. Every movement of the body, from the flicker of an eyelid to the stride of an Olympic runner or the swing of Muhammad Ali's fist, requires at least one muscle to perform it, and usually more. And the way the muscles are arranged gives us a truly amazing variety of movement. How, then, does the system work?

Skeletal muscles—the kind we are concerned with here—are composed of long, parallel **fibers**. But whereas the fibers of cartilage and bone are lifeless, those of muscle are living cells. Each fiber is a single cell, and many of them may be joined end-to-end to run the length of the muscle. Each muscle contains one or several bundles of these fibers, wrapped in a sheath of tough connective tissue. Other connective

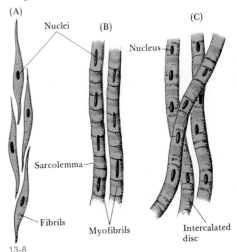

**13-8**
Types of muscle cell. (A) Smooth muscle cells are usually arranged in bundles that are joined by connective fibers. (B) Each striated muscle fiber (cell) is covered by a thin sheath called the sarcolemma. Parallel groups of these cells form bundles that are sheathed by connective fibers. (C) Cardiac muscle exhibits striations. Unlike striated muscle, its fibers form a continuous network.

tissue extends between the individual fibers. At the ends of the muscle, the sheets of connective tissue usually come together to form a strong cord known as a **tendon.** This attaches the muscle firmly to the bone. When the muscle is in action, its fibers contract, causing the whole muscle to shorten. As a result, the tendons at either end pull on the bone, and the body moves.

This simple act of **contraction** is the only one a muscle can perform. But in this case, how can we move a bone in more than one direction? How can we straighten our arm as well as bend it? Obviously, it is because we have two muscles, or sets of muscles, attached to the arm. One set contracts to bend, or flex, the arm. The other set contracts to pull it straight again, or extend it.

If we look at the structure of the human elbow, we may see more clearly how this works. In an engineering sense, the elbow is the fulcrum of a lever. That is, the lower arm is a rigid bar, moving on a more or less fixed point, which is the elbow. The muscles supply force to move the lever, enabling it to do work. The work might be, for instance, lifting a cup of coffee or wielding a hairbrush.

Two muscles are principally concerned with moving this lever. One is the **biceps brachii,** the familiar muscle that bulges when the forearm is flexed. A look at the diagram will show several things about the biceps. Most of it is located in the upper arm. The tendon at its "stationary" end, or **origin,** is attached to the shoulder. Its "moving" end, or **insertion,** is fastened to the radius of the lower arm quite close to the elbow. This placement of the insertion is valuable. It means that the biceps needs to contract only a short distance in order to move the working end of the arm—at the wrist—a much longer distance.

Several muscles assist the biceps in flexing the forearm. The most prominent of these is the **brachioradialis.** This is the muscle that shapes the fleshy part of the forearm on the thumb side, near the elbow. If you flex your forearm while trying to force it out straight with the other arm, the brachioradialis will bulge quite visibly. Most of the other assisting muscles are shorter and not as easy to see. Together, they make possible a smooth, coordinated pull that can flex the forearm, without strain, against quite a strong opposing force.

When it is time to put down that cup of coffee, you need only relax the contracted muscles. Gravity will lower the arm and straighten it. But if you are leaning back with your hands behind your head and you want to reach up and stretch, the **triceps** will be needed. This muscle is located on the back of the upper arm, just opposite the biceps. As this suggests, it works against the biceps. When it contracts, it pulls the arm straight. But why does it not keep right on pulling, and bend the elbow in the opposite direction? In part, the shape of the bones prevents this. But notice where the insertion of the triceps is—right at the elbow joint. This means that when the arm is straight, the triceps is as short as it can possibly get. There is nothing it can bend that would allow it to contract any further. So it stops. The placement of the triceps makes it impossible to exert strong force where it is not wanted.

Similar relationships could be found in any moving joint. Nearly always, there is a **prime mover,** such as the biceps, that provides the main force to move the bone. It is often helped by other muscles, or **synergists,** such as the brachioradialis. Finally, there are **antagonists,** such as the triceps, that work to produce the opposite movement. When one set of muscles contracts,

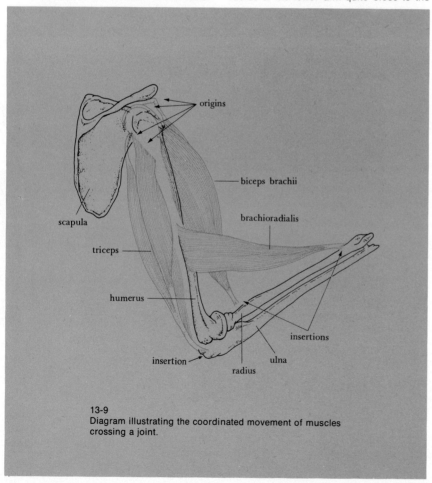

**13-9**
Diagram illustrating the coordinated movement of muscles crossing a joint.

**13-10**
The structural hierarchy of skeletal muscle. Each muscle consists of many individual fibers—long multinucleated cells. The fibers contain a large number of fibrils. These show the light and dark bands characteristic of skeletal muscle. The bands are formed by the overlapping of actin and myosin filaments. (It is the filaments which are the actual contractile elements of muscle.) The filaments are arranged in a linear series of sarcomeres. Each of the sarcomeres shortens as the filaments slide over each other. (See Microscopic structure)

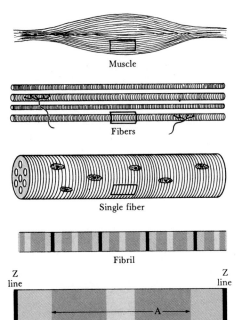

Muscle

Fibers

Single fiber

Fibril

Sarcomere

Myosin and actin filaments

**13-11**
Right: Electron micrograph of an individual sarcomere of rabbit muscle: relaxed (top) and contracted (bottom). From this micrograph it is easy to see that the entire sarcomere (from Z line to Z line) shortens when the muscle contracts.

its antagonists relax, and vice versa.

It might also be noted that many muscles contribute to more than one movement. For instance, suppose you are leaning on your forearm, and your hand is lying palm downward on the table. If you turn the hand palm upward without moving the elbow, you have used both the biceps and the brachioradialis again. More surprisingly, the biceps is also used in two other movements that are precisely the opposite of each other. It works with one set of muscles to move the whole arm out to the side, away from the body. Then it works with another set to move it back.

## Microscopic structure

We said that the only act a muscle can perform is contraction. How does it go about doing this? To begin with, each of the muscle fibers consists of a large number of fibrils. These, in turn, are made up of filaments. The filaments contain two different proteins, actin and myosin, joined in a complex called **actomyosin**.

Under a microscope, a skeletal muscle fiber shows characteristic stripes or striations. These markings are on the fibrils. Most conspicuous are broad, dark stripes known as A-bands. Each of these has a faint, light central section called an H-band. Between the A-bands are wide, light I-bands. Finally, a thin, dark Z-line divides each I-band in two. The part of a fibril between two Z-lines is called a **sarcomere**. Each fibril, then, can be seen as a series of sarcomeres joined end-to-end.

The sarcomere is the functional unit of the muscle. Each sarcomere contains overlapping filaments of myosin and actin. In the I-bands at the ends of the sarcomere, only actin filaments are present. The H-band at the center contains only myosin. In the darker A-bands, the two kinds overlap each other. What happens in contraction is that the actin filaments slide over the myosin. The effect is the same as when the segments of a telescoping TV or radio antenna slide together. The segments stay the same length, but the whole antenna grows short-

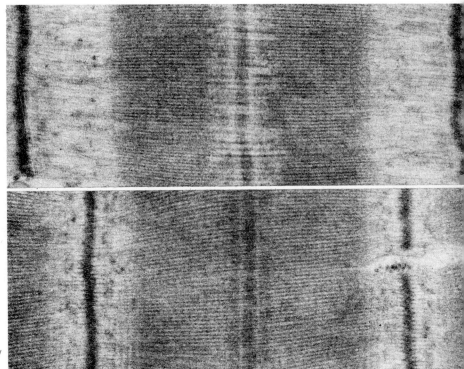

er. Likewise, the actin and myosin filaments remain the same length but the sarcomere grows shorter. And, as all the sarcomeres in all the fibrils in all the fibers shorten, the muscle contracts.

However, the actin and myosin filaments cannot just slide loosely over each other. They need something to pull on. This something is provided by what are known as **cross-bridges.** Tiny protrusions jut out from the myosin filaments. When stimulated, they bind to spots on the actin filaments and pull on them, almost like a rower pulling on an oar. When they have pulled as far as possible, they let go, attach to a new spot, and pull again. All this requires a large amount of energy, which comes from the breakdown of ATP molecules. Some of the energy is dissipated as heat, which is why active exercise makes you feel warm.

## Cardiac and smooth muscle

In addition to skeletal muscle, there are two other types of muscle which serve vital functions in the body. These are smooth muscle and cardiac muscle.

**Smooth muscle** is the kind that occurs in the walls of blood vessels and many internal organs. It is also called **involuntary muscle,** because its action does not depend on the will of its possessor. That is, we do not have to choose to digest the food we have eaten. The muscles in the stomach and intestines go into action when the food arrives, whether we are thinking about it or not. Smooth muscle cells are slender and tapered, and usually have only one nucleus. They lack the light and dark striations of skeletal muscle.

There are two general types of smooth muscle. **Visceral** smooth muscle occurs in large sheets, which contract in unison. It is found in the walls of hollow organs such as the intestines, uterus, and respiratory passages. **Multi-unit** smooth muscle occurs in the walls of blood vessels. It is capable of more localized contractions, and this makes it valuable in regulating the flow of blood to various parts of the body. Unlike

other kinds of muscle, some smooth muscle can remain contracted almost indefinitely. For instance, the sphincter muscle that closes the outlet of the bladder is contracted most of the time. Only when the bladder opens for urination does the sphincter muscle relax.

**Cardiac muscle,** as its name implies, is found in the heart. Like skeletal muscle, it is striated, and its cells have many nuclei. It differs from skeletal muscle in that the fibers are branched. Rather than lying parallel to one another, they form a dense network. This enables the heart to contract inward from many directions at once, as it must in order to pump the blood.

13-12
Electron micrograph of cardiac muscle. Within cardiac muscle are numerous enlarged mitochondria. They provide energy for the contractile activity of the heart.

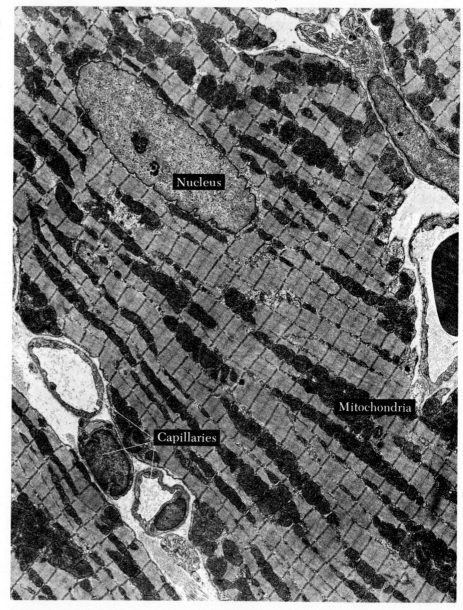

summary

The human skeleton serves three basic functions. It supports the body; it protects the internal organs; and, in conjunction with the muscles, it enables the individual to move. The principal elements in the skeleton are bones and cartilage.

The typical long bone is a long, thin shaft with bulging ends. In the center of the shaft is a cavity filled with fatty yellow marrow. The two ends contain red marrow, which aids in formation of certain blood cells. Tiny blood vessels run all through the bone, penetrating into the marrow.

This design provides maximum strength with minimum weight. The end knobs of the long bone would be too heavy if they were made of compact bone. Instead, they consist of lighter spongy bone. Under the microscope a cross-section of living bone shows many sets of concentric circles, with a small channel at the center of each. The sets are called Haversian systems. The circles are lamellae of nonliving protein fibers and mineral salts, secreted by living bone cells. The central channel, or Haversian canal, contains a blood vessel which brings in needed substances and removes wastes.

The skeleton of the newborn child is largely made up of cartilage. Most of it is gradually replaced by bone in the process of ossification. Permanent cartilage is covered by a layer of tissue called the perichondrium. New cells can form at the inner surface of the perichondrium. This allows growth to continue.

Like bone, cartilage is composed of scattered cells embedded in a noncellular matrix. Bone matrix is rigid, but cartilage matrix is more like a plastic or stiff gelatin. Cartilage contains no blood vessels. Hyaline cartilage, the commonest type, is smooth and milky looking. Fibrous and elastic cartilage are specialized for tasks that require bending and stretching. They are strengthened by fibers interwoven throughout the matrix.

Joints occur where bones meet each other. They hold the bones together, control the amount of movement, and protect the bones from stress and strain. Synarthrotic joints permit little or no movement. They are separated by fibrous cartilage. Ligaments hold the bones tightly against the cartilage. Diarthrotic joints allow relatively free movement. Here the bones are separated by a capsule containing synovial fluid, which lubricates the joint. Many diarthrotic joints are hinge joints (fingers, knees, elbows). Others are ball-and socket joints (shoulders and hips).

Hinge joints bend in one direction only. Ball-and-socket joints allow a wide range of movement. In some parts of the body, such as the wrists and ankles, several types of joint may work together to allow movement in several directions.

Joints would be useless without muscles to move them. Skeletal muscles are composed of long, parallel fibers. Each fiber is a single living cell. Muscles contain one or more bundles of these fibers, each wrapped in a sheath of connective tissue. At the ends of the muscle the connective tissue forms a strong tendon which attaches the muscle to the bone. When the muscle is in action, its fibers contract.

Contraction is the only act a muscle can perform. Movement occurs through the interaction of two or more sets of muscles. In the human arm, the elbow serves as the fulcrum of a lever (the lower arm). Various muscles move this lever. Principal ones include the biceps brachii, the brachioradialis, and the triceps. The biceps serve as a prime mover, providing the main force to move the bone. The brachioradialis is a synergist, assisting the biceps. The triceps is an antagonist that works to produce the opposite movement. When one set of muscles contracts, its antagonists relax, and vice versa.

The sarcomere is the functional unit of the muscle, containing overlapping filaments of myosin and actin. Groups of these filaments make up the fibrils of which each muscle fiber is composed. In muscle contraction, the actin filaments slide over the myosin. In this telescoping movement the actin and myosin filaments stay the same length but the sarcomere grows shorter. The muscle contracts as all the sarcomeres in all the fibrils shorten. Muscle contraction requires a large amount of energy, which comes from the breakdown of ATP molecules. Some of this energy is dissipated as heat.

Smooth or involuntary muscle occurs in the walls of blood vessels and many internal organs. Visceral smooth muscle occurs in large sheets which contract in unison. Multi-unit smooth muscle is capable of more localized contractions. It is valuable in regulating the flow of blood.

Cardiac muscle is found in the heart. Unlike skeletal muscle, its fibers are branched. They form a dense network, enabling the heart to contract inward from many directions at once in order to pump the blood.

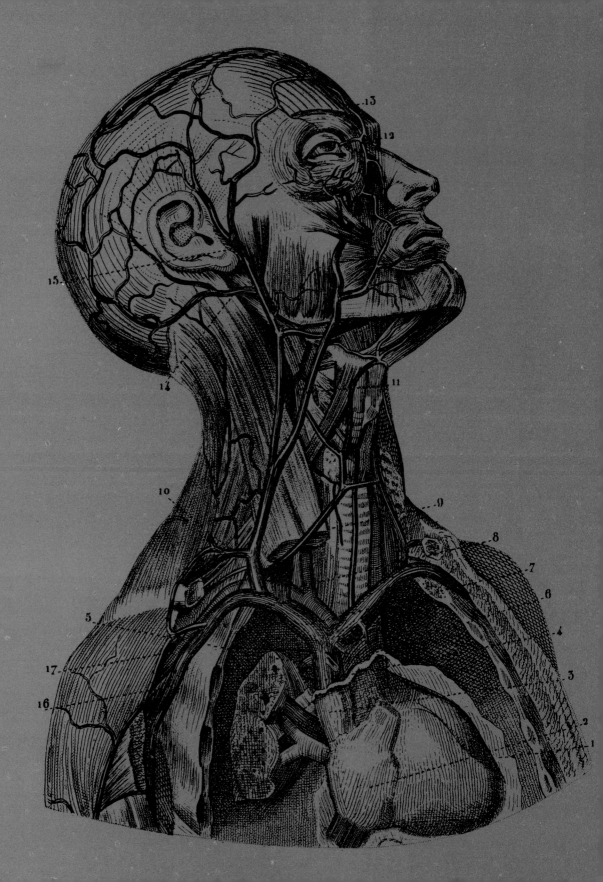

14 human physiology

# h

aving given our human being a framework of bones and muscles, we now have to provide for what goes on inside the framework. In many respects, of course, what goes on is the same as in other vertebrate animals. Food is processed through a digestive system. Oxygen is taken in and distributed by gas exchange and transport systems, and so on. But every animal has its own slight variations on the process. And, being human ourselves, we are likely to be most interested in the human version.

In this chapter, therefore, we shall examine various processes in human physiology. We have already considered the various problems that animals have to solve in order to stay alive. And we have seen, in general, how they solve the problems. But there are many questions we have not yet asked. For instance, we know that hemoglobin in the blood carries oxygen to the cells. But how does it do so? And how does it "know" enough to pick up oxygen at the lungs and drop it at the cells? Clearly, there must be some sort of control process at work here. Likewise, we know that enzymes have something to do with digestion, and that nutrients are eventually absorbed by the body through the intestinal wall. But again, how? And if there are too many nutrients to use, can the body store them for later use? How? Or does it have to discard them? The further we look into physiological processes, the more such questions come to mind.

Ultimately, of course, these questions would carry us farther than we can go here. Hemoglobin and digestive enzymes are chemical substances. So are all the other components of the body. They work together by means of a complex set of interacting chemical responses. And these responses are governed, in turn, by the physical nature of the chemical elements. We can eat, sleep, and engage in work or play partly because a carbon atom has the number of electrons it has, arranged in a certain way. Part of the interest of biology is just this fact that so many "levels of action" go into making the final product. And physiology is, in some ways, a particularly good place to watch it all come together.

## Nutrition and digestion

Living cells are built of an incredible variety of organic compounds, formed from a dozen or so of the earth's elements. Some of these compounds, such as water, are obtained and used directly from the environment. Others must be synthesized from inorganic compounds and energy which are also taken from the environment.

However, human beings, like other heterotrophs, cannot make organic compounds from inorganic chemicals. They receive the energy and carbon "skeletons" they need for synthesis and growth by eating other organisms or the products of other organisms. The organic molecules thus obtained consist mostly of giant molecules—proteins, starches, and lipids. As such, they cannot pass into the cell cytoplasm. These macromolecules must first be digested. That is, they must be broken into components—amino acids, sugars, and fatty acids—which are small enough to pass through cell membranes. Once in the cytoplasm, these small molecules can be bro-

ken down further to obtain energy. Or they can be used to synthesize more complex molecules.

### The human digestive system

Most people would be surprised to learn that the digestion of their most recent meal is taking place outside their bodies. Yet in a sense, this is true. The digestive tract lies inside the body. But its inner surface—the surface with which food comes in contact—is continuous with the outside surface of the body. In effect, the digestive cavity is an extension of the external environment, just as a tunnel through a mountain is an extension of the road that passes through it. This arrangement enables the digestive system to deal with foreign substances—that is, food—and with its own powerful enzymes, without experiencing an immune reaction to the one or being self-digested by the other.

*The upper digestive tract* The **mouth** receives food and prepares it for its journey through the digestive tract. The **teeth** break the food into small pieces. Salivary glands secrete **saliva**. This mucous substance moistens and lubricates the food. In humans, saliva contains the enzyme **amylase**, which begins starch digestion.

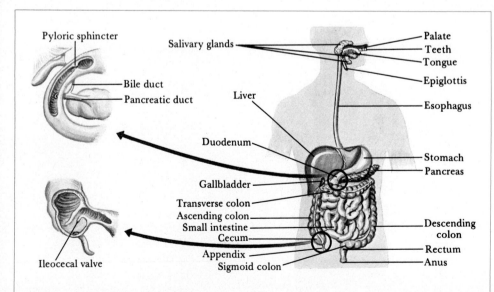

Pyloric sphincter
Salivary glands
Bile duct
Pancreatic duct
Liver
Duodenum
Gallbladder
Transverse colon
Ascending colon
Small intestine
Cecum
Appendix
Sigmoid colon
Ileocecal valve
Palate
Teeth
Tongue
Epiglottis
Esophagus
Stomach
Pancreas
Descending colon
Rectum
Anus

14-1
The human digestive system. Shown are various portions of the digestive tract and the main contributing organs. Note the pyloric sphincter. Just below it is the pancreatic duct at the beginning of the small intestine. Also note the "one-way" structure of the ileocecal valve. It helps to ensure that material once discharged into the colon will not back up into the small intestine. Such one-way valves are common elsewhere in the body.

Herbivore: cow

Omnivore: bear

Carnivore: cat

14-2
Teeth of three typical mammals. The flat surface of the cow's teeth is well suited for crushing and grinding grass. But it would be of little use in tearing up the cat's meat diet.

The **tongue** aids in mixing the food with saliva. It forms this mixture into a ball-like mass which it pushes down into the **pharynx**. Next the food goes to the **esophagus**, a long cartilaginous tube. The muscles of the esophagus move the food toward the stomach by a wave of **peristaltic contractions**. The pharynx and esophagus perform no digestive functions. They merely serve for transport.

*The stomach*   Next, the food enters the **stomach**, a large muscular sac which acts as a storage organ. In humans and in other mammals, the stomach also grinds and mixes food, continuing the breakdown begun in the mouth. It also performs some of the preliminary stages of enzymatic digestion. The stomach wall is composed of an inner mucous membrane containing many glands, a middle layer of smooth muscle, and an outer layer of connective tissue. The glands in the inner lining secrete mucus. This protects the stomach lining and mixes with the food. The glands also secrete highly acid **gastric juice**, containing enzymes which begin the digestion of protein. This high acidity is important, for reasons we will discuss later.

The end result of the stomach's activity is a semiliquid called **chyme**. A valve at the lower end of the stomach, the **pyloric sphincter**, controls the rate at which this chyme enters the small intestine.

*The small intestine*   The **small intestine** is the single most important part of the digestive system. It is here that practically all enzymatic digestion occurs. Here, also, nearly all the absorption of fully broken-down nutrients into the body tissues takes place. Without this absorption, digestion itself would be useless.

The necessary enzymes are produced by glands adjacent to the intestine — particularly the **pancreas** — and by glands in the intestinal wall. Muscular activity mixes the chyme with the enzymes and also moves the mixture through the intestines tract.

*The large intestine*   The main function of the **colon**, or large intestine, is to absorb water and salts from the undigested residue that passes into it from the small intestine. It begins at the lower right side of the abdomen, where it meets the small intestine. At the juncture is a sac called the **cecum**, with a small, finger-like projection — the familiar **appendix**. The cecum is functionally insignificant in humans, though not in all mammals.

The last section of the colon is the **rectum**. It serves as the storage area for feces, which is finally ejected from the body through the **anus**.

## Enzymatic digestion

As we have seen, enzymatic digestion occurs principally in the small intestine, and to a lesser extent in the mouth and stomach. Strictly speaking, the large intestine has no digestive function.

*Carbohydrate digestion*   All digestive enzymes work by **hydrolysis**. That is, they break up complex molecules by inserting a molecule of water between their parts. Most enzymes are highly specific, splitting only one or two types of molecule each. Carbohydrates are hydrolyzed by the various

14-3
The cow chewing her cud is actually taking advantage of an unusually efficient digestive system. Bacteria in the rumen, or first "stomach," ferment cellulose into digestible form. From time to time, the material that is unfermented is returned to the mouth to be chewed again (the cud) before another round of fermentation. After fermentation, the food passes on through the remaining three "stomachs." The last of these (abomasum) is regarded as the true stomach. Bacterial fermentation is not a significant part of digestion in humans.

carbohydrases, or amylases. These enzymes break down long polysaccharide, or starch, molecules. The presence of amylase in human saliva explains why a well-chewed bite of bread begins to taste sweet. But starch digestion is usually still incomplete when the food enters the stomach. There the action of amylase is stopped by the highly acid environment. Once the chyme passes into the small intestine, carbohydrate digestion can resume. Fresh amylase is secreted, along with a substance which reduces the acidity of the chyme. The carbohydrates are reduced to monosaccharides (simple sugars) and disaccharides (double sugars). The double sugars are then further broken down by very specific enzymes inside the cells of the intestinal walls. Finally they are absorbed into the bloodstream. If one of these enzymes is missing—such as lactase, which hydrolyzes milk sugar—then that particular disaccharide cannot be absorbed.

*Protein digestion*  Digestion of protein begins in the stomach. Here an inactive secretion, **pepsinogen**, is converted to the enzyme **pepsin** by contact with the acidic gastric juice. But pepsin splits only a few of the bonds in the complex protein molecules. Protein digestion is completed in the small intestine by additional enzymes. Like pepsin, nearly all of these enzymes are secreted in inactive forms. They are activated by contact with some other substance in the intestinal cavity. This appears to be the body's way of preventing its own substance from being digested by the enzymes. The enzymes are inactive and harmless as long as they are in the cells. By the time they become active and potentially dangerous, they are safely "quarantined" in their proper area of business by the mucous secretions of the stomach and intestinal walls.

*Fat digestion*  Digestion of fats, or lipids, presents special problems. Since fats are not water-soluble, they must first be emulsified. That is, they must be broken up into

droplets small enough to be held in solution. This is the task of the **bile salts**, which are secreted by the liver and stored in the **gall bladder** until needed. Next, the fat is hydrolyzed by yet another enzyme, **lipase**. The resulting substances are absorbed—with some more help from the bile salts—into the cells of the intestinal wall.

---

## Absorption of nutrients

The interior surface of the small intestine is especially adapted for absorption of nutrients. Numerous folds and ridges vastly increase its surface area. The entire surface is covered with finger-like projections called **villi**. The surface of the villi is a layer of cells, each of which is covered by as many as a thousand microscopic projections called **microvilli**. The total absorptive area, then, is about 4500 square meters. It is

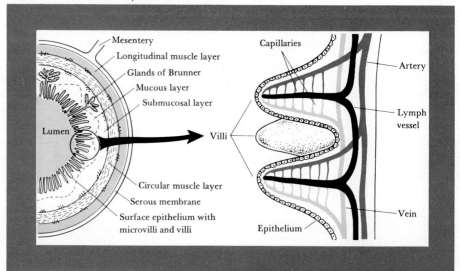

contained within a tube no more than four times the length of a tall man's height, and little thicker than his thumb. Such an extensive surface is needed to absorb nutrients in sufficient quantity and at sufficient speed to meet the body's metabolic needs.

Each villus contains a supply of tiny blood vessels and a lymph duct. Most water-soluble nutrients—mineral salts, simple sugars, amino acids—are absorbed into the bloodstream. Fats, however, are transported mainly by the lymph.

14-4
Interior or generalized small intestine. The enlargement shows the structure of the villi. The epithelium is a type of tissue made of tightly packed cells. These cells line inner and outer surfaces of an animal organism. Secretions from the glands of Brunner help neutralize the acid chyme as it comes from the stomach. Hence, these glands are most numerous in the duodenum, near the pyloric sphincter. Their failure to work normally may contribute to the formation of duodenal ulcers. (See Absorption of nutrients)

### The liver

The body cannot immediately use all the nutrients absorbed by the small intestine. Some of them must be converted into other forms for temporary storage. This task is performed by the liver. One of its particular functions is the transformation of excess glucose to **glycogen**, which it then stores. In this way the liver maintains correct blood sugar levels. It also prevents the overload that would follow a meal if all the absorbed glucose were to pass directly into the bloodstream. Later, when blood sugar levels fall, the liver will convert glycogen back to glucose. When the liver's glycogen storage capacity is exhausted, it converts excess glucose to fat for storage throughout the body.

### Final reabsorption and elimination

By the time food reaches the colon, nutrient absorption is generally complete. But a tremendous amount of water and salt has been secreted into the intestine during digestion. Now much of it must be retrieved. At this stage, the chyme consists of materials which cannot be absorbed. These include cellulose, undigested nutrients, discarded intestinal cells, digestive secretions, and bile residues.

The colon absorbs most of the water and mineral salts. It also absorbs the bile salts for reuse. Large colonies of intestinal bacteria ferment the undigestible matter, reducing it to substances suitable for elimination. An adult on an average American diet usually produces about 150 milliliters of feces per day. About two-thirds of this is water, and bacteria make up from 10 to 20 per cent of the solid portion.

## Gas exchange

Once nutrients reach the cells, they must be metabolized. For this, oxygen is essential. What is needed, then, is a system of gas exchange. This will deliver oxygen to the cells and, equally important, remove the waste carbon dioxide. We have already discussed the elements of such a system, but let us review them here. Gas exchange requires a moist membrane surface with a relatively large area, at which the exchange can occur. There must be some means of moving the oxygen-containing medium across this surface. A transport system between the surface and the body cells is necessary. And finally, there must be a control system that can adjust rates of exchange to meet cell requirements.

A terrestrial environment simplifies respiratory problems by providing a richer oxygen supply than water. But it also creates the new problem of keeping the gas exchange membranes moist. The most satisfactory solution is the lung. Deeply buried within the body, the lung is protected not only against drying but also against temperature change and mechanical damage. So it can function with reasonable efficiency despite wide variations in the environment.

### The human gas exchange system

Before air can be allowed into the lungs, it must be thoroughly saturated with moisture. Otherwise, the lungs would dry out and oxygen could not diffuse through the membranes. So the air must travel a long initial pathway. This begins with the **nostrils**, continuing through the throat or **larnyx**, and on

14-5
The human respiratory system. The epiglottis closes during swallowing to keep food from entering the breathing passage. The mediastinum comprises the heart and other structures that fill the space between the lungs. It is separated from the lungs by its own enclosing membrane. (See Gas exchange)

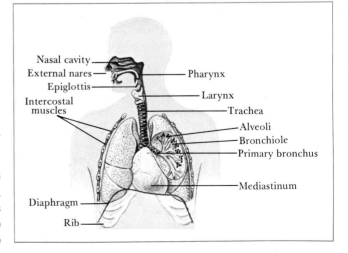

Nasal cavity
External nares
Epiglottis
Intercostal muscles
Pharynx
Larynx
Trachea
Alveoli
Bronchiole
Primary bronchus
Mediastinum
Diaphragm
Rib

into the **trachea**. Throughout this journey the air is continuously moistened, warmed, and filtered by contact with the mucous membranes lining the passages. The trachea is made up of cartilaginous rings, which prevent it from collapsing and cutting off the air supply. It divides into two main branches, the **bronchi**, which lead to the lungs. The bronchi then subdivide repeatedly. After some 20 or more branchings, **terminal bronchioles**—about 20,000 to 80,000 in each lung—lead to tiny air sacs, the **alveoli**.

It is in the alveoli, and only here, that gas exchange actually takes place. The walls of the alveoli consist of a layer of cells covered by a microscopically thin layer of moisture to facilitate gas diffusion, and surrounded by a network of capillaries. Blood is brought to the capillaries by arteries which come directly from the heart. The freshly oxygenated blood is returned to the heart, from which it then goes to the rest of the body.

## Gas exchange and transport

When oxygen diffuses through the alveoli into the capillaries, the problems of delivering it to the tissues are only beginning. Oxygen has a low solubility in water. The amount that can be dissolved in the blood fluids is less than 5 per cent of what the human body needs. Clearly, a more efficient method is called for. The need is met by the red blood cells, which contain hemoglobin. This is a protein containing four iron atoms. Each atom can bind one molecule of oxygen and carry it from the lungs to the tissues. This increases the oxygen-carrying capacity of the blood as much as seventyfold. When the hemoglobin reaches the tissues, it releases oxygen and takes up carbon dioxide for the return journey to the lungs.

Carbon dioxide is 30 times more soluble in water than is oxygen. But only about 5 percent of the $CO_2$ transported by the blood travels dissolved in the blood fluids. About 85 per cent of it combines with water to form

carbonic acid ($H_2CO_3$). This quickly dissociates to form bicarbonate ions ($HCO_3^-$) and hydrogen ions ($H^+$). At the alveoli the reactions reverse, releasing $CO_2$ and $H_2O$. The remaining 10 percent of $CO_2$ is carried by the hemoglobin.

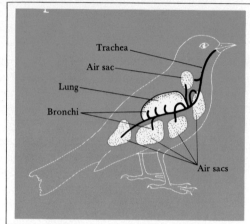

14-6
Mechanics of ventilation in birds. Lung volume in birds is relatively small. But much air passes on into an extensive system of air sacs. Only some of the sacs are shown here. At expiration, some of the air goes back through the lungs. In effect, a fresh supply of oxygen is delivered to the capillaries twice during each breath. In mammals it is delivered only once.

*Partial pressure*    In a mixture of gases at a certain pressure, each gas can be considered as exerting a part of that pressure. This is its **partial pressure**. So we can find the partial pressure of a gas by multiplying the percentage of that gas in the mixture by the pressure of the entire mixture. For instance, atmospheric pressure is measured in terms of the height of a column of mercury (Hg) that the pressure will support—about 760 millimeters at sea level. Air is roughly 79 per cent nitrogen and 21 per cent oxygen. So to find the partial pressure of oxygen we would multiply 0.21 by 760. This gives a partial pressure for oxygen ($PO_2$) of 160 millimeters. But at the top of Mount Everest, total air pressure is only 240 mm Hg. So the partial pressure of oxygen—assuming the percentage remains the same—is only about 50 mm. This is less than one-third the value at sea level.

*Oxygen dissociation curve*    The degree to which hemoglobin becomes saturated with oxygen is determined first by the partial pressures of oxygen in the lungs. At atmospheric partial pressure, hemoglobin

will be 95 percent saturated. At lower partial pressures, such as those in the tissues, it will give up oxygen. It thus becomes less saturated. The ability of hemoglobin to take up or release oxygen at different partial pressures can be shown by an **oxygen dissociation curve**. Such a curve shows that, at certain levels, very slight drops in oxygen pressure—such as occur between lungs and tissues—cause hemoglobin to give up most of its oxygen. At other levels, less likely to be encountered, large changes in pressure have little effect.

An increase in blood acidity will shift the curve to the right. That is, hemoglobin will more readily give up oxygen. Remember that $CO_2$ given up by tissue cells produces carbonic acid. It thus increases blood acidity in the tissues, where oxygen is needed. At the lungs, on the other hand, oxygen must be taken up. Here the loss of $CO_2$ lowers blood acidity, enabling the hemoglobin to hold on to more oxygen. This interdependence of oxygen and carbon dioxide in the blood's gas transport system is one of the wonders of the body's biochemistry. Each promotes the release and transport of the other just where it is needed.

**14-7**
Why do divers need less oxygen than people at sea level? The key to the answer is that the hemoglobin system works on the basis of partial pressure. When mammals abandon the air for the water, they must take an oxygen supply with them. But human divers carry tanks of air. They use a system designed to feed oxygen to their lungs at lower than normal partial pressures. This offsets the extra compression pressure created by the weight of the water. Other diving mammals have natural adaptations. Porpoises can stay under water for twelve minutes or so. They have a blood volume about twice as large, relative to body size, as humans have. The hemoglobin in the extra blood provides "storage space" for reserve oxygen. (See Gas exchange and transport)

**14-8**
Oxygen-dissociation curves of normal human hemoglobin. They show the effects of changes in acidity and in $CO_2$ partial pressure at various levels of oxygen partial pressure.

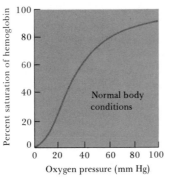
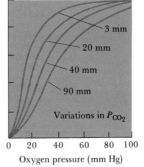
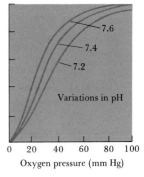

**14-9**
Vicunas typically live at high altitudes where oxygen partial pressure is low. So they have evolved hemoglobin which can absorb large amounts of oxygen at these pressures. On a graph, their oxygen-dissociation curve would be to the left of that for humans. (See Oxygen dissociation curve)

**14-10**
General design of the human circulatory system. It shows the separation of the lung (pulmonary) and systemic circulation. (See Internal transport)

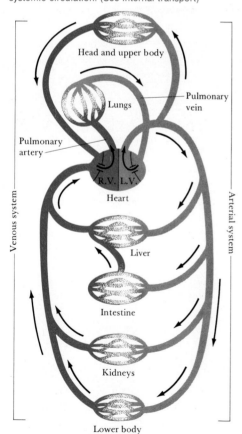

## Control

The respiration rate must be continuously regulated. Adjustments must be made for varying concentrations of blood gases, and for oxygen demands at different levels of activity. This regulation is for the most part involuntary. The control center appears to be in the medulla, in the lower portion of the brain. Chemical receptors in the medulla are highly sensitive to changes in $CO_2$ level. It is these $CO_2$ levels, not $O_2$ levels, which are most important in determining the rate and depth of breathing, just as they are important in regulating oxygen delivery by the hemoglobin molecule. Thus different but interacting systems, both essential to oxygen supply, are regulated by the same mechanism — the presence of carbon dioxide.

## Internal transport

We have seen earlier that both digestion and gas exchange require some means of transport. The transport system must be in close contact with all the cells of the organism. It must be able to move substances — especially oxygen — rapidly. In addition to nutrients and respiratory gases, it must also be equipped to carry a wide variety of other substances, which serve to regulate the internal environment.

As we have already seen, the transport system in humans is closed. That is, it is confined to specific pathways, or vessels. Blood is propelled by a muscular pumping device — the heart — and flows in one direction only. There are two main loops in the system. The **pulmonary circulation** conducts oxygen-poor blood from the heart to the lungs and oxygenated blood back to the heart. The **systemic circulation** carries oxygenated blood from the heart to all the body cells and returns oxygen-poor blood, laden with carbon dioxide, to the heart.

A large **artery** conducts the blood away from the heart. This branches into smaller arteries and then into even smaller **arteri-**

**oles**. From these, the blood is distributed to individual cells by an extensive network of microscopically thin **capillaries**. Nutrients, gases, and other substances are exchanged between blood and tissues through the capillary walls. Blood leaving the capillaries is gathered into small **venules**. These empty into progressively larger **veins**, that eventually return the blood to the heart.

### The human heart

The heart is a pumping organ. In the average human lifetime it will beat approximately 2.5 billion times. It is basically a hollow muscle, divided into right and left halves by partitions called **septa**. Each half is divided into an upper and a lower chamber, the **atrium** and the **ventricle**. In a sense, there are two hearts, since the blood in the left half is entirely separated from that in the right half. Consequently, the oxygen-rich blood from the lungs does not mix with oxygen-poor blood from the body. This is a prime requirement for maintaining the high metabolic rates of warm-blooded organisms.

*Chambers of the heart*    Blood from the systemic circulation is brought to the right atrium. When the atrium is full, it contracts. This forces blood into the right ventricle. The ventricle contracts in turn, driving the blood into the **pulmonary artery** which branches to each lung. After passing through the capillaries in the lungs, the blood is rich with oxygen. It now returns to the heart through the **pulmonary veins**. It enters the left atrium and is pumped — again by contraction of the atrium — into the left ventricle. This chamber is the workhorse of the whole circulatory system. It pumps the blood into the arteries under very high pressure. The initial pressure must be high enough so that the blood will still be under pressure when it reaches the capillaries. So we can easily understand why the left ventricle is the chamber most often damaged in heart attack.

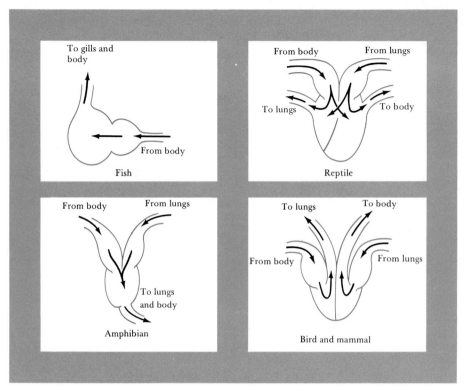

To gills and
body

From body

Fish

From body          From lungs

To lungs
and body

Amphibian

From body          From lungs

To lungs          To body

Reptile

To lungs          To body

From body          From lungs

Bird and mammal

**14-11**
Four types of vertebrate heart. Evolution from two to four chambers allowed the separation of pulmonary and systemic circulation. This permits more efficient oxygen transport. It also makes it possible to maintain strong blood pressure in both circulatory loops.

*Heartbeat*    The heart's rhythmic contractions originate in the heart itself. They are not dependent on the central nervous system. Were this not true, heart transplants would be impossible, since the nervous system of a transplant recipient cannot be effectively connected to the nerves of the transplanted organ.

Although the heart contracts independently, the contractions must be coordinated. They must occur in the proper sequence and rhythm. This task is handled by two nodes of tissue that act as cardiac pacemakers. The first of these is the sino-atrial *(S-A)* node. It generates rhythmic electrical impulses which spread across the muscle fibers of both atria. This in turn generates a wave of contractions. Within less than a second the impulses reach the **atrio-ventricular** *(A-V)* node. The A-V node in turn generates impulses which spread to all parts of the ventricles, causing them to contract.

Each heartbeat cycle consists of a peri-

od of contraction (**systole**) followed by a period of relaxation (**diastole**). The human heart produces, on the average, 72 such cycles or beats per minute.

## The vascular system

Blood leaving the left ventricle moves upward into the **aorta**, which soon gives rise to a number of major branch arteries. Among the first are those which carry blood to the neck and head. In this way, the brain is assured of a fresh and rich oxygen supply. The arteries which serve the arms also branch off before the aorta turns downward behind the heart. After sending out further branches to the organs and tissues of the trunk, the aorta is now much narrower. It finally splits into the arteries which supply the legs and feet.

Blood returning to the heart follows a similar set of pathways through the veins, now converging rather than dividing. But while one artery serves to carry blood out of the heart, two veins finally bring it back. The **superior vena cava** drains the upper part of the body, and the **inferior vena cava** drains the lower.

*Arteries*    Since arteries receive blood under high pressure, their walls are strong, elastic, and muscular. With each new surge of blood from the heart, the artery expands. Then it recoils and returns to normal diameter. The recoil reinforces the heartbeat pressure and sends the blood along in pulsating waves. As the arteries become smaller, their walls become thinner. Finally, in the smallest arterioles the elastic outer layer disappears. The remaining muscular layer allows the arterioles to close completely or to expand, according to the oxygen needs of neighboring tissues.

**Blood pressure** originates in the strong contraction of the left ventricle. It reaches a high point of about 120 mm Hg during systole. During diastole, contraction of the expanded arteries maintains a pressure of about 80 mm Hg. As blood moves from the aorta to the arterioles, the pressure drops

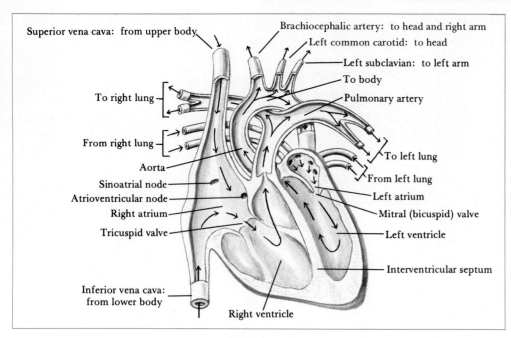

Superior vena cava: from upper body

Brachiocephalic artery: to head and right arm

Left common carotid: to head

Left subclavian: to left arm

To body

Pulmonary artery

To right lung

From right lung

To left lung

From left lung

Aorta

Sinoatrial node

Atrioventricular node

Right atrium

Tricuspid valve

Left atrium

Mitral (bicuspid) valve

Left ventricle

Interventricular septum

Inferior vena cava: from lower body

Right ventricle

14-12
Cross section of the human heart. It shows the chambers, main blood vessels, and path of blood flow. The nodes do not look precisely as shown here. They are drawn to give an idea of their respective locations.

off. But there is great resistance to blood flow in the narrow arterioles. By altering this resistance—through expansion and contraction—the arterioles help to maintain pressure.

*Veins* Veins are constructed similar to arteries, but their walls are thinner. So the veins are easily swollen by a large volume of blood, and easily squeezed by pressure from without.

By the time blood reaches the veins, its pressure is very low. The pumping action of the heart can no longer keep it moving. Some other means is needed to return it to the heart. Here the relative "flabbiness" of the veins is an advantage. As muscles contract in ordinary movement, they press on the veins. This squeezes them and forces blood forward in a "milking action." A system of one-way valves keeps the flow moving in the right direction.

*Capillaries* All exchange between the tissues and the blood takes place through a vast network of capillaries that are in contact with every cell of the body. Capillaries are microscopically thin tubes. Their walls

are only one cell thick, and their diameter is so narrow that red blood cells may be squeezed out of shape while getting through them. The number of capillaries in a given tissue depends on the activity it performs. For instance, muscle, lung, and kidney tissue contain more capillaries than ligament or cartilage.

The capillaries are surrounded by the **tissue fluid** (or interstitial fluid) which bathes all the body cells. This fluid takes an important part in the exchange process.

The flow of blood through the capillaries is partially regulated by the arterioles. By constriction, the arterioles can shut off supplies to the capillary beds extending from them. At any given moment, most capillaries are closed and empty. Blood follows alternate pathways through the capillary beds, depending on demand—in particular, the local demand for oxygen.

Once blood is in the capillaries, two principal factors regulate exchanges between it and the surrounding tissue fluids. One is its remaining hydrostatic pressure. This is what we normally mean by "blood pressure." Blood enters the capillaries at a pressure of about 30 mm Hg. By the time it

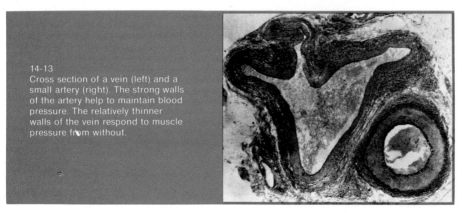

**14-13**
Cross section of a vein (left) and a small artery (right). The strong walls of the artery help to maintain blood pressure. The relatively thinner walls of the vein respond to muscle pressure from without.

reaches the venous end, friction has reduced the pressure to about 10 mm Hg. The pressure at the arteriole end forces water and dissolved materials out of the capillary into the tissue fluid. Alone, this would steadily drain the blood of its water and dissolved materials. At the same time, the tissues would become dangerously waterlogged. But a difference in osmotic pressure develops between the blood and tissue fluid. Capillary walls act as semipermeable membranes, allowing free passage of substances whose molecules are small. But they are less permeable to the large protein molecules, which therefore tend to remain in the blood. As water is forced out by hydrostatic pressure, the protein concentration in the remaining blood becomes higher than that of the tissue fluid. This creates a gradient that tends to draw water back into the capillaries.

## Composition of the blood

The seemingly homogeneous red fluid that spills out of a cut finger is, in reality, anything but homogeneous. It contains highly specialized cells of several types, as well as a rich variety of noncellular materials.

*Blood cells*   Blood takes its color from the red cells, or **erythrocytes**, which make up about 45 per cent of total blood volume. These cells contain the hemoglobin which carries oxygen through the body. In fact, they contain very little else. Although the

young red cell possesses a nucleus and other organelles, it gets rid of them as it matures. This allows the cell to accomodate over 2.5 million molecules of hemoglobin. But it also means the red cell forfeits the capacity to reproduce, or to repair any damage. Red blood cells must be continuously replaced by new cells, manufactured in the bone marrow.

Far fewer than the red cells are the white cells, or **leucocytes**. Their particular job is to defend the body against infection by harmful microbes. Some of them produce antibodies. Others ingest foreign materials by phagocytosis. Both types can move rapidly through the capillaries to threatened areas of the body.

The **thrombocytes**, or platelets, also serve for defense. They are instrumental in blood clotting. Though we are not sure how, they seem to work together with a blood protein called **fibrinogen**. Apparently, when a blood vessel is ruptured, thrombocytes somehow convert fibrinogen into threadlike fibers of **fibrin**. The fibers form a clot and stop the bleeding. White cells and thrombocytes together make up about 1 per cent of the blood.

*Plasma and its components*   The cells we mentioned above account for only a few of the functions performed by the blood. The rest are handled by the liquid **plasma**. While plasma is mostly water, its other components are much more important than

their volume would suggest.

The **plasma proteins** comprise about 7 per cent of the plasma. **Albumin** is the smallest and most abundant of these proteins. Its principal function is to maintain the osmotic potential of the blood. Other such proteins include the antibodies, or **immunoglobins**; a number of substances involved in the clotting process; and a variety of **carrier proteins**. The carrier proteins bind to molecules of other substances to transport them through the blood.

Inorganic ions are essential components of plasma. Calcium, sodium, and potassium are fundamental in regulating nerve and muscle activity. Sodium also has a strong influence on osmotic potential. Bicarbonate transports carbon dioxide and helps to keep the blood slightly alkaline.

Hormones, important regulators of body functions, are transported by the plasma. Nitrogenous wastes given off by the cells are carried to the kidneys for excretion. And in addition to the various materials bound by transport substances, assorted nutrients and gases travel free, dissolved in the plasma water.

## The lymphatic system

We have said that capillary walls are normally impermeable to protein. However, because of the high hydrostatic pressure in the capillaries, there is a constant small leakage of blood protein into the tissue fluid. This leakage could eventually upset the balance of body fluids and cause serious harm. But this does not happen. The protein cannot simply diffuse back into the capillaries, since the tissue fluids do not provide enough pressure. The blood protein must take an indirect route. This is provided by the **lymphatic system**.

The lymphatic system is composed of vessels much like those that carry blood, except that they include no arteries. The walls of the **lymph capillaries** are more permeable to large molecules—particularly proteins—than are those of blood capillaries. They merge into **lymph veins**, which eventually drain into the great veins near the heart.

Since they are more permeable to protein, and since the fluid within them is at a lower pressure, the lymph capillaries can absorb the leaked protein and excess tissue fluid. In due time these are returned to the bloodstream. This retrieval of lost protein is one of the most important functions of the lymphatic system. In fact, lymph consists mainly of this fluid and protein. That is, it is essentially the same as blood plasma. It also contains a group of white cells, the **lymphocytes**, which are important in the body's resistance to infection.

**Lymph nodes** are masses of tissue. They are located either along the lymph vessels or independently of them. Their function seems to be mainly defensive. The lymph nodes contain large populations of lymphocytes. They also act as filters, trapping and storing large particles, such as bits of dust, which the body cannot eject. When infection occurs, they may hold up bacteria until antibodies can be formed to destroy them.

## Chemical regulation

We have already stressed the importance of proper **osmotic balance**. In terrestrial animals, such as humans, the problem is especially complicated. This is because of a constant loss of essential water through respiration, sweating, and elimination in feces and urine.

Osmotic pressure is dependent on the concentration of suspended or dissolved particles in a solution. Animals maintain proper osmotic concentration in body fluids by means of a variety of such solutes—particularly organic molecules and inorganic ions. Proper **ionic balance** is a vital part of the body's chemical regulation. It involves preservation of ions in short supply, and excretion of the excess. A proper **acid--base balance** is equally important.

Breakdown of amino acids by the liver produces nitrogenous wastes, particularly ammonia. In humans, this is quickly converted into urea, which the body can store for a time. But urea must be excreted in liquid form, which depletes the body's water reserves.

The kidney and its associated organs handle much of the regulation of water content, acid-base balance, and osmotic balance within the body. They are also the only means of eliminating the waste products of protein metabolism. The kidneys are therefore vital to maintenance of internal balance.

## The human excretory system

The excretory system in humans consists of two **kidneys**. These are located high in the abdominal cavity, one on each side of the spine. They are reddish-brown in color, and are shaped rather like two kidney beans. On the concave side, toward the spine, is the **renal artery**, which branches directly from the aorta. In the same area are also located the **renal vein** (which leads to the inferior vena cava), lymph vessels, and nerves.

At the same point the kidney connects with the **ureter**, which carries urine from the kidney to the **bladder**. From the bladder, the **urethra** passes the urine out of the body. In males, but not in females, the urethra is also a part of the genital system. Urine is formed only in the kidney. The other organs are concerned with storage and transport.

*The kidney*   The kidney consists of specialized structures for filtering blood and for concentrating and collecting urine. A large cavity on the concave side acts as the initial storage area for finished urine. Around this is the comparatively light-colored **renal medulla**. It consists of cone-shaped tissue masses called **pyramids**, whose tips extend into the pelvis. Outside the medulla is a layer of darker tissue called the **renal cortex**. We will see the importance of this placement of cortex and medulla when we consider how the kidney carries out its functions.

Branches of the renal artery run between the medulla and the cortex. Further subdivi-

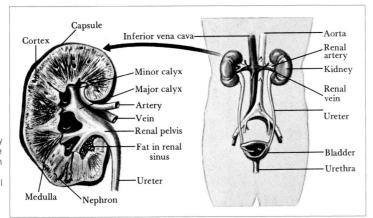

14-14
Human excretory
system. The cross
section shows clearly
the orientation of the
nephrons. They drain
into the calyces, or
branches of the renal
pelvis (a large cavity
on the concave side
of the kidney).

sions produce a network of arterioles and capillaries. This network is intimately linked with the functional unit of the kidney, the **nephron**.

*Structure of the nephron*   Each kidney contains about one million nephrons. The nephron is the structure that actually produces urine. It is a long, microscopically thin tubule. One end of the nephron is closed and folded into a cup-shaped receptacle in the cortex, called **Bowman's capsule**. From the capsule extends the convoluted **proximal tubule**. The tube then straightens, extends downward—toward or into the medulla—and bends up again. This forms a U-shaped section known as the **loop of Henle**. It continues in a second convoluted section called the **distal tubule**. This empties, along with other such tubules, into a **collecting tubule**. The collecting tubule plunges back into the medulla, parallel to the loop of Henle. Eventually it drains into the cavity. All of the nephrons are oriented in the same way. Their capsules and convoluted tubules are located in the cortex, and the loop of Henle and collecting duct point inward toward the tip of the pyramid.

The blood vessels associated with the nephron are as important as the nephron itself. An **arteriole** brings blood to a cluster of capillaries, the **glomerulus**, enclosed in Bowman's capsule. After passing through the glomerulus, the blood is carried by an-

other arteriole to a second capillary network closely surrounding the tubules and loop of Henle. From these capillaries it goes to a small vein which eventually leads to the main renal vein.

## Urine formation

Blood entering the glomerulus has traveled only a short distance from the aorta. Consequently, it is under fairly high pressure. The pressure forces a certain amount of plasma and dissolved substances out through the vessel walls and into Bowman's capsule. When this **filtrate** first enters the capsule and begins its journey through the nephron, it is similar to plasma. It contains all the same ions, glucose, and other substances except protein.

As the filtrate passes through the proximal tubule, it loses most of its water and

solutes. These are reabsorbed into the blood through the surrounding capillaries. The reabsorption is selective. That is, having deposited solutes of all kinds in the tubule, the body takes back only what it can use. Wastes and surpluses are left behind for excretion.

By the time the filtrate reaches the end of the proximal tubule, it has lost about 75 per cent of its water and solutes. But if the remaining 25 per cent were excreted, it would amount to 10 or 12 gallons of urine every day. So there must be a way of getting most of this back into the system. The easiest way would be to move it along a semipermeable tube through very salty surroundings. Osmotic pressure would then draw the water out through the walls of the tube, but leave everything else behind. For this to occur, an osmotic gradient must be established in the tissues through which the tube passes.

This gradient is created by the loop of Henle, and particularly by the second or ascending limb of the loop. As the filtrate passes through this limb, sodium is actively pumped out. Some of the sodium remains in the tissue fluid, making it more concentrated. The rest diffuses back into the descending limb, making the filtrate more concentrated on the way down. Both concentrations are greatest at the bend in the loop.

What happens is that as the dilute filtrate enters the loop, it encounters slightly

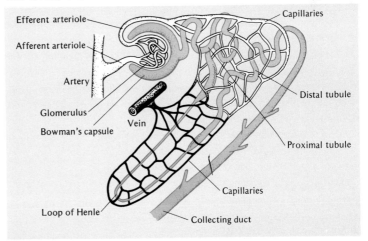

14-15
Structure of
the human
nephron.

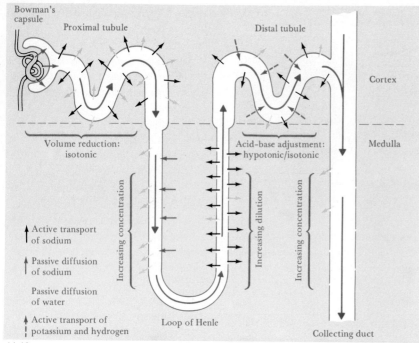

Bowman's capsule

Proximal tubule

Distal tubule

Cortex

Volume reduction: isotonic

Acid-base adjustment: hypotonic/isotonic

Medulla

Increasing concentration

Increasing dilution

Increasing concentration

↑ Active transport of sodium

↑ Passive diffusion of sodium

Passive diffusion of water

↑ Active transport of potassium and hydrogen

Loop of Henle

Collecting duct

14-16
Process of urine formation.

more concentrated surrounding tissues. A small amount of water is therefore drawn off, and a small amount of sodium absorbed. Now the filtrate is more concentrated. But it then moves on into an even more concentrated environment. More water is removed and more sodium absorbed. This continues as far as the bend in the loop. At this point the filtrate has become quite concentrated.

But now, as the filtrate turns the bend and starts upward, it begins to pass back into less concentrated regions. Why does it not simply take back the lost water and become as dilute as before?

Actually, it does become even more dilute than before. But it does so not by gaining water, but rather by the active outpumping of sodium described above. The lost water cannot be recovered, because the walls of the ascending limb are relatively impermeable to water. So the filtrate arrives at the distal tubule somewhat reduced in volume and less concentrated than the blood.

In the distal tubule, more water is lost.

Here the filtrate undergoes a sort of "fine-tuning." A variety of ions are pumped in and out, and the acid–base balance is adjusted to a level slightly more acid than that of the blood. A small amount of ammonia is formed, and the fluid enters the collecting duct. At this point, the fluid is a true urine but still dilute.

As the urine passes down the collecting duct, parallel to the loop of Henle, it encounters the increasing osmotic gradient which was created by the loop. The walls of the collecting duct act as a semipermeable membrane. So water is drawn out of the urine, but all the solutes remain. As the urine passes the tip of the loop, it reaches the same concentration as is found in the renal medulla at its most concentrated point.

As this suggests, the length of the loop of Henle is an important factor in formation of a concentrated urine. The longer the loop, the greater the concentration gradient that can be established, and thus the more concentrated the urine can eventually become.

## Control

The kidneys are subject to both neural and hormonal control. But they can continue to function when nerves are cut. As with the heart, this property makes transplants possible.

The ADH system is one of the most important mechanisms for control of water balance. The collecting tubule has a varying permeability to water, controlled by the amount of **antidiuretic hormone** (ADH) in the blood. This hormone is secreted by the pituitary in response to osmotic concentration in body fluids. An increase of osmotic concentration triggers increased ADH production. This makes the collecting duct more permeable to water and so allows greater reabsorption. The end result is a more concentrated urine. On the other hand, if blood concentration falls, production of ADH also falls. This makes the collecting duct less permeable. Therefore, less water is reabsorbed, and the body rids itself of excess fluid. This explains the well-known effects of drinking large amounts of beer. Alcohol in the blood inhibits ADH production, and body chemistry responds by taking its normal course.

14-17
The kangaroo rat has such efficient water-conservation equipment that it never needs to drink. All the water it needs is produced by metabolism of the dry food it eats. It can be induced to drink sea water. It suffers no apparent ill effects from doing so.

**summary**

The human digestive system must break down macromolecules so that they can be absorbed and used by the human body. The digestive system can do this without damaging its own tissues. This is because the digestive cavity is effectively a part of the external environment.

The mouth breaks the food into small pieces. Saliva lubricates it for easy passage and adds amylase to begin starch digestion. The food then enters the stomach where it is ground, mixed, and broken down further. Gastric juice secreted by glands in the stomach wall contains enzymes that begin protein digestion. The food is now a semiliquid called chyme. It passes into the small intestine, where most digestion and all absorption of digested nutrients occur.

Carbohydrates are digested by enzymes called carbohydrases. They split starch molecules into simple or double sugars. Protein digestion begins in the stomach where pepsinogen is converted to pepsin by stomach acid. It is completed in the small intestine by enzymes secreted by the intestine and the pancreas. Fats are first emulsified by bile salts secreted by the liver. They are then digested by lipase, a pancreatic enzyme.

Digested nutrients are absorbed in the small intestine, whose numerous folds and ridges, covered with villi and microvilli, provide an enormous absorptive area. The villi contain capillaries and a lymph duct. Water-soluble nutrients are absorbed directly into the blood, whereas fats enter the lymph. Excess glucose absorbed by the intestines is converted by the liver to glycogen or fat. Final reabsorption of water and salts takes place in the large intestine. Nonabsorbable and discarded materials are eliminated through the anus as feces.

Metabolism requires intake of oxygen and release of carbon dioxide. This gas exchange requires a moist surface with a large area. The lungs receive air that has been moistened, warmed, and filtered by passage through the nose, throat, and trachea. The trachea divides into two main bronchi that subdivide into bronchioles. These lead eventually to the alveoli, where gas exchange actually takes place.

Upon diffusing through the capillaries, $O_2$ is carried by hemoglobin in the blood to body cells, where it is exchanged for $CO_2$. The $CO_2$ is transported back to the lungs. The exchange of gas between lung and blood and between blood and body cells is governed by the partial pressures of the gases involved. The medulla controls the rate of respiration. It is highly sensitive to changes in $CO_2$ levels.

The human circulatory system consists of two closed loops: the pulmonary and the systemic circulation. The former exchanges $O_2$ and $CO_2$ with the lungs. The latter exchanges these gases and other materials with the body cells.

The human heart consists of four chambers. Systemic blood reaches the right atrium through the superior and inferior vena cava. It passes into the right ventricle, which pumps it to the lungs through the pulmonary artery. The blood returns to the heart through the pulmonary veins and enters the left atrium. It is then pumped to the left ventricle, and out to the body by way of the aorta. The heartbeat is controlled by two nodes of tissue in the heart itself. The sino-atrial node contracts the atria, and the atrio-ventricular node contracts the ventricles.

Blood flows from the arteries into arterioles and then into capillaries. It then passes into venules, into larger veins, and on to the vena cava. Arteries have strong elastic walls. Movement of substances from capillaries to cells is promoted by hydrostatic pressure. Uptake by the capillaries is a result of osmotic pressure.

The blood is a complex fluid. Red cells contain the oxygen-carrying hemoglobin. White cells fight infection, and platelets help in blood clotting. The liquid plasma contains protein and inorganic ions. Also, hormones are transported via plasma.

The lymphatic system parallels the circulatory system but does not have a pumping device. It returns blood proteins that leak out of the capillaries because of hydrostatic pressure. Lymphocytes are white cells of the lymph.

Osmotic, ionic, and acid–base balance and the body's water content balance are maintained by the kidneys. The functional unit of the kidney is the nephron. Blood fluids filter through the nephron, where water and excess ions are removed. A high osmotic gradient produced by the loop of Henle allows much of the water to be removed as urine passed through the collecting duct, leaving the excess ions and urea. This concentration allows the body to preserve water. Concentrated urine passes through the ureter, into the bladder, and out through the urethra.

the terms adaptation and behavior have fairly clear meanings when applied to much of the biological world. But they become problematic when applied to the human race. This is because humans have the capacity for rapid social, cultural, and technological evolution. For example, let us consider an organism which must survive long periods of extreme cold and near vacuum. It is possible that it would evolve some sort of insulated, air-tight carapace. The process, however, would probably take millions of years. Humans, on the other hand, have designed and built space suits for the same purpose. And they have done it in just a few decades. Humans have also accelerated the process of evolution for many other organisms. For example, left to natural selection, the capacity for domestication might have taken wild animals hundreds of millenia to acquire. But the process was enormously speeded up by the fact that humans learned to breed animals selectively for this trait.

Evolution often comes up with similar answers to similar problems. Both the giant kelp, a brown alga, and the water lily, a flowering plant, achieve stability in much the same way. They both anchor themselves firmly to the bottom of their aquatic environment. The latter uses true roots; the former uses a root-like holdfast. To get maximum sunlight, both organisms have ways of keeping parts of their structure above or close to the water's surface. The long, branched stalks of the kelp are buoyed by air-filled bladders. The leaves of the lily float easily on the surface of lakes or ponds.

Plants exhibit a wide range of adaptation to difficult weather conditions. The fuzzy stems of the lousewort, for example, give protection from the cold and drying winds of the northern tundra. Other plants create microclimates suited to their needs. The moss campion *(Silene acaulis)*, another tundra native, forms a dense cushion that holds the sun's warmth and retains moisture. This is very important for the plant during the cool, dry arctic summers. Spanish moss also profits from a microclimate. Spanish moss is really a bromeliad. That is, it is a plant which gets its nutrients mainly from the air and rain, and lives on other trees, such as the cypress. Rainwater and soil particles collect in the crotches of the cypress, providing the bromeliad with nourishment.

Hunters and hunted alike rely heavily on concealment, deception, and clever environmental adaptations. Many predators wait in ambush for their prey. This requires them either to be invisible to potential victims or actually to attract them. For example, the waterbug floats motionless just below the surface of the water. There it waits till small aquatic creatures, such as minnows, come within reach. The flower spider all but disappears into the floral background, waiting for an edible insect. The killer whale is a much more mobile predator. Its white belly and dark back—a common color pattern among marine creatures—make it equally difficult to see from above and below.

Coloration is also an important protective device for animals who are trying to avoid being eaten. The arctic hare, for example, undergoes seasonal color

Humans have affected their own evolution and that of
other organisms. We have designed space suits which
enable us to survive extreme conditions. Left:
Astronaut Garriott on Skylab 3 in orbit. Here on earth,
we can count the domestication of animals as another
human achievement. Above: Norwegian farm horses.

Both the giant kelp (right, bottom), a brown alga, and the water lily (above), a flowering plant, achieve stability in the water by anchoring themselves firmly to the bottom. Another aquatic plant, the mangrove, solves its gas exchange problem by means of air roots (right, top) which project above the water.

Adapting to a given environment is crucial to survival. The moss campion (right, bottom) holds the sun's warmth and retains moisture during the arctic summers. Bromeliads, which often live on cypress trees (above), receive rainwater and soil particles which accumulate in the crotches of the tree. Right, top: Arctic poppy.

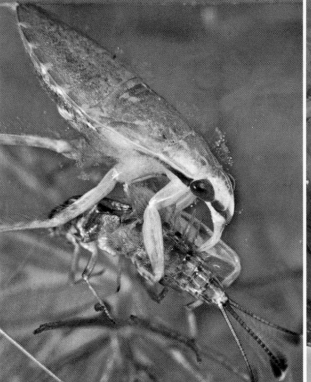

Organisms exhibit a variety of methods for trapping prey and eluding their own enemies. The Venus's flytrap (top, left) lures insects with its attractive scent and coloration. The flower spider (top, right) relies on camouflage. Near right: Waterbug capturing mayfly nymph. Far right: Killer whale, difficult to see from above and below.

Protective coloration is an essential feature of many organisms. Left, top: Arctic hare, vulnerable in its white winter coat. Left, bottom: Sea slug, whose bright colors serve as a warning to predators. Right, top: Aphids. This species comes in pink and green, since members feed on rosebuds for part of their life cycle. Right, bottom: Anole, an adaptable lizard.

Animals engage in a variety of courtship displays and rituals (sometimes involving marked physical changes), without which mating cannot take place. Above: American egret, in its white mating plumes. Right, top: Waved albatrosses "fencing" with their bills. Right, bottom: Rhinoceroses mating.

Rituals and displays are often used to ward off rivals and foes. Left: A short-eared owl tries to look large and formidable when danger threatens. The snarl of the hippopotamus (below, bottom) may replace actual combat. Thompson's gazelles (below, top) engage in relatively bloodless ritual combat.

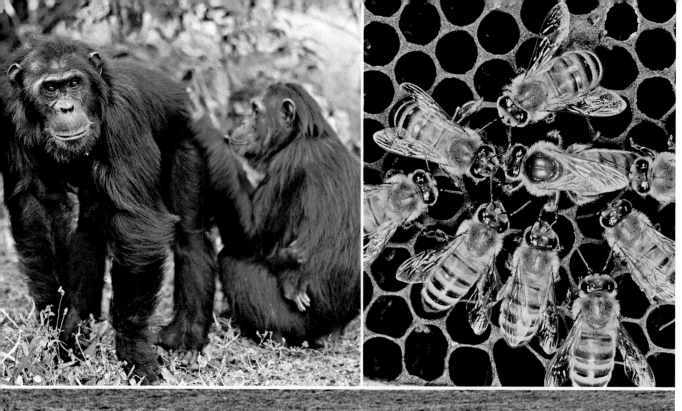

Behavior in animal societies can serve many functions.
Among chimpanzees (top, left) ritual grooming strengthens
social ties and helps to establish a hierarchy of
dominance. Among honey bees (top, right) the dominance of
the queen is ensured by a substance that she secretes.
Muskoxen (above) adopt a circular formation when in danger.

changes. In general, such changes are in response to changes in temperature or the length of the day. But sometimes the schedules fail to harmonize. The hare in the photograph has been double-crossed by nature. Until the snows arrive it will be an easy target. The anole, a lizard, has a more efficient system. Pigment granules in its skin enable it to match the color of any surface it perches on. By contrast, the sea slug is designed to be conspicuous. Its brilliant color warns potential predators that is is dangerous, or inedible, or both.

Humans sometimes wistfully imagine that mating in the animal world is a simple matter. Not so. Many species cannot mate without elaborate courtship displays and rituals. Marked physical changes may appear during the breeding season. An example is the green eye markings and white plumes of the egret. Some birds, such as the albatross, "fence" elaborately with their bills. Other birds touch beaks tenderly. Some rituals and displays serve to assert a claim to a particular territory or to challenge intruders. When danger threatens, the short-eared owl spreads its wings wide and hunches them forward. It is thus able to appear large and formidable. Threat displays and rituals can also be used in place of bloody combat between rivals within the same species. Many horned animals, for example, charge and butt, or lock antlers and "wrestle." This is less costly to the species than if the animals were to slash and gore one another.

Certain insect species live in amazingly intricate societies. This is made possible through rigidly innate behavior patterns that leave little room for changes brought about by learning. The queen bee is the only fertile female in the hive. She keeps her unique position by a purely chemical mechanism: she secretes a substance that inhibits the production of new queens. The workers in the photograph are feeding the queen (center). They are also licking the "queen substance" from her body, and will help distribute it throughout the hive. In comparison, behavior in mammal societies is much more flexible. Social animals tend to develop patterns for dealing with external danger in a concerted way, as well as reducing conflict within the group. For example, when faced with an enemy, musk oxen arrange themselves in a circle. The strong adults face the enemy, while the younger animals are grouped in the center.

15 neurobiology

**W**e have seen that all life requires a continuous interchange between the organism and its environment. But this exchange is not limited to such physical entities as oxygen, water, and nutrients. An organism receives from its environment not only the chemical raw materials of life, and the energy to make use of them, but also something equally valuable and, in a way, even more basic: *information*.

We know that one characteristic of living things is their ability to respond adaptively to their surroundings. But the phrase "their surroundings" is very vague. To respond to its surroundings in a meaningful way, a creature needs a constant stream of information about specific environmental conditions. Organisms have therefore evolved a nervous system for acquiring, conveying, and using information.

This information does not come only from outside the organism. The internal environment must be monitored just as carefully, along with the moment-by-moment performance of the creature's physiological systems. Both of these must be continuously regulated if the organism is to survive. This control is provided by the nervous system.

Information and control are not by themselves sufficient to ensure the survival of an organism. They have no value unless they can be integrated so that the organism can respond correctly to the information it receives. So the third function of the nervous system is to integrate stimulus and reaction. It must evaluate and combine information in such a way that the most adaptive response is made. And it must coordinate all the elements of that response, which may involve complex activities of many different organs in various parts of the body.

To perform these functions, the nervous system has evolved cells and structures which receive, transmit, and exchange information, and stimulate the activity of various effector organs such as muscles and glands. But it is important to realize that all cells possess these abilities to some extent. Irritability is a fundamental characteristic of living matter. Even unicellular creatures with no nervous system can use information from their external and internal environment to regulate their activities. So the cells of the nervous system simply possess one of the universal attributes of life in more fully developed and specialized form.

# Transmission of nerve impulses

We all know that our bodies are full of nerves and that these nerves transmit messages. Some of the messages are very urgent, as anyone who recalls his last visit to the dentist will realize. So it would seem logical to regard the nerve as the functional unit of the nervous system. But this is somewhat misleading. Nerves are rather like massive telephone cables which carry thousands of messages to and from as many different locations. As such, they are more accurately regarded as units of structure rather than function. The smallest functional unit of the nervous system is actually a specialized cell called the neuron.

## The neuron

The **neuron**, or nerve cell, is designed for the transmission of nervous impulses. The largest part of the neuron is the **cell body**. This contains the nucleus and most of the mitochondria and other organelles that are involved in the metabolic function of the cell. Extending outward from the cell body are one or more fibers—long, thin extensions of the cell cytoplasm. In general, there are two kinds of fibers. **Dendrites** are commonly short but elaborately branched fibers. The single **axon**, though, is usually much longer—sometimes many feet in a large animal such as a giraffe or a whale. But the true distinction between the axon and dendrites is in their function and not in their appearance. Dendrites are adapted to receive nervous impulses. Axons are adapted to transmit them to an effector organ

15-1
The structure of a typical neuron. Elaborately branched dendrites receive nerve impulses from other neurons. The long axon conducts the impulses to effector organs such as muscles.

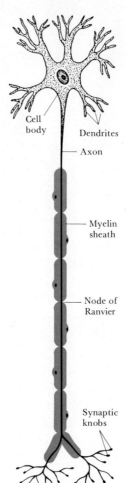

15-1
The structure of a typical neuron. Elaborately branched dendrites receive nerve impulses from other neurons. The long axon conducts the impulses to effector organs such as muscles.

Cell body
Dendrites
Axon
Myelin sheath
Node of Ranvier
Synaptic knobs

such as a muscle, or to another nerve cell. (A nerve, in fact, is simply a bundle of nerve cell axons, each of which carries its own individual impulses.)

What kind of message does the neuron carry, and how is it propagated? Experiments in the early part of this century established that stimulation of a neuron produced an electrical impulse of some sort. But the impulse had certain curious properties. For one thing, it was only generated if the stimulus was above a certain level of intensity, known as the **threshold**. Stimuli

below the threshold produced no response at all. But stimuli above the threshold always produced impulses. These impulses were identical regardless of the intensity of the stimulus. In other words, a stimulus just barely above the threshold produced an impulse with the same speed and strength as did a much stronger stimulus. So the neuron can be described as displaying an "all-or-none" pattern of response. Either a particular neuron "fires" (sends an impulse) or it does not. And all its impulses are the same—it cannot send a half-strength impulse, or an extra-strong impulse, or an unusually fast or slow impulse (though some types of neuron transmit impulses faster than others). The individual neuron also has a limited ability to fire in rapid succession. After each impulse there is a **refractory period** a few thousandths of a second long. During this period the neuron cannot transmit another impulse. Apparently some sort of recharging must take place within the cell before the neuron is ready to fire again.

These discoveries suggest that while the nervous impulse is clearly electrical in nature, the neuron does not conduct a tiny electric current the way a thin wire does. But such a model explains neither the all-or-none response of the neuron nor the refractory period. Moreover, an ordinary electric current diminishes in direct proportion to the distance it travels. But nerve impulses remain constant in strength regardless of how far they are transmitted. In fact, cell cytoplasm has such high resistance to electricity that it is hard to see how an electric current could travel more than a fraction of an inch through a neuron. Finally, nerve impulses, though extremely rapid (up to several hundred feet per second), are far slower than electric currents.

The nerve impulse, then, is not an ordinary electric current. Since it does not lose strength as it travels, the cell must take an active, rather than a passive part in transmission. The basic principles underlying this process were deduced as early as

1902. But it was not until 1939 that scientists developed the experimental techniques that allowed them to discover what really goes on in a nerve cell. In that year, several investigators succeeded in placing tiny electrodes inside the giant nerve fibers of squid. In this way the electrical events associated with the transmission of a nerve impulse could be directly measured and studied in minute detail for the first time. Our modern knowledge of nervous conduction rests largely on such experiments.

## Nature of the nerve impulse

The propagation of nerve impulses is not electrical in nature. It is electrochemical. The process is made possible by differences in the concentration of certain ions inside and outside the nerve cell. Inside the cell, there is a high concentration of negatively charged organic ions and positively charged potassium ions ($K^+$), but with negative charges predominating. Outside the cell, in the extracellular fluid, there is a high concentration of positively charged sodium ions ($Na^+$). When the cell is at rest, the voltage differential between the positively charged extracellular fluid and the negatively charged interior creates a voltage potential of from 60 to 70 millivolts across the cell membrane. This is known as the equilibrium or **resting potential**. It is equiv-

alent to about 1/20 the voltage supplied by an ordinary flashlight battery. The resting potential is maintained because, unless a stimulus is present, the cell membrane is nearly impermeable to Na. That is, the positively charged Na ions cannot penetrate the cell membrane. So the cell interior remains negatively charged, and the voltage differential remains at a constant level.

*The action potential*   The actual nerve impulse is known as the **action potential**. It is triggered by a partial **depolarization** of the neuron membrane. That is, the polarized or asymmetrical distribution of sodium and potassium ions between the inner and outer part of the membrane is temporarily disrupted. This can be caused directly by an electric current, a stimulus often used by scientists studying nerve impulse transmission. As we shall see, it can also be caused by chemical substances from another neuron at the point where neurons make their connection. But perhaps most important in terms of an organism's relation to its environment, depolarization can be initiated by a number of different stimuli acting on various specialized receptor cells, such as those found in the eyes, ears, tongue, nasal passages, and skin. The resulting change in the electrical potential across the cell membrane is called a **generator potential**.

**15-2**
A schematic model of the nerve cell membrane. The sodium-potassium pump is an active transport mechanism. It is powered by metabolic energy stored in molecules of ATP. It moves $Na^+$ ions out of the cell and $K^-$ ions in. In the resting state, pores in the membrane allow some $K^+$ to leak out of the cell. But the larger $Na^+$ ions cannot leak back in. This makes the inside of the cell some 60–80 millivolts more negative than the surrounding extracellular fluid. Upon excitation, however, the membrane briefly changes its permeability. It allows a sudden influx of $Na^+$ ions. (The ions labeled A are negative organic ions. They are also too large to pass through the membrane.)

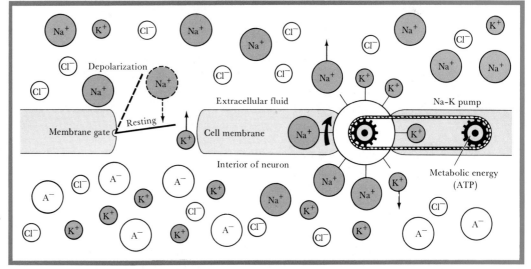

If the generator potential reaches the neuron's threshold level, the membrane undergoes a sudden and dramatic increase in Na permeability. For a brief period it becomes about 500 times more permeable to Na than to K.

The exact nature of this change is not known with certainty. Probably depolarization activates some gate mechanism in the membrane, altering the size or shape of the pores through which ions pass. The change itself lasts less than .001 seconds. But that is long enough for a large number of Na ions to rush into the cell. These ions are driven by a powerful combination of electrical forces (the interior of the cell is negative, the Na ions positive) and the concentration gradient (Na is present in much higher concentration outside the cell than within).

This great influx of Na ions not only fully depolarizes the cell membrane, but actually reverses the previous polarity. For a fraction of a second the interior of the cell becomes more positive than the exterior. Immediately thereafter, the original permeability characteristics of the membrane are restored, so that no more Na can enter the cell. In the meantime, however, the positive charge that the Na ions have given the interior of the cell upsets the K equilibrium. Normally, the tendency of the numerous K ions to pass out of the cell into the extracellular fluid is opposed by electrical forces. That is, the negative cell interior attracts the ions, while the positive exterior repels them. But when the Na influx reverses this polarity, the K ions are impelled both by electrical forces *and* concentration to leave the cell. They pass through the membrane in large numbers.

This outflow of positive charge is great enough to restore the cell's resting potential—the interior of the cell becomes negative again. In fact, for a brief time it actually becomes more negative than normal. This process is known as **repolarization**. Here we face another question. If Na ions rush into the cell interior and K ions rush out

15-3
When an area of the nerve cell membrane is depolarized, its Na⁺ permeability increases. The Na⁺ ions rush into the cell, causing a temporary reversal of polarity. That is, the inside of the membrane becomes positive in relation to the outside. This sudden electrical change constitutes the action potential. The result is a flow of current between the affected area of the membrane and neighboring regions, where the normal resting potential still exists. These areas are depolarized by the current. They become permeable to Na⁺ ions, and so become the site of new action potentials. (A) shows the changes in membrane charge and ion flow as the action potential propagates down the axon. (B) shows the corresponding changes in Na⁺ and K⁺ permeability of the neuron membrane. (C) plots the potential across the membrane during the transmission of a nerve impulse. Excitation of the neuron causes a partial depolarization of the membrane (the generator potential). When the depolarization reaches the neuron's threshold, an action potential results. (See The action potential)

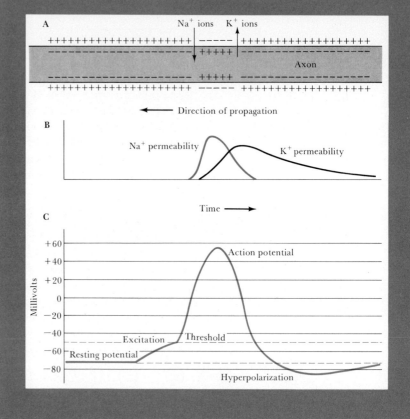

each time a neuron fires, how is the original balance of Na and K ions restored? This is something of a problem. If no other force intervened, the positively charged cell interior would repel the positive K ions and keep them from reentering. However, the cell membrane has a mechanism called the **sodium–potassium pump**. This mechanism uses specific carrier molecules to transport Na out of the cell and K into it. In this way it maintains the resting potential difference across the cell membrane. The pump is an active system. Its operation requires metabolic energy, which must be supplied by the breakdown of ATP. Once repolarization occurs—in a few thousandths of a second—the cell is ready to fire again, and the entire process can be repeated several times over.

Tetrodotoxin is a compound found in the gonads of the puffer fish. This compound interrupts nerve impulse transmission throughout the body by blocking the passage of Na ions through the gates in the neuron membrane. This, in turn, prevents the action potential. The puffer fish is considered a great delicacy in Japan. Although the chefs who prepare it must be trained and licensed by the state, several hundred Japanese die each year from tetrodotoxin poisoning. (It has been suggested that the puffer is so alluring to gourmets partly because of the potential danger involved in eating it.)

*Propagation of the action potential*
When an action potential is generated, it does not occur simultaneously along the entire neuron. At first it is confined to a small area. But the electrical changes which take place in that area affect neighboring regions of the membrane in the millisecond during which the action potential occurs. The result is depolarization and the consequent generation of fresh action potentials in these other regions. In other words, the action potential is continuously regenerated anew in each successive region of the neuron. The propagation of the nerve impulse thus resembles the burning of a fuse, in which the combustion at each point ignites the immediately adjacent regions.

To better understand the advantages of this system, we can consider an analogy. Suppose you wish to send a signal—a series of light flashes—to a remote point. The further away the destination, the more powerful the light needed, and the more energy will be required to send the signal. If the distance to be spanned is very great, it may be impossible to find a single light or a single energy source powerful enough to do the job. And even if these are available, the signal reaching the intended receiver will be very faint. This means the possibility for error in reception will be very high.

At this point another approach might suggest itself. Suppose that, instead of one light and one power source, you use a great many smaller lamps. Each has its own battery and an electric eye device that will turn the beam on whenever light falls on a sensitive photocell. You can then position these units at regular intervals along the path of the signal. When each one flashes it will activate the next one. The signal will thus be transmitted from lamp to lamp until it reaches its destination. Since each lamp has its own battery, the strength of the signal will remain constant no matter how far it has to travel. And its path can be extended indefinitely, without losing strength or fidelity, simply by adding more lamp units. Of course, the signal will reach its destination somewhat more slowly, because of the time consumed by the relays that turn each lamp on and off. But there will be a great gain in the reliability of the system.

In effect, this is how nervous impulses are transmitted along the neurons of an organism. The action potential does not depend solely upon the initial stimulus, but upon the existence of a resting potential at every point along the nerve cell membrane. Therefore it does not lose strength as it travels. The action potentials generated in each succeeding region of the neuron are identical in amplitude, duration, and all other characteristics. This means that the impulse arriving at the end of an axon will be exactly the same as the one initiated a fraction of a second before at the dendrites or cell body, perhaps several feet away.

It is true that the generation of action potentials in successive regions of the neuron takes time. But different organisms have evolved various ways to increase the speed of nerve impulse transmission in those ner-

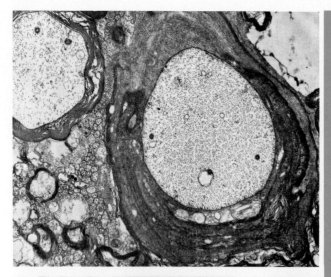

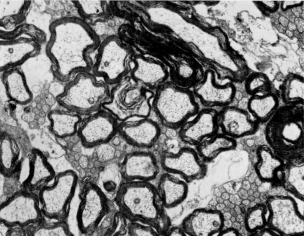

**15-4**
Left, middle: Myelinated and unmyelinated axons in cross section. Left, top: An individual axon at higher magnification. It shows the dark, concentric layers of myelin. Specialized Schwann cells wrap their membranes repeatedly about the axon to create the myelin sheath. This insulates the nerve cell membrane and permits faster conduction of impulses—a great advantage to the organism. (See Propagation of the action potential)

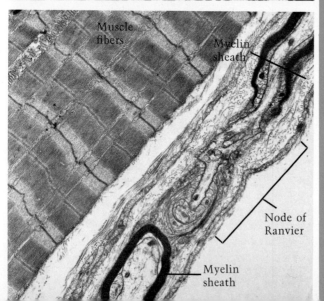

Muscle fibers

Myelin sheath

Node of Ranvier

Myelin sheath

**15-5**
This longitudianl section of a myelinated axon shows a node of Ranvier. It is a discontinuity in the myelin sheath between adjacent Schwann cells. Since ions cannot pass through the myelin insulation, the action potential can occur only at the nodes. Impulses travel rapidly along myelinated axons. This is because the action potential jumps from node to node. It does not need to take place successively at every point along the axon.

vous pathways where rapid response is essential. Many invertebrates such as the squid and the lobster, and some primitive vertebrates such as the lamprey, have giant axons which may reach 1 mm in diameter. The rate at which an action potential can be propagated increases roughly as the square of the axon diameter. So these giant axons function as high-speed conductors. Not surprisingly, they generally control the muscles needed for quick escape from danger.

In vertebrates we find a more economical means of speeding nervous transmission. Most nerve axons in vertebrates are surrounded by a sheath of **myelin**. Myelin is composed of proteins and lipids, and conducts electrical current very poorly. In other words, it is a good insulator. The myelin sheath is interrupted, exposing the axon, every millimeter or two at points called **nodes of Ranvier**. Because of the myelin insulation, action potentials cannot be generated across the membrane of the axon except at these nodes. When an action potential occurs at one node, another is triggered almost immediately at the next node. The action potential thus leaps rapidly from node to node. As a result, conduction by myelinated nerves may be 100 or more times faster than by nerves without myelin.

## The synapse

As we said before, the function of the nervous system is to receive, evaluate, and act on information. In higher animals such as mammals, the amount and complexity of this information is extremely great. If there were no more to the nervous system than the simple impulse-generating neurons which we have just described, the task would be hopeless. It would be comparable to handling the communication needs of a large city with a walkie-talkie set. In order for the nervous system to regulate the enormous amount of information it receives, something more is needed. That something is the synapse.

The axon, or transmitting cell (known as

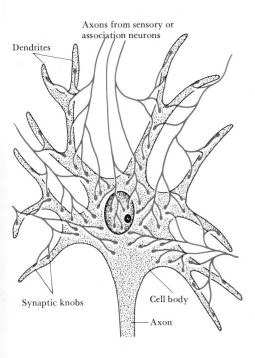

Axons from sensory or association neurons

Dendrites

Synaptic knobs

Cell body

Axon

**15-6**
Synaptic connections allow the transmission of impulses from one neuron to another. The synaptic knob at the end of an axon contains many vesicles. Each holds a chemical neurotransmitter. When an action potential reaches the end of the axon, neurotransmitter is released into the synaptic cleft. It diffuses across to excite or inhibit the postsynaptic membrane. (See The synapse)

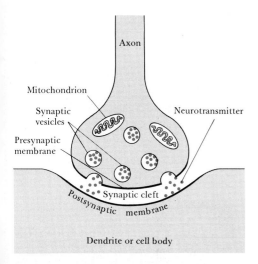

Axon

Mitochondrion

Synaptic vesicles

Presynaptic membrane

Neurotransmitter

Synaptic cleft

Postsynaptic membrane

Dendrite or cell body

the **presynaptic neuron**) usually divides into many small branches toward its end. Each branch terminates in a somewhat flattened bulge called a **synaptic knob** or synaptic bulb. These knobs lie next to the dendrites or cell bodies of the receiving cells (the **postsynaptic neurons**). But between them there is a tiny gap, usually about 20 nm across, called the **synaptic cleft**. Nerve impulses reach the axon terminal as action potentials, but they cannot cross the synaptic cleft in that form. The actual transmission between the sending and receiving cells occurs by chemical means.

The synaptic knobs contain many tiny **synaptic vesicles**. Each vesicle holds a small amount of a chemical **transmitter** substance. An action potential traveling down the axon causes these vesicles to migrate toward the cell membrane and release their contents into the synaptic cleft. The chemical transmitter crosses the gap to the postsynaptic cell membrane by diffusion. Despite the narrowness of the synaptic cleft, this is a slow process as compared with the speed of an action potential along a neuron. Each synapse retards the transmission of the nerve impulse by one or two thousandths of a second.

Molecules of the transmitter chemical react with certain receptor sites built into the postsynaptic cell membrane. Their usual effect is to depolarize the membrane, initiating an action potential. In other words, they cause the receiving cell to fire. But some neurons release transmitters that have just the reverse effect. These increase the polarization of the postsynaptic cell membrane, which tends to inhibit the cell from firing.

In vertebrates, a number of chemicals function as neurotransmitters. The most common of these is **acetylcholine**. It is used in parts of the central, sympathetic, and parasympathetic nervous systems. One of the most important roles of acetylcholine is serving as transmitter at the **neuromuscular junction**—the specialized region at which a motor neuron makes synaptic

connection with a fiber of skeletal muscle.

Certain drugs compete with acetylcholine for a receptor site on the postsynaptic cell membrane and thereby prevent depolarization. Curare is the classical competitive agent. This drug is derived from certain plants and has long been used by some South American Indians for making poisoned arrows. Curare blocks the action of the phrenic nerve on the diaphragm. Respiration is thus inhibited, and the organism dies from asphyxiation. Today, curare and related compounds are used medically in sublethal doses as muscle relaxants prior to certain types of surgery.

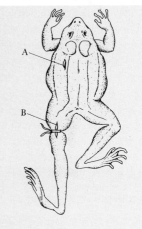

A

B

**15-7**
This illustration from a book by Claude Bernard shows the method he devised for determining the site of action of curare in a prepared frog. Crystalline curare was placed in the dorsal lymph sac (A). From here it could diffuse through the frog's bloodstream. Curare was stopped from flowing to the left leg by a ligature that cut the supply of blood to the muscle (B). But the blood supply could reach the nerves that affected this muscle. The frog became paralyzed except for the left leg. When the opposite leg was pinched, the unpoisoned left leg withdrew. This demonstrated that nerves could conduct impulses despite the presence of curare, but that curare interfered with the transmission at the point of contact between the nerve and muscle in question. (See The synapse)

Other drugs prevent the release of acetylcholine from the presynaptic terminals. A good example is the deadly botulinum toxin, which is responsible for an often fatal form of food poisoning. This substance is secreted by the anaerobic bacterium *Clostridium,* which can grow in canned foods when they are improperly sterilized. Certain diseases also interfere with the operation of acetylcholine. Myasthenia gravis, for example, is caused by the body's inability to manufacture adequate amounts of acetylcholine at the neuromuscular junction. The result is muscular weakness and paralysis.

After they perform their function, transmitter chemicals are quickly deactivated or broken down by enzymes in the postsynaptic cells. If this were not done, the postsynaptic neurons would continue to fire. The organism would lose nervous control, and would soon die. Cholinesterase, for example, is the enzyme which destroys acetylcholine. Many poisons, including certain types of nerve gas and insecticide, work by interfering with the action of cholinesterase.

## The function of the synapse

Transmission across the synapse is always one-way, since transmitter substances can only be released by the synaptic knobs at the ends of axons. But the synapse is more than just a device for passing impulses from one neuron to another. If that were its sole function, it would hardly be needed at all. Two neurons joined by a synapse would offer no advantage over a single longer neuron. (In fact, the synapse would be a distinct drawback, since transmission across a synapse is slower than along a neuron.) Nor are synapses merely a kind of switching system for directing impulses along various pathways in the complex nervous system, though that is part of their function. The key role of the synapse is in the *processing of information.*

At various places in the nervous system the messages represented by the action potentials must be interpreted, analyzed,

evaluated, and a "decision" made about how to react. The urgency of each signal must be weighed, and weak or unimportant signals filtered out. The claims of competing signals must be balanced. Reinforcing and opposing signals must be added and subtracted. Finally, an appropriate response must be initiated.

How is this accomplished? For one thing, synapses act as resistors in the nervous system. In most cases, impulses must reach more than one synapse on a postsynaptic cell at the same time or in quick succession in order to cause the second neuron to fire. Otherwise, not enough transmitter substance is released to cause sufficient depolarization. In such a case, the nerve impulse dies at the synapse without triggering a postsynaptic neuron. This eliminates weak and unimportant signals. The regulatory capacity of synapses is further enhanced by the fact that different postsynaptic cells have different thresholds. Some will fire after receiving only a few impulses from incoming axons. Others will fire only after a great many impulses have been received. These differences in thresholds have a very important influence on the path that impulses will take through the nervous system. The postsynaptic cell may receive inhibitory as well as excitatory influences, which also contributes to the regulatory ef-

Synaptic knob

Synaptic vesicles

Synaptic cleft

Muscle fiber

Neuron membrane

15-8
Electron micrograph of a neuromuscular junction. The synaptic terminal of an axon, with its many vesicles of neurotransmitter, occupies the upper portion of the photo. Below it are specialized projections of the muscle. When molecules of the neurotransmitter reach these membranes, the muscle will be stimulated to contract, if the axon is one that carries excitatory impulses. It will relax if the axon is one that carries inhibitory impulses. (See The synapse)

fect. For example, the effect of a strong excitation from one neuron may be neutralized by a simultaneous strong inhibition from another neuron.

The net effect of all these influences, excitatory and inhibitory, determines whether or not the postsynaptic cell will generate an action potential — and, if the excitation is very great, how many. In effect, each postsynaptic cell is a tiny computer. It performs an intricate calculus, all in the language of action potentials. This process is repeated over and over in the brain, spinal cord, and ganglia, where thousands of axon terminals converge and thousands of cell bodies synapse with them. Thus the high degree of integration and coordination characteristic of vertebrate nervous systems is made possible.

# Receptors

In order to survive, organisms must have some means of receiving information about their environment. Even plants can do this, though the mechanisms they use are not yet fully understood. Animals have evolved specialized structures called **sensory receptors** for this purpose. Information comes in the form of energy — more precisely, changes in energy, for organisms in general can respond only to changes, not to steady-state conditions. Receptors function by changing one form of energy into a different form. This process is known as **transduction**. For example, a microphone is a transducer that changes sound — vibrations in the air — into electrical impulses. These impulses may ultimately be changed back into sound by another transducer, the loudspeaker. Sensory receptors perform the same function. They transduce various forms of environmental energy (sound, light, heat, pressure, vibration, chemical activity) into the language of the nervous system — action potentials.

To monitor the environment adequately, the nervous system must record and interpret a variety of conditions. So different receptors have become specialized to respond to one particular form of energy — the eyes to light, the ears to sound, and so on. Chemical receptors, for example, take the form of taste buds on the tongue, olfactory receptors in the nose, and hormonal and osmotic receptors in the hypothalamus. All of these receptors respond to some form of chemical stimulation, but they do not produce the same sensations. Taste buds elicit sensations of taste and olfactory receptors elicit sensations of smell. Hormonal and osmotic receptors give rise to no conscious sensations at all. Moreover, receptors that are almost identical in form can also elicit very different sensations. For example, the hair cells of the vestibular and auditory systems are very similar in structure. But the vestibular system is responsible for the sense of balance, while the auditory system is concerned with sound perception. So the particular sensation an individual experiences is determined by the neural connections of the receptor involved, not by its structure. In other words, subjective sensation depends upon where the nervous impulses go to in the brain, rather than upon where they come from.

## Smell and taste

Response to chemical changes is probably the most primitive of all. Changes in concentration of nutritive or noxious substances dissolved in a watery medium are fundamental in determining the behavior of one-celled organisms, such as various protozoans. The metabolic output of any small protozoan stimulates engulfing movements on the part of an amoeba. The chemical byproducts of bacteria stimulate feeding behavior in paramecia. On higher levels, the efficiency of detection is increased. The receptor systems are more specialized and the responses are more specific. We see this, for example, in the ability of salmon to distinguish their native stream from dozens

15-9
The antennae of the moth contain chemical (olfactory) receptors and mechanoreceptors. They respond to movements of the air and low-frequency vibrations.

of others by its unique biochemical scent. This ability is also found in certain moths, which can detect chemical mating attractants released by females of their species more than a mile away.

The chemoreceptors responsible for smell and taste occupy different locations in different creatures. They are found on the legs of some insects, on the antennae of others, on the barbels (whiskers) and body surface of various fishes, and on the tongue and nasal membranes of mammals. In general, taste receptors are adapted for the detection of molecules dissolved in liquid. On the other hand, olfactory receptors respond to airborne molecules, often in extremely low concentrations. (Smell receptors may be thousands of times more sensitive than taste receptors.)

In many ways, the distinction between the two senses is artificial. It is obviously meaningless when applied to aquatic creatures. And even in land animals the molecules of odorous chemicals must go into solution on the moist nasal membranes before they can be detected by the olfactory receptors. Moreover, much of what we interpret as the sensation of taste is really the product of our sense of smell, stimulated by food odors reaching the nasal passages from the mouth.

We can discriminate an almost infinite variety of scents and flavors. But in reality, all are produced by different blends of a relatively small number of stimuli. There are only four basic tastes—sweet, sour, salty, and bitter. The receptors for each of these are concentrated on different areas of the tongue. Every taste sensation we experience represents a unique combination of different intensities of these four tastes. Each receptor can register many fine gradations of intensity, so we can distinguish quite a large number of flavors. Our response to odors is more subtle and varied, but it operates on a similar principle. There appear to be seven basic odors, each with its own type of receptor. It has been pro-

posed, though not conclusively proven, that the seven receptors are specific for molecules of different shapes. A particular molecule might fit only one receptor site. Another might fit several, giving rise to a more complex olfactory sensation.

## Vision

Almost all living things can detect and respond to light. Even some unicellular creatures such as *Euglena* possess specialized organelles or eyespots containing a photosensitive pigment that registers the presence of light. Many multicellular animals have photoreceptor cells on their body surface which perform a similar function. For example, the earthworm has light receptors in its skin, enabling it to detect, and avoid, light. Such primitive forms of "vi-

15-10
The snake "smells" by collecting molecules of airborne chemical substances on its tongue, and then inserting the tongue into a cavity in the roof of its mouth, lined with chemoreceptor cells.

15-11
Scanning electron micrograph of a taste bud from the barbel ("whisker") of a catfish. The actual receptors are the elongated, modified epithelial cells clustered at the top.

sion" are also found in various higher species. Certain mollusks and crayfish have specialized neurons that can initiate action potentials in response to light although they are not associated with the eyes or visual regions of the brain. It was determined recently that some birds also possess photosensitive neurons located deep within the brain, which measure the duration of daylight. These receptors synchronize the physiological rhythms of the organism to the daily cycle of dark and light. They may also play an important role in the development of the gonads during seasonal breeding periods, and in signaling the time to begin migration.

Such receptors respond only to gross changes in illumination. They can tell the organism whether light is present, and at best provide some information about its intensity. But they cannot detect the direction the light is coming from, or any movement of the light source. Nor can they form a distinct image. It is obviously advantageous for an organism to be able to extract more of the detailed information potentially available from the light falling on it. The ability to do this has resulted from an evolutionary process in which the photoreceptors have become organized into a sophisticated organ called the eye.

*The eye*   In its most basic form the eye consists of three parts:

1. a structure, usually a **lens**, for focusing the light onto the **receptor** cells;
2. a group of receptor cells, each containing a **photopigment** and organized into an array called a **retina**;
3. a group of neurons that synapse with the receptor cells and transmit visual information to the central nervous system.

Such a system has several advantages. The lens allows light to be concentrated as well as focused upon the receptors. This results in greater sensitivity. Also, the greater the

**15-12**
Various forms of nonvisual light reception are common in the biological world. Many snakes, for example, are equipped with pit organs. These are unique sensory receptors highly sensitive to infra-red (heat) radiation. They enable the snake to locate warm-blooded prey even in the dark. The pit organ, however, can detect only the direction and intensity of the radiation. Since it does not come from an image, it cannot convey as much information about the environment as does the eye.

**15-13**
The compound eye of the fly consists of many individual ommatidia. Each of them forms a separate image. The visual fields of the ommatidia overlap. Partly as a result of this arrangement, the compound eye is especially sensitive to rapid alterations of light and dark, such as might be found at the edge of a moving body (or a static landscape seen by a moving insect).

number of receptor cells, the greater the eye's ability to resolve fine detail in the image.

Two different visual systems have evolved independently in creatures on widely divergent branches of the phylogenetic tree. The **compound eye** is found in arthropods, including insects and crustaceans. The camera-type eye is found among vertebrates and certain mollusks. The compound eye is composed of many individual subunits called **ommatidia**. Each has its own lens, receptor cells, and sensory nerve leading to the brain. The visual field covered by each ommatidium overlaps that of its neighbors. These units are highly sensitive to flicker—that is, to rapid alterations of light and dark. As a result, the compound eye is evidently a very efficient detector of movement. In this respect, it is better than the vertebrate eye.

The compound eye forms hundreds or even thousands of separate images. But the camera-type eye uses a single lens to focus a single image onto the receptor cells of the retina. Although each cell records only a small part of the total image, the brain integrates the information from millions of retinal cells to form a sharp and finely detailed picture of the environment. Like a photographic camera, the camera-type eye can adjust both its focus and the amount of light it admits.

The aperture of the eye is called the **pupil**. Its diameter is regulated by the opening and closing of a structure called the **iris**. The iris is composed largely of smooth muscle controlled by reflex. When bright light strikes the retina, involuntary nerve fibers cause the iris to contract, decreasing the aperture. In dim light the iris is allowed to dilate and admit more light. The muscles that change the thickness of the lens permit the human eye to alter its focus for nearby and distant objects. These muscles are also under the control of the involuntary, or autonomic, nervous system. However, some animals use a different focusing system. Instead of changing the thickness of the lens, they move the lens closer to or further from the retina.

*The retina*    After light passes through the lens and the fluid-filled chambers of the eyeball, it falls on the retina. The human retina contains over 130 million photosensitive receptor cells, which accounts for its high resolving power. It also contains several layers of neurons. These neurons relay information from the receptor cells to the optic nerve fibers and thence to the brain. The presence of this complex network of neurons within the retina itself indicates that visual information undergoes a good deal of processing and interpretation even before it is transmitted to the central nervous system.

The retinas of man and most vertebrates contain two kinds of photosensitive cell, **rods** and **cones**. Each consists of two functional regions, joined by a thin, stalk-like structure. At one end of the cell is an elaborately folded membrane which resembles a

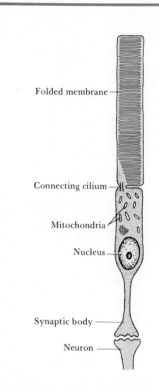

Folded membrane

Connecting cilium

Mitochondria

Nucleus

Synaptic body

Neuron

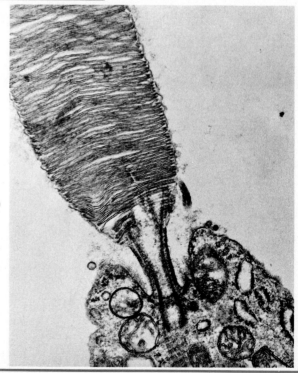

15-14
Diagram and electron micrograph of a rod cell. Light acts on the molecules of visual pigment located in the folded membrane. It creates a generator potential that is transmitted through the connecting stalk to the synaptic body. The sensitivity of the mechanism is remarkable. Even a few photons may cause transmission of a nerve impulse. The connecting structure between the two parts of the cell is a modified cilium. (See The retina)

stack of coins or poker chips when viewed through the electron microscope. This membrane contains light-sensitive pigments. The other end of the cell is similar to a nerve fiber in structure and function. It transmits a generator potential, initiated by the action of light on the visual pigment, to a sensory neuron with which it makes synaptic contact. Partial depolarization of the receptor cell membrane causes the release of transmitter molecules into the synaptic gap. This response is graded, unlike that of most presynaptic neurons. The stronger the light, the greater the depolarization, and the more neurotransmitter is released at the synapse.

Although they are similar in structure, the rods and cones make very different contributions to our visual capabilities. Most of the approximately 6 million cones are located in a region at the center of the retina, only a few millimeters in diameter. Many cones are thus concentrated in a relatively small area. Moreover, each one makes synaptic connection with only a single sensory neuron. In effect, every cone has its own private line to the brain. Because of this anatomical arrangement, the cones can register extremely fine detail. In fact, most of our detailed vision is accomplished by the cones. When we look at an object, we automatically move our eyes so that its image is kept focused on the center of the retina rather than on the surrounding regions.

As we move out toward the edges of the retina, the number of cones diminishes and the number of rods increases. The rods have much more diffuse connections with the sensory neurons than do the cones. Each rod synapses with many neurons, and each neuron receives input from many rods. As a result, their capacity to resolve detail is far coarser than that of the cones. In compensation, the rods are far more sensitive to dim light than the cones. So the cones are used almost exclusively for daytime vision and the rods for night vision. Experienced dim-light observers, such as astronomers,

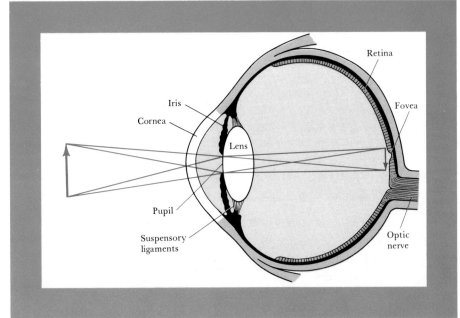

learn never to look directly at a faint object but to place it instead at the edge of their field of vision. In this way they can take maximum advantage of the sensitive rods near the edges of the retina.

*The visual pigments*   The light-sensitive molecules, or visual pigments, of animals are closely related to the plant carotenoids. They contain a carotenoid derived from vitamin A. But the carotenoids cannot be synthesized by the body. They must be obtained from the food we eat—and thus, directly or indirectly, from plants.

The rod cells contain a photopigment called **rhodopsin.** Exposure to light causes the rhodopsin molecule to change its spatial configuration. Somehow, this produces a partial depolarization of the cell membrane. We do not know exactly how this happens. Evidently it is the result of certain chemical reactions that can only be catalyzed by the rhodopsin in its light-altered form. But whatever the mechanism, it is extremely rapid. The electrical impulse is generated within .002 seconds after light falls on the cell. The mechanism is also extremely sensitive. Apparently each molecule of rhodopsin need absorb only a sin-

15-15
The human eye. The space in front of the lens is washed by a watery fluid. Behind the lens, a gelatinous substance fills the eyeball and helps it keep its shape. The lens itself is composed of crystalline fibers of protein. It focuses an image onto the sensitive receptor cells of the retina. The amount of light reaching the retina is regulated by the opening and closing of the muscular, pigmented iris (the part of the eye that gives it its characteristic color). Focus is controlled by muscles which change the shape of the lens. They make it thicker for nearby objects and thinner for those far away.

gle photon (an "atom" of light) to undergo its structural change. And the rearrangement of just a few molecules may cause enough depolarization to trigger an action potential in the postsynaptic neuron. After performing its function, rhodopsin is quickly restored to its original form so that it is again ready to respond to light.

The visual mechanism in cone cells is similar but more complex. Rods are sensitive to a wide range of wavelengths, so they cannot distinguish between colors. Thus no color vision is possible with rods. Their ex-

citation yields only sensations of neutral grey. But human beings have three types of cone, each containing a slightly different visual pigment. One of these is sensitive primarily to blue light, one to green, and one to light in the yellow-red region. We can perceive color because of the presence of these three different receptors, each sensitive to a different part of the spectrum. Few other mammals possess color vision. But a number of birds, reptiles, and fish have it. Insects, too, can apparently distinguish colors, but their visual range is not the same as ours. It includes ultraviolet wavelengths that we cannot see, but excludes the red end of the spectrum. Insects of many species can also detect polarized light, which they use for orientation as a kind of natural compass.

## Hearing and equilibrium

The senses of hearing and equilibrium provide an excellent example of how the same basic biological structures and mechanisms can be adapted for quite varied uses. Although they seem very different at first, both result from the activity of specialized mechanoreceptors that operate in remarkably similar fashion. This is hardly an accident. It appears, in fact, that both types of receptor evolved from a common ancestor. This is the *lateral line organ,* a structure still found in fish today.

*The lateral line*    The lateral line extends along the body and head of the fish. It consists of receptors called **hair cells,** usually located inside a protective groove or canal. Hair cells are specialized epithelial cells with short, protruding hairs (stereocilia). The hairs are embedded in gelatinous membranes. These membranes function rather like the sails of a boat, providing a larger surface area to catch water currents and magnify their effect. When such currents bend the hairs in one direction, the receptor cells are depolarized. They release neurotransmitter, which excites sensory nerve fibers. If the hairs are bent in the

15-16
The night-hunting owl takes advantage of oversized eyes with abundance of rod cells to find its prey in near-darkness. Having few cone cells, however, the owl is color blind. (See the retina and the visual pigments)

opposite direction the cells become hyper-polarized. This inhibits the release of transmitter substances.

Although water currents can be generated in a number of ways, the evidence so far indicates that the lateral line system is used primarily to detect and locate objects near the fish. Another animal swimming nearby—predator or prey—will create currents. In the same way, currents produced by the fish's own swimming movements will be slightly distorted by the presence of local obstacles. The lateral line can detect these subtle deflections. This system helps schools of fish to stay together, since each fish can detect the currents created by the other members of the school. The lateral line is also sensitive to sonic vibrations of low frequency. This makes it, in effect, an organ of hearing as well as touch.

*The ear: acceleration and equilibrium*
The human ear contains three different sensory organs. They are concerned with the detection of sound, acceleration, and spatial orientation. All three utilize receptors that are obviously similar to those of the lateral line system. In each case the basic principle of operation is the same. Hair cells innervated by sensory neurons project hairs onto or into a membrane. The movements of the membrane bend the hairs and thus excite the nerve fibers.

The **inner ear** is a series of fluid-filled channels and sacs. It is called the **labyrinth** because of its complex passageways. Among these are the three **semicircular canals,** each containing a patch of hair cells. Movement of the head causes the fluid in the canals to move, somewhat like liquid sloshing around in a glass that is moved suddenly. This bends the hair cells, generating nervous impulses. The three canals are oriented perpendicular to one another, so that movement in any plane can be detected. The relative levels of excitation of the neurons from each canal inform the brain as to the precise speed and direction of rotation.

Near the base of the semicircular canals are two chambers called the **sacculus** and the **utriculus**. Each chamber contains hair cells. The hairs of these receptor cells are in contact with a gelatinous structure containing crystals of calcium carbonate. Because of their weight, these **otoliths** exert a force on the hairs they touch. If the position of the head changes, so will the direction of the force. Each time the head is moved, some hairs will be bent more and others less. The signals thus generated tell the brain which way the head is tilted with respect to the earth's surface.

These organs are found fully developed in fish as well as in human beings. But in one group of fish, the sacculus has evolved further. It can function as an auditory transducer, giving the fish a much more fully developed sense of hearing than the lateral line provides. These fish are the Ostariophysi, which include the catfish, carp, and herring. They have an air, or swim, bladder. Its main function is to assist the buoyancy of the fish, but it has come to double as a sound receiver. Most fish are nearly equal in density to the water they swim in. So most of them are almost completely "transparent" to water-borne sound. Sonic waves will pass right through them with very little interaction. But when sound waves impinge on the bladder, it expands and contracts with the same frequency as the wave. This pulsation is transmitted through a group of specialized bones to the otoliths in the sacculus, which cause the hair cells to bend. Again, these cells bend with the same frequency as that of the original sonic vibration. The nervous impulses thus generated are interpreted by the brain. Their frequency reveals the pitch of the sound.

In many ways, the hearing mechanism of higher vertebrates resembles that of the Ostariophysi fish. But as animals moved from the water onto the land, certain structural modifications evolved. The swim bladder was replaced as an auditory organ by the eardrum. Also, the role of auditory transducer shifted from the sacculus to a new

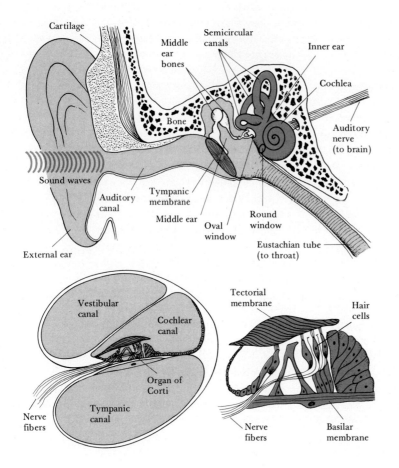

**15-17**
The external ear forms a resonant system tuned to the frequencies of human speech. The tympanic membrane, the small bones of the middle ear, and the oval window together serve to amplify sound vibrations and transmit them to the fluid of the canals of the cochlea. The auditory transducer is the organ of Corti, which sits on the basilar membrane in the cochlear canal. It converts the pressure changes in the canals into action potentials in the auditory nerve. Pressure waves in the tympanic canal bounce the basilar membrane (with its hair cells) up and down. The hairs are bent by this motion. The result is a generator potential which stimulates the nerve fibers. (See The ear: hearing)

structure called the cochlea. This latter change enormously increased the frequency range that could be detected. Fish can hear only frequencies up to a few thousand cycles per second. But human beings can hear frequencies from 20 to nearly 20,000 cycles, dogs and cats can hear up to 50,000 cycles, and some bats can perceive tones as high as 120,000 cycles.

*The ear: hearing*    The anatomical structure of the ear is shown in the accompanying figure. The external ear is the visible fleshy appendage that we ordinarily call the "ear." It serves to funnel sound waves into the ear canal, at the end of which is the **tympanic membrane**, or eardrum. Vibrations of the tympanic membrane are transmitted through the **middle ear** by way of three tiny bones. They next reach a membrane-covered opening in the labyrinth known as the **oval window**. Passage through the middle ear amplifies the original sound wave, partly because of the arrangement of the bones of the middle ear and partly because the area of the oval window is much smaller than that of the tympanic membrane. This amplification makes it possible for the ear to detect very faint noises.

The oval window covers the opening of the **vestibular canal**, one of the three fluid-filled canals of the **cochlea**. The **tympanic canal** connects with the vestibular canal, terminating at another membrane called the **round window**. Between these two lies the **cochlear canal**. All three are coiled together in a shape like that of a snail shell (*cochlea* is the Latin word for snail shell). Together they constitute the auditory portion of the inner ear. The elastic **basilar membrane** stretches between the cochlear and tympanic canals. On it rests the **organ of Corti**, the actual auditory transducer, which contains the receptor hair cells. The hairs of these cells are imbedded in the gelatinous **tectorial membrane**, which overhangs the organ of Corti in the cochlear canal.

By now the mechanism of transduction should be familiar. Movement bends the hairs of the receptor cells, which are thus stimulated and in turn excite the sensory neurons with which they make synaptic contact. The only difference is that in this case it is the tectorial membrane that is relatively fixed. The hairs are bent by the movements of the basilar membrane, which vibrates up and down like a trampoline in response to pressure waves in the fluid of the tympanic canal. These pressure waves originate at the oval window. Sonic vibrations cause the membrane to move in and out, pushing the fluid back and forth in the vestibular and tympanic canals. (This movement is possible only because the round window is present at the opposite end of the canal system. Its membrane bulges inward or outward in response to the changing pressure of the fluid caused by the pulsations of the oval window.)

15-18
Bats have big ears. They rely heavily on their sense of hearing for information about the environment. By emitting loud ultrasonic (high-frequency) pulses and detecting their echoes, the bat is able to locate its prey. It thus can orient itself during flight.

The basilar membrane is constructed so that its vibration characteristics vary along its 35-mm length. One end responds best to high-frequency vibrations. The other is most responsive to lower frequencies. So the frequency of the sound waves transmitted by the fluid in the cochlear canals determines which hair cells are most strongly stimulated, and which sensory neurons are most intensely excited. From this "geographical" information the brain can infer the frequency of the sounds.

*The war between the bats and the moths*
Bats use hearing the way humans use sight to gain information about their external environment. Contrary to popular belief, most bats are not blind. However, their sense of vision is very poorly developed. In the early 1940s, experiments showed that many bats emit loud ultrasonic pulses, far beyond the range of human hearing. The pulses rebound off environmental objects, and the bats can detect the echoes. This enables them to locate and capture prey, avoid obstacles during flight, and accurately orient themselves within their surroundings. This sensory capacity of bats is called echolocation.

Bats are remarkably successful creatures. They have survived and flourished for some 60 million years. To a great extent this success results from their ability to exploit a nocturnal food supply for which there is little competition. Moths, for example, make up a good part of the bat's diet. In fact, bats have created such tremendous pressure on moth populations that some species have evolved special organs to detect the bat's echolocation cries and avoid capture. For instance, noctuid moths have two tympanic organs, one on each side of the body. Each of these is supplied with two nerve fibers. One fiber is sensitive to low-intensity ultrasonic sounds, the other to loud ultrasonic sounds. These neurons inform the moth of the location of the bat. A faint pulse would indicate that the bat is still probably at some distance. The moth would

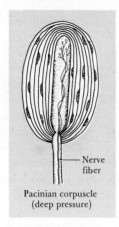

Nerve
fiber

Pacinian corpuscle
(deep pressure)

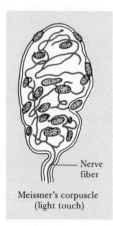

Nerve
fiber

Meissner's corpuscle
(light touch)

15-19
Two of the several
types of tactile (touch)
receptor distributed
through the skin and
underlying tissues.
Pacinian corpuscles
respond to deep
pressure. Meissner's
corpuscles are sensitive
to light touch. (See
Physical sensations)

then steer a course away from the bat's effective echo range. A loud pulse would excite both nerves and signal that the bat is close. The moth then initiates a complex evasive maneuver, sometimes diving straight to the ground.

## Physical sensations

The skins of most animals, including human beings, possess a variety of specialized sensory receptors. These receptors respond to temperature and various forms of physical contact. When stimulated, they give rise to the sensations we call touch, pressure, warmth, cold, and pain. The receptors vary widely in their relative abundance (human beings have many more pain receptors than receptors for warmth or cold). Their distribution also varies (the fingers, face, and tongue, not surprisingly, contain more touch receptors than such areas of the body as the back). They vary also in structure. For example, Pacinian corpuscles lie deep inside the body tissues. They take the form of onion-like layers of connective tissue wrapped around a nerve ending. When pressure is applied to the enclosing tissue the neuron is excited. The fine hairs that cover much of the human body surface also function as part of a very sensitive touch receptor system. The base of each hair is surrounded by a network of nerve fibers. The nerve endings register even a tiny displacement, such as might be caused by the gentle breeze of an insect alighting. Other receptors are similarly specialized for detecting heat, cold, and touch.

Pain is not itself a specific stimulus. It is a sensation that can be caused by many different stimuli. Pain can result simply from the overstimulation of an ordinary heat, cold, or pressure receptor. But the body also possesses specialized pain receptors. These take the form of free nerve endings, and appear to function in two ways. If the neuron itself is hurt—for instance, cut or crushed—it will transmit nervous impulses which the brain interprets as pain. But even

if the neuron is not directly affected, it may still respond if other tissues in the vicinity are damaged or destroyed. Cells that are burnt, wounded, or otherwise injured apparently release certain chemical messengers. These excite neighboring free nerve endings, causing them to fire. This mechanism accounts for the fact that the sensation of pain often builds up slowly, and is relatively nonspecific. Different sorts of injury can produce similar feelings of pain.

## Sensing the internal environment

We are most familiar with the senses that give us information about the outside world. But sensory receptors must also monitor the complex world within our bodies. Two kinds of receptor sense the internal environment. The first are specialized receptors located in the viscera. They signal the brain when the lung is stretched in breathing, when the blood pressure is too high or too low, or when changes occur in the oxygen or carbon dioxide levels in the blood. This information guides the brain in its automatic regulation of bodily functions. (Unlike heartbeat and blood pressure, breathing is partly subject to conscious control as well—but only partly, as you can see if you try to hold your breath indefinitely. The rise in carbon dioxide levels in the blood will eventually cause the part of the brain that regulates respiration to override your voluntary efforts not to breathe.)

Receptors of the second type are unique in that they are simply neurons in the brain with no specialized structure to indicate their role as sensory receptors. Their specialty is sensing the blood. Specifically, they sense its temperature, oxygen and carbon dioxide content, osmotic pressure, ionic composition, and the levels of certain hormones. Each group of cells seems to be specialized for sensing only one of these factors. The information these internal receptors gather often gives rise to no conscious sensation. For instance, we are not aware when receptors send messages that monitor the level of carbon dioxide in the blood. But there are exceptions. The sensations of hunger, thirst, and nausea are obvious examples. Between these extremes is a vitally important area of sensory perception of which we are partially aware but to which we usually pay little conscious attention. This is the realm of **proprioception**, or self-perception. It informs us about the state and position in space of our limbs and other body structures.

Proprioceptors are specialized mechanoreceptors located in joints, tendons, and muscles. They transmit information about the angles of various joints, and the state of tension or relaxation of various muscles. For example, if you shut your eyes you can still bring both of your index fingers together until they touch, without very much effort. You can even do this with your hands behind your back. In terms of sensory processes this means that you know at all times the exact positions of your arms, hands, and fingers. Furthermore, you know exactly how fast and in what direction they are moving. This information is sensed by special receptors in the joints which are sensitive to very small movements of the limbs.

The maintenance of proper muscle length is performed by stretch receptors called **muscle spindles**. These spindles monitor the contraction of the muscle fibers in which they occur. Such information is essential for the proper regulation of all our muscular activities. People who lose their senses of sight or hearing can, with proper training, lead reasonably normal lives despite their handicap. But if an individual were to lose the function of his muscle spindles he would not be merely handicapped, but completely incapacitated. Muscular movements could still be initiated, but there would be no feedback, and consequently no control. It would be impossible for such a person to make the movements appropriate in both distance and degree of force. He could not effectively speak, focus his eyes, chew his food, walk, or execute any other motor act.

# Nervous systems

One of the most striking aspects of animal behavior is that the entire organism operates in a coordinated fashion. In such a commonplace activity as locomotion, for example, many muscles work smoothly together. They work so smoothly, in fact, that the act of taking a step or sweeping the tail in swimming appears to be a single continuous movement of the whole animal. All this locomotor activity is constantly guided by the sense organs. The environmental information they receive is instantaneously sifted, reorganized, and interpreted in the light of internal physiological states and current external requirements.

We usually attribute such integrated behavior to the operations of the nervous system. But unicellular animals have no nervous system, and yet display remarkably complex behavior in certain respects. Paramecia, for example, are propelled through the water by the synchronized beating of their cilia. When the animal contacts an undesirable object or substance, ciliary beating is reversed and the animal moves backward. The animal turns slightly, and then moves forward again. But if food is detected, the cilia will respond appropriately by producing water currents that sweep food through the oral region and into the interior of the animal.

The paramecium, then, can respond to stimuli in its environment. We may also note that the animal's response is both discriminative and adaptive. It approaches and ingests food but avoids other substances. Furthermore, the activities of the cellular structures are coordinated, enabling the creature to move forward or backward and ingest food. This behavior suggests that the protoplasm of the paramecium is highly organized and differentiated, which is indeed the case. Cellular organelles are specialized to detect stimuli, transmit excitation to various regions of the cell, and respond appropriately in the form of ciliary movement. Thus a single cell can function as receptor, conductor, integrator, and effector.

## Evolution of nervous systems

With the appearance of multicellular animals, a serious problem arose. If each cell were to function independently, the organism's activity would be uncoordinated and chaotic. Clearly, the various parts of the organism had to be integrated somehow. This need was met by the evolution of the nervous system.

The evolutionary level of sponges (Porifera) is just barely above that of an unintegrated colony of cells. Sponges do not possess nerve cells. Communication from one cell to another results from a direct domino-like effect in which the response of one cell stimulates adjacent ones. In this way a strong stimulus applied to one part of the sponge is eventually transmitted to all parts. But sponges also possess some rather curious cells that appear to be glandular in function. The structure of these cells is remarkably similar to that of neurosecretory cells in higher animals. It has been theorized that true nerve cells evolved from glandular cells. It is also clear that all nerve cells have a secretory function, at least at the presynaptic membrane. So it is quite possible that these glandular cells in sponges represent the ancestral form of true nerve cells. The additional property of nerve cells is their ability to conduct an impulse. The development of this property is a quantum jump into a new level of organization. It confers on the organism new and different capacities for behavior.

We see the first true nervous system in the coelenterates. The hydra, for example, has both specialized sensory cells that convey information about the environment and specialized effector cells (muscle-like cells which contract when stimulated) that respond to this information. These components are linked by a **nerve net**—a diffuse, unstructured network of interconnecting nerve fibers. An impulse entering the net does not travel along a specifically defined pathway. It simply moves outward in all directions, diminishing in intensity as it spreads. All parts of the animal are in contact with all other parts through the neurons of the nerve net. But no central control or specialized response is possible.

Jellyfish have a nerve net system which is significantly more advanced than that of the hydra. In jellyfish there are two nerve nets—a giant fiber net and a diffuse net. The periphery of the "bell" is encircled by two **nerve rings**, each containing axons of neurons in one of the nerve nets. These provide a conduction system considerably faster than the nets themselves. **Marginal ganglia** are aggregations of cell bodies situated in the nerve rings. The two nerve nets make synaptic contacts through these ganglia. Adjacent to each ganglion there is a light-sensitive organ called an **ocellus**, and an equilibrium organ called a **statocyst**. These are the first true sensory organs found in the animal kingdom.

Jellyfish display two particularly interesting forms of specialized behavior. The first is swimming movement caused by rhythmically forcing water out of the bell. The other is their feeding behavior, which in some species consists of swimming to the surface, turning upside down, and floating to the bottom with tentacles fully spread, thus fishing for food. Experiments show that the swimming movements are initiated by impulses from the ganglia, conducted over the giant fiber net. The diffuse nerve net plays no role in this activity, but is important in feeding behavior. So in the jellyfish we can see the beginning of specialized nervous pathways which respond to specific stimuli and elicit specific behavioral responses.

*The great leap forward*    The advent of organisms with bilateral symmetry was accompanied by profound changes in the organization of nervous systems. An animal with this sort of body plan is designed to move chiefly in one forward direction. As a result, it has a permanent, specialized front

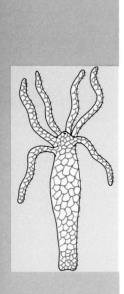

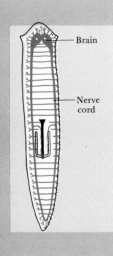

15-20
Two organisms with relatively primitive nervous systems. The diffuse nerve net of the hydra allows only limited response to stimuli. The planarian has a more complex system, with the beginning of a brain.

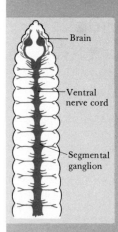

15-21
In the earthworm the anterior ganglion, or "brain," is still primarily a processing center for sensory data.

15-22
Insect nervous system.

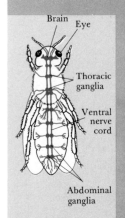

end. But if the animal moves forward, it needs to have some knowledge of the environment directly ahead. This statement sounds innocent enough, but it has profound implications. In effect, it says that the animal must have its sense organs placed up front. This adaptation requires that a large mass of neural tissue be located near the front to receive the neurons from the sense organs. In other words, the evolution of a bilaterally symmetrical body plan also requires the development of a **brain**.

We can see the beginning of this process in certain flatworms. The brain or **anterior ganglion** of the primitive flatworms does not function as a center for correlating information and initiating activity. Instead, it is merely a region that receives information from the anterior sense organs and conveys information to other body regions by a system of longitudinal **nerve cords** (bundles of axons). In more advanced flatworms we can see considerable evolutionary progress. For example, the number of longitudinal nerve cords is reduced to two, whereas the more primitive organisms may have as many as eight. The brain becomes increasingly developed and assumes a larger role as control center for the animal's activities. The invertebrate brain reaches a peak of development in the hymenopteric insects (ants, bees, and wasps) and the cephalopod mollusks (squid and octopus). With their highly developed brains, these animals are capable of behavior patterns far more sophisticated and complex than the other invertebrates. The intricately organized social behavior of bees and the problem-solving ability of octopuses are cases in point.

The same direction of development persists in the vertebrate nervous system. Even the most advanced insects have doubled nerve cords, in which large **ganglia** (masses of nerve cell bodies) play an important role. In certain functions these ganglia sometimes rival the dominance of the brain. This is quite understandable. The fact that legs, wings, and often sense organs are at-

tached to the thoracic body segment of the insect makes the presence of a local control and coordination center very convenient. But in vertebrates, the main nerve cord or **spinal cord** is single. Its division into alternating ganglia and connecting fibers is much less apparent. The brain has developed further, and is now clearly the dominant integration center for the activities of the entire nervous system.

## The vertebrate nervous system

All but the simplest nervous systems have three components. The first comprises the **sensory neurons**, which transmit information about the environment. (In some cases these neurons make synaptic contact with specialized receptor cells, as in the eye. In other cases they are themselves the receptors, as with the free pain receptors in the skin.) Second, there are the **effector** or **motor neurons**. These neurons transmit some response to an effector organ, generally a muscle or gland, enabling the organism to act upon the information arriving via the sensory neurons. Sensory and motor neurons are usually linked by at least one, and often very many, **intermediate** or **associative neurons**. Such neurons make possible all the more complex forms of behavior of which various organisms are capable. This means not only intricately coordinated muscular movements, but also memory, learning, and decision-making—characteristics of the higher animals.

When we compare organisms at different levels of phylogenetic development, we see that the most dramatic neurological differences are in the number of intermediate neurons. The more advanced organisms have many more intermediate neurons. Most of them are massed in the spinal cord and brain. For example, the total number of brain cells in a higher primate is estimated to be about ten billion. But only a few million of these are motor neurons. So there may be a thousand or more associative neurons for each motor neuron. This suggests that the vertebrate nervous system is not merely a structure which receives sensory information, or which initiates motor activity. Rather, it is a system for *integrating* and *evaluating* sensory information, and for effecting an *appropriate, coordinated response.*

*The reflex arc*    We can best illustrate certain features of the structural and functional organization of vertebrate nervous systems by means of an example. The **reflex arc** is the simplest of all nervous pathways. It produces a rapid and automatic response to some sensory stimulus. The knee-jerk response which the doctor tests with a rubber hammer during a physical examination is an example of a reflex arc. The most basic reflex arc involves only two neurons—one sensory and one motor. In the vertebrate nervous system, the sensory neuron is usually very long. It carries the sensory information all the way from the receptor site to the spinal cord, often a distance of several feet. The axon of the sensory neuron projects into the spinal cord, but the nerve cell body lies outside, in a nearby spinal ganglion. Inside the spinal cord the sensory neuron synapses with a motor neuron. The cell body of the motor neuron lies within the spinal cord, and its axon projects out to make contact with an effector organ (generally a muscle).

On the basis of this anatomical arrangement we can divide the nervous system into two components. The **peripheral nervous system** consists of the sensory neurons, plus the axons of the motor neurons that project out into the bodily organs. The **central nervous system** includes the associative neurons of the brain and spinal cord, along with the cell bodies of the motor neurons that are also found there. Axons enter and leave the central nervous system in bundles called nerves. These are simply convenient groups of nerve fibers going to or coming from a particular region of the body. The human nervous system has 31 spinal nerves, all of which include both

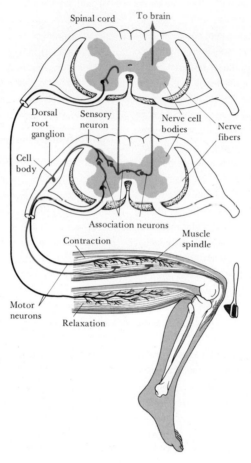

Spinal cord    To brain

Dorsal root ganglion    Sensory neuron    Nerve cell bodies    Nerve fibers

Cell body

Association neurons    Muscle spindle

Contraction

Motor neurons

Relaxation

15-23
A reflex arc. Striking the knee tendon stimulates the muscle spindles. A nerve impulse is then sent via a sensory neuron to the spinal cord. Association neurons transmit the message to motor neurons. This causes the muscle to contract. Meanwhile, the information is relayed to another level of the spinal cord. Here an impulse is sent by way of a second motor neuron to inhibit contraction of the antagonistic leg muscle. Other association neurons "report" what is taking place to the brain.

sensory and motor axons. Twelve cranial nerves connect directly to the brain. Some consist solely of motor axons, some solely of sensory axons, and some of both.

In reality, pathways as simple as the one described above are probably very rare. In most cases at least one intermediate neuron will intervene between the sensory and motor neurons. These intermediate neurons channel the incoming information along additional pathways of the nervous system. In particular, they pass the information to various parts of the brain. The brain may then modify the initial reflex response, countermand it, or issue supplementary instructions. For example, if you stub your toe while carrying a tray of food, several different regions of the brain may come into play. They inhibit your reflex reaction to quickly raise your foot. They prepare the muscles of your other leg to take the extra strain and balance your body as you shift your weight from the bruised foot. And at the same time they arouse your bodily systems (both by direct nervous action and by eliciting the release of certain hormones) to cope with the crisis, and they decide which nearby surface will most safely hold the tray and can most easily be reached.

*The autonomic nervous system*    Reflex arcs like the one described above usually involve skeletal muscle as the effector organ. Often the individual is aware of the reflex action, and may be able to exercise some voluntary control over the response. The system of motor neurons that control the visceral organs and glands is called the **autonomic nervous system**. We are seldom aware of its operation, and usually quite unable to influence it. (Persons using ancient yogic or modern biofeedback techniques reportedly can control certain autonomic functions after intensive training. But the extent of such control is uncertain and the entire area is only now being rigorously investigated.) The autonomic nervous system is divided into the **sympa-**

thetic and the parasympathetic. These differ in both their anatomical arrangements and their effects. Each visceral organ receives nerve impulses from both divisions, but the responses they evoke are functionally opposed.

In general, the sympathetic system is called into action during emergency states. It helps mobilize the organs of the body to meet a crisis. Its effects have been termed "fight-or-flight" responses. Priority is given to those tissues which can help the organism deal with the dangerous situation, at the expense of those whose function is not immediately required. For example, blood flow to the muscles is increased while the blood supply to the intestines is cut back. Heartbeat and respiration are accelerated, while peristalsis is inhibited. Glycogen reserves are converted into glucose and released into the blood, along with extra blood cells. The pupils of the eye are dilated, and resistance to fatigue is increased. All these reactions are generally provoked by stress, exercise, pain, cold, fear, anger, or other strong emotional excitement.

By contrast, the parasympathetic system works mainly to protect the organism and conserve its resources. Its effects are generally just the reverse of those of the sympathetic system. They include decrease in heartbeat, constriction of the pupil (to protect it from bright light), and stimulation of the digestive processes. Another difference between the two systems is their pattern of innervation. The sympathetic system is diffusely organized. A fiber from the spinal cord can project for a considerable distance along the chain of ganglia, thus activating neurons that contact a variety of different organs and structures. Consequently the system tends to go into action as a whole. By contrast, nerve fibers of the parasympathetic division go directly to ganglia in the vicinity of their target organs. There is little or no interconnection among these ganglia, so a parasympathetic fiber has a discrete effect confined to a specific organ.

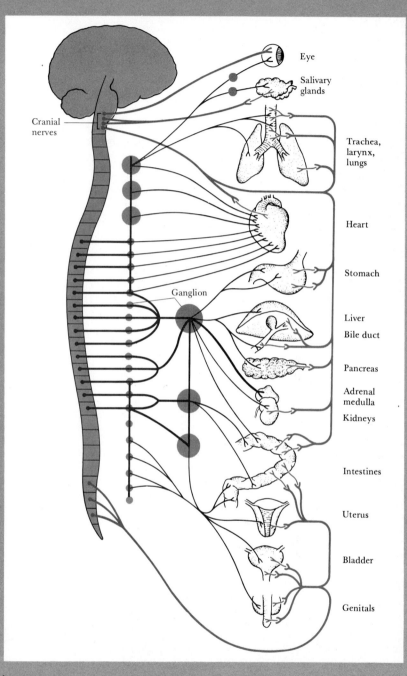

15-24

The sympathetic nervous system is activated in situations of great stress. It puts the various systems of the organism on an emergency basis to deal with the crisis. It also imposes a special set of priorities. That is, some organs are mobilized, some suppressed. Respiration, for example, is increased, but digestion is inhibited. The parasympathetic division is involved in conservation and restoration of bodily activities. Its effects are generally the opposite of those of the sympathetic division. The sympathetic neurons (black) are interconnected through a series of ganglia outside the spinal cord. As a result, the system tends to function as an integrated unit. The parasympathetic (colored) fibers by contrast generally follow individual and unconnected pathways. They form synapses only when they arrive at their target organs. (See The autonomic nervous system)

## The brain

We saw earlier that in most primitive bilaterally symmetrical creatures, the "brain" is merely a front-end ganglion, serving mainly as a receiving center for information from the sensory organs. But as the brain grew in size, complexity, and importance, different regions became specialized for various functions. Even in the most primitive vertebrates, the brain is seen to consist of three distinct regions, which can also be recognized in the human embryo during its early stages of development. These regions are the forebrain, the midbrain, and the hindbrain. Each region has undergone a great deal of additional evolution, and more highly specialized structures have emerged. Quite early in this process (that is, in relatively primitive vertebrates such as fish and amphibians) we can observe the following adaptations:

1. The lower portion of the hindbrain gave rise to the medulla oblongata, which oversees and regulates such automatic visceral functions as heartbeat and respiration. It also links the spinal cord with the other regions of the brain.

2. The upper portion of the hindbrain became enlarged and specialized as the cerebellum. This control center is largely concerned with muscular coordination, balance, and equilibrium.

3. The optic lobes, integrating centers for visual information, developed from the midbrain.

4. The posterior region of the forebrain divided into an upper part, the thalamus, and a lower part, the hypothalamus.

5. The anterior region of the forebrain evolved into the cerebrum.

As we move up the evolutionary ladder, there are changes in the relative size, importance, and even the functions of the various parts of the brain. In higher verte-

brates such as birds and mammals the cerebellum increases greatly in size. The consequent gain in muscular coordination enables these animals to move much more quickly while exercising very precise control of their movements—for example, think of a cat chasing a mouse. The midbrain, which is the dominant integration and control center in the most primitive vertebrates, diminishes in size and significance. In higher vertebrates it is chiefly a link between hindbrain and forebrain. Even its role as a visual center has been largely taken over by the cerebrum.

The cerebrum itself is at first little more than an olfactory center (sometimes called the "smell brain"). But it now acquires a multitude of additional functions while increasing its domination over all other regions of the brain. These changes are reflected in its progressively greater volume

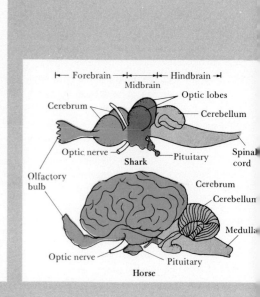

15-25
Changes in relative size and importance of different parts of the brain. Mammals such as the horse have a better-developed forebrain than do lower vertebrates such as the shark. The midbrain, by contrast, dwindles in importance. The most prominent part of the human brain is the neocortex, the outer layer of the cerebrum.

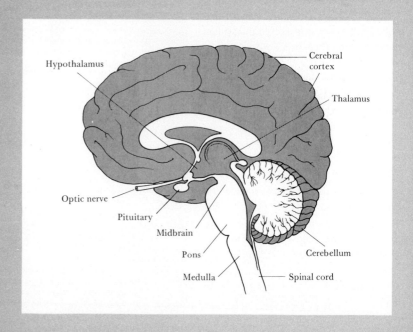

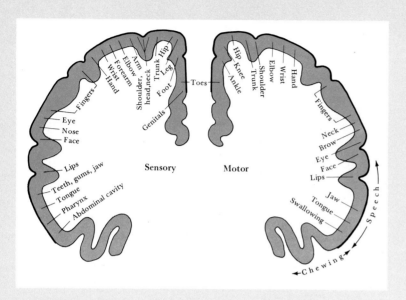

**15-26**
Experiments involving direct electrical stimulation of the brain have made it possible to map both the sensory and motor areas of the cerebral cortex. It is easy to see from such a map that the "geography" of the cortex corresponds roughly to that of the body itself. But the relative sizes of the parts are very distorted. This is because the brain area devoted to each part is proportional, not to its actual body size, but rather to its neurological importance and complexity. More neurons are needed to control the intricate movements of which our fingers are capable than the much simpler ones of the toes. Similarly, there are more sensory receptors on the face than on the legs.

as well as in its greater structural complexity. As the number of cell bodies (grey matter) in the cerebrum increased, they migrated gradually outward. In time, most of them came to form a layer on the surface of the cerebrum known as the **cerebral cortex**. A new cortical layer, the neocortex, then evolved. Eventually it grew larger to cover the entire cerebrum, so that the old cortex now lies inside the neocortex. The neocortex has continued to expand. In higher mammals its surface area is increased by extensive wrinkling and folding. This accounts for the familiar convoluted appearance of the human brain. The neocortex never developed in birds. This may account for their less flexible, more rigidly "programmed" behavior patterns, since in mammals the neocortex contains the associative areas that make possible such higher functions as speech, memory, and learning.

*The hypothalamus and thalamus* The hypothalamus is concerned mainly with the internal functioning of the body. It regulates body temperature, blood pressure, water balance, and sexual activity. Through direct electrical stimulation of different regions of the hypothalamus, experimenters have been able to elicit a variety of sensations and emotions in animals—hunger, thirst, rage, pleasure, pain, sexual desire. In this way researchers have located the control centers for many basic drives. We will see in the next chapter that the hypothalamus also coordinates the body's nervous and chemical control systems by regulating the release of many different hormones.

In lower vertebrates the thalamus plays an important role in integrating sensory data. It retains some of this function in higher organisms as well. In addition, it includes part of a structure called the **reticular system**, which also extends into the midbrain and medulla. This intricate network of neurons performs several related and vitally important functions. Basically it seems to serve as a kind of monitoring system. All channels into or out of the brain— both ascending sensory pathways and descending motor pathways—contribute side branches to the reticular system. The reticular system is like an executive assistant who decides which messages should be seen by the boss and which can safely be ignored, which matters require immediate action and which can wait, which visitors must be seen and which put off. This system evaluates the importance and degree of urgency of incoming impulses. It amplifies some and suppresses others. It also filters out irrelevant and distracting stimuli such as background noise when you are trying to concentrate on a conversation, or hunger when you are taking an important exam. Even pain or injury can be suppressed when you are intensely absorbed in more pressing concerns—as athletes and soldiers know from experience. On the other hand, the reticular system can also alert the other regions of the brain to urgent stimuli. It functions as a kind of arousal or warning system, like a buzzer or flashing red light on a control panel.

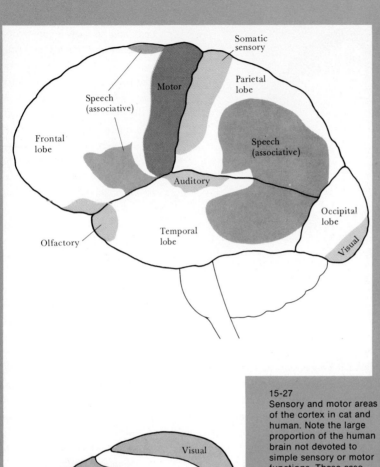

**15-27**
Sensory and motor areas of the cortex in cat and human. Note the large proportion of the human brain not devoted to simple sensory or motor functions. These associative areas enable us to remember and to think. That is, we can make meaningful interpretations of our experiences. The left cerebral hemisphere contains the sensory and motor areas for the right side of the body, and vice versa. The speech association areas, however, seem largely concentrated on the left hemisphere.

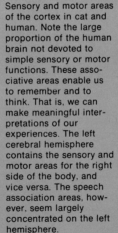

*The cerebral cortex* In the course of its rapid evolution, the cerebral cortex has at least partially taken over many functions once performed by other areas of the brain. In addition, it has acquired some functions all its own. Some of these, such as judgement, memory, and imagination, are still mysterious. Others, such as motor and sensory coordination, are better understood. The sensory and motor areas of the cortex have been mapped in some detail using such techniques as direct electrode stimulation. These areas lie adjacent to each other. Curiously, though, the motor and sensory regions for the right side of the body are on the left side of the brain, and vice versa. The areas concerned with the different parts of the body are arranged in a way that roughly reflects their actual anatomical relationship. For instance, the motor area for the forearm lies between the areas that control the wrist and the shoulder. But the amount of space associated with each organ is in proportion to its sensory or motor function rather than to its size. The motor area for the hand is much larger than that for the foot, since the hand must perform so many complex muscular movements. The mouth also requires a large area to control its intricate activities of speech, chewing, and swallowing. The mouth and face, with their great sensitivity, command almost as large an area of the sensory region as all the rest of the body together.

In lower animals almost the entire surface of the cortex can be accounted for as motor or sensory areas for various parts of the body. But in man, much of the cortex is not concerned with these functions. Instead, it appears to consist of associative areas that make possible such higher functions as speech, emotion, imagination, memory, and learning. Three speech areas have been discovered. These regions are concerned not with the actual muscular coordination necessary for making sounds, but with the mental processes needed for coherent utterance. These include the association of words with their correct mean-

15-28
Electron micrograph of skeletal muscle from a deep-water ocean fish, caught at a depth of about 8,000 feet. The parallel arrangement of the muscle fibrils, and the characteristic stripes or striations, are clearly visible. The roughly circular structures are sections of the sarcoplasmic reticulum, which transmits electrical impulses from the muscle cell surface to the interior fibrils. It also serves as a repository for calcium ions. These ions play a crucial role in the contraction of muscle.

ings, and the command of proper syntax.

An interesting discovery of recent brain research is that there are remarkable differences in function between the left and right cerebral hemispheres. The left half of the cerebral cortex seems to be involved primarily with the conceptual and intellectual side of our natures. Its specialty is the handling of abstract ideas and language. (The speech areas described above are found principally on the left side.) By contrast, the right side seems associated with the esthetic and intuitive faculties—emotion, imagination, artistic creativity, grasp of spatial relationships. Apparently one side or the other is more fully developed and therefore dominant in most people. So we tend to be either "left-brained" or "right-brained." Research in this area may eventually enable us to use both halves of the brain more fully and more equally.

## Effectors

In most higher organisms, coordinated movements are necessary not only for mobility but for many other activities such as eating and digestion. These movements are effected by a specialized tissue called muscle. Like nervous tissue, muscle tissue is excitable. That is, it can initiate and conduct action potentials.

### Skeletal muscle

In chapter 13, we noted that muscle contraction requires energy. This energy, is derived from breaking down ATP molecules. Interestingly, it has been found that the reaction can be catalyzed by the protein myosin itself. So myosin plays a dynamic as well as a structural role in the process of muscle contraction. But this catalytic activity also seems to require the presence of many calcium ions within the cell. And, in turn, the influx of calcium into the cell is triggered by the depolarization of the muscle membrane.

In other words, the conduction of an action potential is a precondition for muscle contraction. An action potential must sweep over the muscle and excite every fibril before the filaments will shorten. But how does the wave of depolarization penetrate the surface muscle tissue and invade the deep fibrils? The answer lies in a special system of membranes, the **sarcotubular system**. This system consists of a grid of transverse tubules, known as **T tubules**. They are continuous with the cell membrane, and are connected by an irregular system of membranes called the **sarcoplasmic reticulum**. The T tubules seem to function in the rapid transmission of the action potential from the cell membrane to all of the fibrils. The sarcoplasmic reticulum acts as a storage and release site for calcium ions.

## Cardiac muscle

Skeletal muscle cannot contract unless an action potential is transmitted to it. But, as we saw in chapter 14, specialized regions of heart muscle, called nodes, generate

their own action potentials spontaneously. They do not need any stimulation from the nervous system. The nodes act as pacemakers to regulate the cycle of cardiac contraction. Moreover, the branched structure of cardiac muscle enables an action potential initiated anywhere in the heart to spread rapidly through all the fibers.

## Smooth muscle

The mechanisms that trigger the contraction of smooth muscle fibers are more complex than those of other kinds of muscle. In the walls of the gastrointestinal tract, smooth muscle cells can function to some extent without stimulus from any nerve. On the other hand, some smooth muscle cells are stimulated by neurons from several different parts of the nervous system. All smooth muscle cells, however, are highly sensitive to circulating hormones, such as the adrenalins. Some smooth muscle can sustain contraction almost indefinitely.

15-29
What appear to be thick tubes of a cloth-like material are actually striated muscle cells of skeletal muscle. And the "ropes" which are coming down and passing across these cells are actually some of the nerve fibers which stimulate contraction of the muscle tissue. (See Skeletal muscle)

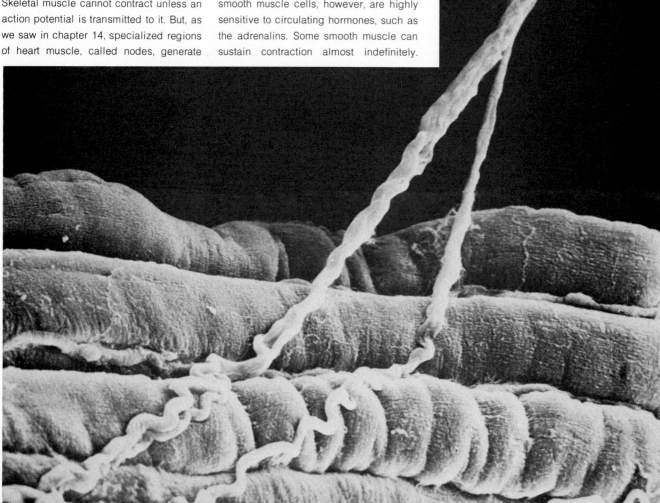

summary

The nervous system receives information about both the external and internal environment of an organism. It then uses that information to regulate body functions. The functional unit of the vertebrate nervous system is the neuron. These long thin cells are adapted to transmit electrochemical impulses. The impulse is generated because of a difference in the number of potassium ions inside the neuron and the number in the fluid that surrounds it. This difference creates an electrical potential. The nerve impulse, or action potential, takes place when something depolarizes the membrane, and potassium ions rush out of the neuron. The resulting change in the cell's electrical potential is called the generator potential.

At first the action potential is localized in a small portion of the neuron's membrane. But the electrical changes associated with the process cause nearby areas to depolarize also. The impulse is thus quickly transmitted throughout the entire length of the cell.

When the impulse reaches the end of one neuron, it is carried to the adjoining one by chemical rather than electrical means. An action potential traveling down the axon causes synaptic vesicles to migrate toward the cell membrane. They release their contents—the transmitter substance is usually acetylcholine—into the tiny gap (synaptic cleft) between cells. The transmitter substance stimulates depolarization of the membrane of the adjoining cell, and is then broken down by enzymes. The synapse is the point of transmission between cells. It provides a mechanism for coding messages as to their degree of urgency. The action potential of a single neuron is an all-or-none phenomenon. It does not vary quantitatively. But not every neuron fires, because it may not be stimulated to the necessary level, or threshold. The amount of transmitter substance released by one action potential may not be enough to cause threshold depolarization. But when a second action potential releases another dose, the combined effect may be great enough to cause the cell to fire.

Sensory receptors are specialized structures in the nervous system. They receive energy in one form—such as sound or electricity—and transduce it into another form, that of the action potential. Receptors may be chemical, as is the case with taste buds and olfactory receptors. They may be electromagnetic, as in the case of visual receptors that respond to light. They may also be mechanical, as in the case of receptors for sound, pressure, spatial orientation, and muscle extension.

A true nervous system is first seen in the coelenterates. But the great leap forward came with the advent of bilateral symmetry, which in effect necessitated a brain. Nervous systems of higher vertebrates have three components. Sensory neurons transmit information about the environment. Effector or motor neurons transmit some response to an effector organ. Intermediate or associative neurons make possible delicately coordinated movements, memory, learning, and decision-making. A sensory neuron and a motor neuron are connected in a pathway called a reflex arc. Often an intermediate neuron processes information from the sensor before it is passed along to the motor neuron.

Most reflex arcs involve skeletal muscles. The individual is aware of the reflex action and can usually exert some control over it. The autonomic nervous system controls the visceral organs and glands. We are seldom aware of its operation and usually cannot influence it. This system has two divisions. The sympathetic division helps to mobilize the body to meet a crisis. The parasympathetic division mainly serves to protect the organism and conserve its resources.

The brain of even the most primitive vertebrates is divided into three parts. The hindbrain includes the medulla oblongata and the cerebellum. The midbrain includes the optic lobes. The forebrain includes the thalamus, hypothalamus, and cerebrum. In higher vertebrates the cerebellum becomes larger. This permits more precise control and coordination of movements. More significantly, the cerebrum also acquires many additional functions while coming increasingly to dominate all other regions of the brain. In mammals, there has been great expansion of the cerebral layer called the neocortex. Its surface area has been increased by extensive folding. This center of the brain—especially well developed in humans—contains the associative areas that make possible such higher functions as speech, memory, and learning.

16 chemical coordination

II

IV

III

I

VI

**a**s we have seen, there is a complex and ever changing chemical environment within each living cell. The number and variety of reactions that occur within the cell are quite astonishing. Because these reactions are close both in space and in time, they influence each other strongly. For example, the product of one reaction—call it substance A—might promote the rate of a second reaction, X, while inhibiting a third reaction, Y. So reactions X and Y will be controlled to some extent by the concentration of A. If this regulatory mechanism proves useful to the organism, natural selection is likely to further increase the sensitivity of these reactions to substance A. This is the basis of chemical control.

Some form of chemical control exists in all organisms. In many simple microorganisms, the metabolites themselves perform the regulatory functions necessary to their activity. When enough of a particular metabolic substance is present, any further buildup of that substance inhibits or "turns off" the reaction by which it is synthesized—perhaps by deactivating a necessary enzyme, or preventing its formation. Similarly, the accumulation of a substrate may "turn on" the reaction in which it will take part. It does this by inducing creation of the appropriate enzymes. These are examples of **feedback control**, a vitally important principle in biological systems.

But even in microorganisms, some substances seem to function solely for regulation. They do not take a direct part in the metabolic process. In higher organisms, specialized cells have evolved to secrete such regulatory chemicals. Their effects will usually be experienced by cells of other kinds, often in widely scattered parts of the organism. These agents of intercellular chemical control are called **hormones**.

In 1902, the English scientists William Bayliss and E.H. Starling isolated a substance, secreted in the small intestine, that stimulates the flow of pancreatic juice. They named it secretin. Starling proposed that chemicals which promote reactions in this way should be called hormones, from the Greek word meaning "to excite." Secretin was, in fact, the first hormone to be discovered. But it later became evident that hormones can inhibit chemical reactions as well as excite them.

## Hormones

The cells that produce secretin are scattered through the intestinal mucosa. Many other hormonal secretions are produced by localized groups of cells, called **glands**. All hormone-secreting tissues are known as **endocrine** tissues, whether they are organized into glands or not. Endocrine means "secreting internally." Hormones do not leave the endocrine tissue through tubes or ducts, as do the secretions of such **exocrine** glands as the gall bladder. Instead, they enter the circulatory system directly from the secreting cells. Because of this, the endocrine glands are also commonly called "ductless glands." Hormones are transported through the extracellular fluids to their various **target cells**. These are the cells whose activities they influence.

The effects of hormones on the organism fall into two broad categories: **developmental** and **regulatory**. The developmental functions bring about long-lasting or permanent changes. Examples are growth, molting, and metamorphosis. The French scientist Berthold performed a classic experiment in 1840 that demonstrated the developmental control deriving from an endocrine gland—long before it was conceived of as such. A castrated rooster ordinarily does not develop secondary sexual characteristics. But Berthold showed that these characteristics would develop if the testes were reimplanted elsewhere in the rooster's body. He concluded, correctly, that the testes must secrete some substance that provoked these physiological changes. The actual discovery of many endocrine glands, and the roles of their respective hormones, resulted from studies of the developmental abnormalities often

produced by endocrine malfunction. These included such conditions as giantism and dwarfism.

The regulatory functions of hormones are many and varied. They maintain homeostasis in the internal environment by controlling metabolic processes. They permit the organism to respond to the external environment, particularly stress situations. And hormones control periodic activities such as the reproductive cycle.

Chemically, hormones comprise a large and diverse group of substances. The sex hormones are steroids, which are synthesized in the body from lipids such as cholesterol. Many other hormones—insulin, for example—are modified proteins or amino acids. Hormones that have the same biological activity may differ chemically in different species. Some affect only one species. Others have different effects on different organisms. For example, prolactin causes lactation (milk production) in animals. But in certain birds, such as pigeons, it stimulates the production of "crop milk," a secretion in the bird's crop that is regurgitated to feed the young. In all species, though, prolactin seems to evoke maternal behavior. Similarly, thyroxin injected into a tadpole will change it into a frog prematurely. But removal of the tadpole's thyroid glands will prevent metamorphosis altogether. Thyroxin in humans is a metabolic stimulator, and metamorphosis is very closely associated with accelerated metabolism. So we can see that the functions of this hormone are analogous in the two species.

The endocrine system shares its responsibility for control and coordination with the nervous system. The two systems possess many similarities. Both systems control processes that may occur far from the control center. And both operate on feedback principles, with the controlling mechanism itself controlled by the product of the activities it regulates. There are also distinct differences between the two. The messages of one system are nerve impulses, traveling

16-1
The hormone thyroxin acts as a metabolic accelerator in many different organisms. Administered to a tadpole, for example, it will cause it to develop into a frog. Such metamorphoses is closely linked with speeded up metabolism. This "frogpole" is half way between the two stages.

over well-defined pathways and acting on specific structures—for example, on a particular muscle. The messages of the other system are hormone molecules that are transported through the circulatory system. Their action is usually more general, and may affect large areas of the organism. Nerve impulses are rapid and usually of short duration. Hormonal action is much slower and longer lasting. This is why chemical control is adequate for plants, with their limited mobility and slowness of response. Animals, though, have evolved nervous systems more suited to their active lifestyles.

But within the endocrine system, several adaptations increase the speed and specificity of hormonal action. Target cells, for instance, are extremely sensitive to particular hormones. In most instances only a few molecules are necessary to elicit a response. The time required for the synthesis of hormone molecules is further reduced because the key components are often stored in the cells of the organism. These **precursor** molecules can be changed very rapidly into specific hormones when needed. Cholesterol, for example, is a precursor of several human hormones.

In actuality, we separate the endocrine and nervous systems only for convenience in studying them. We have seen that nervous transmission depends upon chemical action—impulses are propagated across synapses by chemical agents. Conversely, nervous stimulation will often induce chemical secretions. In fact, the adrenal medulla, commonly considered an endocrine gland, is in essence a part of the sympathetic nervous system. We should view both methods of control simply as different aspects of a single integrated system.

# Invertebrate hormones

Some type of hormonal activity probably occurs in all plants and animals. But it is exceedingly difficult to isolate hormones from most invertebrates because of the complexity of the reactions and the minute quantities of chemicals produced. So our knowledge of invertebrate hormones is limited to only a few varieties. The arthropods—in particular the insects—have been most widely studied. At least six hormones have been isolated from arthropods. Most of these control growth and development. But others have been found that are involved in homeostatic regulation of the internal environment in insects. For instance, a hormone discovered in cockroaches seems to take part in regulating blood-sugar levels.

## Molting hormone

Immature insects grow by periodically shedding or **molting** a hard exoskeleton. The pressure of the rigid exoskeleton on the growing tissues within initiates the molt. During the 1930s a brain hormone was isolated that stimulates glands in the insect's prothorax (the body segment lying just behind the head). These prothoracic glands respond by secreting the hormone **ecdysone**. This, in turn, causes the release of an enzyme from glands in the outer body layer. The enzyme promotes the digestion of the exoskeleton, which is then shed.

16-2
Two principle hormones regulate the growth and development of insects. When the insect starts to outgrow its rigid exoskeleton, the resulting pressure stimulates production of the hormone ecdysone. This hormone causes secretion of an enzyme to digest the old exoskeleton. Juvenile hormone controls the insect life cycle. When its concentration is high, the insect remains immature. When the hormone level drops, it enters the pupa stage. When secretion of the hormone stops, the insect develops into an adult. Recently, a scientist isolated antihormones, which he called precocenes, that block production of the juvenile hormone. One of several effects of these antihormones is that the insect may bypass one or more stages in the immature part of its life cycle and becomes a "precocious" and sterile adult. The use of these and similar substances to curb commercially harmful insects is now being investigated. (See Molting hormone and Juvenile hormone)

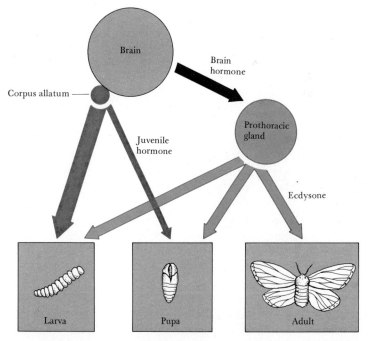

This molting mechanism is significant because it involves a sequence of hormonal activities similar to those found in higher organisms, including man. The pressure on the exoskeleton signals the brain, via the nervous system, to release a neurosecretion. This secretion has no direct physiological action, but stimulates the action of other glands. The affected gland then releases its own particular hormone to induce a specific reaction—in this case, the secretion of an enzyme. The many steps in the process definitely slow the response. But they also have advantages to the organism. They constitute a kind of "fail-safe" mechanism. That is, the steps insure that the process is not likely to be triggered accidentally. At the same time, the various steps provide a number of stages at which control can be exercised.

### Juvenile hormone

Insects go through several immature or nymphal stages after each molt before they become adult. V. B. Wigglesworth, the English scientist who did much of the early work on insect hormones, studied the mechanisms involved in the metamorphosis from larva to adult. He isolated a hormone secreted by a pair of glands located behind the brain—the **corpora allata**. The concentration of this juvenile hormone controls the insect's developmental cycle. When the hormone is present in high concentrations, it leads to another immature stage after the molt. But when the concentration is low, the insect enters the last larval stage. This is known as the pupa stage. For the pupa to finally molt into an adult, juvenile hormone must be totally absent. We should note how intimately the brain is involved in these endocrine mechanisms. The prothoracotropic hormone is secreted directly by the brain. Juvenile hormone is secreted by glands that are located very near the brain and are closely associated with it. The nervous and endocrine systems overlap, functioning in close cooperation.

16-3
This adult moth is emerging from the pupa stage. The spherical bead of liquid at the base of its antennae is an enzyme that helps dissolve the cocoon. (See Juvenile hormone)

## Vertebrate hormones

This same overlapping pattern exists in the control systems of vertebrates. The hypothalamus is a region in the lower portion of the brain, just above the pituitary gland. It plays a key role in regulating the output of many hormones. The anterior pituitary has been called the "master gland." It secretes at least four tropic hormones which regulate the activity of other endocrine glands, as well as several hormones which act directly on the body. But the anterior pituitary itself is directly influenced by chemical secretions from the hypothalamus. So the hypothalamus is in effect the master of the master gland. This is another example of how the two chief regulatory systems of living beings are closely integrated.

There are about a dozen endocrine glands in the human body. In some cases they seem to have little anatomical relationship to each other or to their function. For example, the four small parathyroid glands are not related to the thyroid either functionally or developmentally, though they lie on its surface. But the endocrine glands nonetheless function together as parts of a well-coordinated system.

### The pancreas

Diabetes is a disease characterized by abnormally high blood-sugar levels. It has been recognized since the time of the Roman Empire. But it was not associated with the malfunction of a body process until 1899. In that year the German physicians J. von Mering and O. Minkowski made an interesting and quite accidental discovery. They had been studying pancreatic enzymes. The physicians found that the urine of dogs whose pancreas had been removed attracted ants. But the urine of normal dogs did not. Analysis showed that the urine of the surgically altered dogs contained high concentrations of sugar. This is a symptom long associated with diabetes. Furthermore, the dogs soon developed other symptoms of diabetes.

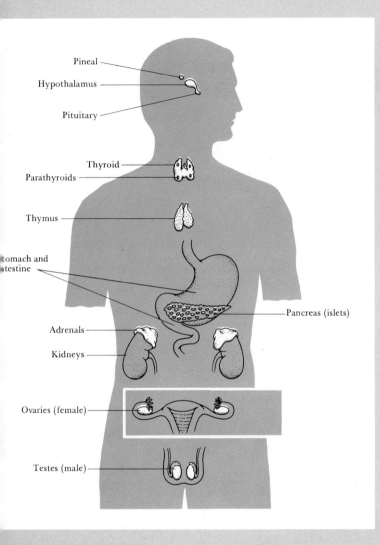

**16-4**
The endocrine glands form a highly coordinated system. This system is further integrated with the nervous system through the pituitary, or master gland. The hypothalamus in the brain controls the pituitary. In turn, the pituitary controls the function of several glands. In addition to endocrine glands, there are endocrine tissues located in other organs, such as the lining of the stomach and intestine.

Experiments indicated that the onset of diabetes was not associated with the absence of pancreatic digestive enzymes. But the pancreas contains several types of cell that appear to function independently. Cells clustered like small islands had been discovered by the German anatomist Paul Langerhans in the mid-nineteenth century. They were named **islets of Langerhans**. It seemed plausible that these cells might secrete a hormone controlling blood-sugar levels.

In 1922, Frederick G. Banting and C. H. Best tied off the pancreatic duct of dogs. The enzyme-producing section of the pancreas soon atrophied. But the islets remained viable—and diabetes did not appear. The researchers concluded that the hormone sought was produced by the islets, and called it **insulin**. By this method, they were able to isolate the hormone. When they injected it into diabetic dogs, the insulin produced a definite reversal of symptoms. Several years later insulin was analyzed. It was shown to be a protein, consisting of two linked polypeptide chains. This was the first time that the structure of a hormone had been determined. It also marked one of the great advances in the medical application of biochemistry. Countless diabetics formerly condemned to suffering and early death could now lead almost normal lives through the administration of insulin.

Insulin lowers blood-sugar concentrations, apparently through several mechanisms. It inhibits the liver from producing glucose, stimulates the muscles and liver to convert glucose to glycogen, and causes more rapid oxidation of carbohydrates in the cells—probably by increasing membrane permeability to glucose.

An insufficient supply of insulin produces the symptoms of diabetes. An individual with this disease can have normal or even excessive blood-sugar levels. But he is in serious trouble nonetheless, since the sugar cannot gain access to the interior of the cells where it is metabolized to produce energy. Diabetes thus leads to a kind of paradoxical "starvation in the midst of plenty." Glucose cannot be converted into glycogen without insulin. Thus glycogen reserves in the liver and muscles are depleted. At the same time, excess glucose in the blood is excreted through the urine. To obtain energy, the body must metabolize its protein and fat reserves. This excessive fat metabolism creates toxic by-products (ketones). Eventually it can lead to a dangerous rise in the acidity of the blood.

Insulin shock can be caused by an acute overproduction of insulin. Insulin increases the transport of glucose into muscle cells. So excessively high insulin levels cause the blood-sugar level to fall so low that the brain cannot function. Coma and death may follow. A less severe but chronic overproduction of insulin leads to **hypoglycemia**—low blood sugar.

Though insulin is the more famous because of its role in the treatment of diabetes, the pancreas also secretes **glucagon**. This hormone is equally important in the regulation of blood-sugar levels. Glucagon functions as an antagonist to insulin. The two work together to keep the amount of glucose in the blood within a physiologically normal range. After a meal or whenever blood glucose levels rise, the pancreas responds by secreting insulin. Insulin facilitates the movement of glucose into the cells of the body. This allows the glucose to be used as a source of energy by the cells, and lowers the concentration of sugar in the blood. A decline in blood glucose levels depresses insulin secretion and promotes glucagon output. Glucagon causes the liver to secrete glucose, thus raising the level of glucose in the blood. This seems to be a particularly important mechanism for maintaining normal or near-normal blood glucose levels during starvation. So the pancreas can be described as a "glucostat." It monitors and responds to changes in the amount of glucose in the blood. Such systems using two antagonistic hormones are very common in the biological world.

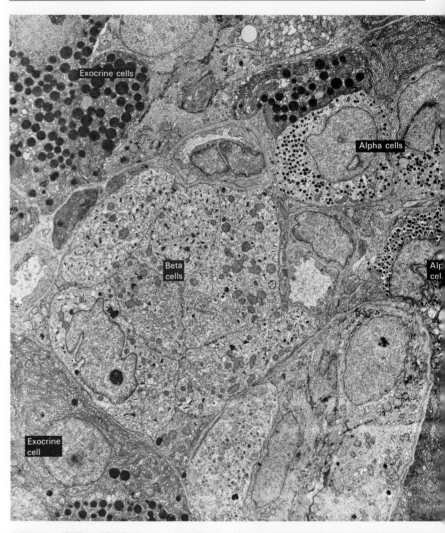

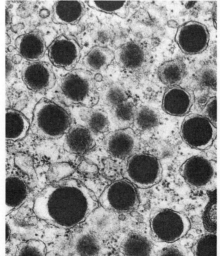

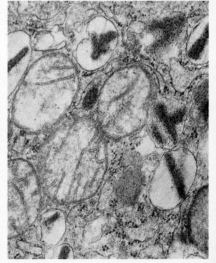

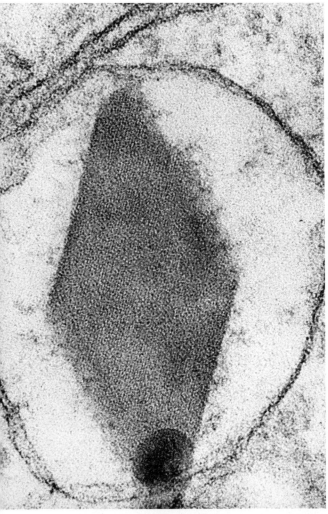

16-5
The endocrine part of the pancreas consists of small clusters of cells called Islets of Langerhans (far left, top). There are two types of islet cells. Alpha cells secrete glucagon. Beta cells secrete insulin. The lower photos show detailed views of the tiny vesicles that hold the granules of glucagon (opposite page, left) and insulin (opposite, right). From the photo to the left of this caption one can see that insulin is stored in crystalline form. The photo below shows insulin granules just inside a beta cell, ready for release into an adjacent capillary. The basement membrane of the endocrine cell runs across the picture, separating the granules from the capillary wall.

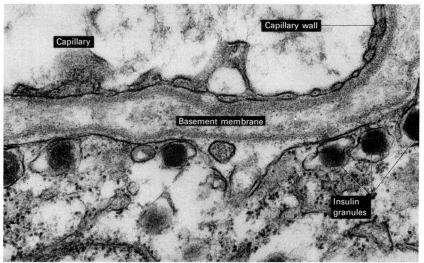

## The thyroid

The thyroid is an H-shaped gland located in the neck. Unlike the pancreas, it is highly specialized. Its only function is to secrete its hormone, thyroxin. The gland appears to have evolved from a primitive structure in the pharynx that served to filter food particles. But in modern vertebrates it is totally unconnected with the pharynx. The actual secretory elements of the thyroid are the **follicles**—spherical structures of epithelial cells surrounding a globule of gelatinous material. Thyroxin is produced by these cells and stored in the gelatinous material.

The first clue to thyroid function came from the study of goiter. This abnormal enlargement of the thyroid often causes noticeable swelling in the neck. The condition was especially prevalent in the Swiss Alps and the Great Lakes region of the United States. Sufferers usually showed signs of decreased metabolism—lethargy, obesity, slow heartbeat, and mental dullness. Such symptoms were also observed in patients whose thyroids were completely removed. This suggested that the thyroid normally secretes a hormone which prevents these symptoms. Presumably, then, those patients with goiters were suffering from the same lack despite the enlargement of the thyroid. This condition is known as **hypothyroidism**. It was successfully treated with extracts of animal thyroids as early as the 1890s. This provided further evidence for the hypothesis of a thyroid secretion.

There was no explanation of the action of the hormone, and it had not yet been isolated. But it was discovered that the thyroid did contain noticeable concentrations of iodine. A relationship was also noticed between goiter and the lack of iodine in the food and water of some geographical regions. When iodized salt was eventually introduced into the diet of these areas, goiter disappeared almost totally. The explanation for this became clear when thyroxin was isolated. It proved to be an amino acid containing four iodine atoms.

16-6
The thyroid hormone, thyroxin. Note the four iodine atoms in the molecule's structure.

Thyroxin controls metabolism, the oxidation and energy-producing reactions in the body. An excess of thyroxin, or **hyperthyroidism**, naturally leads to an unusually high metabolism, with high body temperature, high blood pressure, weight loss and irritability. Hyperthyroidism can be treated by partial removal of the thyroid. More recently, it has been treated with thyroxin-inhibiting drugs. A lack of thyroxin in infants produces cretinism, a condition characterized by malformation and mental deficiency. Fortunately this condition is reversible if thyroxin is administered immediately.

## The parathyroids

The four pea-sized **parathyroid** glands are located on the surface of the thyroid, but are completely independent of it. They secrete the hormone **parathormone**, which regulates the calcium-phosphate balance between the blood and tissues. Parathormone is a modified polypeptide. It acts on target organs to raise the calcium ion concentration in the blood. It also inhibits the excretion of calcium by the kidneys and intestines, and stimulates its release by the bones. But calcium in the bones is bonded to phosphate, and so the phosphate level increases whenever calcium is drawn from the bones. To compensate for this, parathormone induces the kidneys to excrete phosphate and thus reduce its level in the blood. Calcium ions play an extremely vital role in the innervation of cardiac and skeletal muscles. So a complete absence of parathormone, with the consequent reduction in calcium ions, leads to convulsions and death.

It has recently been found that the thyroid secretes **calcitonin**, an antagonist to parathormone. Calcitonin lowers the concentration of calcium in the blood, both by increasing its rate of excretion and by depositing it in the bones. Thus a feedback mechanism exists between the two that maintains the calcium balance between blood and tissues.

## The adrenal glands

The two adrenal glands lie just above the kidneys. Each consists of an outer layer called the **cortex** and an inner core known as the **medulla**. These are two distinct glands. They function independently despite their close physical relationship. They also develop from different embryonic tissue. The cortex is derived from the epithelium covering the main body cavity. The medulla, though, is essentially a part of the sympathetic nervous system. Its cells are similar to nerve cells, though they lack axons and dendrites. They also are directly controlled by presynaptic sympathetic neurons.

*The medulla* The close kinship between the adrenal medulla and the nervous system is evident in the hormone it secretes. One of these is **noradrenalin** (also called norepinephrine). This is the same chemical that carries the nervous impulse across the synapses of the sympathetic nervous system. The other hormone secreted by the medulla is **adrenalin** (epinephrine), a closely related compound. Both hormones are derived from the amino acid tyrosine. The two have similar, though not identical, functions. Adrenalin produces the "fight-or-flight" reactions. These include rise in blood pressure, increase in the rate and force of heartbeat, and increased consumption of oxygen. Also included are accelerated conversion of glycogen into glucose by the liver and its rapid release into the bloodstream, and vasodilation of blood vessels in the heart and skeletal muscles, which results in an increased blood supply to those organs. All of these mechanisms serve to mobilize the bodily systems most needed to deal with a potentially dangerous situation. At the same time, other bodily processes not needed to meet the emergency (such as digestion) are inhibited. For example, peristalsis is slowed or arrested, and blood flow to the smooth muscles of the

Aldosterone

Adrenosterone

16-7
Adrenosterone and aldosterone, two steroid hormones secreted by the adrenal cortex. Despite their small structural difference, the two have very diverse functions. The former is a male sex hormone. The latter plays a role in maintaining proper ion balance in the body fluids.

intestinal tract is decreased. All of these reactions can be triggered by powerful physical exertion, fear, pain, anger, or any other cause of stress. But we have seen earlier that they can also be induced by the nervous system directly, without the mediation of the adrenal medulla. They can occur even if the medulla has been removed. The body thus possesses two overlapping systems that participate in its response to crisis.

*The cortex*   The adrenal cortex secretes a remarkable number of hormones. Over fifty have been identified so far, and more may yet be discovered. Some of these appear to be relatively inactive. But several play essential roles in regulating a wide range of body processes. An insufficiency of these cortical hormones, or **corticoids**, produces a variety of adverse effects. There may be a rise in the concentration of potassium in the blood, with a corresponding decline in the levels of sodium and chloride ions. Blood volume and blood pressure may be lowered. Carbohydrate metabolism and kidney function may also be impaired, resulting in weakness, weight loss, and an increase in toxic wastes in the blood. And there may be browning of the skin. These symptoms are typical of the corticoid deficiency called **Addison's disease**. In fact, removal of the adrenal cortex (unlike removal of the medulla) always results in death unless hormone replacement therapy is provided.

Most hormones are amino acids, short peptide chains, or proteins. But the corticoids are all steroids. (The only other steroid hormones in the human body are those secreted by the gonads.) Their chemical makeup is therefore very similar, varying only by a few atoms in their side chains. But their actions are remarkably distinct and specific. Two hormones with almost identical structures may have vastly different effects. Several classes of corticoids have been distinguished. The first comprises sex

hormones, which closely resemble the hormones secreted by the gonads in both chemical structure and function. The corticoids secreted by the adrenal cortex are for the most part **androgens**—male sex hormones such as **adrenosterone**. These tend to cause development of male secondary sexual characteristics.

A second and more important class are the **mineralocorticoids**, of which **aldosterone** is the most important in humans. These act primarily on the kidneys to regulate the balance of sodium, potassium, chloride, and water in the blood and body tissues. They are thus an important part of the body's intricate mechanism for maintaining homeostasis in the internal fluid environment. These hormones stimulate the tubules of the nephrons to reabsorb less potassium and more sodium. This also causes increased reabsorption of chloride and water. As a result the volume of blood increases.

The third class of cortical hormones is also the largest and most complex. These are the **glucocorticoids**, of which the chief representatives are **cortisone**, **hydrocortisone**, and **corticosterone**. Glucocorticoids have a variety of important effects. They regulate the metabolism of fats, proteins, and carbohydrates. And they stimulate the conversion of amino acids into carbohydrates and the formation of glycogen by the liver. These hormones also affect the smooth muscle of the blood vessels. We have seen that in times of stress both the adrenal medulla and the neurons of the sympathetic nervous system secrete adrenalins. But the vascular muscles cannot respond to these hormones unless glucocorticoids are also present. In addition, the absence of glucocorticoids causes severe degenerative changes in the capillary walls.

In large doses the glucocorticoids have two actions which are of particular interest. First, they inhibit the inflammatory response to tissue damage. For this reason athletes who sustain injuries are given injections of cortisone. This relieves the swelling and related symptoms, and enables them to participate in a game in spite of injury. Second, the glucocorticoids suppress manifestations of allergic reactions caused by the release of the hormone **histamine** from the tissues. So they are often used clinically to relieve symptoms of asthma and other allergic reactions. Unfortunately, these valuable hormones also have extremely severe side effects when used in large quantities or over a long span of time. They have been shown to cause stomach ulcers, high blood pressure, psychological changes, brittle bones, excessive hair growth, retarded healing of wounds, and decreased resistance to certain types of infection. So their medical usefulness is limited in many cases. The doctor prescribing them must always evaluate their potential for harm along with their possible benefits to the patient.

### The pituitary

The **pituitary**, or **hypophysis**, is a pea-sized gland located in the center of the head—that is, at the base of the brain just below the hypothalamus. (This is the most protected part of the body.) Like the adrenals, the pituitary is a double gland. It has a posterior lobe (the neurohypophysis) and an anterior lobe (the adenohypophysis). The two are connected by a third or median region, and the anterior lobe is partially wrapped around the posterior lobe. But the two lobes remain functionally separate. In the pituitary we can see most clearly the delicate feedback mechanisms already mentioned. And because the pituitary is controlled by the hypothalamus, it is here that neurological and chemical regulation of body processes are ultimately integrated.

*The posterior pituitary*    Like the adrenal medulla, the posterior pituitary is really a specialized part of the nervous system. It is composed mainly of axons and axon termi-nals. Their cell bodies lie in the hypothalamus, to which the posterior pituitary is joined by a stalk-like structure. The hormones of this gland are actually produced by cell bodies located in the hypothalamus. These secretions migrate down through the axons into the posterior pituitary, where they are stored at the axon terminals. Their release is triggered by nerve impulses from the hypothalamus. The posterior pituitary, therefore, is not really an endocrine gland. Rather, it is a storage area for neurosecretions from the hypothalamus.

There are two such secretions: **oxytocin** and **vasopressin**. Chemically the two are very similar. Each is a small peptide containing eight amino acids, six of which are common to both. Nevertheless, their functions are very different. Oxytocin causes smooth muscle contraction. It acts on the muscles of the uterine wall during childbirth, and for this reason is often used clinically to induce labor. This hormone may also cause uterine contractions after coitus, which help sweep the sperm up the genital tract toward the ovum. Oxytocin is also released in response to suckling. It causes certain cells of the mammary glands to contract, forcing milk through the nipple of the breast. Vasopressin raises blood pressure by stimulating constriction of the arterioles. It also acts on the tubules of the kidneys to cause reabsorption of more water.

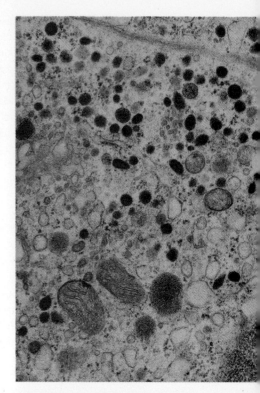

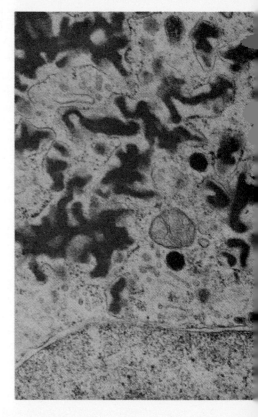

16-8
The anterior pituitary contains a number of different types of cell. Each secretes a different hormone. At least three can be seen in this survey electron micrograph of a bat pituitary: TSH cells, GH cells, and FSH cells. The smaller photos show the hormonal secretions within four types of pituitary cell: (top) TSH, which stimulates the release of thyroxin by the thyroid; (bottom) LH, which affects the ovaries; (opposite, bottom, right) GH, which regulates growth; and (opposite, bottom, left) FSH, which stimulates the development of the ovarian follicles.

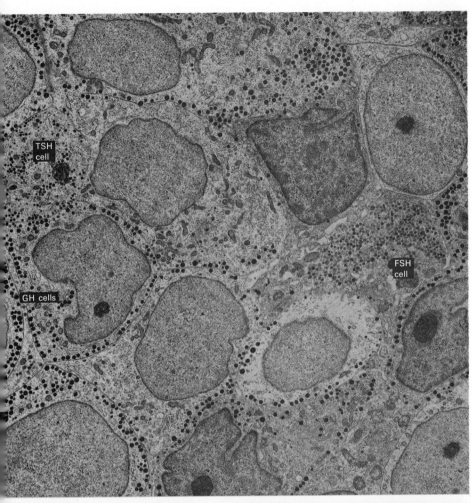

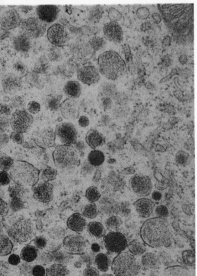

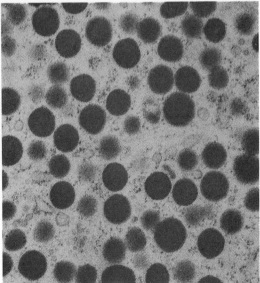

*The anterior pituitary* The anterior pituitary develops from embryonic tissue that forms the roof of the mouth. It is composed of several different types of cell. Each type is thought to be responsible for secretion of one of the major hormones produced by the anterior lobe. These fall into two major categories:

1. the **nontropic hormones,** which act directly upon certain tissues of the body, and
2. the **tropic hormones,** which have little or no direct physiological effect, but instead regulate the activity of other endocrine glands. (The neurosecretion released during molting is a tropic hormone.)

The principal nontropic hormone is **growth hormone** (GH, also known as somatotropic hormone, STH). As its name implies, growth hormone regulates the growth of the long bones in the body. Overproduction of this hormone results in giantism, whereas undersecretion will produce a midget. Growth hormone also has certain metabolic functions. The second nontropic hormone, **prolactin,** plays a major role in the initiation and maintenance of milk secretion from the mammary glands. A third nontropic hormone, **melanocyte-stimulating** hormone (MSH), causes darkening of the skin in some animals. This provides them with protective adaptation to a dark background (the chameleon is a familiar example). But since this mechanism does not function in mammals, the role of MSH in these creatures is not clear.

There are four known tropic hormones. **Thyrotropic hormone** (also called thyroid-stimulating hormone, TSH), causes the thyroid gland to release thyroxin. **Adrenocorticotropic hormone** (ACTH) activates the adrenal cortex. Two **gonadotropic hormones,** follicle-stimulating hormone (FSH) and luteinizing hormone (LH), affect the gonads.

The anterior pituitary controls these glands but its activity is in turn directed by the hypothalamus. The hypothalamus does not innervate the anterior pituitary, but there is an intimate connection between them by the way of the hypothalamic–hypophysial portal system. Capillaries in the hypothalamus empty into veins which run into the anterior lobe of the pituitary. There they divide once more into a second bed of capillaries, forming a system similar to the hepatic portal system. Neurons in the hypothalamus produce a number of neurosecretions, called **releasing factors**. These secretions reach the anterior pituitary by way of the portal system. There appears to be a different releasing factor for each hormone synthesized by the anterior pituitary, which stimulates the pituitary to secrete that particular hormone into the bloodstream.

We see that the hypothalamus can secrete releasing factors upon neural stimulation. Therefore a major feature of this system is that it creates a direct connection between the endocrine and nervous systems. For instance, a stress signal from the external environment—such as extreme cold—is transmitted to the brain by the sensory organs. The hypothalamus responds to the signal by secreting the releasing factors that stimulate the pituitary to produce ACTH and TSH. Circulating in the bloodstream, ACTH provokes the adrenal glands to secrete cortical hormones which prepare the organism to respond to the

stress situation. At the same time, TSH causes the thyroid gland to secrete more thyroxin. This raises the body's rate of metabolism, which generates additional warmth, adapting the organism for survival in a cold environment.

In addition to direction by the hypothalamus, the pituitary is also highly sensitive to negative feedback from the glands that it regulates. For example, thyroxin is synthesized and secreted by the thyroid gland upon stimulation by TSH from the anterior pituitary. The elevated level of thyroxin in the blood inhibits both the anterior pituitary and the hypothalamus which controls it. This results in a decreased output of TSH. Less TSH in the blood causes a decline in the secretion of thyroxin. When the level of thyroxin in the bloodstream falls, the pituitary and hypothalamus are no longer inhibited. TSH is released again, and the cycle is repeated. Under normal conditions, this feedback system sustains an optimal level of thyroxin at all times. The same sort of delicate balance is maintained in this way between the pituitary and other endocrine glands under its control.

## The thymus

The thymus is located in the upper part of the chest. We have already mentioned it as part of the lymphatic system. But recent discoveries show that the thymus also func-

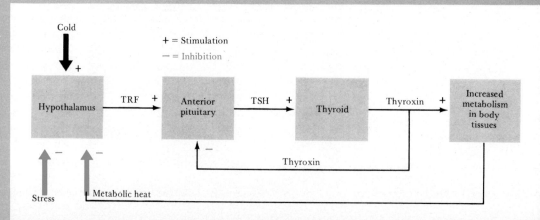

16-9
The regulation of the production of thyroxin is a typical example of feedback control, a common mechanism in the body's endocrine system. TSH secreted by the anterior pituitary stimulates the production of thyroxin. A high level of thyroxin in the blood inhibits the secretion of TSH. (See The anterior pituitary)

tions as an endocrine gland. It releases a hormone called **thymosin** which is vital to the development of the body's immune system. The lymphocytes, which play a key role in cell-mediated immune responses, cannot mature without thymosin.

## The pineal gland

The pineal gland is located in the rear portion of the forebrain. It has recently been found to secrete a hormone called **melatonin.** In lower vertebrates, this hormone is released in response to light, and causes adaptive color changes. In birds it may play a role in photoperiodic behavior. But in mammals the pineal is apparently not photosensitive. Since mammals do not have the specialized cells that produce color changes in creatures such as frogs and amphibians, its role in mammals is a mystery.

## Other hormones

Some hormones and hormone-like substances are secreted by tissues other than those of the principal endocrine glands. These include the various digestive hormones, hypertensin, and histamine.

*Digestive hormones* In addition to secretin, mentioned earlier, there are several other digestive hormones. Early in this century, Ivan Pavlov discovered that secretion of digestive juices was only partially controlled by nervous stimulation of the digestive system. He postulated that partially digested foods—meat, in his experiments—released substances that somehow triggered further gastric secretion. It was later found that compounds in the digested meat do indeed stimulate the pyloric mucosa to secrete a hormone called **gastrin.** Gastrin, in turn, induces the secretion of gastric juice. A later discovery showed that fats stimulate the duodenal mucosa to secrete the hormone **enterogastrone.** Enterogastrone inhibits the secretion of gastric juice, and is thus an antagonist to gastrin. The secretion of bile from the gall bladder

is stimulated by still another hormone, **cholecystokinin,** released in the small intestine.

*Hypertensin* The kidney has the ability to regulate its own blood supply. It does this by means of a hormonal homeostatic mechanism. When blood flow to the kidneys is restricted for any reason, a rise in blood pressure soon occurs. The kidney cortex responds by releasing a protein called renin. Renin combines with a blood protein to form **hypertensin.** In turn, hypertensin stimulates constriction of the smooth muscles of the small blood vessels. This leads to a rise in blood pressure. More blood is forced through the renal arteries, thus compensating for the original constriction.

*Histamine* Unlike many other hormones, histamine is secreted locally, and exerts its effects locally. Histamine is secreted by the cells of damaged or traumatized tissues. It causes the muscles in the walls of the blood vessels to relax. Thus the permeability of the vessels is increased. This promotes the flow of white cells into the damaged area. It also promotes the increased flow of fluids which cause the congestion associated with colds and allergies such as hay fever. Histamine also causes constriction of the bronchioles, a factor in asthma attacks.

## Hormonal control of reproduction

Fertilization in vertebrates, whether external or internal, generally involves complex activity and intricate cooperation by the parent organisms. This is needed to ensure successful joining of the gametes. To a large degree, this synchronization is achieved by endocrine control. Only in human beings has voluntary control to some extent superseded hormonally dictated patterns of behavior.

*The gonads* The male gonads are the testes. Gonadotropic hormones released by the anterior pituitary at puberty stimulate their development. FSH promotes the maturation of the spermatogonia in the testes, which then produce sperm. LH promotes maturation of the interstitial cells, which then secrete the male sex hormone **testosterone**. Testosterone brings on the secondary sex changes of puberty. These include growth of beard and pubic hair, muscular development, maturation of the seminal vesicles and prostate, and deepening of the voice. Castration before puberty will prevent these characteristics from appearing. However, castration after puberty will only cause them to diminish slightly. Castration may also cause the sexual urge to disappear entirely in most animals. But the sex urge in man is affected by many psychological factors, and thus it does not diminish.

Releasing factors from the hypothalamus stimulate the pituitary to secrete the gonadotropic hormones. The onset of puberty in the female follows the same pattern. FSH and LH cause the ovaries to mature. The ovaries then secrete **estrogen** and **progesterone**, the female sex hormones. Estrogen promotes development of the female secondary sexual characteristics. These include pubic hair, breast development, enlargement of the uterus and vagina, and the beginning of the menstrual cycle.

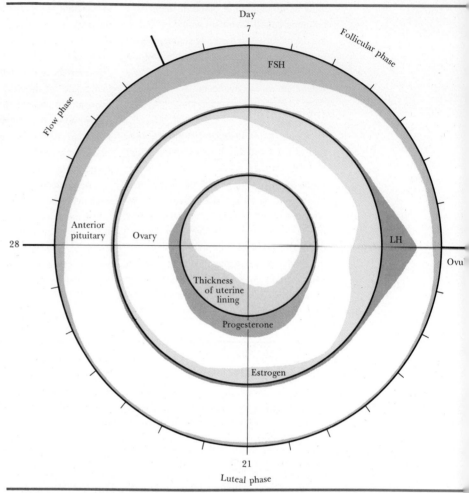

*The estrous cycle* The secretion of the two gonadotropic hormones by the pituitary is not constant. It varies in a regular pattern, producing cyclic changes in the condition of the reproductive tract and in the female's sexual responsiveness. This is known as the **estrous cycle**. Most female animals are sexually receptive to the male only during that part of the cycle when ovulation—the release of the egg cell—occurs. This period is called **estrus**, or heat. The length of the estrous cycle varies in different species. Some animals have only a few periods of estrus each year. Others experience them as frequently as every few days.

The cycle begins when FSH is secreted by the anterior pituitary. In response, many ovarian follicles begin to grow. These are

the structures that contain the egg cells. In humans, one follicle develops at a faster rate than all the others. That one continues to mature, while all the others soon cease their growth. This part of the cycle is called the **follicular phase**. It lasts about 10 days. During this time a small amount of LH is present in the system. The LH stimulates the follicle to produce estrogen, which causes thickening of the lining of the uterus. The increase in estrogen level also initiates a complex feedback mechanism. Estrogen slows the production of FSH by inhibiting the secretion of FSH-releasing factor by the hypothalamus (negative feedback). At the same time, it promotes LH production by stimulating the secretion of more LH-releasing factor by the hypothalamus (posi-

tive feedback). With the resulting increase in LH, the cycle enters the **luteal phase** around the thirteenth day.

When the concentration of LH reaches a certain level, the developing follicle **ovulates**. That is, it ruptures and releases the egg. After ovulation, LH causes a change in the ruptured follicle. The follicle is converted into a yellowish body called the **corpus luteum**. The corpus luteum continues to secrete estrogen, though in smaller amounts than before. But its main function is to secrete the luteal hormone, progesterone. Progesterone prepares the uterus to receive the embryo. It causes maturation of the glands already in the thickened uterine lining. A fertilized ovum cannot implant in a uterus that has not been altered by the se-

16-10
The estrous cycle is regulated by a complex feedback system, involving the hypothalamus, the anterior pituitary, and endocrine secretions of the reproductive organs themselves. During the flow and follicular phases, the hypothalamus secretes a releasing factor that causes the pituitary to produce FSH. This stimulates the growth of a follicle in the ovary. The follicle in turn produces estrogen. This causes thickening of the uterine lining. It also slows secretion of LH releasing factor. The pituitary then produces LH. The result is ovulation—the follicle ruptures, and develops into the corpus luteum, which produces progesterone. This hormone inhibits the secretion of both FSH and LH releasing factors. As the level of LH declines, the corpus luteum atrophies, progesterone production stops, and the uterine lining is sloughed off in the flow phase.

cretion of progesterone. The presence of progesterone in the blood also inhibits the secretion of FSH, which would trigger new follicle growth and a new cycle.

If no fertilized ovum implants, another negative feedback mechanism now occurs. The high progesterone level inhibits the secretion of LH. The consequent reduction in LH level leads to atrophy of the corpus luteum. Progesterone production is thereby halted. The uterine lining can then no longer be maintained. In many animals it is reabsorbed. But in the human female it is sloughed off during the **flow phase**, or menstrual period. With progesterone now absent, FSH secretion begins again and with it a new cycle.

During the flow phase there is a brief but total absence of sex hormones. This situation sometimes causes physiological and psychological disturbances during the menstrual period—nausea, cramps, irritability, and depression. The entire menstrual cycle averages about 28 days in length. But this figure varies from individual to individual, and even from cycle to cycle in the same individual. Within the cycle, the luteal phase appears to be relatively constant in duration—about 14 or 15 days. The follicular phase, however, may vary in length by a week or more.

*Pregnancy* If an ovum is fertilized, it becomes implanted in the lining of the uterus. But ordinarily, high progesterone levels lead to the onset of menstruation, as we have seen. How, then, is pregnancy maintained? The answer is that if a fertilized ovum implants in the uterine lining, the corpus luteum does not atrophy. It is maintained by the secretion of a gonadotropic hormone, similar to LH, from the placenta. The negative feedback mechanism is thus circumvented. Progesterone production continues, and menstruation is prevented. The quantity of this chorionic gonadotropin is so great that it shows up in the urine and forms the basis for pregnancy test. In humans, both estrogen and progesterone are also secreted by the placenta. This provides a backup system to the secretions from the corpus luteum.

*Childbirth* Progesterone apparently inhibits contractions of the smooth muscles in the uterus during pregnancy. Estrogen, on the other hand, stimulates contractions. Just before birth the placenta increases its estrogen production. This brings the onset of uterine contractions. The posterior pituitary aids this process by secreting oxytocin. The placenta and ovaries secrete a hormone called **relaxin**. This hormone also helps to facilitate birth by expanding the mouth of the uterus and loosening the bones of the pelvic girdle.

*Lactation* The growth of the mammary glands appears to be affected by a complex combination of hormones. These include the sex hormones, growth hormone, insulin, prolactin, and certain adrenal hormones. Several of these same hormones control the initiation and maintenance of lactation. They are aided by the disappearance just before birth of the sex hormones, which ordinarily inhibit lactation. The release of milk is stimulated by both neural and hormonal action. Sucking by the infant produces neural stimulation of the hypothalamus. This, in turn, stimulates the secretion of oxytocin from the posterior pituitary. As we have seen, oxytocin causes contraction of the alveoli in the breast, forcing milk to the nipple.

## Hormone mechanisms

Hormones appear to act in several ways to provide chemical regulation of body processes. One such mechanism is the stimulation of enzymes that increase the rate of certain chemical reactions. For example, adrenalin facilitates the action of an enzyme that converts glycogen to glucose. This increases the energy supply available to the organism. Hormones can also affect the rate at which certain protein compounds are synthesized. It is believed that insulin assists in the formation of molecules needed for active transport of glucose across the cell membrane. It seems likely that hormones can operate directly upon the genes to influence the synthesis of protein molecules. For example, we know that RNA synthesis can be accelerated by thyroid and sex hormones. Further evidence for this is provided by the discovery that some hormones can elicit the activity of genes that are ordinarily repressed by other, more dominant genes.

Most vertebrate hormones can also increase membrane permeability. Specifically, they increase the rate at which water and certain solutes are transported across cell membranes. For example, the antidiuretic hormone vasopressin increases the permeability of kidney tubule membranes to water and a wide variety of inorganic solutes, sugar, and amino acids. Recently a very interesting class of compounds called **prostaglandins** has been discovered. It is suspected that these compounds may be synthesized at cell membranes by the operation of hormones. The cell membrane is composed largely of phospholipids, which are chemically related to prostaglandins. The latter, in turn, may alter the structure of the cell membrane, changing its permeability characteristics.

Research on the prostaglandins has attracted great interest, for these substances have many remarkable properties. Chemically they are fatty acids—compounds not previously known to play any part in metabolic regulation. Prostaglandins seem to function in many of the same roles as do hormones. But unlike hormones, they can be synthesized by many different kinds of tissue. They are effective in very minute quantities. However, they are broken down rapidly by enzymes, and thus have very short lifespans within the organism. This has made their study quite difficult for biochemists. The known physiological effects of different prostaglandins are remarkably varied. They include increased excretion of sodium by the kidneys, with a consequent drop in blood pressure, relaxation of the smooth muscle of the gastrointestinal tract and respiratory passages, and constriction of blood vessels. Prostaglandins also seem to act as antagonists to certain metabolic hormones, and inhibit nervous transmission within the sympathetic nervous system. Moreover, they appear to influence the reproductive system in a number of ways. They can induce labor, cure certain kinds of sterility, or prevent conception. This last property has raised hopes that prostaglandins may eventually become the basis of a truly safe, reliable method of birth control. These and many other medical uses for prostaglandins are now under intensive investigation.

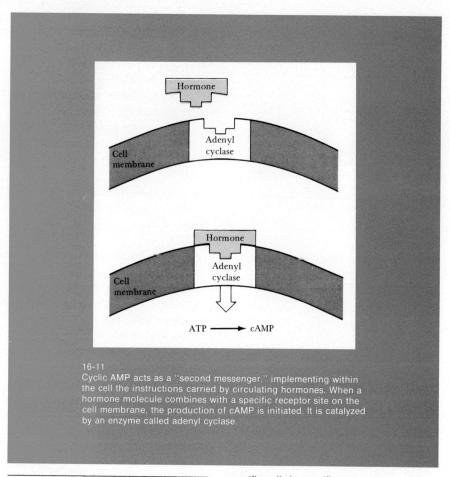

16-11
Cyclic AMP acts as a "second messenger," implementing within the cell the instructions carried by circulating hormones. When a hormone molecule combines with a specific receptor site on the cell membrane, the production of cAMP is initiated. It is catalyzed by an enzyme called adenyl cyclase.

## Cyclic AMP

During experiments concerned with the hormonal control of blood sugar in rats, Earl Sutherland discovered that adrenalin increases the concentration of cyclic adenosine monophosphate (cAMP) within liver cells. This higher level of cAMP activates an enzyme which converts glycogen into glucose. It has since been found that a very large number of hormones stimulate the production of cAMP by their target cells. If we think of the hormone as a chemical messenger, we can regard cAMP as a "second messenger" which acts directly upon the enzymes within the cell to help bring about particular reactions. In other words, the hormone carries the directions, and cyclic AMP causes them to be executed.

The ability of hormones to affect only specific cells in specific ways is apparently a property of the target cell rather than the hormone itself. The cell membrane of each target cell is thought to possess receptor sites which are hormone-specific. That is, they will accept only hormone molecules of one particular type and no other. When the appropriate hormone molecule combines with the receptor site, an enzyme in the cell membrane (adenyl cyclase) catalyzes the synthesis of cAMP within the cell. The cAMP then stimulates the response for which that cell is peculiarly adapted. For example, a thyroid cell which is chemically equipped to produce thyroxin will be activated to do just that by the presence of cAMP. Thus cAMP can evoke a variety of different activities within different cells. This makes it a kind of universal mediator of hormonal function.

summary

Hormones are regulatory chemicals produced by endocrine or ductless glands. They are secreted directly into the circulatory system, affecting cells in distant parts of the organism.

The endocrine system shares its responsibility for control of the organism with the nervous system, although they differ in their action. The nervous system acts over well-defined pathways. Action is of short duration and usually affects very localized areas. Hormones travel through the transport system. They act much more slowly and usually for longer periods of time, often stimulating larger areas of the organism.

Hormonal activity among invertebrates has been determined most accurately for the insects. Among the hormones isolated is the molting hormone ecdysone. This hormone is secreted by glands in the prothorax upon stimulation by a neurosecretion from the brain. The latter is a tropic hormone. That is, it exerts no direct physiological effect, but stimulates the activity of specific endocrine glands. Tropic hormones are also found in vertebrates. Juvenile hormone is another important invertebrate hormone. When present in large quantities, it produces immature nymphal stages. In small amounts it induces a final larval state, the pupa. When juvenile hormone is completely absent, the pupa molts into an adult.

In vertebrates the nervous and endocrine systems are closely interconnected. The anterior pituitary is itself under direct control of the hypothalamus. Thus, those glands that are influenced by the pituitary are indirectly controlled by the hypothalamus. There are about a dozen major endocrine glands situated in various places in the body. Usually there is no functional relation between the gland and the structure to which it is attached.

The pancreas contains clusters of cells called islets of Langerhans. These cells produce the hormone insulin. Insulin lowers blood sugar by inhibiting glucose production in the liver. This stimulates rapid conversion of glucose to glycogen in the liver and muscles, and more rapid oxidation of glucose in cells by increasing membrane permeability to glucose. A lack of insulin causes the disease diabetes. Overproduction of insulin may cause hypoglycemia, or, in larger amounts, insulin shock.

The thyroid, located in the neck, produces thyroxin. This hormone controls metabolism. A lack of it—hypothyroidism—causes lethargy, obesity, slowed heartbeat, and mental dullness. An excess of thyroxin—hyperthyroidism—leads to unusually high metabolism. The parathyroids are functionally independent of the thyroid. They control the calcium—phosphate balance in the body fluids by secreting parathormone.

The adrenals, located above the kidneys, consist of two independent glands: the outer cortex and the inner medulla. The medulla produces noradrenalin and adrenalin. Adrenalin is responsible for the "fight-or-flight" reactions of the organism. The cortex secretes a large number of hormones. Among the most significant of these steroid cortical hormones are the androgens, or male sex hormones. The cortex also produces the mineralocorticoids, which maintain homeostasis of the body fluids, and the glucocorticoids, which regulate metabolism of fats, proteins, and carbohydrates, and stimulate the conversion of amino acids into carbohydrates.

The pituitary is located at the base of the brain under the hypothalamus. The posterior pituitary is a specialized part of the nervous system. It stores neurosecretions from the hypothalamus: oxytocin, which stimulates contractions of the smooth muscles of the uterus, and vasopressin, the antidiuretic hormone.

The anterior pituitary secretes many hormones. Some are nontropic hormones such as the growth hormone and prolactin. The tropic hormones include thyrotropic hormone (TSH), adrenocorticotropic hormone (ACTH), follicle-stimulating hormone (FSH), and luteinizing hormone (LH). Anterior pituitary hormones are produced under the stimulation of releasing factors secreted by the hypothalamus. This process permits the organism to respond hormonally to external stimuli.

All of the glands affected by tropic hormones exert a direct influence on the pituitary by negative feedback mechanisms. The reproductive cycle operates under a complex arrangement of positive and negative feedback between the reproductive organs and the pituitary. This interaction produces the estrous cycle, composed of the follicular and luteal phases.

Hormonal action appears to occur by affecting protein synthesis, by operating directly on the genes, and by increasing membrane permeability to certain solutes. A secondary messenger—cAMP—may actually stimulate the desired response within the target cell. It thus acts as a universal mediator of hormonal function.

17 plant development

**t**he development of an organism involves all the changes it undergoes from its beginnings until its death. The development of the form and structure of an organism is called **morphogenesis**. It requires carefully orchestrated interaction by a large number of processes and influences.

In plants, unlike in many animals, growth continues throughout the life cycle. **Cell division** provides the potential for growth but is not growth itself, since the two new cells it produces occupy the same volume as the original parent. Division is followed by **cell expansion**, as the newly formed cells take up water and increase in size. Finally comes **cell differentiation**—changes in the cell structures to fit them for various specialized tasks. Why cells differentiate as they do is still one of the unanswered questions in biology. But some of the signals are known, and we shall examine several of the principal ones. The reason a cell becomes what it does must lie in the way its genetic programming interacts with its physical and chemical environment. For example, a cell on the surface of a leaf becomes an epidermal, not a xylem cell. And this is at least partly because of its exposure to the environment. Similarly, the reproductive organs develop later, responding to a signal from the rest of the plant. As we shall see, the signal itself results from an interaction of various internal and external factors.

The phenomenon of **cell totipotency** is an intriguing and important feature of plant development. Even though a cell has matured and is no longer naturally dividing, it still has the potential not only for cell division but for giving rise to any other type of specialized cell. This shows that each cell contains all the genetic information common to all cells. None of this information has been lost during development and specialization.

The first part of this chapter is a survey of the stages in the plant life cycle. It is followed by a discussion of the influences which control the life cycle. These include environmental stimuli and the mechanisms by which a plant responds to these stimuli.

# Life cycle of the plant

Just as an animal begins life with the fusion of two sex cells, so does a plant. We have already seen how this occurs at all levels in the plant kingdom. In this chapter, we shall deal exclusively with the angiosperms. In these plants the zygote develops into an embryo which is protected and endowed with a food source, forming a seed. By the time the seed is mature, we can distinguish an embryo shoot or **plumule**, an embryo root or **radicle**, and seed leaves or **cotyledons** (one in monocotyledons, two in dicotyledons). The rudiments of the next few leaves may be present as part of the shoot, but this is a far cry from the completeness of a mammalian embryo. Most of the plant is not present in the tips of the root and shoot, the **root apex** and **shoot apex**.

In animal embryos, part of the tissue has already become delineated as the sexual reproductive cells, or the **germ cells**. But no role of this kind can be ascribed to any cells in a plant embryo. Reproductive organs are formed only after the plant is mature.

## Germination and early growth

Certain conditions, both external and internal, must exist for a dormant seed to "waken" and begin growing. We shall discuss the internal ones a little later. The external requirements for growth are sufficient water and oxygen, and a favorable temperature (10–30° C). Under such conditions the seed starts to take up water, and swells greatly. Soon the embryo plant starts to grow.

The germinating embryo is very active metabolically. Cellular respiration occurs in dormant seeds, but at a very low rate. As the seed takes up water, respiration increases, to provide the energy needed for growth.

*The stem apex*    The earliest growth in the

young plant takes place by cell division and elongation. Cell division initially occurs at only the root and shoot (or stem) apex. These apices are composed of **meristematic** tissue—immature, undifferentiated cells. The stem apex, or tip, is basically a dome. Its shape and size vary according to the species. On the edges of the dome, just below the peak, are small bulges called the **leaf primordia**. They mark the beginning of differentiation in the plant structures. The base of the leaf primordia remains fixed, but their cells divide faster than those on the dome. As a result they grow up and over the dome, forming the **apical bud**. Meanwhile, the cells in the apical dome divide continually and expand, increasing the surface area and the bulk of the apex. These dividing cells are known collectively as the **apical meristem**. They are very active in DNA synthesis, and do not have the vacuoles typical of older plant cells.

At the base of the stem apex the cells start to differentiate. Long **procambial strands** of cells can be seen just below each leaf primordium. They occupy regions where the vascular tissue will develop. These cells differentiate further as the apex grows farther away from them. Eventually they mature into primary xylem and phloem, and then into the vascular bundles of the mature stem.

The cells continue to grow in length in the region immediately behind the apical bud. But a few centimeters back from the apex, this elongation ceases. Each cell wall has only a limited capacity for growth, and thickening also makes the wall more rigid. This is particularly true of the xylem elements.

*The root apex*    The structure and function of the root give it a somewhat different apical structure. There is still a dome, but it is much more pointed than that in the stem, since it must be able to push through the soil. To protect the growing tip, the apex is covered with a **root cap**. Cells in the outer-

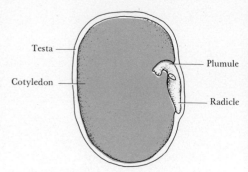

**17-1**
The pea is a fairly typical dicotyledon seed. The cotyledons occupy most of the space. Eventually they supply nutrients for the growing embryo. The point of attachment of the second cotyledon (here removed to show the embryo) is marked by the small oval between plumule and radicle. (See Life cycle of the plant)

*Labels: Testa, Cotyledon, Plumule, Radicle*

**17-2**
Stages of germination in the bush bean *(Phaseolus)*. Here the cotyledons come above ground and are able to photosynthesize. In some other species, the cotyledons remain below ground.

most layer divide vigorously. They produce cells which are pushed to the outer side of the apex. These cells enlarge and then are worn away at the outer edge of the cap, as newer cells expand and push outward to replace them. In the apical meristem, cells divide and add to the bulk of the root. They develop into the different layers of the root, with the vascular tissue in the center. Root hairs form as outgrowths of epidermal cells in the region just behind the most rapidly elongating area of the root.

## Formation of vegetative organs

The length and bulk of the plant are increased by growth at the root and shoot apices. Further growth and development lead to the formation of the vegetative organs—leaves, stem branches, and root branches. These will carry on the various physiological functions which are needed for the plant to survive.

*Leaves*    The leaf primordia do not form at random, but in an ordered pattern. Such patterns are governed by the genetic programming of the plant, and are known as **phyllotaxy**. The new leaves may occur singly at each node (the point where the leaf and stem join), in pairs, or in whorls of three or more.

As the new leaves begin to enlarge and flatten into the shape typical of the species, procambial strands develop. Eventually these strands mature into the veins of the fully formed leaves. In many plants a petiole, or leaf stalk, joins the leaf to the stem of the plant.

*Stem branches*    Branches in the stem develop from axillary or lateral buds. These are small meristematic areas, left in the axil (the angle between the upper side of the petiole and the stem from which it arises) of each leaf as the apex grows away from the formed leaves. This meristematic area itself becomes organized into an apex with leaf primordia. The primordia may remain dormant or grow out as a stem, lateral to the

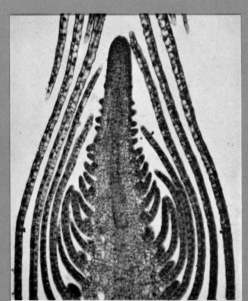

17-3
Longitudinal sections of two stem apices. Shown is the overlapping arrangement of leaf primordia and young leaves (bottom) and the procambial strands of the primordia (left). (See Germination and early growth)

original stem. The phenomenon known as **apical dominance** limits the growth of stem branches to a greater or lesser degree, according to how close they are to the shoot apex. Within a certain distance from the apex, lateral stem branches usually cannot grow at all.

*Root branches*  Branch, or secondary, roots do not develop near the tip of the root but grow from inside the primary root. The outermost tissues in the central vascular cylinder undergo cell division and bulge

17-4
Beginnings of a new root branch. (See Formation of vegetative organs)

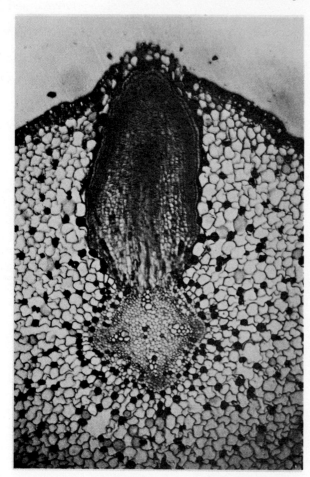

out laterally. They then break through the cortical tissues of the root, forming a new branch. This branch possesses its own apical meristem, which forms all the tissues of the branch.

## Reproductive growth

We mentioned earlier the complete absence of reproductive tissue in the embryo and the young plant. Cells only start development into germ cells and the related reproductive organs upon the induction of a reproductive stage. The onset of this stage is controlled by either the age of the plant or the environmental conditions, or both. The point at which the reproductive stage begins depends on the species. Some species—mustard, for example—will flower as soon as they come above ground if the day length is right. Others must reach a certain stage of development before they can flower after producing a certain number of leaves, regardless of day length. Still others, including many trees, go through a juvenile phase, and will not flower until they are several years old.

When the plant changes from vegetative to reproductive development, it stops producing vegetative leaf primordia. Cell division in the stem apex changes so that the apex broadens. Instead of leaves, the primordia form the floral organs—sepals, petals, stamens, and ovaries. (Details of flower structure and pollination were discussed in chapter 8.)

*Fruit growth and ripening*  After flowering occurs, the fruit and seeds develop from the ovary and ovules of the flower. Both pollination and fertilization cause the ovary wall, or the receptacle in "false" fruits such as the strawberry, to grow, creating the tissues of the fruit. The fruits grow initially by cell division, later by cell expansion. After the fruit has reached its full size, biochemical changes occur which we term **ripening**.

Ripening is closely connected with respiration of the fruit. When the carbon dioxide output from a ripening fruit is measured at intervals, it will often rise sharply for a short period and then sharply decline. The period of increased carbon dioxide output is called the **climacteric**. It derives from increased cellular respiration. Once the

**17-5**
Dormant twig of horse-chestnut tree *(Aesculus hippocastanum)* and bud split to show the protective cottony insulation (See Dormancy)

climacteric begins, the fruit rapidly goes through the changes that transform it from a fully grown unripe fruit to a ripe fruit ready to be eaten. The climacteric was once thought to be a degenerative process. However, it is now seen as a positive change which requires the expenditure of energy. It can be prevented by respiration inhibitors, by high carbon dioxide or nitrogen concentrations, or by the low temperatures used in fruit storage. By contrast, application of the gas ethylene promotes both the climacteric rise and ripening in mature fruit. This method can be used to ripen fruits that are shipped before they are fully ripe.

## Dormancy

To survive in a world of changing environment and constant challenge, the plant must be able to stop as well as to start its various physiological processes. Not only must buds be able to grow when the favorable weather of spring arrives, they must also be able to cease activity and prepare for such unfavorable conditions as a freezing winter or a long dry spell. Preparation for these unfavorable periods must be made well in advance of their arrival if the plant is to survive. This is because some of the adaptations involve the formation of new substances, tissues, or organs.

An examination of a dormant winter twig reveals the extent of these preparations. The tender terminal growing point is protected from the outside world in several ways. It is usually surrounded by a tuft of cottony insulating material, modified from leaf primordia in the bud. Instead of leaves, there are small, thickened **bud scales.** These overlap in shingle fashion and are closely pressed together, to form a tightly fitting protective cap over the insulated growing point. The scales are also covered by a protective varnish-like material that effectively waterproofs the bud. Below the terminal bud, all the leaves have neatly fallen off. A leaf scar is left where they were attached to the stem. But it is well protected by a corky layer that seals the broken vas-

cular bundles and the cells around them. Finally, deep within the trunk, the cambium has become dormant. The parenchyma cells of the xylem and phloem have undergone chemical changes that make it possible for them to withstand freezing without injury—a sort of built-in antifreeze system.

The **abscission,** or shedding, of leaves also helps the plant, by getting rid of these delicate organs, to survive a period of cold or drought. Leaves which are unproductive due to age or excessive shading are shed even at other times of year, as they may be a drain on the plant's resources. Waste products are also discarded in the shed leaves.

Seed dormancy, like the winter dormancy of buds of deciduous trees (trees which shed their leaves at the end of a growing season), has great survival value for the plant. Obviously, if the seed were to germinate as soon as it matured in the autumn, it would almost certainly be killed by the first frost. Lack of activity during the winter, or during dry periods, can be guaranteed by incorporation into the seed of a critical quantity of **abscisic acid,** a growth inhibitor. Many seeds are known in which germination is prevented by such inhibitors. Other seeds may have impermeable seed coats, which prevent entry of water and oxygen until after a period of microbial breakdown. Only then can the seed germinate.

Seed dormancy is uncommon in cultivated plants. It has been eliminated during the selection of species and varieties for man's use. Also dormancy is probably not common in areas of continually favorable climate, such as the tropical rain forest. Germination sometimes can be induced in seeds showing dormancy. This is done by washing the seeds in large amounts of water in order to wash out the inhibitor. Such a "triggering" mechanism is important in desert plants, whose seeds must germinate quickly after rainfall.

Provided that a viable seed is ready to germinate, and any inhibitor has been broken down or counteracted, the seed will germinate when warm conditions return in

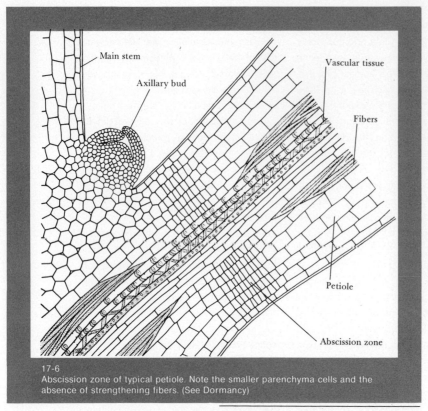

17-6
Abscission zone of typical petiole. Note the smaller parenchyma cells and the absence of strengthening fibers. (See Dormancy)

Plant growth is also influenced by light. We have all seen plants in a window bending toward the light. This bending is actually an asymmetrical growth of the stem. Greater growth occurs on the dark side, so that the stem curves toward the light. Such a growth response to a unidirectional stimulus is called a **tropism**. The response to light is called **phototropism** and the response to gravity is known as **geotropism**. If the growth is toward the stimulus, it is termed positive; if away from the stimulus, it is negative. Thus stems are positively phototropic and negatively geotropic. Roots, on the other hand, are the exact opposite. Leaves tend to orient themselves at right angles to both light and gravity.

## Photoperiodism

A green plant growing in the changing seasons of a temperate zone must synchronize its activities to suit the changing weather. It is particularly important that the plant develop to a reasonable size before it invests a large part of its photosynthetic product in the formation of fruits and seeds. Obviously, a large plant can produce more seed, and thus improve the distribution and the chances for survival of the species. At the same time, it must allow enough time after flowering for adequate fruit and seed ripening before the start of winter.

It has long been known that most plants, when grown at a particular latitude, flower at roughly the same date each year. Thus we have come to expect violets in the springtime, roses in the summer, and chrysanthemums in the fall. Why? Is there an irreducible and unalterable number of days that must elapse before the vegetative plant initiates floral primordia? Or is there some environmental "signal" for flowering? That is, is there some environmental variable that has a given value at a given date?

A simple experiment answered this question. Soybeans of a single variety were planted at different dates. Surprisingly, all the plantings came into flower at the same time. It is clear, then, that the flowering be-

the spring. Water is taken up, metabolic processes are activated, food reserves are mobilized, and the embryo begins to grow.

# Responses to stimuli

The more we consider all the stages of plant development, with their carefully timed interaction of many different cellular events, the more we may be led to wonder how it all comes about. What controls when or how much a plant grows, or the nature of this growth? The age of the plant dictates some of its characteristics. For example, the plant may be a juvenile, or an adult capable of reproduction, or it may be dying.

Internal secretions, or **hormones**, within the plant are one part of the system of growth controls. **Environmental stimuli**, such as light and gravity, make up a second important part. These stimuli may operate by changing the internal level of the hormones.

## Tropisms

Place a plant on its side, and its growth pattern is soon altered. The roots curve down, pointing toward the center of the earth. The stem curves upward, pointing away from the center of the earth. The petioles of the leaves readjust their positions, orienting the blades parallel to the surface of the earth. Each of these changes in response to gravity has a built-in survival advantage for the plant. The roots, which anchor and support the plant and absorb water and nutrients from the soil, obviously function best by growing downward. The stem, supporting the leafy photosynthetic organs, serves the plant best by elevating the leaves above the surface. There they are less likely to be shaded from the light. The leaves themselves, which are light receptors for photosynthesis, obviously function most efficiently in light absorption if their broad surfaces are oriented perpendicular to the sun's rays.

17-7
Lay a coleus plant on its side in normal light, and in 18 hours the stem has bent upward at right angles. (See Tropisms)

havior of this plant is not regulated solely by internal events. There must be an external trigger—but what is it? Experiments were then performed with a tobacco mutant known as Maryland Mammoth. It was demonstrated that flowering in this plant is controlled by the day length. If Maryland Mammoth plants are grown in long days with more than 14 hours of daylight, they do not flower. If grown in short days, with fewer than 14 hours of daylight, they flower. They were therefore referred to as **short-day plants**. The length of the day that was barely short enough to cause them to form floral primordia was called the **critical photoperiod**.

Later it was discovered that there are also **long-day plants**, which will not flower in short days but will flower in long days. Examples of this type are spinach and many cereals. There are also **day-neutral plants**, such as the tomato. In these, flowering is relatively unaffected by the length of day, but depends instead on internal or structural features. Actually, it is the length of darkness, not of light, that matters. A short-day plant is really a long-night plant. It requires a certain minimum length of uninterrupted darkness for flowering to occur.

Day length affects not only flowering behavior but also many aspects of vegeta-

tive development. In addition, leaf fall and dormancy, at least in deciduous trees, are usually triggered by decreasing day length (or, more accurately, increasing night length). These general responses of plants to the relative length of day and night are referred to collectively as **photoperiodism**.

## Circadian rhythms

Certain internal rhythmic changes in a plant indicate its capacity not only to perceive light but to measure time. In the day-length experiment already mentioned, it was found that even a brief flash of light in the dark period prevented flowering in a short-day plant if it occurred during the normal night length. But if, after a light period, the plant was kept in continuous darkness, a flash during what would normally be the next day permitted flowering. Even later, in a period

17-8
Photoperiodic behavior of short- and long-day plants under various lighting conditions. The dashed line marks the critical photoperiod This may, of course, be of different length for different plants. (See Photoperiodism)

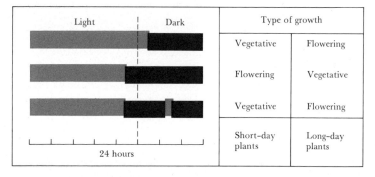

| Light | Dark | Type of growth | |
|---|---|---|---|
| | | Vegetative | Flowering |
| | | Flowering | Vegetative |
| | | Vegetative | Flowering |
| 24 hours | | Short-day plants | Long-day plants |

equivalent to the following night, flowering was again inhibited by light. Discovery of these reactions showed that the plant had an **endogenous rhythm** (one originating within the plant) with a cycle approximately 24 hours in duration. Such **circadian** ("about a day") rhythms are well known in many systems. ("Jet lag" in humans is the result of interference with such a rhythm.) It is clear that some form of biological clock operates to control many responses of living things. The nature of this clock, however, remains a mystery.

## Vernalization

While flowering is controlled by the length of days (or more precisely, of nights), biennial plants germinate one year and flower the next. This is because they require a period of cold before flowering can be triggered by long days. The application of this cold period is referred to as **vernalization**, which means "making spring-like."

The requirement for a cold period—several weeks just above freezing—is important in agriculture. It allows the time necessary for fruit or seed production to be shortened from two growing seasons to one by sowing the crop in the autumn. Once the plants have sprouted and begun to grow, the winter cold induces vernalization. The plants then flower the following summer instead of taking up growing space for two summers. Winter wheat is a prime instance of such a crop. On the other hand, some biennial plants, such as carrots, make a food reserve such as a swollen root during their first season. The stored food is then utilized in growth during the second season, when the plants flower. These plants form our main root crops. Since first-year rather than second-year growth is desired, they must be planted when spring is fairly well under way. If sown too early and thus exposed to a cold period, they will flower in the long days of summer without ever forming any food storage. So if a farmer is too eager to sow his root crop, he may end up without one.

# Perception of light

Before a plant can respond to environmental stimuli, it must perceive them. In the case of light stimuli, detection must involve some sort of pigment. One such substance has been studied extensively. This is the pigment **phytochrome**, by which the plant perceives the light/dark cycles involved in photoperiodism.

We said above that if a dark period long enough to induce flowering in a short-day plant is interrupted near its midpoint by a flash of light of sufficient intensity, then the effect of darkness is negated and flowering

17-9
Germination of lettuce seed after exposure to red and far-red light in sequence. (See Perception of light)

| Irradiation | Germination (%) |
|---|---|
| None (dark control) | 8 |
| R | 98 |
| R + FR | 54 |
| R + FR + R | 100 |
| R + FR + R + FR | 43 |
| R + FR + R + FR + R | 99 |
| R + FR + R + FR + R + FR | 54 |
| R + FR + R + FR + R + FR + R | 98 |

(From Borthwick, et al. Proc Nat Acad Sci US 38:662–666 (1952)).

does not occur. It was found that red light (about 660 nm wavelength) was the most effective color in preventing flowering. The specificity of this reaction to light of a particular color suggested a pigment which absorbed precisely this color. But many attempts to extract and identify such a pigment failed. Finally a clue was found in an apparently unrelated problem. This concerned the effect of light on the germination of certain varieties of lettuce seeds. These seeds germinate poorly in darkness, but do better if exposed to red light. If, however, after exposure to red light, they are then exposed to far-red light (more than 700 nm wavelength), germination is inhibited. This effect of far-red may, in turn, be counteracted by a new dose of red light. It is as if there were a two-way switch capable of being pressed any number of times without marked effect on its operation. The plant responds only to the most recent press of

**17-10**
Mimosa leaflets (top) were placed in darkness after brief exposure to far-red light. After 30 minutes they were still open. Others (bottom) were exposed to red light and then placed in darkness. After 30 minutes, all the leaflets were closed (See Perception of light)

the switch. Not only does this system work in lettuce seed germination, but it is also effective in the control of flowering.

From these data, it was proposed that the pigment involved exists in two mutually reversible forms. Form 1 absorbs red light but not far-red light. Form 2, on the other hand, absorbs far-red but not red. The first form, called $P_r$, absorbs red light of 660 nm wavelength and is thereby transformed to $P_{fr}$, the second or far-red-absorbing form. $P_{fr}$ can be transformed back to $P_r$ by far-red light of 730 nm wavelength. Photoperiodic behavior apparently depends on interaction between a circadian rhythm and the relative amounts of the two forms of phytochrome in the plant.

What does phytochrome do to induce chemical changes? Phytochrome is a protein molecule, so a change from the $P_r$ to $P_{fr}$ forms probably involves a change in protein structure, and this could change its effects. (For instance, different protein structures account for different enzyme actions.) The most likely situation is that phytochrome is located in a membrane, perhaps including the plasma membrane, and controls the movement of substances across the membrane.

Some sort of biochemical change must occur after phytochrome in the leaves has received the inductive dark and light periods. We know that it is the leaves which perceive the photoperiod. If even one leaf of a short-day plant is exposed to short days while the rest of the plant is kept in long days, flowering will occur. Since the leaf perceives the stimulus but the flowering response is in the apex, some chemical message must pass between the two sites. Named **florigen** by researchers, this substance must be made in the leaves under the control of phytochrome. However, it has not yet been identified.

## Hormones and their action

A plant must not merely be able to perceive environmental stimuli. It must also be able to react to them. And this, as the preceding paragraph suggests, requires some sort of chemical messenger. Something chemical has to happen inside the plant, as a result of the stimulus, to change its patterns of growth. The substances through which this happens are the hormones.

Hormones can almost be considered more important in plants than in animals, since plants do not have a nervous system. The job of control and regulation falls to the hormones alone. So it is not surprising that we find a variety of plant hormones. The most widely active are the groups known as auxins, cytokinins, and gibberellins.

### Auxins

Over a century ago, Charles Darwin was studying the phototropic behavior of young grass shoots. He found that the light stimulus was perceived by the extreme tip of the

**17-11**
The effect of light on coleoptile (young grass shoot) growth. Plant at extreme left is growing in darkness. Darwin demonstrated that even though the point of growth is a centimeter or so below the tip of the coleoptile, it is the tip itself that receives the light stimulus. He showed this by first shading the tip so that it did not receive the light from the side, while leaving the growing area illuminated. The plant continued to grow straight. But then he reversed the conditions. He shaded the growing area and illuminated the tip from the side. Bending occurred. Apparently, a signal was passing from the tip to the growing zone. (See Auxins)

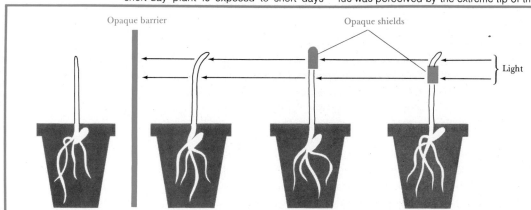

Opaque barrier     Opaque shields

Light

17-12
The camellia cutting at left was placed in plain water. The one on the right was placed in water containing synthetic auxins. The effect on root formation is evident.

shoot. However, when the plant turned toward the light, it did so by means of growth at a point a centimeter or so below the tip. Evidently, some chemical substance must be carrying a message from the shoot tip to the growing point. That substance has since been identified as indole-3-acetic acid, a simple derivative of the amino acid tryptophan. It is one of the hormones we now call **auxins**.

Auxins have many roles to play in the plant. In general, they stimulate growth. Plants bend toward the light because auxin tends to concentrate on the dark side, causing more growth there and producing a curve in the stem. Cut stems often can be made to grow roots by being dipped in a solution of auxin. (This is an effect which gardeners find very useful when they want to start new plants from cuttings.) And a small flower ovary swells up into a large fruit partly because large amounts of auxin are present in it after fertilization.

But too much auxin can inhibit growth. How much is too much depends on the tissue involved. The amount that stimulates growth in a stem, making it bend toward the light, will stop growth in a root, bending it away from the light. And enough of it will kill the plant, apparently by completely upsetting its metabolism. In fact, some important weed-killers, such as 2,4-D, are essentially synthetic auxins.

We do not yet know just how auxin achieves its effects. Probably it somehow softens the rigid cell wall, enabling it to stretch and therefore permitting the cell to grow. Researchers continue to look eagerly for the answer. Auxin could be even more valuable to agriculture than it already is, if we fully understood how it works.

## Cytokinins

One of the most intriguing problems in biology involves the regulation of cell division. Why do cells divide at one time and stop at another time? Why do meristematic cells retain their ability to divide, while other cells in the mature organism normally do not? And why, in case of injury, do some of these other cells suddenly resume division?

It seemed clear to researchers that some substance in plants must be regulating cell division. The final isolation and identification of such substances stemmed from attempts to induce development in isolated plant tissues. Experiments were performed with pith parenchyma cells from tobacco stems. These cells do not normally divide. However, when coconut milk was added to the sterile culture in which they were grown, they began to do so. Coconut milk is a liquid endosperm—a natural growing medium for an embryonic plant—so it was a logical choice for the early work on cell division. But it is also quite a complex substance. Any one of its components might have been the active factor. So a number of related pure materials were tested. By chance, a sample of autoclaved DNA (sterilized by steam under pressure) was found to contain a substance highly active in promoting cell division. The new substance formed from the DNA by autoclaving was named **kinetin** (from *cytokinesis,* the technical name for cell division). Later, researchers found a whole group of compounds, the **cytokinins**, which occur naturally in plants.

The availability of kinetin ( which does not occur naturally in the plant) opened up great new fields for investigation. When kinetin was added, together with auxin, to cultures of plant callus (undifferentiated tissue), all sorts of things happened. If the concentration of kinetin was higher, buds were formed. If the two hormones were about equal, more callus was produced. And if the auxin was in higher concentration, roots appeared.

In some cases, auxin and kinetin worked against each other. For instance, in plants which display strong apical dominance, auxin produced by the terminal bud prevents nearby lateral buds on the same stem from growing. But when kinetin was applied to such auxin-repressed lateral buds, they began to grow.

Cytokinins also seem to control another important feature in plants. Apparently they prevent senescence, or aging. If the petioles of detached leaves are placed in cytokinin the leaves remain green, but if placed in water the leaves yellow. Cytokinin, then, apparently prevents the breakdown of proteins and nucleic acids. Another interesting observation comes from these detached leaves. If the petioles develop roots, the leaves do not yellow. This suggested to experimenters that the roots supply cytokinins—a suggestion which was later proved to be correct.

It is still not understood how cytokinins produce their effects. They occur in transfer

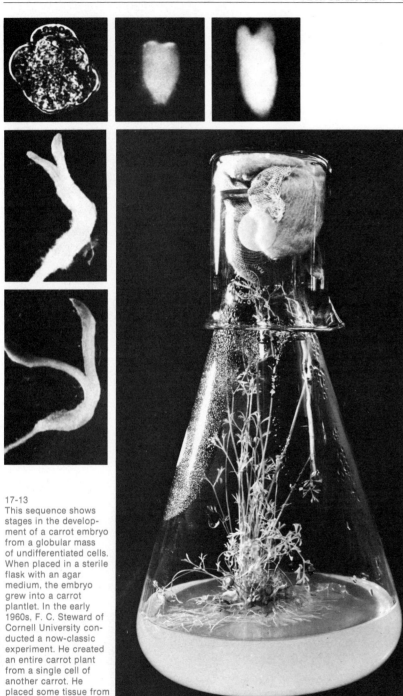

RNA, but they seem to cause cell division independently of it. Their effect on senescence may have something to do with maintaining the integrity of cell membranes, and preventing protein breakdown.

## Gibberellins

Early in this century, oriental rice farmers noted that some of their seedlings were growing abnormally fast. Unfortunately, these fast-growing plants were not much use. They rarely flowered, and never produced viable seeds. Examination showed them to be infected with a fungus, which was named *Gibberella fujikuroi*. A filtered culture of this fungus caused other plants to show the same symptoms.

**17-13**
This sequence shows stages in the development of a carrot embryo from a globular mass of undifferentiated cells. When placed in a sterile flask with an agar medium, the embryo grew into a carrot plantlet. In the early 1960s, F. C. Steward of Cornell University conducted a now-classic experiment. He created an entire carrot plant from a single cell of another carrot. He placed some tissue from a carrot root in a solution with various nutrients, including hormones and coconut milk. (The milk nourishes the carrot culture, and certain of its hormones induce cell division.) Though mature, the carrot cells began dividing. They formed a mass of undifferentiated cells called a callus. Individual cells were removed from the callus and successively placed in two new mediums of coconut milk and different hormone mixes. Some of the cells developed into rootlets and these then produced shoots. That is, they became carrot embryo cells. When placed in earth, one of the embryo cells grew into a seedling and finally into a whole plant.

**17-14**
Witch's brooms form when many lateral buds close together suddenly sprout. They grow into a crowded clump of weak, dwarfed shoots which may drain the strength of the plant. They are usually caused by a fungus, virus, or other invading organism. The plant is stimulated to produce cytokinin, overcoming the normal inhibitory effects of auxin. (See Cytokinins)

The substance in the culture which caused these effects was finally isolated in the 1950s, and was named **gibberellin.** More than forty different gibberellins are now known. Many are naturally produced by the plants themselves rather than by an infecting agent such as a fungus.

Gibberellins work in general by enhancing cell division and cell elongation. This was what caused the rapid stem growth of the farmers' rice seedlings. Another instance of such growth is the bolting of long-day plants such as cabbage. Many long-day plants spend most of their vegetative growth period in a rosette stage—a low-growing compressed shoot. But in summer they bolt—that is, the stem shoots up very rapidly—and flower. Gibberellins can be used to induce bolting without exposing the plants to long days.

Like auxin, gibberellin may induce formation of **parthenocarpic** fruits—fruits produced without fertilization—in some species. Apples, for example, cannot be parthenocarpically produced with auxin alone, but they can be by using auxin and gibberellin together.

In seeds, gibberellin may enhance germination, substituting for cold or light. In cereal grains it also controls the digestion of starch reserves in the germinating seed, so that they can be made available to the embryo. Interestingly, this gibberellin is synthesized by the embryo itself—so the embryo is, in a sense, in control of its own food supply.

## Ethylene

The effects of hydrocarbon gases on plants have been known for a long time. **Ethylene** is the most active of these gases, generally producing abnormal effects. These may include loss of geotropic sensitivity, a downward bending of petioles, and the development of adventitious roots on stems. For a long time, ethylene was regarded as an alien and unhealthy substance.

Recently, however, ethylene has been recognized as a normal substance in plant metabolism. In fact, it is the agent which induces ripening, being produced just before the onset of the climacteric. Ethylene can, therefore, be termed the ripening hormone.

This effect can produce storage problems. As a ripening fruit produces ethylene, it causes surrounding fruits to ripen also. But it does not cease production when it is fully ripe. A rotting apple continues to produce ethylene, and will cause all the surrounding stored apples to ripen and spoil (hence the proverb about "one bad apple in a barrel"). Carbon dioxide, though, opposes the action of ethylene, and so helps in fruit storage.

Ethylene also interacts with auxin to bring about leaf abscission. While the leaves are active they produce auxin, but this slowly declines as the leaves age. As the cells of the abscission zone age, they no longer respond to auxin. Instead, they respond to the ethylene which is continually produced by the cells. The ethylene stimulates production of an enzyme which degrades the cell walls. In consequence, the cells of the abscission zone separate, the petiole breaks, and the leaf falls.

## Abscisic acid

Abscisic acid is an inhibitor substance. We have already seen its role in keeping seeds dormant during seasons unfavorable for growth. It is also involved with the cessation of cell elongation and formation of dormant buds. In fact, tree dormancy is controlled by a balance between an "on switch" consisting mainly of cytokinins and gibberellins, and an "off switch" consisting of abscisic acid. Abscisic acid is synthesized in the leaves throughout the year. However, its effects are suppressed until production of the "on" hormones decreases in the fall. At this point the inhibitor moves into the stem and to the growing point. There it begins to prepare the plant for its period of dormancy.

17-15
Any normal cabbage plant will bolt when the weather gets hot. But these have distinctly overdone it. Gibberellin treatments are to blame. (See Gibberellins)

**summary**

Growth occurs throughout the life cycle of plants. Cell division is followed by cell expansion and then cell differentiation. Reproductive organs appear only in the mature plant. Earliest growth is characterized by cell division at the root and shoot apices. Leaf primordia mark the beginning of cell differentiation. They appear at the shoot apex and form an apical bud. Below the apex, procambial cells differentiate and become primary xylem and phloem. The root apex, pointed so it can push through the soil, is covered with a root cap. Rapid cell division thickens the root, forming root hairs and vascular tissue. Growth of both these apices increases the size of the plant. Eventually leaves, stem branches, and root branches appear.

Leaf primordia form in an orderly pattern, or phyllotaxy, owing to genetic programming. Stem branches develop from lateral buds, which are meristematic areas that become apices with leaf primordia. Apical dominance limits the growth of stem branches close to the shoot apex. When the reproductive period begins, leaf primordia form floral organs. Subsequently, fruits and seeds develop from the ovary and ovules. When the fruit is full-sized, it undergoes a short, sharp rise in cellular respiration and $CO_2$ output, known as the climacteric. This brings on the changes which produce ripening.

Plants must be able to stop growth processes in response to unfavorable environmental conditions. Twigs form bud scales coated with a varnish-like substance as a protection against winter cold. Leaves cannot be protected, and are shed to conserve the plant's resources. Seeds are kept dormant by the presence of inhibitors such as abscisic acid. This dormancy is broken in the spring by light, or by warmth after the long period of low winter temperature.

Environmental stimuli—especially light and gravity—affect plant growth. A growth response to a unidirectional stimulus is called a tropism. Tropisms are positive or negative, depending on whether the growth is toward or away from the stimulus. A stem growing upward exhibits negative geotropism and positive phototropism. Roots growing downward display just the opposite.

Plants also demonstrate photoperiodic behavior. Many of them begin or end certain growth cycles by responding to changes in the length of darkness. There are short-day plants, long-day plants, and day-neutral plants. Plants are capable of measuring time, and exhibit circadian rhythms.

Plants must contain substances which can perceive these environmental stimuli. In the case of photoperiodism, the substance is a pigment called phytochrome. It is found in two forms, responding to red and far-red light respectively. Photoperiodic behavior apparently depends on interaction between phytochrome and a circadian rhythm.

Phytochrome influences flowering as well as other reactions, including germination of some seeds. But another chemical substance must be present, to carry messages from the tissues which perceive the stimulus to those where the reaction takes place. In the case of flowering, this is thought to be a substance called florigen, which has not yet been identified.

Florigen is only one of many hormones which control and regulate plant behavior in response to environmental stimuli. More widely important are the groups of hormones known as auxins, cytokinins, and gibberellins.

Auxin stimulates cell growth. It is the hormone mainly responsible for phototropic behavior, and for growth of fruits to full size after fertilization. It can be used to induce root formation on cut stems. But in high concentrations it may inhibit growth. Synthetic auxins are used for this purpose in weed-killers such as 2,4-D.

Cytokinins help to regulate cell division and differentiation. Working together with auxin, they induce formation of buds and roots from undifferentiated callus. Cytokinin works against auxin to release lateral buds from the repression caused by apical dominance. It also helps prevent aging.

Gibberellins enhance cell division and elongation. They promote rapid stem elongation, such as bolting. Gibberellins can be used to induce parthenocarpic fruit development, and can sometimes help in the germination of seeds.

Other hormones include ethylene and abscisic acid. Ethylene is the ripening hormone, produced just before the climacteric. It also works with auxin to help bring about the shedding of leaves. Abscisic acid, an inhibitor substance, helps to prepare plants for dormancy, and keeps seeds dormant during seasons unfavorable for growth.

# HOUSEPLANT FUN

You can learn to be a green thumb by growing plants indoors

Daniel Schiler

# Basics for brownthumbs

Daniel Schiler

Plants are among our best friends. In fact, we literally can't live without them—although they can live without us and did so for millions of years before the first humans appeared in their tranquil world. Besides being a physical necessity—they put us in touch with nature. Plants affirm our ancient contact with the earth and the forest which our ancestors venerated as deities. And, last but not least, they are sources of beauty which delight the eye and calm the mind. The great American poet, Ralph Waldo Emerson had this to say about the joys of meditating with the plants in his garden:

> There I feel that nothing can befall me in life, no disgrace, no calamity which nature cannot repair. Standing on the bare ground, my head bathed in blithe air, and uplifted into infinite space, all mean egotism vanishes. I become a transparent eyeball: I am nothing: I see all; the currents of the universal being circulate through me; I am part or particle of God.

If plants can do this to so great a man as Emerson, imagine what they can do for you! You will appreciate the words and feelings of the poet all the more when you adopt a houseplant for your own. You will find that the plant becomes an increasingly important part of your life as you witness the changes it goes through during its growth and development.

Of course, the human-plant relationship is not all one-sided. In exchange for the physical and spiritual benefits it gives you, the plant must receive something in return—it must receive kindness, care, even love. After all, this fellow living thing, taken from its natural habitat, is more or less at your mercy. If you don't nourish it, make sure it has the proper living conditions—even sing and talk to it as some enthusiasts claim—the plant will shrivel and die. So when you get your new plant, you must match the living conditions it's used to.

If you want to become involved with plants on an intimate daily basis, but are afraid that you might be all brown thumbs, don't despair. There are an enormous number of plants that require very little effort on your part. Indeed, they seem to thrive in an atmosphere of benign neglect. Some easy-to-care for plants include dieffenbachia, philodendron, Chinese evergreen, and grape ivy. Any one of them will make a rewarding first plant.

Buying a plant The first piece of advice on plant buying is simple: buy your plant from a reputable florist, garden center, or nursery—a store that specializes in plants and has a stake in their quality. Try to avoid supermarkets, discount stores, and other such places which carry plants only as a sideline to make extra money. How do you know whether a plant dealer is reputable? It's easy if you use your eyes and ears. Does he have a wide selection of plants? Is the store clean and well organized? Do all the plants look green and healthy? Are the salespeople knowledgeable? Question one of them about the plants that interest you. Plant people are some of the friendliest and most helpful people around. If the salesperson wants to know what kind of home you plan to bring the plant into (that is, if he's more concerned about the green on the plant than he is about the green in your wallet) you can be sure you're in good hands.

Next, look at the plant you intend to buy. Don't take it if it shows any of the following symptoms:

1. Discolored or faded leaves
2. Drooping or limp leaves
3. Roots growing from the pot's drainage hole
4. Signs of insects or disease
5. Soil that is dry to the touch
6. Leaves too far apart

A healthy plant, on the other hand, should:

1. Be green and vigorous
2. Have moist soil that is very porous
3. Have buds and tender young leaves that indicate growth
4. Have a pleasing shape

Now, let's examine the factors in the plant's environment—the pot, nutrition, light, temperature, and humidity.

Pots and soil. The best kind of pot for the beginner is the old-fashioned terra cotta, or claypot. Because this type of pot is porous and has drainage holes, water and nutrients can pass through it, thus lessening the chance of your overwatering or overfeeding it (the two biggest sins of the novice indoor gardener). The earthy color of the clay pot also lends a natural accent to your green plant. The other kinds of pot—those made of plastic or glazed ceramic—are not recommended for beginners because they are not very porous and lack waterholes. In this kind of pot, the plant can easily become water-logged as a result of overwatering or develop indigestion from overfeeding.

As for the soil, you can buy the various ingredients and mix them yourself, or you can purchase soil that has already been mixed and sterilized. Such soil typically is composed of equal parts of peat moss, garden loam, and coarse sand. It's best to buy the pre-mixed variety until you learn more about the subject.

When you buy your plant, it should come in the soil of its natural habitat. Desert plants, for example, thrive in coarse, sandy soil. Tropical plants, on the other hand, do best in soil rich in humus (decayed animal, vegetable, and mineral remains). Subtropical or temperate-zone plants are used to a mixture of coarse soil, clay, and silt with humus.

Light. Before you actually buy your plant, you should carefully examine the condition of the home you're going to give it. The amount of light it will receive is crucial because it is the condition you are least able to control (unless you use artificial illumination.) And the situation is not helped by the fact that it is very difficult to determine how much light any given plant needs for a long happy life. If anything is certain about light, however, it is this: it is a rare plant that can withstand full sun or total darkness all day long. Nearly all plants require something in between. Generally speaking, the great majority of houseplants thrive near windows. Plants that are used to the sun grow well in southerly or westerly exposures, whereas those that like shade prefer northerly or easterly exposures. However, many of these latter plants do just as well in dark areas away from windows—on mantels, in wall niches, in alcoves, and such.

As in most human disciplines, indoor horticulture has its own jargon, especially where light conditions are concerned. So perhaps it would help to translate some of the more popular terms here. High-level light, or strong sun, is the light that pours unobstructed into windows facing south. Avocado, cactus, and geraniums grown well in this kind of light. Medium, bright diffused, or semi shady light is found in unshaded east and west exposures, or in south exposures that have just a wee bit of shade. This type of light is best for begonias, orchids, and gesneriads. Direct reflected light and shady light is found in northern exposures or in those facing west or east. Plants that like this kind of light include the Chinese evergreen, philodendron, and dieffenbachia. Finally, dark or deep shade light prevails where there are no shadows. Sansevieria and aspidistra are best adapted to this light.

How can you tell when your plants are suffering from too much or too little light? They will send out unmistakable distress signals. If the lower leaves are dying, and all the leaves are smallish, the plant is starving for light. Too much light causes the plant to turn yellow and shrivel. If not corrected, both conditions can be fatal.

You can prevent green deaths from inadequate lighting by following these simple rules:

1. Every two weeks or so move plants from sunny spots to more shady ones, and vice versa.
2. Shade small plants with larger ones.
3. Every day, rotate your plant about a quarter turn; this assures equal distribution of sunlight and straight growth.

Finally, if all else fails, you can illuminate your plant by means of a fluorescent light or a plant-gro light. The latter is a special kind of fluorescent light that, in many cases, is better than natural sunlight.

Water. Watering is the trickiest job for the indoor horticulturist, and most plants that die do so because they have been watered too much or too little by the beginner. How can you tell if your pot is dying of thirst or drowning? The answer is not cut-and-dried, but generally a thirsty plant begins to droop, whereas a drowning plant shows rotting stems, soggy soil, and yellow leaves.

How much and how often you water your plant depends upon the plant itself, the size of its pot, the type of soil, the atmosphere, the time of the year, and other factors. For example, the soil around a tropical plant should be kept moist, whereas the soil of a desert plant should be given sufficient time to dry before re-watering. During winter, when the days are short, plants need less water than in the long days of summer.

If your room is hot and dry, you must water your tropical plant frequently and you must mist it daily as well—just give the plant a couple of spritzes from a spray can full of warm water. Moreover, a plant in a small pot needs more frequent watering than one in a large pot because it dries faster. Similarly, a plant in a plastic pot requires less frequent watering because plastic is less porous than clay. You can tell whether soil in a plastic pot is dry by tapping the side of the pot with a metal object, such as a knife or a pair of scissors. If you get a hollow, ringing sound, add water. If your pot answers with a thud, wish it good health and leave it alone.

If your plant is small or medium-sized, you can immerse it pot and all (up to the base of the stem) in a bathtub or a pail of water until the soil stops bubbling. Then let the pot drain for an hour or so. Give it this treatment once every one or two months, but, at the same time, don't forget to water it regularly. How often is regularly? A good rule of thumb is to water the plant thoroughly whenever the uppermost inch of the soil feels dry to your prodding fingers. Don't water too often—if the soil is soggy or feels wet, leave the plant alone. Fill the pot until the water reaches its rim. If you see water flowing from the drainage hole, stop watering because the plant

has had enough. It's better to water thoroughly once a week than to give the plant a tiny drink once a day or so. Water in the morning, rather than the evening, because the plant needs moisture during the warmer hours when the rate of evaporation is high. Incidentally, the water should be room temperature rather than cold—cold water makes the plant wilt and even worse, slows its growth.

Avoid water softeners because the chemicals in them can murder the plant. The same goes for chlorinated water—let it sit overnight before using to give the chlorine a chance to evaporate. If you have placed a saucer under the pot, don't let the pot sit in the water that has run out of the drainage hole. Empty the saucer because this water can cause the plant to become water-logged, rotting the roots.

Food. When you buy your plant, it will be potted in highly nutritious soil that has been sterilized to ward off infection from bacteria and fungi. After a month or so, it will have eaten all the minerals and other food in the soil and will be ready for another helping. What should you feed it?

Any fertilizer prepared specifically for houseplants is okay, but the label should say that it contains six parts of nitrogen, eight parts of phosphorus, and six parts of potash. Make sure you read carefully and follow the label instructions exactly. Whatever you do, don't gorge the plant—overfeeding can burn the roots and kill the plant. How can you tell when you're making a glutton of the plant? The usual signs of overfeeding are a greenish scum on the outside of the pot and a whitish-greyish crust on the soil.

Set yourself a written schedule (don't rely on your memory) and feed the plant about once a month. A new plant should not be fed for at least a month and a half after purchase. You can tell when an old plant is hungry by its appearance—it looks droopy and scraggly and does not produce new buds. If the younger leaves start turning yellow, the plant may not be getting enough nitrogen.

Plant foods are available in many forms—powdered, granulated, liquid, and tablet. The powdered and liquid varieties can be dissolved in water and either sprayed on the plant or poured on. The most recent development in plant food is the timed-release fertilizer which automatically feeds the plant after it has been placed in the soil. Some indoor gardeners also swear by the inner membranes of eggshells, but it is recommended that beginners not use these as plant food. The same goes for used tea bags and coffee grounds. Both contain caffein, and you don't want your plant to become an insomniac.

Don't feed your plant when it is ailing because you only make

Daniel Schiller

Daniel Schiller

Courtesy of Westinghouse Electric Co.

matters worse. And don't feed it during its winter dormant period when it stops growing. Feeding at this time—which for most plants is the months of December and January—will force the plant to grow when it should be resting. Start feeding the plant in March or so, when it wakes up and starts going again.

**Temperature and humidity.** Most house plants do well in temperatures of 65 to 70 degrees during the winter months. Like us, plants love fresh air. So try to put the plant in a spot where it gets a little air every day. But don't go overboard. Keep plants out of direct blasts of cold air and don't place them near a radiator where warm air can reach them.

Although there is a good deal of debate on the subject, some experts believe that plants do well in air-conditioned rooms. However, air conditioning removes the humidity, or moisture, that houseplants vitally need. If the humidity is too low, the plant will let you know—the leaf tips and edges will turn brown and wilt, and the new leaves will not grow to normal size. If the situation is not corrected, the plant will die. You can generally tell when the humidity is low in your home because it affects you too—hot dry air causes congested noses and parched, aching throats.

There are several things you can do to increase humidity. Buying a humidifier will benefit you and your plants or you can mist the plants every morning. Another way to increase humidity is to group plants so they are in breathing range of one another—this lets them exchange moisture among themselves. Finally, you can use a pebble tray, or dry well, to provide more moisture for plants. Buy one of these from a garden store, or you can make one yourself in a few minutes. Get a cake pan, tray, or similar container and pour a one-inch layer of pebbles, gravel, or marbles into it. Put your pot on the pebbles, then fill the tray with water almost to the bottom of the pot. But be sure that the water does not touch the base of the pot. Add water every day to replace that lost by evaporation.

# Spotting plant pests

Enemy number one for plants is the human being. By overfeeding, overwatering, and neglecting them altogether, people cause more trouble for plants than any other living thing. But insects also occasionally attack your plants, so it's nice to know what they are, what they look like, and how to get rid of them. The best way to deal with insects is to prevent them from attacking in the first place. To do this, examine plants carefully every day, and give them a bath and thorough cleaning at least once a month. If your plant falls prey to one of these pests, isolate it in the intensive care room because whatever it has is catching—for other plants, that is. Here are the most common houseplant pests to watch for.

| Pest | What it looks like | How to get rid of it |
|------|-------------------|---------------------|
| Mealybug | A sticky, white, fuzzy-looking insect that creates clusters resembling angel hair | This is the most common houseplant pest. For mild cases, pull off individuals with tweezers or fingers, or spray with warm water. For severe cases, swab with a Q-tip dipped in alcohol. |
| Red spider mite | Appears as a red dust or web on the undersides of leaves. After a while, leaves turn silver-grey, then yellow as the mite sucks the life out of them.. | Virtually impossible to control because it has usually done its damage by the time you detect it. Bathe plant in warm soapy water about twice a week. If you see no signs of improvement, start making funeral plans because the plant is doomed. |
| Aphid | This one is easy to spot. It is a small, winged insect about one-eighth of an inch to one inch in length. It can be grayish-white, black, or red. | Wash off with warm soapy water, pick off with tweezers or fingers, or dab with a Q-tip dipped in alcohol. |
| Scale | This is really the skeleton that covers the body and eggs of the insect. It protects the beastie while attaching itself to the plant and sucking the juices. Scale can be white, brown, or black, and attacks the stem as well as the leaves of the plant. | Usually found on ferns, this pest is difficult to get rid of. Wash with warm soapy water, using a Q-tip or soft toothbrush, then rinse with warm water. |

# Four plants for brown thumbs

**1** Dieffenbachia. This attractive plant, which comes from Brazil, is sometimes called dumb cane, or mother-in-law's tongue. It gets its peculiar name from the extraordinary effect it has on the human tongue—it causes temporary muteness when eaten. There are more than 18 species of dieffenbachia. The hardiest, the Ameona, boasts large dark green leaves with a dash of white in them. The leaves can grow as long as 18 inches. The Rudolph Roehrs variety has small yellow-green leaves, whereas the Exotica has small white, yellow, and green leaves. When dieffenbachia grows up, it can be four feet tall. It prefers homes where the temperature is warm to medium and the humidity is moderate.

Soil. A premixed, all-purpose soil containing sand, loam, and peat in equal parts is fine.

Light. Dieffenbachia can grow under virtually any conditions. All species thrive in spots that are warm and receive indirect light.

Care. The points and edges of the leaves turn brown and the plant begins to droop melancholically if you forget to water it. Dieffenbachia loves baths—so it's a good idea to dunk it in your bathtub once every month or two. Once a month, you should sponge warm soapy water on the leaves, then rinse—this opens the pores and lets the plant breathe. Snip off the bottom leaves when they turn yellow.

**2** Philodendron. This is the most common of houseplants, largely because it is attractive, easy to care for, and economical. Its Greek name means "tree-loving"—it thrives in the shade of tall trees on the floor of the Central American rain forest. It's a good idea to train it to climb up a stake which you can plant right in your pot. Tie the newly growing vines to the stake with string or twine, but be very gentle about it. When the roots have taken a strong hold, you can cut the string. However, the plant looks just as nice on a shelf, trailing out of its pot, or hanging from a basket. It grows just about anywhere—indoors, outdoors, in a south window, in a north window, in warm and cold homes, in dry and moist homes, in bathrooms, in kitchens . . . and so on.

Soil. Any of the commercially prepared, all-purpose or high-humus soils will do.

Light. The philodendron does best in good indirect light—near a bright window. The glossy leaves should grow to a nice size; if they don't, the plant is probably not getting enough light and should be moved.

Care. Water two or three times a week to keep the soil damp. If you have trained the plant to climb a stake,

water the roots on the stake too. Dunk the plant in lukewarm water, sponge the leaves with soapy water, then rinse with warm water once every month or two. If the humidity in your home is low, give the plant a good misting every morning.

**3** Chinese Evergreen. This plant is a cinch to care for. Generically known as Aglaonema, it is a native of tropical Asia. It's really an herb which grows quite slowly, often reaching a height of four feet. Its leaves have a leathery texture, and come in green or variegated colors. There are a number of Chinese evergreen species, including Aglaonema modestum, simplex, marantafolia, treubli, and pseudobracteatum. Some produce red berries and flowers that resemble lilies.

Soil. Use any good all-purpose soil mix.

Light. This herb flourishes in virtually any light.

Care. Water thoroughly about twice a week or when the soil seems dry. From time to time, a leaf or two may turn yellow. This is no cause for alarm because it's part of the plant's natural cycle. Just cut the offending leaf off.

**4** Grape Ivy. Virtually indestructable, this plant grows in the West Indies and in the northern regions of South America. It will thrive even in places considered impossible by most plant experts—in the corner of a room, in any window, anywhere except places where the sun is intensely hot or the temperature unbearably high. Its shiny, dark green leaves grow in clumps of threes. Like most ivies, it grows well in hanging planters or up a stake or trellis. It prefers cool to medium temperatures, and medium to high humidity.

Soil. Use a good all-purpose mixture.

Light. The grape ivy likes good indirect light and grows well under artificial light.

Care. Water when the top inch of soil feels dry, which will probably be about once every two weeks. If the humidity is low, mist daily so the roots can cling better. Keep the plant clean and healthy by bathing in soapy water every other month, being sure to rinse well and drain. Grape ivy tends to grow very fast and become scraggly, a situation you can correct by a technique known as "pinching back." This is done by using your thumb and index finger—or a pair of scissors—to pinch off the tip of the bud growing at the top of the plant's main stem. This prevents the stem from growing more leaves and permits the growth of branches from the side of the plant. Of course, when these branches become too unruly, they too must be pinched back. The result of pinching back is a bushier, healthier-looking plant.

# Pharmacy in your garden

The medicinal value of wild plants has long been understood by those who live close to the earth. The five plants described here, for example, were used by American Indians and early settlers to ward off or treat physical ailments of various kinds. You can get information on many more similar plants in *A Guide to the Medicinal Plants of the United States* by Arnold and Connie Krochmal. However, a word of warning is in order—you should not attempt to treat yourself with any of these plants because many are poisonous until properly processed.

**Common Foxglove** (Digitalis purpurea). This biennial grows to a height of about four feet and has drooping, bell-shaped purple flowers. It is found in Pennsylvania, along the Eastern seaboard from New York to North Carolina, and in many Western states. It serves chiefly as a heart stimulant, but has also been used to treat neuralgia, asthma, and fever.

**Feverfew** (Chrysanthemum parthenium). This perennial grows to a height of three feet. Its tightly-grouped flowers are white or yellow. It is found throughout the United States, along roadsides next to wooded areas, and in places that are very dry. It has been used to treat hundreds of ailments throughout the ages. The leaves are used most. Chewing them, for example, is said to relieve colic, and tea made from them is used for indigestion, colds, and diarrhea. Suppositories have been made by mixing soap and honey with the leaves. Potions made from the flowers have been employed to eliminate intestinal worms, to bring on menstruation, and to induce abortion.

**Checkerberry Wintergreen** (Gaultheria procumbens). This creeping evergreen shrub is known by many names, including aromatic wintergreen, boxberry, checkerberry, and ground ivy. Its branches reach two to six inches in length and its leaves have a waxy shine. The unusually shaped white flowers dangle from the axilla, the place where the branch of the leaf joins the stem. Red berries replace the flowers in fall and winter. It is found in the southern states, particularly in dry wooded areas of Virginia, West Virginia, Kentucky, and North Carolina. The leaves are boiled to make a tea that relieves the pain of rheumatism and general body pain. The plant has also been used to treat toothache, dysentery, and delayed menstruation and milk flow in women. Oil from the wintergreen plant is used to perk up the taste of many foods and as an aid to digestion. Rubbing it on muscles reduces swelling and soreness.

**Common Yarrow** (Achillea millefolium). A perennial that is also known as blood wort, green arrow, nosebleed, and soldier's woundwort. Yarrow reaches a height of three feet and has sharp-smelling, feathery leaves. The stems are branchless and the white or purple flowers are found tightly grouped at the top of the plant. To a casual glance, they may suggest a small Queen Anne's lace. It grows throughout the United States on roadsides, as well as in fields and pastures. Indians brewed a tea from the plant to treat stomach ailments, and early settlers made a tea that increased sweating to break a fever. They also used it to relieve headaches and to treat tuberculosis. Some people have used the yarrow plant as a pick-me-up or to increase urine flow. Skin rash and simple skin diseases are other ailments that have responded to treatment by this plant.

## Many plants have undisputed medicinal value; others, we're not so sure about.

**Witch Hazel** (Hamamelis virginiana). This well-known plant is also called pistachio, long boughs, spotted alder, and winterbloom. It grows either as a shrub or as a tree, ranging in height from eight to fifteen feet. The branches have many forks and the bark is smooth and brown. The thick leaves, which grow on a short stalk, are more or less round and vary in length from three to five inches. In the late fall, spindly yellow flowers emerge. Witch hazel grows throughout the United States in woods and along stream banks. Lotions are made from the twigs, leaves, and bark to treat bruises, cuts, and sprains. The plant was a general cure-all for the Indians. The bark was used to treat tumors, skin inflammation, and eye ailments. It was also boiled and used to limber up the legs of athletes and to relieve back pains. And the extract to the plant has been distilled to reduce swollen hemorrhoids. It is available in drugstores without prescription.

# How to trans-plant

1. Hold the pot in one hand and the plant in the other. Turn the pot on its head and gently tap it against the edge of a table, or chair.

2. When the rootball falls out in your hand, examine it carefully. If it is compact enough to stand alone, or if there are more roots than soil, it is rootbound and needs repotting.

There are certain times in the life of every successful plant when it needs a new home. When this happens, you must become an instant doctor and give it a transplant, or repotting. Generally, you should repot if—

1. The plant grows too large for the pot and becomes top heavy
2. The plant seems eternally thirsty
3. The roots start peeping from the drainage hole

You'll have no trouble at all if you follow these simple steps.

3. Select a larger pot. A good rule of thumb is to get a pot that is about two inches wider than your old pot. If you really want to be exact, measure the height of the plant (or the width, if it is wider than it is high), then get a pot whose diameter is approximately one-third of this figure.

4. If the new pot has a drainage hole, place a shard (a piece of broken pottery) or a bottle cap over the hole. This prevents soil from washing out with the excess water. If your pot has no drainage hole, fill the bottom fourth of it with pottery shards or small pebbles and some charcoal.

5. Place a layer of sphagnum moss over the shards. Then add about an inch of potting soil.

6. Now place the plant in the center of the pot. You can get it the right height (that is, at the same level it was in the old pot) by adding or subtracting soil. Add a bit of potting soil and tap it down. Repeat this step until the soil reaches to within a half-inch of the rim of the pot.

7. Water thoroughly with lukewarm water until you see the water flowing from the drainage hole. Allow plant to drain.

Photo sequence: Rodelinde Albrecht

# Recycling your Christmas tree

What do you do with your Christmas Tree when the Yule season ends? Throw it in the garbage, right? If you do this—as millions of Americans do—you're wasting money and adding to environmental pollution.

Have you ever thought of recycling your tree? Well, some ecology-conscious people have. *Science Digest* reports that students at the State University of New York College of Environmental Science and Forestry at Syracuse have devised a model recycling plan which you and your neighbors can also set up.

At Syracuse, practically the entire community got into the act. A recycling center was established at the school's parking lot and manned by student volunteers. Trees were collected and delivered to the center by the local Chamber of Commerce, by a Boy Scout troop, and by individual residents. At the center, the trees were cut into wood-chip mulch with two wood chipping machines that had been donated by an alumnus. Each person who delivered a tree was given a shopping bag full of mulch, which can be used as an ingredient of soil compost or as a covering to protect flower bulbs from freezing. Each participating family was also given a coupon for a free lunch at a local restaurant. The project was so successful that 3000 coupons were distributed and some 4500 Christmas trees were ground into mulch in one weekend. Not bad, hm? Have you ever considered starting a recycling project in your community?

**Across**
2. Plants get much of their food from this
3. Technique that makes plants bushier
5. Useful in removing scale
6. Captain of Biblical boat
9. These prevent soil from washing out of pot's drainage hole
10. Do this to plants when the humidity in your home is low
12. Nice way to say "gorge"
14. Kind of mushroom
15. A perennial almost as long-lived as Chairman Mao: Chinese _____ (abbr.)
17. Citrus fruit that is used when green
18. The most fragrant of seasoning herbs
20. What the Italian lover said to his *Donna*
21. With 22 down, this plant is associated with a practitioner of the occult
23. A creature that sometimes ends up as plant food
24. It's important to keep these plant parts free of dust
26. An ingredient of potting soil
27. Surname of author of terrific plant book
30. This fruit needs lots of sun
31. A type of mushroom that has an umbrella-like cap
32. An enemy of your plants

**Down**
1. What every plant should have once a month
2. An ingredient of potting soil
3. The star of this magazine
4. This Christmas favorite produces bright red berries
7. To diffuse by osmosis
8. When you adopt a plant, make sure you give it a good _____
11. Liquid moving at a snail's pace (one word)
13. An herb that's particularly good with shellfish
16. What's happening in farming: the _____ Revolution
19. Latin name for basil
20. Latin name for genus to which yarrow belongs
22. See 21 across
25. This vegetable is supposed to be good for your eyes
27. Too much fertilizer can cause plant roots to do this
28. Plant haircut
29. Keep the soil of most herbs _____

Wild edible mushrooms are among the most delicious plants in nature. Their taste is quite different from the soggy, commercially produced fungi you may be used to. So it is well worth the time required to gain the expertise that will enable you to identify the various species of mushrooms. But be sure to get the expertise before nibbling. In this area, what you don't know can kill you. There are hundreds of edible species, and hundreds more that are not only inedible but poisonous as well. One of the best guides on the subject is the Department of Agriculture circular, number 143, "Some Common Mushrooms and How to Know Them," by Vera Charles, available from the Superintendent of Documents in Washington, D.C. for under one dollar. Meanwhile, here are four groups that are easily identifiable; among fungi enthusiasts, they are known as "the foolproof four."

## The "foolproof" four are easy to spot

# Identifying edible mushrooms

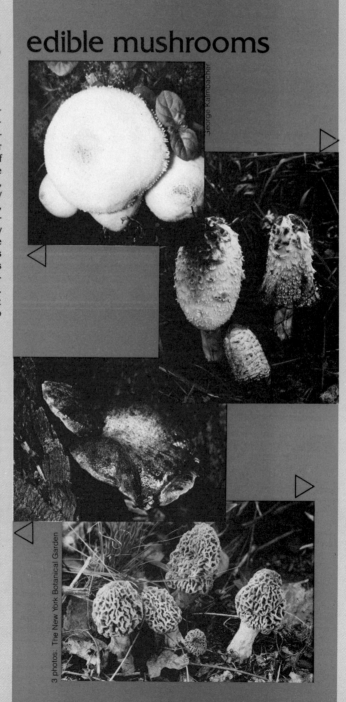

George Kalmbacher

3 photos: The New York Botanical Garden

**Puffballs.** The most delicious mushrooms of this group are the Calvatias, which have a number of varieties. The Calvatia gigantea, or giant puffball, for example, is of superior quality. It is unmistakable in that it has no stalk; it has smooth, white flesh, and resembles a puffy oval basketball. Occasionally, specimens up to five feet in diameter have been found. It has powdery olive spores that spurt out when the cap is prodded. Giant puffballs grow in wet areas and on the banks of streams in the central and eastern parts of the United States. Gather in spring and fall. Don't eat when the flesh has aged to yellowish-brown.

**Beefsteak mushroom (Fistulina hepatica).** This delectable fungus gets its name from the beefy texture of its flesh and the red liquid that oozes from it. The moist, reddish cap is quite wide—ranging from four to twelve inches in diameter. It looks like a hand fan or a liver lobe. The flesh of the cap is also rather thick—from one to two-and-one-half inches thick. The stalk, the same color as the cap, is attached to the side of the cap rather than the center. It ranges in length from one-and-one-half to a little over three inches. On the underside of the cap and embedded in it are numerous whitish tubes which resemble drinking straws; they turn red when squeezed. The beefsteak grows on the dead stumps and logs of hardwoods and at the base of the oak tree. It is found in all areas of North America, and is ripe for harvesting in the fall.

**Inky caps (Corprinus).** There are three edible species of this genus—the shaggy mane (C. comatus), the inky (C. atramentarius), and the early inky (C. micaceus). The most prized is the comatus, which features a distinctive conical cap having numerous scales and measuring two to four inches in height. The soft flesh of the cap is white, and the scales that cover it are reddish-brown. The scales closest to the top of the cap curve upward. The fibrous stalk is white and stands from three to eight inches high. The comatus grows throughout the United States, in grassy areas and along roadsides. Harvest in late spring or in the fall.

**Morels (Morchells)** are also called sponge mushrooms because of their resemblance to that marine animal. Their distinctive appearance and choice quality make them a favorite among mushroom hunters. The delicious esculenta species, for example, is high on the lists of all mushroom enthusiasts. The stalk of this variety is greyish-white and attaches directly to the cap. The ridges of the cap are light brown, and the pits between them are dark brown. Gather only in the spring, so you won't mistake it for the false morel. The latter fruits only in summer and early fall, and resembles the morel in its wrinkled cap. The cap of the false morel, however, lacks definite ridges and pits. The *esculenta* is found throughout the United States in woodland clearings, in old fields, and especially in areas that have been burned.

# Do plants have mystical powers?

Plants have played important parts in the legends and folk tales of every society. Some plants have been worshipped as deities. Others have been venerated because of their supposedly evil powers. Poets—ancient and modern—have extolled plants as things of immense beauty and power. The British poet Alfred, Lord Tennyson, for example, saw plants as a key to human identity:

Flower in the crannied wall,
I pluck you out of the crannies,
I hold you here, root and all, in my hand,
Little flower—but if I could understand
What you are, root and all, and all in all,
I should know what God and man is.

Throughout history, people have attributed mystical powers to certain plants. Once such plant is the mandrake, the Mandragora officinarum, a member of the nightshade family which grows in Mediterranean countries. The plant grows about a foot high, and its root is sometimes branched, resembling the legs of a human being. In the past, some enthusiasts even claimed to be able to distinguish between male and female mandrakes because of their distinctive shapes.

The mandrake also was believed to be useful in matters pertaining to sex. Some people considered it an aphrodisiac; others relied on it to cure sterility. Still others said it could be used to make one person fall madly in love with another. Figures were carved from mandrake roots and used in all sorts of rituals to help believers gain secret knowledge or large sums of money.

Whether the plant does indeed possess such mystical powers is best left to witches, sorcerers, and others who dabble in the black arts. It is certain, however, that the mandrake is a powerful narcotic. Chemically, it is composed of scopalamine, mandragorac, and hyoscyamine, all of which are sleep-producing alkaloids. Since it does induce sleep, it may once have been used as an anesthetic. Indeed, the Greeks were known to add it to wine, as a sort of Mickey Finn, to neutralize enemies or to silence boring dinner guests.

The mandrake is not used by modern pharmacists. However, a close relative, belladonna, is. The next time you purchase a package of 24-hour cold capsules, read the ingredients. You'll find belladonna alkaloids prominently listed.

Belladonna (which means "beautiful lady" in Italian) has been known variously as deadly nightshade, sorcerer's herb, devil's herb, poison cherry, and naughty man's cherries. It belongs to the genus Atropa, and is poisonous. In his book "Nightshades," Charles Heiser states that this plant may have been added to wine served at orgies where it drove participants into frenzies of sexual excesses. It was also one of the staples of brews, potions, and other such concoctions served up by medieval witches and sorcerers.

Exactly what effect does belladonna have on the human body? There have been reports that people who have eaten a single berry from the plant have died. However, these reports have been challenged. It has been demonstrated that it takes quite a lot of belladonna to produce death. A healthy helping of belladonna berries will produce the following symptoms within half an hour: thirst, dizziness, double or blurred vision, delirium, convulsions, general paralysis, and finally, death.

Another plant which is believed to possess mystical healing powers is ginseng, which has been called the first miracle drug. Used by Chinese physicians and herbalists since before the time of Christ, ginseng root has reportedly cured an enormous number of human ailments. It has been said to soothe nerves, improve concentration and memory, add years to life, and increase and prolong sexual powers.

Ginseng (Panax ginseng) grows in many parts of the world. Russian scientists have reported that rats which had been administered the plant were virtually immune to cancer, the effects of X-rays, and minor infections. An English physician has claimed that ginseng has significantly increased the energy and endurance of athletes. Paradoxically, a Swedish researcher says that the plant also makes an excellent sedative. And a New York research facility is reported to have used ginseng successfully to treat impotence in males.

Is there any truth to these claims? Apparently some scientists believe there is. In 1974, for example, about 70 percent of all Swiss doctors were reported to be prescribing ginseng to their patients. Some American practitioners say there may be something to this, but many agree that much more research must be done before they add ginseng to their prescription lists.

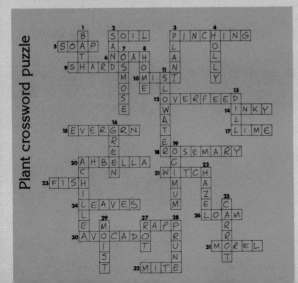

## Plant crossword puzzle

18 animal development

Imost all animals begin life as an egg. This single living cell divides over and over, forming a cluster of cells which begin organizing themselves into the shapes and structures that will comprise the adult body. The science of development is the study of how cells, tissues, and organs change their nature over a period of time, either intrinsically or in response to environmental alterations. Development focuses mainly on the mechanisms which cause change. It examines changes at all stages of life, from birth until death. In this chapter we shall concentrate mainly upon embryonic events. But we will also look for basic principles and mechanisms which apply equally well to later stages of life. Before we examine these principles, let us make a survey of the main events in the development of a representative vertebrate embryo, the frog.

**Embryogenesis** is the development of the embryo. It begins when a sperm fuses with a mature egg, forming a **zygote**. As the sperm enters the egg it releases its nucleus, which migrates toward the egg nucleus. When the two nuclei come together they fuse, and their membranes dissolve. This allows the nuclear materials to intermingle. After an interval of DNA replication, a spindle is formed. Both sets of chromosomes mix, line up, and begin to separate, just as they do in a typical mitosis. But once the chromosomes have separated, a special type of mitosis occurs. This is called **cleavage**. In this process, the zygote undergoes several divisions, which produce daughter cells. But these cells do not grow. That is, they do not form new cytoplasmic materials, as they would during normal mitosis.

The unfertilized egg of the frog, while somewhat spherical, is not homogeneous. One half, the **vegetal hemisphere**, contains most of the nutritive material known as the yolk. The other half, the **animal hemisphere**, contains the nucleus of the cell but almost no yolk. The point on the surface of the egg closest to the nucleus is called the **animal pole**. The point on the opposite side is called the **vegetal pole**. When the egg is

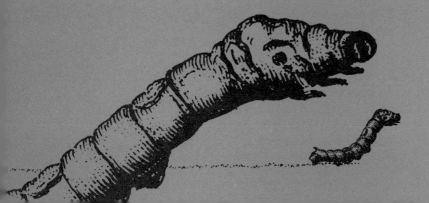

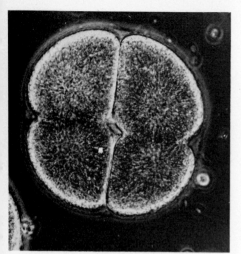

18-1
This fertilized egg has divided once to form two cells. The furrow along which the second cleavage will occur and the mitotic spindle apparatus are visible in the picture.

sliced from pole to pole (**meridional cleavage**) the two halves are virtually mirror images of one another. For one thing, both receive almost the same amount of yolk. But if the egg divides at the equator (**equatorial cleavage**) the resulting halves, animal and vegetal, are quite different. As we will see, the latter type of cleavage affects the future course of development for the daughter cells. But first, let us consider another factor which affects development.

Soon after the frog egg is fertilized, a **gray crescent** appears slightly below the equator in the vegetal hemisphere. It stretches almost halfway around the egg. The first cleavage is meridional. It therefore divides the gray crescent more or less equally between the daughter cells. When this happens, each cell can, if isolated, form a completely normal embryo. Once in a while, though, the cleavage is such that one daughter cell gets almost all of the gray crescent. When the daughter cells are separated, the cell with the gray crescent continues to divide and develops normally. The cell without this material also goes through a series of cleavages, but it does not develop. It remains a simple undifferentiated cluster of cells. Thus the gray crescent material seems crucial in determining the future pathway of development that cells will take.

Now let us see the effect of cleavage on development. The second cleavage of the frog zygote is also meridional. That is, each of the daughter cells from the first cleavage divides from pole to pole. The result is four cells, each of which can form a completely normal embryo if separated. But in the third cleavage, each of these four cells divides at the equator. There are now four animal cells and four vegetal cells forming the embryo. If the animal and vegetal halves of the embryo are separated, neither develops into a whole embryo. Instead, each half forms only those structures which would derive from it in a normal embryo. The ultimate fates of the animal and vegetal regions are now **determined**. Each is headed on a specific

18-12
Early embryology of a sea urchin. If the two daughter cells of the sea urchin zygote are separated each will form a completely normal embryo. This is also true at the 4-cell stage. But in the third cleavage the cells divide along the equatorial plane. Thus the four cells in the animal half of the embryo contain very little yolk and no pigment. The four cells of the vegetal half possess most of the yolk and all of the pigment.

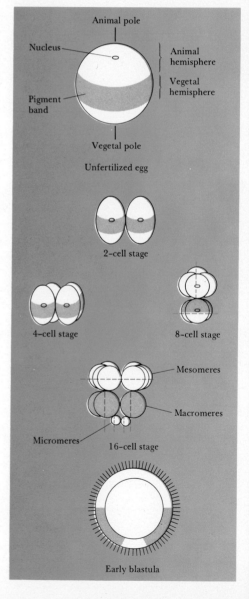

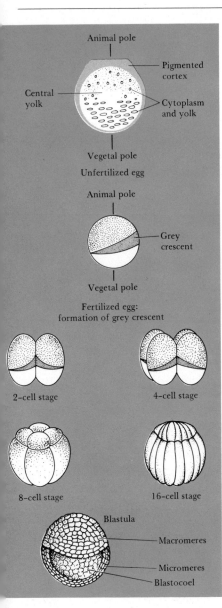

Early embryology of a frog. The first three cleavages in the frog egg are much like those of the sea urchin. But there are differences. By the 8-cell stage the four animal cells of the frog are somewhat smaller than the four vegetal cells. Thus equatorial cleavage does not produce equal-sized daughters. More important, soon after fertilization in the frog egg, a gray crescent appears.

and different pathway of development. Since the two types of cell—animal and vegetal—are different in composition, they differ in developmental capability. Their fates will be determined by the components they possess and restricted by those they lack.

# Early changes in development

The fourth cleavage of the vegetal region produces four large cells and four very tiny cells. These are called **macromeres** and **micromeres**, respectively. In the animal region, the cells formed are of medium size. They are called **mesomeres**. By the end of the sixth cleavage (64-cell stage) there is a top layer of mesomeres. Below this is a double layer of cells, also mesomeres. These mesomeres will form the **ectoderm**, or outer skin. They will give rise to the mouth and cilia. The macromeres now form two layers. These cells will create the **endoderm**, or inner skin. They will give rise to the gut. The **mesoderm**, or middle skin, will develop from a single layer of micromeres. These cells will eventually form the skeleton.

## Gastrulation

As cleavage continues, a cavity called the **blastocoel** forms in the center of the embryo. The cells arrange themselves around it in a single layer. This is known as the **blastula** stage. The micromeres form a cluster at the vegetal pole, while the macromeres locate in the middle part of the embryo. At the top or animal half are the mesomeres.

Cell division now largely stops. The process which follows is known as **gastrulation,** and the embryo resulting from it is called a **gastrula.** A slight indentation forms at the boundary between the gray crescent and the vegetal region. Its rim is called the **blastopore**. Cells in the surrounding regions on the surface of the embryo now begin to migrate toward the blas-

Gastrulation. Shown here is the development of (A) the blastopore; (B) the archenteron; and (C) the dorsal and ventral lips.

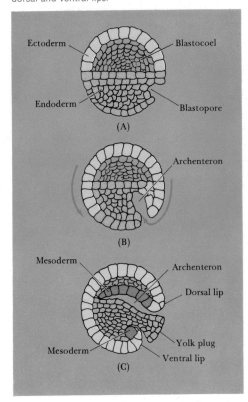

topore. As they arrive, they stream into the interior of the embryo. The original indentation quickly enlarges. And the cavity which it encloses becomes the primitive gut, or **archenteron**.

The blastopore grows in size and forms a large ring. Its animal portion is called the **dorsal lip**. This part of the embryo will become the back. The roof of the archenteron is formed by mesodermal cells which migrate inward over the dorsal lip. Endodermal cells form the floor of the archenteron. A second region of mesoderm forms just inside the vegetal rim of the blastopore. This rim is called the **ventral lip**.

As the archenteron grows, the blastocoel all but disappears. When gastrulation is completed, the entire surface of the embryo is covered by ectoderm. In the interior is a large mass of endodermal cells. The blastopore begins to shrink and is gradual-

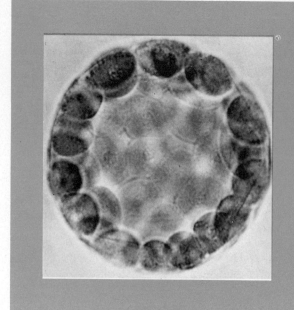

18-5
In its 64-cell stage, or sixth cleavage, the dividing starfish egg has a transparent appearance. The blastocoel, or cavity in the center of the cluster of cells, has begun to form. (See Early stages in development)

ly reduced to a small slit. Later it will close off entirely, leaving only a depression which will become the anus. The inner end of the archenteron, farthest away from the blastopore, will eventually form the mouth. Thus we see that an **anterior–posterior axis** is beginning to form.

## Neurulation

In the center of the archenteron roof, the frog mesoderm differentiates into a long rod parallel to the developing axis. This is the **notochord**. Above the notochord ectodermal cells form a thickening called the **neural plate**. At the edges of this plate, **neural folds** are thrown up. These folds move toward one another, meet, and fuse, forming a **neural tube**. The tube will eventually give rise to the brain and spinal cord. This process is called **neurulation**, and the embryo is now referred to as a **neurula**.

As neurulation proceeds, the edges of the frog endoderm also migrate upward, meeting and fusing to form a tube. This tube is the gut. At the same time, the mesoderm spreads. It largely, but not totally, covers the gut. This mesodermal layer thickens in the vicinity of the notochord. The upper part of it forms segments called **somites**. They will later differentiate into muscle and cartilage. The inner and outer portions of the mesoderm split, forming a body cavity known as the coelom.

At this point, the first phase in embryonic development has been completed. The three basic types of tissue are now formed and situated in their proper locations. From these tissues all other embryonic structures will derive. The ectoderm forms the outer layer. It is separated from the inner endoderm by a middle layer of mesoderm.

Now begins the second major phase of development, called **organogenesis**. The foundations of the nervous system already exist in the neural tube. This tube, along with the nearby ectoderm, will differentiate into the brain, spinal cord, and nerves. The rest of the ectoderm will differentiate into such structures as the epidermis, hair, eye lens, and inner ear. The gut also exists. It will differentiate into the various regions of the digestive tract. Eventually, it will give rise to such organs as the liver, pancreas, and bladder, and to the respiratory system. The somites will form voluntary muscle,

18-6
Neurulation: (A) differentiation of the neural ectoderm; (B) upward migration of the edges of the endoderm; beginning differentiation of the mesoderm into the notochord; (C) fusion of the edges of the endoderm into the gut; thickening in the dorsal ectoderm to form the neural plate; (D) development of the neural tube from folds in the neural plate which have moved together and fused; splitting and separation of the mesoderm to form the coelom.

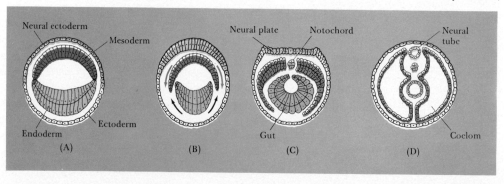

dermis, and skeletal material. The mesoderm enclosing the coelom will produce excretory organs, heart, circulatory system, sexual organs, and visceral muscle. It will also form the **peritoneum**. This is the membrane which lines the abdominal cavity.

# Gametogenesis

The **primordial germ cells**, which will some day become eggs or sperm, are themselves formed during **gametogenesis**. This occurs early in the development of the embryo. Those which differentiate into eggs are called **oogonia**. Those destined to produce sperm are called **spermatogonia**. In the first stage of gamete formation, the oogonia and spermatogonia increase their numbers by a series of mitotic divisions. When this period ends, the cells are termed oocytes and spermatocytes. In their next transition to eggs and sperm, the DNA will be reduced from diploid to haploid quantity.

## The egg cell

In the frog's ovary, newly formed oocytes are only $50\mu$ in diameter. But over the next three years they grow steadily in size. Eventually they reach a diameter of about 2,000 $\mu$, increasing their volume over 60,000 times. We can see the necessity for this extraordinary growth if we consider the events which occur after fertilization. Throughout the entire development period from fertilization to hatching, the embryo of an egg-laying animal is incapable of feeding. It therefore receives no food or other material from the environment. To grow and differentiate, it must convert substances already present in the unfertilized egg. So all of the necessary nutrients and raw materials for early development must be formed and stockpiled before fertilization. Until the tadpole hatches and acquires the ability to feed, embryonic development is dependent on conversion of preexisting materials. Placental mammals, however, can provide the embryo with maternal nourishment. They can also thus make do with a smaller egg.

And they can delay birth until a later stage of development.

*Stockpiling*    As the oocyte grows, it accumulates and stockpiles large reserves of lipids, proteins, and carbohydrates. These are known collectively as the **yolk**. The oocyte synthesizes some of its own yolk material, but experiments strongly indicate that most of the yolk is made within maternal tissues. It is later transferred to the oocyte for final processing. For instance, as the chicken egg passes down the hen's oviduct, its yolk increases more than a hundred times, reaching a value of about 20 grams. This is an immense amount of material. The egg itself could not possibly synthesize so much protein and lipid. It follows, then, that most of the yolk is made by the hen and later transferred to the egg.

Soon after fertilization, eggs enter a prolonged phase of very rapid division and differentiation. This phase is critically dependent upon the synthesis of large amounts of many types of protein. The productive facilities of embryonic cells are severely taxed during this period. So we might expect that ribosomes, the cellular protein factories, might be stockpiled before fertilization occurs. And, in fact, during egg formation, there is a roughly thousandfold increase in the genes involved in the production of ribosomal RNA, a crucial component of ribosomes. By the time oocyte growth ends, it has stockpiled in the cytoplasm large numbers of ribosomes for later use.

But yolk and ribosomes are not the only materials stockpiled during oogenesis. There is a continual synthesis and buildup of both transfer and messenger RNAs, mitochondria, and many enzymes. This process usually ends when the oocyte finishes its growth stage. Messenger RNA, however, is an exception. Its synthesis increases briefly in response to the pituitary hormone that triggers maturation of the egg. After this, though, the egg is almost completely inactive metabolically. It is in a state of suspended animation. Even many of its enzymes stop functioning. They will remain this way until activated by the sperm. After fertilization, the conversion of stockpiled materials permits embryonic development and differentiation to occur.

# Fertilization

The egg is stationary and has no power of self-motion. But the sperm is a stripped-down and streamlined cell, specialized for only two things. They are transportation of the paternal chromosomes and fast movement. Once the sperm cell is released, its flagellum beats rapidly, propelling it along a random path. If it approaches an egg, the sperm encounters chemicals released by the egg. These stimulate it to even faster movement, increasing the likelihood of sperm–egg collision.

The nuclear material of the sperm is condensed and organized into a **head**. It is partially covered with a cap or **acrosome**. The acrosome contains enzymes vital to the fusion of the sperm with the egg. When the sperm contacts the outer envelope which surrounds and protects the egg, its acrosomal tip breaks down. This releases one or more **lytic enzymes**, which catalyze the hydrolysis of complex molecules to simpler ones. Such enzymes disrupt the envelope and enable the sperm to penetrate. Once inside the egg envelope, the acrosomal membrane of the sperm makes contact with the egg plasma membrane. As contact occurs, the egg surface rises up to form a **fertilization cone** that partially surrounds the sperm head. The egg plasma membrane then fuses with the acrosomal mem-

brane. This makes the sperm and the egg effectively a single cell. The sperm nucleus can now migrate through the egg cytoplasm. It fuses and mingles its chromosomes with the egg nucleus. The entire process is surprisingly rapid. When eggs and sperm are mixed together in sea water or saline solution, the membranes fuse within a few tenths of a second. Mingling of the two chromosome sets requires only minutes more.

## The cortical reaction

The triggering event in the activation of the egg seems to be electrical changes in its membrane, caused by the sperm. The egg cytoplasm alters as a result. And this change induces the next event, known as the **cortical reaction**.

In eggs, as in many cells, the cytoplasm bordering the membrane differs in consistency from the more central body of cytoplasm. The central cytoplasm is rather fluid. But the outermost part is thick and gelatinous. It is called the **cortex**. Often, it contains a layer of granules which lie near the plasma membrane. As the egg surface becomes activated, there is a temporary disruption of the cortex. During this period, the cortical granules fuse with the egg plasma membrane. They rupture and release part of their contents into a space between the plasma membrane and the **vitelline membrane**—a nonliving, protective layer around the outside of the egg. The vitelline membrane becomes a thicker and harder **fertilization membrane**. It now serves two very important functions. First, it prevents **polyspermy**. This is penetration of the egg

**18-7**
Formation of the fertilization membrane. In the eggs of many species, the cortex contains cortical granules. In the outer half of the granule, there is a large globule known as the dark body. The inner portion contains several smaller hemispherical globules. As the egg becomes activated, there is a brief disruption of the structural organization of the cortex. The granules fuse with the egg plasma membrane, then rupture. The dark bodies are released into the perivitelline space. They drift outward, and stick onto the vitelline membrane. The plasma membrane remains as a series of crater-shaped depressions. The hemispherical globules remain in the craters, but absorb water and expand to form a mucous material. This is the hyaline layer, within the lower portion of the perivitelline space. In consequence of these surface changes the vitelline membrane becomes thicker and harder. It is now called the fertilization membrane. (See The cortical reaction)

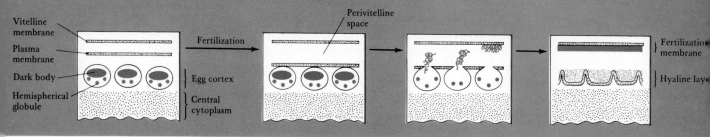

Vitelline membrane
Plasma membrane
Dark body
Hemispherical globule
Egg cortex
Central cytoplasm
Fertilization
Perivitelline space
Fertilization membrane
Hyaline layer

by more than one sperm. Such an event would cause complications and interfere with development. Second, the fertilization membrane helps to protect the egg.

## Cellular communication

**Differentiation** is the process by which cells and tissues of different types develop from common ancestors. Or, to put it another way, it is the process by which similar cells become different from one another. It allows each type of cell to become progressively more specialized for the role it must play in later life. During the earliest stages of development, differentiation is programmed spatially and biochemically by the events that occur during oogenesis.

Preprogramming is an example of what is known as **open loop control**. A system with open loop control has a fixed course of action. It cannot deviate from this even when it needs to. A bullet fired from a gun is a good analogy. Once the trigger is pulled, a marksman can neither change nor control the course of the projectile. The preprogramming of early development is similar. It is an inflexible system that cannot be changed except by accident.

Open loop controls have the advantage of simplicity. But they cannot cope with changing circumstances. When they are applied to a complicated mechanism or used in complicated circumstances, they lead almost inevitably to failure and breakdown. By the time gastrulation occurs, an embryo is already a moderately complicated system. As such, it needs a more flexible and adaptable means of regulating its own affairs. And so it changes its control policy from open loop to **closed loop**. The essential feature of closed loop control is that it monitors both itself and its surroundings. It also feeds back upon itself to make adjustments to any relevant changes that are detected. A spacecraft with steering rockets is a good representation of a system with the capacity for closed loop control.

Long before a cell becomes, for example, part of muscle tissue, its fate has been determined. It has been committed to that specific pathway of development. If the cell is removed from the embryo and grown in isolation, it will continue to develop toward becoming a muscle cell. But usually its development will be either incomplete or defective. We can draw three conclusions from this. First, when a cell becomes determined, it behaves as if it has a fixed objective or goal to reach. Second, when taken out of its normal environment and grown in isolation, it will make a number of adjustments (closed loop regulation) to cope with these disturbances. It will then continue toward its original objective. Finally, proper differentiation does not usually occur unless the cell has access to the other cells and cell types of its normal biological environment. In other words, cells influence one another's differentiation. This influencing of one cell by another is called **coupling**.

## Coupling mechanisms

Cells can influence one another by several mechanisms. One requires direct cell-to-cell contact (**contact coupling**). Another operates over very short distances (**proximity coupling**). And a third operates over longer distances (**remote coupling**). When cells are in direct contact, small molecules can be passed from one to another (**metabolic coupling**). So can large molecules such as enzymes and RNA (**macromolecular transfer**).

So far, two types of remote coupling have been discovered. In **diffusion coupling**, a chemical released in one part of the body diffuses, often through the bloodstream. It moves to other regions and there influences target cells. Hormones are one example of diffusion coupling. A second example is the nerve–muscle synapse. This is the place of juncture where the nerves release a chemical transmitter which causes the muscle to contract. In the other type, **indirect coupling**, two cells interact through a chain of one or more intermediates. In metamorphosis, for example, brain cells secrete a chemical which trig-

Metabolic coupling

Macromolecular transfer

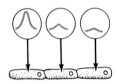

Electrical coupling

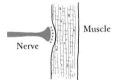

Diffusion coupling

18-8
Some coupling mechanisms. Many types of cell are electrically coupled. That is, any change in the electrical membrane potential of one will cause a flow of ions that will produce similar though slightly smaller changes in an immediately neighboring cell.

gers the pituitary to produce a certain hormone. This hormone then causes the thyroid gland to release thyroxine. The thyroxine eventually diffuses throughout the body, causing a variety of effects in different tissues.

## Tissue differentiation

We have called organogenesis the second major phase of development. The first true event in this phase occurs at the neurula stage, when the primitive nervous system begins to form. The ectoderm will not fold up to form the neural tube unless it is directly associated with the underlying mesoderm. (This is the layer of cells that lines the archenteron roof.) If this mesoderm is destroyed, or separated by a barrier from the ectoderm, neurulation does not occur. The process by which one tissue stimulates another, either near or in contact with itself, to differentiate is called **induction**. It is probably the single most important way that vertebrates initiate and control the development of organ differentiation. The most common type of induction involves the interaction between **mesenchyme** and **epithelium**. Mesenchyme is embryonic connective tissue derived from mesoderm. It usually lies beneath the epithelium. Epithelial tissue consists of sheets or tubes of cells lining cavities and exposed body surfaces. Its density and capacity for secretion make it a highly protective covering. The epithelium also serves as a filter between the organism and its external environment.

In the chick, the nephrons which develop first are an anterior group known as the **pronephros**. The middle part of the body trunk later gives rise to the **mesonephros** units. Finally the posterior part of the trunk generates the **metanephros**. The pronephros does not develop to any great extent. The mesonephros develops a little more. But it is the metanephros that creates the bulk of the adult kidney.

The mesonephros does not form a collecting duct of its own. Instead, its tubules join up with the pronephric duct to form the Wolffian duct. A ureter bud forms on the Wolffian duct and begins to elongate. The base of the bud forms the ureter, or main collecting duct for the metanephric kidney. A loose layer of mesenchyme lying on top of the ureter bud slips to one side. In the process, it induces the bud to elongate and branch to form one collecting tubule for each of the network of nephrons. At the same time, the epithelium induces the mesenchyme to differentiate. It becomes the glomerulus, convoluted tubules, and (in birds and mammals) Henle's loop.

We can examine the relationship between the mesenchyme and the ureter bud epithelium by surgically removing pieces of each and culturing them separately or together. When grown in isolation, neither differentiates. When they are cultured together, both differentiate normally. Neither the epithelium nor the mesenchyme can develop by itself. Each must be induced by the other in order to differentiate.

Clearly there are two kinds of specificity involved in mesenchyme induction. The

18-9
Tissue induction of liver epithelium and mesenchyme, showing their effects on each other at different stages.

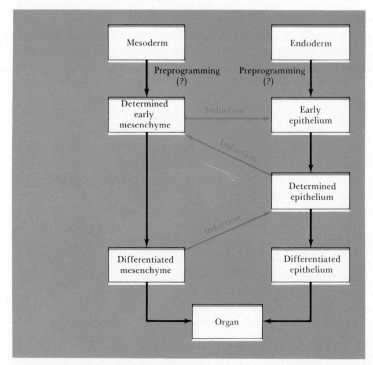

mesenchyme will not differentiate by itself. If it is associated with epithelium, its differentiation will be at least partially determined by the epithelium. But not all mesenchymes can respond to induction by a particular epithelium. Only after the mesenchyme is already partially differentiated in a particular way does it become competent to respond to a particular inducer.

Since mesenchyme and epithelium each require induction by the other, how is it that differentiation occurs in the first place? We can answer this question by going back to an earlier stage in development, before the mesoderm differentiates into mesenchyme. In the three-day chick, the part of the mesoderm that will help form the liver has already become determined, even though it has not yet differentiated. (How this determination arises is unknown, but preprogramming may well be involved.)

But at three days, the endoderm that will become liver epithelium is not only undifferentiated but also undetermined. If isolated and cultured with liver mesenchyme, it will not differentiate. In the embryo, the endoderm is located next to mesenchyme of the precardiac region. This mesenchyme apparently induces determination of the endoderm to a liver pathway of development, though it does not cause differentiation. By the fifth day, the endoderm is sufficiently determined so that it can be induced by liver mesenchyme to differentiate into liver epithelium. Thus, development involves two types of induction—first of determination, and then of differentiation.

During the three-to-five-day period of development, a basic change occurs in the mesenchyme. At the earlier stage the mesenchyme supports the survival and growth of various determined epithelia. But because of its weak inductive powers, it induces only undetermined epithelium.

At the fifth day, this situation changes. In the liver, the determined epithelium invaginates into the surrounding determined mesenchyme and induces it to differentiate. As the liver mesenchyme differentiates in

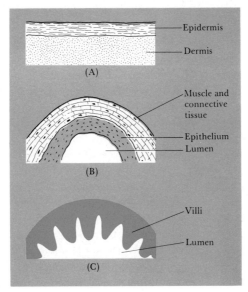

**18-10**
Tissue arrangement: (A) parallel sheet design; (B) concentric shell design; (C) multiple fold design. Tissues do not only differentiate. They also become organized and shaped in certain ways. When two tissues must each remain discrete but need to interact moderately with one another, the parallel sheet design is ideal. The skin, with an outer layer of epidermis and an inner layer of dermis, is a good example. The dermis contains hair follicles and sensory nerves to monitor the outside environment through the epidermis. The epidermis in turn provides physical protection. If two tissues need to be in close proximity to one another but do not need to interact to any great extent, the concentric shell design is one possible arrangement. It minimizes the surface area at which communication between the two tissues takes place. The lining of the gut uses this design. The innermost tissue is an epithelial tube that either secretes material into the gut lumen, or absorbs nutrients. Surrounding this is a shell of muscle and connective tissue which generates movement. The muscle and epithelial layers, however, have little need for interaction. Therefore they are well suited to the concentric shell design.

response to the epithelium, its own inductive powers increase greatly. It can now induce the determined epithelium to differentiate into liver epithelium. In fact, the inductive capabilities of the mesenchyme become so great that it can cause other types of epithelium (lung, gizzard, intestine) to change their pathways of development and differentiate into liver epithelium. The entire process is a cooperative one. It involves a sequence of mutual inductions. The end result is the formation of an entire organ made up of both mesenchymal and epithelial tissues.

## Later stages of development

In some organisms, such as mammals, organogenesis leads directly to a fully formed adult. In many other species, including the frog, organogenesis produces a larva. Larvae have nearly all of the functional capabilities of the adult, but with one exception. In most species, the larvae cannot reproduce. The reason for the existence of a larval form is basically ecological. Larvae typically live in different habitats and eat different foods than adults. So larval and adult phases do not compete with each other for resources. When the adult population is as large as the environment will allow, the species can still expand in numbers. It simply increases its larval population. Eventually, the larva undergoes a major reorganization of its tissues and organs. This is known as **metamorphosis**. In the process, the larva becomes transformed into a young but adult form.

Other stages of later development involve the repair of injuries and senescence. The repair of injuries includes the ability of animals to replace cells or tissues which no longer function properly. In some cases, whole organs or limbs are regenerated. The last phase in development is **senescence**, or aging. It is characterized by typical cellular and tissue changes whose causes are not yet fully understood.

## Metamorphosis and larval development

When frogs and most other amphibians emerge from hibernation in the early spring, they make their way to a nearby body of water. This may be a lake or a stream. Or perhaps it is only a small puddle that will quickly evaporate as the days warm. Here frogs lay eggs which eventually develop into almost fish-like larvae. They are perfectly adapted to their aquatic environment. But as the season progresses, these larvae must go through a basic and profound transformation. They must abandon all of the attributes which have enabled them to live under water. And they must build from scratch all of the organs required for their terrestrial, air-breathing adult stage.

Frogs, like many species, are born or hatched before larval organogenesis is complete. Thus embryonic development continues during the first part of the larval stage. In one sense, metamorphosis is only the last part of a process that has been going on since fertilization. Immediately after it hatches, the tadpole's muscle coordination is still very poor. The mouth has not yet made connection with the gut, and the gills are still poorly developed. Thus, even though the embryo is free from its egg capsule, it cannot fend for itself yet.

The tadpole swims jerkily to a nearby rock or aquatic plant, attaching itself by means of an oral sucker. It remains attached for several days, while its gills develop and are infiltrated by capillaries. By the time the tadpole reaches 7 mm, its sex organs have begun to develop. At 8 mm the mouth begins to make contact with the gut. And at 9 mm teeth begin to develop, and so does a horny beak. When the embryo reaches 11 mm, it has developed enough to be capable of active swimming. The oral sucker begins to disappear, the corneas have become transparent, and a flap of skin has begun to cover the gills. The embryo also displays limb buds that will develop into the hind legs.

The tadpole is now a self-reliant free-swimming larva. Still its development continues. It begins to prepare itself for metamorphosis into a terrestrial frog.

The first phase of this transition is the **limb bud stage**, so called because the stumps of the hind legs are beginning to grow. During the **paddle stage**, the end of each limb bud flattens into a paddle-shaped structure. Indentations appear on the paddle, forming an outline of the toes. Knees and ankles form, and become capable of bending. During the **foot stage** which follows, the toes become well developed, and the formation of the hind limbs is completed. The tadpole is now ready to metamorphose into a young froglet.

As metamorphosis occurs, the front legs develop and the beak is shed. The mouth widens and loses the embryonic parts which were specialized for vegetarianism. The gills are resorbed, and so is the tail. The excretory system reorganizes to handle urea instead of ammonia. When metamorphosis is completed, the animal has been transformed into a small frog. The next to the last stage in development is growth to full adult size.

Timing and coordination are immensely important in the restructuring of a creature as complex as a tadpole. For instance, it would be disastrous if the tadpole lost its tail, which propels and steers it through the water, before developing the legs it will need on land. Differentiation in this case must be sequential. First, the tadpole must grow legs. Then it can afford to resorb its tail. But in switching from ammonia to urea excretion, the situation is entirely different. The tadpole must shift the relative amounts of several different enzymes for the change to be made. And unless all of them are properly readjusted, the chemical processes of excretion will not work properly for either ammonia or urea. In this case it is necessary to adjust a whole series of enzyme levels almost simultaneously. Finally, all of the changes involved in metamorphosis must be carefully coordinated with one another.

(A)

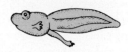
(B)

(C)

(D)

18-11 Amphibian metamorphosis in a frog. (A) Premetamorphosis stage. The tadpole is a free-swimming larval form. (B) and (C) Growth of the hindlimbs and start of development of the forelimbs. (D) Climax stage. The mouth of the tadpole widens, the ears form, and the tail is resorbed.

Both urea and legs are needed for terrestrial living. So the development of one must occur in step with that of the other.

*Silkworm hatching*    The hatching of a silkworm pupa from its cocoon occurs during the final step in metamorphosis to the adult form. The silkworm cocoon is made up of two proteins. One is the silk itself, or fibroin, and the second is sericin, which serves as a glue. To escape from its cocoon, the silkworm manufactures a digestive enzyme, **cocoonase**. This breaks down the sericin, leaving the fibroin fibers in a flexible state.

Cocoonase is made in a pair of structures called **galeae**. Each galea consists of units made up of a duct cell and a giant cell in which zymogen, the inactive precursor to cocoonase, is produced and stored.

On the ninth day after the pupa begins to metamorphose, the Golgi bodies of the zymogen cell start to synthesize large amounts of a single zymogen protein. This protein moves out of the Golgi bodies and into the zymogen vacuole of the cell. Synthesis accelerates and continues from the ninth to the fourteenth day. During this peri-

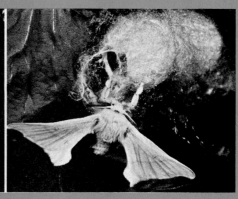

**18-12**
The larva of the silkworm moth has a growing period of about 45 days. During this period it reaches a length of 3 inches. But it still looks very different from the adult form it ultimately assumes. Toward the end of its period of growth, the silkworm spins a cocoon that is the place of pupal development. (It is also the major source of commercial silk.) During pupation, the internal and external structures are replaced by those typical of the adult form. Finally, the adult silkworm moth with its hairy body and wings emerges from the cocoon. It looks very different from the larval silkworm.

od, the zymogen accounts for more than 70 percent of all protein synthesized within the giant cells. The vacuole itself contains almost pure zymogen. On the fourteenth day, the galeae secrete tiny droplets of concentrated cocoonase onto the face of the moth. These droplets quickly evaporate. They leave behind a crystal of virtually pure cocoonase, which is not yet active.

The cocoonase crystals sit on the moth's face for one to two days after deposition, until metamorphosis is complete and the moth is ready to escape from its cocoon. Then the labial gland, strategically located between the two galeae, starts to secrete large amounts of virtually pure potassium bicarbonate buffer. The cocoonase promptly dissolves and begins digesting the sericin. When it has finished, the moth need only push apart the remaining fibroin fibers and step out into the world in adult form.

### The repair of injuries

All animals have at least some power to repair the injuries that they receive. The simplest type of repair process is **cell replacement**. In many tissues, cells continually die and are sloughed off or otherwise disposed of. So there must be a continuing renewal process that replaces those lost cells, in order to maintain proper tissue geometry and function. But when an animal suffers a cut or a burn, a certain amount of tissue destruction occurs. To repair this,

more than mere cell replacement is needed. The local structure and organization must be built. This process is called **tissue restoration**. Finally, a whole limb or organ may be lost or destroyed. The process which restores such a complicated structure is known as **regeneration**.

The process of repair is much the same as that of development and differentiation. The major difference is that the repair builds on a foundation of already developed tissues and organs. With development that foundation is missing. The process uses the same basic mechanisms as does embryonic development. This tells us that once a structure is completed, the developmental forces which produced it do not disappear. Instead, they persist to some extent throughout adult life. And they can be reactivated when the need arises.

*Cell replacement* The epithelium serves as a good example of cell replacement. Epithelial cells are subject to damage by environmental forces. For example, the outermost epithelial cells of our skin are exposed to dehydration by the air. They also

**18-13**
Cell replacement in skin epithelium.

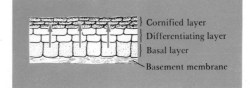

Cornified layer
Differentiating layer
Basal layer
Basement membrane

are exposed to lethal ultraviolet radiation from the sun, and to heat, cold, and mechanical disturbances. The epithelial cells which line our stomach and intestines are exposed to strong acids and digestive enzymes. As we might expect, the outermost epithelial cells die rather quickly. When they do, they are sloughed off and must be replaced.

The skin epithelium rests upon a basement membrane. It is composed of three separate layers. Next to the basement membrane is a single layer of **basal cells.** Above this is a layer of **differentiating cells.** At the top is a **cornified layer.** This is made up of dead or dying cells that are continually sloughed off.

To replace cells which die in the cornified layer, the basal cells undergo continual cell division. This active division produces extreme crowding. Thus it generates mechanical pressures which force excess basal cells upward into the next layer. Here the cell stops dividing. It begins differentiating into a cornified epithelial cell. As it becomes progressively more cornified, it is gradually pushed upward into the top layer by the upward flow of cells from the basal layer. Once in the top layer, it replaces an older cell which has died and been discarded.

*Tissue restoration*   The ear of a mouse is a very thin structure. If a wound is made in the ear, epithelial cells from the periphery of the wound migrate into the wounded area and cover it. As they do this, both these cells and epithelial cells in undamaged regions near the wound increase their rate of division. Basal cells divide more rapidly than usual. Cells in the differentiating layer, which normally do not divide at all, begin division. As this continues, the wounded area fills up with fresh cells. These cells now begin to change into basal, differentiating, and cornified cells.

Why is it that cells suddenly begin dividing when an injury occurs? One possible explanation is that under normal conditions a growth inhibitor is produced which prevents most cells from dividing. Injury would destroy some of the cells which produce this inhibitor. Therefore, there would be less inhibitor available. This would tend to release cells from growth inhibition and permit them to resume cell division.

Such an inhibitor exists, and is called a **chalone.** Many tissues put out their own unique type of chalone. Each type inhibits a particular target tissue from dividing. Since most cells tend to divide unless repressed, a decrease in the amount of chalone as a result of injury will favor a resumption of division.

For some reason, chalones do not greatly affect the cells which produce them. Instead, they inhibit nearby cells of a different type. Thus, in skin epithelium, the chalone is produced by basal cells. But it is the differentiating and cornified cells that are prevented from normally dividing.

*Regeneration*   With wounding, tissue organization is destroyed locally. But nearby regions remain intact. They can serve as a foundation for reconstruction. With severe damage such as amputation, whole organs or limbs may be destroyed. When this happens the entire structure must be completely re-created, much as it was first created during embryogenesis.

The ability to regenerate varies enormously from one type of animal to another. In general, simpler organisms have a better regenerative capacity than complex ones. But there are numerous exceptions. For

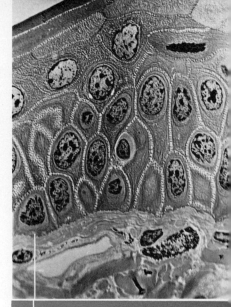

Basement membrane

18-14
(A) Stratified squamous tissue from the skin of an amphibian. Stratified tissues are named according to the cell type closest to the surface. The lower cells replace surface ones as they are destroyed or sloughed off. Cell shrinkage during preparation of the specimen accounts for the unusually wide intercellular spaces and reveals the strands of cytoplasm which connect adjacent cells.

18-15
Tissue restoration, showing the high rate of cell division at the site where the injury occurs.

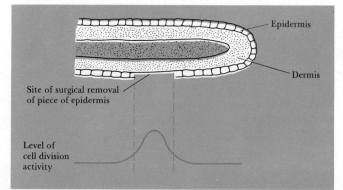

Epidermis

Dermis

Site of surgical removal
of piece of epidermis

Level of
cell division
activity

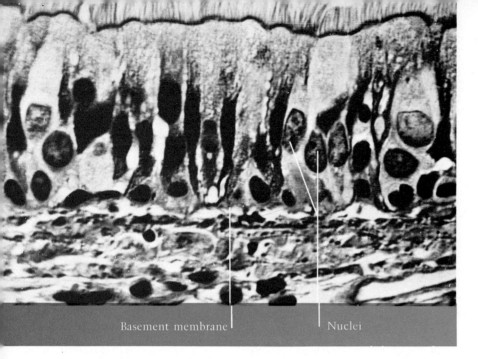

Basement membrane | Nuclei

(B) Ciliated columnar cells from the trachea of a mouse. The tissue shown here is termed pseudostratified. True stratified consists of layers of cells. But the tissue shown only seems to have several layers because the nuclei of the cells occur at different levels. Actually, all the cells are touching the basement membrane. (See Cell replacement and Tissue restoration)

18-16
Regeneration: tail of a 2-tailed southern fence lizard; arm of a starfish.

example, many coelenterates can regenerate an entire organism even after 80 or 90 percent of the animal has been destroyed. But their close relatives, the ctenophores, have almost no regenerative capacity at all. Most adult vertebrates cannot regenerate organs other than the liver. Yet frog tadpoles and even adult salamanders have enormous powers of regeneration.

When a salamander's leg is amputated, a stump is left behind with a raw wound. The first step in regeneration is wound healing. Epidermal cells from the intact epithelium of the stump migrate across the open amputation surface. They provide a protective covering. Several days later, dermal cells from the stump also migrate. They

form a layer underneath the epidermal cells. The epidermis which covers the wound thickens into an **apical cap**. It is similar to one formed during the normal development of the limbs. If this cap is removed, the limb will not be restored.

Regeneration, like development, must take place in part through the differentiation of cells into new specialized tissues. This process, in turn, requires the presence of undifferentiated mesenchymal cells as "raw material." But after amputation there are no mesenchymal cells left in the limb stump. They have all long since differentiated into such tissues as muscle or bone. To overcome this difficulty, tissues in the stump near the amputation site undergo **dedifferentiation**. They lose their differentiated characteristics. They become, in form and function, like embryonic mesenchyme that has not differentiated.

These dedifferentiated cells now begin to group just beneath the apical cap. Here they form a new cone-shaped mass called the **blastema**. Once the blastema is formed, dedifferentiation stops. The blastema cells now begin to divide.

If the apical cap is killed by ultraviolet irradiation, blastema formation stops. If the apical cap is moved to a new location on a limb stump, the blastema cells migrate away from their original location. They then group beneath the apical cap in its new location. Thus the apical cap organizes the mesenchyme-like cells just as it organizes primary mesoderm in normal limb develop-

18-17
Increased susceptibility of organs with age. Collagen makes up 25–30 percent of total body protein in mammals. With aging, collagen becomes harder, more rigid, and less soluble. Since collagen surrounds muscle fibers, its hardening makes contraction more difficult and less efficient. This is also true for cardiac muscle. The capacity of the heart to pump blood becomes diminished. The inner layers of large blood vessels are supplied with small blood vessels surrounded by collagen. As the collagen hardens, lipids and other substances accumulate in the blood vessel. This produces an inflammatory reaction which causes the lesions associated with arteriosclerosis. The hardening of collagen also makes the large blood vessels more rigid. This in turn causes high blood pressure.

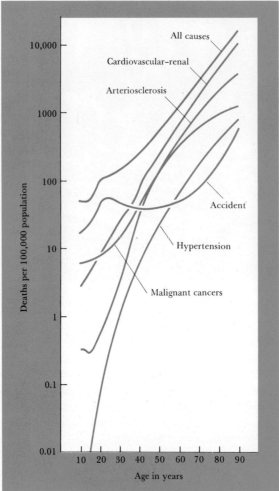

## Senescence

Senescence is the process of growing old. In one sense, many of the simpler living organisms of our planet are immortal. That is, they may be killed by accident or an enemy, but they do not ever suffer old age. Such creatures as bacteria live indefinitely unless killed by outside forces.

But as one moves up the evolutionary tree, there is a transition from immortality to mortality. Higher plants and animals grow old and die. Of course, germ cells are effectively immortal. Human germ cells faithfully carry their genetic information from one generation to the next. Time after time they use it effectively to create human beings. Yet the human dies even though his germ cells—providing they can successfully engage in the reproductive process—do not. So while the human species lives indefinitely, individual humans die after a few decades.

Why did evolution grant eternal life to simple animals yet deny it to more advanced creatures? It would seem for the sake of ecological stability. Many higher animals are reasonably well protected against death by predators. If they did not age and die, their numbers would increase rapidly. In time they would exhaust the supply of food and space in their respective environments. Death by aging, then, prevents serious overpopulation. It also ensures that individual organisms controlling the status quo at a particular moment will eventually be eliminated. This creates the opportunity for them to be replaced by new individuals with slightly different genetic endowments. In turn, this promotes evolution and the development of new species.

The wearing down caused by aging is well known. But the mechanisms underlying senescence remain largely a mystery. Many theories have been advanced, but evidence exists to support only three of them. Even this evidence is limited. Perhaps research will soon clarify the process and its relation to development.

ment. One reason that frogs do not regenerate limbs is that they do not form an apical cap.

We must now look at one of the few aspects of limb regeneration that differ from normal limb development. If the nerves of an amputated limb stump are destroyed during the first week of regeneration, regeneration immediately stops. Evidently, nerves are required for limb regeneration. As noted, adult salamanders regenerate limbs readily. Adult frogs and lizards cannot regenerate at all. Comparison of these animals shows that salamanders have many nerve fibers in their limbs. But frogs and lizards have far fewer. If extra nerves are surgically rerouted from other parts of the body into the stump of an amputated

frog limb, the limb can then regenerate. So we note a second reason why some animals do not normally regenerate. It is that they do not have a sufficient supply of nerves.

How is it that nerves promote regeneration? The answer is not yet clear. We do know that for limb regeneration to occur, nerve endings must make contact with the epithelium. In frogs, the dermis forms over the wound before nerve endings can make this contact. In salamanders, though, nerve endings are able to reach the epithelium before the dermal barrier forms. So regeneration of a limb requires three conditions. (1) adequate innervation, (2) apical cap formation, and (3) nerve—epithelium contact before the dermal layer covers the wounded surface.

summary

The development of a vertebrate embryo begins when a sperm fuses with a mature egg, forming a zygote. The sperm and egg nuclei fuse and their membranes dissolve. This allows the nuclear materials to intermingle. After an interval of DNA replication a spindle is formed. Both sets of chromosomes mix, line up, and begin to separate. Cleavage then occurs, dividing the zygote into two daughter cells. As cleavage continues, a cavity called the blastocoel forms in the center of the embryo. The cells become arranged in a single layer around the blastocoel. In gastrulation, an indentation forms along the vegetal region of the embryo. Its rim is known as the blastopore. Cells on the surface of the embryo migrate toward the blastopore. They enter the interior of the embryo. Now the indentation enlarges. The cavity which it encloses becomes the primitive gut, or archenteron. As the archenteron grows, the blastocoel collapses, forming a neural tube. Neurulation is followed by organogenesis, the differentiation of the endoderm, mesoderm, and ectoderm layers.

Gametogenesis is the formation of germ cells destined to become eggs or sperm. It occurs early in embryogenesis. The nuclear material of the sperm condenses into a head which is capped by the acrosome. This contains enzymes vital to the fusion of sperm and egg. A powerful flagellum is developed for propulsion. Before fertilization, the maturing egg cell stockpiles reserves of lipids, proteins, and carbohydrates (the yolk). It also stores ribosomes (for protein production), enzymes, and mitochondria. The egg cell then remains metabolically inactive until stimulated by a sperm cell.

When the sperm contacts the outer envelope of the egg, its acrosomal tip breaks down, and lytic enzymes are released. Inside the egg envelope, the acrosomal membrane makes contact with the egg plasma membrane. This forms a fertilization cone. The egg plasma membrane then fuses with the acrosomal membrane to make sperm and egg effectively a single cell. A fertilization membrane forms to protect the egg and to prevent penetration by additional sperm.

After the early stages of development, when differentiation is preprogrammed, cells begin to react to their environment. The process by which cells influence one another's differentiation is called coupling. Coupling may involve direct cell-to-cell contact.

Development of the primitive nervous system is the first true event in vertebrate organogenesis. But the ectoderm will not fold up to form the neural tube unless it is directly associated with the underlying mesoderm which lines the archenteron roof. The process by which one tissue stimulates another, either near or in contact with itself, to differentiate is known as induction. The most common type of induction involves the interaction between mesenchyme—the embryonic connective tissue derived from mesoderm—and epithelium. Differentiation involves a sequence of mutual inductions.

In some organisms, organogenesis leads directly In some organisms  organogenesis leads directly to a fully formed adult. In many others, organogenesis produces a larva which has nearly all the functional capabilities of an adult except reproduction. Eventually the larva undergoes metamorphosis—a major reorganization of its tissues and organs—and assumes the form of a young adult.

All animals have at least some power to repair the injuries that befall them. In many tissues, cells continually die and are sloughed off. Cell replacement is the simplest type of repair process. But when tissues are damaged, tissue restoration must occur. Some animals can restore entire limbs or organs through regeneration. Simpler organisms usually have a better regenerative capacity than more complex ones.

Senescence is the process of growing old. Death by aging not only controls overpopulation but ensures that dominant individual organisms will eventually be eliminated. This gives new individuals with slightly different genetic endowments the opportunity to replace them. In turn, this promotes evolution and the development of new species. The deterioration caused by aging is well known. But the mechanisms underlying senescence remain largely a mystery.

19 human growth and development

**d**espite its wonderful complexity, the human body is much like that of other animals. It develops, as they do, from a primitive assortment of lumps, tubes, and cavities. These, in turn, originate in the union of a tiny egg or ovum, 1/175 of an inch in diameter, with an even smaller sperm cell, 1/500 of an inch long. It has been estimated that all the eggs from which the earth's present human population grew could be contained in a shoebox. All the sperm cells which fertilized them would only fill a thimble. Eggs and sperm are collectively known as germ cells. They are solely responsible for carrying on reproduction. Once they join into a fertilized egg or zygote, they begin a process of development according to chromosomal information in their nuclei. This process finally results in the formation of trillions of specialized somatic cells. The somatic cells make up all body tissues exclusive of the germ cells. They provide the framework of the human body and enable it to carry on its life functions.

Even before the zygote begins to form such vital organs as the heart and brain, it has taken the first step toward ensuring the continued reproduction of the human species. It forms a yolk sac, approximately the same size as the embryo itself. But instead of providing nourishment as it does in other animals, the human yolk sac prepares the embryo for distant parenthood by producing about a hundred primordial germ cells. About twenty-one days after the union of sperm and egg, or conception, these germ cells migrate toward the future abdominal region of the embryo. Upon arriving there about seventeen days later, they begin to form two gonads, or germ-cell-producing organs. In the male, the gonads differentiate as testes. In the female, they become a pair of ovaries.

Responding to chemical cues, an embryo which will become female develops a uterus in which her own children will one day take form. Also developed at this time are the fallopian tubes which provide a passageway from the ovaries to the uterus.

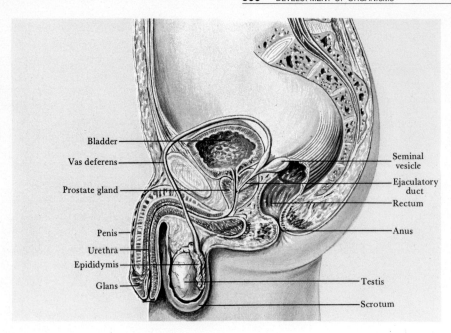

19-1
Male reproductive system.

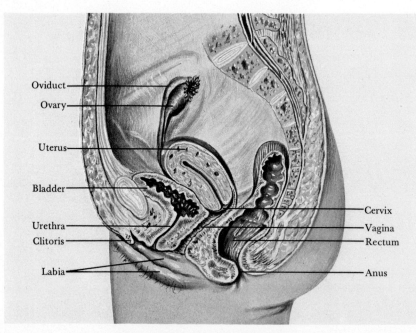

19-2
Female reproductive system.

The **cervix** forms a narrow channel plugged with mucus which permits selective passage in and out of the uterus. It connects the uterus with the flexible, tubular **vagina**, which serves as an opening to the outside.

The male testes originate in the abdomen. About 8 weeks before birth, they drop down into the **scrotum**. This is an external sac in which the testes are cooled by temperatures outside the body. Within each testis is a convoluted 20-foot passageway called the **epididymis**. This passage will collect spermatozoa from many smaller ducts and conduct them to the **vas deferens**, a canal which leads to the **seminal vesicles**. Here the millions of male germ cells or **spermatozoa**, produced each day by the mature male will be stored just before **ejaculation**, their forceful expulsion from the body through the **urethra** of the **penis**. Also formed in the tiny embryo are glands such as the **prostate**. Together with the seminal vesicles, this will produce a whitish alkaline fluid called **seminal plasma**. This viscous material mixes with and activates the previously motionless spermatozoa during ejaculation, forming **semen**.

## Pregnancy

Around the age of twelve, the female reproductive system begins to produce mature eggs, or ova, in response to hormonal cues. Of the 2 million oocytes with which the female was born, only about 400 will actually become ova. The others never mature. They function instead as **nurse cells**, surrounding and protecting each mature egg until it is released from the ovary.

The **menstrual cycle** is an egg-releasing process. It repeats itself approximately every 28 days from the time of puberty when **menarche**, the onset of menstruation, occurs. **Menopause**, the cessation of menstruation, usually takes place between the ages of 40 and 55. During the first part of each cycle, one mature ovum and its nurse cells form a **Graafian follicle** on the surface of one of the ovaries. On about the fourteenth day of the menstrual cycle, **ovulation** occurs. The Graafian follicle bursts, spewing forth the ovum and its nurse cells into the body cavity. In most cases, they are drawn into the trumpet-shaped mouth of the nearby fallopian tube by its finger-like projections and cilia. If the ovum is not fertilized at this time, it will continue down the tube and into the vagina, and be passed from the body. The blood-rich mucous membrane which lines the uterus each month in preparation for a possible pregnancy also is eventually passed from the body.

Under sufficient sexual and psychic stimulation, hundreds of millions of spermatozoa are mixed with seminal plasma and propelled forcefully by muscular contractions through the penis of the man. Few of these sperm cells will survive the trip to the ovum. Out of the vast number moving randomly in every direction, some must make their way through the nearly lethal acidity of the vagina, the mucus of the cervix, and the long-distance swim through the uterus to reach the fallopian tubes. Only those sperm cells which happen to head down the tube containing that month's egg stand a chance of fertilizing it. These must swim upstream against the muscular and ciliary waves which are carrying the egg toward the uterus. Many will be trapped in bends along the way, and disposed of as foreign matter by white blood cells. The spermatozoa are also short-lived. They can only survive for 72 hours at most in the female's upper reproductive tract.

Despite these obstacles, there are a number of factors working in favor of fertilization. For one thing, the sperm are somewhat protected from the acid female secretions by the alkalinity of the seminal plasma. During ovulation, the female passage-ways also become more alkaline than usual. The mucus plug in the cervix becomes less obstructive. Contractions of the uterine muscle apparently help to draw the

sperm cells toward the fallopian tubes. And, by a mechanism not yet understood, the few thousand spermatozoa which finally enter the fallopian tube may be somehow guided toward the ovum.

## The embryo

If a sperm cell chances to collide with a viable ovum, it must penetrate the outer covering of the egg—the **zona pellucida**—in order to effect fertilization. As it enters the inner cytoplasm of the ovum, the sperm cell loses its tail and head covering. It leaves only the 23 chromosomes from the father which are contained in its nucleus. The arrival of the sperm cell stimulates the previously immobile ovum to activity.

For the first month or so after fertilization, the **embryo** develops at a remarkable rate. It grows from a single fertilized germ cell the size of a needlepoint into a quarter-inch being composed of millions of cells. These cells are organized into primitive nervous, digestive, muscular, circulatory, and skeletal systems.

*Cleavage* The first **cleavage** occurs in the fallopian tube, about 36 hours after fertilization. The chromosomes from the original zygote nucleus double, split, and pull apart, as furrows begin to grow between the two halves. But even when they have completely disengaged, the daughter cells are usually held together within the zona pellucida by some cohesive force. Rarely, the first cleavage results in splitting of the zona pellucida and complete separation of the daughter cells. In such cases, twins of identical genetic makeup are produced. Fraternal twins are somewhat more common than identical twins. They are dissimilar siblings who originate with the simultaneous fertilization of two eggs by two different sperm cells.

By about 48 hours after the pregnancy has begun, the two cells produced by the first cleavage have divided again. Now the pace of cleavage accelerates. Within a few hours of the 4-cell stage, the cluster of pro-

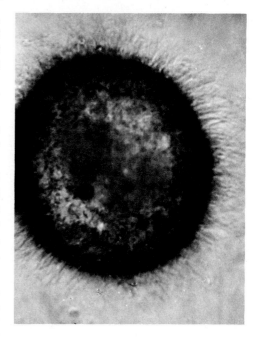

19-3
Zona pellucida. The zona pellucida can be seen here as the clear, gelatinous membrane surrounding the ovum. Its name means "an area that admits light." What looks like a thick coat of hair on it is actually the hundreds of sperm needed to soften it with their enzyme secretions. Only one of this horde will penetrate the zona pellucida and fertilize the egg. (See The embryo)

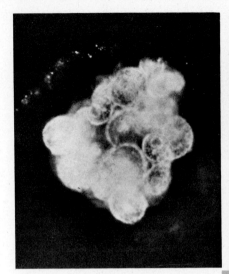

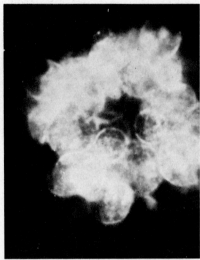

liferating cells—perhaps 16 to 32 of them— forms what is called a **morula**. This descriptive term is derived from the Latin word for "mulberry." Still cleaving, the morula passes down from the fallopian tube into the more spacious uterus.

*Blastulation*   The identical cells of the morula stage now begin to take on different functions, following their chromosomal blueprint. The cluster of cells reaches the uterine cavity about four days after conception. By this time it has formed a hollow ball, or **blastocyst**. At the center is a liquid-filled cavity called the **blastocoel**. As this cavity grows larger, most of the cells group themselves to one side of it. There they form the **embryonic disc** or **blastoderm**, which will become the embryo. The remaining cells are spread thinly around the rest of the sphere. They will develop into the **chorion**, or covering for the embryo.

Within the blastoderm, cells differentiate into two layers. The thicker outer layer, or ectoderm, will become the nervous system, skin, and sensory organs. The inner layer, or endoderm, will develop into the lining of the digestive tract. In humans, as in most other animals, a third layer will form later. This layer, the mesoderm, will give rise to many organs and the skeletal and muscular systems.

**19-4**
Late morula and late blastocyst. (A) At the late morula stage, the embryo is still in the fallopian tube. It shows a typical berry-like shape. (B) The blastocyst, or mammalian blastula, is here seen to have organized itself around the central blastocoel, which is normally filled with fluid. The cells are beginning to differentiate into those that will become the embryo (blastoderm), and those that will form its protective covering (trophoderm). (See Blastula)

*Implantation*   Seven to nine days after the pregnancy begins, the free-floating blastocyst is now composed of several hundred cells. It burrows deep into the lining of the uterus, rupturing blood vessels. This stimulates the mother's tissues to regroup protectively about it. This **implantation** is a gradual process which lasts several weeks. During this period, glycogen from the bleeding maternal blood vessels bathes the embryo and provides it with its first food. The pinpoint-sized embryo begins to grow rapidly, at first doubling its size every day.

At the same time, cell differentiation creates two new cavities within the blastocoel. The **amniotic cavity** is located near the outer wall. It fills with amniotic fluid, which will cushion and protect the floating embryo. The other becomes the yolk sac.

Twelve days after fertilization, the chorion develops fingered projections, or **villi**. These enable it to break the uterine blood vessels during implantation, capturing some of the mother's digested food and oxygen for the embryo. The villi also return waste products to the ruptured uterine capillaries, from which the mother's unruptured blood vessels absorb and dispose of them. This important exchange mechanism formed from the fetal chorion and part of the uterine lining later develops into the **placenta**, an intermediary organ attached to

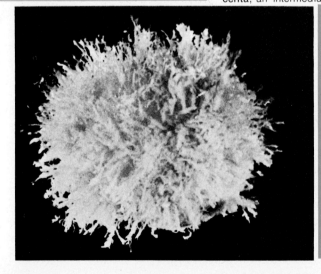

**19-5**
Trophoblastic processes. The trophoblast is the epithelial tissue that forms the fetal side of the placenta and the outer layer of the chorion. The villi are visible as the finger-like projections. They rupture blood vessels in the uterus to obtain from the mother's blood the substances needed by the developing human. (See Implantation)

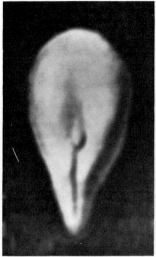 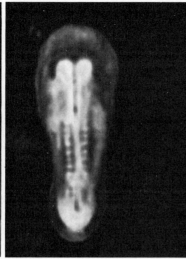 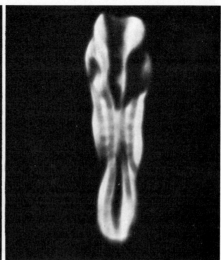

**19-6**
(A) Embryonic disc, about 13 days after conception. The bulge of cells visible in the photograph and the nearby groove running lengthwise to it form the "primitive streak." This is the main axis of the embryo. (B) and (C) Human development at 19 and 21 days. Neural folds have risen on either side of the primitive streak. They have joined to form the neural tube. By the twenty-first day, a primitive brain has formed at the anterior end of the neural tube. Smaller depressions on either side of it are the rudiments of eyes. The short, horizontal bands near the middle of the neural tube are the somites, or segments, which will develop into the muscular and skeletal systems.

the baby's body by the umbilical cord.

The placenta allows the mother's body to carry on digestive, excretory, circulatory, and respiratory functions for the immature embryo and fetus. Following the laws of diffusion, nutrients dissolved in the blood move from a region of high concentration to one of low concentration, or from mother to fetus. This exchange takes place across membranes without actual mixing of fetal and maternal blood. The embryo therefore receives only selected materials from the mother. For instance, it absorbs antibodies against infection, but not the infections themselves. The exceptions are diseases carried by viruses small enough to slip through the placental filters.

The period from 18 to 28 days after conception is extremely important. It is called the neurula stage because the critical development of the nervous system takes place at this time. Earlier in the first month, a thickening of cells appears along the main axis of the embryo. During the neurula stage, neural folds rise on either side of this groove. They soon join above it to form a neural tube. This tube becomes a spinal cord with rudimentary eyes, a primitive brain which begins to control movements six weeks after conception, and early neurons reaching all parts of the body. Alongside the neural tube, 40 pairs of segments,

or **somites**, develop. They form the basis of the skeletal and muscular systems.

Development in this critical early period is so complex that failures often occur, and embryo growth stops. Perhaps 30 to 50 percent of all fertilized eggs never develop into babies. Many stop growing during the first two weeks when the mother is not even aware of having conceived. During a **miscarriage**, the mother experiences lower abdominal pain and vaginal bleeding. The embryonic tissue is then expelled from the uterus and through the vagina.

## The fetus

About five weeks after conception, the rapidly developing embryo begins to assume human features. It is no longer indistinguishable from embryos which will become chicks, mice, or elephants. It is now called a **fetus**, its name until birth.

*Period of development*    From embryonic beginnings, the fetus develops rapidly. One month after conception, the quarter-inch embryo is one-third faceless with a jelly-like trunk. What appears to be a tail is the protruding tip of the future spinal column. It is curled into such a tight curve that the head and tail almost touch. At thirty days, arm and leg buds, pelvic muscles, optic stalks for eyes, a stomach, an esophagus,

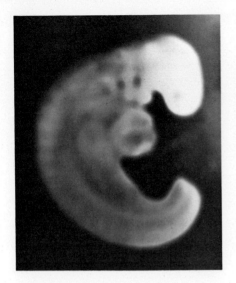

19-7
(Top) Human development at 28 days. By
the end of the first month, the embryo is a
quarter inch in length and curled up
tightly. At one end of it we can see the
faceless head region. The vestigial
structure at the other end looks like a
tail, but is an extension of the neural
tube. Beneath the head of the embryo and
barely visible is the bulge of the
incomplete, S-shaped heart. It contains
primitive veins and arteries. (Bottom)
Human development at 35 days. The arm
and leg buds (short, squat projections
from the body) have formed. Because the
digestive organs are growing so rapidly,
they protrude as a very noticeable pouch
from the abdominal region. (See
Implantation and The fetus)

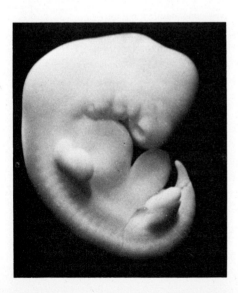

heart valves, and nerve root fibers make
their appearance. The fetus begins to look
distinctly human as its tail gradually disappears, the back straightens, and hand and
foot plates develop fingers and toes. A face
develops with jaws, nostrils, pigmented
eyes, and ears formed from the gill arches.

Inside, changes are occurring at a very
rapid pace. So it is less confusing to follow
the development of the major vital systems
individually than to follow the day-to-day
changes in the fetus as a whole.

Despite the effective functioning of the
placenta, the fetus cannot continue to grow
unless it begins to circulate its own food
and waste products. At the end of the first
month, the developing fetal heart bulges
visibly beneath the head. By the end of sev-
en weeks, the heart is functionally complete, with mature valves and chambers. By
the fourth month, it is circulating 25 quarts
of blood a day through the fetus. (In contrast, the adult heart will pump 72,000
quarts of blood each day through the equivalent of 100,000 miles of blood vessels.)

The digestive tract develops from a
simple food canal which runs from the
mouth area to where the anus will be. A
stomach, intestines, liver, and pancreas all
differentiate from this primitive tube. At first
they take up so much space that they protrude pot-bellied from the fetus's abdomen.
The anus opens during the eighth week,
when the rectal passage is completed.

Three distinct sets of kidneys evolve.
The first set, or **pronephros**, is a pair of non-
functioning structures similar to those of
primitive eels. These are supplanted by the
**mesonephros**, frog-type organs which
temporarily perform some excretory functions. During the second month they are
gradually replaced by the tubules of the
permanent mammalian kidneys, or **metanephros**. In the third month, the metanephros begins to filter wastes from the fetal
bloodstream, occasionally passing urine
into the amniotic fluid through the newly
developed bladder. By the eighth or ninth
month, the fetus may be swallowing the

continually replenished amniotic fluid at a
rate of 6 to 8 pints every day, deriving some
nutrition from it. The mother's body will continue to perform most excretory functions
until birth. But the fetus must be prepared
to take over completely once it is born.

The lungs also must be fairly well developed for their function in the newborn, so
they develop early. They are not needed for
intrauterine life, since the fetus receives
oxygen through the placenta from the mother's bloodstream. If the fetus swallows a
bit of amniotic fluid early in its development, some will go into the normally col-
lapsed fetal lungs. This stimulates them
to expand and contract as though they
were receiving air.

By the end of the third month there is a
clear difference between the sexes. Certain
reproductive structures begin to form
around the thirty-eighth day after conception. **Milk lines**, the precursors of mammary
glands, develop in fetuses of both sexes.
The mother's hormones give boys as well
as girls the initial ability to produce milk.
However, boys will lose this potential once
they are separated from the maternal hormones at birth. By the forty-sixth day, the
testes and ovaries have developed far
enough that boy and girl fetuses can be distinguished with the aid of a microscope.
During the third month, the lumps which will
be a clitoris or penis become better defined, and related glands begin to form.

The fetus begins to make small coordinated movements during the third month. At
first it responds totally to any stimulus.
When it is touched at any point, the whole
body jerks. But by the end of the third
month, its developing brain and musculature enable it to react locally and appropriately to stimuli. If we could stroke its lips,
it would make sucking motions with its
mouth, just as it will after birth when nursing. It can kick its feet, turn its head, curl its
toes, make a fist, and open its mouth. These
abilities result from the extending and maturing of its muscular system, which was
laid down only a few weeks before as 40

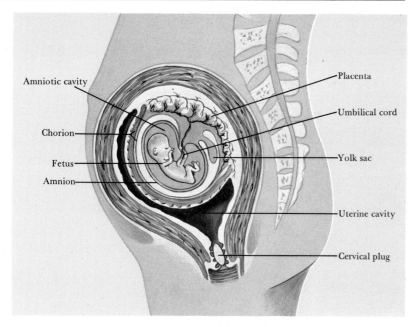

**19-8**
Human embryonic membranes. Shown here are the embryo's protective covering (the chorion) and other structures associated with it (the amnion, yolk sac, and placenta). The umbilical cord is an outgrowth of the gut. It connects the fetus to the placenta. Initially this is done through a network of embryonic blood vessels. Ultimately it is through two fetal arteries and a fetal vein.

crude somites along the spinal column. The growth of the brain is so important that, like the protruding digestive system, it enlarges faster than the rest of the body. At two months, almost half of the fetus is head, giving it a markedly top-heavy appearance.

*Period of growth*    Despite the phenomenal development of its vital systems, the fetus grows very little in size during the first three months. By the end of the first three-month period, or **trimester**, it weighs only an ounce and measures about 3.5 inches from the crown of its head to its rump. During the second trimester, the fetus gains weight to about 1.5 pounds. The body elongates, and it assumes more adult proportions.

Its heart is now pumping regularly, the hardening of its bony skeleton is well under way, and its reproductive structures are organized. Lungs, digestive tract, nervous system, and musculature are developed in miniature. We might suppose that the fetus is ready for independent life if it had to leave the uterus at this time. But if delivered during the second trimester, it would almost surely die for want of a number of finishing touches. At this stage, for instance, the fetus

has no temperature-regulating mechanism. The **hypothalamus** of the brain, which controls temperature regulation, develops early, but it does not begin to function until the end of the third trimester. The sweat glands which will help to cool the body through evaporation have formed. But they will not open to the outside until the fetus is seven months old. The fat deposits which insulate the newborn against heat loss will not accumulate until the eight month.

*Period of intelligence*    The fetus continues to grow rapidly, putting on weight to an average at birth of 7.5 pounds. During the third and last trimester, development is centered on the growth and refinement of the central nervous system. This system will receive a complex variety of stimuli from all parts of the body and coordinate the baby's activities, both voluntary and involuntary.

The fetal brain begins as simply the larger end of the central neural tube, but it gradually fills with nerve cells. They form on either side of the **brain stem**, a central liquid-filled cavity which is continuous with a similar canal in the spinal cord. The brain receives messages from the primitive neurons, relaying instructions to appropriate muscles through the developing spinal cord. The two hemispheres or **forebrain**, located in the upper part of the brain stem, grow enormously. In human fetuses they cover all the other brain structures. Deep convolutions form in the **cerebral cortex**, the covering of the forebrain. These greatly increase its surface area without necessitating a larger skull. Specific sections of the cortex will initiate voluntary movement and provide awareness of sensations in specific parts of the body. The cortex is the seat of logical thought, memory, and imagination. The intellectual activities which occur here will distinguish the child from lower animals.

The synaptic pathways established before birth represent only a part of those present in the adult brain. The neural network of the fetal brain is wired according to chromosomal directions for innate responses and abilities, which are similar in all humans. After birth, many other paths will form among the brain's cells as a result of the child's learning experiences. But it already "knows" how to see and hear.

The number of neural linkages in both an adult and a fetus is highly speculative. But a few instinctive responses are presumably facilitated by fetal brain connections. These have been noted in newborns immediately following birth, and also in premature babies born seven months after conception. The **sucking reflex** is triggered in the baby when its lips are touched. A **rooting reflex**, in which the head turns in search of food, is stimulated by touch on the baby's cheek. If its body position is suddenly changed or if it is surprised by a loud sound, the baby throws its arms and legs out in a startled **Moro reflex**. If placed on its feet it tries to walk in a **step reflex**. If given something to hold on to, it will show a strong **grasp reflex**, and the toes will curl if the sole of the foot is stroked. Babies born seven months after conception have such a strong grasp that they can support their own weight while hanging from a clothesline by their hands. Perhaps the grasp reflex is left over from the days of a hairier simian ancestor whose babies had to cling tightly to the mother's fur as she moved about.

*Damaging prenatal influences* Since the critical refinements of the last few months prepare the fetus for extrauterine life, babies born before fullterm (about 266 days after conception) have decreased chances of surviving. Ninety-nine out of 100 fullterm babies delivered in the United States live. But only 70 percent born at 8 months and 10 percent born at 7 months survive. Even fullterm survivors may have problems of improper development which show up after delivery as birth defects. In this country, one out of every sixteen babies is born with some defect. Among the most common are Mongolism, cleft palate, clubfoot, and heart malformations.

Many of the 250,000 yearly incidences of birth defects in this country could have been prevented by proper prenatal care. Only 20 percent of the total are **inheritable anomalies**, genetic disturbances such as cystic fibrosis and sickle-cell anemia which were passed on from the parents. The rest are **congenital anomalies**. Some of these result from the combination of an inherited tendency and exposure to a certain damaging influence.

Destructive environmental prenatal influences are known as **teratogens**. A number of these have been pinpointed as possible causes of congenital birth defects. Certain infectious diseases in the mother, such as rubella or "German" measles, mumps, syphilis, and polio, may reach the fetus. They are caused by viruses small enough to pass through the placental filter. These diseases may be responsible for abnormalities including blindness and deafness. Whether they affect the fetus at all, and in what way they alter it, often depends upon its stage of development. The first 3 months are the most critical period. For instance, if the mother has a fever during the third month while the fetus's hearing is developing, the child may be born deaf. Unfortunately, the central nervous system is always vulnerable to damaging influences, since it continues to develop from embryonic stages until birth.

A number of drugs may be teratogenic. Thousands of deformed babies were born in West Germany during the 1960s to mothers who had innocently used the tranquilizer thalidomide. Cigarette smoking may have damaging effects, dangerously altering fetal circulation, lowering the oxygen content of the blood, stunting growth, and often causing premature birth. If morphine is used, fetal addiction and respiratory problems may result. Heroin use can cause convulsions and even the death of the newborn.

Exposure to radiation from radioactive materials and diagnostic X-rays may cause irreversible chromosomal abnormalities,

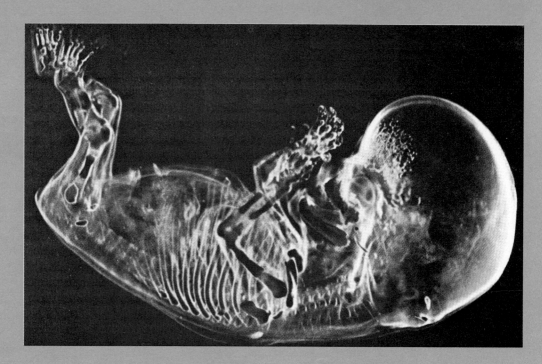

19-9
For many years, the only means of examining the fetus *in utero* was by X-ray pictures taken through the mother's abdomen. The X-ray is now used with caution because of its possible harmful effects. It is being replaced in many medical centers by ultrasound. Sound waves far too high to be heard by humans are beamed at the mother's abdomen. As they bounce back off certain surfaces, the echoes are recorded on a screen. The dot-picture they form reveals whether the fetus is alive or dead, whether it is mature enough to survive early delivery to counteract developing problems, and whether it suffers from any of 40 detectable defects.

leukemia, or brain damage in the embryo or fetus. It is not certain just how much radiation the human fetus can tolerate at various stages. But as a precautionary measure, some physicians recommend aborting a pregnancy if the mother has been exposed to 10 roentgens or more of X-rays. This is 100 times the normal radiation received from one X-ray.

Many other destructive prenatal influences have been found to cause congenital abnormalities. Extreme pressure or temperature change may damage the fetus despite the protection offered by the uterus. Its growth may be affected by too much carbon dioxide, too little oxygen, anesthesia, diabetes, or inadequate nutrition in the mother. Deficiencies in most vitamins, proteins, and minerals all can hamper development.

Recent research has uncovered teratogens in startlingly common substances. If blighted potatoes containing an antifungus chemical are eaten during the first month of pregnancy, two known defects may result. The first, spina bifida, is a crippling and

sometimes fatal gap in one of the vertebrae which allows the spinal cord to protrude. The other, anencephaly, is a fatal defect in which the brain and the top of the head do not develop.

## Childbearing

There seem to be hundreds of possibilities that something may go wrong somewhere during the development of the fertilized egg into a 9-month-old fetus. In spite of this, 93 percent of the babies born in this country appear normal and healthy at birth. The expulsion of the fetus during the process of childbearing marks the time when protected intrauterine life gives way to independence in the outside world.

During the ninth and last month in the uterus, growth slows. The placenta begins to degenerate as the fetus prepares for the critical moment of birth, when it must take over its own breathing, digestion, and excretion. The fetus is now 14 to 15 inches from crown to rump, and weighs from 6 to 8 pounds. It fills the entire grossly enlarged uterine cavity, and can no longer move freely. Nonetheless, the fetus somehow manages to reverse its position shortly before birth. Upside down, with its head well down into the mother's widening pelvic area, it is oriented to squeeze through the narrow birth canal.

A major deciding factor in the newborn baby's survival is the ability to take its first breath. This is second in importance only to its capacity for temperature regulation. The tiny unused **alveoli**, or air pockets within the lungs, must inflate with air within 30 seconds after birth. The oxygen they take in must then be traded for carbon dioxide in the blood sent from the heart. The gasping reflex which results in the start of breathing is apparently triggered by the effects of an intolerable buildup of carbon dioxide in the bloodstream.

## Labor

The first and longest stage of childbearing is appropriately called **labor**. The mother's body must work hard to push a 6-to-8-pound baby out through the narrow opening in the bony pelvis and vaginal canal. To make the baby's passage possible, the muscular cervix guarding the neck of the uterus gradually dilates from its normal one-half-centimeter diameter to perhaps 10 centimeters. It is further stretched by downward pressure from the baby's head. The vagina prepares for the birth process by secreting glycogen, which turns into antibacterial lactic acid and thus sterilizes the birth canal.

As the cervix begins to dilate, the muscular walls of the uterus begin involuntary rhythmic contractions. At first these may be 10 to 15 minutes apart, lasting only 15 to 25 seconds. But they will eventually increase to about 1 minute in length and occur every 2 or 3 minutes. The contractions will generate an average pressure of 25 to 30 pounds during the first stage, and up to 60 pounds in the second, or expulsive, stage.

The change to the expulsive stage takes

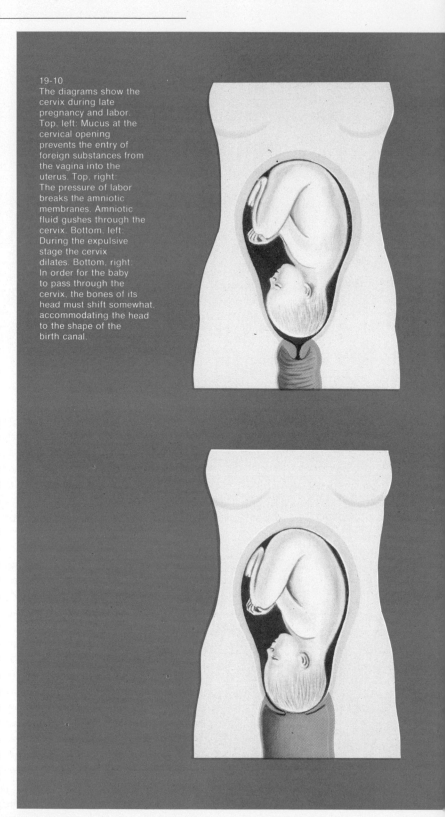

19-10
The diagrams show the cervix during late pregnancy and labor. Top, left: Mucus at the cervical opening prevents the entry of foreign substances from the vagina into the uterus. Top, right: The pressure of labor breaks the amniotic membranes. Amniotic fluid gushes through the cervix. Bottom, left: During the expulsive stage the cervix dilates. Bottom, right: In order for the baby to pass through the cervix, the bones of its head must shift somewhat, accommodating the head to the shape of the birth canal.

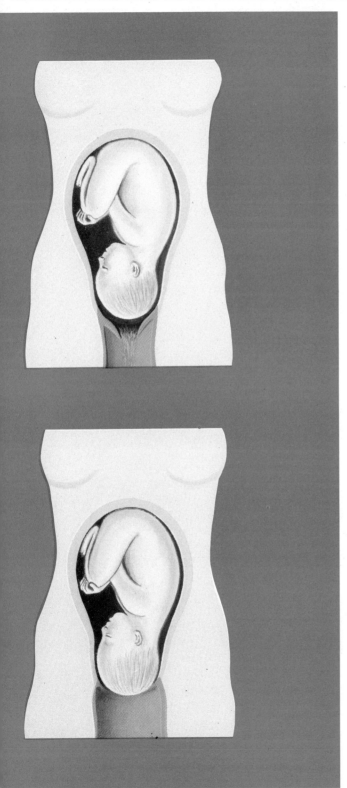

place suddenly when full dilation of the cervix allows the baby to pass through. It is usually preceded by a gush of amniotic fluid when the pressure of labor breaks the amniotic membranes. Now the head presses against the lower vagina and bowel, triggering terrific bearing-down efforts by the mother to move the mass out of her body. The baby is forced downward by the combination of uterine and abdominal contractions. Its head rotates to present its narrowest facet, the crown, to the birth passage. The bones of the baby's skull are not yet fully fused, so they can shift slightly to accommodate themselves to the structure of the birth canal.

## Delivery

Labor averages 7 to 12 hours of contractions. It is ended by **delivery**, the passage of the baby through the birth canal and its emergence from the mother's body. Its head will begin to appear in the vaginal opening, normally facing toward the mother's back.

Once the head has negotiated the tightest parts of the birth canal, the doctors tugs gently at it. The rest of the body slips out with relative ease. But if the baby has somehow failed to turn upside down in the uterus, it may present itself rump-first. Such **breech births** account for only 3.5 percent of all vaginal deliveries, and extend the duration of labor by about an hour. They present the danger that the baby might start to breathe before he is out of the mother's body, and thus suffocate. In about 1.5 percent of vaginal births, the baby presents itself either crosswise—shoulder-first—or face-first, with the front, rather than the small back of the head, leading the body down the birth canal.

About 6 to 7 percent of all births in this country are performed by **caesarean section**. In this procedure the baby is surgically removed through an incision in the mother's abdomen and uterus. Named after Julius Caesar, who is said to have been born this way, the caesarean section may be required if the baby is too large to pass

## Nursing

If the mother is awake during the delivery, she may hold the baby after its examination. Depending on hospital procedures and the mother's own preference, she may be encouraged to try **lactation**, or breast-feeding. If she elects not to breast-feed, she will be given medication to halt milk production. A formula will then be prescribed for bottle-feeding of the baby.

Women who breast-feed their babies have no milk in their breasts at first. Instead, the breasts secrete a yellow fluid called **colostrum**. Colostrum supplies few calories, but it is rich in antibodies which give the baby a share in its mother's resistance to disease and infection until it can develop its own. The fluid also furnishes the newborn with protein, minerals, and vitamin A, and acts as a gentle laxative.

Unless the baby is sleepy from depressant drugs given to the mother for pain relief, it will suck vigorously when put to the mother's breast. The sucking stimulates impulses to the mother's hypothalamus. This brain center immediately signals the pituitary gland to release the hormone **oxytocin**, which is carried rapidly through the bloodstream to the breasts. There it induces contraction of the alveoli, tiny milk-producing sacs. The sacs squeeze out their contents into ducts which lead to pores in the nipples of the breasts. Within a few days, the alveoli are producing milk as food for the newborn. They are stimulated by the baby's sucking and by another hormone released by the pituitary gland at delivery.

The mother's diet influences the quality of her milk. She must have a balanced diet rich in protein, vitamins, iron, calcium, and fluids, to ensure ample production of high-quality milk as well as to meet her own nutritional needs. Severe malnutrition in a nursing mother may cause mental retardation in her baby since her milk is its only food at first, while its nervous system is still developing.

through the mother's pelvis, or for considerations of maternal or fetal health. Caesarean sections are usually done before labor is expected to begin. However, they are sometimes performed as an emergency measure if the fetal heartbeat drops dangerously low during an attempted vaginal delivery.

As soon as the baby emerges from the mother's body, mucus is sucked from its mouth and nose with a syringe to clear its breathing passages. Its first cry is a reflex gasp as its lungs fill with air, and it begins to breathe. The baby is still attached by the umbilical cord to the placenta, which has not yet left the mother's body. This allows it to receive the last few surges of blood from the placenta before the cord is clamped and cut.

In normal hospital procedure, an attendant cleans and dries the newborn and injects it with vitamin K to prevent hemorrhaging. Silver nitrate drops are put in its eyes to prevent infection. The baby is then checked to see that it is capable of normal, healthy, independent life. Newborns are rated on a scale called the **Apgar Scoring System**, according to their pulse rate, breathing, muscle tone, reflex irritability, and color. Very low scores may call for life-saving measures.

## Afterbirth

Meanwhile, mild contractions continue in the mother. The placenta, or afterbirth, is finally expelled about five minutes after the baby is born. As the placenta tears away from the walls of the uterus, the uterine cells bleed briefly before they are closed by the muscles of the uterus. The uterus begins to shrink to its former size, no longer containing baby, placenta, or amniotic fluid. Breast-feeding will stimulate uterine contractions to continue for some time. This forces the discharge of lingering wastes and helps the organ to shrink to one-tenth to one-twentieth of the size it had reached before delivery.

# Family planning

The most ancient methods of avoiding unwanted children were abortion and infanticide. But eventually it was understood that intercourse was the cause of conception, and a variety of ways were suggested to prevent pregnancies before they happened. Methods of **contraception**, or prevention of conception, have been reported from nearly every society and every period of history. They include plugging the vagina to block the opening of the cervix with everything from feathers and grass to crocodile dung, attacking the sperm through vaginal applications of substances such as lemon juice and gum arabic, and even slitting the penis so that semen seeps out before it can enter the vagina.

Modern contraceptive measures today require more than simple pregnancy prevention. Couples want contraceptives which will not disrupt intercourse or make it less pleasurable, will not require inconvenient equipment or frequent trips to the doctor, will be aesthetically satisfactory, harmless, inexpensive, and close to 100 percent effective. But no current method meets all these requirements. Up to one-third of the babies born in this country are still unplanned for. Some are also unwanted, which creates a variety of social problems. Family planning advocates hope eventually to ensure that every child added to the world's population is born to parents who genuinely want and are prepared to care for it.

## Natural methods of contraception

The only completely reliable natural method of contraception yet devised is total **abstinence**, or avoidance of intercourse. Ova are viable for 12 hours after ovulation, and sperm for up to 72 hours after ejaculation. So the time to be avoided is the three days before ovulation and the half-day following it. This form of contraception by partial abstinence is called the **rhythm** method. The period when conception is most likely has traditionally been calculated by recording the length of the menstrual cycles over a year's time, and then guessing when ovulation must be taking place. It usually occurs about midway between periods, or more accurately, 12 to 16 days before menstrual bleeding starts. But 99 percent of all women have irregular menstrual cycles. This makes it very difficult to be sure when intercourse is safe, and the ban must be extended to cover a large part of the menstrual cycle.

In a new technique, the woman keeps a meticulous daily record of her basal body temperature (BBT) taken before she gets out of bed in the morning. The temperature will show a rise of $0.50°$ to $0.75°F$ at the onset of ovulation. Three days after this rise, intercourse is presumed safe until the next menstrual period. It is not allowed at all before ovulation. But even if these methods are supervised by a physician and strictly adhered to, the rhythm method based on body temperature still fails to prevent conception in 7 out of 100 women every year. The failure rate of the calendar rhythm method is 16 out of 100. Both limit intercourse considerably, as well as requiring extreme self-discipline and exacting computations.

The oldest of all contraceptive methods appears to be **coitus interruptus**. This involves withdrawal of the penis from the vagina before ejaculation. It is perhaps the most common form of contraception in the world today, though not very popular in this country. Withdrawal requires extreme control on the part of the man. Pregnancy can result from failure to withdraw in time, from seepage of even a few drops of semen before ejaculation, or from semen deposits on the external female genitals. Coitus interruptus may limit the woman's sexual satisfaction and relief of congestion in her erectile tissues through orgasm. It may also have negative psychological effects on the man. But it is 78–85 percent effective, requires no equipment or elaborate calculations, and allows intercourse at any time. It appears to be largely responsible for the slow population growth in Europe.

## Mechanical methods of contraception

Various mechanical means have been devised to prevent the passage of semen to the fallopian tubes or to prevent implantation if conception has occurred. The **condom** is usually a thin rubber sheath. It is fitted over the erect penis before ejaculation to trap semen. The condom not only keeps sperm from entering the vagina, but also inhibits the spread of venereal infection from one partner to the other. Unless it tears, as it may once in 150 to 300 times, or slips off and spills semen into the vagina, the condom will effectively prevent pregnancy, especially if used along with a sperm-killing vaginal lubricant. It is harmless and from 83 to 88 percent effective. But drawbacks to its use include interruption of foreplay and possible dulling of sensation.

In another mechanical method, the woman uses a **diaphragm** or a **cervical cap**, which must be fitted by a doctor. The device is placed by the user over the cervix, preventing the entrance of sperm into the cervical canal. The diaphragm is a rubber hemisphere on a flexible metal ring. It must be inserted before intercourse and left in place for at least eight hours after. The smaller cervical cap is more difficult to place accurately, but it may be left in place for almost the entire time between menstrual periods. If used with spermicidal chemical preparations, these devices are about 88–90 percent effective, and harmless to women who are not allergic to rubber. But because of the nuisance factor, many women fail to use them with every copulation. Diaphragms can slip out of position when sexual excitation causes ballooning of the upper part of the vagina.

The **IUD**, or **intrauterine device**, is a very effective but controversial mechanical contraceptive. It is now used by about 6 mil-

lion women around the world. Made of plastic or stainless steel in a variety of shapes, the IUD is surgically inserted into the uterus and can be left there indefinitely. The woman can check for its presence by feeling for the ends of a string tied to the device and left protruding slightly from the cervix. It is not yet certain just how IUDs work. But they apparently prevent implantation by irritating the uterine lining, creating an environment hostile to the fertilized ova. However, this constant irritant may disturb the uterus so much that the device is expelled from the body, sometimes without the user's knowledge. An expulsion rate of 10 to 12 percent lowers the effectiveness of the IUD, and it may not always prevent pregnancy even when properly in place. Depending on the type of device, the age of the woman, and her number of previous pregnancies, IUDs are 92 to 98 percent effective. They prevent conception without requiring motivation or self-discipline on the part of the user. But in some women they may cause severe bleeding, pelvic inflammation, infection, or perforation of the uterus. Questions on other side effects, such as a possible link between IUD use and cancer, must be answered after long-term usage by large numbers of women.

A new prospect for mechanical male contraception is a removable clip, plug, or microvalve designed to shut off the vas deferens. This would prevent passage of sperm from the male's body, without damaging surrounding tissue. The dangers of such methods are the impairment of male sexual behavior, and the production of a partially damaged sperm whose defects are congenital.

## Chemical methods of contraception

There is a chance that conception can be prevented if the vagina is flushed immediately after intercourse with a **spermicidal** (sperm-killing) solution. Vinegar in water or prepared spermicidal solutions are often

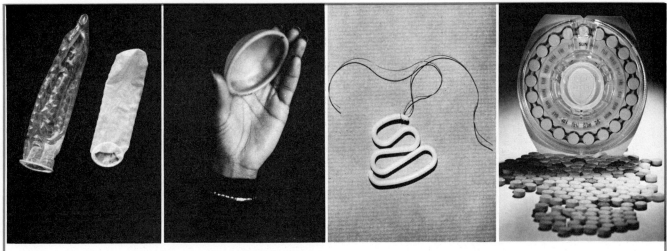

19-11
From the left: condom, diaphragm, I.U.D., and birth control pills.

used in this **douche** method. However, the spermicidal douche method is only 40 to 66 percent effective. This is because sperm cells can disappear up the cervical canal within 90 seconds of ejaculation.

Strongly spermicidal creams, jellies, foam, or suppositories inserted *before* intercourse are far more effective than emergency douching after the fact. They can be up to 90 percent effective when used in sufficient quantity. But they often lead to messy drainage from the vagina. They are much more likely to prevent pregnancy when used with mechanical barriers such as condoms, diaphragms, or cervical caps.

An entirely different sort of chemical intervention is now available in the form of **oral contraceptives**, or birth control pills, which are taken daily for most of the menstrual cycle. The pills contain synthetic hormones resembling estrogen and progesterone. They prevent ovulation but allow monthly shedding of the uterine lining through menstrual bleeding. "Combination pills" contain both estrogen and progesterone. Taken as directed, they are about 99.7 percent effective. "Sequential pills" (in which those taken at the beginning of the

cycle contain only estrogen) are 98–99 percent effective. But while they are the most effective birth control method ever created, oral contraceptives have a number of undesirable side effects. They create a hormonal situation similar to pregnancy. This may cause weight gain, breast tenderness, headaches, nausea, light bleeding between periods, and water retention, especially during the first few months of their use.

The sequential pills have proved helpful to women who experience unpleasant side effects from the combination pills. However, there appears to be a high correlation between a certain type of cancer and use of the sequential pills. The most severe problem defintely associated with oral contraceptive use is abnormal and sometimes fatal blood clotting caused by the estrogen. Of every 100,000 women using oral contraceptives, 3 will die every year from blockage of blood vessels by blood clots. This rate is several times as high as deaths from blood clotting among non-users. Advocates of birth control pills point out that 25 out of every 100,000 women who become pregnant die from the effects of childbearing, concluding that pill use is the lesser evil. The long-range effects of continuous suppression of ovulation are still uncertain. However, they may involve changes in carbohydrate metabolism, and liver and thyroid gland functioning.

Progress has been slow in the search for a chemical method of male contraception to inhibit either the production or the function of sperm. One method now under thorough investigation is the suppression of gonadotrophic hormones. This would be done by administering progesterone to inhibit sperm formation and testosterone to maintain normal sex characteristics. However, progesterone is believed to induce the loss of libido. Large amounts of testosterone may also cause metabolic or cardiovascular complications.

## Radical methods of birth control

Increasing numbers of people are now resorting to extreme measures to prevent unwanted births. Where liberalized laws permit, many women are choosing to end their pregnancies by **abortion**, or surgical removal of the fetus when it is too young to survive outside the mother's body. The old method of abortion is by dilation and curettage under anesthesia. The cervix is stretched and a loop-shaped **curette** is used to scrape the uterine cavity. **Aspiration** is a newer method of abortion. It involves a virtual vacuuming of the uterine contents by a suction device. Both methods of abortion are occasionally subject to complications. These may include perforation of the uterus, hemorrhaging, incomplete removal of fetus and placenta, and infection.

**Sterilization** is permanent surgical prevention of the release of germ cells. This method may be chosen by men and women who no longer want to be able to create pregnancies. In men, one such method is **vasectomy**, a relatively simple procedure which can be performed in a doctor's office. Small incisions are made in either side of the scrotum. The vas deferens from each testicle is tied in two places, and the part in between is cut out. No sperm cells can then reach the urethra, but erection is unimpaired and the volume of semen will diminish only slightly by the subtraction of spermatozoa. Sperm cells continue to form but they degenerate and are reabsorbed in the epididymis. The operation is 100 percent effective in preventing pregnancy, unless the two ends of vas deferens form a new canal for the passage of sperm. This occurs in 1 out of 100 vasectomies. and can be detected by analysis of the semen. After vasectomy, there is an initial waiting period for the structures leading to the urethra to be completely emptied of sperm cells.

Until recently, sterilization of women was a major surgical procedure, since it involves cutting into the body cavity. Interruption of conception is usually achieved by tying off and cutting the fallopian tubes. Eggs continue to be released but they cannot reach the uterus. Access to the tubes requires an incision either in the abdomen or through the top of the vagina. Female sterilization by **laparoscopy** is a relatively new technique requiring only brief hospitalization. The laparoscope is a tube with a magnifying glass and a light source. It is inserted through a tiny abdominal incision and the abdomen is inflated with carbon dioxide to push the intestines out of the way. The revealed fallopian tubes are then cut and cauterized by slender instruments inserted through the laparoscope. Although not yet fully tested, another technique for sterilization has been developed which promises to be safe, effective, and simple. It requires only a few hours of hospitalization. In this procedure, a piece of rubber called a **fallope ring** draws up each fallopian tube and holds it tightly. The tube becomes fibrous once its blood supply is cut off.

Both male and female sterilization operations are largely irreversible. But they are 100 percent effective, and offer a final solution to preventing undesired pregnancies.

summary

Unlike other animals humans have a yolk sac that produces primordial cells which differentiate into sperm-producing testes and egg-producing ovaries. The female menstrual cycle begins at about the age of twelve. Midway through this cycle, the egg bursts from its protective covering in a process called ovulation. If not fertilized, it passes from the body through the vagina.

Four days after fertilization in the fallopian tubes, the zygote migrates to the uterus. It is now called a blastocyst. It differentiates into the blastoderm, or future embryo, and the chorion, a protective membrane. Implantation is a gradual process. The embryo grows rapidly, burrows into the lining of the uterus, and breaks down uterine capillaries. It captures some of the mother's digested food and oxygen through the placenta.

During the neurula stage, 18–20 days after conception, the nervous system begins to develop from a primitive streak along the lengthwise axis of the embryo. It gives rise to a primitive spinal cord, eyes, and brain. About five weeks after conception, the developing embryo is called a fetus.

During the first three months, the fetus begins to develop its vital systems. By the end of seven weeks, the fetal heart can pump blood in and out of the placenta. The digestive tract develops from a food canal that runs from the mouth to the anal area. Kidneys and lungs develop during the latter part of this period. At the end of the development period, there are clear differences between the sexes. The fetus also reacts locally to stimuli, by means of its brain and muscle systems.

During the period of growth (3–6 months), the fetus gains weight, the head becomes less prominent, and the legs grow longer. But it still lacks a temperature-regulating mechanism, and cannot yet live independently. During the period of intelligence (6–9 months), the nervous system grows and differentiates. The forebrain is covered by the convoluted cerebral cortex, where human thought processes occur. Instinctive responses have been observed in newborns, but many other synaptic paths are formed after birth as the result of learning. In the ninth month, fetal growth slows, and the placenta starts to disintegrate.

Births defects can be divided into two types. Inheritable anomalies are genetic disturbances. Congenital anomalies result from both inherited tendencies and damaging environmental influences. These influences include drugs, radiation, and disease.

Childbearing, the expulsion of the fetus, occurs through involuntary uterine contractions. Labor is the first and longest stage of childbearing. The cervix dilates through contractions that grow more frequent and violent until full dilation of the cervix allows the baby to pass through. Delivery usually begins with the emergence of the baby's head. During afterbirth the placenta is expelled through mild contractions.

Lactation, or breast-feeding, begins after childbirth with the secretion of colostrum. This is a yellow fluid rich in antibodies and vitamins. Within a few days the alveoli, stimulated by the hormone oxytocin, empty their contents into pores leading to the nipples, and begin to produce milk.

Contraception is the prevention of pregnancy. Abstinence is the total avoidance of intercourse. The rhythm method involves abstinence during the most fertile part of the menstrual cycle, which usually varies. Coitus interruptus involves the withdrawal of the penis from the vagina before ejaculation.

Mechanical means of contraception prevent passage of the semen to the fallopian tubes, or prevent implantation if conception occurs. Condoms, thin rubber sheaths, fit over the penis to prevent semen from reaching the vagina. Diaphragms, large rubber hemispheres on flexible metal rings, and the smaller cervical caps, prevent the entrance of sperm into the cervical canal. IUDs are metal or plastic devices inserted into the uterus. They appear to prevent implantation by irritating the uterine lining.

In the douche method of chemical contraception, the vagina is flushed with sperm-killing solutions. Oral contraceptives suppress ovulation through hormonal means. Except for abstinence, they are the most effective birth control method.

An ultimate contraceptive method is sterilization, the permanent surgical prevention of the release of germ cells. In men the operation is called a vasectomy. It is relatively simple to perform and 100 percent effective. Sterilization in women once involved major surgery. Simpler methods have now been developed. Abortion is a means of terminating pregnancy rather than preventing conception. It involves the removal of a fetus from the uterus before it is old enough to survive on its own.

# 20 basis of evolution

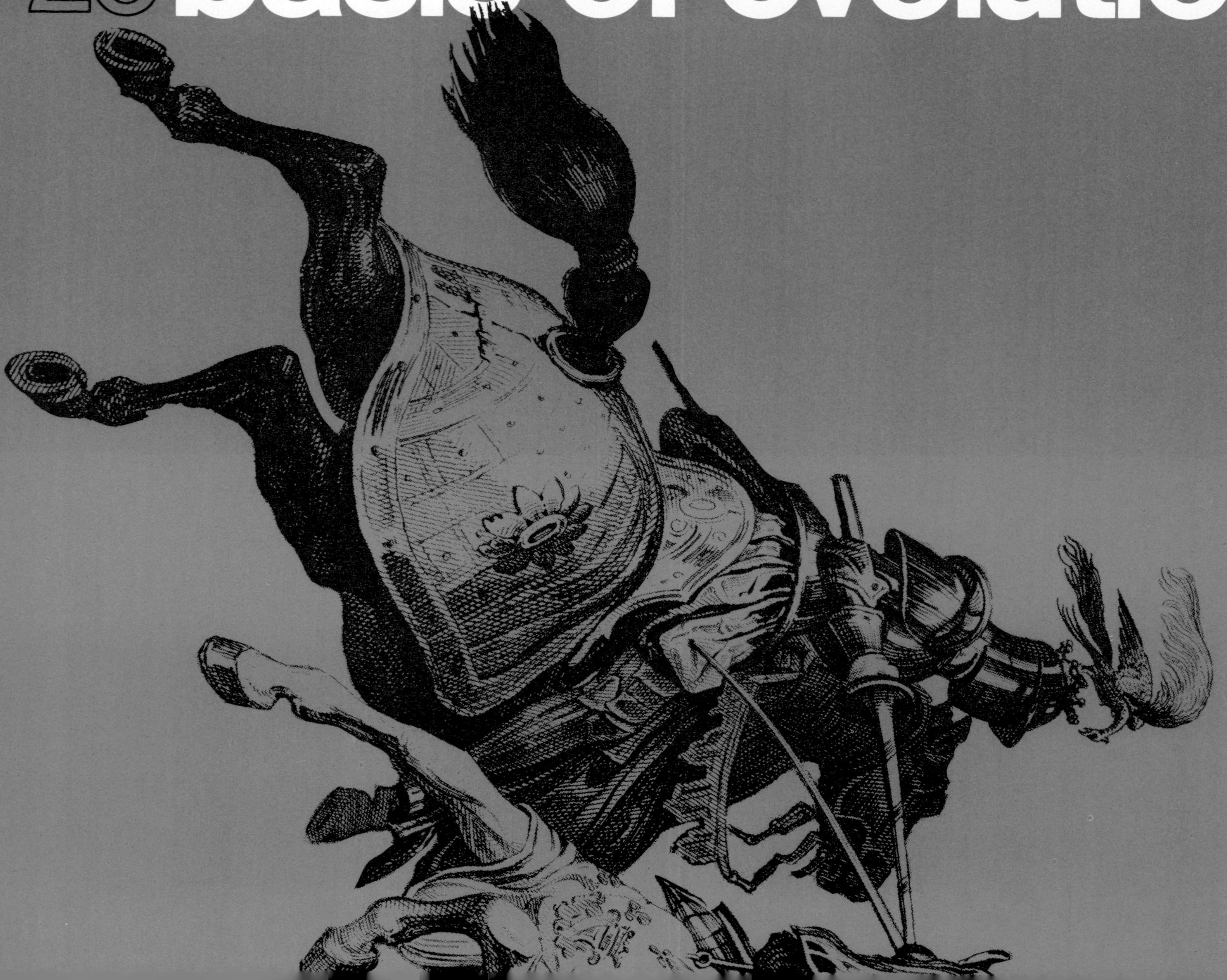

**t**he biological history of all of the earth's organisms and the geological history of the earth itself have one thing in common: constant change. The changes that occur during the relatively brief life of an individual organism are generally referred to as developmental changes. Evolutionary changes are the long-term directional changes in one or more characteristics of a group of individuals, or population. Such changes are slow and spread over many generations. So we can only rarely watch evolution take place. But when we compare the many forms of life on earth today with the fossilized forms of only a million years ago, we see that very few living things remain unchanged. And when we study forms with very short individual life spans, such as the insects, we can observe changes over as little as 20 or 30 years. An example of such change is the evolution of insecticide-resistant pests during recent years. Finally, the creation of entirely new species by plant and animal breeders shows that new forms of life can be produced from previous forms.

But these discoveries are relatively recent. Before we could bring about such changes in life forms we had to understand the process by which change occurs. And before that we had to accept the idea that change occurs at all. The evolutionary process is slow, and the life span or "observation time" of the human being is short. These factors both contributed to scientific acceptance of Aristotle's concept of fixed and unchanging nature. Until the end of the eighteenth century, his ideas were rarely questioned throughout the Western world.

But in 1809, the French scientist Jean Baptiste de Lamarck formally proposed that life on earth evolves slowly and continuously. His theory of evolution was based on the notion that individuals have an internal need to achieve perfection, and that the characteristics which they succeed in developing in themselves are inherited by their offspring. So each generation would start off in a better position than the pre-

**20-1**
Support for Darwin's ideas came from the work of his friend and contemporary, Charles Lyell (1798-1875). Lyell believed that the forces of change operating on the earth's surface were constant and gradual, rather than catastrophic. Equally important, Lyell himself supported and encouraged Darwin in formulating his theory.

**20-2**
Charles Darwin (1809-1882).

**20-3**
Dutch botanist Hugo De Vries (1849-1935) devised the first mutation theory. (See Rediscovering Mendel)

vious one, and in turn would pass on its own improvements. Lamarck suggested that one mechanism by which individuals evolve was the "use or disuse" of certain traits. Giraffes, he said, grew long necks as a result of stretching to reach leaves on the higher branches of trees. These giraffes passed on their relatively longer necks to their offspring, who continued to stretch, and so on. Similar reasoning is sometimes used to describe the process of human evolution. For example, primates who began to live on the ground no longer needed long tails and so the tails atrophied. This sort of reasoning—that individual needs or desires can bring about inheritable biological change—is often referred to as Lamarckian.

Almost fifty years later, in 1858, Charles Darwin and Alfred Wallace each independently proposed a new theory to explain how organisms adapt to their environment over time. This was the theory of natural selection. Darwin's *The Origin of Species* was published in November of the following year.

## Natural selection

The Darwin–Wallace hypothesis borrowed an idea from British economist Thomas Malthus. Malthus had proposed that for each kind of organism there is usually a vast overproduction of offspring in relation to the life-sustaining resources of the environment. Darwin's own observations convinced him that all organisms of a certain type vary among themselves as well as being different from any other kind of organism. He suggested that with an overproduction of offspring there is competition, or struggle, for survival. And in this struggle, some traits would be more useful than others. The theory of natural selection states that every species consists of a great variety of individuals engaged in the struggle for limited resources. Those organisms whose inherited characteristics best fit

them to adapt to their environment will survive and produce fertile offspring. Because more offspring thus result from the organisms with the best-adapted characteristics, they will increase in numbers in future generations.

Darwin's theory further suggested that in early giraffe populations, some had longer necks than others. All of them, however, were suited for browsing on the ground and nibbling low branches. But during periods of recurring drought, those animals with the longest necks would be best adapted to eating leaves from the higher branches. So they would obtain more food than those with the shorter necks and would more often survive to reproductive age. They would therefore produce offspring in greater numbers. This capacity is what Darwin called "fitness."

There is no absolute meaning for "fitness." It does not necessarily involve strength, or character, or intelligence, as some people have claimed. Instead, it refers simply to those characteristics that best enable an organism to leave behind fertile offspring. For example, if a fire were to destroy most of the tall trees, the long-necked giraffe would no longer be particularly fit.

Darwin's theory did away with the need to invoke a notion of progress, or striving, to explain evolutionary progression. But it did not explain how the offspring of the best-adapted individuals inherited their characteristics. Nor did it explain variation. If each individual inherited a "blend" of its parents' traits, as Darwin believed, why did the species not all gradually become uniform? Darwin's observations convinced him that variation remained relatively constant in successive generations of a population, despite the action of natural selection. But the question of how it originated puzzled him for years. Like Mendel, he experimented with crossing garden peas. He noted the three-to-one ratio of original traits that appeared in the second generation of hybrids.

Unlike Mendel, Darwin did not perceive the significance of this. And since Mendel's work had fallen into obscurity, he never did.

### Rediscovering Mendel

Near the end of the nineteenth century, Hugo DeVries, a Dutch botanist, made extensive observations of hothouse flowers. He noted how they could be bred for a wide range of colors. DeVries found that slight variations, such as shades or intensity of one particular color, could be produced by selective crossing. But he also noted that totally new colors or forms were always sudden and accidental. He referred to changes of this type as "mutations."

After years of studying primroses, DeVries discovered several totally new types. But he observed that changes did not occur in every trait at once. For instance, tulips that changed from red to purple did not also change the shape of their leaves or the size of their flowers. From this, DeVries deduced that heredity involved multiple and separate units. Next he delved into existing research to see if anyone else had thought along these lines. He came upon Mendel's long-neglected work concerning the laws of particulate inheritance. That same year two other scientists, Karl Correns in Germany and Erich Tschermak in Austria, also came upon Mendel's discoveries, and confirmed their validity.

Mutation, and the resulting success or failure of the mutant trait, soon formed the basis of the geneticists' theory of evolution. It explained both the source of variation and the mechanism of inheritance. Some geneticists even believed that every mutation instantly created a new, or potentially new, species. But Darwin's observations had indicated that most sudden changes, which he called "sports," were of themselves harmful, and thus were not selected for over time. He insisted that the process of evolution was long and gradual, taking place through a large number of very slight variations.

Naturalists supported Darwin's view. But none of them could explain how the variations originated. A synthesis of the two opposing viewpoints became possible only when geneticists began to study populations rather than individuals. This synthesis forms the basis of the modern theory of the process of evolution: (1) continuous change in the genetic makeup of a population from one generation to the next as a result of (2) natural selection acting upon (3) genetic variation. Once such a change occurs, some degree of (4) isolation is necessary to maintain and continue genetic change. We will discuss this latter aspect of evolution in the next chapter, when we consider the formation of species.

## Populations and evolution

The theory of evolution is based on the fact that it is **populations** that evolve, rather than individuals. Most organisms live in

**20-4**
Giraffe browsing among high branches. As food competition intensified the long-necked giraffes gained a survival advantage over their shorter-necked relatives. (See Natural selection)

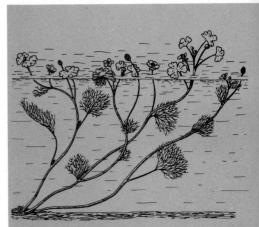

The water buttercup (*Ranunculus aquatis*) with finely divided leaves submersed and more nearly entire leaves above the water. (See Kinds of variation)

populations. A population is defined as a community of sexually interbreeding individuals at one locality. A single dog may harbor a population of fleas, an aquarium a population of goldfish, or a game forest a population of deer. For the purpose of studying evolution, the population is considered to be randomly mating. That is, each of its sexually mature members is equally likely to mate with any other of the opposite sex and produce offspring.

Every population is characterized by a common **gene pool**. This includes all the genes of all the gametes of a population. Normally, genes are not exchanged between gene pools of different species. But they may be exchanged among gene pools of different populations within a species. So each individual in a population holds only a small part of a gene pool for a very short time. But only in the entire gene pool do genes interact in the multitude of combinations that supplies the population with the variation necessary to evolution. The contributions of all individuals together invest the population with the ability to change over time.

## Types of variation

No two individuals of a sexually breeding population are identical, with the exception of monozygotic twins. In populations of plants or animals most individuals will hold a unique combination of genes called a **genotype**. Each one is unlike any other genotype in the population. If the genotype affects the size, shape, or some other visible or measurable characteristic, the organism will also have a unique appearance, or **phenotype**.

Changes in the genotype are manifested in various ways in the phenotype. But many organisms also have some traits that can be modified by the environment rather than by changes in the genotype. For example, a number of aquatic plants have finely divided leaves on the part of the stem that is under water but undivided leaves on the part that is out of water. All of the leaves

20-6
The American short-tailed weasel (*Mustela erminea*) changes the color of its coat with the northeastern seasons.

have the same genotype, since they come from the same plant. So this kind of variation is influenced primarily by the environment. This is not to say that leaf structure is not influenced by the genotype. It is the genotype that determines the range of variation.

Phenotypic variation provides the basis for the individual to adapt within a certain range. It enables the individual to respond, to a limited extent, to its environment. But genotypic variation reflects adaptation of the members of a population, enabling the population as a whole to respond to environmental changes over time. Genotypic variation can be divided into **continuous variation** and **discontinuous variation**. All populations show a range in a number of traits, such as size and weight. These are controlled by the interaction of several different genes. The more genes that are involved, the more regular, or continuous, the variation throughout the population. Continuous variation in traits such as body size and skin pigmentation often follows geographical variation. We shall examine this further in the next chapter, when we discuss the subject of races, or subspecies.

When sharp, dramatic differences characterize individuals or populations, the variation is called discontinuous. It usually occurs in traits which involve fewer genes, in some cases only one. Discontinuous variation can occur from one population to another in a species, or from one individual to another in a population. When individuals within a population differ strikingly from each other in one or more traits the population is considered **polymorphic**. Red and silver foxes, black and red ladybugs, and different patterns on the shells of snails are all examples of polymorphism.

## The Hardy—Weinberg principle

Mendel's theory explains why parental traits are not obliterated by "blending" but simply reassorted in the next generation.

at Stanford
El. 30 m

at Mather
El. 1400 m

at Timerbline
El. 3050 m

20-7
Phenotypic variation due to environmental factors. *Horkelia californica* grows wild at 700 feet. It flourished at sea level but became dwarfed at higher altitudes. (See Types of variation)

We have seen that genes influence the individual organism or phenotype. But the genetic potential of a population is determined by their proportionate representation, or frequencies, in the population's total gene pool. Because each gene may occur in two or more alleles, **gene frequencies** of a population are defined as the proportions of the various alleles of each gene represented.

Consider a cattle population of 10,000 head. In this population, color is determined by one gene, with two alleles, $R$ and $R'$. Of the total population, 5,500 cattle are red and have the genotype $RR$, 1,500 are white, with genotype $R'R'$, and the other 3,000 are mottled red and white, with the genotype $RR'$.

The easiest way to look at the gene frequencies of these cattle is to count the $R$ alleles from all 10,000 animals. There will be 11,000 $R$ alleles from the 5,500 $RR$ cattle plus 3,000 from the 3,000 $RR'$ cattle, for a total of 14,000 $R$ alleles. Since there are a total of 20,000 alleles in this population, the gene frequency of $R$ is 14,000/20,000 = .7. In the same way, we may compute that the gene frequency of the $R'$ allele is 6,000/20,000 = .3. Note that the sum of the gene frequencies for the two alleles for the same characteristics is equal to one (.7 + .3 = 1).

If we know a particular set of gene frequencies for a specific population at a given time, we can predict what will happen to the gene pool in the second generation and all future generations. We might assume that recessive genes would gradually be lost in a population, as dominant genes increase in frequency. But Mendel's experiments show that recessive genes do not disappear, even when their existence is not apparent in the phenotypes. They coexist unchanged with dominant genes in a genotype. And they are as likely to be passed on to the next generation as are their dominant alleles.

Even in cases where there is no dominance, it might seem that an allele with a lower frequency in a given population than another allele must disappear. Thus in our hypothétical cattle population, white cattle would inevitably become fewer and fewer and eventually all the cattle would be red. But in fact, the distribution of red and white cattle will remain about the same, if there are no mutations and no selective advantages, and if no new cattle join the herd. This observed pattern of constant variation was formalized in a principle developed independently in 1908 by a British mathematician, G. H. Hardy, and a German physician, W. Weinberg.

The Hardy–Weinberg principle states that under certain conditions gene frequencies in a population will remain constant generation after generation—that is, at **equilibrium**. This equilibrium implies that given these same conditions, genotypic frequencies will reach equilibrium in one generation. After that, they will remain constant. The conditions under which gene frequencies will remain in equilibrium are as follows:

1. the population is large enough to prevent errors in sampling;
2. there are no mutations;
3. there are no selective advantages,

so that all offspring will be equally viable and fertile;
4. the population is randomly mating.

When these conditions hold, the gene frequencies of the population will remain constant from one generation to the next. It is important to note that *genotypic frequencies* may alter during the first generation. But after that, they, too, will remain constant. We can illustrate this principle with our example of the red and white cattle. For simplicity, we will assume that there are 5,000 heifers and 5,000 bulls, and that each pair produces two offspring.

To find out what the gene frequencies of the second generation will be, we first determine their genotypic frequencies. A Punnett square will show every possible result of a random mating process in a parental population with the genotypic frequencies .55 *RR,* .30 *RR'*, and .15 *R'R'*. There are nine possible combinations. The frequency with which each occurs is shown in the relevant box. For example, 16.50 percent (.55 × .30) of the matings involve an *RR* father and an *RR'* mother (box 2). Another 16.50 percent (.55 × .30) involve an *RR'* father and an *RR* mother (box 4).

The mating of an *RR'* female with an *RR* male is genetically identical to that of an *RR* female with an *RR'* male. So the total num-

## The Hardy–Weinberg principle

| Parental frequencies | Males | | |
| --- | --- | --- | --- |
| | **RR** **.55** | **RR'** **.30** | **R'R'** **.15** |
| *RR* .55 | .3025 ① | .1650 ② | .0825 ③ |
| *RR'* .30 | .1650 ④ | .0900 ⑤ | .0450 ⑥ |
| *R'R'* .15 | .0825 ⑦ | 0.450 ⑧ | .0225 ⑨ |

20-8
Results of a random mating process in a given parental population.

## Genotypic frequencies of second generation of cattle

| Parental Combinations (1) | Frequencies (2) | Genotypic frequencies | | |
|---|---|---|---|---|
| | | RR (3) | RR' (4) | R'R' (5) |
| RR × RR | .3025 | .3025 | — | — |
| RR × RR' | .3300 | .1650 | .1650 | — |
| RR × R'R' | .1650 | — | .1650 | — |
| RR' × RR' | .0900 | .0225 | .0450 | .0225 |
| RR' × R'R' | .0900 | — | .0450 | .0450 |
| R'R' × R'R' | .0225 | — | — | .0225 |
| Totals | 1.0000 | .4900 | .4200 | .0900 |

20-9
The offspring of each mating receives one allele from its father and one from the mother.

ber of offspring from $RR' \times RR$ is 33 percent of the total, or 3,300. $RR \times R'R'$ is identical to $R'R' \times RR$, and $RR' \times R'R'$ is identical to $R'R' \times RR'$. So we are left with six possible parental combinations and their frequencies, as shown.

We can now use these frequencies to determine the genotypic frequencies of the second generation. Since the offspring of each mating receives one allele from its father and one from its mother, the offspring of $RR \times RR$ matings must be $RR$. The offspring of $RR \times RR'$ matings can be either $RR$ or $RR'$, and will be equally divided between the two types. So the 3,300 offspring of $RR \times RR'$ matings will include 1,650 $RR$ animals and 1,650 $RR'$ animals. When the results of the other matings are calculated similarly, we find that the $F_1$ frequencies are .49 $RR$, .42 $RR'$, and .09 $R'R'$. These are significantly different from the parental genotype frequencies of .55 $RR$, .30 $RR'$, and .15 $R'R'$.

But when we look at the gene frequencies of this generation, we find 9,800 $R$ alleles from the 4,900 $RR$ calves and 4,200 $R$ alleles from the 4,200 $RR'$ calves. This total of 14,000 $R$ alleles produces a gene frequency of .7 (14,000/20,000). We also find 1,800 $R'$ alleles from the 900 $R'R'$

calves, plus 4,200 $R'$ alleles from the 4,200 $RR'$ calves, for a total of 6,000 $R'$ alleles and a gene frequency of .3. Thus the gene frequencies have not changed from one generation to the next, although the genotypic frequencies have. The latter have now reached equilibrium. They will remain constant from generation to generation so long as the gene frequencies do not change.

### The Hardy–Weinberg law

The Hardy–Weinberg law allows us to determine the equilibrium genotypic frequencies for a given set of gene frequencies. This law states that in a random-mating population, the genotypic frequencies will be in accord with the following:

$$p^2, 2pq, q^2$$

where p and q represent the frequencies of the respective alleles. The sum of the gene frequencies is equal to unity—that is, $p + q = 1$. Now, let p represent the frequency of the $R$ allele and q represent the frequency of the $R'$ allele. In diploid, random-mating populations at equilibrium the genotypic frequencies for $RR$, $RR'$, and $R'R'$ will be equal to $p^2$, $2pq$, and $q^2$. So in our example, given the gene frequencies $R = .7$ and $R' = .3$, we know the equilibrium genotypic frequencies are .49 $RR$ ($.7 \times .7$), .42 $RR'$ ($2 \times .7 \times .3$), and .09 $R'R'$ ($.3 \times .3$).

The Hardy–Weinberg law is useful for determining gene frequencies, especially where one allele is dominant and the heterozygotes are indistinguishable from homozygous dominant individuals. The frequency of the homozygous recessive genotype, $q^2$, is, of course, the same as the frequency of recessive individuals in the population. And the frequency of the recessive gene, q, is simply the square root of $q^2$. For example, if the frequency of cattle with the $R'R'$ color genotype in a population is 0.0004, the $R'$ gene frequency (q) is 0.02. By subtracting q from 1, we find p. In this case, $p = 1 - 0.02 = 0.98$. Thus if we know how many homozygous recessives there are in a population we can determine how many heterozygotes there are, as long as the population conforms to the equilibrium conditions required by the Hardy-Weinberg principle.

But we must remember that, according to the principle, gene frequencies will remain constant only *under certain conditions*. If gene frequencies have changed, one or more of these conditions must not be operating. Several factors can upset equilibrium gene frequencies. These include mutation, selection, migration, and genetic drift. These factors, alone or in combination, influence genetic variation in a number of ways.

## Sources of variation

Genotypic variation in a sexually reproducing population originates in **recombination** and in **mutation**. However, most natural populations are not completely isolated. So a third source of variation is provided by new immigrants, or by **migration**.

### Recombination and mutation

Sexual reproduction allows recombination of genetic material by the process of crossing over. Recombination also occurs when paternal chromosomes pair with maternal chromosomes during zygote formation, forming entirely new chromosome combinations. Together these processes generate enormous variation. Once a gene pool has been established, new combinations of existing genes are usually more effective in evolution than new mutations. For example, most of the many varieties of dogs—miniature dogs, long-legged dogs, hairless dogs—have been produced by recombining genes of an existing gene pool rather than by the formation of new genes.

But another source of new chromatids—and the only source of new genes—is mutation. Mutation can occur through changes in the DNA of the genes themselves, known as point mutations. It can also occur through changes in chromosome number and changes in chromosome structure.

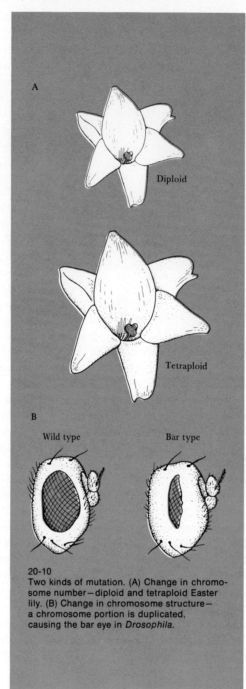

20-10
Two kinds of mutation. (A) Change in chromosome number—diploid and tetraploid Easter lily. (B) Change in chromosome structure—a chromosome portion is duplicated, causing the bar eye in *Drosophila*.

## Migration

Changes in gene frequencies resulting from migration occur through the process of interbreeding between the original population and the new immigrants. So migration provides another source of new genotypes, and thus of variation. Normal exchange of genes is still possible between the divergent populations. Therefore, migrants from one population can contribute new alleles to the gene pool of their adopted population. This passage of alleles is called **gene flow**. Its effect is to increase variation within a population.

Gene flow through migration can be a significant evolutionary force only when it occurs between relatively isolated populations with distinct gene pools. Thus the counterpart to evolutionary migration is a certain degree of isolation. This isolation need not be geographical. Individuals within a common gene pool often select mates with characteristics similar to their own. This is known as positive **assortative mating**. Both geographical and behavioral factors influence assortative mating within a population. For example, among a single fruit-eating insect population, some may feed on the fruit from one type of tree, and others on that from a different type. Individuals of both types may tend to select mates with similar preferences, simply because they encounter them more frequently. So assortative mating limits the size of the effective breeding population. The ratio of homozygous to heterozygous individuals is increased, and the Hardy–Weinberg equilibrium is disrupted.

## Restraining variation

Estimates of mutation rates vary widely. They range from one in 50,000 per gene per individual per generation to one in 1,000,000. But if we accept the conservative estimate, we can conclude that in a species of reasonable size—several million individuals—mutation occurs at a rate of at least

**20-11**
Japanese onaga-dori cock—an example of
artificial selection. (See Selection pressure)

two mutations per gene locus per generation. Together with the enormous variation provided by gene flow and recombination, this would produce a constantly accelerating degree of diversity that we do not find among most natural populations. Two forces operate against a steady increase in random diversity. The first is natural selection. The other is fluctuation resulting from accidents of sampling, known as genetic drift.

## Selection pressure

We can define **selection** as anything that systematically tends to produce differential reproduction of the genotypes in a population. If humans do the selecting, as in the breeding of certain plants and animals,

selection is said to be **artificial**. However, it involves the same biological principles as selection in nature, or **natural** selection.

In both cases, selection does not act directly upon the genes. Rather, it acts on the phenotypes which the genes produce. Phenotypes that are better adapted to their environment will survive in greater numbers than those less well adapted. Thus, the genotypes which they carry will be reproduced with greater frequency.

Selection operates to eliminate harmful genotypes produced through either mutation or migration. Consequently, it serves as a stabilizing factor. A continuous level of variation is essential in most populations, especially among species with a relatively long lifespan. This enables the population to survive under fluctuating environmental pressures. Selection that eliminates extreme forms in a population thereby favors the continuation of an average set of phenotype characters. This is called **stabilizing** selection.

Most of the action of selection is of the stabilizing type. So how can selection be considered an evolutionary force?

The fact is that selection acts in two ways. It conserves variation in a population, and it directs the population toward an optimum range. The environment is always changing, however slightly. And in a changing environment, the criterion of adaptedness also changes. If the change is such that individuals at one extreme of the population can no longer survive, selection is considered **directional**. This kind of selection is deliberately practiced by animal and plant breeders who favor extremes of productivity, yield, or appearance. Another instance of directional selection is the increase of disease-resistant strains. Insects became resistant to DDT, and rabbits to myxomatosis. This was largely due to strong selection against most of the phenotypes in a population which favored the increase of those carrying a previously rare recessive trait.

When environmental change operates

20-12
Melanic and light forms of *Biston betularia,* against lichen-covered tree trunk (left) and against soot-blackened tree trunk (right).

against the average phenotypes of a population, it begins to produce two or more extreme forms of a species. This is called **disruptive** selection. Two directional lines are established by this type of selection, each suited to a different environmental condition. We will see in the next chapter that this is significant in the formation of new species.

An excellent example of directional selection is seen in the evolution of dark populations (industrial melanesia) in the English pepper moth *(Biston betularia).* This species normally has a light color pattern resembling the lichens on the trees and rocks where it rests during the day. But during the nineteenth century, smoke pollution began to kill the lichen and blacken the tree trunks in industrial areas of Britain. As a result, a number of dark (melanic) forms began to appear among the pepper moths. The dark form, known as *carbonaria,* was

first recorded in the area around Manchester about 1845. Fifty generations later, by 1895, this form had almost completely replaced the light form in the Manchester industrial area. However, the light form remained predominant in the nonindustrial countryside.

Color in the pepper mouth is determined by a single gene. Some form of mutation, then, must have been responsible for the original appearance of the dark pepper moth. But this does not account for its rapid increase or its uneven distribution. It has been found that birds that prey upon this species are more likely to see and capture the light moths than the dark ones on the blackened tree trunks. Constant selection against the light variety in industrial areas leaves increasingly more dark moths in each generation relative to light moths. This allows more dark moths to reproduce. Conversely, the dark moths are at a selective disadvantage in the countryside where bark and lichens are light-colored. So the frequency of the light moths remains high in these areas.

The interaction of different types of selection probably accounts for most of the history of evolutionary change. In some cases, the two forces may conflict with each other. L. W. Taylor describes an experiment in which artificial selection was applied to increase the number of blades on chicken combs. The experiment was begun in 1940, using a population of chickens with one, two, and three blades on their combs. Offspring with one and two blades were separated out and only those with three blades were allowed to reproduce. After several generations, as single- and double-bladed combs decreased in frequency, chickens with four-bladed combs began to appear. By 1944 single- and double-bladed combs had disappeared entirely. But a number of five-bladed combs had joined the population. Two years later this mixture of three, four, and five blades had reached equilibrium frequencies, and thereafter remained

20-13
Directional selection overcome by stabilizing selection for blade number on chicken combs. (See Selection pressure)

constant. This example illustrates the tendency of most populations to maintain a constant level of variation, even while they are yielding to the directional forces of selection.

## Genetic drift

Selection operates toward stability in a large population, where variation is maintained by the large number of possible recombinations. In a small population, though, there is a much greater possibility that some genes might be carried by so few members that they become lost by chance. Moreover, harmful mutations may be eliminated more rapidly in a small population than in a large one, due to more frequent pairing of recessive alleles. But at any one time, small populations may contain a relatively high percentage of deleterious homozygous recessives because of this more frequent pairing. Such random changes in gene frequencies are known as **genetic drift**. They may occur in a population of any size. But they produce the greatest fluctuations in small populations characterized by little or no migration.

The frequency of **inbreeding** within small isolated populations also contributes to the operation of genetic drift. Inbreeding is a form of assortative mating that involves close relatives. The result of inbreeding, like that of assortative mating, is an increase in the frequencies of homozygous phenotypes. These are then operated on by selection, thereby changing gene frequencies.

Genetic drift is of particular interest to observers of human populations. We generally regard modern populations as comfortably large. But is is important to determine the size of the **effective breeding population** when we look at the effects of random selection. In all cases this is much smaller than the population itself—generally about one-third the size. When a rural population of anywhere from 500 to 5,000 individuals is considered apart from children and people

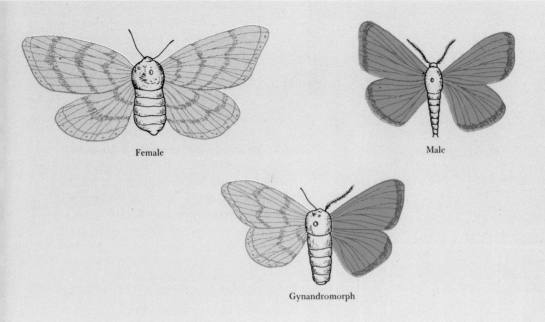

Female

Male

Gynandromorph

20-14
Mistakes on genetic direction of sexual development often result in gynandromorphs. These are organisms which have the characteristics of both sexes of their species in various parts of the body. Here a gypsy moth gynandromorph has light-colored wing and thin antenna of the female on one side of its body and brown wing and feathery antenna of the male on the other. Errors like these are usually eliminated by selection. (See Preserving variation)

who can no longer reproduce, it becomes small enough to be affected by random drift. And even in the much larger city populations, the effects of assortative mating due to religious, economic, educational, and racial preferences considerably reduce the chances of random mating. The city population is thus broken into a number of smaller effective breeding populations.

*Founder effect*    One form of random drift is known as the **founder effect**. It is often illustrated in inbreeding populations. Founder effect describes the presence of one or more harmful alleles in relatively high frequencies. It results from a nonrepresentative sample in the founders of a population. This often occurs in bird or insect colonizers of offshore islands, which may number only a single pair or even one fertilized female. Founder effect may also apply to the surviving members of a population greatly reduced by plague, famine, or some other catastrophe.

Among the Old Order Amish community in Lancaster County, Pennsylvania, the recessive Ellis–van Creveld syndrome has a frequency of 0.07. This disease causes dwarfism and polydactylism (extra fingers and toes) and often heart malfunctions in the homozygotes. Of the 100 cases reported since 1860, over 55 have belonged to this community. All of them can be traced to a man and woman who came to the United States in 1744.

## Preserving variation

The example of blade number in chicken combs illustrates that opposing selection forces protect the continuation of variation in a population. Since the environment changes constantly, the adaptive value of the genotype also changes constantly. So it is advantageous for the population as a whole to maintain as many genes as possible in the population. This allows the production of viable combinations in the face of environmental changes, chance, and migration. In addition to opposing selection

20-15

An example of hybrid vigor is hybrid corn. Different types have been produced for different growing conditions by crossing four inbred strains. Strain 1 is crossed with strain 2. Strain 3 is crossed with strain 4. The resultant hybrids are then crossed with with each other to produce new hybrid seed. This procedure must be repeated each year. This is because hybrid vigor decreases when the hybrid is inbred. (See Heterosis)

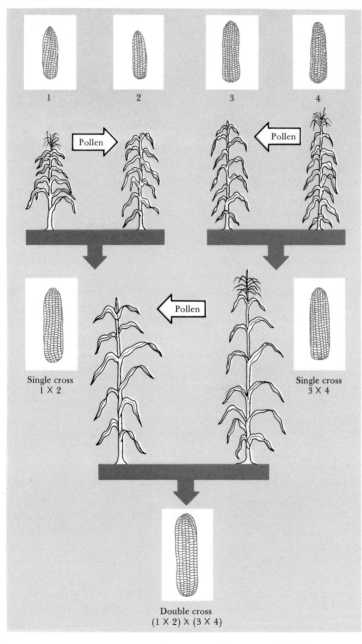

1    2    3    4

Pollen →    ← Pollen

← Pollen

Single cross
1 X 2

Single cross
3 X 4

Double cross
(1 X 2) X (3 X 4)

forces, a number of other factors contribute to the preservation of genetic variation in a population.

The adaptive value of a particular gene varies depending on its interaction with other genes with which it is combined in a genotype. Thus a great many potentially harmful genes can be tolerated within a gene pool despite the action of selection. The less effect a particular gene has on a phenotype, the less likely it is to be either favored or disfavored by selection. So it will remain at a constant frequency in a population through many generations.

If there is such a high degree of genotypic variation in a sexually breeding population, why do we not observe greater diversity in natural populations? The fact is that survival and reproduction of a species requires a fairly high degree of phenotypic similarity. Because selection operates directly upon the phenotype, it efficiently "weeds out" structurally unfit members of a population. As a result, development of every member of the species is carefully controlled along prescribed pathways.

## Heterosis

**Heterosis** is sometimes referred to as superiority of the heterozygote. It is another reason for the preservation of genetic variety in a population. This adaptive superiority may be due to the fact that the heterozygote has the benefit of two kinds of metabolite, one produced by each allele. It has the capabilities of both homozygotes. So in certain conditions, it is better adapted than either.

We should distinguish heterosis from the phenomenon of **hybrid vigor**. It is not unusual for a hybrid to be somewhat larger and more vigorous than either of its parents. Apparently this results from gene interactions that produce the phenotype luxuriance so useful in agriculture and horticulture. Hybrid corn is a well-known example. But hybrid vigor in itself does not imply any increased evolutionary fitness. On the contrary, many extremely vigorous hybrid indi-

20-16
Polymorphic variation in one species of snail, *Helicella virgata:* different banded and unbanded forms on one plant. (See Balanced polymorphism)

20-17
Blue goose and snow goose together in Squaw Creek Refuge, Mo. The two color forms were once regarded as two separate species, because of their nonrandom breeding preferences. They are now known to be an efficient form of balanced polymorphism in a single species *(Chen caerulescens).* The two plumage colors are most likely determined by a single pair of alleles. Since males of both types tend to prefer mates of the same color as one or the other of their parents, the polymorphism is preserved in relatively constant ratios. Its adaptive value apparently lies in extending the breeding season of the species.

viduals are completely sterile. They thus have no evolutionary significance. This is especially true of the first generation after crossing. Moreover, hybrid vigor decreases as the hybrid is inbred. It often disappears after three or four generations.

Heterosis, though, is an agent of evolutionary change. It is defined as a condition in which the heterozygotes have *adaptive* superiority over the homozygotes. This requires the ability not only to survive but also to reproduce.

## Balanced polymorphism

Greater fitness of the heterozygote ensures the maintenance of both alleles in populations operated upon by opposing selective forces. This results in **balanced polymorphism**, a stable proportion of two or more forms. Any imbalance in either direction will be disadvantageous for the population as a whole. But selection against the homozygotes will tend to restore equilibrium. Polymorphism is particularly useful to

species living in a variable environment. It enables one or another form to thrive under various local conditions. For example, the two forms of the British pepper moth allow it to survive in both rural and industrial areas. We can also see such variation in the different patterns of snails and butterflies, each one favored for protection in a different environment.

Balanced polymorphism is not limited to structure or behavior. Recent analysis of enzymes and other proteins reveals a previously unsuspected number of genetic polymorphisms in protein chains. Richard Lewontin and his colleagues discovered different forms of the same enzyme in numerous different species of plants and animals. In almost all species examined so far, two or more alleles exist at fairly high frequencies at about 30 to 40 percent of all loci tested. An average individual is heterozygous at some 12 to 15 percent of its loci. The same polymorphism often exists in each of several closely related species.

summary

The theory of evolution developed independently by Charles Darwin and Alfred Wallace states that natural selection favors those individuals whose traits render them best able to survive and reproduce. Their offspring will thus be represented in greater numbers in future generations. This theory proposed the concept of constant and gradual change as characteristic of all life. Geneticists later found that characteristics favored by selection are passed on from generation to generation according to Mendelian laws of particulate inheritance, thus preserving genetic variation in a population.

Populations comprise groups of individuals in one locale capable of freely interbreeding. All of the genes of these individuals form a single gene pool. The way in which each allele is represented in the gene pool determines a population's gene frequencies, or variation.

Variation is both phenotypic and genotypic. The range of both is ultimately determined by the individual genotype. Phenotypic variation represents adaptation by the individual. Genotypic variation, however, represents adaptation by the population, enabling it to change over time. Genotypic variation may be continuous, or regular, or it may be discontinuous, or sharp. When the latter occurs among individuals within a single population, it is called polymorphism.

The Hardy–Weinberg principle states that under certain conditions gene frequencies in a population will remain at equilibrium—that is, constant generation after generation. Factors that can upset equilibrium and influence genetic variation include mutation, selection, migration, and genetic drift. Sexual reproduction allows recombination of genetic material and generates enormous variation. The passage of alleles between relatively isolated populations with distinct gene pools is called gene flow. It increases variation within a population.

Forces of selection and genetic drift operate upon genetic variation. Selection acts upon the individual phenotypes to increase or decrease the representation of the corresponding genotype in a population. If selection acts to eliminate less well-adapted phenotypes at either extreme of a certain trait in favor of the average, it is called stabilizing. If it acts against one extreme only, it is called directional. If it favors both extremes at the expense of all intermediate types, it is called disruptive. Directional selection is probably most significant in terms of evolution, especially when combined with stabilizing selection.

Genetic drift, or random changes in gene frequencies, is most likely to become an evolutionary factor in a small population. This is particularly true of one characterized by a high degree of inbreeding. Due to more frequent pairing, homozygous recessives may appear in relatively high frequencies. On the other hand, some genes may be carried by so few members that they become lost by chance. Founder effect causes such changes to occur as a result of a nonrepresentative original population.

Variation is protected in any population by the combination of a deleterious recessive gene in heterozygous form. Selection favors modifying genes that render the heterozygote phenotypically similar to the dominant homozygote. Moreover, standard patterns of development are imposed upon genetic variation for traits essential to survival. Heterosis, or heterozygote superiority, has a demonstrable influence on continued variation. Geneticists increasingly believe that heterosis may explain most instances of balanced polymorphism, a stable proportion of two or more forms in a population.

Creatures of past ages: a forest of the Carboniferous Period; the woolly mammoth of
ancient northern Siberia; case of coelacanth,
a primitive fish long thought to be extinct but
rediscovered in the present century; cave
painting by the prehistoric inhabitants of
Lascaux, in southern France.

# Biological and geological evolution

| Era (and duration) | Period | Epoch | Major biological events | Major geological events | Millions of years before present |
|---|---|---|---|---|---|
| Cenozoic (70 million years) | | Recent (Holocene) | Human beings and higher animals | | 0.1 |
| | Quaternary | Pleistocene | Early *sapiens* appear; many large mammals become extinct | Glacial advances and retreats | 3 |
| | | Pliocene | Large carnivores, many modern mammals appear | Cascades uplifted | 7 |
| | Tertiary | Miocene | Grazers appear | Cooler climates; Himalyas formed | 26 |
| | | Oligocene | Many modern animal families appear | Warm climates; Pyrenees uplifted | 37 |
| | | Eocene | Modern mammals appear | Climates fluctuate | 54 |
| | | Paleocene | Modern birds appear; hoofed animals diversify | | 65 |
| | Cretaceous | | Conifers dominant; flowering plants appear; giant reptiles become extinct | Rockies uplifted | 130 |
| Mesozoic (150 million years) | Jurassic | | Primitive birds appear; insects radiate; reptiles and ammonites abundant | Warmer climate; Sierras rise | 180 |
| | Triassic | | Primitive dinosaurs, labyrinthodontamphibians | Warm, semiarid climate | 225 |
| | Permian | | Reptiles displace amphibians; insects abundant | Widespread glaciation | 280 |
| | Pennsylvanian (Carboniferous) | | Primitive reptiles and trees; amphibians dominant in great coal swamps and forests | Glaciation in some parts of the world | 310 |
| Paleozoic (380 million years) | Mississippian | | Seed ferns and lycopsids dominant; sharks, amphibians abundant | | 345 |
| | Devonian | | Primitive gymnosperms appear; amphibians appear; fishes dominant | Appalachians uplifted | 400 |
| | Silurian | | Ostracoderms; bryophytes and vascular spore-bearing plants, terrestrial animals | Appearance of shallow seas in North America | 440 |
| | Ordovician | | First vertebrates (primitive fishes) appear; marine invertebrates dominant | | 500 |
| | Cambrian | | Algae diversify; invertebrates abundant | | 600 |
| Precambrian (?) | Periods not definitely known | | Soft-bodied invertebrates; very few fossils | Glaciation on most continents | 4.5 billion years (?) |

In the grasslands, buds stay close to or beneath the soil. In this way, they manage to withstand destruction by fire or grazing. Some plants are more daring. They thrust flowers above the grass layer on tall stems to attract insect and bird pollinators. Some birds, such as the roadrunner and the secretary bird, have adapted to the lack of trees by growing long legs for fast running. (The ostrich can run up to 40 miles per hour.) Smaller animals find protection by living in underground burrows. Only the cats are solitary hunters. Most animals travel in protective herds in the open country of the grasslands. One such animal is the wild horse, or mustang. At one time, the horse's major enemy was the wolf. Today, it is people. The mustangs, along with their one-time companions, the bison and the American antelope, are nearly extinct in the wild.

Human populations are not so dominant in the tropical habitats. The rain forest has a year-round warm and moist climate. It thus supports a broad diversity of plant and animal life, much of it highly specialized to fit specific ecological niches. However, there are few duplications, especially among the plants. This is because survival is a matter of intense competition, and sometimes the niches support only one individual of a species. Flowers grow on tree trunks and branches, or dangle from long stalks. In this way they can be seen by the forest pollinators—insects, bats, and birds. Some of the plants, such as the orchids, have developed aerial roots. This enables the plants to take in nutrients without touching the ground. Between floor and canopy (the treetops) is a region of woody trunks and vines, and nonwoody parasites and epiphytes. Epiphytes are plants which usually rely on trees only for physical support. They obtain nutrients from rainwater and organic matter collected in their roots. Many normally terrestrial animals never need to come down from the trees. Tree frogs, for example, make water supplies for their tadpoles in the cup-shaped structures of the bromeliads, or in pools of water that collect on the broad leaves. In South American rain forests, the monkeys have specially adapted tails by which they can move easily among the branches and vines. Sometimes it is hard to detect animals below the canopy. Dull-colored birds hide in the woody environment. And ants and termites, two of the litter collectors in this environment, stay in their nests by day. So do their predators—owls and tarsiers, for example, which have huge eyes for seeing at night.

The barren tundra discourages all but the hardiest—or most ingenious— plants and animals. Plants crouch close to the ground. In winter, animals go under the snow or else go south. Snow is a good insulator, especially for the small animals. Hares, for example, nest under alders bent into snow-covered tents. Lemmings and voles actually dig tunnels beneath the snow. Animals with larger body mass can withstand the cold. Polar bears drift with the ice packs, stalking careless seals and swiping up fish with their huge paws. Furry soles on their feet protect them from cold and keep them from slipping. Perhaps nowhere is spring so welcome as in the tundra. Long daylight hours follow the spring thaw. The result is a burst of plant growth, which provides food for swarms of insects and birds. Many birds are migratory breeders. They

During much of the year, the grasslands can be a
difficult environment. Animals are often subjected
to cold winds and lightning fires. The openness
of the grasslands also makes it imperative that
many animals, such as the African impalas (above),
travel in herds for protection from predators.

The grasslands are home to a great number of plants and animals. Top, left: Goldfinch and chicory. Small animals, such as the prairie dog (top, right), mice, and rabbits, avoid their enemies by living underground. Only the cats hunt alone in this wide open biome. Above: Lion cubs at water hole.

Some birds have adapted to the lack of trees by
growing long legs for fast running. Top, left:
Secretary bird, Kenya. Mustangs (bottom) keep in
disciplined herds for protection while grazing,
one stallion taking charge of a harem of mares.
Top, right: Buffalo on Montana wildlife refuge.

The climate of the rain forest supports a broad
range of life. Left: Below the canopy, El Yunque,
P.R. The Puerto Rican tree frog (right, bottom)
often draws its water from pools that collect on
the leaves. Right, top: Three-toed sloth hanging
from a branch in a South American rain forest.

Most of the really colorful life is up in the treetops, or canopy, of the rain forest. Right, top: Gould's hummingbird. Right, bottom: Spider orchid, Borneo. Some animals, such as the big-eyed tarsier (left), are hard to detect below the canopy because they stay in nests by day.

Far to the north of the grasslands and rain forests is the windswept tundra. With their large body mass, caribou (above) can stay warm all winter. But they are obliged to migrate enormous distances to find enough food to accomodate their large herds.

The barren tundra discourages all but the
hardiest plants and animals. Left, top:
Ptarmigan in late winter. Left, center: Lynx
watching for beavers. Left, bottom: Purple
saxifrage, the Canadian tundra's first spring
flower. Right: The well-protected polar bear.

Life in the coral reef is very competitive, and all the animals seem to have a color trick. Left, top: Clown fish and sea anemone. Left, bottom: Scorpion fish. Right, top: Four-eyed butterfly fish. Right, center: Trumpet fish, which can look like a waving alga frond. Right, bottom: Parrot fish.

must prepare their nests, lay their eggs, and nurture their young while the summer lasts. One year-rounder is the ptarmigan. In spring and summer this bird's brown and white plumage enables it to forage undetected for berries and new shoots. In winter it turns white. Heavy feathers on its feet serve as cushions for walking.

The coral reef is an extraordinary water biome. It presents a vivid motion picture in living color. Green no longer dominates the spectrum: even the algae are disguised in hues of purple, red, and brown. As photosynthesizers, the algae provide the basic food source for life on the reef. But life in this rich environment is highly competitive. All the animals seem to have a color trick— for protection or concealment, for warning and confusing, and even for recognition. Carnivores such as the cuttlefish and the scorpion fish are almost indistinguishable from the algae. Angelfish and saddlebacks conceal their outlines against the algae, seaweed, or barnacles. The parrot fish gets its name from its beak, with which it scrapes the corals for food. An intriguing deceiver is the butterfly fish. As prey, smaller fish are usually grabbed head first. This is so that they cannot dart away when the predator fish pauses to swallow. But the butterfly fish has extra "eyes"—one on each side, just above the tail fin. This often fools the predator into snatching at the wrong end, thus improving the victim's chances of escape. But predators, too, are deceiving. The sea anemone, for example, looks like a harmless flower. But it quickly paralyzes fish who stray too near to its beckoning tentacles, then ingests them whole. Only the bright-colored clownfish is safe. The anemone allows this fish to swim freely among its tentacles. In return for this protection, the anemone receives the larger fish who are attracted by the clownfish's bright colors. How the anemone "knows" not to attack the clownfish is still somewhat of a mystery. It is one of many that marine biologists are only beginning to unveil.

# 21 species and speciation

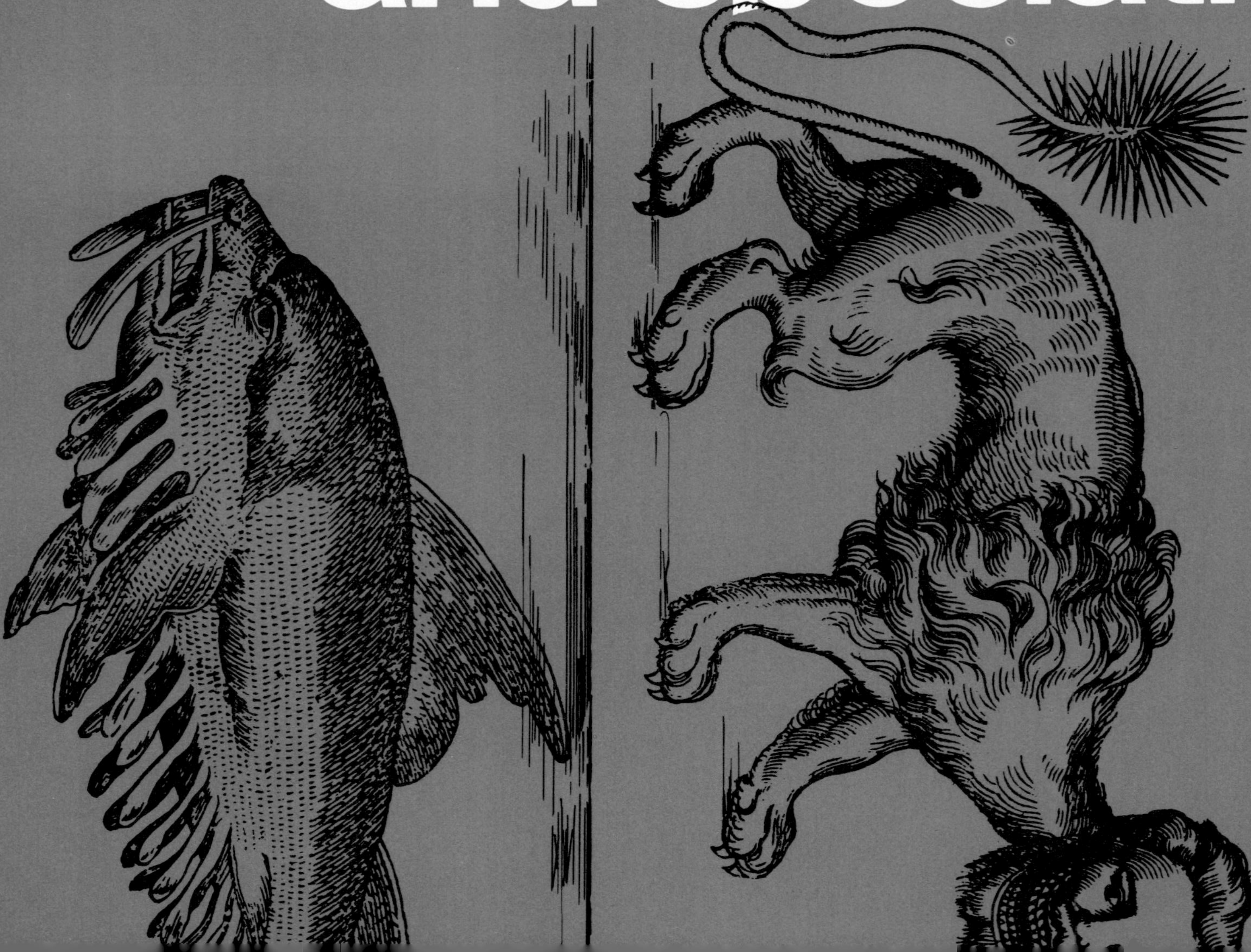

n the last chapter we looked at the way evolution can affect the gene pool of a population. But what does this have to do with the origin of new species? The evolution of a population takes its pattern from the interaction between recombination and expansion of the gene pool in the ways that we have just discussed. But this is only one part of the process. The other aspect of evolutionary change involves the isolation and restriction of the population's gene pool. Once populations have begun to adapt in different ways to different environments, various barriers tend to restrict interbreeding and recombination between them.

When a population adapts to a local environment, genetic changes inevitably occur. Some of these may result in gene combinations that do not cross successfully with gene pools of other local populations. When gene flow between two populations is limited to the point where new mutations in either population affect only that population, and the forces of natural selection and genetic drift act differently on each of them, the groups will become genetically isolated from each other. They will form new and separate species. This process as known as speciation.

We have stressed that the population is the basic unit of evolutionary change, to emphasize that populations evolve but individuals do not. However, populations of the same species can interbreed. This ensures continued gene flow between them. Populations of different species cannot interbreed with one another—at least, not in nature. So by definition, when members of two populations cannot freely interbreed, they form separate species. Isolation of a population and evolutionary change within it results in a new species.

There are many definitions of "species" depending on the purpose for which the word is used. Thus we have taxonomic species, paleontological species, and morphological species. But to understand the way species form, we need a definition of a **biological species.**

# Biological species

In 1940, zoologist Ernst Mayr defined a biological species as follows: "Species are groups of actually or potentially interbreeding natural populations, which are reproductively isolated from other such groups." As Mayr pointed out, the word "potentially" is necessary to distinguish reproductive isolation from isolation in time and place. For example, the life of a fruit fly is very short. A population of fruit flies born in 1975 are therefore reproductively isolated from those born in 1965 by a complete time barrier. However, they are still members of the same species. Spatial isolation often may lead to species divergence, but the mere fact of separation in space is not enough to differentiate two species. The remains of once numerable populations of Indian lions, for instance, are now protected in a sanctuary at Gir Forest. None of them will have an opportunity to interbreed with any African lion population. But the phenotypic similarity of the populations suggests that they are genetically similar—certainly close enough to both be lions. This similarity would be further confirmed by bringing the two populations together. If a number of Indian lions were transported to an African plain, they would probably begin to interbreed with the African lions.

This illustrates a very important fact of evolution. If populations retain the ability to exchange genes, they will merge into a single species when they are brought together, regardless of the passage of time. But if genetic divergence is such that they can no longer exchange genes, they will remain distinct biological species.

However, the idea of breeding potential must not be carried too far. We are still discussing "natural" populations, whether actually or potentially interbreeding. The method of lion "migration" from India to Africa in the example above is artificial, but the conditions under which mating occurs are nevertheless "natural," give or take a few lions. However, both biologists and animal and plant breeders have contrived conditions under which organisms of two distinct species will successfully interbreed. Lions and tigers provide the most fanciful examples. When separated from their own species and placed under conditions of intense association (in zoos, for example), lions and tigers have successfully mated. The offspring are ligers (if the male is a lion) and tiglons (if the male is a tiger). But although their ranges overlap in India, no liger or tiglon has ever been spotted in the wild.

The above example helps to clarify that the ability to interbreed is not the same as the ability to crossmate. Successful breeding involves the capacity to reproduce viable, fertile offspring, in numbers typical of the particular species.

The biological species definition is most useful when we compare two contemporary populations in contact with each other. When we look at those which are isolated in time or space, we must draw upon morphological (form and structure) and behavioral comparisons to determine the interbreeding potential of the two groups. Genetic differences are generally correlated with structural and behavioral differ-

21-1
What do you get if you cross a male tiger with a female lion? A tiglon— but only in zoos.

ences. Such differences thus provide an essential clue in species identification. But we can observe a wide range of structural and behavioral variation between members of the same species — for example, between the two sexes, or among organisms at different developmental stages. On the basis of structure alone, a tadpole and a frog appear to be farther apart than a bullfrog and a tree frog. But the tadpole is simply an early stage of development for both species. So in the determination of different species, structural or behavioral differences are always subordinate to the condition of reproductive isolation, or failure to interbreed freely.

## Speciation

At this point, we have some idea of how to determine whether or not two populations form two distinct species. We can now ask, echoing Darwin: How do species originate? In theory, speciation can occur both among populations that are separated by a geographical barrier, and among those that are not. These are known, respectively, as **allopatric speciation** and **sympatric speciation**.

### Allopatric speciation

In the process of allopatric speciation a single population becomes divided by a physical barrier. So we can deduce the history of allopatric speciation by comparing living populations in various stages of divergence across a geographical border. We generally find a range from freely interbreeding populations, to intermediate or relatively infertile breeders, to completely isolated populations. Allopatric speciation frequently occurs when members of a plant or insect population are taken to offshore islands on debris carried by floods, or when birds are transported by severe winds. Once they arrive on the island, they lose contact with the mainland population. Normal gene flow between the two populations is blocked. The founder population already

constitutes a slightly unrepresentative gene pool because of its small size. Its gene pool will develop differently from the mainland population because of different selection pressures.

Islands are sometimes populated by a process called **multiple invasion**, in which successive groups of the original population invade the new territory. Once the original colonizers have had time to diverge from the mainland population, new invaders from the mainland may be unable to interbreed with the first. This results in the coexistence of two distinct species.

Other physical barriers may divide a population more equally, so that the two resulting gene pools more closely represent the original. An original population may be split in this way by formation of a canyon due to an earthquake, or by the divergence of a river into a new course. This process is called **fission**. Eventually, the two new populations will diverge, because of their different environments.

We may ask whether the existence of a physical barrier necessarily creates two different environments. The answer is that it does, even if the differences cannot be seen immediately. Different selective pressures are created by subtle differences in climate, soil character, and plant and animal life. They may also result from differences in the types and numbers of predators, and even in the types and numbers of competing species.

Physical barriers need not be so dramatic as mountains, canyons, or rivers. They can also be ecological divisions, such as that between the forests and the neighboring plains. Once isolated, the new populations diverge for several reasons. It may be due to chance, or drift, resulting from the nonrepresentative nature of the founder population. Moreover, each population will obviously be affected differently by mutation and by new migrations. Finally, selection in the different environments will favor one gene combination over another, and these differences will increase.

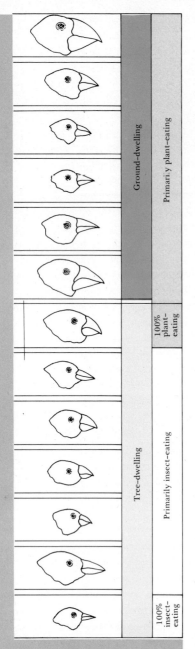

Ground-dwelling

Primarily plant-eating

100% plant-eating

Tree-dwelling

Primarily insect-eating

100% insect-eating

**21-2**
Beak adaptations to various food sources among the thirteen Galapagos finches. Not shown is the tree-dwelling Cocos Island finch, which brings the total number of adaptations to fourteen. (See Darwin's finches)

*Darwin's finches* Darwin discovered many types of finch on the Galapagos Islands off the coast of Ecuador. These provide a classic example of allopatric speciation. The Galapagos Archipelago is far away from the mainland, so it is unlikely that more than one excursion of the same species from the mainland could have occurred. Thus a total of fourteen different finch species are thought to have evolved from a founder population which might have consisted of only a single pair. These first colonizers were probably ground-dwelling seed-eaters that were carried the 600 miles from the mainland by storm winds.

The colonizers found a very harsh environment on the islands. On most of them, dryness restricts the vegetation to the hardy, leafless thornbush and occasional tall cacti. But a few of the larger islands are more humid. Their highest peaks are covered with a damp cloud mist, sustaining trees, ferns, lichens, and some orchids. When the original finches arrived, there were almost no other land birds on these islands. So the newcomers could take advantage of all the different food sources. These birds successfully colonized all of the various islands over the course of a few centuries. But once they had done so, they were in effect reproductively isolated, because of the fairly large water barrier between the islands. Eventually each island population adapted to a slightly different habitat, depending on what food was available.

In the adaptation process, the finches evolved different types of bill, ranging from large, heavy, seed-cracking bills to thin pointed ones for drawing nectar from cactus flowers. Six species dwell and feed on the ground, three of them cracking and eating the various seeds that have dropped there. The beaks of these seed-eaters are mostly stubby. Their size depends on the size of the seed they favor. Two ground-dwellers feed on fruit or cactus flowers, for which their beaks are more pointed. The

same range of beak sizes characterizes the tree-dwellers, most of which eat insects of various sizes. The beaks of the ground-dwellers are generally larger than those of the tree-dwellers. Further specialization depends on the nature of the food.

One species, the cactus finch, has adapted to fill the ecological niche that is occupied in most places by a woodpecker. Like the woodpecker, this finch digs insects out of cactus crevices and from beneath the barks of trees—but not with its beak. Instead, it uses its beak to chip a hole in the bark, then grasps a cactus spine to do the digging. Only the absence of woodpeckers on the islands has allowed the cactus finch to evolve the way it has. The "genuine article" would beat out its imitator in any competition.

The honey creepers are even more spectacular in terms of differential development. These birds colonized the islands of Hawaii, 2,000 miles from the nearest mainland in any direction. Since the chances of many birds being carried so far are very slight, all of the thirty-nine different types probably developed from a very small founder population, perhaps a single pair. Like the finches, the honey creepers diversified in bill structure, and one of them specialized to fill the woodpecker niche.

In both cases, the birds were able to diversify to fill different niches because they did not have to compete with an already adapted species. As a result their descendants will vary in both structure and behavior. Eventually, though, a group of finches from one island will colonize another island, presenting the resident species with stiff competition for some food sources. For example, if some birds which have adapted to feeding on the ground on Island A happen to colonize Island B, where the residents are better suited to feeding in the trees, the newcomers will eliminate ground food sources for these resident birds. The residents will be forced to become even more efficient at getting food from the trees. This additional specialization takes the

21-3
The cactus finch
demonstrates tool use,
probing for insects
with a cactus spine.

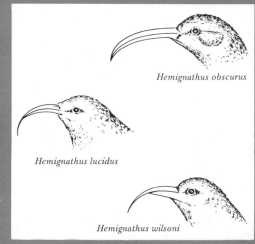

*Hemignathus obscurus*

*Hemignathus lucidus*

*Hemignathus wilsoni*

21-4
Character displace-
ment in the Hawaiian
honey creepers. Three
insect-eaters that
evolved from the
insect and nectar-
feeding *Hemignathus*:
*H. obscurus* picks insects from crevices in tree trunks and branches with
its matching long, curved bills. *H. ludicus* uses its thick, shorter lower
bill to chip away loose bark and expose insects. *H. wilsoni* uses its
extremely stubby lower bill like a woodpecker. It pounds into soft wood
for less accessible insects.

form of **character displacement**. Two populations can coexist in the same range only
after they have diverged to the point where
they occupy different ecological niches—
eating different food and nesting on different territory. But such coexistence nar-
rows the environment niche of each population. The result is further specialization—
and thus further speciation—of each. In
both the finch and the honey creeper populations, the character displaced was the
beak.

Character displacement occurs in two
ways. The one we have just mentioned occurs when two divergent populations come
together in the same territory but still share
the same food or nesting preferences. The
result is that they compete with each other.
For both populations to survive, selection
must favor those gene combinations that
are most divergent in each case. This eliminates competition and allows both populations to share one environmental range.

Character displacement also occurs
when two reunited populations have not yet
developed structural or behavioral mechanisms which will prevent them from occasionally trying to interbreed. Matings between divergent species sometimes fail to
produce any offspring at all. This may result
in the waste of a complete breeding season—in the case of birds as much as a
quarter or a third of their lives. Even if offspring are produced, they often cannot
develop properly or reproduce successfully. This is because they are imperfectly
adapted to either parental habitat. Consequently, individuals of the two populations
that do not attempt to interbreed will be favored over those who do. This gives the
evolution of each a further push toward
complete speciation. The process continues over time, as groups from each original
island population colonize other islands. In
the long run, the result is a type of allopatric
speciation called **adaptive radiation**—the
formation of many ecologically diverse
species all descended from a common
ancestor.

## Sympatric speciation

Speciation that occurs in the absence of geographical barriers is much more controversial, because it is so difficult to demonstrate. We can deduce allopatric speciation, but we must hypothesize sympatric speciation. Two conditions are necessary for it to occur. First, a strong nonrandom mating tendency must develop between members of a polymorphic population. Second, a selective force must operate against the formation or viability of hybrids between the two forms. For instance, in a study of the polymorphic population of geese that breed in the Canadian Arctic, it was noted that blue geese seem to favor other blue geese for mates, as white geese prefer their own lookalikes. It was found that this results from an identification with one of the parents at birth, which influences the future choice of a mate. (We will examine this behavioral phenomenon in chapter 23.) But interbreeding between the two populations is still possible, and apparently occurs in nearly 50 percent of the cases. However, if some selective force should eliminate the heterozygotes—such as a form of environmental pollution that puts them at physiological disadvantage—the blue and white forms would be unable to produce viable, fertile offspring. They would thus be effectively isolated reproductively.

21-5
A new primrose species by polyploidy. *Primula kewensis* (below, right) is a hybrid between *P. floribunda* (right) and *P. verticillata* (below, left). It has twice as many chromosomes as either parent. (See Sympatric speciation)

Most advocates of the theory of sympatric speciation believe that nonrandom mating based on habitat preference, rather than color or morphological characteristics, will favor a strong disruptive selection against intermediate forms. A variety of British tree moth lays eggs on both apple and hawthorn trees, upon which the larvae feed. All of the moths tend to stay put on their preferred types of tree. Thus they mate with and give rise to offspring with similar habitat preferences. The result is intense inbreeding, which in time may result in genetic divergence. If this happens, hybrid offspring may not be able to feed successfully on either apple or hawthorn trees, and this would constitute a force against interbreeding.

Questions remain as to whether any of these divergent selective conditions could exist in nature long enough to produce reproductive isolation. Polyploidy is the only form of sympatric speciation which has been successfully demonstrated. Polyploids are formed by the addition of one or more complete sets of chromosomes to a cell. This occurs either through the fusion of unreduced gametes or by the failure of a cell to divide after its nucleus has divided. Mating between polyploid offspring and the diploid parents is restricted, because at meiosis the polyploid gametes will contain twice as many chromosomes as the diploid gametes. This will result in pairing difficulties in the formation of daughter cells. Such difficulties usually block the process of meiosis altogether, so no offspring are produced. But no such difficulties arise when polyploid individuals mate with other polyploids: new polyploid offspring will result. Thus the polyploid species are reproductively isolated from the parent diploid species after only one generation.

Polyploidy appears to account for about 70 percent of the existing species of higher plants. It is extremely rare among animals, however, since the XY mechanism of sex determination is upset when chromosome sets are accidentally doubled.

## Clines and subspecies

We have emphasized that time, often millions of years, is one of the important aspects in species formation. Because the process is a gradual one, it goes through many stages, from a single species, to subspecies, to two or more distinct species. In order to decide which of these stages defines two populations, we can apply the biological definition of species and determine what degree of reproductive isolation characterizes the two. When populations vary in one or more traits in regular gradations from one locality to the next, they comprise what is known as a **cline**. Members of a cline can all interbreed freely. Clines are characterized by continuous variation, which often follows environmental variation. In fact, a number of general observations or rules govern geographical variation.

**Bergmann's rule** states that the average body size of members of populations in cooler climates tends to be larger than that in warm climates. We can see this, for example, in sparrow populations of the eastern United States. Birds in New England are heavier than those in the South. In general, this is because large body mass conserves heat, as less surface area per unit of volume is exposed to the cold. But for burrowing mammals such as lemmings and voles, the depth of the soil is the significant factor. Populations of such animals in cold, high areas were found to be smaller than those in low, warm areas, due to the relatively shallow soil in high, windswept areas.

An extension of Bergmann's rule is **Allen's rule**, which holds that protruding body parts such as ears, tails, and bills are relatively shorter in cold climates. Once again, this allows greater conservation of heat. The exceptions are wings and tails of birds, which do not contribute to heat loss.

A third general rule is **Gloger's rule**, which states that pigmentation is darker in warm, humid areas and lighter in cold or cool dry ones. Some other observations are true only for certain species. Among birds that feed their young, those in areas of high latitude produce more eggs (because of the longer hours of daylight) than those near the equator, and their wings are relatively longer. Mammals in cold climates have lusher coats than those in warm areas, with both longer hair and heavier underfur.

All of these rules apply only to populations, not to species. For example, we do not find all the large animals in the Arctic and all the small ones in the tropics. Moreover, continuous variation of this type characterizes populations within a species rather than populations themselves. On the other hand, discontinuous variation occurs both within a population (polymorphism) and from one population to another within a species. When sudden gaps or sharp, discontinuous variation occur in several traits between two breeding populations in a species—and yet some degree of interbreeding still exists—the populations are regarded as **subspecies** or **races**. While interbreeding is still possible between different subspecies, each one represents a distinct group within a species, which primarily mates internally for geographical or cultural reasons. So we can define a subspecies or race as a breeding population which has gene frequencies unlike those of other populations in the species.

Subspecies are breeding populations, not individual members of those populations. So not all members of a subspecies will display every trait that characterizes the group as a whole. Some wide-ranging species have thirty or more described subspecies which can interbreed. Each race is distinguished from other races by population averages or characteristics. But the range of individual variation in one race often overlaps that of another. Therefore, it may be difficult to assign an individual to a particular subspecies, unless we know its origin.

The several races of the human species are clearly of geographical origin. Population movements and gene flow, however, have modified their characteristic gene frequencies, especially during the last 500 years. Evidence indicates that a number of human racial differences represent adaptations to original environmental conditions. Skin color is an example. Dark skin pigmentation of African and Melanesian populations protects the body from sunburn caused by intense equatorial ultraviolet radiation. Moreover, the amount of pigmentation in the outer layer of skin regulates the amount of ultraviolet radiation that penetrates into the deeper layer where vitamin D is synthesized. In effect, then, pigmentation controls the production of vitamin D. Some vitamin D production is essential to supply enough calcium to the body and prevent such diseases as rickets. But too much vitamin D production results in the overcalcification of the body. So in areas of intense sunlight, a dark pigmentation prevents the formation of excess amounts of vitamin D.

A chain of subspecies often develops as populations adapt to different local environments over a wide area. Each population is characterized by a broad range of distinct traits, and each mates predominantly within itself. But each can interbreed to some degree with neighboring populations. Biologist Robert Stebbins discovered such a chain among populations of the California salamander, *Ensatina eschscholtzi*. Comparing a number of traits in the different populations, he noted sharp variations from one population to the next, instead of the regular gradations that characterize a cline. Gene exchange was possible between each two successive populations, but the salamanders at the two ends of the circular chain did not interbreed, even though their distribution overlapped. At this point we still have a series of subspecies—or what Mayr has called a "circular overlap" of geographic races. Despite the reproductive isolation of the two ends of the ring or chain, gene flow between them is possible indirectly by way of the intermediate subspecies. If environmental change should cause harsh selection against one or more of the intermediate subspecies and result in their extinction, the ring would then be completely separated. Gene flow between the two ends would be totally cut off, and the process of speciation would be complete.

We must not assume that subspecies always represent a transitional stage in the process of speciation. All subspecies are

21-6
A chain of subspecies of the California salamander, *Ensatina eschscholtzi*. Based on data of R. C. Stebbins.

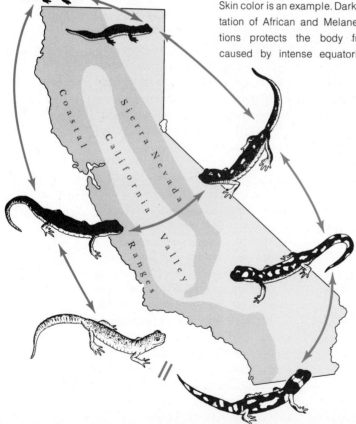

potential new species, but this is not their inevitable destiny. Their fate is dependent on their degree of isolation, as well as the operation of selection, mutation, genetic drift, and gene flow. Some will remain subspecies, some will become separate species, and some will form a single wide-ranging population, characterized by a free exchange of genes.

## Isolating mechanisms

Subspecies or race formation is always potentially reversible. The genetic differences which arise as a result of adaptation to local conditions will disappear if gene flow is reestablished. To avoid being swallowed up into the same gene pool, divergent populations must develop some degree of reproductive isolation. The mechanisms by which they do this are collectively known as **isolating mechanisms**, barriers to the free flow of genes between divergent populations.

Isolating mechanisms can be broadly categorized as those that operate before mating occurs and those that operate after mating occurs, as shown in the accompanying chart.

1. *Seasonal isolation*. Two divergent populations often evolve different breeding seasons because of differences in local food supplies or climate conditions. In some cases, this seasonal difference involves only a few weeks or days, or even a few hours. In the slime molds, for example, the swarm cells of different species aggregate at different times of the day. Thus only a few hours' difference isolates a basic step in the reproductive cycle among the several species of slime mold that may occur in a single rotting log.

2. *Habitat isolation*. In the course of adaptation, members of two related populations may exist more successfully in two different habitats within the same geographical area. Unless they are fairly mobile, individuals in each habitat will tend to mate with others of the same habitat. This

---

**21-7  Isolating mechanisms**

### PREMATING

1. Seasonal isolation: divergent populations breed at different seasons, which can be defined as days or weeks or simply different times of the day.

2. Habitat isolation: divergent populations adapt to different habitats, or sometimes they merely breed in different habitats.

3. Behavioral isolation: divergent populations evolve different patterns of courtship and mating behavior to aid in species identification.

4. Mechanical isolation: divergent populations evolve differences in size or structure that prevent interbreeding.

### POSTMATING

5. Gamete isolation: the male gamete fails to reach or fertilize the female gamete.

6. Zygote mortality: the zygote never develops due to genetic incompatibility.

7. Hybrid mortality: the hybrid dies before reaching reproductive age.

8. Hybrid sterility: the mature hybrid is sterile, due to failure of the reproductive organs to develop or failure of the gametes to develop.

9. $F_2$ hybrid mortality of sterility: the $F_1$ hybrid is only partially sterile, resulting in $F_2$ hybrids that die before maturing or are completely sterile.

---

kind of isolation is characteristic of many plant species. Often habitat preferences reinforce seasonal isolation. Since breeding seasons can vary from year to year, breeding season preference is most effective when it occurs in conjunction with habitat preference. For example, the flowers of two plant species, *Tradescantia canaliculata* and *T. subaspera*, bloom at different seasons. This is partly because one species has adapted to sunny growing places and the other to areas of deep shade.

3. *Behavioral isolation*. For animals, differences associated with courtship and mating behavior are more important than seasonal or habitat adaptation. These differences facilitate species recognition and therefore reproductive isolation, even at the lower levels of organization. During the August twilight, Caribbean fireworms leave their burrows on the ocean floor and swim to the water's surface. There they turn phosphorescent, spreading the surface with tiny green blinking lights. Males blink on and off about once or twice a second. Females turn

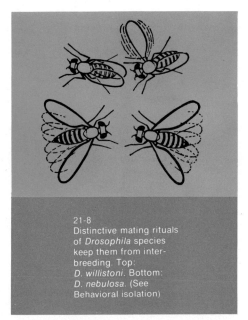

21-8
Distinctive mating rituals of *Drosophila* species keep them from interbreeding. Top: *D. willistoni*. Bottom: *D. nebulosa*. (See Behavioral isolation)

on a brighter light that stays steady for at least ten seconds. When a female lights up, males converge upon her to mate, blinking as they swim.

4. *Mechanical isolation.* In many cases, obvious size differences between different populations prevent either copulation (for internal fertilization) or clasping (necessary in species such as toads and frogs for external fertilization). A secondary form of mechanical isolation may operate in related mammals of different size, such as the horse and the donkey. If the female is of the smaller species, she would be unable to give birth to the proportionately larger hybrid offspring. Many animals show differences in the genitalia which interfere with attempts to mate, even when they are similar in size. This is common in insects, and some rodents.

In animals, mechanical isolation is now generally considered to be secondary to behavioral isolation, as mating between structurally different animals is never seriously attempted in nature.

In higher plants, on the other hand, differences in floral structure often play the most important part in reproductive isolation of related species. In some plants these differences function to attract different pollinators. For example, various species of beard tongue *(Pentstemon)* attract different bees—large bees, bumblebees, and solitary bees—depending on their size and shape. A few are shaped to fit only the beaks of hummingbirds. Other flowers, such as the milkweeds, are structured so that even if a pollinator does visit two different species, the pollen will not be transferred into the stigma of the female flower.

5. *Gamete isolation.* When members of different species do attempt to mate, the sperm often fails to reach the egg. This can happen in plants if pollen grains are unable to grow pollen tubes in the style of a different species. In animals, some chemical incompatibility can immobilize or destroy the sperm after it enters the vagina. For instance, in some *Drosophila* crosses, insem-

21-9
The male satin bower bird prepares a wedding-night suite unlike those of any other bower bird species. In it, he will sing loudly and display brightly colored feathers in species-typical ways. Ritualized displays of color patterns are some of the most widespread means of assuring that the female chooses a member of her own species as a mate. (See Behavioral isolation)

ination causes the reproductive tract of the female to swell and destroy the sperm.

6. *Zygote mortality.* Successful fertilization does not always lead to successful development. In crosses between a leopard frog and a wood frog, for instance, one experimenter noted that in some cases the zygote never reached the cleavage stage. In others, gastrulation never occurred. The failure of zygote development is apparently caused by incompatibility of genes between individuals of two different species.

7. *Hybrid mortality.* If zygotic development is arrested at a later stage, abnormalities may prevent the hybrid offspring from surviving to reproductive age. Malformations which prevent it from eating or defending itself will result in an early death. Examples can be seen in crosses between different species of leopard frog. These crosses produce tadpoles with huge heads and no tails, or huge tails with almost no heads. Neither hybrid will survive to pass these defects on to the next generation.

8. *Hybrid sterility.* Some crosses between individuals of two separate species result in hybrid offspring which are normal in every way except that they cannot reproduce. Hybrid sterility usually occurs because the reproductive organs, especially the testes, fail to develop. For example, the major problem in the ten-year effort to successfully cross cattle and buffalo was that the hybrid "beefalo" could not reproduce themselves. The breeders have not yet revealed how this problem was overcome.

None of these isolating mechanisms operates separately. Instead they combine, usually sequentially. If one is circumvented, another will operate to prevent interbreeding. The two sibling species of *Drosophila* mentioned earlier provide a good illustration. Both are found in the same range in the western United States. But *D. persimilus* usually lives in cooler, higher regions than does *D. pseudoobscura,* resulting in habitat isolation. This is reinforced by courtship activity. *D. persimilus* is much more active in the morning, but *D. pseudoobscura* be-

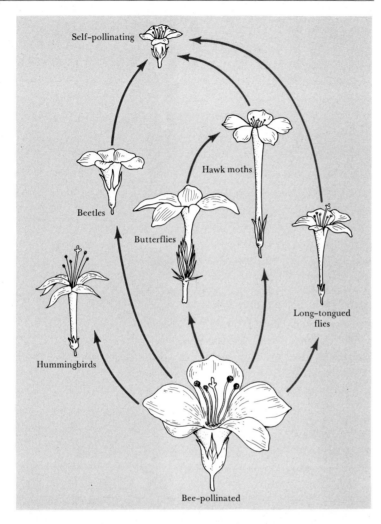

Self-pollinating

Hawk moths

Beetles

Butterflies

Hummingbirds

Long-tongued flies

Bee-pollinated

**21-10**
The diversity of floral structure in the *Polemoniaceae* resulting from adaptation to different pollinators. Arrows indicate possible direction of evolution. Not shown here is a much larger flower adapted to bat pollination. (See Mechanical isolation)

ful. Thus selection acts strongly against any morphological or behavioral aspect of a species that would lend itself to interbreeding attempts. In this way, the isolating mechanisms themselves are maintained and often strengthened.

Isolating mechanisms are far less precise in areas not inhabited by other closely related species. For example, a song bird species *(Parus)* coexisted with a number of related species on the Northwest African mainland. But when *Parus* moved to the offshore island of Tenerife, where it was the only one of its genus, it lost both structural and behavioral traits related to mating, most notably its characteristic song.

If such a species later moves back to the mainland or is joined by other related species, the nonspecific isolating mechanisms which had maintained species identity on the island might no longer be sufficient. Even without such travels, isolating mechanisms are not always perfectly efficient. Failure and breakdowns do occur. The interbreeding which results produces a number of hybrids. As we have noted, most of these are partially or completely sterile. Also, the hybrids may be so inferior to either parental species in their ability to adapt to an existing environmental niche that they are at an immediate competitive disadvantage and fail to reach maturity. Occasionally when stable habitats are disturbed, either by natural forces or by human presence, new or different habitats will be created very near to the old. These can be somewhat intermediate in nature, providing suitable sites for the survival of the hybrids of otherwise ecologically separated populations.

Biologist G. L. Stebbins has pointed out that when the first settlers came to this country they cut down much of the dense forest for cultivation or grazing lands. These new fields and pastures were quickly invaded by several different species of the sturdy hawthorn shrub, previously isolated by their location in relatively infrequent forest clearings or along river banks. Habitat

comes more active in the evening. Even if these two mechanisms are bypassed by placing both species together under artificial conditions, the females of both species still show a preference for males of the same species. In the relatively few cases in which premating isolation has been overcome, the hybrid offspring cannot mate, as the males are completely sterile.

## Hybridization

One observed aspect of isolating mechanisms is that they are most precise and efficient in areas where a number of closely related species exist. Mistaken courtships, unsuccessful mating attempts, and the production of inviable offspring are all waste-isolation had served earlier to prevent hybridization among the different species. But the close proximity of the shrubs over a wide area led to the formation of a vast number of different hybrids. Many of these were better adapted to pasture life than any of the parent species.

By far the greatest number of habitat disturbances have resulted from human enterprises of one sort or another. But natural forces also have been at work. We can see a good example in the case of three species of beard tongue, a floral plant found in southern California. Originally only two species existed. The mountain pentstemon was adapted to the moist, forest-covered mountain slopes, and the scarlet buglar was adapted to the steeper, dryer slopes. Despite the fact that the forest plant is pollinated by large bees and the scarlet buglar by hummingbirds, occasional cross-pollination occurred. This produced a few fertile hybrids with some of the characteristics of each type. The hybrids were ill-adapted to either slope, so they never established themselves as a separate species. But gradually the mountain climate became dryer. Much of the dense forest gave way to brush, forming a transitional

habitat that particularly suited the hybrid form. As the hybrids spread into the new habitats they were soon favored by still a third pollinator, the wasp, thus ensuring a degree of isolation from either parent species.

## Rates of evolution

The history of evolution indicates that many organisms evolve to the point where they are fully adapted to a particular environmental niche. They then change very little, if at all. For instance, there are some 1,200 species of cockroach, and they are much the same today as they were 300 million years ago at the beginning of the Carboniferous period. But most of the mammals have shown a much greater rate of evolution, changing rapidly over a period of some 70 million years. These different rates are due primarily to different selection pressures. Once the cockroach had established a form best suited to survival in a number of different niches, it had reached an **adaptive peak**. Selection therefore favored its continued stability. Mammals, on the other hand, faced greater challenges, from competitors as well as predators.

21-11
The horseshoe crab is related to the extinct trilobites. It is sometimes called a living fossil. This is because it has changed little from fossil representatives dating back 190 million years. (See Rates of evolution)

Selection is not the only factor in differential rates of evolution. Every major change in the earth's environment has been followed by a burst of evolution in one or more groups of organisms. But not all organisms have had the adaptive capacity for survival. The fossil record is strewn with evidence of thousands of different plant and animal species that evolved, survived for a few millennia, then became extinct.

Since selection acts upon variation in a gene pool of a population, the amount of variation becomes important, and so do the size and reproductive rate of the population. The more gametes a particular population produces the more likely it is that new mutations or recombinations will actually occur. And the more offspring the population produces the more likely it is that some phenotypes will be better adapted to a changed environment and new selective pressures. But large population and high rate of gamete production will not by themselves ensure a high rate of evolution. Generation time is also important. Given comparable population sizes, the shorter the generation time the higher the potential rate of evolution.

The environment to which a population adapts is as important as evolutionary potential in determining the degree and speed of a population change. In most cases, for evolution to continue after a population has reached an adaptive peak, the environment to which it has adapted must usually undergo a change or series of changes. Otherwise, new environmental niches must become available. Evolution has been most explosive and diverse where species could occupy a new and uncolonized territory, filling a variety of niches in a series of adaptive radiations. In fact, evolution may take the form of a series of adaptive radiations. This occurs if an evolutionary line has adapted to an environment that is not stable but changes progressively over a long period. However only a few of these radiations may be ultimately successful, or adaptive over the long term.

This is apparently what happened in the evolution of the modern horse, for which we have a fairly complete fossil record. During the Eocene period, over 60 million years ago, a small form about the size of a beagle lived in the moist forests of North America. This was *Hyracotherium,* sometimes called *Eohippus.* It has four toes and padded feet for browsing—that is, eating leaves of trees and shrubs. Slowly this evolved into *Miohippus,* a three-toed forest browser the size of a great dane. Two different radiations developed from this form during the Oligocene and Miocene, involving a total of ten different genera. One radiation contained four different forms of browsers, still three-toed and still small for horses. All of them became extinct as the forests receded. The other radiation was more successful. Its members evolved into larger beasts, with specialized grinding teeth for grazing on the tough, abrasive grasses of the expanding plains environments. These six genera had no foot pads and had a sort of arched foot resembling a hoof. The most successful, *Pliohippus,* had only one toe, and five new forms of this line radiated again. Three of the new radiations migrated from North to South America. There all of them, including the modern form *Equus,* became extinct. But at some time during the Pleistocene era, 2.5 to 3 million years ago, *Equus* had also migrated to central Asia. From there it spread eastward into east Asia and west-

21-12
The whale is a mammal that has readapted to the sea. It shows the impossibility of reverse evolution in a genetically complex structure. Whales evolved from four-legged carnivores. So they did not redevelop the musculature and fins of the fish to propel themselves through the water. Instead they evolved tail flukes, which move up and down to achieve the same results.

21-13
Marsupials in Australia have radiated to fill many ecological niches elsewhere occupied by placental mammals. Left, top: a marsupial cat, a threat to birds and their eggs. Left, bottom: a Tasmanian devil, similar in color and build to a small bear.

21-14
Another marsupial from Australia is the sugar glider, shown at rest (below) and taking the role of a flying squirrel (right).

ward into the Mediterranean countries. It was finally reintroduced in America by the Spanish colonists in 1519.

Fossil records indicate that the modern horse developed through sudden, rapid changes, with no continuous trends. This example illustrates the fact that adaptive radiation is not always permanently adaptive. During the first stages of evolution, character displacement and lack of competition from other species result in considerable diversity. Eventually, natural selection eliminates the less well-adapted forms. So evolution is always forward, even if it leads to extinction.

Among the marmosets and tamarins (small monkey-like primates) of the South American rain forests, some populations are now evolving toward progressive bleaching of the hair or coat color. The whiteness increases with the distance, in both time and space, that a colony travels from the dark-colored parent population. Since these animals live in dark forests, their whiteness renders them far more vulnerable to predation than any of their darker relatives. The lighter races may therefore become extinct unless they can establish themselves in a niche where coat color has no survival value.

The tendency to overspecialize goes along with adaptation. It is accompanied by loss of flexibility. In fact, the organism which has adapted perfectly to a particular environmental niche is the one most likely to be overspecialized and so unable to survive a new, rapid environmental change. This gives the human species a special responsibility, since we can tailor the environment to some extent to our own specifications. If we do not protect the specialized environments of the world from destruction or homogenization, our distinctive and varied forms of plant and animal life may give way to an unspecialized set of "weedy" organisms such as rats, mice, sparrows, starlings, crabgrass, and poison ivy—all suited to life in unspecialized environments.

Summary

Biological species have been defined as "groups of actually or potentially interbreeding natural populations which are reproductively isolated from other such groups." As long as populations can exchange genes, they will merge into a single species when brought together. On the other hand, if genetic divergence is such that they can no longer exchange genes, they will remain distinct biological species. The biologist may draw upon morphological and behavioral comparisons to determine the interbreeding potential of the two groups. But ultimately such comparisons are less important than the condition of reproductive isolation.

In theory, speciation can occur both among populations that are separated by a geographical barrier (allotropic speciation) and among those that are not (sympatric speciation). Multiple invasion occurs when successive groups of an original population invade a new territory and find themselves unable to interbreed with previous colonizers. Fission is the splitting of a population by such barriers as an earthquake-formed canyon or a shift in the course of a river. Subtle differences in climate, soil, and plant and animal life in each new habitat create different selective pressures. These will eventually favor one gene combination over another. Two populations may diverge to the point of occupying different ecological niches. They can then coexist in the same range. The additional specialization needed takes the form of character displacement. The formation of a large number of ecologically diverse species descended from a common ancestor is called adaptive radiation.

When populations vary in one or more traits in regular gradations from one locality to the next, they comprise a cline. Members of a cline can interbreed freely and are characterized by continuous variation. General observations or rules govern geographical variation from one population to another. Bergmann's rule states that the average body size of members of populations in cooler climates tends to be larger than that in warm climates. Allen's rule states that protruding body parts are relatively shorter in cold climates; and Gloger's rule that pigmentation is darker in warm, humid areas than in cold or cool dry ones. When sudden gaps or discontinuous variation occur in several traits between two

breeding populations in a species, yet some interbreeding still exists, the populations are regarded as subspecies or races.

As populations adapt to different local environments over a wide area, a chain of subspecies often develops. Each population mates predominantly within itself but is capable of interbreeding with neighboring populations. Depending on their degree of isolation, selection, mutation, genetic drift, and gene flow, some subspecies will remain subspecies, others will become new species, and others will form a single wide-ranging population with a free exchange of genes.

To maintain their gene pool, divergent populations must develop some degree of reproductive isolation. Barriers to the free flow of genes between divergent populations are called isolating mechanisms. These include the evolution of different breeding seasons, habitational differences, distinctive courtship behavior, physical barriers to copulation, incompatibility of gametes, inability of zygotes to develop, or the failure of hybrids to live to reproductive age or to be fertile. Because of the wastefulness of unsuccessful mating attempts and the production of inviable offspring, selection acts strongly against any aspect of a species that would lend itself to species interbreeding.

The history of evolution indicates that many organisms evolve to a point of optimum adaptation to a particular environmental niche. After they reach this adaptive peak, selection favors continued stability of the organism. Evolutionary potential is also determined by the nature of the organism itself and the genetic structures of its populations.

The environment to which the population adapts is as important as evolutionary potential in determining the degree and speed of a population change. The environment to which an evolutionary line has adapted may have changed progressively over a long period. In this case, evolution may take the form of a series of adaptive radiations. Adaptive radiation is not always permanently adaptive. At first, character displacement and lack of competition may result in considerable diversity. Over time, natural selection eliminates the less well-adapted forms. Evolution is always forward, even if it leads to extinction.

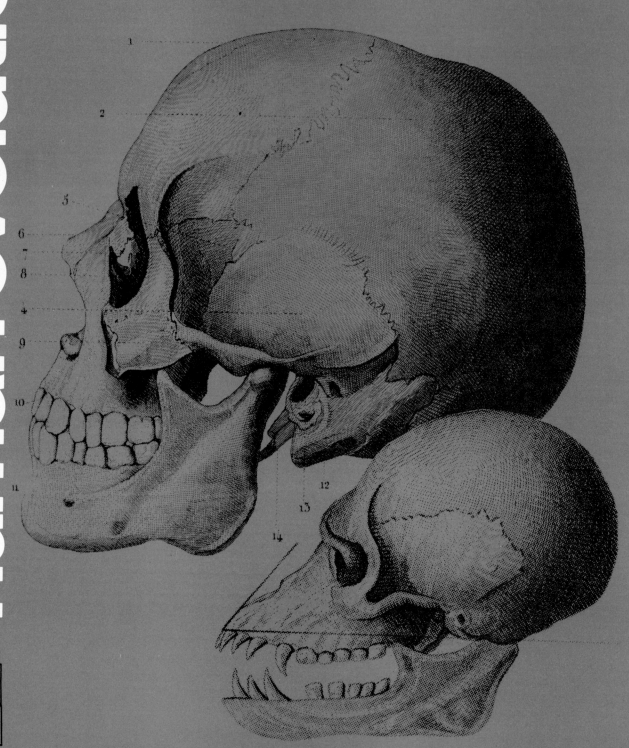

the story of evolution begins in the Precambrian era, the earliest era of geologic time. Not much is known about the Precambrian, because the earliest forms of life had no hard body parts which could be preserved as fossils. But during the following Paleozoic era, both plant and animal life began to diversify a great deal. This was probably due to the greater environmental variation produced by separation of the continental land masses. It was also affected by certain tectonic (earth-building) events which occurred at the ocean floor. The Paleozoic witnessed the appearance of the arthropods, fishes, and reptiles.

Higher forms of plant and animal life, including both the flowering plants and the mammals, first arose during the Mesozoic era. This was followed about 65 million years ago by the Cenozoic, in which the primates and finally the humans appeared. Both the present-day position of the continents and the zone divisions based on differences in climate were probably established during this era.

The first period of the Cenozoic was the Tertiary. During this period mammals proliferated rapidly and replaced the reptiles as the dominant form of life. Because of this, the Cenozoic is sometimes called the Age of Mammals. Some mammalian radiations, notably seals and whales, readapted to the sea during the Tertiary period. The divisions of geologic time date from the formation of the earth about 4.5 billion years ago. They are shown on the chart that appears after chapter 20.

During the Cenozoic era a number of changes occurred. The seas retreated, exposing new bodies of habitable land. The climate of the earth also became milder. This resulted in the formation of large forest belts in many parts of the world. Insectivores and other small mammals now began a shift to tree-living. They were escaping larger predators on the ground, and were also seeking more plentiful sources of food. From these tree-dwelling insectivores the first primates evolved.

# The early primates

Unfortunately, we have not discovered many early primate fossils. The acid soil of their tropical habitats destroyed their bones shortly after death. Most investigators believe that the earliest primates date back to the beginning of the Cenozoic era in the Paleocene epoch. The earliest known form was a rodent-like creature which resembled the modern tree shrew. It is called *Plesiadapis*. It was native to the lush African forests, and lived on insects and seeds. *Plesiadapis* had a long, pointed snout for digging, and flexible digits for grasping limbs and branches. Its front teeth were large, and may have been used for gnawing. The position of the eye sockets indicates a lack of stereoscopic vision. That is, it could not see objects three-dimensionally. And it did not have a postorbital bar, the protective ring of bone around the eye socket that other primates have. *Plesiadapis* resembled the tree shrew so closely that for years it was considered an insectivore.

Paleontologists specialize in the study of human evolution as manifested in fossils. How do they decide when they have discovered a primate fossil? Primates have marked characteristics that distinguish them from other mammals. First and foremost, primates are arboreal, adapted to life in the trees. All of their physical characteristics, including dentition, sensory apparatus, and skeleton, reflect this fact.

Dentition refers to the number, kind, and arrangement of teeth. Because of their omnivorous diet—seeds, nuts, insects and fruits—early primates required less specialized dentition than the ancestral mammal from which they probably evolved. Early in their evolution the primates lost an incisor tooth from either side of both jaws, which differentiates them from other mammals. Their third and fourth molars grew larger and added another cusp. (A cusp is a point on the surface of a tooth.) This increased their chewing ability by combining in a single tooth the functions of grasping,

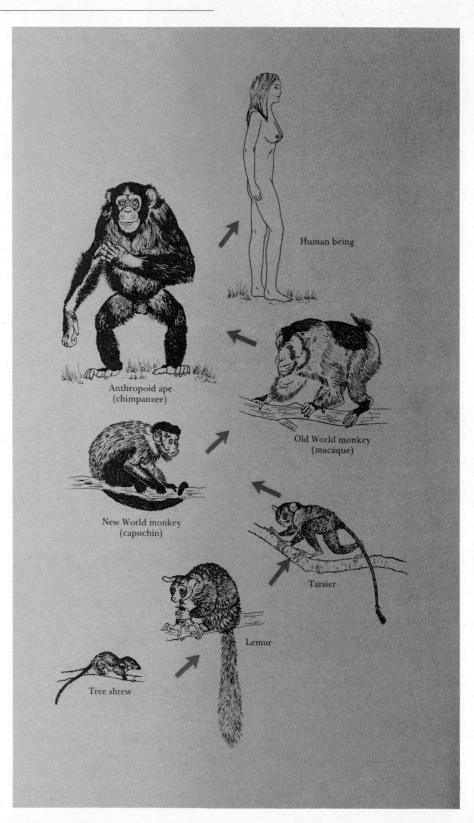

Human being

Anthropoid ape
(chimpanzee)

Old World monkey
(macaque)

New World monkey
(capuchin)

Tarsier

Lemur

Tree shrew

grinding, and cutting.

Life in the trees also favored a sharper sense of vision. Primates with eyes that could accurately judge distance, depth, and direction were better able to leap rapidly from one branch to another. Not surprisingly, higher primates evolved stereoscopic vision, requiring a forward positioning of the eyes. This probably contributed to an increase in brain size, particularly in the visual cortex area. There the number of nerve cells and pathways increased with greater use of the eyes. Other parts of the brain also increased in size and complexity as primates developed greater muscular control, better coordination, and a better sense of balance. Survival in the arboreal environment requires a highly complex nervous system to coordinate the thousands of sensory messages which are received. With a keener sense of vision, primates no longer had to sniff out their food on the ground, and long snouts had no particular advantage. Therefore, snouts became shorter and the sense of smell less acute.

On the other hand, the primates evolved a more acute sense of touch and an improved ability to grasp tree limbs and other objects. Flattened nails replaced awkward claws. The forelimbs became more important in locomotion than the hindlimbs. This development would have important consequences for later primate evolution. Posture became more upright, and the foramen magnum was shifted forward. The **foramen magnum** is the opening at the base of the skull through which the spinal cord is attached to the brain. The further forward and downward-facing this opening, the higher the primate is on the evolutionary scale.

22-1
The primate order, from tree shrew to human being, illustrates the direction of human evolution. Each of the modern primate groups represents the culmination of a separate evolutionary branch.

## Primate evolution

For most of the Eocene epoch, which lasted from about 54 to 37 million years ago, most of the earth had a warm, damp climate. This favored the evolution of a number of different prosimians. Fossil lemurs from this period possessed a primitive dentition. But each of their species showed the postorbital bar, with eyes set well forward in the head. Like the modern lemur, early lemurs were adapted to leaping and grasping.

About 36 million years ago, during the Oligocene epoch, small monkeys and primitive apes appeared. The remains of the earliest known monkey have been found in the Fayum, near Cairo, Egypt. This creature is called *Parapithecus*, or "near ape." *Parapithecus* had dentition much like that of modern Old World monkeys, but the number and kind of teeth differed slightly. Other remains belonged to *Oligopithecus*, or "recent ape." From the generalized features of both these primate fossils, investigators concluded that later primates descended from these or similar forms.

The most important finds at Fayum were the skull and limb of an ape called *Aegyptopithecus* or "Egyptian ape." It is thought to be about 30 million years old and is regarded as the earliest known ape skull. It is probably an ancestor of *Dryopithecus*, discussed below. The dentition of *Aegyptopithecus* reveals affinities with apes. But certain aspects of the limb bones and skull are more primitive. The Fayum finds indicate that the primates were becoming more specialized and more numerous during this period.

During the Miocene epoch which followed, the great apes evolved. The earliest known gibbon-like ape was *Pliopithecus*, which ranged through both Africa and Europe. Nearly the entire skeleton of one of these animals was unearthed in Czechoslovakia. Its dentition, snout, eye sockets, and parts of the collarbone and long bones show definite gibbon affinities. Some aspects of the upper limbs are monkey-like.

22-2
An Eocene primate more recent and more advanced than *Plesiadapis* was the prosimian *Smilodectes*, with shorter snout, enlarged front brain, and forward-facing eye sockets.

22-3
The mandibles and
lower jaws of (top)
*Parapithecus*, (middle)
*Pliopithecus*, and
(bottom) a modern
gibbon.

22-4
Side view of the maxilla
of *Ramapithecus*.

## Dryopithecus

Perhaps the first important find in the primate fossil record was *Dryopithecus*, or "tree ape." Most of its fossil remains have been found in Africa, but others have been found in Europe and Asia. *Dryopithecus* exhibits features that suggest it was an ancestor not only of the pongids, or great apes, but possibly also of humans. The wrist bones indicate that it may have been able to use its arms to swing from one tree limb to another. But the facial bones, spinal cord, and foot bones suggest affinities with the gorilla. Its body size was comparable to that of contemporary African apes. But the most significant feature is the dentition. While the size of the canines resembles that of the monkey, the lower molars show a pattern found only in gibbons, the great apes, and humans.

Because *Dryopithecus* is a transitional specimen, it varies in many specifics. Some forms are closer to monkeys and orangutans. Others are closer to chimpanzees and gorillas. The dental structure indicates that *Dryopithecus* was chiefly herbivorous. The larger specimens may have spent a good deal of time on the ground.

## Ramapithecus

A primate of the later Miocene and early Pliocene is *Ramapithecus*, of the same subfamily as *Dryopithecus*. Many investigators believe that *Ramapithecus* is a member of the Hominidae, the family which includes modern and extinct human species. But the remains are not sufficient for positive classification.

Fossil remains of this form found in East Africa and India are upper and lower jaw fragments. They suggest that *Ramapithecus* was a transitional form between *Dryopithecus* and *Australopithecus*, the earliest undisputed hominid. The dental arch formed by the arrangement of both rows of teeth is like that of humans, but not of other fossil primates. As in humans, there is no **diastema**, or gap between the incisor and canines of the upper jaw. (The diastema is found in most primates, and allows for excellent cutting action.) The proportion of front to back teeth suggests that *Ramapithecus* fed on the ground, eating a variety of tough morsels. It is known that *Ramapithecus* lived in the forests of northern India. These forests began to recede about 10 million years ago, giving way to open country and grasslands.

The small canines, which led to a reduction in the face size, have led some investigators to theorize that *Ramapithecus* used tools. Most primates use their canines as weapons, as well as for shredding tree bark and other foodstuffs. Without large canines a primate is almost defenseless, and would not survive long in its hostile environment. Therefore *Ramapithecus* may have used small objects both for aggressive display and for obtaining food. For this, of course, they would have needed to use their hands. This assumption suggests that *Ramapithecus* may have been **bipedal** like later hominids. That is, it could walk on two feet. This would have freed the hands to carry and manipulate tools. But this is only a guess, based on a few jaw fragments. Paleontologists must have bones from the rest of the skeleton—especially those of the leg, foot, and pelvis—before they can be sure. These bones would also indicate whether *Ramapithecus* was arboreal, like most primates, or terrestrial, like later hominids including humans.

An interesting theory to account for the small size of the canines has been advanced by anthropologist Clifford Jolly. This theory is known as the seed-eating hypothesis. It suggests that reduction in the tooth size is explained by diet rather than weapons or tools. Jolly studied a Pleistocene baboon species, *Theropithecus*, which is related to the modern gelada baboon inhabiting an African grassland. He compared this form to *P. papio*, a baboon that lives in the African woodland and forest. Jolly found that the canines of *Theropithecus* were smaller and shorter than those of the woodland baboon. Jolly suggests that this is because *Theropithecus* fed on seeds, grass, and other plant tissues, like the gelada baboon. Chewing these foods requires a powerful side-to-side jaw action, and animals with large canines cannot chew in this way because the canines would interlock. Thus, ground-dwelling individuals with smaller canines were better able to obtain food. They survived in greater numbers, and so passed on this trait in greater frequencies. As they began to feed increasingly in open country, *Ramapithecus* and early hominids also consumed tough plant foods, and perhaps small animals, which favored the evolution of smaller teeth.

It is still possible that early hominids did use weapons, just as do contemporary grassland chimpanzees and baboons. Use of weapons may even have been a secondary force permitting evolution of even smaller canines. Small-toothed individuals favored for their advantage in obtaining food would be at a defensive disadvantage without some alternative weapons.

*Ramapithecus* is important not only because it may be the first hominid. It is also an example of the evolutionary progression resulting from dryopithecine radiations toward the end of the Miocene. It is now virtually certain that apes and hominids branched off from a common ancestor during this period. *Ramapithecus* gives us possible evidence of this important event.

## Early hominids

After *Ramapithecus,* there is a gap in the fossil record of human evolution. The gap covers about 10 million years during the Pliocene epoch, from which few fossil remains have been found. A number of atmospheric changes occurred during this period. The result was a cooler, drier climate that speeded up the reduction of lush forest land in favor of woodlands and open savannahs. *Ramapithecus* and its successors may have been increasingly obliged to adapt to a new, open environment.

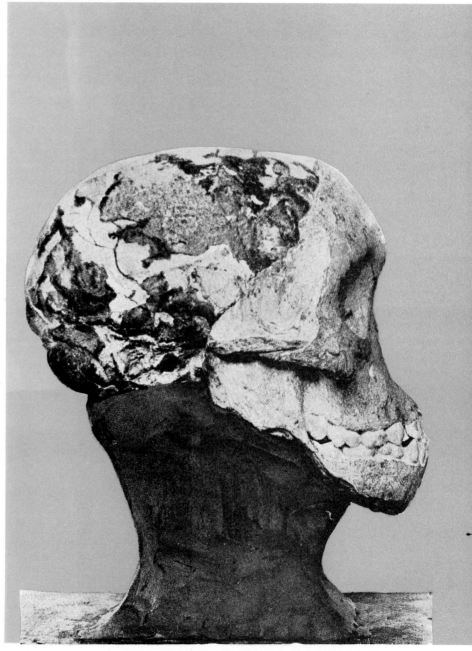

22-5
This child's skull from Taung, Africa, was the first discovery of *Australopithecus.*

## Australopithecus

The fossil discoveries which follow the gap in reconstruction of human evolution reveal definite evidence of a hominid form. It was characterized by a large brain, bipedal locomotion, erect posture, the consumption of meat in its diet, and possibly even the manufacture and use of tools. This fossil hominid is the controversial *Australopithecus*, or "southern ape."

Paleoanthropologists have unearthed the remains of about 300 australopithecines from sites in South and East Africa. It has tentatively been concluded that these hominids came in two varieties. One is *Australopithecus africanus*, a slight form weighing about 50 to 100 pounds. It is believed to have included meat in its diet. The stockier form is *Australopithecus robustus*, weighing 100 to 150 pounds. It probably fed mostly on plant foods.

Skulls, pelvises, and limb bones indicate that *Australopithecus* had both primitive and more advanced characteristics. It stood about four and one-half feet tall. It had massive jaws, no chin, a low cranium, and huge brow ridges. But the dentition has evolved further, and there is no diastema. Tooth wear also suggests that chewing was from side to side, as in humans. The skull is ape-like, but the foramen magnum is set forward and downward-facing. This is the same position found in *Homo sapiens*. The cranial capacity is small compared to that of humans. But the ratio of brain size to body size approaches that of later hominids. One of the most important facts to emerge from the study of *Australopithecus* is that hominids stood erect before they possessed a large, complex brain. Examination of fossil remains confirms that *Australopithecus* was definitely bipedal.

*A. africanus* and *A. robustus* also differed in ways other than those noted earlier. For example, *robustus* had a raised crest running the length of the top of the skull. Also found in apes, this crest anchors heavy jaw muscles needed for chewing tough

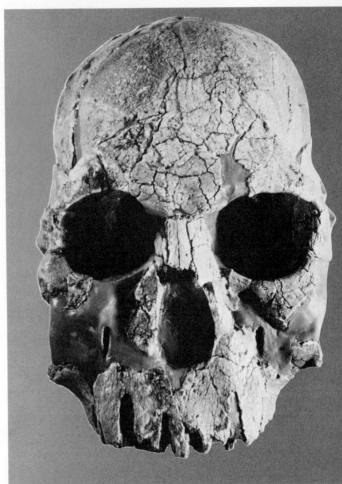

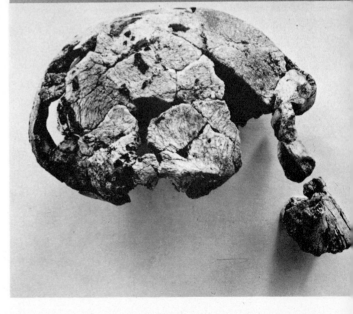

22-6
Front and side views of "1470," Richard Leakey's "Third Hominid Model" from Lake Rudolph, pieced together by his wife, Dr. Maeve Leakey.

plants. The cheek teeth of *robustus* increased in size, and the chewing surface of its molars expanded. These features suggest a reason for the extinction of the *robustus* form. It probably became too specialized too soon. Those forms which had not developed specialized jaws may have been forced to learn a more efficient use of tools. Thus they became better adapted over the long run. Furthermore, the eventual trend of human evolution was toward smaller teeth with less chewing surface. Thus *A. robustus* seems to represent an evolutionary dead end.

Considerable controversy among paleoanthropologists surrounds the question of whether or not *Australopithecus* was in fact a tool-maker and user. Raymond Dart, for example, believes that *Australopithecus* had a bone–tooth–horn culture, using these items as tools and weapons. However, no artifacts have yet been found that can be clearly identified as tools. Louis Leakey found what he believed to be crude pebble tools at Olduvai Gorge in Africa. However, he ascribed them not to *Australopithecus* but to a more advanced hominid called *Homo habilis*. The remains of this form were found with the tools. They include cranial bones dated to about 1.75 million years ago.

Where does Leakey's *Homo habilis* fit into the scheme of human evolution? At present, the situation is very confusing. Recently Leakey's son Richard discovered a skull called simply "1470." This skull is more advanced than any australopithecine fossil known. The cranial capacity of 1470 approaches that of the later *Homo erectus*. Yet it existed some 2 million years earlier. If the date of the 1470 specimen is correct, this means that a more advanced hominid existed before the less evolved *Australopithecus*. Leakey suggests that specimen 1470 outcompeted *Australopithecus* and evolved into *Homo erectus*. Leakey has classified 1470 as a member of the genus *Homo* and identifies it with the *Homo habilis* form.

## The genus Homo

Most anthropologists disagree with Leakey's classification. They believe that the australopithecines showed considerable variation, some dying out and others evolving into the genus *Homo*. To evaluate the two positions, we must know the characteristics of *Homo* and how they evolved. The traits that characterize both humans and human-like primates can be grouped into four general categories. These are dentition, brain, skeleton, and sexual reproduction and care of the young.

When early hominids left the trees and entered the woodlands and savannahs, their diet became omnivorous. It included

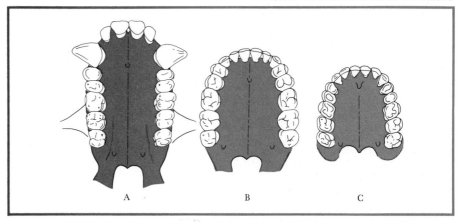

22-7
The palate and upper teeth of (A) a gorilla, (B) *Australopithecus*, and (C) a large-toothed human.

meat and fruit as well as plant foods. As a result, human dentition has evolved toward fewer, more generalized teeth. The mammal from which *Plesiadapis* is thought to have evolved, for example, had teeth which were specialized for cutting, tearing, and grinding. With the evolution of later primates the canines became smaller. A number of premolar teeth were lost, and the remaining teeth became more generalized and efficient. Human beings have 32 teeth, arranged in a U-shaped dental arch and all in line with one another.

As the teeth became smaller and fewer, the size of the jaw and face were reduced accordingly. Eventually they reached the compact facial structure seen in modern man. The switch from a primarily vegetable diet to one based on meat may also have favored an increase in the size of the brain. Early vegetarian primates met few challenges in the getting of food. Plants, fruits, and shrubs were theirs for the nibbling. The change to meat-eating, however, required new adaptations. Some of these may have led to the development of certain cranial areas. To catch smaller game such as lizards and rabbits, primates needed great speed. To bring down larger game such as young antelopes and baboons, they required foresight and planning. And when they began to pursue even larger adult animals, they required all of these, plus the ability to cooperate with each other. The pursuit of fast-moving large animals often involved problems that had to be solved immediately. This demanded flexible, non-stereotyped responses.

Manufacture and use of tools also made increased brain size and complexity more adaptive. Tool-making requires a preconceived notion of the shape and use of the tool. It is done in a standardized manner, following prescribed steps, and requires coordination of the hand, eye, and brain. While other animals have been seen to make and use tools, only humans use tools to make other tools. These selective pressures led to a fairly rapid increase in brain size. They also resulted in a more complex organization of the nerves and nerve pathways and connections.

Thus cranial capacity is a good indicator of a specimen's position on the evolutionary ladder. The cranial capacity of humans ranges between 1,000 and 2,000 cc. That of apes ranges from 350 to 650 cc, and of *Australopithecus* from 450 to 650 cc. However, brain size alone cannot be considered a valid criterion of intelligence. The average brain of *Homo neandertalensis,* for example measures 1,500 cc—larger than the average human brain. Bigger bodies require bigger brains simply to coordinate muscle activity. Whales and elephants have the largest brains of all.

A number of skeletal changes accom-

panied erect posture and bipedal locomotion. These form the third category of traits which characterize the genus *Homo*. The human species today has a broad pelvis and straight legs. The foot has a crosswise as well as a lengthwise arch, forming a complex spring for transmitting tension in walking. The spine is S-shaped.

Several theories attempt to explain the evolution of bipedalism and erect posture. One theory suggests that they conferred a selective advantage by allowing early hominids to see farther over the tops of tall grasses that may have concealed predators and prey. But this would explain only temporary bipedalism, a characteristic possessed by other primates. It does not indicate why humans became permanently bipedal. The suggestion that bipedalism developed because it enabled early hominids to carry their food with them also does not seem a sufficient explanation. Other primates have been observed to carry their food while walking erect for considerable distances.

A more promising theory, suggested by anthropologist John Pfeiffer, centers around increased hominid eating and sharing of meat. A lone hominid who had killed a large animal would find himself with a quantity of spoilable meat. It could not all be eaten on the spot, nor could it be successfully stored. Since it would be too precious to abandon, the hominid may have carried it back to camp to share with others. The survival advantage of the ability to carry food for long distances may have led to the selection of groups of individuals able to walk several miles, carrying an animal carcass in their hands or slung over their shoulders.

Finally, a variety of sexual reproductive features distinguish hominids from other primates. Human females, for example, do not have a seasonal estrous cycle. Instead, they have a menstrual cycle that makes mating possible at any time of the year. Humans do not possess a sexual skin—an area around the breasts or genitalia that changes color to signal the onset of the es-

**22-8**
Femur from a *Homo erectus* form found in Java (left) is closely similar to that of Homo sapiens (right).

trous period. Nor do they secrete specific sexual odors. Sexual attraction is based partly on secondary sexual features. Human infants are born almost completely helpless, their nervous systems not yet fully developed. As a result, they must depend upon parents and other adults for at least the first ten to twelve years of life. The selective advantage of this unique situation is that human offspring experience a long learning period. During this time they learn complex techniques of physical and social survival. These, in turn, contribute to the ability of the human species to dominate nearly all other forms of life.

Two final hallmarks of the genus *Homo* are tool-making and language. Both represent primarily cultural adaptations. As such, they probably appeared more or less simultaneously with the physical adaptations in a system of positive feedback, each new characteristic reinforcing others. Culture simply means that which is learned and, as we have seen earlier, the ability to learn is a biologically inherited characteristic. Moreover, the conditions which favor learning developed as part of our evolution as sexually reproducing, social mammals. Cultural evolution cannot occur without the biological changes that make it possible. On the one hand, physical evolution of brain size and capacity was necessary to the ability to communicate by language. On the other hand, the development of language provided a catalyst for further evolution of the brain. It made the physical and social environment more complex simply by defining it.

## Homo erectus

The first hominid form to possess all the characteristics of the genus *Homo* is *Homo erectus*. The fossil remains for this first true member of the genus were discovered in 1891 by Eugene Dubois in Java. He came upon the skull cap, thighbone, and some teeth of a hominid that had both ape-like and human features, including bipedalism. Dubois named his 500,000-year-old discov-

ery *Pithecanthropus erectus* (erect ape-human). The name has since been changed to *Homo erectus,* reflecting the specimen's somewhat more evolved status.

In 1927, near Peking in China, Davidson Black discovered a tooth in a limestone cave, along with stone tools including choppers and flakes. The young anatomist realized that the tooth belonged to a human ancestor. He named it *Sinanthropus pekinensis* (the Chinese human of Peking). Later expeditions unearthed the skull, teeth, jaws, and limb bones. These confirmed it as another *Homo erectus*.

On the basis of fossil discoveries, we can make a number of generalizations about the appearance of these very early

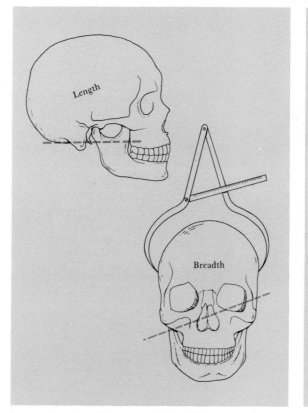

22-9
A much-studied but as yet unexplained example of ongoing human evolution is increasing brachycephaly (broad-headedness). Both Neanderthal and Paleolithic Europeans were primarily dolichocephalic (head width below 76 percent of length). As late as the 8th century A.D. no more than 30 percent were brachycephalic (head width more than 80 percent of length). But by the nineteenth century the balance had shifted: brachycephaly became the rule. A similar change has been noted among American Indians. In central and southeast Asia. Central Europe, the Near East, and America, the majority of native populations are brachycephalic. But the trend is not universal. Brachycephaly remains a rarity among present-day native populations in Africa, Melanesia, Australia, and Greenland.

human ancestors. They were all about five feet tall, roughly the same as the australopithecines to whom they are related. Their skulls, averaging about 1,000 cc, were low and wide at the base. Modern human skulls, by contrast, are widest in the area over the ears. The teeth of these *Homo erectus* forms are large, as are the jaws. In all of them the chinless jaw is somewhat prognathous (outward-projecting). The limb bones are as fully evolved as those of modern humans, and there is no doubt that *Homo erectus* stood and moved just as we do.

*Cultural remains*   Cultural items found with the physical remains are as important as physical appearance in determining the human status of *Homo erectus*. This is particularly true of the Chinese specimen. The discovery of a number of different tools, for example, shows that these individuals used tools for several purposes. One of these

22-10
Cast of reconstruction of *Sinanthropus pekinensis* found at Choukoutien, China. Classed as a *Homo erectus*, its cranial capacity is slightly larger than that of forms found in Java and other locals.

was certainly hunting, and the bones of numerous large animals indicate that they were skillful hunters. Among the bones were also a number of human skulls. In each of these the foramen magnum had been cracked in such a way as to enlarge it. The number of such cracked skulls suggests that these early humans were cannibals. Enlarging of the foramen magnum is the standard means used by contemporary cannibals for extracting the nutritious brain. Human long bones were found together

with the skulls. These were also smashed, probably to obtain the protein-rich marrow.

Perhaps most interesting was the discovery of hearths, evidence of the use of fire. The ability to use fire suggests a major adaptation to a cold environment, such as that which prevailed in China during the Middle Pleistocene. It also helps explain why the facial features of *Homo erectus* were not so massive as those of its forbears. If meat was tenderized by cooking, large teeth and jaws for chewing would no longer have any survival advantage. Indeed, their interference in chewing would probably put their owners at a slight disadvantage. Fire, of course, had many other uses. It could be used to heat and light caves, to frighten away animal predators, and to harden the wooden points of spears and other weapons. All of these factors would have increased the ability of *Homo erectus* to survive in greater numbers. They would also favor its evolution as a social being.

The capacity for culture increased along with the ability to learn and to communicate. *Homo erectus* remains in Europe reveal more about the cultural adaptations of these individuals. They hunted large animals together, in small groups, apparently using a good deal of cunning. Stone tools were found at the site of a bog at Torralba, Spain, for example, together with the remains of mammoths and other large animals. The animals are thought to have been driven into the bog and slaughtered by bands of *Homo erectus* hunters. This would have required cooperation and at least rudimentary communication. It also indicates the ability to solve problems by planning. A hunting camp on the French Riviera near Nice provides the earliest evidence of huts, apparently built by *Homo erectus*. These huts were made of thatched roofs supported by wooden posts, and ranged from 26 to 49 feet in length and 13 to 20 feet in width. They contained hearths, tools, a wooden bowl, and a quantity of red ocher, a paint used for religious and burial purposes among later human populations.

## Homo sapiens neandertalensis

The earliest fossil specimen of *Homo sapiens*, the species which includes present-day humans, was found in the Neander Valley of Germany, in 1856. *Homo sapiens neandertalensis* ranged throughout Europe and other areas during the upper Pleistocene.

Because large glaciers covered much of the earth during this period, the Upper Pleistocene is known as the Great Ice Age. Between 600,000 and 10,000 B.C., a series of glacial advances and retreats occurred in many parts of the world. The most recent, called the Würm, began about 70,000 to 40,000 years ago—at the time of the evolution of the Neandertal forms. Advancing glaciers caused dramatic changes in the surface of the earth and in the life which the earth supported. Seas and rivers were frozen or partly frozen, altering coastlines and changing the shapes of continents. Climatic changes included the movement of heavy rainfall regions toward the equator, changing deserts to grasslands. These extreme environmental changes resulted in comparatively rapid evolution and a number of different adaptive radiations.

The earliest Neandertal forms date from before this period, between 70,000 and 100,000 years ago. During the Würm glaciation, however, two distinct types evolved: the "classic" Neandertals and the more generalized forms. Both exhibit the rather large average cranial capacity of 1,500 cc. But the classic form was much stockier, with a low skull and heavy brow ridges.

Like the forms from which they evolved, Neandertals lived by hunting and gathering plant food. There is evidence that they lived in single-family groups or in small multi-family bands. They buried their dead, often with gifts. And they seem to have practiced a form of worship, centering around the cave bear.

The difference in appearance between the two Neandertal forms was probably the result of adaptation to different environ-

22-11
One sculptor's conception of Neanderthal man, whose unselective techniques of hunting may have hastened the extinction of all the great Pleistocene mammals.

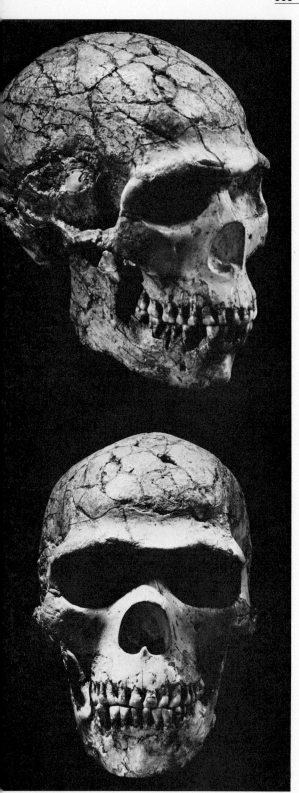

ments. The classic form lived in the severe, tundra-like environment of Western Europe. Its unusually heavy build would have helped it to survive the frigid cold. The classic Neandertals possessed a large nose, which may have functioned to warm the icy air they breathed. In addition, they had massive jaws, large brow ridges, and huge neck muscles. These features could have evolved as a result of hide chewing, a hide-softening technique practiced by modern Eskimos.

The generalized Neandertal possessed facial and skeletal features closer to those of its modern descendants. This was probably a result of the more moderate environment in which it evolved. As the glaciers retreated, this form would have been able to migrate to areas throughout Europe. Exam-

22-12
Two views of a skull (left) of one of the earliest *Homo sapiens sapiens*, found at Skhūl, Israel. The skulls were reconstructed by Hillel Burger, Harvard University.

22-13
What some early humans may have looked like. The second from left is the Piltdown man, once a scientific puzzle, now known to have been a hoax. From the left, the others are Pithecanthropus, Neanderthal, and Cro-Magnon. The restorations are by Dr. J. H. McGregor.

ples of this type have been found in Africa and China. Later fossils found in Yugoslavia and Czechoslovakia show evidence of their migration northward. Some anthropologists, however, classify these specimens as a more advanced form of *Homo sapiens*.

The generalized form of Neandertal is more closely related to the modern types that followed. It is believed that because of the harsh climate of the early Würm glacial period, classic Neandertals were relatively isolated from other *Homo sapiens* populations. This would have resulted in restricted gene flow and a considerable degree of inbreeding, emphasizing their distinctive characteristics. Isolation and inbreeding may also have resulted in reduced fitness, leading to the extinction of these European forms.

Another theory suggests that classic Neandertals did not die out, but interbred with later modern types. Fossils unearthed in Israel are believed by some to be hybrids between classic Neandertals and more modern types. Early human populations apparently migrated to a far greater extent than other animals, thus ensuring a fair amount of gene flow between them. Because of their bipedalism, their range was wider. And because of their large brains, they could adapt to many different environments. As they added more meat to their diet, longer hunting expeditions were required. This contributed to their increased mobility.

Some anthropologists believe that the Israeli specimens represent transitional forms between classic Neandertals and

modern humans, or *Homo sapiens sapiens*. It is believed that modern Europeans evolved from this Middle Eastern line, as migration increased with the retreat of the glaciers. A few anthropologists have even classified the Israeli specimens as *Homo sapiens sapiens*.

## Upper Paleolithic forms

The Würm glaciation advanced and retreated three times. The first was about 35,000 years ago and the last about 9,000 to 10,000 years ago. The period between retreats was marked by increasingly temperate conditions which coincided with a cultural epoch known as the Upper Paleolithic (Old Stone) Age. During this period an evolved human form appeared in Europe. It possessed a

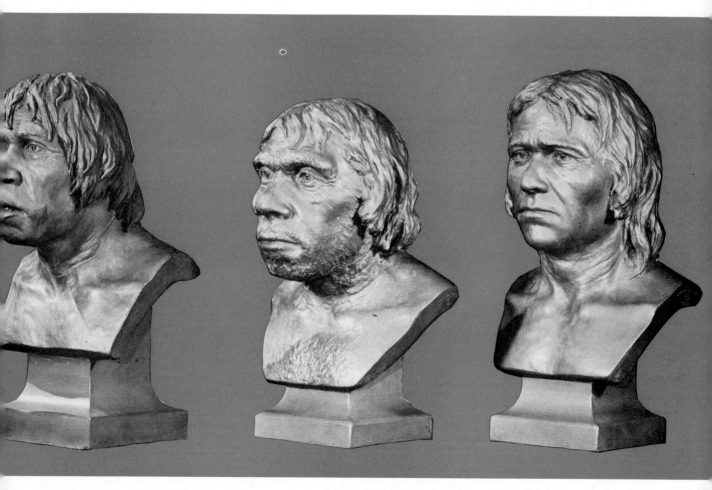

brain, skeleton, and overall physical appearance much like those of modern Europeans. This superior form was named Cro-Magnon, after the rock shelter in France where the best-known remains were discovered in 1868. Since then, a number of similar modern forms have been found, primarily in Europe. All of these are now classified as Upper Paleolithic forms belonging to the species *Homo sapiens sapiens*.

What were the physical adaptations of these Old Stone Age forms? For one thing, their facial structure was quite similar to our own. The brain had grown in size and complexity, a result partly of increased tool use and partly of the use of language. As these populations produced more efficient and specialized tools, the tools performed the cutting and tearing previously done by the massive teeth and jaws. Greater use of fire probably put those forms with large teeth and jaws at a selective disadvantage even more quickly.

For a long time it was believed that the Upper Paleolithic forms replaced the Neandertals by conquering and killing them. This theory was used to explain the lack of transitional forms so far found in Europe. It was suggested that modern forms developed in the Middle East and travelled to Europe at the last retreat of the Würm, where they conquered the existing generalized Neandertals.

Recently some anthropologists have begun to doubt this theory. Archaeological records show no sudden replacement of Neandertal tools by Upper Paleolithic tools. If the Upper Paleolithic types were so much superior to Neandertals in intelligence, we would expect to find more advanced tools than have been found with their remains. These investigators believe that transitional forms did exist in Europe but have simply not been found, for three reasons. One is that the search for fossil remains has traditionally been concentrated in caves, rather than in the open areas where transitional forms would have spent most of their time. Moreover, the archaeological record for the three retreat periods within the Würm glaciation is not well understood. Finally, it is quite possible that transitional Upper Paleolithic specimens have been discovered and are tucked away in museums or other collections, unrecognized for what they really are.

With the appearance of Upper Paleolithic populations, the morphological evolution of the human species seems to be com-

22-14
Cave drawing from Les Trois Frères, France. It is a beautiful example of Upper Paleolithic culture.

plete. Structurally these forms differ very little from present-day human populations. The ability to use fire and make tools, along with the ability to communicate, enabled them to adapt to a variety of environments. Gradually human beings began to migrate to all parts of the earth. The most recent migration was across the Bering Straits from Asia to the New World. During the last period of the Würm, sea levels averaged about 400 feet lower than they do now. A land bridge lay open which permitted movement to this continent by early nomadic societies from 25,000 to 11,000 years ago. From this period forward the many differences that distinguish human populations have been caused by biological and cultural adaptations to different localities. They come within the subject of human variation.

# summary

Some of the characteristics that distinguish primates from other mammals include arboreal habits; an omnivorous diet, leading to reduced and less specialized dentition; sharp, stereoscopic vision; increased brain size; an acute sense of touch and grasping ability; a tendency toward upright posture; and a foramen magnum which is shifted forward.

During the Cenozoic era of the Paleocene, the first primate forms evolved. The Eocene epoch favored the evolution of prosimians. During the Oligocene, small monkeys and primitive apes appeared. *Dryopithecus*, dating from the Miocene and early Pliocene, may have been an ancestor of the great apes and humans. A related primate of the later Miocene and early Pliocene is *Ramapithecus*. Its small canines suggest that it may have used tools and thus been bipedal. *Ramapithecus* may have been a transitional form between *Dryopithecus* and the earliest known hominid, *Australopithecus*.

*Australopithecus* closes a 10-million-year gap in the fossil record. It had a large brain, bipedal locomotion, erect posture, and perhaps tool-making ability. Remains found in East Africa and India suggest that two varieties existed—*A. africanus* and *A. robustus*. They show that hominids stood erect before they possessed large, complex brains. Crude pebble tools found by Louis Leakey may have been made by a more advanced form called *Homo habilis*, which outcompeted its contemporary *Australopithecus* and evolved into *Homo erectus*. Many doubt this.

The traits which characterize both humans and protohumans can be grouped into four categories: dentition, brain, skeleton, and sexual reproduction and care of the young. An omnivorous diet caused human dentition to evolve in the direction of fewer, more generalized teeth. The resulting decrease in the size of the face and jaw allowed for increased brain size. Tool-making and language both depended on larger brain size and capacity, and provided impetus for these evolutionary steps. Thus cranial capacity is a good indicator of a specimen's position on the evolutionary scale.

Skeletal modifications accompanied erect posture and bipedal locomotion. The most important of these were in the direction of a broad pelvis, straight legs, feet with a crosswise as well as lengthwise arch, and an S-shaped spine. Lack of an estrous cycle and sexual skin, and extended parental care of newborns, also provided selection advantages.

All of these characteristics were first displayed in *Homo erectus,* which used tools for hunting, engaged in cannibalism, used fire, and built huts for shelter. Its 500,000-year-old remains were found in Java and Peking. The earliest fossil of *Homo sapiens,* the species that includes present-day humans, was found in Germany. *Homo sapiens neandertalensis* hunted mammoths and other animals, gathered edible plants, and probably lived in single-family groups or small multifamily bands. The Neandertals, classified as either "classic" or generalized in form, were the dominant hominid during the Great Ice Age.

During periods when the glaciers retreated, the rising temperatures coincided with the Upper Paleolithic Age. In Europe, there evolved a human with a brain, skeleton, and appearance much like that of modern man: Cro-Magnon, now called *Homo sapiens sapiens*. The Cro-Magnons had large, complex brains and used tools in a highly specialized way. Able to adapt to a variety of environments, they eventually migrated to all parts of the earth.

ne of the most important ways of coping with the environment is behavior. All behavior represents an attempt by an organism to adapt to a stimulus—that is, a change in the environment. An underlying principle of adaptation is that organisms tend to react in ways which favor their survival.

The term "behavior" usually refers to responses to environmental change that involve the integrated functioning of the entire organism. Plants react to stimuli at the cell level, as do unicellular organisms. In multicellular animals, genetically inherited sensory and nervous systems form the framework within which all adaptive behavior evolves. Within this framework, the way the animal experiences its environment also influences its behavior. Even simple organisms—such as the flatworm—show behavior variations. Such variations depend on how the organism is influenced by experience. The interaction of inheritance with experience—the way experience affects inheritance—is the nature of adaptive adjustment. Animal behavior, therefore, is an important part of evolution.

On one level the study of behavior includes a search for the mechanisms that produce and control it. That is, we look for the underlying physical and biochemical processes. On another level the study of behavior seeks to analyze the interaction of learned behavior with that which is inherited. Both these studies contribute to an understanding of how behavior patterns are acted upon by selection in the process of evolution.

In order to study behavior we must understand the principle known as **Morgan's canon:** "In no case may we interpret an action as the outcome of the exercise of a higher psychical faculty, if it can be interpreted as the outcome of the exercise of one which stands lower in the psychological scale." By following this principle we avoid ascribing human characteristics, such as emotion, reason, decision making, or anticipation, to the behavior of nonhuman animals.

## Levels of organization

Along with searching for the simplest explanation for a given phenomenon, we must consider the level of organization on which that phenomenon occurs. Each group of organisms possesses some unique features that give it capabilities not present among organisms in the level below it. When we compare animals of different kinds, we find that the structural, physiological, and behavioral capacities of insects, for example, are considerably more complex and varied than those of flatworms. Insects thus represent a higher level of organization, which their behavior capabilities reflect.

The concept of levels also applies to the development of an individual organism. Development represents a fusion of hereditary and environmental factors. While some distinction between inherited and learned behavior is useful for purposes of study, it is not a case of either/or. It is not simply heredity versus environment, or nature versus nurture. Perhaps it is just a matter of when the learning process begins, or what sort of stimuli can be called experience. In any case, all adaptive behavior has an inherited component. This component interacts with the experience of the organism in a changing environment. The interaction is complete at all levels of organization. The more complex the organism, the more complex the interaction.

The feeding behavior of ring doves is a good example. In these birds, both sexes cooperate to build the nest and incubate the eggs. When the young birds hatch, both parents begin to produce a substance called "crop milk." When the chicks clamor to be fed, the parents take turns feeding. Grasping the bill of each chick in its own, the adult regurgitates the contents of the crop into the chick's mouth. Crop milk production is stimulated by the secretion of the hormone prolactin from the pituitary gland. Secretion of prolactin depends, in turn, upon the presence of the mate in the environment. Since the mate is present before the young are hatched, the production of crop milk "on time" is guaranteed.

The pattern of feeding behavior is also influenced by the amount of practice the adult birds have had. This was shown in a series of experiments conducted at Rutgers University by the late Daniel Lehrman and his colleagues. Adult birds were injected with prolactin. They produced milk and began to feed the young, but their first attempts were clumsy and ineffective. The young chicks were similarly inefficient at receiving food. But with repeated feedings, parents and offspring became more adept. Lehrman also showed that injection of prolactin elicited proper feeding behavior far more easily in adults who had previously raised chicks than in birds with no prior parental experience.

A final influence on this behavior pattern is the growth of the young. As they grow, their size stimulates the parents' pituitary glands to discontinue prolactin secretion. The crop milk content of the regurgitated food is thus reduced, allowing an increase in the proportion of adult foods such as seeds and grain. In this way the chicks are prepared to start feeding themselves.

## Sign stimuli

Biologists are increasingly reluctant to categorize behavior patterns in rigid frameworks. They recognize that it is hard to draw sharp lines between the effects of heredity and those of experience. But it is clear that many animals lack the sensory and neural equipment to sort out a confused set of stimuli, and so must respond quickly to a few key signals. These responses are species-typical: that is, they can be seen in every member of a species. Often they are sufficiently characteristic to be used as a means of classifying the species. Again, we have the example of the secretion of prolactin which initiates feeding behavior in the ring dove. It is a direct, immediate response to a single stimulus—the presence of the

23-1
Care-soliciting behavior in young yellow warblers. The young birds are blind at birth and direct gaping mouths straight upward. Only after ten days do they point toward the parent. The wide-open orange mouths act as a sign stimulus for parental feeding behavior.

mate. Signals which produce such responses are called **sign stimuli**, or **releasers**.

Often, merely identifying the source of a stimulus does not tell us much. In the case of the ring dove, a number of physical or behavioral traits of the mate could have provided the stimulus for secretion of prolactin. These include its odor, shape, sounds, or gestures. Lehrman tried separating the parents with a glass partition. He found that one bird produced prolactin as long as it could see the other sitting on the egg. When the glass was darkened, the bird stopped producing prolactin, although both sounds and smells circulated freely through the room. Thus the stimulus was visual. However, just what quality of the visual appearance caused the response is not yet known.

This does not mean that the ring dove has no receptors for scent or touch, or that it cannot respond to these stimuli. When it is selecting suitable food, for example, sensations of touch are especially important. Other sensations are taken in, but some of them are somehow blocked between the receptors and the motor centers. At another time, during a different activity, the stimulus which produces a response may be something else. Sign stimuli, then, are particular sensory cues. They are selected from among other sensory stimuli in a given situation.

Occasionally a single stimulus will provoke conflicting responses at the same time, such as the impulse to escape and that to attack. Male turkeys and fighting cocks are stimulated to attack each other, but inhibited by the equally strong urge to flee. Since they are thus prohibited from doing either one effectively, they peck vigorously at the ground. Such behavior is often called **displacement activity**. It is evoked by the conflict situation itself rather than by an appropriate object (such as food in the case of pecking).

The reproductive behavior of the stickleback fish is a well-known example of the importance of sign stimuli in triggering

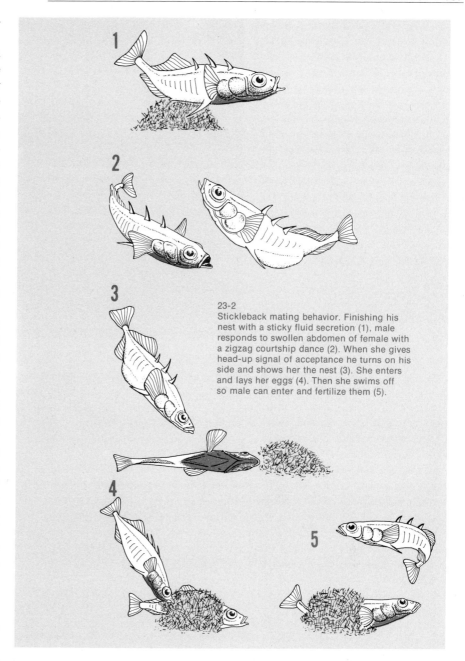

23-2
Stickleback mating behavior. Finishing his nest with a sticky fluid secretion (1), male responds to swollen abdomen of female with a zigzag courtship dance (2). When she gives head-up signal of acceptance he turns on his side and shows her the nest (3). She enters and lays her eggs (4). Then she swims off so male can enter and fertilize them (5).

behavioral responses. When ready to reproduce, the male stickleback develops a bright red belly. He aggressively displays it to other males when staking out his nesting territory. This signals to the other males his intention to defend that territory, and they react by staying clear. As soon as the nest is ready, the fish changes color again. He keeps his red belly but acquires a pale blue back in place of the normal grey-green camouflage colors. This color change attracts a prospective mate. Her appearance, in turn, triggers the next stage in the male's courtship. This is a zigzag dance, during which he may touch the female with his stickles. If she lifts her head in acceptance, the male shows her the nest, pointing to it with his head. When the female enters the nest, her mate prods her on the tail. This is a tactile stimulus that provokes spawning. The male repeats this sequence with several mates, fertilizing each deposit of eggs as the female leaves the nest. It is also his responsibility to protect the young fish. When the eggs hatch he assumes his original protective coloring, both top and bottom.

## Inappropriate responses

Chains of stimuli and responses such as that shown by the stickleback fish clearly depend upon a large inherited component, despite the complex interaction with the environment. This is most clearly demonstrated by studies of inappropriate behavior, when the animal responds to one aspect of reality, such as shape, color, or sound, despite the absence of other characteristics that make up the whole. For example, ornithologist David Lack has noted that the male robin will attempt to repel a small red feather as vigorously as it will a convincing stuffed replica or even a real male robin. It seems that the patch of red at a certain height triggers the response. The warbler is a more poignant example. It will incubate and hatch the much larger egg of a cowbird that has pushed the warbler's own eggs out of the nest. Moreover, the wide-open mouth of the hatched intruder stimulates feeding behavior in the mother warbler, regardless of the fact that the chick is not her own.

In some cases artificial stimuli are even more effective if they enlarge upon reality rather than imitating it exactly. Faced with two painted wooden eggs, the female herring gull will try to incubate the larger one

23-3
Female herring gull tries to incubate a dummy egg several times larger than her own egg beside it. (See Inappropriate responses)

despite difficulty in sitting on it. The warbler's response to the cowbird egg may be a similar example.

## Orientation behavior

One of the simplest components of behavior is **orientation**. This term refers to ways in which organisms move their bodies in response to environmental stimuli, especially gravity, heat, and light. An orientation response is thus a steering reaction. Like the simplest form of response to a stimulus—the reflex—orientation can be modified by experience. In lower organisms, orientation takes one of two forms, taxis or kinesis.

### Taxis

Some organisms have a receptor system which enables them to find out the direction from which a stimulus is coming. The resulting orientation is called a **taxis**. For example, a flatworm will move toward a light source by positioning itself so that both eyespots are equally stimulated. We note that when movement is toward the stimulus (as in the example), the taxis is termed positive. When the movement is away from the stimulus, the taxis is negative.

Taxis responses occur in various ways. The simplest organisms appear to compare repeatedly the relative intensity of the stimulus, first on one side of the body and then on the other. They do this by swaying. Other organisms with paired receptor organs can compare the stimulation on both sides of the body at the same time.

Many factors can modify or even reverse the taxis response. In most cases a low-intensity stimulus evokes a positive taxis. The same stimulus at a high intensity evokes a negative taxis. Amoebas, for example, will move away from a strong light but toward a weak one.

The fact that a response can be modified is adaptive. Biologist John Paul Scott performed a series of experiments with newly hatched fruit flies. Fruit flies generally move toward a light source. But Scott discovered that when they were placed in a dark tube and then exposed to light from one end of the tube, the young fruit flies did not crawl toward the light. They simply stayed still or wandered around. However, when the experiment was performed again, the flies did crawl toward the light. Repeated tests elicited both types of response, with no apparent explanation for either.

Then Scott noticed that the positive response occurred at times when heavy trucks were passing, shaking the building and the tubes. In further experiments, light combined with jarring resulted in consistently positive responses. In natural surroundings, of course, relentless pursuit of light would exhaust the flies. But when they are foraging for food in dark places such as trash cans or rotten logs, flight toward the light in response to a jolt would increase their chances of escape from sudden danger.

## Kinesis

Some organisms do not have the means for locating the source of a stimulus. In such cases, orientation takes the form of **kinesis**. This is a change in the rate or probability of

motion. It is not specifically directed toward or away from a stimulus. Sowbugs, for example, tend to move away from lighted areas and toward shady spots. The reason seems to be that they simply walk faster when in light. In the dark, they move very slowly, or even stop completely. In other words, their motion is not specifically directed toward or away from light. Instead, they simply increase or decrease activity according to the intensity of the stimulus.

Some kinds of stimulus, such as slowly diffusing chemicals, convey direction poorly if at all. A chemical stimulus consists of material particles with which an organism actually comes in contact. For example, we become aware of an odor only after it has reached us. The problem is that its strength is the same no matter what direction we turn in. This is because the particles of the stimulus are evenly distributed around us. Only by first moving in one direction can we determine the relative intensity of the stimulus and thus its likely source. Sharks, for example, swim in figure-eight patterns when they detect the odor of food. The movement is not specifically directional, but the increased activity adds to the probability of locating the source.

## Sonar

Another method of navigation involves a complex form of orientation by **sonar**. This is the process of sending out sonic and ultrasonic waves and listening to their echoes as they bounce off an object. Most animals that hunt at night have good vision, but not the bat. Instead, a bat emits repeated ultrasonic cries. Their echoes are reflected off objects in the bat's path. Sonar detectors enable the bat to navigate by picking up these echoes, much as sonar devices in submarines allow them to avoid running into things. Bats also detect food with these devices, as their screams are reflected off the bodies of flying moths. It is interesting that this has apparently exercised a selective pressure on moths. It has favored the development of ultrasonic listening devices

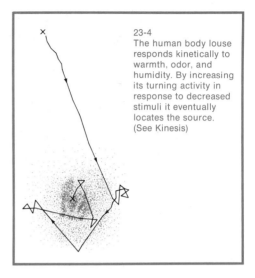

23-4
The human body louse responds kinetically to warmth, odor, and humidity. By increasing its turning activity in response to decreased stimuli it eventually locates the source. (See Kinesis)

23-5
The serotine bat in flight. It emits repeated cries that echo off objects in its path. (See Sonar)

23-6
Nocturnal migrants—
among them thrushes,
warblers, buntings, and
geese—navigate
apparently by the
position of the moon
and stars. Here a
flock of snow geese
fly across a full moon.

on the moths' midsections. These pick up bat cries and so provide a warning that a bat is on their trail.

## Homing and migration

Some of the most complex interactions of orientation patterns are displayed by migratory birds. Homing and migratory behavior is often reinforced by previous experience with an area recognized as "home." Many animals identify with a particular locality quite early in their lives. In birds, the act of nest-building apparently creates an attraction to one spot. Some birds come back to the same place every year. Naturally this sort of attraction means that they must be able to find their way home if they leave it. All birds have good eyesight and doubtless use familiar landmarks just as humans do. A person can see 100 miles at bird altitudes, but a bird's ability to pick up details at such distances is two to three times greater than ours. Most birds have a regular feeding or hunting territory. This ranges from an area of five or six square miles for small titmice to several hundred for birds of prey. If they are released outside of this territory, the birds are less likely to return to the nest than when they are released within it.

Migratory birds also depend on wind and weather conditions, often waiting for good weather before migrating. European woodcocks pick up southwest winds arising from areas of low pressure over Britain

and follow them to Hungary. Starlings leaving from the northeast United States make a wide detour out to Bermuda in order to catch the trade winds to South America. A drop in temperature and reduced daylight signal the autumn migrants that it is time to go south.

But clearly more is involved. Migratory birds also seem to follow a sun compass. Ornithologist Gustav Kramer placed starlings in a windowed enclosure which was otherwise free of landmarks. He altered the apparent angle of the sun by means of mirrors outside the windows. At the time of the spring migration the starlings all moved to the direction they perceived to be southwest, which varied as the sun's angle was altered with the mirrors. When the sky was overcast the birds did not orient in any direction.

## Magnetic fields

Homing pigeons are attractive subjects for testing navigation theories. They reveal more complex behavior patterns each time biologists sort out a piece of the puzzle. Although he accepted the theory of sun compass navigation, William Keeton of Cornell University observed that as the birds became used to flying under cloudy skies, they became much better at it. To rule out any possibility that the birds were following landmarks, he fitted them with frosted contact lenses. This made them unable to distinguish any outlines but did not plunge them into darkness. The birds' success rate was reduced considerably, but they all appeared to correct for direction en route, and none came down more than a mile from the home loft. Keeton next wondered if the birds might be picking up faint signals from the earth's magnetic field. He outfitted them with small magnets and set them off on a totally overcast day, calculating that the magnets, together with the lenses, would throw the birds completely off. They did. Then he altered the birds' perception of the magnetic field with magnetic coils that reversed the north-south orientation. This caused them to fly in a completely opposite direction. The experiment explained why earlier use of magnets with normally sighted birds had not thrown the birds off course. These birds had simply followed the sun compass on fair days and visual landmarks in cloud. In fact, birds follow many clues. Recent experiments in Pisa, Italy, have indicated that they may even orient by smell. When one signal system is frustrated they switch to another.

## Biological clocks

The ability to sense time is an orientation related to biological rhythms. Such rhythms are changes in metabolic activities that match periodic environmental changes. Many animals respond to seasonal changes in the relative length of day and night. Animals alter the color of their fur or plumage for seasonal camouflage. Birds go south when the days get shorter. And a vast number of organisms control their reproductive cycles according to the time of year. In some organisms, such as the fruit fly *(Drosophila)*, the biological rhythms will persist indefinitely under artificial conditions, such as constant darkness. This happens if the rhythms are first established under natural conditions. Higher animals, however, show an ability to adjust their rhythms, over time, to new conditions.

# Learning behavior

The term "orientation" usually describes behavioral responses that are innate. But it is clear that the more complex the organism, the greater the influence of experience in affecting, or even modifying, these responses. The process of modifying behavior as a result of experience of the environment is known as **learning**.

We noted earlier that the stimulation of crop milk production in the ring dove depends upon external factors in the environment for its timing. But this sort of response is hormonally, or internally, controlled. It is not the same as learning by experience.

The simplest form of learning is known as **habituation**. This is a waning of a response when a particular stimulus is repeatedly or continuously presented. The crawling snail *(Helix albolabris),* for example, characteristically withdraws its tentacles when mechanically shocked or jolted. But if the shock is repeated over and over, the withdrawal response eventually stops. In other words, the snail has become habituated to the stimulus.

Habituation occurs at all levels of organization, including the protozoa. But the length of modification at the lower levels is quite limited. For example, if a day goes by, and the snail is again jolted, it will retract its tentacles as usual. Efforts to modify behavior permanently at the lower levels have in fact proved futile. If learning is to take place, experience must be retained and become part of the development of behavior. For this to happen, a central nervous system seems to be necessary.

## Learning by association

One of the best-known categories of learning, **association**, is based on the ability to respond to sign stimuli. If a different or secondary stimulus is repeatedly produced together with the sign stimulus, the animal learns to associate the two stimuli with one another. Presenting the secondary stimulus alone will then produce this response. The secondary stimulus is usually presented immediately before the primary one. Thus the contractions of flatworms normally produced by an electric shock can be stimulated by a beam of light. It is achieved by exposing the worm to 50 or 100 experiences of shock immediately following the beam of light.

This is the type of learning response which Russian behaviorist Ivan Pavlov studied so thoroughly in his experiments with the feeding behavior of the dog. After repeatedly sounding a bell before presenting the dog with meat, Pavlov then sounded the bell without producing any meat. The dog started salivating as soon as he heard the bell, even though no meat was present. This indicated his association of the bell with food.

## Learning by discrimination

Pavlov also experimented with bells that varied considerably in pitch and volume. At first he fed the dog after ringing each type of bell. In time, all the bells produced the same response, salivation. Then he fed the dog after only one of the types of bell. Eventually, the dog would not respond to any bell but the one that had been followed by food. This type of behavior is known as **discrimination**, and requires two abilities. The first is to generalize all variations of a class of stimuli. The second is to discriminate among the variations.

## Learning by trial and error

Experiments were devised by B. F. Skinner of Harvard University to confirm the effects of association of stimuli in both voluntary and involuntary feeding behavior. He used what came to be called a Skinner box, which contained a food-releasing lever and a food slot. A hungry rat placed in this box learned to associate the receipt of food with the pressing of a lever. The association differs from that made by Pavlov's dog because it involves the association of a response with a later event rather than a preceding one. Thus the association becomes a means of learning by trial and error.

The process by which an insect learns a maze is more complicated. An ant in a maze with several T-choices and U-turns learns to find the shortest route to the food box through a series of three stages. At first, the ant displays a good deal of general activity and erratic behavior. This decreases with repetition, but with no improvement in avoiding blind alleys or taking shortcuts. Gradually, however, the ant shortens its runs into blind alleys. Finally it eliminates the blind alley turns completely. It runs through the entire maze quickly and smoothly. This gradual improvement occurs

as the ant learns from its experience. But such learning seems to take place within an individual series of problems. Given a new series of problems, the ant must start over again. That is, it does not seem to be able to apply its previous experience to a new situation.

In similar mazes, rats learn the correct pathways with fewer errors in fewer runs than do insects. They shorten the blind alley runs much sooner. Subsequent alterations of the maze show that rats can modify their behavior readily in response to new situations and can profit from their initial learning experience. Ants, however, apparently face each new maze as a new problem. It is clear that this type of trial-and-error learning can occur only when the organism is capable of sufficiently variable behavior to begin with. As variability increases, so does the ability to modify behavior on the basis of past experience. When animals hunt for food under natural conditions, their rewards are usually uncertain and infrequent. So the ability to learn from past errors avoids wasted energy and represents an adaptive modification of behavior.

## Problem-solving behavior

The ability to solve problems is a more complex type of learning than the simple trial-and-error method. German psychologist Wolfgang Koehler made a study of the behavior of chimpanzees. He noted that they appeared to perceive the problem first, then proceeded immediately to solve it. Koehler placed some bananas high out of reach in their cages, in which he had scattered a number of boxes. After examining the dilemma and without trying alternative approaches first, the chimps stacked the boxes one on top of the other and climbed up to the fruit. Later they managed a more complicated task. By fitting together several short poles placed in their cage, they succeeded in pulling in bananas from the ground outside the cage. Both tasks were done quite quickly.

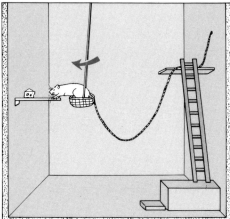

**23-7**
A white rat is faced with the problem of getting cheese from a shelf high above it. The rat climbs the ladder to the shelf on the opposite wall and locates the cord tied to the basket hanging between the two shelves. The rat pulls the basket over to it by means of the cord. It then climbs into it and swings across to the cheese.

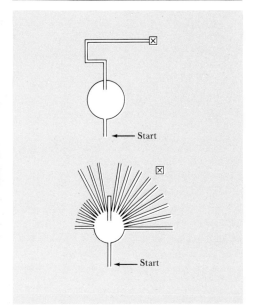

**23-8**
Tolman's "sunburst maze" experiment. In both mazes, the rat reached its goal at the point marked X.

Such problem-solving behavior involves the ability to visualize both the problem and the solution. This avoids wasting time and effort on many false tries. A brain is necessary for such conceptualization, but the ability apparently is not limited to the relatively complex brains of anthropoid apes and human beings. Loh Seng Tsai at Tulane University showed that specially bred white rats could be trained to solve problems such as the one shown in the accompanying diagram. Edward Tolman probed more deeply into aspects of rat behavior that appear to go beyond trial and error. He noted that rats placed in a new environment invariably explore it immediately. Further, if a change in the environment occurs, they will investigate the change at once, regardless of what they are doing. Their apparent ability to conceptualize spatial relationships was even more interesting. Taught to run down a series of turns to reach a goal, rats will identify the location of that goal even when the route to it is completely altered. In the altered version of the maze, many directional choices are possible. However, the rat does not repeat the progressive directional turns, but goes straight to the goal (see diagram). This sort of behavior is closely associated with memory, as we saw in the neurobiology chapter. It is controlled by the hypothalamus.

Not all animals can solve problems in this way, even those as far up the evolutionary ladder as the raccoon. But we cannot conclude from this that some animals are more "intelligent" than others. Behavior ability depends as much on what stimuli the animal is able to receive, as it does on how it reacts to sensations. Moreover, the ability to conceptualize problems depends on how important that ability is to the survival of the species. Animals that are used to living in holes, such as earthworms, have no need to run on horizontal surfaces or turn corners, either to find food or to avoid predators. They are therefore likely to perform poorly in mazes. So, also, are sheep, whose terrain is vastly different from that of mice. Cats cannot perform manipulative tasks—not only because their paws are not constructed to do so but because they exist quite efficiently without them.

## Imprinting

All of these types of learning can take place while the animal is in isolation. There remains one type of learning behavior that can take place only in group settings. This is a special type of species recognition known as **imprinting**. It is so named because in it an image of the parent is apparently imprinted on the brain of the new offspring.

Soon after it hatches, the duckling or gosling waddles after the first moving thing it lays eyes on, usually the mother. It watches her behavior and learns what she looks like. The period of imprinting usually starts very soon after birth—in ducks it starts within a few hours—and lasts for a very short time, usually no more than a couple of days. But the species-image imprinted during this critical time is permanent. Konrad Lorenz first studied this phenomenon with geese. He noted that if another parent-figure is substituted during the imprinting period, the young bird will follow that figure rather than its natural parents or another member of its own species. Moreover, the

23-9
Imprinting functions mainly as a means of recognition—in this case not for the young seal pup but for its mother. Right after giving birth the female nuzzles her pup, imprinting its special smell and sound. Later, searching among the thousands of newborn seals, she listens for the cries of her own. Then she completes the identification with a nuzzle.

substitute parent image usually influences the animal's future choice of a mate. This is true regardless of whether the substitute was an inappropriate species such as a dog or a human being, or even an inanimate object. All that is necessary is that the image-object move, and make noise.

# Social behavior

Social behavior in any population involves competition and cooperation. Both of these require the ability to communicate. Although aspects of competitive behavior represent adaptation and will be mentioned in this chapter, the function of competitive behavior within a population is treated in more detail as it relates to population control in chapter 24. In this chapter we are concerned with one result of competition: cooperation.

Cooperation within a group results in increased ability of the group to compete with other groups. The ability to share experience greatly speeds up and expands the process of individual adaptation, and ultimately that of the population. As members of a species specialize their behavior, some of them can perform one task and some another. Thus each specialty group extends its activities in one direction while remaining part of the group. Broader feeding territories can be discovered and defended, and more efficient protection can be organized. Perhaps most important are the expanded possibilities for learning, based on the experience of the entire population and not simply that of a single individual.

## Communication

To interact socially, animals must learn to recognize, and identify themselves with, fellow species members. Effective communication, then, involves the ability to send identification signals, and to receive and respond to them. Moreover, the signal or stimulus is normally supplied by a specialized structure of the sender. Thus flies receive a signal of warmth from the bodies of large mammals, including humans, but this cannot be regarded as communication.

We tend to think of verbal communication as the most sophisticated method of transmitting information, perhaps because it is potentially the most precise. But the types of animal communication are extraordinarily varied. Some of them are immensely complicated, involving all of the senses.

### Chemical communication

Pheromones are chemicals produced by individuals of a population which affect the social behavior of the group. Pheromones convey messages from a distance, and function as stimuli in a number of ways. For example, individual worker ants forage on their own, but when one finds a food particle that is too big to carry alone, it leaves the particle and returns to the nest. On the way it deposits a chemical substance along the trail by touching the tip of its abdomen to the ground at regular intervals. The odor of this substance attracts other worker ants to the food source. If a number of ants find a very large quantity of food, all of them do the same thing, thus making the trail wider. This odor lasts for only a short time, so that when food sources are exhausted the trails are extinguished. This is an example of a well-developed system that functions more simply among other animals. Flies alighting on a food source for the first time, for example, touch the food with a particular scent which makes it known to other flies at a greater distance.

Many animals use chemical signals to transmit alarm or distress warnings. Ants have glands near the mouth and the anus that secrete alarm-giving substances, bringing large numbers of fellow ants to the rescue. Fish secrete chemicals from the skin that function in the same way. And odors produced from glands in the hooves of deer spread fear among the others and signal them to flee from danger.

Possibly the widest use of chemical communication is in sexual attraction. Some examples of this will be discussed as they function in courtship behavior. Chemical communication is found at all organizational levels, since chemical responses are possible for even the simplest organisms. This type of communication tends to become an auxiliary system for those animals able to communicate visually or aurally.

### Auditory communication

Animals can produce sounds in a variety of ways, but require hearing organs to receive them. The more developed hearing any animal has evolved, the more it tends to rely on sound for communication. Sound signals allow for considerably more variation than chemical signals. Unlike chemical communication, auditory communication can convey a sense of direction, especially at high frequencies. Moreover, once chemical signals have been sent out they permeate the medium in which they are diffused. Auditory signals, though, can be suddenly stopped if they are no longer appropriate.

Since sounds are made by vibration, they can be produced in many ways. In order to mate, the male spider must approach the female in her web. To distinguish himself from a possible prey and be accepted as a mate, he plucks the strings of the web in recognized rhythms. Most insects communicate by nonvocal sounds of one sort or another. Grasshoppers scrape their legs together, moths and mosquitos vibrate their wings, and beetles and ants tap their bodies against solid objects.

All vertebrates can produce sounds, even the fish. Puffers, for example, make bumping noises, as do some fresh-water minnows. Among the reptiles, male alligators and crocodiles roar to attract mates, and gecko lizards chirp loudly at night. Noisier still are the amphibians, including toads that rattle, frogs that croak, and tree frogs that whistle.

In sexual communication, usually the male makes the signal, and the female responds to it. Both sexes, however, send out warnings. Many mammals, including elk, wolves, and chimpanzees, give distress calls to summon other members of their species population. Other animals, such as rats and many birds, use distress calls to warn the others away.

### Visual communication

Visual signals are most common among animals at the high levels of organization, especially ar-

**23-10**
A cricket produces the familiar rasping chirp by rubbing together file-like structures on its elevated wing covers. (See Auditory communication)

**23-11**
Some birds can give two kinds of alarm signal. The herring gull, for example, warns of marginal danger with a low intensity call. It warns of serious danger with sharp, staccato shrieks.

thropods and vertebrates. This is because well-developed eyes are needed for effective visual communication. Color signals, such as those shown by the stickleback fish, reach their greatest variation in the birds. In almost all bird species the males are more brightly colored than the females, since the male does not usually have to stay by the nest to protect the young. Instead, he warns off other birds by displaying his colors. Some males do in fact require camouflage for protection. In such cases the color spots are usually displayed only under certain circumstances. For example, the robin is perfectly camouflaged from above. It is only his red stomach that is threatening, usually to other males of his species. Both protective and warning coloration usually require corresponding behavior patterns. Often the behavioral gesture required to show off color adds to the threats. Lizards, for example, stand on their back legs to display their colored undersides. Thus they appear threatening in gesture as well as in color.

## The dance of the honeybee

One of the most intricate examples of social behavior is displayed by colonies of honeybees. It involves chemical, auditory, and visual communication. The group cooperates to obtain food, using an elaborate system in which foraging worker bees communicate the location of their finds to the other hive-dwellers. This system was first described by Karl von Frisch in 1946. When the worker bee locates an area rich in pollen and nectar, she first feeds, picking up the scent on her body. Then she returns to the hive, where she bumps against other bees and thereby spreads the scent. If the food is odorless, she deposits pheromones at the source for identification by other bees. After this she performs one of two dances, either the round dance or the waggle dance. In the round dance, the bee simply circles, counterclockwise, then clockwise. This stimulates the others to look for food nearby. The waggle dance consists of

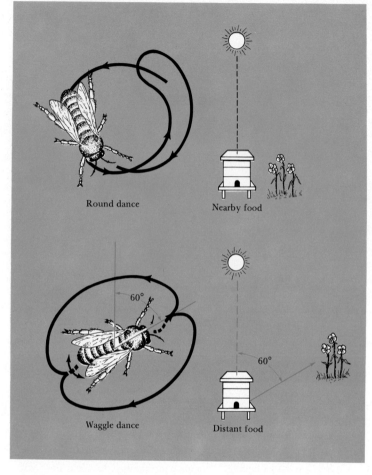

Round dance

Nearby food

Waggle dance

Distant food

figure-eight sweeps around a center run, during which the bee also waggles her abdomen. She conveys the distance from the hive by both tempo and duration. The faster the dance the closer the food, and the longer it is, the farther the food. She also indicates its direction by the line formed by the center of the figure-eight pattern. Outside, where the sun is visible, she can point straight toward the food. When the dance is done inside the dark hive, the degree off from the vertical indicates the angle to the sun at which the other bees should fly. In addition to sun compass orientation, the dance shows the use of a biological clock. As the worker bee repeats her dance periodically, she must change the direction of the center run as the sun moves across the sky.

23-12
Honeybee dances. Above: round dance, indicating nearby food. Below: figure-eight "waggle" dance, indicating the precise location of more distant food. Straight run with wagging abdomen is shown by broken line in middle of figure-eight.

**23-13**
Some animals deceive would-be predators by displaying outsized eyespots, as shown by the eyed click beetle. (See Defensive behavior)

**23-14**
Some behavioral disguises serve the predator. The insectivorous sundew lures insects by secreting nectar-like droplets on its leaves to trap the unsuspecting visitors until they are dissolved by digestive juices.

Bees can orient themselves by the sun's position on overcast days or even inside the darkened hive, so long as there is a patch of blue sky visible. Compound eyes allow them to perceive the amount of polarization of the sun's rays reflected off dust and gas particles in the atmosphere. These eyes, unlike human eyes, are also sensitive to ultraviolet light. By detecting the plane of polarization in any patch of blue sky, they can locate the sun's position in the sky.

## Defensive behavior

Animals use all of the three sensory channels to communicate threats or warnings, to members of other species as well as to their own. Many poisonous or harmful animals employ warning signals. This allows them to avoid potentially injurious conflicts in which they would have to use their primary defenses. Cobras make use of their identifying shapes, spreading their hoods as a warning to any who invade their territory. Scorpions go through elaborate posturing to warn trespassers of their deadly stings. Other animals use sound warnings. The rattle of a snake, the buzz of a bee, and the growl of a dog are three familiar examples.

*Mimicry* Some less well-armed animals have profited from such danger signals by imitating them. In this **Batesian mimicry**, harmless animals imitate one or more aspects of a distasteful or poisonous species. Thus they avoid predation themselves. Such mimicry is displayed by robber flies, which provide tasty meals for toads. The flies are colored to look like the stinging wasp, and can also imitate the buzz of the wasp to complete the disguise. They are therefore avoided by toads who have been stung once. Viceroy butterflies, a favorite meal for many birds, have color patterns closely resembling those of monarch butterflies, which birds find inedible. This protects Viceroys from birds who have sampled monarchs.

But a number of different butterflies which all taste unpleasant also look alike. In

this case they are exhibiting **Müllerian mimicry**, first described by German naturalist Fritz Müller. All of these species benefit from avoidance by predators who have tasted only one. Bees, wasps, and hornets all sting, but because they all look more or less alike, a predator has to be stung by only one to shun them all.

A Florida biologist recently noted that the females of some firefly species apparently can reproduce the flashing mating signals of other species. This attracts unsuspecting alien suitors. Once having lured these males, the female mimics grab and consume them. Such behavior is known as **aggressive mimicry**. The zone-tailed hawk is not only shaped much like the turkey vulture, but also displays a similar flight pattern. This enables it to catch small rodents and other prey that mistake it for the harmless carrion feeder. The evolution of a behavior pattern for predation, rather than for defense, is probably due to its value in increasing the food supply of the species.

*Territoriality* Another form of defensive behavior, territoriality, occurs among members of the same species. Many animals have evolved ways to allocate the sources of their food supplies. Too many feeders on one source would result in starvation for all of the contenders. On the other hand, fighting to the death over food is destructive also. This is true both for the individual who loses and for the species as a whole. In many species, therefore, fighting is symbolic or ritualized and is rarely harmful. In some cases it is reduced to aggressive, or **agonistic**, display, often involving the same mechanisms seen in interspecies behavior. Snakes and scorpions, for example, threaten trespassers of their own species with the same visual and auditory signs they use to warn potential enemies. In this case, though, they are signaling their presence in a certain territory rather than their poisonous nature. Less well-protected animals are fiercely aggressive toward potential rivals. But when faced with a potential ene-

**23-15**
Fiercely territorial are the Siamese fighting fish. When two males encounter each other on a disputed territory, they flash bright-colored patches in warning. Then they dart aggressively at each other. They often lock jaws and jockey for position.

**23-16**
The cheetah leaves a scent trail to show where it has gone to hunt. After following the urine trail for a short distance, the newcomers will branch off and go in a different direction to avoid competition. (See Territoriality)

my or predator, they usually flee or hide. Many lizards, for example, defend their territory vigorously against a fellow lizard. They arch their backs. Circling the intruder and then facing it, they raise their bodies off the ground on stiffly stretched legs. If the newcomer fails to go away, the defender will rush at it and often nip it until it scurries off. But in the face of an enemy, a lizard will keep still for effective camouflage.

Methods of communicating territorial claims vary from animal to animal. Birds usually indicate territory by a loud call, repeated as often as necessary. However, some also display themselves visually. Gulls stand very upright and snap their bills. Birds with colored wings or tail feathers wave them vigorously. Mammals often use chemical signals to mark off hunting and feeding territories, since most of them have a highly developed sense of smell. Rabbits, foxes, dogs, and wolves leave small amounts of urine at regular intervals. Rhinos and hippos deposit piles of dung for the same purpose. A more elaborate pattern is that of the bison. First carving out grooves on trees with its horns, it then urinates and rolls in the urine so that it can rub the odor into the tree trunk with its back.

Territorial displays often occur near a nesting or breeding site. Usually the male is the one who shows such behavior. It serves as a warning to other males that he intends to defend his property from rivals. Also, it is a way of inviting females to enter into courtship. Occasionally, the female defends the territory for her future family. A female Venezuelan frog, for example, goes straight up to an intruder and raises her head to display a bright yellow throat, which she pulsates rapidly. Often such behavior does not go unchallenged. But if the intruder fails to go away, the female will pounce.

Many species have evolved ways of indicating that they have renounced a claim. When a displaying stickleback is placed in a tank occupied by another, he will suddenly give up his display posture and lose his red belly color. When two hermit crabs fight,

23-17
Fighting? No, courting. Such "loveplay" is part of the lion's courtship ritual. (See Reproductive behavior)

the loser falls on its back, a symbolic posture also seen in vertebrates.

When fighting does occur among animals, it is almost always the animal on home ground who wins. The selective advantage of this is clear—it assures protection of young.

### Reproductive behavior

Territorial behavior is probably the simplest form of social interaction. Often, it requires only the ability to communicate. Once an animal has successfully established a territory, it is ready for more cooperative behavior—reproduction. There are two aspects to this. One is **courtship** and **mating**. Its purpose is to attract and mate with a sexually mature individual of the same species and opposite sex. Such behavior occurs among animals that reproduce either by internal or external fertilization. The second aspect is **parental behavior**—to aid the survival of the young once they are born. It is more often found where fertilization is internal.

In many cases, territorial display may actually serve as a stimulus for reproductive behavior. For example, female elephant seals are attracted to the fiercely defensive males. And almost immediately after repelling a rival, the male elephant seal starts to mount the female. In other cases, territorial and courtship displays are more clearly marked off. The male goby (a small fish) defends its territory—an empty shell, a crevice, or even a beer can—by darkening its body colors, gaping, and puffing its throat. But if the intruder is a gravid female goby, the male's behavior changes sharply. The gravid female exudes a chemical that excites courtship behavior in the male. He changes to a light body color with a black chin. Then he proceeds to dart about the female, intensely fanning his body and tail. At first the female holds her ground. Then, seemingly aroused by low grunting noises from the male, she responds. With the male, she moves into the shelter he has been defending. Once there, she lays her eggs.

If reproductive behavior is to begin, animals must be able to identify and attract the opposite sex. For simple organisms, chemical stimuli may serve both functions. In the case of the goby, the chemical given off by the female is the primary stimulus. But visual signals also help the female goby to identify the male. Most mammals recognize species mates by way of both scent and sight. In many cases, the female signals her fertile season by giving off a strong scent. But in a few cases it is the male who gives off the scent. The male chamois, for example, marks his territory by rubbing his antlers against trees. This releases odors from scent glands, which serve the double purpose of warning off other males and attracting females.

Mammals also rely on touching each other for successful mating, much as humans do. Rabbits, horses, cows, deer, and cats lick each other and nuzzle and rub necks. Elephants tangle their trunks. All of this requires a long period of socialization. Reciprocal stimulation between mother and young and among littermates is essential to the development of normal sexual behavior.

**23-18**
Parental behavior. Physical contact between mother and young forms an important part of parental behavior among higher animals, including the hyenas. Below: mother elephant nurses her young. (See Reproductive behavior)

As higher organisms tend to rely less on chemical attraction, more elaborate **bond-forming behavior** develops. Such behavior establishes ties to keep the parents together during the long nurturing period required for offspring at these levels. It thus aids in species survival. Apart from depositing their eggs in a safe place, most animals that fertilize externally—such as the stickleback—display little or no parental behavior. The newly hatched young must immediately feed and protect themselves. But those that reproduce by internal fertilization produce offspring that need some period of parental care. Young birds, for example, hatch from their eggs long before they are capable of flight. They require the provision of food as well as shelter. Often, as we saw with the ring dove, both parents share in the jobs of incubating the eggs and providing food. In other cases, these tasks are divided. Sometimes the male protects the eggs while the female goes after food for the chicks, as in the case of the emperor penguins. More often, though, it is the other way around. Nurture is a female job among mammals, whether marsupials or placentals, because only the female can do the nursing. So among these animals the male more often hunts food and defends the breeding site.

## Animal societies

In some social animals cooperation reaches a high degree of organization, for provision of food, defense of the group, reproduction, and care of the young. Tropical American army ant colonies, numbering hundreds of thousands of individuals, cling together in a hollow log or under an overhanging bush. The queen forms the center, from which irregular columns of raiders move out and bring back other insects or even small rodents for food. At certain periods the entire bivouac decamps nightly, usually following the trail of one of the raiding columns. Then, after a few weeks, the colony settles for a while in one place, and raiding columns are sparse.

23-19
It is not only the mother who cares for the young.
Here, care-giving is shared between male and female
gorillas. And among the social primates, all females
seem to share an interest in the young of others.
(See Animal societies)

The queen and each worker in the colony stimulate and are stimulated by each other, mainly through chemical and tactile senses. Food also excites the ants. Returning raiding parties stimulate raiding activity by other colony members. This complexity of interactions is known as **reciprocal stimulation**. It is central to the control of the colony's cyclic behavior. The queen's primary function is to lay eggs. When these hatch into helpless larvae, workers feed them with the food procured in raids. Since the larvae are constantly hungry, raiding activity reaches a high point, resulting in nightly moves. As the larvae mature and begin to go into the nonfeeding pupa stage, the colony settles down. But in the meantime, the activity of the nomadic phase has stimulated the queen to produce new eggs. At about the time when the new workers emerge from their pupal cases and begin to feed, the new brood of eggs begins to hatch. Thus, the cycle continues, with the queen's egg production rate acting as a sort of clock.

Despite the intricate social organization of insects such as ants and bees, the range of variability of their behavior is extremely limited. But in higher vertebrates—especially mammals—much behavioral development is guided by the variable interaction between parent and young. The longer this interaction continues, the more variable the experiences and stimuli that the young encounter. The development of social behavior in the domestic cat is a good example. A newborn kitten operates primarily on the basis of tactile and chemical stimuli. As its eyes open and its locomotor coordination improves, reciprocal stimulation between the mother and the kitten increases. Soon the activity of its littermates provides new stimuli. The kitten is thus influenced by experiences beyond simple metabolic effects. All of these experiences are integrated into its development as an individual. The cat's behavioral range is thus highly variable and adaptable, compared to that of an ant.

### Hierarchy, dominance, and leadership

Most social animals recognize patterns of authority. The two most basic are parent—child, or provider—dependent, and the relationship of the stronger to the weaker. Some societies, such as the bees and ants, are more centrally organized, and depend on more hierarchical patterns of authority. Hens provide the classic example. They establish a specific "pecking order" in which the dominant hen pecks or otherwise threatens all her subordinates. Thus, she secures the right to eat first. Among the subordinates, each dominates those beneath her.

Similar behavior occurs in wolf packs for the consuming of scarce food. Dominant males always eat first, and the others take what is left. Moreover, dominant males have sexual rights. They can interfere in the sexual behavior of weaker males. Such behavior patterns are adaptive. They ensure that the strongest will be the best fed and so remain strong and successfully reproduce. The weaker, on the other hand, are less likely to survive. Social behavior is encouraged at an early age. As soon as the pups are old enough to play with their peers, the mother begins to attend to them less. This encourages social bonds between agemates that form the basis of adult pack solidarity.

An interesting form of dominance organization is that of savannah baboons. These primates live mainly on the ground, where they cover a wide area, feeding on a variety of plants and animals. At the center of the group is the dominant male. He is surrounded by subordinate males and females with their young in widening concentric circles. The youngest males, who are the most mobile and alert, form the perimeter. Their task is to spot the big cats—their predators—and alert the others for group defense. As a group they successfully drive off all the cats except lions. When a lion is sighted, cooperation breaks down, and the baboons head for the trees.

Females, who are smaller and weaker than the males, are subordinate to them. They usually seek out the strongest males for sexual relations. But dominance does not depend only on relative strength. It also involves the ability to enlist the support of others in intraspecies contests. Females can enlist the aid of males in competition with other females. Both sexes help to establish appropriate behavior patterns in the young. They encourage the young baboons to play, tussle, and tumble together in mock battles. And they discipline them by chasing them up trees, and frightening them without hurting them. Thus young baboons quickly learn their places in the dominance order.

23-20
Mutual grooming is an important part of primate socialization. Here, an olive baboon removes fleas from the fur of her young. (See Hierarchy, dominance, and leadership)

23-21
Primates are not the only animals that groom each other. Here, a penguin obligingly scratches the neck of its mate.

23-22
Through rough play with littermates (above) young polecats learn neck-biting techniques for killing prey (below) as well as successful mating. When raised in isolation, the animals try to bite prey wherever they can, leaving it free to bite back. And males grasp ineffectually at resistant females when trying to mate. (See Hierarchy, dominance, and leadership)

Other species of baboon, the forest-dwellers and those who live by raiding farms and gardens, have different sexual patterns. The males do not protect the females, and the females mate with whomever they choose. Among the other primates, even differences in physical appearance are not pronounced. This is especially true among those such as the chimpanzees and gibbons who live in the trees and have no need for group protection.

In many animal social groups, the behavior of the entire group is directed by one or more leaders, who determine feeding or defense movements. Leaders may be of any age, and of either sex. Thus leadership does not always fall to dominant individuals. Among the red deer, for example, protection of the herd from danger falls to the most experienced female rather than to a dominant stag. Dominant rhesus monkeys, however, are those who are the best fighters, and these become the leaders in group territorial defense.

At the University of Wisconsin, Harry Harlow observed how young Indian rhesus monkeys develop into "normal, well-adjusted" adults in steps, beginning with complete dependence on their mothers. Through stages of mouthing and handling, the young monkeys gradually develop species-typical patterns of play and playful aggression with their peers. This fosters their ability to cooperate in a group. Eventually, social hierarchies form within the peer group, in which the young monkeys find appropriate sex roles. Monkeys raised in complete social isolation were never capable of any kind of social adjustment. While they could be sexually aroused, they were unable to assume correct positions for mating. And animals deprived of contact with peers at early stages had difficulty adjusting to the group. They lacked normal cooperative behavior and sex-role patterns.

Thus for all of the primates, as for the wolves, socialization is very important. Both playing and mutual grooming serve this purpose, not only for the primates but for many other social creatures. Lambs as well as lions are encouraged in social play, and many birds engage in ritual preening behavior.

## Evolution of behavior

This chapter has tried to demonstrate that the evolution of behavior, like the evolution of form and structure, is primarily adaptive. It enables individuals of a species to survive and reproduce and so increase the possibilities for species survival. However, history is full of examples of overspecialization—adaptations to one environmental change that reduced the flexibility of a population and so its chances of adapting to the next change. Many of these instances concern the predator populations, large animals who have few natural enemies and who once seemed likely to flourish in a particular environmental niche forever. Now that their habitats are being threatened by human beings, they are proving less capa-

ble of adjusting to new environments than some of the less specialized species.

The development of social behavior in the wolf is such an example. The species *Canidae* includes coyotes, jackals, wolves, wild dogs, and foxes. Most of these hunt singly or in pairs, reserving more social behavior for mating or caring for the young. In the cases of the wolf and the Cape hunting dog, hunting in packs probably evolved so that the animals could capture large herbivores. In the course of this evolution, patterns of social behavior, generally unspecialized among the *Canidae,* began to specialize for social cohesion, in order to have a workable hunting group. The Cape hunting dog apparently relies on communal feeding rituals for this purpose. But the wolf developed a social hierarchy, involving ranked privileges for both feeding and mating. In a society where sexual rights are thus strictly marked out, the breeding potential of the population is considerably reduced.

Hunting in packs, moreoover, may not be adaptive in environments where humans have become dominant. Not only are the packs often seen as a menace, but their social cohesion makes them very vulnerable. Group defense behavior, by which a wounded or threatened wolf summons the aid of the entire pack, exposes the whole group to human predation. And the mere fact that wolves live and move in groups makes them more visible to hunters than a solitary animal would be. Studies indicate that the coyote, a close relation of the wolf, never developed such a complex pattern of social organization. The coyote has thus been more successful in reverting to a more isolated existence. The measure of adaptive behavior, then, is that it increases or sustains the ability of a population to survive and successfully reproduce. Evidence seems to show that, in an environment which includes humans, the development of a highly structured system of social hierarchy in the wolves has been nonadaptive in both respects.

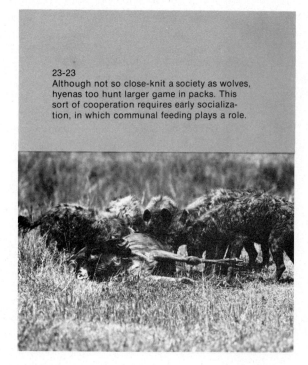

23-23
Although not so close-knit a society as wolves, hyenas too hunt larger game in packs. This sort of cooperation requires early socialization, in which communal feeding plays a role.

summary

Behavior includes responses to environmental change that involve the integrated functioning of the entire organism. Behavior is produced and controlled by physiological and biochemical processes, which are inherited. But it is also controlled by the interaction of these processes with the organism's experience. According to Morgan's Canon, behavioral action may not be interpreted as the outcome of exercising a higher psychical faculty if it can be interpreted as the outcome of exercising a lower one.

Genetically determined behavior interacts with experience in a changing environment. The more complex the organism, the more complex the interaction. Signals which produce direct, immediate species-typical responses are called sign stimuli, or releasers. Conflicting responses to a single stimulus cause displacement activity, which is facilitated by the conflict situation itself rather than by an appropriate object. Inappropriate behavior occurs as a result of extreme alterations in the natural environment.

Orientation refers to the ways in which organism move their bodies in response to environmental stimuli. While orientation is innate, it can be modified by experience. In its simplest forms, orientation occurs as kinesis or taxis. Kinesis is change in the rate or probability of motion. It is not specifically directed toward or away from a stimulus. Taxis is the receiving of directional information through a receptor system. Migratory birds show complex interactions of orientation patterns. Their migratory and homing behavior is reinforced by previous experience with a "home" area. It may also use a sun compass, magnetic field orientation, and smell orientation. The ability to sense time is an example of temporal orientation related to biological rhythms. Such rhythms involve fluctuations in metabolic activities. These fluctuations correspond to periodic environmental changes.

Learning is the process of modifying behavior as a result of experience with the environment. The simplest form is habituation, a waning of response upon repeated presentation of a particular stimulus. In learning by association, a secondary stimulus is repeatedly produced in close association with the sign stimulus. In learning by discrimination, the organism first generalizes all variations of a class of stimuli. It then discriminates among the variations. Trial and error involves an association of a response with an event which occurs after the stimulus. Problem-solving behavior requires a brain and the ability to visualize both the problem and the solution.

One type of behavior can occur only in group settings, in a species-typical environment. This is imprinting, a special type of species recognition in which the parental image is apparently imprinted on the brain of the new offspring.

Social behavior involves competition and cooperation. Both require the ability to communicate. Sharing experience speeds up and expands individual adaptation and ultimately that of the population. Effective communication depends on sending, receiving, and responding to identification signals. Pheromones are chemicals produced by individuals that affect the behavior of the group. Auditory communication allows for variability in pattern, volume, regularity, and frequency. Visual communication uses color, gesture, body shape, and movement.

In Batesian mimicry, harmless creatures imitate a distasteful or poisonous species, thus avoiding predation. In Müllerian mimicry, different members of a species look alike, and are avoided by predators who have tasted only one. Aggressive mimicry uses imitation for predation.

Territoriality is another kind of defensive communication. In aggressive display, species trespassers are threatened in the same way as potential enemies. Such display often serves as a means to avoid actual fighting, which might be destructive to the species.

Reproductive behavior is cooperative. Its two aspects are courtship and mating, and parental behavior. Bond-forming behavior aids in species survival by keeping both parents together during the long nurturing period needed by offspring at these levels.

In some social animals, reciprocal stimulation creates a highly organized way of providing food, defending the group, and reproducing and caring for young. Patterns of hierarchy, dominance, and leadership emerge.

The evolution of behavior is primarily adaptive. But overspecialization may occur. Adaptations to one environmental change may reduce the flexibility of a population, and thus its chances of adapting to the next change.

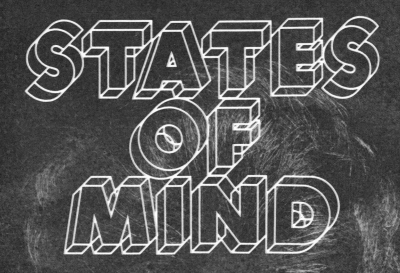

# STATES OF MIND

The facts about meditation . . . and a free lesson in TM
Does your right brain know what your left brain is doing?
Glimpses of sleep learning, déjà vu, and behavior control
Find out if you have ESP
Test your knowledge of hypnosis
Are brain transplants possible?

"Left-brained people are good at science and math. Right brainers do better in art and fantasizing."

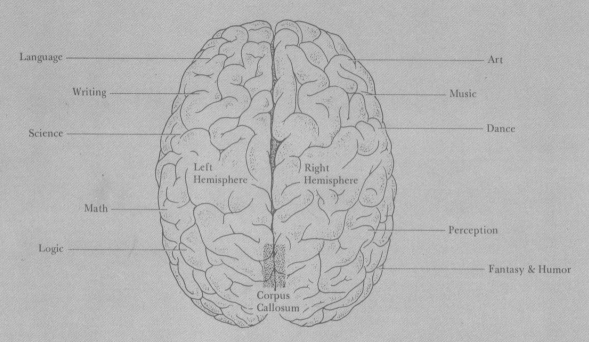

Language — Art

Writing — Music

Science — Dance

Left Hemisphere — Right Hemisphere

Math — Perception

Logic — Fantasy & Humor

Corpus Callosum

# The human braincase houses two distinct minds

One evening during the heat of a family argument, a man tried to throttle his wife with his left hand. Suddenly, to the astonishment of both, his right hand came to his wife's rescue, trying to pull the left hand away from her neck. Sounds like something straight from Woody Allen or Mel Brooks, doesn't it?

Well, it's not. Recent experiments on brain-damaged individuals have shown that all of us — not only those who have sustained brain injuries — actually have two brains in our skulls. Each works independently of the other. And each, says researcher Robert Sperry, "has its own private sensations, perceptions, and learning experiences."

Virtually everyone is aware that the behavior of the left hand, and the entire left side of the body, is governed by the right hemisphere of the brain. Conversely, the right side is controlled by the left hemisphere. Until now, researchers thought the left hemisphere to be dominant over its partner. Since most people (13 out of 14, some researchers say) are right-handed, and the speech center is known to be located in the left cerebral hemisphere, this conclusion was quite logical.

Now, however, Sperry and others have amassed overwhelming evidence that indicates otherwise. According to Sperry:

. . . both the left and right hemispheres of the brain have been found to have their own specialized forms of intellect. The left is highly verbal and mathematical, performing with analytic, symbolic, computerlike, sequential logic. The right, by contrast, is spatial and mute, performing with a synthetic spatio-

temporal and mechanical kind of information processing that cannot yet be simulated by computers.

In other words, a left-brained person is apt to be good in skills such as writing, language acquisition, and the logical activities of math and science. Conversely, right-brained people are strong in art, music, dance, perception, and fantasy.

## STUDY OF EPILEPTICS

Sperry discovered the split brain when he tested brain-damaged patients at the California Institute of Technology. These people had undergone operations during which the corpus callosum — the bundle of fibers that links the two cerebral hemispheres — had been severed. This procedure was performed because it reduced the physical effects of epilepsy. The behavior of these patients is normal in all respects save one: their right hands literally do not know what their left hands are doing. In effect, the hands act independently of one another. Hence, the bizarre behavior of the irate husband above.

The discovery that there were actually two separate consciousnesses in his patients intrigued Sperry. Attempting to learn how the two hemispheres differed in terms of function, he designed a number of experiments. In one of these, several objects were placed behind a screen. The subject was seated on the other side, in such a way that he could pick up the objects but could not see them. If he picked up an object such as a pencil in his right hand, he could easily identify it — tactually and

M.C. Escher
Escher foundation
Haags Gemeentemuseum
The Hague

## Do the eyes tell all?

The eyes are the windows of the mind, says the ancient proverb. One way you can test this piece of conventional wisdom has been devised by James Austin of the University of Colorado Medical Center. Here's how it works: Look directly into the eyes of a friend while you ask him questions that you think might be dealt with by one cerebral hemisphere or the other. For example, you might ask him to explain how biorhythms work. You will see that your friend's eyes will glance to the right or the left as he ponders the question. If he glances to the left, says Austin, he is usually more introspective (that is, he is a right-brained, intuitive person). The "left glancer" probably is more interested in art or humanities than in science or math. A right glancer, on the other hand, tends to favor analytical subjects.

The reason for this phenomenon, observes Austin, is that one cerebral hemisphere is physiologically biased, or set, to spring into action a millisecond before its partner. "It is plausible to think, then," says Austin, "that when left movers start their movement of internal reflection, they are revealing the greater facility in function with their right cerebral hemisphere." Just the opposite is true, of course, for right glancers, who are left-brained.

---

verbally. However, when he used his left hand — connected to the right hemisphere where there is little or no speech facility — he could not describe the pencil. When presented with an array of objects that included the pencil, and asked to pick out the object he previously held but could not describe, the subject was able to select the pencil every time.

### INTERPRETING THE WAVES

The split-brain phenomenon has also been tested in normal people. In San Francisco, for example, Drs. David Galin and Robert Ornstein are measuring waves produced by the cerebral hemispheres in an attempt to determine the respective analytical or intuitive capability of each. The researchers presented subjects with various tasks — writing a letter to test analytical ability, and arranging colored shapes into a given pattern to test intuition. The tests supported the hypothesis that normal people also have specialized cerebral hemispheres. During the test for analytical ability, for example, recording devices detected electrical changes in the left hemisphere which indicated that cerebral activity of some sort was occurring there. For the right hemisphere, by contrast, the device picked up only alpha waves, which suggest a state of relaxation. The tests for intuition revealed the exact opposite — only the left hemisphere generated alpha waves. Thus, the hemisphere being tested for its specialized activity did all the work, while the other relaxed.

What does the discovering of the split brain mean? In practical terms, it means that in western cultures at least, one half of the brain is being over-educated while the other half remains virtually illiterate. As Sperry points out:

> Our educational system and modern society generally (with its very heavy emphasis on communication and early training in the three R's) discriminates against one whole half of the brain. I refer, of course, to the non-verbal, non-mathematical minor hemisphere, which, we find, has its own perceptual, mechanical, and spatial mode of apprehension and reasoning. In our present school system, the attention given to the minor hemisphere of the brain is minimal compared with the training lavished on the left, or major, hemisphere.

The next step in this intriguing story? Obviously to probe the right hemisphere in an attempt to unlock some of its secrets. The most recent research on this hemisphere reveals that it may not be as mute as had been thought. For example, Dr. Eran Zaidel, an associate of Sperry at Cal Tech, has shown that the adult right hemisphere does possess language capability. Indeed, it has the sentence-forming ability of a 5-year-old, and the vocabulary of a 14-year-old. And other work with stroke patients suggests that the right hemisphere may be the seat of our emotions. Such discoveries begin to cast shadows on Sperry's hypothesis about hemisphere specialization. Perhaps future work will erase these shadows. Then we can learn how to educate both hemispheres in order to maximize our intellectual capabilities more fully.

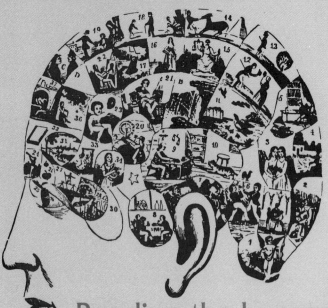

# Reading the bumps

The science of the brain has come a long way since its shaky beginnings in the cramped, makeshift laboratories of the last century. Consider, for example, one of its immediate forbears, phrenology. Phrenology might well be dubbed a testament to the excesses of the human imagination. Introduced at the end of the eighteenth century by the Viennese anatomist, Franz Gall, this discipline purported to analyze the bumps and hollows of the human skull in order to determine personality, talents, and disposition. According to Gall, the skull was divided into 27 definite regions, each of which controlled or was associated with certain characteristics. Later followers, notably J.W. Redfield, expanded this number to no fewer than 186, which he carefully numbered or lettered on ivory models of the skull and sold for a modest fee. Each of Redfield's figures indicated some cranial region and human quality. Thus, region Z was the site governing economy, submission, and, paradoxically, independence. Region 65 A was the center of wave motion (whatever that was), and region 149 governed Republicanism. The neighboring areas, 148 and 149A, were associated with faithful love and responsibility, respectively.

By taking the mystery out of character analysis, phrenology threatened to put the fortune tellers and novelists out of business. The phrenologist had only to run his hands over an individual's skull to determine his intelligence, artistic ability, or predisposition to criminal activity. Phrenology has since been dismissed as a pseudo-science, of a piece with palmistry, astrology, and tea-leaf reading. Yet, it did contribute to scientific knowledge by focusing on the fact that particular physical and intellectual faculties are associated with the cortex and are located in definite regions of the brain. Says one modern psychologist, "The theory of Gall . . . is, however, an instance of a theory which, while essentially wrong, was just enough right to further scientific thought."

# Brain transplants

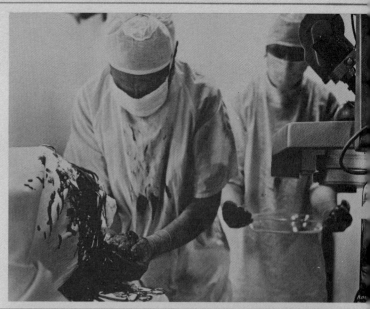

Nearly everyone is familiar with the scene shown on the late night movie: the dedicated but slightly mad surgeon, aided by his loyal assistant, operates on a patient in a secret surgery. The operation? A brain transplant. The surgeon makes it look like a snap, almost routine. But in real life, such an operation is virtually impossible — at least with today's technology. As Erwin Lausch points out in his book Manipulation, even a team of the world's fastest surgeons could not possibly transplant a human brain from one skull to another. For one thing, they could not attach all the nerves and blood vessels of the donor brain to those of the receiving body. Even if this could be done, the operation would not succeed because the severed nerve endings would not heal. A person with such a brain would not be able to see, hear, feel, or speak, and his body would be paralyzed. Transplanting an entire head is much easier — it involves connecting only several large blood vessels. But this too would be useless because the millions of nerves in the spine could never be connected to the new brain.

# What do you know about hypnosis?

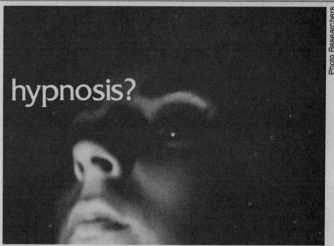

Photo Researchers

Hypnosis is a sleeplike state in which the mind of the subject appears to be under the control of the hypnotist. Much nonsense has been written on hypnosis. It is not surprising, then, that there are numerous popular misconceptions about it. Test your knowledge of hypnosis by taking the following True-False quiz.

| | |
|---|---|
| 1. Major surgical operations can be performed without anaesthesia on a patient who is under deep hypnosis. | T/F |
| 2. Posthypnotic suggestion rarely works for a person who wishes to stop smoking. | T/F |
| 3. Women are more easily hypnotizable than men. | T/F |
| 4. The practitioner of hypnosis requires much training and skill. | T/F |
| 5. An individual can be hypnotized against his will. | T/F |
| 6. Cold sores, skin blisters, and other similar physiological changes have been induced by hypnosis. | T/F |
| 7. A hypnotized individual can be induced to see people and objects that are not present. | T/F |
| 8. Hypnosis cannot be faked — a subject cannot pretend that he is hypnotized. | T/F |
| 9. A deeply hypnotized individual can be induced to commit crimes and even deliberately harm himself. | T/F |
| 10. It is possible to hypnotize oneself by listening to the voice of a hypnotist on a tape recorder. | T/F |

Mystics have long known the benefits of meditation. Now, scientists, delving into its mysteries, are turning up some surprises.

# "Sit back, relax, breathe deeply, tune out . . ."

The technique is simple enough. It doesn't cost a cent, and it's easy to learn. It requires only forty minutes of your time a day. Thousands of Americans swear by it. And some scientists say it can do you a world of good. The "it" is Transcendental Meditation — TM for short.

For ages, mystics have claimed that meditation has given them peace of mind and enabled them totally to relax and enrich their lives. Sparked by these claims and others, Dr. Herbert Benson and his associates at Harvard Medical School have probed the techniques of meditation, attempting to discover what makes them tick. They examined meditation as practiced by mystics of various religions — Christianity, Zen Bhuddism, Islam, and Judaism.

The Harvard researchers noted that these techniques have four things in common. First, the believer employs some kind of mental device, such as the continued repetition of a sound or word. Second, all distractions are screened out, to keep the environment as quiet as possible. Third, the individual assumes a completely passive attitude during meditation. Finally, the practitioner gets into a comfortable position so that the muscles are totally relaxed.

## Physiological changes

With this information in hand, Benson attempted to duplicate these techniques in the laboratory. What he found tends to support the claims of the mystics. He discovered, for example, that meditation brings about a number of important physiological changes. Among the most significant of these is the reduction in the amount of oxygen consumed by the body — typically about 10 percent. Predictably, this is accompanied by a drop in the carbon dioxide output. In addition, the rate of respiration — the number of breaths per minute — decreases, as does the production of perspiration. Finally, the brain produces telltale alpha waves, electrical patterns which indicate a state of relaxation. In effect, the body's most important housekeeping systems — all controlled by the autonomic nervous system — are virtually shut down during meditation.

It is for good reason, then, that Benson has dubbed this symphonic group of changes "the relaxation response." He has experimentally shown that it can be effective in controlling hypertension, or high blood pressure, the disease behind strokes and heart attacks. This silent killer affects one out of ten persons in America today. In real numbers, this translates to between 20 and 30 million people.

In their experiment, the Harvard scientists chose 14 subjects who suffered from high blood pressure — six females and eight males, with a mean age of about 53 years. Although they had been taking drugs to control hypertension, the group's blood pressure averaged about 145 millimeters — just 15 millimeters shy of the danger point.

## Benefits — and disadvantages

Enter Transcendental Meditation (see box for the Harvard technique). After 20 weeks of meditation — and continued drug use — group blood pressure fell to 135 mm, which is considered normal by most physicians. Although Benson sees TM as an aid to the control of hypertension, he issues a caveat: meditation should not be used by laymen to treat themselves because very few can accurately determine their own blood pressure. Those suffering from hypertension should see their physicians regularly. Although the doctor may recommend meditation, he will probably also prescribe drugs to help keep blood pressure down.

There is also good evidence that too much of this good thing can be harmful. Thousands of Americans practice TM for 20 minutes twice a day, with no apparent detrimental effects. But those who engage in it for several hours a day have reported experiencing hallucinations. Pink elephants, green snakes, flying autos — all the stock-in-trade visions of alcoholics — have been seen by some overenthusiastic meditators. Although the reasons for these visions are not clear, it appears that the sensory deprivation which accompanies extended meditation induces individuals to create their own dream worlds to replace the real world from which they are temporarily isolated.

But individuals who practice TM in moderation — even those who do not suffer from high blood pressure or similar diseases — can enjoy the peace of mind that meditation apparently brings. Many claim, for example, that TM has helped them come to terms with who they are, decrease anxiety, increase energy and creativity, do better in school, sleep better, and discontinue the use of drugs, alcohol, and tobacco. Most researchers agree that our modern environment, constantly battering away at the nervous system, may be largely responsible for hypertension and similar conditions. It has, in effect, made many of us "nervous wrecks." Any technique which promises deliverance from this wretched situation, even if only for 40 minutes a day, deserves attention.

"TM may be effective in treating hypertension, migraine, and a host of related diseases."

Herbert Benson has elaborated his work on TM in his book "The Relaxation Response." He describes the following simple techniques for "turning off":

1. Pick out a nice quiet room where there are no distractions.
2. Sit in a comfortable position. Loosen your clothes and take off your shoes if you like. Close your eyes.
3. Relax all the muscles of your body, beginning at the feet and progressing up to your head. Try to keep them deeply relaxed.
4. Breathe through your nose. Focus entirely on breathing. As you breathe out, say the word "one" to yourself silently. For example: Breathe in . . . breathe out . . . say "one" . . . In . . . out . . . "one" . . .
5. Continue this for 20 minutes. If you wish, you may occasionally open your eyes to check the time. After 20 minutes are up, sit quietly for a few minutes — first with eyes closed, then with eyes open.

During meditation try to keep an entirely passive attitude. Stay as relaxed as possible. Don't worry if you are not succeeding at first, and don't try to force yourself into meditation. If distracting thoughts pop up, try to ignore them by repeating "one" and concentrating on your breathing. Try to meditate twice a day — 20 minutes in the morning and 20 minutes in the afternoon or evening. Avoid meditating for two hours before or after meals because digestion interferes with the physiological processes involved in meditation.

# Brain briefs

**Instant replay?** "Déjà vu" is the bizarre sensation that you are reliving exactly an experience that took place in the past. No one has yet pinpointed the cause of this phenomenon, but some scientists feel that it may be connected with our split brains. For example, R. Efron, a British researcher, notes that in the brain, incoming sensory data is not handled by both cerebral hemispheres simultaneously — there is a lag of as much as six milliseconds between the time the dominant hemisphere receives the stimulus and passes it on to the minor hemisphere for processing. On some occasions, this time lag is longer; by the time the minor hemisphere gets the news, its dominant partner has already received and processed it to its side of the body. When the minor hemisphere transmits the information, the individual gets the impression that he is experiencing a particular event the second time around, somewhat like instant replay.

**Sleep learning.** Is the brain idle during sleep? Can you actually learn certain kinds of materials while you sleep? Although most scientists scoff at the idea, there is some evidence that you can learn some simple things, such as vocabulary, while you lie slumbering. Two American scientists, Wilse Webb and C. Michael Levy, tested this hypothesis by playing tapes of Russian words to 20 subjects for five nights running. Each night, after the subjects had gone to sleep, a dozen Russian nouns, together with their English meanings, were repeated over and over in their ears. Most subjects learned one new noun a night, and a few could recall up to four. The scientists found that the subjects learned the words best during light sleep. And the amount of words learned increased with practice: scores rose, on the average, about seven points after the first three nights. So apparently sleep learning, like most other things, can be improved with practice.

**The psychocivilized person?** Current research on the brain is raising the possibility of the control of human behavior by the electrical and chemical stimulation of the brain. For example, one of the outstanding researchers in the field, Jose Delgado, predicts a future when aberrant human behavior can be therapeutically controlled by such methods. Thus, manic depressives and others who suffer from mental diseases thought to be caused by brain disorders, can be helped. Already, epileptics and those suffering from arthritis have been treated by implanting electrodes into the brain and equipping the victims with portable electro-stimulators. When an individual feels an attack coming on, he simply presses a button on the device. This stimulates certain areas of the brain and subdues the pain. Delgado thinks such techniques can also be applied to normal individuals to improve performance in certain areas. He sees the day when "psychocivilized" people will walk the earth. "Because our brains, as well as our cultures, can be modified," he says, "we now have the unique capability to direct our own evolution."

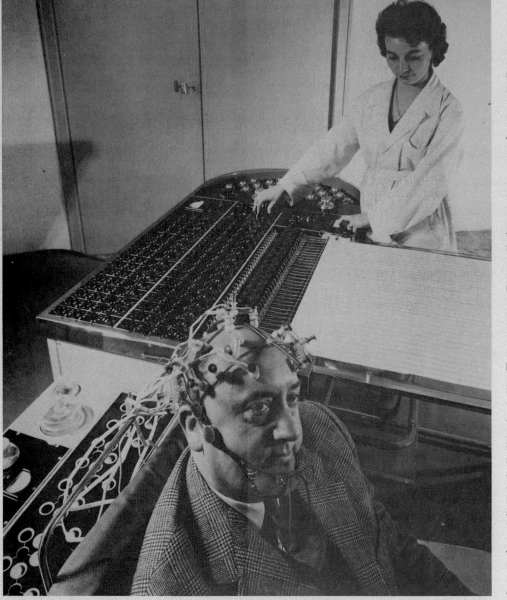

Robert Doisneau/Photo Researchers

## Book review

**Manipulation:** dangers and benefits of brain research. Erwin Lausch. New York: Viking, 1974. 283 pp. (illustrated). $8.95.

This book, translated from the German, is a lively summary of brain research. It offers a glimpse of the history of man's interest in his own mind, beginning with the Egyptians and extending down to the present day. Topics include the split brain, memory, electrical and chemical manipulation of the brain, sleep, and dreams. Particularly interesting are the sections on brainwashing, brain transplants, the effects of certain drugs on the human brain, and the account of experiments in relatively stupid flatworms that ate brighter worms and got smarter.

Lausch's smooth style makes the book eminently readable — even the most complex subjects, such as neuroanatomy and the brain as a computer, are very clear. For example, the author explores the fallacy that the human brain and the computer are alike in structure and function. At first blush, this may seem true — both appear similar in that they are fed coded information which they process and pass on. But certain phenomena of the brain — creative thinking, will power, consciousness, emotions — make this analogy useless.

The illustrations, which are mostly drawings and diagrams, further clarify the subject matter. All in all, a good book for anyone interested in the mysteries of the human mind.

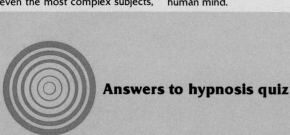

## Answers to hypnosis quiz

1. True. But only a small percent of individuals can be so deeply hypnotized.
2. False. Posthypnotic suggestions have been found effective for treating this habit, but success depends on how strongly the person wants to quit.
3. False. However, younger people of both sexes appear to be more readily hypnotizable than others.
4. False. Nearly anyone can become a hypnotist in a very short time.
5. False. No one can be placed into a hypnotic trance unless he or she wishes to be.
6. True. But only for those who are prone to transfer emotional upsets into the symptoms of these skin conditions.
7. True. Other hallucinations, such as a feeling of warmth or coldness, may also be experienced.
8. False. Some people are so good at this that they have even been able to withstand a needle passing through the arm, without moving or crying out.
9. False. Hypnotized people will not do things that they don't normally do when awake.
10. True. One who engages in self-hypnosis often finds it much easier to be induced if he listens to his own taped voice.

# Do you have ESP?

G.W. Gardner/Photo Researchers

Extrasensory perception, or ESP, is considered by many to be a capability of the human mind that enables some individuals to see the future, read minds, or be aware of events that occur elsewhere. Do you have ESP? Take the following test, designed in part by Hans Holzer of the New York Institute of Technology, and see.

1. Ask a friend to form a mental picture of any number between one and ten for about a half a minute. Try to tune in to your friend's thoughts, then jot down the number you think he or she is picturing. Very few people will get the number. If you do, you make a good candidate for more testing.

2. Ask each of three or four people to place a personal object — a comb, ring, or watch — into an envelope. Have one of them number the envelopes and place them in a basket or bag, mixing them up thoroughly. During the numbering process, you are to close your eyes or turn your back, so you won't see what number belongs to whom. Now, choose one of the envelopes. Hold it in your hands, concentrate on the contents, and try to tell as much as you can about the owner of the contents. Score this test by giving a point for each true fact. The total number of points should not exceed ten. A score of five or better qualifies you for further testing.

3. Get ten pillboxes or matchboxes. Place them on a table in a semicircle — about two or three feet apart. Ask a friend to secretly place an object in one of the boxes. Next, tie a weight (a key or other metal object) to the end of a six-inch string, and tie the other end of the string to a pencil. Hold the pencil over the box in the center of the semicircle, and let the weight swing gently back and forth over the other boxes — like a pendulum. If the pendulum finally comes to rest over the box with the object, you are a good subject for more ESP tests.

24 patterns in the ecosystem

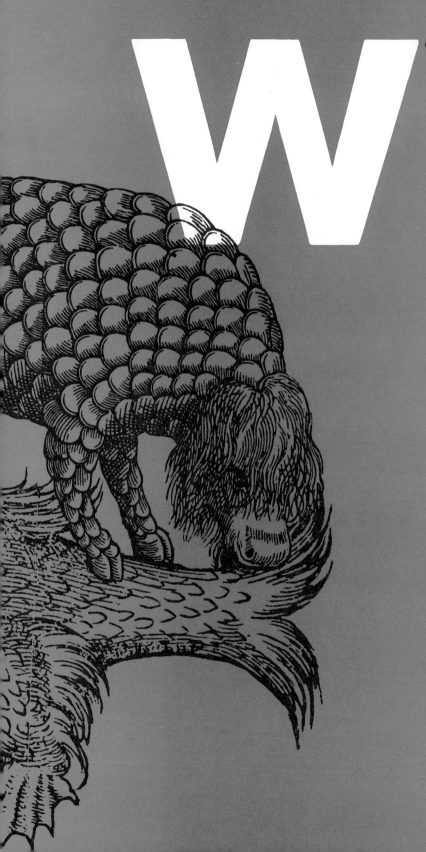

**W**e are discovering that individual organisms or particular species cannot be fully understood by themselves. **Ecology** is the study of the complex ways all living and nonliving things are related to each other. The total of all living things, all inorganic materials, and all physical forces, is called the **ecosphere**. The concept of ecosphere includes the interactions between living things and their environment, the transfer of food, the flow of energy, and the exchange of inorganic nutrients and organic compounds. Like other organisms, humans depend on the delicate balance of ecological processes for the fulfillment of their needs. Therefore, it is crucial that we learn to predict the consequences of human activities which might interrupt these essential patterns.

Ecologists have a twofold task. They must explore the natural patterns in the ecosphere. Then they must try to determine how these patterns affect the balance and survival of the system as a whole. The science of ecology began as a series of alarming discoveries about DDT, atmospheric testing of nuclear weapons, artificial fertilizers, and pesticides. It is now becoming a science of the future. Ecologists work to compile all the available evidence of interrelationships among organisms and nonliving factors. This gives them the background material they need in order to predict the consequences of proposed environmental changes.

Global relationships are extremely complex. So we often try to uncover the patterns in areas smaller than the ecosphere. An **ecosystem** consists of organisms and the relatively self-contained environment in which they live and interact. It might be a pond, a lake, an ocean, or a forest. Whether the ecosystem is small or large, it has two parts. These are the **biotic**—or living—component, and the **abiotic**—or nonliving—component. The biotic part of an ecosystem consists of plants, animals, and microbes. These interact with each other and with the environment. The abiotic part is the environment itself. It includes inorganic elements and compounds such as carbon, hydrogen, oxygen, water, phosphates, and carbonates, along with physical factors such as moisture, currents, light, and heat.

Within a given ecosystem, there may be a number of different **habitats**, or places where each type of organism is normally found. The concept of habitat is an important one. For an organism to prosper, it must locate itself in the appropriate physical, chemical, and biotic environment. For example, snakes and lizards cannot exist in Alaska. The short Alaskan summer is not warm or long enough for them to breed. Fish need oxygenated water. They cannot live in waters heavily polluted by organic wastes. This is because microorganisms consume the oxygen in such areas as they feed upon the organic material.

Less obvious is the need for an organism to locate where there is a job that needs to be done. In ecological terminology, **niche** refers both to the place where an organism lives and to the function it serves. For example, one niche is filled by vast numbers of tiny crustaceans called copepods, which live in the sea. By eating plant plankton, they concentrate their nutrients in an amount which can support small fish. Large niches can accomodate a variety of organisms. The aphid-eating function is shared by ladybird beetles, spiders, and lacewing fly larvae (sometimes known as aphis lions). Mosquitoes may be preyed upon by swifts during the day, dragonflies at dusk, and bats at night.

The plants, animals, and microbes in a self-sustaining ecosystem form the **biotic community**. Great numbers of species are found even in such forbidding habitats as the desert or frozen tundra. In every case these organisms are interacting. Each is making some contribution to the survival of the others and of the system as a whole.

Despite the complexity of the ecosystem, several essential patterns of interdependence appear. All of these are subject to seasonal alterations in the physical—

chemical environment and to occasional unpredictable climatic changes. The climate and soil in an area determine the plant life. The plants, in turn, support the animal life.

The net effect of the diverse interrelationships among organisms is a beautifully balanced ecosystem. Within it, food and nutrients cycle continuously. Only sunlight must be added to fuel the energy flow and make the entire ecosystem self-supporting.

## Food and energy flow

Movement, organization of cellular processes, synthesis of compounds, and conduction of nerve impulses all require energy. Directly or indirectly, organisms receive this energy from the sun. Animals can bask

24-1
Monkey in tropical rain forest habitat. The canopy of a tropical rain forest is the uppermost layer of branches. It forms the habitat for a variety of animals. Many of them have adhesive pads, grasping paws, and prehensile tails. This equipment leaves these animals well adapted for their arboreal habitat by enabling them to cling to trees.

in the sun for warmth, but they cannot convert its rays to the chemical energy needed to drive cellular processes. Only green plants can do this. So animals must obtain the energy they need by eating either plants or plant-eating (herbivorous) animals.

We see, then, that plants form the only link between the biotic and abiotic communities. They draw water and minerals from the soil. They combine these with sunlight and carbon dioxide from the air to make carbohydrates, fats, proteins, vitamins, and (usable) minerals. This nutrient-rich vegetable material is then consumed and converted to animal material by small herbivorous organisms such as caterpillars, field mice, and copepods. These organisms may then serve as food for meat-eating animals, who, in turn, may be eaten by larger carnivores. This sequence of eating and being eaten, with the resultant transfer of energy, is called a **food chain**. When plants and animals die, their remains become food for scavengers and the microorganisms of decomposition. This keeps carcasses from piling up and also returns their nutrients to the food chain for reuse.

In many habitats, one or more species may dominate the other members of the community by virtue of sheer numbers. These organisms constitute the greater part of the **biomass**—the total weight or volume of the organisms in a biotic community. An "oak forest" or an "oak-hickory" forest is named for the dominant species, oak and hickory trees. These trees protect the forest animals from harsh weather as well as furnishing them with food.

## The flow of food

No single viewpoint gives a complete picture of the complexity of food flow in an ecosystem. Trophic levels, food chains, and food webs are all useful concepts in tracing the movement of food. Together, they provide a helpful framework for understanding and appreciating the multiplicity of relationships which comprise so much of life on earth.

**24-2**
Badger killing prairie dog. Grass is well adapted for life on the prairie. Its narrow, elongated leaves grow straight up. This provides each leaf with clear access to sunlight. One acre of grass offers ten acres of photosynthetic surface. This provides a great deal of energy to such herbivorous animals as the prairie dog. The prairie dog burrows out extensive underground communities as refuge from both harsh weather and marauding predators. Its sandy-brown color enables it to blend with the grass and earth mounds surrounding its burrows. Prairie dogs are, in turn, eaten by such carnivores as the badger, a highly competent digging animal which is able to pursue and catch a burrowing prairie dog. The badger is a fierce fighter rarely pursued by other carnivores. (See Trophic levels)

*Trophic levels* The **biota** are the flora and fauna of an ecosystem. They can be divided into several categories based on the way they obtain their nourishment. **Primary producers** are plants that produce food through photosynthesis. **Consumers** are organisms that depend on producers either directly or indirectly. **Herbivores** are animals that feed on plants. **Carnivores** are animals that feed on herbivores or on smaller carnivores. **Detritivores** are organisms that feed on all kinds of dead plant and animal tissue. Each of these categories is a **trophic level** (from the Greek *trophe*, meaning nourishment). All organisms with patterns of nourishment that serve a similar function belong to one trophic level. Cattle, grasshoppers, and mice feeding on grass, birds feeding on buds, and sea urchins feeding on algae are all members of the same trophic level: primary consumers.

Carnivores and herbivores alike may become prey. They may succumb to the effects of weather, accidents, or parasites. But in a self-supporting community, nothing is wasted. Much of the body tissue of animals and almost all the tissue of plants is eventually consumed and recycled by detritivores. The detritivores are so important and widespread that they include several subdivisions. **Scavengers**—animals such as hermit crabs, crows, and earthworms—eat dead animal and plant remains. Fungi, bacteria, and yeast are microscopic **decomposers** which break down carcasses and excrement into simpler compounds. **Transformers** are organisms that convert these products into forms which plants can use again to produce food.

A few species fill niches not covered by any of the trophic levels. Among these are the **parasites**. These organisms derive their nourishment from the living bodies of larger plants or animals, usually without killing them.

*Food chains* Patterns of eating and being eaten can be shown in linear fashion for study purposes. A simple food chain is

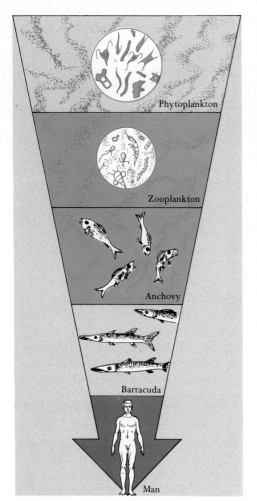

24-3
A simple food chain.

found on the Arctic tundra. Grasses are eaten by lemmings, which in turn are eaten by snowy owls. Food chains begin with green plants. They move through a series of animals in gradations which usually correspond to increasing size of the predators. Predators generally confine themselves to organisms which they can overpower. However, humans are a significant exception to this rule.

Aquatic food chains are generally long ones, because the primary producers are very small. So it may take several steps for phytoplankton to proceed through the food chain and reach a size which larger fish can even see to eat. In a pond, a food chain might have six links: algae→protozoan-→small aquatic insect→larger aquatic insect→black bass→pickerel. But some organisms shortcut the long aquatic food chain. The 100-ton baleen whale is a notable example. With its mouthful of massive bony strainers, it sieves through tons of water to obtain the plankton-eating euphausids or krill, tiny shrimp-like animals which constitute the baleen whale's only diet.

*Food webs* Trophic levels and food chains are artificial conveniences. These abstractions may help us understand certain patterns. However, they ignore the many links between trophic levels and food chains which form the **food web**. This term designates the total pattern of relationships in a community. Lemmings eat grass and are preyed upon by snowy owls in what we called a food chain. But they are also preyed upon by foxes, weasels, short-eared owls, jaegers (another type of bird), and gulls.

To represent more accurately the flow of food in a community, we must take into account the facts that most predators eat several different kinds of food. Also most foods are eaten by many different kinds of animal. An organism can belong to more than one trophic level and/or food chain simultaneously. A further complication is that some animals are **omnivorous**. Their diet includes both plants and animals. Variations in available food bring changes in their eating patterns. In the summer, when berries are abundant, fully half the diet of

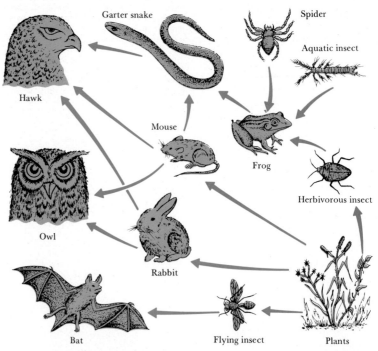

24-4
Food web.

the red fox may consist of fruit. But during the winter he subsists mostly on rabbits and small rodents, occasionally supplemented by whatever shriveled fruits are left. Depending on what he can find and catch, he will also eat birds, chipmunks, and insects.

## The flow of energy

Living cells are constantly active. They absorb, process, and excrete materials, change shape, and move about. To fuel these activities, they require energy. As food is produced by plants and consumed at successive trophic levels, light energy from the sun is converted to chemical energy. This is passed along to fuel the biological processes of each organism in the chain. The same amount of energy that enters the system leaves it. The total energy needs of all organisms in a food web exist in dynamic equilibrium. But along the way, some of the energy is used in respiration and dissipated as heat energy. In this form the energy is no longer available to the biota. Energy passing through a food web follows the principles expressed in the first and second laws of thermodynamics. The First Law of Thermodynamics states that energy cannot be created or destroyed. It can only be changed from one form to another. In an ecosystem, light energy is converted to chemical energy, which is gradually changed to heat energy. This process follows the Second Law of Thermodynamics. At every transformation of energy, some of the energy available for doing work is converted to heat energy. So the available energy would soon be used up if more were not continually being added from outside the system. The source of this added energy is the sun.

*Primary productivity* Green plants form glucose through photosynthesis. They can immediately use the glucose for respiration, the oxidative process by which organisms use chemical energy to fuel their activities. It can also be converted into other compounds necessary for support, protection,

and other functions. Alternatively, the energy trapped in the plant's compounds can be intercepted and used by other organisms. This is most important to animals who cannot themselves trap and fix light energy.

It is sometimes useful to know how much energy the plants in a certain ecosystem are producing. **Primary productivity** refers to the amount of energy produced by plant photosynthesis in a given area (ordinarily one square meter) in a given amount of time (ordinarily one year). This energy is expressed in terms of calories per gram. Methods for measuring productivity often take advantage of the fact that carbon dioxide from air or water is taken in by the plant, and oxygen is released.

Primary productivity varies widely from one region to another. Only a small percentage of the world is very fertile. Deserts, grasslands, deep lakes, mountain forests, and deep oceans are not very productive as compared to estuaries, coral reefs, tropical forests, and intensely managed agricultural lands. On land, water is often the factor lim-

24-5
The gross primary productivity of different habitats, measured in kilocalories per square meter per day. Gross productivity is the total amount of energy produced regardless of how much is used by the plants themselves in respiration.

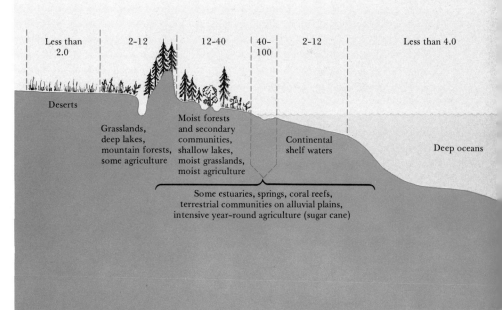

| Less than 2.0 | 2-12 | 12-40 | 40-100 | 2-12 | Less than 4.0 |

Deserts

Grasslands, deep lakes, mountain forests, some agriculture

Moist forests and secondary communities, shallow lakes, moist grasslands, moist agriculture

Continental shelf waters

Deep oceans

Some estuaries, springs, coral reefs, terrestrial communities on alluvial plains, intensive year-round agriculture (sugar cane)

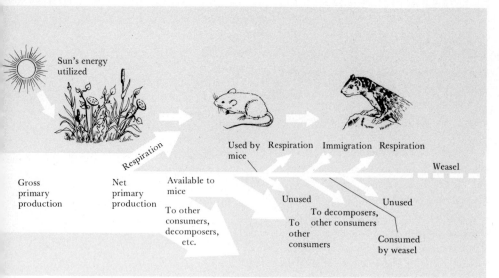

24-6
The flow of energy.

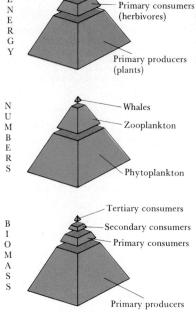

24-7
Pyramids of energy, numbers, and biomass. Pyramidal models can be used to show certain ecological relationships. The pyramid of energy shows the loss of energy along a food chain. The greatest quantity of energy is in the photosynthetic producers. As energy passes through herbivores and carnivores, significant quantities are lost through respiration and excretion.

The pyramid of numbers shows the relative numbers of organisms at each level in the food chain, extending from phytoplankton to the whale. This pyramid tapers from bottom to top because the consumed organisms are smaller than their consumers. The larger numbers of consumed organisms are necessary to support the larger consumers.

An aquatic ecosystem in Silver Springs, Florida shows that the less energy there is at a trophic level, the less biomass can be supported at that level. The largest amount of energy is found in the producers which constitute the largest concentration of biomass. The numbers represent grams of dry biomass, a standard form of measurement. (See Secondary productivity)

iting primary productivity. There is much greater productivity in regions that receive heavy rain, such as the Indian subcontinent, than in those lacking it, such as the Sahara and the Arabian peninsula.

*Secondary productivity*    It has been estimated that over 99 percent (by weight) of the earth's living substance is composed of green plants. When this biomass of green plants passes to the herbivore or detritivore trophic levels, not all the material is assimilated to serve as an energy source. Much of the tough cellulose of plants is excreted. Digestion and assimilation of the plant material use up some energy, leaving less for growth and reproduction. Waste materials from cellular processes cause the loss of more energy. They may disrupt the flow of energy, and may prevent the use of the organism by the next predator level. The flow of energy through a trophic level is measured in units called kilocalories (Kcal). One kilocalorie is the energy necessary to raise the temperature of one kilogram (one liter) of water one degree centigrade. (For example, a loaf of supermarket white bread contains approximately 1250 kilocalories.) **Secondary productivity** is the rate of energy transfer from producer to consumer and

detritivore trophic levels. It drops appreciably at each link in the food chain. Some part of the original energy input is directed to the detritivores even in an essentially non-detritivore trophic level.

Combining the diagrams for several trophic levels gives us a so-called "pyramid model" of energy flow through an ecosystem. A model of the energy flow of Silver Springs, a Florida River community, shows that about one-half of the incoming solar energy is absorbed. But only about 1 percent (20,810/1,700,000) is actually converted to gross productivity. The efficiency of gross primary productivity typically ranges from 0.1 percent to 2 percent, so this 1 percent is representative. Over half of this gross productivity is lost as heat during respiration. This leaves a net primary productivity of 8833 kilocalories per square meter per year (figures from Odum, 1959).

Along with the absorption of solar energy used in photosynthesis, 486 Kcal/m²/year are imported into the Silver Springs community from outside in the form of bread fed to the fishes. But only 6 Kcal/m²/year are available beyond the top carnivores. Where have all the calories gone? Plants generally are rather inefficient at capturing and using light energy. Animals are usually more efficient energy converters. But they cannot use all the energy theoretically available in prey organisms. For example, plant cell walls, insect skeletons, bones, and hair all contain energy. However, these are not used as food by most organisms. And before they are eaten themselves, animals in a food chain may expend a considerable amount of energy in their daily activities. These include moving about, converting food into tissue, avoiding predators, and, in the case of warm-blooded animals, producing body heat. So we see that a good deal of the food energy transmitted at lower levels is dissipated before it can reach the top of the chain.

With so little energy per square meter available to them, carnivores at the higher trophic levels must be large and active, with an extensive range. Otherwise they cannot gather enough food energy to survive.

## Biogeochemical cycles

Energy travels a one-way path through the ecosystem. But nutrients are constantly cycling within it. The air you just inhaled contained oxygen that previously may have been in the body of a dinosaur or of Adolf Hitler. The 30–40 elements basic to life are used again and again. They follow complex circuits between living organisms and the earth's water, air, soil, and rocks. These circuits are called **biogeochemical cycles**.

For the most part, productivity in an ecosystem is determined by the rate of nutrients recycling from the abiotic to the biotic community. If nutrients are trapped for long periods of time in inaccessible places or unusable forms, productivity will be low. Natural processes may bury or consume valuable nutrients. Human activities also remove large amounts of materials from the nutrient cycles. Such practices as logging, harvesting, and mining withdraw vital elements from the nutrient supply in one area. When those elements are eventually deposited in other ecosystems, their unusual con-

centration may cause a severe imbalance.

An example of such disruption is seen in our use of phosphate rock. This rock is excavated at a current rate of three million tons a year. It is treated with acid to make it soluble, and then spread over fields as fertilizer. When it rains, much of the phosphate dissolves and runs downhill into streams, ponds, and lakes. There the out-of-place phosphorus nourishes the rapid growth of algae which would ordinarily be limited by the normally low phosphorus level of freshwater systems. In the chain of events which follows, the bacteria which feed on dead algae also increase. Their increasing demand for oxygen causes a depletion of oxygen in the water. Decreasing oxygen levels, in turn, cause a buildup of undecomposed plants and the death of fish and other organisms whose survival depends on normal oxygen levels. This is the process of **eutrophication**. It is essentially a defeat of the natural biogeochemical cycles, which hold nutrients where they are needed and provide for their continued reuse.

### The carbon cycle

All living things require a carbon source. The basic carbon chain is from carbon dioxide. In photosynthesis, plants combine hydrogen from soil water with carbon dioxide from the air to make energy-rich compounds. When these carbohydrates are used by the plants or intercepted by plant predators, most of their energy is lost as heat. Through respiration or decomposition, the carbon is returned to the atmosphere as carbon dioxide. About 100 billion metric tons, or 14 percent, of the carbon dioxide in the atmosphere is incorporated into living organisms by photosynthesis each year. The atmosphere is also the main reservoir for usable carbon. A small portion of the 20,000,000 billion metric tons of carbonates in the earth's crust is constantly eroded, or recycled by volcanic processes.

When carbon follows a complete, or "**perfect**" cycle, it moves through biogeochemical processes and returns to its origi-

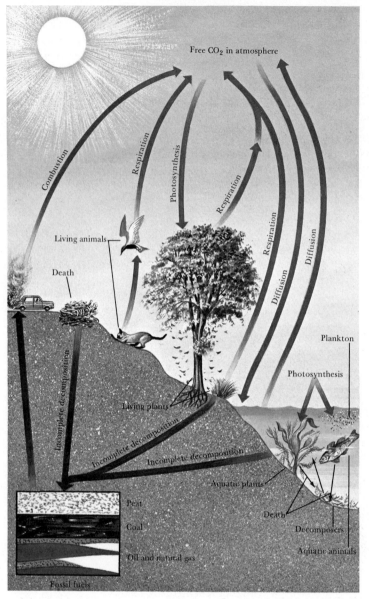

24-8
The carbon cycle.

tons of carbon. But it has been estimated that there may be 35,000 billion metric tons of it in the sea.

## The nitrogen cycle.

Our ocean is 79 percent nitrogen, but in an inert form which few organisms can use. The nitrogen must first be "fixed," or combined into some chemical compound that plants or animals can use. In terms of energy, it is expensive to fix nitrogen. Moreover, most organisms lack the necessary enzymes to do so. A few plants—alder trees, and legumes such as peas, beans, and alfalfa—have nitrogen-fixing microorganisms on their roots. Microscopic *Rhizobium* bacteria penetrate the roots and multiply, causing rounded **nodules** to form. All life depends on these bacteria, along with certain free-living bacteria, blue-green bacteria, and fungi, for the nitrogen needed to produce proteins and amino acids.

In soil, water, and root nodules, these nitrogen-fixing microorganisms change atmospheric nitrogen ($N_2$) to ammonia ($NH_3$). Some of this ammonia is excreted into the soil or water. Some is used to make organic nitrogen compounds, mostly amino acids. The bacteria in root nodules retain very little for their own use. They may release up to 90 percent of the nitrogen they have fixed into their host plant. An acre of alfalfa can fix up to 400 pounds of nitrogen in one season. Since much of the nitrogen is eventually returned to the soil in usable form, farmers often rotate their fields between planting of legumes and other crops. In this way they replace the nitrogen consumed by crops such as corn, which do not fix it themselves.

Specialized **decomposer bacteria** and fungi use fixed nitrogen compounds as energy sources. These organisms complete the nitrogen cycle by returning nitrogen to its inorganic form. When an organism dies, these bacteria break down its living matter into amino acids, organic residues, and (in the case of animals) urea. **Ammonifying bacteria** change the amino acids to am-

nal gaseous state within minutes, hours, or perhaps a few years. But sometimes it is trapped in the bodies of organisms which fail to decompose for one reason or another. Some parts of dead organisms in the ocean are not completely broken down. This is especially true of their carbonate-containing skeletons. These may accumulate to form huge deposits of calcium carbonate such as the White Cliffs of Dover. The atmosphere contains about 700 billion metric

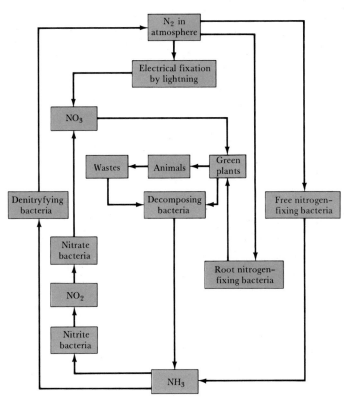

24-9
The nitrogen cycle.

## Other cycles

In contrast to the gaseous cycles such as those of carbon and nitrogen, some nutrients follow "imperfect" cycles, ending as sedimentary rock. Such nutrients can be reclaimed very slowly through natural processes for use by organisms. For example, phosphorus is a key element in the ATP needed for energy-using processes. If it is effectively lost to the ecosystem, plant growth may be seriously limited by its absence. Phosphate rock is the chief reservoir for this nutrient. It is normally available to plants through rain erosion and stream runoff. Plants take up the dissolved phosphorus through their roots. When death occurs or phosphorus is excreted by the plants or their predators, the phosphorus returns to the soil. But in its dissolved state, much of it is washed away. Eventually it is deposited on the sea bottom. There it may be buried by marine sediments and lost to living organisms unless geological activity of the upwelling of deep ocean waters carries the sediments to the surface. Some phosphorus is returned to land by fish-eating birds. Their droppings, called guano, are gathered as fertilizer on South America's west coast. Additional phosphorus is retained by some organisms which have developed hoarding mechanisms. In salt marshes, mussels filter substantial amounts of phosphorus from the water. They deposit it as sediment on the marsh's surface, where it is taken up by marsh plants.

Less plentiful elements may be just as necessary to life. Sulfur, for instance, is a minor but key element that ties proteins together. Magnesium forms the central atom of every chlorophyll molecule. Like carbon, nitrogen, and phosphorus, these elements follow cyclic paths through the ecosystem. Some nutrients are needed only in tiny quantities. But their absence produces major effects. Molybdenum, for example, is a key element in the nitrogen-fixing enzyme nitrogenase, which is found in symbiotic nitrogen-fixing organisms. The

monia, which is then broken down into nitrites by **nitrite bacteria. Nitrate bacteria** decompose the nitrites to make nitrates. Nitrates can be used directly by green plants in protein synthesis. **Denitrifying bacteria** act to return some of the nitrates to the atmosphere. The work of these microscopic organisms is immensely important. The American Chemical Society has warned that extinction of as few as twelve species of bacteria involved in the nitrogen cycle could mean death for all life on earth.

Natural terrestrial and marine plant processes fix about 40 million metric tons of nitrogen each year. An additional 7.6 million tons are produced by lightning and other atmospheric processes. Several million tons are added by human planting of legumes such as clover and alfalfa, with their valuable nitrogen-fixing bacteria. Another 30 million tons of nitrogen is added to the soil each year by means of industrially fixed nitrogen fertilizers.

addition of two ounces of molybdenum per acre can make land capable of sustaining legumes.

## Biological interactions

Plants and animals do not merely coexist in an ecosystem. They affect each other either directly or indirectly in an immense number of ways. They may feed on, hitch rides on, cross-pollinate, shelter, pick ticks and parasites from, compete for food with, stabilize the population of, join in hunting with, mate with, and even cooperate with each other in complicated social structures. Such associations are important to each species in ways we are only beginning to understand.

To make some sense of the variety of plant and animal relationships which have been discovered, we may divide them into general groups. Intraspecific relationships occur among organisms within the same species. Interspecific relationships occur among organisms of different species. We can examine predator–prey relationships to see what effect they may have on the survival of species. Some organisms form close associations with creatures unlike themselves. For these, we can try to determine whether the relationship is one-sided or mutually advantageous. Finally, we can look at the effects which competition and cooperation, both intraspecific and interspecific, have on the whole ecosystem.

In the long run, intraspecific relationships serve to determine the fitness of a species as a whole. They may also determine the fitness of individual members of the species. Competition for food, living space, mates, or other limited resources regulates population sizes, balancing them with the carrying capacity of a region. For instance, male birds that sing define their territory in song and defend it against occupation by others of the same species. Those who are squeezed out and left with no territory cannot breed and raise young. This prevents overcrowding and direct competition within the species for food.

Not all intraspecific relationships are competitive. Often the survival of a species requires cooperation among its members. Parents care for and defend their young. Birds flock together to breed and migrate. And predators such as wolves band together to capture prey larger than themselves. When fish swim in schools they are safer than when swimming alone. They may be unable to defend themselves against attack by predators. But they can collectively watch for them in more directions at once. At the same time, their mass movements are visually confusing. This makes it difficult for predators to aim precisely at a single target. Cooperation reaches an apex in the division of labor we observe among social insects such as bees, termites, and ants.

Organisms from different species may also exist in cooperative associations with each other. However, we do not know the extent to which they "understand" the ef-

24-10
Coyote. The coyote has long been considered a pest. In America, it has been trapped, shot, and poisoned in efforts to control its population. But in fact, coyotes help farmers and ranchers by controlling rodent populations. Without coyotes, rodents would multiply rapidly and devour grain and vegetation. Also, coyotes are scavengers. They often drag carcasses away from human water supplies. They thus prevent contamination of the water. Also, they help keep deer, elk, moose, and other animal populations strong by eliminating old, weak, and feeble members. (See Biological interactions)

fects of these relationships. Natural selection often seems to favor those organisms which have evolved such cooperative living arrangements. Ostriches, antelopes, and zebra often share a feeding ground. The long-necked, large-eyed ostrich alerts the others to the approach of distant predators. The antelope and zebra, with their acute sense of smell, can detect lions hidden nearby in the bushes.

Interspecific relationships may be cooperative, competitive, predatory, or symbiotic. Like intraspecific cooperation and competition, these various types of interaction usually balance out. They may lead to death for individuals, but rarely to extinction for whole species.

## Symbiosis

**Symbiosis** is a broad term which literally means living together. It covers any close association between two or more members of different species. At least one of the participants, or symbionts, must benefit from the relationship. In many cases both do. Some symbiotic associations may be almost accidental, giving only a slight advantage to one and none at all to the other. For example, barnacles can settle on rocks or pebbles and often do. But those which attach themselves to the shells of crabs, mussels, or oysters have a slightly better chance for survival. Their hosts help to stir up food for the barnacles by moving about or by circulating water through themselves.

The various symbiotic relationships range from casual to life-or-death interdependence. In an effort to identify the exact nature of the relationships, we generally subdivide them into three categories. These are commensalism, mutualism, and parasitism.

*Commensalism*    When one species benefits from a symbiotic relationship while the other is neither helped nor harmed, the relationship is called **commensalism**. The Spanish "moss" which hangs in grey beards from trees in the southern and western United States is a seed plant which makes its own food and can absorb water from the humid air. It uses its host tree only for support and exposure to sunlight. This is a commensal relationship because the moss benefits from the tree without significantly affecting it for better or for worse. Arboreal orchids are also commensals. They grow on the trunks of rain forest trees from which they gain living space but do no harm to the tree.

Animals often take up residence near other species for protection. The drongo is an aggressive, crow-like African bird. When drongos begin to build their nest in a tree, smaller birds such as orioles and doves rush to establish nesting sites in the branches below. Whenever nest-robbers such as hawks and crows appear, the drongos can be counted on to drive them off with great flapping of wings and noisy calls. Obviously the proximity benefits the smaller birds by safeguarding their eggs and young. But the relationship is commensal because it has no effect on the drongos.

Cockroaches, pigeons, and house mice have become commensal with human beings. Our leftovers and waste products provide a ready source of food for them.

*Mutualism*    When both species benefit from the interaction, the symbiotic relationship is called **mutualism**. Lichens are a classic example of mutualism. They are a composite of algae (which carry out photosynthesis) and fungi (which absorb water and nutrients). Together they can live in places where neither could survive alone. Often they live where nothing else can survive, as on bare rock. Earlier in this chapter we mentioned another plant partnership which is mutually beneficial. Nitrogen-fixing bacteria live in nodules on the roots of legumes. The bacteria gain a favorable and relatively protected environment. The legumes, which like most other plants cannot use the nitrogen in the air, receive usable nitrogen compounds in return.

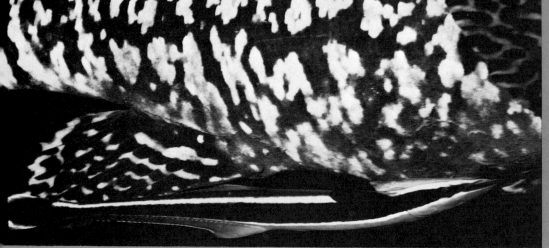

24-11
Commensalism. The remora fish has spinous dorsal fin modified into a sucking disc to attach itself to the body of a shark, swordfish, tunny, barracuda, or sea turtle. While the relationship neither benefits nor harms the host, it benefits the remora, which sweeps up scraps of food produced while the host is eating.

24-12
Mutualism. The tickbird finds a food supply—skin parasites—on rhinoceroses. The tickbird relieves the rhinoceros by eating the irritating parasites. It also provides warning of danger by suddenly flying off to the security of a nearby tree.

24-13
Parasitism (left). Ticks, fleas, lice, mites, leeches, and this bedbug are examples of the external, or ecto-parasite. They use suckers, clamps, or adhesive surfaces to attach themselves to the skin of a host. They use cutting, biting, or sucking mouth parts to extract the host's internal body fluids. Also, they carry protozoa, bacteria, and viruses which can cause serious disease in the host.

Insects are essential to the reproduction of flowering plants. They cross-pollinate the plants by transporting male reproductive cells from one plant to the female structures of another plant of the same species. One such pollinator is the bee. It benefits from this interaction by gathering nectar from the flowers for food. It has adapted to its role by gathering nectar from only one plant species on each trip.

Our own mutualistic interdependence with domesticated animals such as cattle, sheep, goats, chickens, and pigs is echoed in the insect world, where ants tend herds of aphids. The aphids benefit by being carefully carried to good feeding places on plants. The ants receive sugar-rich droplets of honeydew to drink when they "milk" the aphids by stroking their abdomens.

*Parasitism* When one species benefits to the detriment of the other species, the relationship is called **parasitism**. The species that benefits is known as the **parasite**. The species that suffers is called the **host**. Parasitism differs from predation. The host, unlike prey, is killed very slowly, if at all. It is to the parasite's advantage to siphon off food from the larger host in, on, or near whom it lives, without actually killing it. In the long run, if the host were killed before the parasite had a chance to reproduce, the latter would die without offspring. This pattern would eventually lead to extinction for the parasite species. In the short run, killing the host would destroy the parasite's food supply.

Ticks, bedbugs, lice, and fleas have evolved specialized structures for attaching themselves firmly to their hosts' outer body surfaces. They are called **ectoparasites**. **Endoparasites** live inside the host, often in its digestive tract. They have developed means of resisting the pull of food currents and peristaltic movements and of preventing themselves from being digested. Tapeworms, for instance, have a hard outer skin that is not affected by powerful digestive secretions and enzymes.

There are even parasites which parasitize parasites which are parasitizing a host. This relationship is aptly named **hyperparasitism**. For example, certain wasp larvae live on fly larvae which live on moth caterpillars. Such situations inspired Augustus de Morgan in 1872 to pen the couplet: "Great fleas have little fleas upon their backs to bite 'em,/And little fleas have lesser fleas, and so ad infinitum."

## Predation

"How to get something to eat" and "How to avoid being eaten" are two of nature's most basic problems. Broadly speaking, **predation** is the feeding of one organism on another. Each ecosystem has many different kinds of predators at every level of the food chain. Rabbits and caterpillars are plant predators, and may themselves be preyed upon by hawks and jays, respectively. These birds, in turn, are preyed upon by internal parasites. (However, we are considering parasitism separately from predation, as a slower process which may or may not lead to death.)

Predators aid in population control by feeding on other organisms. They also assist the flow of food and energy through an ecosystem, ensuring the recycling of essential nutrients. Like parasitism, predation plays an important role in maintaining ecological balance. It serves to weed out those members of a prey species that are weaker than their fellows.

*Minor impact on prey* Many predators have little or minor impact on their prey. The green environment is evidence that herbivores seldom consume much of the available food. For instance, several large predators, including the hyena, hunt on the Serengeti plains of Africa. The hyena is an effective predator, second only to the lion. But the available evidence suggests that hyenas do not control any prey species. Rather, they feed on a doomed surplus of animals. Destruction of all hyenas would not increase the number of zebras, ga-

**24-14**
Predator. The piranha is well adapted for preying upon other fish, animals, and even humans. It has short, wide jaws with extremely sharp, strong, triangular-shaped teeth which fit tightly together. Its powerful jaws can snap a fishhook in half and shear the fingers from a person's hand. The presence of blood triggers a savage reaction. It causes the fish to snap wildly in any direction, even that of other piranhas. Piranhas have been known to strip the flesh from a 400-pound hog in less than 10 minutes.

**24-15**
Prey with defensive adaptation. The skunk's best defense consists of the two large musk glands at the base of its tail. They contain a foul-smelling fluid capable of repelling most predators. When endangered, the skunk contracts the muscles surrounding the glands and forces out a fine spray. Besides offending the sense of smell, the spray can irritate eye, nose, and mouth membranes. (See Major impact on prey)

zelles, and other ungulates. They would inevitably succumb to something else.

*Major impact on prey* Occasionally predation may be so heavy or major that the prey becomes extinct. The predator is thus left without enough to eat. For example, this occurs when lemming migrations severely upset the balance of life on the tundra. Their sudden absence results in a major loss of prey. In turn, the organisms which remain are forced into new feeding patterns. Often this results in drastic changes in the whole food web.

The effects of overpredation can be experimentally simulated. One ecologist (Paine, 1966), acting as a superpredator, removed all the starfish from a section of the rocky intertidal coastlines of Washington. The normal food web had been composed of fifteen species. But it was soon reduced to a system of eight species. Six species in addition to the starfish became locally extinct.

Some biologists have studied predator–prey interactions in laboratory situations where variables are easier to control. The Russian biologist G. F. Gause (1934) used ciliated protozoans in test-tube experiments. *Paramecium* fed on bacteria in the culture vessels and functioned as prey. *Didinium* functioned as the predator. The prey population grew quickly, providing food for a rapidly increasing number of the predators. The predators ate all the prey and starved shortly thereafter. In another experiment, Gause provided hiding places for the paramecia. *Didinium,* the predator, starved again, after which the size of the prey population increased. Trying to prolong the existence of both populations, the experimenter added one of each organism every third day. This permitted the populations to coexist almost three times as long. This additonal complexity was intended to simulate the immigrations which might occur in nature.

Not surprisingly, prey evolve ways to avoid being preyed upon. Moose are large enough and fast enough that wolves, even in a pack, can seldom kill any but the very young, sick, injured, or relatively old moose. Many animals develop some form of camouflage to avoid becoming prey. They may look like sticks, leaves, flower parts, bird-droppings—anything but what they are.

Under natural conditions, complete extinction of one species by another occurs only rarely. Instead, a more efficient predator pressures the prey to evolve a better strategy of avoidance. This puts the predator population under greater pressure to become more efficient, and so on. In natural

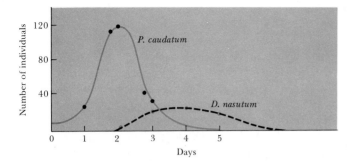

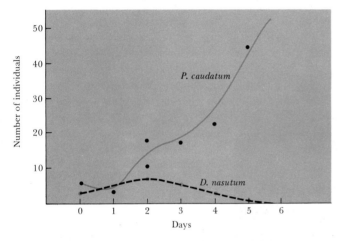

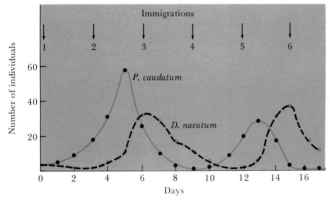

24-16
Gause's experiments
with *Didinium (D.
nasutum)* and *Parame-
cium (P. caudatum).* (See
Major impact on prey)

situations, predators and prey have generally interacted in this way for long periods
of time. They have coadapted or coevolved
with each other. Instances of excessive
predator impact usually occur under unnat-
ural conditions. This may happen, for example, when a new predator is introduced into
an environment. There it has few or no enemies, and its prospective prey have never
had the opportunity to adapt to it. Extinction
or severe reduction of the prey often results.

24-17
Gypsy moth. Calosoma
beetles, parasitic
wasps and flies, white-
footed mice, cuckoos,
and certain flocking
birds all prey on the
gypsy moth. These
predations have not
prevented periodic gypsy
moth population
explosions. Only when
the gypsy moth
population becomes
extremely dense does an
internal wilt disease
virus cause it to
collapse.

## Competition

Competitive interactions may occur when
two or more species use the same resources. If resources such as food, space,
light, and nesting sites are abundant, intense competition does not occur. There is
no competition for oxygen in the atmosphere, for instance, because it is not in
short supply. But there may be competition
for the limited amount of dissolved oxygen
at the bottom of a lake. Competitors are
usually members of the same trophic level.
Herbivores and primary producers do not
compete for the same ray of sunlight, but
two plant species often do. However, herbivorous insects give omnivorous man his
greatest competition for an adequate food
supply.

During the past three decades, many
laboratory experiments have tested competition between two species in a simple environment. The results have usually been the
same. One species has persisted, and the
other has died out. For example, in one
experiment (Gause, 1934) two species of
*Paramecium* were first grown separately in

a rich culture medium to show that they grew well in the medium. They were then cultured together to determine the results of competition. When grown together, both populations showed the same growth curve. Growth was slow at first. It then became more rapid, and finally leveled off when an equilibrium was reached. Eventually, one species perished. Similar results occurred when two species of flour beetles were grown together. One scientist (Park, 1938) discovered that two flour beetle species could coexist if he provided some broken wheat kernels in the flour. The kernels gave the insects a physical refuge. The researcher showed this by replacing the kernels with pieces of fine glass tubing, which also permitted coexistence.

24-18
Intraspecific competition. Koalas feed exclusively on the eucalyptus leaf. The size of the koala population is dependent upon the supply of leaves and the competition for them.

Experiments in nature, whether natural or directed by man, tell us that competition is a potent force in ecology and in evolution. When sheep and rabbits were introduced into Australia, the native herbivore populations of kangaroos and wallabies were significantly reduced. Prickly pear cactus rapidly became dominant over grasses on 60 million acres after it was introduced to Australia in 1839. In marshes of western Canada, male redwings establish breeding territories in the center of the marsh. Here the water is deep and predation is less likely than near the shore. Days later, yellow-headed blackbirds arrive and drive the redwings off the central marsh zone, establishing their own breeding territories there.

Intense competition for choice feeding sites has been observed between two species of barnacles which live together on rocky intertidal shores. *Cthamalus* is invariably found higher on the rocks than *Balanus*, and can better withstand drying. But the high intertidal is not a choice feeding site. Young *Cthamalus* occupy the lower part of the intertidal but are outcompeted by young *Balanus* which settle in greater numbers and grow faster. *Balanus* will even smother, undercut, or crush individual *Cthamalus* when they come into contact. This causes a very high mortality rate for *Cthamalus*.

Many species seem to be constant losers in competitive interactions. The question therefore arises of how it is possible for these species to survive. We note that the flour beetles do prosper in their refuges. Kangaroos formerly prospered when geographically separated from sheep by thousands of miles. Redwings breed successfully at marsh edges where yellow-headed blackbirds do not. And *Cthamalus* can tolerate drying out better than their competitors. These species thus employ many different strategies to reduce or avoid competition. Why? According to Gause's principle, this is because two species cannot occupy the same niche simultaneously. Alliteratively rephrased, this means that "complete competitors cannot coexist." Where pairs of species are too similar to each other in their requirements, one of three things is likely to occur: extinction of one species, character displacement (discussed in chapter 21), or competitive exclusion.

*Competitive exclusion*  In competitive exclusion, one species is squeezed out of a habitat by another. However, it may survive nearby under slightly altered circumstances. This niche diversification permits the coexistence of the two barnacle species discussed earlier. Another example is five warbler species which were studied in a northern coniferous forest in Maine. These species belong to the same genus, are of similar size, eat insects, and live in trees of the same kinds. But they manage to coexist by avoiding direct competition. By using different feeding locations on the trees and by feeding in different manners, they uncover and eat different kinds of insect food.

## Cooperation

To cooperate means to act or work together with others toward a common end and for mutual benefit. It is difficult to separate interspecific cooperative behaviors from patterns of mutualism and commensalism. Indeed, there is some overlap here. In mutualism, organisms of two species may be completely dependent on each other for survival. Since participation in such arrangements is obligatory, perhaps we cannot really call this cooperation. But in commensal relationships, any cooperation involved generally seems to be gratuitous. The cooperative patterns are favored by evolution but not by individuals. When ostriches, antelopes, and zebras graze together, they do not deliberately alert each other to the approach of predators. By showing fright or by running away, they just happen to draw the attention of the others to approaching danger.

Perhaps the major problem in interspecific cooperation is that different species are relatively unable to communicate with each other. But occasional cases do occur which appear to be true interspecific cooperation. For example, a small African bird known as the honey guide lures a honey badger to a bees' nest. It waits quietly while the larger animal tears the nest open to feast on the honey. Then it enters the nest to gather honeycomb wax for itself. Flying ahead of the honey badger and perching occasionally to urge it on with a churring call, the honey guide may lead it as far as a quarter of a mile to a bees' nest. At times the bird has used the same calling method to guide Africans to the bees, waiting for them to perform the same function as the honey badger. But where the humans have taken up other pursuits and stopped gathering wild honey, the birds have come to ignore them. The relationship between the bird and the badger may not be obligatory. Honey badgers can and do find bees' nests on their own. While they benefit from their cooperation with the honey guide, they are not absolutely dependent on it. Likewise, nine out of eleven species of honey guides manage to tear open bees' nests without the help of badgers. So it is possible that the two species which do invoke the badgers' assistance might be able to survive without it. Braving the swarm of bees to open the hive is apparently no problem—the birds' tough skins are reported to be resistant to insect stings.

**24-19**
Intraspecific cooperation. Army ants live in colonies of up to 22 million members. They show a remarkable degree of intraspecific cooperation. Most colony members join the hunting parties which conduct organized raids to obtain food. Army ants do not have permanent homes. They bivouac in temporary nests, which they form with their own clustered bodies on a branch, in a hollow in the ground, or inside a hollow log. The ants provide these nests with passageways, regulated temperatures, and a protective pocket for the young and the queen. In time of flood, army ants have even been known to form clusters which float.

We find many true instances of cooperative activities among animals of the same species. During cold or rainy weather sparrows, titmice, swallows, and rodents frequently clump together to conserve heat. Territorial defense is often cooperative. Group hunting is found among army ants, wolves, hyenas, dogs, eagles, crows, cormorants, and pelicans. For example, a pelican group will form a large ring and then swim closer together. This forces their prey into a tighter circle from which the birds can more easily make their kill. Many animals group together for mutual protection against predators. Musk oxen on the tundra form a circle, facing out, to fend off attack by wolves. Examples of the care of young by other than parents are found among birds and mammals.

Recently, more biologists are watching specifically for cooperative behavior. As a result, cases of cooperative control of social interactions are starting to be observed. In the Serengeti, male lions need at least one male companion in order to be permitted to remain in a pride. This form of cooperation is essential to the male if he is to have access to prey usually captured by the females, and to the females when they are in heat. A pair of younger male lions may turn a pair of older males out of the pride. If the companion of an older male dies, a cooperating pair of lions will soon drive him off and take over the pride.

Not surprisingly, the most advanced forms of cooperation occur among the primates. Parental "aunt" and "uncle" behavior toward young infants is often seen, and it has great survival value. For instance, a mother rhesus monkey died when her baby was only eight months old. But the baby was quickly adopted by the "aunt" (a behavioral rather than genealogical term) who had been the mother's "best friend." Japanese investigators have observed that middle-caste male macaques will display "uncle" behavior toward high-caste infants. In return for hugging, grooming, and protecting an infant from other monkeys and

from dangerous situations, the "uncle" may be tolerated by leaders and their females, and may rise in rank within the troop.

Structural complexity in the social interactions of a species seems to be a prerequisite for much cooperative behavior. So instances of cooperation are most often found in species living in dense colonies, in mobile troops, or in groups with long-term social bonds. There is little need for complex social interactions in the simple mother—young social unit of solitary burrow dwellers. But the situation is different for many animals—marsupials, ungulates, carnivores, and primates. These animals have adapted to open habitats, such as savannahs, by forming more highly structured groups. Here we find dominance hierarchies with characteristic display behavior. This behavior is triggered by increased proximity.

As the young animal of a species matures, he takes on different roles and passes through varying status levels. He comes to know other members of the relatively stable group as individuals. This enables him to engage in predictable interactions when competing for food, safety, and mates.

24-20
Lemmings in migration.

## Population dynamics

Individual organisms within an ecosystem are born, live for a while, perhaps reproduce themselves, and inevitably die. A population is made up of all individual organisms of the same species which occupy the same area and share the same resources. The populations of different species display different patterns of birth rates, death rates, fluctuations in population size, and density. Population ecologists are concerned with observing these characteristics of organisms at the population level of organization rather than at the individual or community level. They can then predict the implications of the patterns observed in a particular population. Their predictions may help us to anticipate an explosive growth of pest populations, or a decrease in

plant and animal populations which we rely on for food. Population ecologists also give us a picture of our own future: how fast the global human population will increase, and whether or not it can continue to do so *ad infinitum.*

Groups of organisms never persist in exactly the same numbers year after year. The size and distribution of populations always fluctuates to some extent. This is due partly to environmental changes and partly to the characteristics of the populations themselves. The ways they respond to both internal and external factors are referred to as **population dynamics**. These factors include growth rates, density, population controls, immigration, emigration, and long- and short-term fluctuations in population size.

Population ecology is concerned both with the species members within a population and with how they space themselves. This latter factor may be important to a population's ability to perpetuate itself. The most common pattern of distribution is **clumping**. This occurs when individuals within a population congregate for mating, food-seeking, protection from predation or harsh weather, or similar purposes. Overcrowding or undercrowding may limit the size of populations by increasing death rates, decreasing birth rates, or both.

Lemmings provide an unusually dramatic example of how population dynamics work. These small arctic and subarctic rodents are prolific breeders. A female may produce three to six litters per year, with the major breeding taking place during the short summer. One theory traces the famed growth and mass deaths of lemmings to climatic factors. These include a temperature cue in the spring. Weather conditions may allow mating to occur early enough that the babies can mature before winter. This means that the numbers which can breed in underground burrows during the winter will be greatly increased. The weather may also permit a second successful breeding season the next summer. In

this case, the population may grow enormously over the following winter. It may grow to as much as a hundred times its average size during previous years. Severely overcrowded, widespread colonies of lemmings then burst from their underground confinements in the spring, and set out on a mass migration. Their behavior may be a frantic search for new feeding grounds, a reaction to social pressures, a type of adrenal shock, or a population-controlling response triggered by some other factor as yet unknown. As they leave the security of their burrows, the lemmings are exposed to many predatory birds and mammals, and are eaten in vast numbers. Lemmings normally do not swim. But those who survive predation often cross rivers and lakes in their migrations. Death by drowning is the fate of those who jump into the sea instead. A few lemmings do not join the mass migration. This helps ensure the survival of the species. The remaining lemmings reproduce, renewing a boom-and-bust cycle which recurs approximately every four years. Since the lemming population fluctuates wildly, populations of their predators are trapped in feast-or-famine cycles.

## Birth and death rates

To predict the future size of a population, we must first know the rates at which members enter into the population at birth and leave at death. Whether the new individuals are live-born, hatched, or germinated, the **birth rate** is the number of offspring born per individual in a population during a specific time period, such as one day or one year. We usually calculate birth rate by dividing the number of births by the total size of the population. The birth rate of human populations may also be expressed as the number of births per 1,000 of the total population. This estimate is called the **crude birth rate** because it is an average for the whole population. It ignores the finer distinctions of age and sex ratios, and their effects on the breeding capabilities of a population.

The **crude death rate** is the number of individuals dying in a specific time period per individual in the population. It includes all deaths, whether by predation, disease, parasites, accident, or old age. Like the crude birth rate, the crude death rate for humans is usually calculated somewhat differently than for other populations. It is the number of deaths per 1,000 people in the population. For instance, the 1970 death rate in the United States was expressed as 9.6 deaths per thousand.

It is not surprising that the best population census data available are for human populations. Human birth and death statistics are published annually. Local or colony-wide census figures for the white population date back to 1650. Demographers specialize in the study of human population characteristics. They find from statistics that the death rate in the United States has gradually declined from 1875 to the present. There are only two major interruptions in this trend. The first variation occurred in 1918, reflecting World War I casualties and a severe influenza epidemic. In 1943 a second increase in the death rate resulted from World War II casualties. But death rates in the United States show an overall downward trend from 20 or 25 per thousand in 1800 to 9.4 per thousand in 1972. This decline is generally attributed to greater medical knowledge and improved medical care. During the same period, U.S. birth rates also show a decline, from 51 per thousand in 1800 to 15.6 per thousand in 1972. However, a sharp *increase* in births occurred after World War II.

*Life tables*    Toads may live to be 36 years old, eagles may reach 80, and men may live for 115 years or more. But few individuals in a population live to these maximum ages. Ecologists calculate the average life expectancy in a natural species population by constructing a **life table** of death rates at particular ages. This is based on information about the deaths of individual members of the population.

Life tables for difficult-to-observe species can be constructed by examining the remains of individuals. In this way we determine their ages at the times of death. A classic study was made of the skulls and horns of 645 Dall mountain sheep carcasses found in Mount McKinley National Park in Alaska. The study showed that although the sheep's maximum lifespan was fifteen years, the average age at death for this population was seven years. Statistically, for every 1,000 sheep born, 199 would have died by the end of their first year. Those who survived had a good chance of living up to seven years, after which their chances of staying alive dropped sharply. Biologists search for survivorship patterns both for management of economically important animals—such as deer, fish, and houseflies—and for an understanding of their life history strategies.

*Survivorship curves*    The survivorship curve is another useful way to look at how long individuals may be expected to live. We plot on a logarithmic scale how many of each 1,000 born into a population are still alive at every year between birth. Then we plot the maximum lifespan for the species. The results produce a downward curve. The

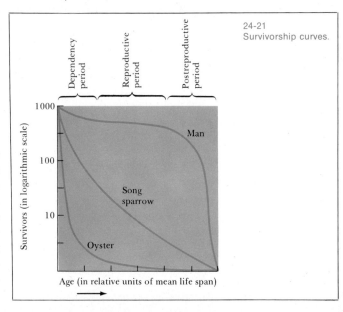

24-21
Survivorship curves.

shape of a survivorship curve for a particular species is as characteristic of that species as is its anatomy or its behavior. At one extreme of survivorship, a laboratory population of experimentally starved fruit flies will almost all survive for a while and then all die at about the same time. In human populations, a certain number die at birth. But stable food supplies, improved sanitation, and modern medical techniques have significantly lowered mortality in the youngest age groups. Most people in advanced industrial societies live for 70 to 80 percent of the average population lifespan.

The survivorship "curves" of organisms such as the hydra, herring gull, and American robin are basically straight diagonals. They indicate an equal chance of living or dying at every point between birth and the maximum possible age. The survivorship curve of many fish and oysters is exactly the reverse of that of starved fruit flies. It involves an extremely high initial mortality for the vulnerable young, followed by a very long life for the few organisms that do survive. For example, oysters give off millions of eggs. Very few of these will ever become adult oysters. But by using this seemingly wasteful strategy, the species has continued to exist for hundreds of millions of years.

## Population growth curves

More individuals may be born into a population than are leaving it by death at a particular time. In such a case, there will be a net increase in numbers. The **population growth rate** is the rate a population increases or decreases in numbers over a certain period of time.

To look at the relative rate of growth over several generations, population ecologists graph their increasing or decreasing numbers as lines which may take one of two general forms. The lines may form an upward curve in the shape of a "J," usually followed by a downward plunge. Or the lines may form a curve in the shape of a forward-leaning "S".

*J-shaped curves*    All populations have a potential for explosive increase in numbers. Thomas Malthus was the first to point out that this is because population size increases by a multiplication factor rather than by simple addition.

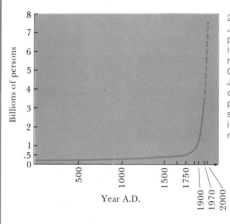

24-22
J-shaped curve. Human population growth rate in the first two millenia of the Christian era forms a J-shaped curve. The dashes along the upper portion of the curve show what will result if the present growth rate continues.

After reading Malthus, Charles Darwin calculated that, barring accidents, the descendants of one pair of slow-breeding elephants (even given their long 22-month gestation period) would constitute a population of 15 million elephants after only 500 years. This kind of dramatic growth, in which individuals increase population growth by multiplying themselves, is called **exponential growth**. It is unlike **linear growth**, in which a quantity increases by the addition of a constant amount over a constant period of time—one pound per year, for instance. Quantities growing exponentially increase by a constant percentage of the whole over a constant time period:

Linear growth: 3 + 3 + 3 + 3 = 12
Exponential growth: $3^4 = 3 \times 3 \times 3 \times 3 = 81$

Compounded interest in a savings account grows in the same way. On a graph, exponential growth produces a J-shaped curve. It grows slowly at first and then rises almost vertically as the multiplying base increases. Then, as in the case of the lemmings, a J-curve may "crash" sharply downward when a population exceeds the life-supporting limits of its habitat.

*S-shaped curves*    If many natural populations are observed for a sufficient time, the numbers of individuals show an exponential increase at first. But then at some point the rate of increase tapers off. Eventually it reaches a stable plateau. In nature, populations do not continue to increase indefinitely. Instead, there seems to be a maximum number of individuals for each species in a habitat. This is called the **carrying capacity** of the habitat. It is the maximum number of individuals which can be supported over a long period of time by the available resources, principally food and space. If a population overloads its environment's carrying capacity, excess members may die from starvation. The only other options are restricted breeding or **emigration**, the migration of individuals out of a population. But rather than persisting in exactly the same numbers, year after year, most such populations perpetually fluctuate slightly above and below their environmental carrying capacity. Thus their population curve appears slightly S-shaped, rather than as a straight horizontal line.

## Population density

The total number of species members in a given area at a particular time is called its **population density**. Population density can be expressed as the number of individuals per unit of area. It can also be expressed as biomass per unit of area or of volume. Measurements of this kind give ecologists an important way of studying the interactions both within and between species. Large top predators must distribute themselves over a wide area in order to obtain enough food energy. But smaller creatures lower in the food chain may exist quite satisfactorily in enormously concentrated groups.

The way in which the members of a population space themselves is an important aspect of population ecology. In **random distribution**, individuals neither attract nor repel each other. This is rather uncommon in nature. It occurs when environmental conditions are uniform, and individuals do not either group together or show intense antagonism or competition. Plants which propagate themselves by seed-scattering techniques are among the few examples of random distribution.

**Uniform dispersion** often results from situations where space or resources are scarce. Individuals within a limited area then tend to antagonize or compete with each other. For example, desert plants such as the creosote bush crowd into areas where moisture is available. But an even spacing is maintained between the bushes. This is because their roots secrete antibiotics which prevent the growth of other plants within their radius.

We have already noted that clumping is the most frequent pattern of distribution. **Allee's principle** states that there is an optimal degree of clumping for each species. If organisms are more or less tightly packed than this **optimum density**, they will not thrive. On the one hand, oceanic birds gather in fantastic numbers for nesting. Apparently the sight and sound of so many like themselves is a stimulus to breed. Colonies of Peruvian cormorants, for instance, seem to require a density of three nests every ten square feet and a total population of at least 10,000 birds for successful breeding. On the other hand, when snowshoe hares become too densely spaced, the stress of frequent interactions causes their livers to degenerate. Then, with insufficient glycogen avilable for emergency reactions, sudden danger may trigger convulsions in the hares rather than flight.

### Population growth factors

Suppose you were to pluck a bacterium from your hair and place it in an unrestricted environment where it and all its descendants could grow and reproduce. Within a month the bacterial mass would weigh

Uniform distribution

Random distribution

Clumped distribution

24-23
Types of population distribution.

more than the visible universe and would be expanding at the speed of light. The intrinsic rate of increase in the absence of any restrictions is known as the **biotic potential** of a species.

Fortunately, the growth of most species is held in check by **environmental resistance**. This includes restraints such as predation and competition for food or space, which increase death rates, lower birth rates, or both. When a J-curving population increasing exponentially overloads the carrying capacity of its habitat, it will run up against environmental resistance. Eventually it will crash, or fall back dramatically in numbers. Large crashes are typical of lemmings, predator-free deer herds, and many insects. They reduce populations to well below carrying capacity. Those individuals who survive seem to be left alone by predators, who emigrate or switch prey species when their usual victims are scarce. In the relative absence of competition for food and space, as well as of predation, the population begins to multiply anew. The increase in numbers once again takes a J-curved exponential shape, eventually overloading the carrying capacity and crashing as before.

**Limiting factors** are environmental characteristics which by their inadequacy prevent populations from exploding in the first place. The factor most responsible for checking a population's potential or actual exponential rise is called its **primary limiting factor**. It is the weakest link in the population's life-support system. The study of limiting factors has been especially helpful to farmers. In 1840 the German agricultural chemist Justus von Liebig discovered that crop yields could be significantly increased by adding one nutrient previously available in insufficient amounts. Adding more nitrogen to a cornfield already well supplied with this element would have little effect. But by experimentally adding other nutrients one at a time it might be found that insufficient phosphorus was the primary factor limiting productivity. If enough phos-

phorus were applied to the land, yields would increase to a certain point and then level off, indicating some other limiting factor. This might be the lack of a different nutrient, or of water.

Liebig's "Law of the Minimum" states that population regulation is imposed by a nutrient or other ecological factor available in the least amount. But there is also Shelford's "Law of the Maximum": populations may also be limited by too much of a factor. For example, certain amounts of nitrogen are essential to plant growth. But the addition of too much nitrate fertilizer can burn plants and even kill them. Each species has a range of tolerances for environmental factors. For example, heat from the sun may be an essential requirement to all forms of life. But too much heat or too little may both be disastrous.

## Changes in population size

The size of natural populations is rarely constant. Some invertebrate populations fluctuate in size by factors as great as 10,000. Vertebrate population size may vary

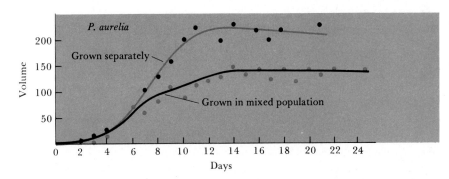

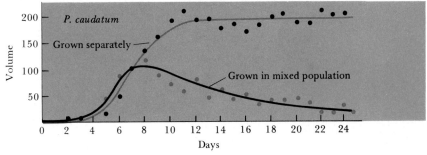

**24-24**
The effects of competition on population size. Gause's experiment involving two species of paramecium, was discussed earlier. It provides an example of the effects of competition on population size. Two species, *P. aurelia* and *P. caudatum*, were first raised separately. Each population showed a typical S-shaped growth curve. But when they were placed together, *caudatum* gradually diminished, while *aurelia* increased to a level lower than that which it reached separately. (See Population growth factors and Density-dependent factors)

24-25
Muskrat. This rodent is found over much of North America. It builds its nest in the shallow portion of a stream, lake, or pond. Droughts intensify competition for food and space. They have considerable effect on the muskrat population in America's midwestern states. As a drought worsens, their shallow-water homes dry up and their food supply—mostly herbs, grains, and water animals—decreases. Savage fighting ensues and many muskrats emigrate. The emigrants have adaptations for an aquatic environment such as webbed hind feet. They are therefore left more vulnerable to predators and the elements as they travel over land in search of new homes and sources of food. Thus, droughts serve to reduce the population by exposing it to increased predation and intense competition for food. Humans, by killing millions of muskrats each year for their pelts, also have a considerable effect on the population. (See Population growth factors and Population controls)

by a factor of up to 100. What triggers these dramatic fluctuations has long been something of a mystery. The removal of some previously limiting factor is often hypothesized. In some instances, ecologists have found that rapid increase can occur only under a complex combination of circumstances. The so-called "red tide" is a case in point. Every so often, a normally rare member of a group of microscopic marine organisms called dinoflagellates suddenly multiplies so rapidly that one drop of seawater may contain 6,000 of them. In such concentration, they discolor the water and secrete a toxic chemical which kills vast quantities of marine life and is also poisonous to humans. Red tides may leave millions of dead fish on seacoasts, seriously threatening fishing industries. Such outbreaks have been traced to the simultaneous occurrence of at least four factors. These include a heavy rainfall which washes precise amounts of certain trace elements into the offshore waters from the land; a drop in the salt content of the water; a certain water temperature; and a lack of wind. Under this rare combination of conditions, a single dinoflagellate can produce 33 million descendants in only 25 brief divisions.

Many population fluctuations seem to follow regular cycles. For example, we are uncomfortably aware of seasonal variations in the numbers of mosquitoes. Many such populations enter dormant states during months of unfavorable weather. But many populations experience surprisingly regular cycles of increase and decrease in numbers which seem to span several years. Three- to four-year cycles of abundance and decline have been observed among small rodents around the world, including rats, hamsters, gerbils, mice, and lemmings. Such cycles may be linked to environmental cycles of rainfall, temperature change, nutrient cycling, or sunspot activity, for instance. Or, they may be simply an average of random fluctuations.

## Population controls

All populations have the potential for engulfing the world with their progeny. But none have yet done so. Their numbers are held down by a broad spectrum of **population controls**, natural checks on increase.

Even in simple organisms with limited activities, a number of factors may be at work to control population growth. For instance, extensive laboratory studies (Park, 1938) of flour beetles have revealed many population-checking mechanisms. These small pests spend their lives wandering through and fouling the flour they both eat and inhabit. But they are limited to a density of 4.4 beetles per gram of flour by the negative effects of overcrowding. Even when there is plenty of flour to eat, the cannibalistic beetles have the habit of eating any beetle eggs they encounter. The more eggs there are, the more beetles will hatch to eat them, and the greater the possibility that a beetle will randomly come upon an egg. As the numbers of beetles and eggs rise, the percentage of eggs eaten before they can hatch will also rise. Finally an equilibrium is reached in which the number of eggs being eaten equals the number of eggs being laid. At this point the S-shaped growth curve of the beetle population levels off.

24-26
Density-dependent relationship between the coyote and the jackrabbit in Curlew Valley, Idaho.

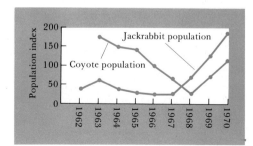

Flour beetle population controls are all functions of relative density. Other population checks have nothing to do with density. But they can increase deaths just the same. For example, hurricanes and flooding wipe out large segments of the populations of everything from snakes to trees. It makes no difference how sparsely or densely packed they may be. These two kinds of control—density-dependent and density-independent—combine to prevent the earth and its available food and space from becoming overwhelmed by living things.

### Density-dependent factors

When a factor limits dense populations more than sparse ones, we say that the factor is **density-dependent**. Density-dependent factors generally tend to hold populations near a steady state. Additions to the population either through birth or through **immigration**, the migration of individuals into a population, are exactly balanced by the loss of individuals through death or emigration. Many density-related population checks result from the finite nature of the earth. All organisms tend to increase exponentially. So eventually they confront shortages of some essential resources, directly or through increased interactions with other organisms. There is also a finite physiological limit to a species' subsistence activities. For instance, Tibetan sheep have to feed at a run because their grass supply is so sparse. Sheep population growth is thus held in check both by their barren habitat and by the impossibility of their ranging any farther in search of food.

Several important density-dependent factors cause population growth to start tapering off before habitat carrying capacity is exceeded. Perhaps the most significant of these is competition. Obviously, when population numbers are increasing, available resources must be spread thinner and thinner. Other major density-dependent factors are predation, disease, and physiological reactions to overcrowding.

### Density-independent factors

Some limits on population growth have nothing to do with density. Weather may limit or determine the size of populations.

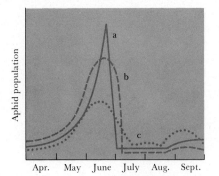

**24-27**
Density-independent factors. The aphid population in the northern California walnut orchards is affected by temperature and leaflet condition, as shown by line *a*, and the predation of coccinellid beetles, as shown by line *c*. The combined effect of both of these factors is shown by line *b*.

This is particularly true of yearly differences in rainfall, severity of the winter, or similar changes beyond the range of tolerance of certain species. A sudden drought will affect a certain percentage of a population, regardless of whether it is high or low in density. So the drought is an example of a **density-independent** population control. Other such factors include the rate of evaporation, temperature levels, wind velocities, light intensity, soil structure, nutrient levels, fire, and human activities.

Density-independent environmental fluctuations affect all populations. But they are most effective in controlling small, rapidly breeding organisms with high biotic potentials—for example, some insects and plankton. Such populations generally lack the stabilizing influences of density-dependent controls. Instead, they careen up and down by factors of up to 10,000. They grow exponentially until they collide with a

harsh environment, die back, and repeat the cycle the next season.

Intentionally or not, people often control populations by acting as a major density-independent factor. Many people engage in dam-building, blacktopping, clear-cut logging, marsh-draining, wetlands-filling, and/or field-clearing. When they do, they disrupt animal populations. Habitats may be destroyed or the nature of the vegetation may be changed. This forces native organisms to compete for diminished food supplies and space. Their alternative is to try to subsist elsewhere. Technology often creates situations toxic to all but the most tolerant species, such as weeds, rodents, and sparrows. As we extract petroleum from the earth's crust and transport it by sea, our accidental oil spills may have devastating effects on marine populations. Spillage from one ship, the grounded *Torrey Canyon,* killed 25,000 seabirds in 1967.

**24-28**
East Pakistani refugees receiving rationed rice at the Salt Lake Camp in West Bengal, India. Human population growth can be seen in terms of the same dynamics which operate among plant and animal populations. Two hundred to three hundred generations ago, domestication of plants and animals raised the carrying capacity of the environment. Humans controlled and increased the food supply in what is now referred to as the agricultural revolution. And as life became safer and the food supply more stable, a larger number of babies survived. Then, starting about 1650 A. D., the scientific-medical revolution significantly increased survivorship rates. With more people living longer, there began an exponential rise in human population growth, which is still a soaring J-curve today. Unless the J-curve meets substantial environmental or cultural resistance, the number of people on earth will double within 35 years.

Despite the gains of the agricultural revolution, world food production is showing signs of being unable to keep up with population growth. In less developed countries, the high birth rates, increasing urbanization, and growing food shortages are already causing escalating numbers of deaths. These occur from starvation, malnutrition, and diseases to which the hungry are easy victims.

But birth rates are dropping. This is due to a variety of circumstances, which make large families less desirable and contraception easier to achieve. The zero-growth movement urges each couple to limit its children to two—the replacement rate—or fewer. If global family size could drop well below the replacement rate for several decades, then level off at the replacement rate, population stability at a tolerable density level could be achieved.

**summary**

Ecology deals with the complex relationships among organisms and their environment. One reason ecologists study these relationships is to predict the effects of environmental changes upon the ecosphere or on an individual ecosystem. The ecosphere includes all organisms, inorganic matter, and physical forces. An ecosystem is limited to a relatively self-contained environment and the organisms living within it. An ecosystem can be seen as a number of habitats, or places where individual organisms are found. It also can be viewed in terms of niches. A niche refers to the place an organism is found, and the function it performs there.

The study of organisms and their interrelationships requires some attention to the transfer of food and energy. The direct or ultimate source of all energy is the sun. Only photosynthetic plants can convert the sun's rays to chemical energy. This chemical energy is necessary to drive an organism's metabolic processes and enable it to do work. Animals obtain their energy from the food produced by plants through photosynthesis. The flow of food and energy through a series of organisms can be traced along food chains and food webs.

Within the ecosystem, nutrients are constantly being recycled. Thirty to forty elements essential to life move back and forth between living organisms and the earth's water, air, soil, and rocks in what are known as biogeochemical cycles. The carbon and nitrogen cycles are, perhaps, the two most important of the numerous biogeochemical cycles.

Ecologists observe two types of relationship among organisms. Intraspecific relationships occur among organisms of the same species and may be either competitive or cooperative. Interspecific relationships occur among organisms of different species and may be competitive, cooperative, predatory, or symbiotic.

Symbiotic relationships are close associations between two or more members of different species. The three types of symbiosis are commensalism, mutualism, and parasitism. In commensalism, one species is helped, while the other is neither helped nor harmed. In mutualism, both species benefit. In parasitism, one species is helped, and the other is harmed.

Predatory relationships involve the feeding of one organism on another. Predations helps to control populations and move food and energy through the ecosystem. By removing the weaker members of a prey species, predators strengthen the species and help to maintain ecological balance.

Competitive relationships may involve two or more species which use the same resources. If the competitors are too much alike in their needs, one of three things is likely to happen. First, one of the species may become extinct. Second, one species may leave the competitive habitat and survive in a slightly different one. A third possibility is that one species may evolve means to use different resources in the same habitat.

In cooperative relationships, two or more organisms act or work together for mutual benefit. Intraspecific cooperation is much more common than interspecific. This may result from the fact that members of different species are relatively unable to communicate with one another. Intraspecific cooperation often involves hunting or protection.

Population size and distribution of species within an ecosystem are not constant. Instead, these two factors fluctuate in response to both population characteristics and to environmental changes. The ways in which they do so are referred to as population dynamics.

Birth and death rates are important to a population's future size. Life expectancy is another important factor. The population growth rate is determined by subtracting the average death rate from the average birth rate and multiplying the result by the initial number of population members. When a population's growth rate is charted over a series of generations, it usually produces either a J- or an S-shaped curve.

The number of species members in a given area constitutes the population density of a species. The survival of a species is closely related to its achieving an optimum population density, around which normal fluctuations occur. Optimum population density is that number of members best suited to ensuring the survival of the species.

Factors which prevent populations from increasing are either density-dependent or density-independent. Density-dependent controls are factors which come into operation when the population density increases to a certain level. The major density-dependent population controls include competition for food and space, predation, disease, and stress syndrome. Controls on population which have nothing to do with density are said to be density-independent. Significant density-independent controls are weather and human-made environmental changes.

25 biotic community

biotic community exists when at least two—but usually many more—species of organism live together within the same habitat. The number of species and the number of individual members of those species are not important in understanding the concept of biotic community. Nor is the size of the habitat. What is important is the interaction among the various species. In sharing the same habitat, organisms develop complex interrelationships and patterns of interdependence. These interactions ultimately determine the survival of individual organisms and the community at large.

A biotic community does not contain equal numbers of all its plants and animals. Often one or more species will have a particularly strong influence on the nature of the overall community. Such species are referred to as **dominant**. The dominant species of the community are usually the chief producers or consumers of energy at each trophic level. Thus, on a stretch of grassy field, certain grasses might be the dominant plants, plant-eating insects the dominant herbivores, and insect-eating birds the dominant predators. Simple ecosystems often have just one dominant species. On the other hand, it is very difficult for one species to be dominant in complex ecosystems.

The organisms within a given species share a similar ability to obtain energy from food, sunlight, and other sources. The rate at which a species can gather organic matter from these sources is called **species production**. This organic matter is either immediately converted to energy or stored for later use. As we might expect, some organisms are better energy accumulators than others. They are therefore more productive. These organisms also tend to be dominant within the community. However, genetic and environmental factors may limit this tendency.

Another mechanism that helps maintain the subtle system of ecological balance is **species diversity**. This refers to the number of different plant and animal species con-

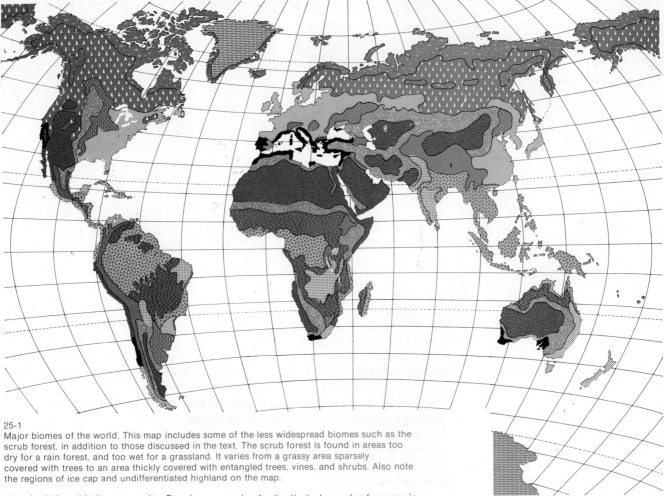

**25-1**

Major biomes of the world. This map includes some of the less widespread biomes such as the scrub forest, in addition to those discussed in the text. The scrub forest is found in areas too dry for a rain forest, and too wet for a grassland. It varies from a grassy area sparsely covered with trees to an area thickly covered with entangled trees, vines, and shrubs. Also note the regions of ice cap and undifferentiated highland on the map.

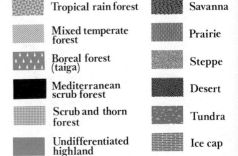

| | |
|---|---|
| Tropical rain forest | Savanna |
| Mixed temperate forest | Prairie |
| Boreal forest (taiga) | Steppe |
| Mediterranean scrub forest | Desert |
| Scrub and thorn forest | Tundra |
| Undifferentiated highland | Ice cap |

tained within a biotic community. Species diversity is linked to the concept that two species cannot occupy the same niche. Plants and animals which differ in their position in the food chain, their use of resources, and their interactions with other species must find a special combination of habitat and function. Greater species diversity is often correlated with increased stability in the biotic community as a whole.

The **predator-prey relationship** is linked to species diversity. This relationship is another factor that helps maintain balance. Predators suppress the growth rate of their prey populations, thus helping to maintain the balance between species size and food supply.

Competition exists among and within species for the limited supply of energy in each habitat. This competition is an essential part of the biotic community. Success in competition determines which species will become dominant.

## The biome

Similarities in climate among various geographic regions of the world seem to produce similar vegetation patterns. Animal life and community forms are, in turn, partially regulated by vegetation.

A **biome** is made up of the total of all biological communities interacting within a single life zone where the climate is similar. Communities maintain themselves and the entire biome of which they are a part by means of complex relationships between organisms and environment. Plant and animal life interact with each other and with climate, topography, and natural occurrences such as floods and fires. These interactions make the biome a unit which contains both stable and unstable communities.

Terrestrial or land biomes are the most often described, and so are the most commonly known. But in recent years we have learned much about water biomes. Some biologists even propose that there are manmade or city biomes and natural or country biomes. In this chapter we will limit discussion to the natural biomes of land and water.

## Land biomes

Different biologists classify land biomes differently, depending on their points of view. Some list only five, others as many as thirty. So there is no absolute number. The descriptions below deal with the six major biomes generally acknowledged throughout the field.

*Tundra*   The tundra is the biome farthest from the equator. It takes its name from the Siberian word meaning "north of the timberline." The tundra comprises 10 percent of the earth's surface. It is found in a narrow belt that circles the Arctic Ocean in such areas as Canada, Siberia, and Alaska. The tundra is often called the "frozen desert" because of its temperature and limited precipitation. Tundra climates have a variable range of temperature, extending roughly from 5°C in midsummer to −32°C in midwinter. The average annual precipitation is only 10 inches, of which 8 inches falls as rain and the remainder as snow. A short growing season and poor soil are also characteristic. The alternate periods of freezing and thaw cause the top layer of tundra soil to heave and change its shape. Below is the permanently frozen layer of subsoil called **permafrost**.

Both the Arctic and Antarctic Circles

25-2
Tundra during the thaw. Pleistocene glacial action smoothed out the arctic tundra and left it with a poor drainage system. During the tundra's brief annual thaw, this causes water to accumulate in low places. Because of this, and the low evaporation caused by cold temperatures, almost 50 percent of the tundra's surface is covered by water during the thaw.

have direct sunlight only six months of the year. But in those six months, life on the tundra flourishes amazingly. The short summer extends from late May to late July. During this period the land is dotted with lakes and cut through by streams. The higher and drier areas tend to be bare rock outcroppings with scant vegetation. But the lower areas blossom forth with relatively lush plant life. Insects by the millions hatch and feed about the marshy ground. In turn, they become food for the sandpipers, plovers, and other migratory shore birds which arrive in great numbers for the brief summer breeding season.

Plants in the tundra are almost all less than 4 inches tall, and grow in dense patches. Even the stunted survivors of willow, birch, and alder trees are likely to grow horizontally. Stunted shrubs, seed plants, lichens, and mosses stay close to the ground, where it is relatively warm and shelter is provided by rocks. Plants supply food for the herbivorous musk oxen, caribou, hares, and lemmings. These, in turn, become food for the carnivorous wolves, bears, foxes, and owls.

The physical structure and habits of ani-

25-3
Lichens growing on rock. Lichens serve as pioneer communities on barren rock surfaces, which they mechanically disintegrate in two ways. During dry spells, lichens lose water and contract. In doing so they pull up the small bits of rock to which they had tightly adhered when moist. The other way lichens disintegrate rock is through the excretion of corrosive carbonic acid. These processes leave small, loose rock particles which combine with bits of dead lichen to form a substratum in which other plants can grow. (See Tundra)

25-4
Timber wolf. The timber wolf is a well-equipped boreal forest predator. It has long, dagger-like canine teeth to hold its prey; sharp, shearing carnassial teeth to cut through flesh and sinew; and strong, thick molars to grind bones. Also, it is swift and has good eyesight, a keen sense of hearing, and an exceptional sense of smell. The wolf generally hunts in packs of no more than a dozen related wolves. Wolves fill an important ecological niche in the boreal forest. By killing off old, sick, and feeble members of deer, mountain sheep, caribou, and moose populations, they help maintain the overall strength of these populations.

mals in the tundra favor the conservation of heat, needed for their survival. They may have layers of fat under their skin, thick fur, or feathers to provide insulation. During sleep or inactive periods, they curl up their bodies to help conserve heat. Body shape and size are also adaptive. Animals in the polar regions generally have bodies with smaller surface areas relative to their internal mass.

*Boreal forest*    The boreal is the world's most northern forest. This is the biome of needle-leaved evergreens. It borders the tundra and often the deciduous forest in high latitudes of the Northern Hemisphere, where these three biomes come together. The boreal forest on the continent of North America extends from Alaska through Canada. It also includes northern parts of Minnesota, Michigan, and New England. Another belt runs across the Eurasian landmass from northern Scandinavia to the Pacific Ocean.

The climate of the boreal forest is cold and humid. Precipitation varies between 15 and 40 inches per year, much of it falling as snow. The boreal forest is variously called the taiga or, in literature, the "great northwoods." It is characterized by almost pure stands of trees such as fir, spruce, hemlock, and pine. The energy produced by the plant life is five to six times greater than that of the tundra.

Since the forest is so dense, little light can penetrate to the forest floor. Consequently, few shrubs or small plants grow there. Needles and other litter on the forest floor decompose slowly because of the cold temperatures. They form a thick needle bed which is springy underfoot.

With its higher productivity, the boreal forest can support a larger and more diverse animal population than the tundra. Moose, deer, caribou, muskrats, beavers, snowshoe hares, mice, and porcupines are typical herbivores. Their chief predators are timber wolves, lynx, and foxes. Here, as in the tundra, a great influx of migratory birds comes to feed on the summer insects.

*Deciduous forest*    The deciduous forest exists in both hemispheres. It contains more species of animals and plants than do the northern biomes. Deciduous forests are located in the middle latitudes of the temperate climate zone, largely in the United States, Eastern Asia, and Central Europe. Their moderate, humid climate contributes to their diversity of plant and animal species. Rainfall averages between 30 and 60 inches a year. Decomposing leaves and other organic matter enrich the topsoil layer.

Deciduous plants adapt to unfavorable conditions such as cold weather or scarcity of water by shedding their leaves. Leaves have a high degree of metabolic activity which requires a great deal of water. They are also likely to suffer the most serious damage from cold weather. The remaining parts of the plant undergo changes which lower their freezing point and prevent drying, considered to be the greatest threat to winter survival.

The dominant plants of the biome are broad-leaved, deciduous trees. Their name derives from the Latin word *decidere,* meaning "to fall off." Because of the wide range in latitude and altitude, there are three belts of dominant trees running in an east–west direction in the American deciduous forest. Sugar maple, commonly associated with beech, is in the north. Oak, often found with hickory, occupies the middle area. The southern region is largely pines, intermixed with hardwoods. In contrast to the boreal coniferous forest, sunlight does penetrate to the floor of the deciduous forest. This permits a thick layer of small plant and shrub growth.

The greatest concentration and diversity of animal life in the deciduous forest is just below the ground layer. Here, humidity and temperature are relatively constant. Beetles, snails, spiders, ants and termites may occupy the area under a fallen branch, often along with snakes and lizards. The mammals in a deciduous forest are usually ground dwellers. However, mice, shrews, ground squirrels, and foxes burrow into the ground to find both food and shelter. The squirrels nest and scamper in the treetops.

Today the most numerous large mammals of the region are deer. But bears and mountain lions also were important before man destroyed them as "vicious predators." There are many year-round bird residents such as warblers, finches, nuthatches, woodpeckers, owls, crows, and turkeys. During the summer these are joined by flycatchers, thrushes, thrashers, ovenbirds, and other species traveling from the warmer climates.

*Grassland*    Large, open areas of grassland are distributed throughout the temperate and tropical zones of both hemispheres. Grasslands occur on every continent where

25-5
Southern Appalachian highlands. About 80 inches of rain fall on the southern Appalachian highlands each year. This rainfall gives the highlands the densest and most luxuriant vegetation of any deciduous forest. Trees adapted to a moderately moist climate (such as oak, hickory, walnut, birch, beech, and chestnut) form climax communities in this region. The region includes the Cumberland Mountains of West Virginia, the Blue Ridge Mountains of Virginia, and the Great Smoky Mountains of Tennessee and North Carolina. (See Deciduous forest)

**25-6**
The woodchuck adjusts to the cold winter in its deciduous forest home by hibernating. To prevent death by freezing, or starvation, the woodchuck secludes itself in a sheltered place. It then "sleeps" as its temperature falls almost to that of its surroundings. Its rate of heart beat, oxygen consumption, and metabolism drop to extremely low levels.

**25-7**
The zebra is a running herbivore, well-equipped for life on the African savannah. Long legs and sharp senses enable it to detect and flee from fires and predators. Its horny hoofs are adapted to travel on hard, sunbaked ground. The zebra can thus cover the long distances often required in finding food and water during the dry season.

annual rainfall averages between 10 and 30 inches, except for the Arctic and Antarctic regions. The bulk of them, however, are found in Eurasia and Central North America.

Seasons in the grasslands are marked by changes in the availability of water and by changes in temperature. Winters are bleak, windy, and cold. In spring and early summer the warm, moist weather leads to a high production of plants in the rich topsoil. This period is followed by a scorching dry season. Birds and the large mammals that cannot go underground migrate to escape the summer.

**Prairies** and **steppes** are two kinds of temperate grasslands. Their vegetation once was lush but has now been destroyed. Prairie grasses are thick, generally growing from 2 to 3 feet high. But on the drier steppes, the grasses are distributed less densely and grow to between 5 and 10 inches. In the United States prairie grasses once occupied roughly the area now known as the corn belt. The steppe, however, lies adjacent to deserts. Originally it covered the area we now call the Great Plains.

The **savannah** is a tropical or subtropical grassland which may also contain a few scattered trees. Savannahs are warm all year long and subject to frost in limited areas. They are found adjacent to tropical rain forests in South America, Africa, and other small areas of several continents. Animal life on savannahs includes elephants, buffaloes, wart hogs, and antelopes. Many of these are preyed upon by lions, leopards, and cheetahs. Hyenas and vultures are among the scavengers of this region.

Many grassland plant species overcome the water shortage with roots that extend into the ground some 6 to 8 feet. Plants in the drier grasslands tend to absorb even the smallest amount of water through branched root systems. Such grasses can be cut quite short and still send up new shoots. They can also withstand a lack of water without suffering extensive damage to their tissues. This is possible because they have a thick cuticle and can curl up their leaves to retain moisture in dry weather. Buffalo grass, wheatgrass, fescue, and needle grass are common grasses.

Animals in the grassland often are adapted to life on the surface of the ground, rather than beneath it. Herbivores have long legs and horny hooves. These enable them to run quickly from fire or predators and travel far for food and water during the dry season. Those that graze on the land have teeth suited for chopping up bulky plants. They also have strong digestive systems to process these materials.

Animal life in the grasslands of the United States was vastly altered as man expanded westward. Many of the grassland mammals group together in flocks. Presumably this provides protection against predators in an environment with few places to hide. But this grouping together renders them especially vulnerable to man and his weapons. For instance, the bison almost became extinct before a bill to protect it was passed during the middle of the nineteenth century. The pronghorn antelope, with its swiftness, good vision, and group life style, is well suited to the grasslands as they are now. Other animals found are antelope, wild horse, deer, jackrabbits, prairie dogs, ground squirrels, gophers, porcupines, skunks, squirrels, and foxes.

Many birds inhabit the grasslands. Without trees to fly into, they have frequently evolved into good runners. Some examples are quail, secretary birds, road runners, and meadow larks. Emus, rheas, and ostriches have adapted so well to grassland running that they have completely lost the ability to fly. Like their mammal neighbors, many of the bird species—finches, grouse, ostriches—flock for safety. Others, such as the burrowing owl, nest underground.

*Desert* The desert biome occurs in regions of low rainfall. It includes the typical hot desert as well as cold desert lands, where snow can fall during the winter. Deserts are found principally in two large belts near the tropics of Capricorn and

Cancer. They are best defined by the distribution of life and the kinds of organism found within them. Soil in the desert is coarse. It is composed partly of small, dust-like particles that blow away, especially during windstorms, and partly of the heavier meaterials that are left behind.

Deserts tend to lie on the western parts of landmasses. Their climate is dry. The little water that does fall is rapidly lost. This is because of the high evaporation rate and the torrential overflow from the dry and almost nonabsorbent soil. The common view regards deserts as nearly lifeless. But in fact, most of them contain many organisms which are adapted to the harsh life of a low-water environment. In order to conserve water, desert plants are small and thick, with a heavy layer of cuticle. To reduce the competition for water, they are usually spaced far apart. Cacti have vestigial leaves. They use their stems to carry on photosynthesis. Some plants have leaves that fall off during dry periods and grow back after a rain. Others die all the way

25-8
The sidewinder (horned rattlesnake) is found in the Mojave and Sonoran deserts, among other places. It has developed a form of locomotion particularly useful in the shifting desert sands. The snake lifts its head, extends it forward, and drops it to the sand. As the head drops, the body swings to the side in an S-shaped looping motion and lands in front of the head. The snake progresses in a series of body motions at right angles to its course. To protect its eyes from sunlight and sand, the sidewinder has a "horn" of thickened skin to shade each eye. Sidewinders eat lizards and small desert rodents. (See Desert)

25-9

Desert plants. There is little precipitation in the desert. In addition, low humidity and a high rate of evaporation limit the amount of rainwater plants can obtain. Most rainwater runs off the hard desert surface into temporary streambeds. Only some seeps into the ground. Below 6 feet, however, there is moisture all year round. Plants such as the creosote bush and mesquite have roots which reach depths of 30 feet or more, and can draw water from underground accumulations. Other plants, such as the cactus, develop extensive shallow root systems to soak up as much of the limited rainfall as possible.

down to the ground and regenerate themselves via their roots.

Successful desert animals have learned to deal with the problems of their climate. However, their adaptations are not as specialized as those of plants. Many desert animals come out at night, when the weather is cooler. They thus conserve the limited water available to them and also avoid the heat. During the day, insects go into crevices or burrow into more moist, cooler soil. As a rule, mammals do poorly in the desert. American desert mammals include rabbits, skunks, foxes, badgers, bobcats, deer, and coyotes. Many Australian marsupial species have also adapted to desert life.

*Tropical rain forest*  To biologists, the tropical rain forest biome seems like the Garden of Eden. It generates hosts of organisms. The tropical rain forest occurs in the lowland regions of Central and South America, Africa, the East Indies, and parts of southern Asia. The growth and reproductive patterns of tropical rain forests are influenced by factors different from those in the deciduous forest. The most important of

these is high rainfall throughout the year. In some places the annual rainfall reaches four or five hundred inches.

Like their temperate kin, tropical rain forest trees lose most or all of their leaves. But this does not occur in the synchronized seasonal manner of deciduous trees. The tropical forest remains green all year round. As individual leaves die, they are replaced immediately by new ones. The tropical rain forest possesses the most luxuriant vegetation of all the biomes. It also displays an astonishing variety of plant organisms. A deciduous forest may have fifteen or twenty species of tree. But the tropical forest may have anywhere from five hundred to three thousand tree species, plus hundreds or even thousands of additional woody plant species.

Life in the tropical rain forest is obviously more stratified than in the temperate forest. Occasional giant trees called **emergents** jut one hundred to two hundred feet above the canopy of branches, leaves, and vines. The flowers and fruits of the forest grow below their tops, in the brightly lit canopy where most of the sunlight is trapped and transpiration is slowed. Most mammal life in the deciduous forests is found on or below the ground. But tropical life is concentrated in this upper stratum. Many animals have adapted to life in the trees by developing grasping paws with adhesive pads and prehensile tails. Monkeys and other animals travel the canopy highways up to the narrowest branches to feed on fruits and insects. Bats and a few other mammals have developed skin folds which allow them to glide or fly. Snakes loop and undulate among the branches. Brightly colored birds—macaws and parrots—also dwell in the canopy, along with the more somber hawks, eagles, and vultures.

In the intermediate layer of tropical forest life are bromeliads, orchids, mosses, and ferns. The light is dimmer here, and color often serves as a camouflage. The birds which dwell at this level—wrens, pi-

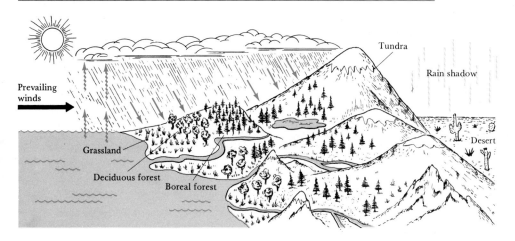

25-10
Topography and climate. The surface features of a region, including its mountains, hills, valleys, lakes, and rivers are called topography. Topographical features can have a considerable effect on climate and environment. For example, mountains block winds. They may therefore cause excessive moisture to fall on the windward side and produce "rain shadows." Or they may cause desert areas with little moisture, on the leeward side. Many mountain ranges are located near the edges of a continent. When such ranges block the wind, deserts and grasslands form in the continental interior.

geons, woodcreepers, and the turkey-like curassows—are less colorful than the birds of the canopy.

The third stratum, or ground layer, of tropical forest life is the darkest of all. Because there is little light, it is not the impenetrable jungle shown in tropical adventure movies. Instead, it is open like a park, constantly dripping with humidity, and oppressively quiet. Fewer birds live here than in the upper layer. Those that do are dull-colored species such as partridges, rails, tinamous, and antbirds. Scavenger insects abound, looking for dead matter. Insects such as beetles and ants are longer-bodied than their kin in more open, windy spaces.

### Water biomes

These are two basic types of water biome—ocean and fresh water. Each of these can be further subdivided.

*The ocean* An **estuary** is any place on a coastline where fresh and salt water meet and mix. Silt and decayed organic material are deposited here by fresh, inland water. Estuaries are thus extremely fertile areas. They also produce great amounts of nutrients, beginning with the photosynthetic phytoplankton and microphytes. This abundant food supports large populations of fish. The environment of the estuary is varied. There is a wide range of saltiness, temperature, and degree of tidal rise and fall.

So the estuary is characterized by diversity as well as density of organisms. It is the habitat of crabs, scallops, clams, and oysters; eels, turtles and frogs; rushes, pickleweed, cordgrass, and eelgrass.

A second marine zone begins at the low tide mark. This zone is usually called **neritic** (from Nereus, the ancient Greek god of the sea). It encompasses all the waters above the **continental shelf**. This shelf is formed by the edge of a continent continuing out under the sea. It may slope gently down or may extend for two or three miles before plunging down abruptly. The shallow water above the continental shelf remains at moderate temperature. This makes the neritic zone one of the most densely populated regions in the ocean. The entire neritic food chain—indeed, the abundance and distribution of all ocean life—depends on the availability of the predominantly single-celled drifting **phytoplankton**. These tiny organisms are photosynthetic. So they must stay near the ocean's surface to have adequate light for photosynthesis. **Zooplankton** are the animal counterparts of the phytoplankton. About 70 percent of zooplankton are tiny crustacean species. Such drifting animals prey either on phytoplankton or on one another.

The bulk of marine plants on the continental shelf are algae such as seaweed and smaller algal forms. Huge kelps can be rooted to the bottom as deep as 350 feet.

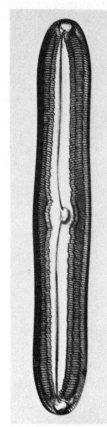

25-11
Diatom. There are more diatoms floating near the ocean's surface than any other organism. They are photosynthetic and play an important role in many ocean food webs. Walls filled with silica often cause diatoms to glisten in the sunlight. Diatoms are classified according to wall characteristics. Different species of diatom show a remarkable variety of shapes. (See The ocean)

But seaweed often floats freely. Many people are familiar with the *Sargassum* variety, which has small, round sacs filled with gas that allow it to float.

Near the tide line, the plant and animal populations of the estuary and the neritic zones may be almost indistinguishable. But as the neritic zone extends into deeper water, it gradually becomes a more distinct environment. In warm regions it often includes **reefs**. These may be the remains of islands that have been taken over and built upon by colonies of coral polyps. Or, they may be sheer stretches of coral and similar organisms.

Many animals are commonly found near the reef or attached to it in some way. These include sea anemones, sponges, clams, sea snails, starfish, and shrimp. Predators such as sharks and barracudas and several varieties of poisonous fish usually are not far off.

Bottom-dwelling life in the neritic zone includes barnacles, sea squirts, scallops, crabs, sand dollars, and sea urchins. Mollusks and annelids burrow into the floor of the sea and use siphons or tubes to extract oxygen and food from the water. Deeper yet, but still in the relatively shallow waters of the continental shelf, fish of commercial value begin to occur. Among these are the bottom-feeding flounder and fluke, which are predators of the burrowing worms and crabs.

Near the continental shelves are **banks** or shallows which can be found in water from 20 to 30 feet deep. The zooplankton and phytoplankton found here provide enough food to support large populations of fish. Ocean currents often contribute to this food supply. For example, the abundant food sources on the fishing banks near Newfoundland are the result of two converging currents. The Gulf Stream, a warm body of water, comes from the south. The colder Labrador Current comes from the north. Each current carries along its own set of organisms.

A great variety of other fish—from sea robins to herring—inhabit these shallower neritic waters. They, in turn, draw sharks and other large predatory fish.

Fish and other **nektonic** or free-swimming animals are found throughout the ocean. But they are most abundant where food and light enable photosynthesis to occur. This is generally between 100 and 300 feet below the surface. Free-swimming animals that would be visible near the surface use movement and color camouflage as adaptive mechanisms. Fish often have blue or green on the top of their bodies, which blends in well with the surface of the water. Their bellies are frequently white or silver, making them virtually invisible from underneath. Air bladders or layers of body fat help free swimmers maintain the proper depth at which they move. Their streamlined body shape makes movement easier by reducing the resistance they encounter from the water.

Along with the light needed by phytoplankton, all drifting plankton populations must be constantly replenished with nutrients such as nitrogen and phosphorus compounds. These needs are partly supplied by anaerobic bacteria which live in the bottom sediment. These bacteria release nutrient-rich particles and gases that are carried upward in the constantly circulating vertical currents of the ocean. Other sources of nutrients are the salts carried into the ocean from rivers, and the droppings of shore and oceanic birds.

The third major marine zone is the deep or **open sea**. The uppermost part of the open sea is usually called the **euphotic layer** (literally, the layer of good light). It extends from the surface down to the limit of light penetration where photosynthesis ceases, at about 650 feet. The **aphotic layer** ("lightless") lies beneath the euphotic layer. As in the neritic zone, large numbers of phytoplankton and zooplankton drift near the surface. The relatively large, shrimp-like krill are particularly noteworthy among the zooplankton. They form an extremely important food source for many

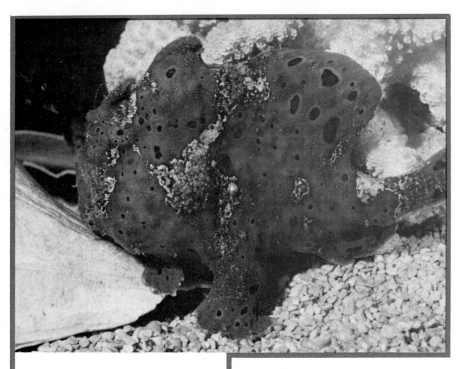

**25-12**
Angler fish in the deep sea. Fish living in the aphotic zone have adapted to this fiercely competitive deep-sea habitat. Food is scarce and special equipment is needed to find and devour it. A well-developed sense of pressure enables many fish to detect nearby turbulence in the pitch-black water. Depending upon the nature of the turbulence, the fish will either pursue a source of food or flee a predator. Huge mouths rimmed with razor-sharp teeth enable many deep sea dwellers, including this angler fish, to eat prey larger than themselves.

large fish of the open sea, as well as for oceanic birds such as albatrosses. Like the desert, the open sea is not very fertile. On the average, it is only about 1/20 as fertile as an estuary.

No photosynthesis can occur in the aphotic layer. So the creatures which inhabit it could not exist without the organic debris—dead or dying organisms and pieces of them—that falls from above. The organically rich discharges of major rivers provide another source of nutrients at these lower depths. Some of these rivers have cut deep submarine canyons through the continental shelf. Adaptations to the extreme scarcity of food, and to other factors such as darkness and pressure in the aphotic environment, have resulted in some of the strangest-looking creatures on earth. For example, luminous organs and enlarged eyes are common in these depths.

*Fresh water biomes* Fresh water biomes can be separated into types occurring in standing water and in running water.

The term lake generally designates a major body of standing water of some depth, with a relatively large expanse of unbroken surface water. A typical lake contains three more or less distinct environments or **regions**. The **littoral region** is comparable to the neritic zone in the ocean. It comprises the shallowest water, through which light penetrates all the way to the lake bottom. The **limnetic region**, analogous to the euphotic layer in the ocean, comprises deeper water penetrated by a small amount of light. The deepest waters make up the **profundal region**, penetrated by no light at all. Like the corresponding ocean zones, the limnetic and profundal regions have no large organisms as permanent residents. But they serve as important storehouses for food and nutrients. The limnetic zone is populated mainly by photosynthetic algae and diatoms. These, in turn, are preyed upon by microscopic animals such as rotifers and copepods.

As in the oceans, the depth to which light penetrates determines to what depth photosynthesis can occur. Population density is always greater in regions occupied by photosynthetic organisms. So the littoral region is the most densely and diversely populated in the lake. Animals on the surface of the lake include beetles and water striders. Mosquitoes also lay their eggs there. Just below the surface are mosquito larvae, small snails, hydras, and several kinds of small worm. Many seed plants root in the nutrient-rich bottom mud of the littoral zone. These include plants with leaves that rise above the surface of the water, such as rushes, cattails, and even large shrubs and trees. There are also plants such as water lilies whose leaves float on the lake surface, and plants with submerged leaves. Underwater leaves are typically thin. This provides maximum surface for absorbing carbon dioxide and other nutrients from the water.

From these large seed-bearing plants, the photosynthesizers scale down to the blue-green bacteria. These bacteria are the

**25-13**
Youthful lotic stream. Streams, which account for a very small amount of the earth's water supply, are subdivided into lotic or flowing, and lentic or slow-moving (or standing) water. Because the stream shown flows in a more or less straight path it is called lotic. It is also classified as youthful. Youthful streams flow swiftly down steep slopes. Thus they cause considerable erosion. Plants and animals which live in these streams must be adapted for survival in rapidly flowing water. For example, immature blackflies and some other larvae are equipped with hooks which serve them as anchors.

basis for the animal populations of the lake biome. They fix free nitrogen into nitrates, and thus make essential nitrogen compounds available to other lake organisms. The trouble is that the nitrogen-fixing bacteria do not know when to stop. They will over-fertilize with nitrates, thus using up oxygen and causing other organisms to die. This happens especially when man-made pollutants—such as phosphate detergents—enter the lake and give the bacteria a superabundance of raw materials.

The blue-green bacteria and other tiny photosynthesizers of the littoral zone support the populations of zooplankton. These, in turn, are eaten by larger animals. The littoral zone supports species from every animal phylum. There are insects in every stage and of every description; snails, leeches, and worms; snakes, salamanders, frogs, and turtles; and fish from tiny minnows to the large predatory species such as bass, perch, pike, catfish, sunfish, and lake trout. Other than fish, most nektonic animals either move in and out of the water or inhabit it only at certain stages of their development. This group of part-time lake

dwellers includes water scorpions, diving beetles, water scavengers, giant water bugs, turtles, snakes, frogs, and rats.

The ooze at the deepest part of the profundal zone is a receptacle for organic debris falling from the surface layers of the lake. Certain organisms—mosses, protozoans, hydras, and algae—attach themselves to rocks or plants on the lake bottom. Populations are sparse, and the organisms living here are microscopic—protozoans, copepods, and ostracods or mussel shrimp. Bacteria and fungi break down the organic debris, turning it once again into the nutrients needed by photosynthetic plants. These nutrients are then distributed by the circulating water.

## Succession

Biomes are relatively stable and uniform. But the communities within them are much less so. Biotic communities pass through stages in their evolutionary growth from simple to complex. This process is called **succession**. Succession of communities can be caused by changes in the environment—wind, water, and soil—or on the surface of the earth. Both of these kinds of change are usually directly influenced by the community of organisms, which thus help to contribute to their own succession. As communities pass through successional stages, such as that from farmland to hardwood forest, their suitability as habitats for different animals is altered correspondingly.

At every stage of succession, one community within a biome is replaced by another. The successive communities are each integrated units. They function successfully as long as they can resist or adapt to the environmental changes around them. If they cannot withstand these changes, the communities are replaced by new ones, and then these, too, are later replaced. This process continues until a community arises that can maintain long-term equilibrium with the environment and continue to reproduce itself. This relatively stable com-

25-14
Pond succession. During
the initial seral stage
in pond succession, the
bottom is sandy and
rather bare. As the years
go by, decaying plants
and animals form a layer
of humus. The humus
provides a substrate for
a type of bottom-
anchored algae called
Chara. Chara gives rise
to a new community of
plants and animals,
called the submerged
vegetation stage.
Continuing decay adds
sufficient humus to
support plants which
emerge from the surface
of the pond along its
edges. These plants
provide a habitat for
oxygen-breathing
animals. They give rise
to a community called
the emerging vegetation
stage. Later, as the
humus layer builds, a
marsh or swamp
develops. When the
bottom of the pond is
finally above the water
level at the pond's edges,
the temporary pond
stage has been reached.
The pond in this stage
dries entirely during the
summer. The pond
eventually reaches the
low prairie stage. Either
prairie or beech/maple
forest may be the
climax stage.

Stage 1: Sandy bottom

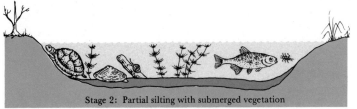

Stage 2: Partial silting with submerged vegetation

Stage 3: Increased silting with emerging vegetation

Stage 4: Temporary pond and prairie

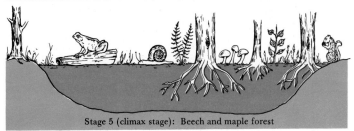

Stage 5 (climax stage): Beech and maple forest

munity of indefinite length is called the
**climax community**. The total of all the successive communities in the series is called
a **sere**. Each individual community is referred to as a **seral stage**. To understand
the biomes, we must recognize that each is
dominated by typical climax communities
surrounded by other communities which
are at different seral stages.

For example, when a piece of farmland
in North Carolina is abandoned, it undergoes rapid successional changes. During
the year of abandonment, crabgrass is the
dominant plant. The next year, horseweed
shares the dominance with the crabgrass,
and sometimes also ragweed. The third
year finds asters so profuse that the horseweed plants are barely noticeable. Then
comes broomsedge, which flourishes until
the pine seedlings which have begun to
appear are able to take over. After five years
the pines are usually taller than the broomsedge. And after fifteen years, they have
formed closed stands.

Experiments were conducted to discover why the succession follows this pattern. It
was found that crabgrass throws off many
small, light seeds. These tend to arrive first
on a sunny field and quickly grow to cover
it. Horseweed seeds are also light and efficiently dispersed. This is why the plant
codominates during the second year. But
decaying horseweed roots inhibit the continued growth of horseweed seedlings. The
stage is thus set for the biennial asters. Aster seedlings, however, cannot tolerate
shade. Their tall parents eventually shade
them out of existence. In addition, the
broomsedge competes with the aster for
water.

The succession occurs because each
establishment of a new species modifies
the environment. The horseweed makes the
field environment less acceptable for horseweed. Adult asters shade out aster seedlings, and the broomsedge is eventually
shaded out by the pines. Another important
factor is the rate at which the habitat is colonized, since plants have to reach the field in
the first place. As we noted above, broomsedge could be dominant earlier in the
abandoned field if its seeds arrived sooner.
This is also true of the pines. But their seeds
are larger and heavier and disperse more
slowly than those of the crabgrass and
horseweed.

The pine communities, however, are not
the climax of the succession. Growing in
the soil for many years, these softwoods
feed it with great amounts of organic material. This enriches the soil and also helps it
to hold moisture. These pine-produced

changes in the soil, combined with the fact that pine seedlings do not grow well in the deep shade of adult trees, contribute to the demise of the pine communities. But oak and other hardwood seedlings can grow in these deeply shaded areas. They thrive on the organic matter and moisture produced by the pines. So in time the softwoods give way to the hardwoods. The hardwood forests continue to replace themselves, and thus become the climax of this plant community.

Succession takes place in all communities. But a climax community may fail to form because an essential resource is only temporarily available. Such a resource is quickly consumed by the community that develops on or around it. The organisms dependent on it then either die or disperse, ending the progression without producing a relatively permanent community.

Succession, of course, also occurs in freshwater and marine environments. A lake may go through three successive stages— "young" (**oligotrophic**), "middle-aged" (**eutrophic**), and "old" (**dystrophic**). The oligotrophic lake typically has "clean, clear" water and sides which slope deeply to a V-shaped, rocky bottom. Little vegetation is present on the lake's shores or bottom. Dissolved nutrients are scarce. In time, silt-producing erosion and plant growth may nudge this relatively sterile lake into the eutrophic phase. This stage could be described as the lake's prime of life. At the bottom is an ooze rich in nutrients. Dissolved nutrients and oxygen are abundant, supporting a great variety of animal and plant populations. Gradually—thanks to the very success of the lake-living plants and animals—the lake may become clogged with a welter of organisms living off the plentiful decaying plant and animal matter. It becomes dystrophic—a swampy, bog-like area (often the forerunner of a peat bog). The superabundance of organic matter in a dystrophic lake makes the water highly acid and low in oxygen. This new environment eliminates some species but

25-15
Oligotrophic lake. During the summer season, photosynthetic organisms in the upper region of the lake produce organic matter. Organic residue settles into the lower region, or hypolimnion. There it decays and depletes the oxygen supply. A lake can be designated oligotrophic, eutrophic, or dystrophic according to its productivity as indicated by hypolimnion oxygen content. Oligotrophic lakes have an abundance of oxygen and little productivity. A eutrophic lake is by far the most productive, and a dystrophic lake the least productive.

offers opportunities for colonization by others. The succession from a "young" to an "old" lake normally occurs over hundreds or thousands of years. It is rarely well defined for a particular lake. Different parts of the same lake may display oligotrophic, eutrophic, or dystrophic features. A lake also may remain in one stage for thousands of years, if the forces that push it toward old age are balanced by environmental influences that tend to keep it young.

The rise and fall of a coral reef is an example of succession in a marine environment. But here the succession proceeds at a much slower pace, over many millions of years. A reef begins with a colony of millions of tiny, carnivorous coral polyps, which secrete exoskeletons of calcium carbonate. As individual polyps die, their skeletons remain. Eventually they form a vast structure of which only the surface layers are composed of living animals. But like many living systems, the mature coral reef can be destroyed by forces at work in the new environment it has created. Mollusks and marine worms find the reef a highly suitable environment. Their burrowing

weakens and crumbles its structure. The **crown of thorns** is a large, reef-living starfish. It feeds on living coral polyps and can destroy whole stretches of coral reef. Even an undisturbed and thriving coral reef is in danger of dying from its own success. Through geological time, it may build up to such proportions that it will sink under its own great weight. With this sinking, the living corals' critical limits of water temperature and depths may be exceeded. Without the addition of new coral, the reef begins slowly to be eaten away by erosion and the activities of other marine organisms.

**summary**

A biotic community consists of two or more species of organism living in the same habitat. Two mechanisms which help maintain the ecological balance in a biotic community are species production and species diversity. Species production refers to the rate at which a species can accumulate organic matter. Species diversity is the number of different plant and animal species in a community.

Biotic communities interact within larger life zones called biomes. The boundaries of a biome are climatically determined. Therefore, each biome has distinctive types of plant and animal life. The biotic communities within a biome interact with each other and with climate, topography, and natural occurrences. This interaction makes some communities stable and others unstable. The six major land biomes are tundra, boreal forest, deciduous forest, grassland, desert, and tropical rain forest. The two principal water biomes are ocean and fresh water.

The tundra is characterized by low temperatures and a little precipitation. These conditions give the tundra poor soil and a short growing season. Plants have adapted to these conditions by growing close to the relative warmth of the ground. Animals in the tundra have adapted to conserve heat.

The boreal forest is characterized by coniferous trees. Its climate is cold with moderate precipitation. Though few shrubs or plants grow in this biome, its productivity is greater than that of the tundra.

The deciduous forest is noted for its trees which respond to unfavorable conditions by shedding their leaves. It possesses a moderate, humid climate. Decomposing leaves and other organic matter produce a rich topsoil. Beneath this topsoil lies the greatest concentration and variety of deciduous forest animal life. The grassland also has a rich topsoil, but most of its animal life has stayed above ground. Deciduous forests and grasslands both lie to a large extent in the temperate zone. This gives them cold winters and warm summers. The grassland, which also lies partially in the tropical zone, has a long dry season. Many grassland animals herd together for protection. They also are adapted for travel on the open, flat terrain, especially during the dry season.

The desert is extremely dry. Its soil consists of small, windblown sand particles and heavier materials which form the desert pavement. Desert plants and animals are adapted to the dry environment. Like the tundra, the desert features rapid plant and animal reproduction.

The tropical rain forest is the exact opposite of the tundra and desert. It features high rainfall throughout the year. It has luxuriant vegetation and an enormous variety of plant organisms. Most of its plant and animal life is found in the brightly lit canopy just beneath the tops of forest trees. However, some organisms have become specially adapted to the dimmer areas below.

The ocean can be divided into three zones: the estuary, the neritic zone, and the open sea. An estuary is a coastal area where fresh and salt water mix. The extremely fertile estuaries have large numbers of photosynthetic phytoplankton and fish. The neritic zone also is densely populated. It begins at the low-tide mark and extends out beyond the continental shelf. The open sea can be divided into the euphotic ("with light") layer, near the surface, and the deeper aphotic ("without light") layer. Though it has large numbers of phytoplankton near its surface, the open sea is not very fertile.

There are two types of fresh water biome: standing water and running water. A lake is a body of standing water with three regions: the littoral, or shallow water; the limnetic, or deeper water; and the profundal, or deepest water. The littoral region, with larger numbers of phytoplankton, is the most densely populated.

Though biomes are relatively stable, biotic communities are often unstable. In a move from the simple to the more complex, biotic communities evolve through seral stages called succession. The total of all the successive stages in a biotic community is called a sere. A relatively stable community of indefinite duration is called a climax community. Each biome is dominated by typical climax communities.

# THE ODD
## AND THE EERIE !

Talking to the animals
The Loch Ness Monster lives!
All you need to know about shark attacks
Take our test on dangerous creatures
Computer dating among zoo animals, chimps who paint, more
The truth about vampires
Strange but true

"King Kong," RKO Pictures, 1933

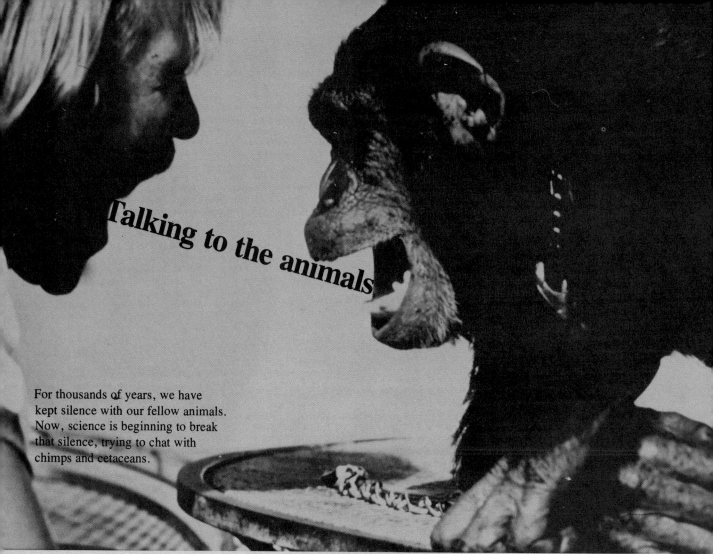

# Talking to the animals

For thousands of years, we have kept silence with our fellow animals. Now, science is beginning to break that silence, trying to chat with chimps and cetaceans.

Paul Fusco/Magnum

Scientists are discovering that talking to animals is not really that difficult—if one goes about it the right way. For example, in the 1960s Beatrice and Allen Gardner adopted a chimp whom they named Washoe, so they could teach her to communicate with them. Accepting the fact that human language is vocally impossible for chimps, they hit on the idea of teaching Washoe to use the hand signals of the American Sign Language for the deaf. The approach worked dramatically well; Washoe could put together whole series of words in requests, questions, and statements. Incredibly enough, Washoe has also invented her own signs. The first time she saw a swan, for example, the chimp, who had never been taught the sign for swan, signed to her human companion the two signs for "water bird." On another occasion, the Gardners had been unable to discover the ASL sign for "bib," so they taught the chimp a sign of their own creation. One evening at the dinner table, Washoe, forgetting the sign that had been taught her, made her own—she drew an outline of a bib on her chest with both index fingers. Five months later, the Gardners learned that Washoe's sign was the correct ASL sign for bib!

## Does anybody here speak Yerkish?

A more rigorous experiment is being carried out by Duane Rumbaugh with his chimp Lana at the Yerkes Primate Research Center in Atlanta. Lana uses symbolic shapes representing words and relationships, printed on a pushbutton panel connected to a computer. Using a special computer language he calls Yerkish, Rumbaugh is in a position to control and monitor all of Lana's language behavior. Lana lives in a large Plexiglas room with the computer panel, which includes an electronic display board. Her computer is connected to another outside the room. When she wants something, such as water or fruit, she presses certain buttons on the panel in the proper sequence. A technician then brings her whatever she asks for. Recently, for example, Lana used the panel to ask the technician "?Tim tickle Lana." This message was flashed on Tim's display panel. He tapped out "yes" on his computer, then entered Lana's room and tickled her. When he was finished, Lana, in a playful mood, asked "?Lana tickle Tim." Tim agreed, and allowed the chimp to tickle him. Since Lana used the same three words but in a different order, she apparently knows that different word order carries different meaning. How much more can she, or other chimps, learn? Frankly no one is yet sure.

### Voices in the depths

While Rumbaugh and the Gardners have been talking to chimps, other scientists have been trying to talk to cetaceans—whales and dolphins. What they have found is quite astounding. For one thing, the brains of cetaceans are larger and more complex than those of chimps and all other primates except man. For this reason, scientists believe that these great beasts may have something important to say.

In terms of size, for example, the brain of the bottle-nosed dolphin is significant. The ratio of this animal's brain weight to its body weight is about 90 to 1. This compares with a figure of 50 to 1 for man and 150 to 1 for chimps. As for complexity, the dolphin brain is revealing. According to Myron Jacobs, a neuroanatomist specializing in cetacean nervous systems, the structure of the dolphin's brain rivals our own in complexity. For one thing, the cerebral cortex shows a high degree of folding, with the result that the surface area is greater than that of humans. Moreover, the cerebellum comprises as much as 20 percent of the total brain weight, compared to twelve percent in human brains. Finally, the intricacy of the nerve patterns is similar to that found in the brains of monkeys and humans.

### Two kinds of sounds

What does all this mean for cetacean communication? Scientists have discovered that cetaceans have a complex communication system based on sound. Animal behaviorist Peter Warshall, writing in the book *Mind In the Waters*, states that the sounds of dolphins and whales are divided into two kinds—pulsed sounds and pure tones. The pulsed sounds include those used for echolocation, or sonar; clicks used for social chatting; and repetitious, nonrhythmic sounds which can be compared to human humming and which resemble squeaks, squawks, and grunts. "The pure tones," says Warshall, "sound to us like clear whistles. They are beautiful birdlike sounds with trills and arpeggios, glissandos and sitarlike bends in the notes. Each whistle is particular to the species that makes it". Scientists using hydrophones—underwater microphones—have eavesdropped on dolphins conversing with one another in the ocean. In one experiment, for example, a number of aluminum poles were placed at the entrance to a bay that was often visited by whales and dolphins. As a group of bottle-nosed dolphins approached the entrance to the inlet, they produced a whistling sound which grew increasingly louder. The group suddenly stopped swimming and whistling, and one of them swam up to the poles. After examining the structures, the animal returned to its companions. Whistling in the group resumed for a moment or so, then stopped again as the dolphins continued swimming past the poles and into the bay. In human terms, the single dolphin, acting as a scout, reported to its friends that the poles were not dangerous and that it was safe to enter the inlet.

Dolphin communication has also been studied in captivity. On one occasion, for example, two dolphins who had shared the same pool were placed into separate pools by their keeper. The two solitary animals began emitting long continous whistles, presumably as a sign of loneliness. If a dolphin becomes ill, it produces a certain kind of mournful whistle; a friend responding to the distress signal answers with another kind of whistle. Young dolphins and their mothers produce distinctive whistles, each of which is clearly recognizable by the other. Like humans, two dolphins do not whistle to one another simul-

*"In terms of complexity, the dolphin brain approaches our own"*

"The Day of the Dolphin"/Avco Embassy Pictures, 1973

taneously; one waits until the other has finished before responding. Each individual within the species has a unique whistle, much like human surnames or signatures.

*Can dolphins speak in human voices?*

Since dolphins do have a large number of sounds at their disposal—some 2000 different whistles have thus far been detected—some think that the animals may have a relatively evolved language. Indeed, scientists have even attempted to teach them human language. On one occasion, John Lilly, who pioneered the study of cetacean communication, placed a microphone over the blowhole of a dolphin to amplify and tape the sounds coming from the animal. When the tape was played back, Lilly was astounded. "We discovered that (in a very terse shorthand quacking sort of way) the dolphin had been mimicking some of the things I had been saying," states Lilly. He described the mimicry as "a very high-pitched Donald Duck quacking-like way."

In a key experiment, two dolphins were taught to produce human sounds which consisted of nonsense syllables. Although this experiment failed, the two animals had succeeded in changing their voices in an attempt to mimic those of humans. However, Dr. Lilly believes that scientists may one day succeed in establishing vocal communication with these animals. But first it may be necessary to use electronic amplification to produce and understand the high-frequency messages of dolphins in order to converse with them.

Is Lilly right? Judge for yourself. The following is a conversation between Peter Dolphin (PD) and one of his trainers, Margaret Howe (MH), recorded by Lilly and reproduced in his book, *The Mind of The Dolphin*. In the dolphin's "speech," the symbol "x" indicates a "humanoid" sound which cannot be clearly distinguished.

MH   Now you think, Peter, 'cause you used to do this. Listen. BA BEE BLOCK
PD

MH                    Yes! (clapping) That's better. Now do the other
PD          mxx xxx

MH   one. Say . . .BA SKET BALL      No, BA SKET BALL
PD               xx   xx xx xx          xxxx xx xx

MH   Better.  shhh! MAGRIT      No. It's EMMMMMM (ends with a kiss
PD           xxx       xxx xxx

MH   on Peter's head) say . . . MMAGRIT      no, not EH. It's MMM.
PD                    eh xxx

MH   Eh . . . MMM MMMMMM MMAGRIT                Yes! Yes! (clapping)
PD           (softly) Mxx xxx

MH   That's an EM. Let's do it again. Say . . . MMAGRIT      Yes, that's
PD                          mxxx xxx

MH   better. (clapping) Good! Say . . . BALL      No, not MAGRIT.
PD                     xxx xxx

MH   BALL  with  a BEE. Say . . . BALL   Yes! BAWL! Good! Say . . .
PD               baww

MH   MMAGRIT      No . . . not EH. MMMMM. MMMMM.
PD   eh xxx

MH   MMAGRIT          Yes . . .that's better . . . that's better, Peter . . .
PD               mxx xxx

MH   Good! Yes, you can muffle it (clap)
PD

*The song of the whale*

Researchers have not attempted to talk to whales yet, but they have overheard these giant animals talking to one another. Like dolphins, whales use sonar for navigation and to find food. They also use special sounds for social communication. It has been reported that sperm whales have tried to talk to the beeps emitted by the sonar equipment on ships. The beasts replied to the signals, apparently mistaking them for the sounds of fellow whales.

And then of course, there are the beautifully haunting songs of the humpback whale. The songs last for seven to thirty minutes; on occasion, the whale will sing a single song for a half-hour, then repeat it for two or three hours. One musician has found these songs so beautiful that he has incorporated them into a symphony entitled "And God Created Great Whales." According to Roger Payne and Scott McVay, the songs have three main sections: (1) trains of rapidly repeated pulses that frequently alternate with sustained tones; (2) many short, high-frequency units, most of which suddenly rise in frequency; and (3) lower, more sustained notes that are repetitious in rhythm and contain many units that fall in frequency.

Payne thinks the songs are used for communication rather than self-expression. Quoted in Daniel Cohen's book, *Talking With The Animals*, Payne observes: "We already know there's a deep sound channel in the ocean. This is a layer of water that, for various reasons—temperature, density, and so forth—has acoustical qualities which permit the transmission of sound over very long distances, in some cases more than a thousand miles. I'm not saying that whales sit on two sides of the ocean and chat with each other, but it's possible they produce sounds either in or out of the sound channel, which may allow them to flock together. This could take the simple form of 'Humpback whale here!' or maybe even a more sophisticated 'George here!' "

Cetaceans, chimps, humans—each has a language which is unintelligible to the other. Perhaps the work of future scientists will provide the rosetta stone that will enable the three to understand one another. Such a discovery would be more than welcome, for the animals undoubtedly have much to say to us. After all, they've been around a great deal longer than we have.

## Homers among the humpbacks?

I calculate that the approximate number of bits of information (individual yes/no questions necessary to characterize the song) in a whale song of half an hour's length is between a million and a hundred million bits. Because of the very large frequency variation in these songs, I have assumed that the frequency is important in the content of the song—or, put another way, that whale language is tonal. If it is not as tonal as I guess, the number of bits in such a song may go down by a factor of ten. Now, a million bits is approximately the number of bits in *The Odyssey* or the Icelandic *Eddas*.

Carl Sagan
*The Cosmic Connection*

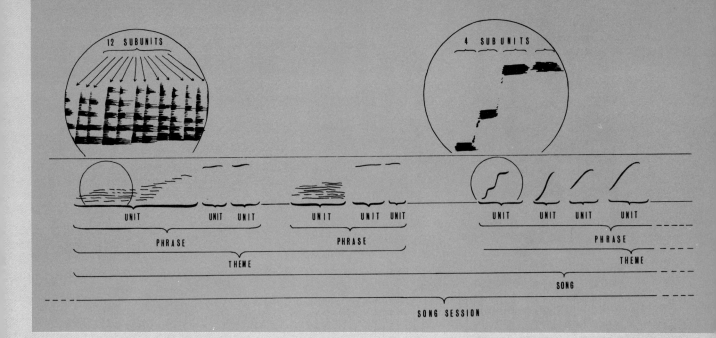

12 SUBUNITS      4 SUBUNITS

UNIT    UNIT UNIT    UNIT   UNIT UNIT    UNIT   UNIT UNIT UNIT

PHRASE      PHRASE      PHRASE

THEME      THEME

SONG

SONG SESSION

## Strange facts about plants and animals

1. The tiny hummingbird lays only two eggs during its lifetime.
2. Crocodiles don't want to miss a thing—they sleep with their eyes open. So do pigeons.
3. Apples have a soporific effect on cut flowers. When the fruit is placed next to a vase of flowers, the flowers doze off and wilt.
4. The average chicken grows about 8,000 feathers during its lifetime.
5. A Brahma bull purrs like a kitten when it is content.
6. In Venezuela there is a tree that gives milk which tastes just like cow's milk. Appropriately enough, it is called the cow tree.
7. Butterflies use their feet, not their mouths, for tasting food.
8. The double coconut produces the world's largest seed, which can weigh as much as 40 pounds.
9. A newborn hippopotamus weighs about 100 pounds.
10. The wood of the cypress tree is so strong that it can last longer than concrete.
11. The General Sherman tree in California is the earth's tallest living thing. This giant redwood stands 272 feet high.
12. Flies and frogs are like humans in one minor respect—they too can contract athlete's foot.
13. Fish sometimes become seasick.
14. It takes about four hours to hardboil an ostrich egg.
15. Plants are like us in that their temperatures rise when they become ill.

For more interesting facts, see *Salted Peanuts: 1800 Little-Known Facts*, by E. C. McKenzie.

## The deadly vampire bat?

Because of its blood-sucking ways, the vampire bat has probably been one of the most maligned creatures in animaldom. The bat has fired the imagination of many writers who have depicted it as a murderous beast that flaps forth on moonless nights from its gloomy Middle-European castle to drain the lifeblood from some helpless human—usually a beautiful woman fast asleep.

The monster could be held at bay by flashing a crucifix at it. Sleeping with a wreath of garlic around the neck also helped. The truth about the vampire, however, is a bit more mundane. For one thing, the nocturnal mouselike creature—which has a three-inch long reddish brown body, 12-inch wings, and razor-sharp teeth—is found only in Latin America. It lives in caves and abandoned railroad tunnels and mines. Only one of the five vampire species—*Desmodus rotundus*—will attack a sleeping human. Since the creature can drink only one ounce of blood at one sitting, it is highly unlikely that it can kill its victim in a single attack. It can however, transmit rabies. Indeed, this species—

"Vampire Circus"/20th Century-Fox, 1972

along with two other vampire species—has caused considerable damage to Latin American cattle and horses by transmitting the disease to these animals. For example, before 1968, when a method was devised to control the bats, some two million cattle and thousands of horses died each year from rabies. So the next time a bat brushes past you in the night, don't run for your garlic or crucifix. Chances are, the beast is more interested in fruit or insects than you.

What a whale song looks like. *This figure, called a spectogram, shows the elements that comprise a whale song. A unit is the shortest continuous sound perceptible to the human ear. A subunit is one of a series of discrete tones, emitted in rapid sequence, which can be detected only by mechanical means, usually by replaying a tape of the subunit at very slow speed. A phrase is a series of units. Similar phrases, emitted in an unbroken sequence, make up a theme. A number of themes comprise a song.*

"Songs of Humpback Whales," R. S. Payne & S. McVay.
*Science*, Vol. 173, pp. 585-97, 13 Aug. 1971

## Book Review

*Mind in the waters: A book to celebrate the consciousness of whales and dolphins.* Joan McIntyre, Assembler. New York: Scribner's, 1974. 240 pp. (illustrated). $14.95 (5.95 in paperback).

This excellent book is more than a celebration of the minds of cetaceans, as the title proclaims. It is also a protest against the irresponsible practices of those nations who are hunting the whale into extinction. The book consists of contributions by 23 authors, plus seven essays by the editor. Cetaceans are celebrated in poems, scientific treatises, historical treatments, pieces of folklore, gorgeous full-color photographs, and even drawings. There is, for example, a poem by D.H. Lawrence, an article on the whale brain by Myron Jacobs, an essay on dolphin communication by John Lilly, a Kwakiutl poem about a man finding a dead whale, and a plea by Victor Scheffer for saner whaling practices. It is, as the flap copy says, ". . . a basic compendium of information about whales and dolphins and a picture of the new understandings that seem to lie just beyond our present knowledge. It is also a call to action. Today a whale is being killed every fourteen minutes. Thirty-six thousand whales are killed every year. The reasons for stopping this slaughter are humanitarian, biological, ecological . . ."

The book is beautifully written and put together. Ms McIntyre deserves highest praise for her sensitivity to these beleaguered fellow mammals, and the selections reflect this sensitivity. If the book succeeds in its purpose—to get readers involved in the struggle to save the whales—it will have accomplished much.

Even if you don't have time to become actively involved in this cause, you can help by purchasing a copy of the book—royalties from its sale will go to Project Jonah, a group devoted to the protection and understanding of cetaceans. The funds will be used in the Project's campaign for a world moratorium on the commercial killing of whales and dolphins.

# Animal round-up

*Matchmaker, matchmaker, make me a match. . . .* It used to be that computer dating services were used exclusively by humans. Not anymore. *National Wildlife* magazine reports that the Minnesota Zoo at St. Paul has established something called the International Species Inventory Systems (ISIS). ISIS's chief job is to get together individuals of rare species that are located in different zoos around the United States. In so doing, it eliminates the tedious task of contacting zoos, one at a time, in an attempt to mate rare or endangered individuals. ISIS is currently in the process of collecting information on 50,000 mammals in North American zoos. The program will eventually include reptiles, amphibians, birds, and fish. About 200 zoos in the country are plugged into the system, but officials hope to expand it to cover those all over the world. The matchmaker behind ISIS is Linda Murfeldt. "ISIS will do more than simply tabulate the total number and kinds of animals" she says. "One of our primary objectives is to determine how many animals listed as endangered species are in captivity." Meanwhile, dozens of mammals are meeting their ideal mates, and surplus animals are being relocated in new homes.

*I knew I shouldn't have eaten those daffodils!* Most paleontologists think that cooling temperatures were primarily responsible for the downfall of the dinosaurs. But *National Wildlife* magazine reports that a British scientist has come up with another villain—poisonous plants. T. Swain, a botanist with the Royal Botanical Gardens, has pointed out that the dinosaurs died out 65 million years ago—about the same time that the angiosperms began their rise. It seems that two chemicals synthesized by the plants—tannins and alkaloids—were poisonous and so protected the plants from being eaten by animals. But Swain believes that the prehistoric behemoths, unlike other animals, may have gorged themselves on the flowering plants. Swain's evidence is impressive enough. For example, he points to dinosaur fossils which were discovered in "contracted positions suggestive of alkaloid poisoning." Then too, dinosaur eggs dating from the

Cretaceous Period were discovered to be thinner than eggs found in earlier periods. (DDT has the same effect on bird eggs.) Finally, the British researcher says that his studies of reptilian diets indicate that they may not have possessed the sensory apparatus necessary for distinguishing toxic alkaloids. If Swain's hypothesis is true, then the dinosaurs may have been the first living things to have eaten themselves into oblivion.

Photo courtesy of Portland Zoological Gardens

*Arty Apes.* Remember the old saw that says if you give a chimp a typewriter and enough paper, it would eventually crank out another *Hamlet*? Well, now there's a twist to that. This one goes, if you give a chimp a paintbrush and enough paint . . . Two years ago, the Portland, Oregon zoo initiated an art therapy program to help relieve boredom in chimps. The result? Apparently the zoo has a bunch of budding Michelangelos on its hands. Each animal works in its own unmistakable style. One female, for example, paints standing up. "We don't push them," says Lucy Wilson, the person in charge of the art studio, "they have a short attention span—about ten minutes each session. They're apt to drink more of the paint—it's nontoxic—than they put on the paper. And sometimes, if they don't like what they've painted, they'll tear it up and eat the whole thing." Some of the paintings appear to be quite good. In fact, the zoo has raised about $2000 by selling their masterpieces in its souvenir shop. Now, if the folks at the zoo could only get the chimps to sit down to a grand piano. . . .

Friends and enemies quiz

Many animals that are thought to be dangerous to us are actually harmless, and vice versa. In the following true-false quiz, can you identify your friends and enemies?

| | | |
|---|---|---|
| 1. | A bull will charge anything colored red. | T/F |
| 2. | Vampire bats can kill humans by sucking their blood. | T/F |
| 3. | Rats have been known to eat people. | T/F |
| 4. | The venom of most spiders is not dangerous to man. | T/F |
| 5. | Gorillas are vicious killers, often attacking humans on sight. | T/F |
| 6. | Wolves frequently attack people. | T/F |
| 7. | Killer whales have reportedly sunk ships and devoured their passengers. | T/F |
| 8. | The venom of a Gila monster is poisonous to humans. | T/F |
| 9. | A cobra snake can blind a human by spitting into his eyes. | T/F |
| 10. | The urine of toads can raise warts on a person's hands. | T/F |

# The truth about shark attacks

A spate of reported shark attacks on humans—and the film *Jaws*—has generated a great deal of curiosity about these "silent savages," as they have been called. But are sharks really that dangerous to us? In reply to this, here are some key questions and answers about shark attacks, compiled by the editors of *Science Digest* magazine.

*Q. Are all sharks dangerous to humans?*
A. No. Of the 250 known species of sharks, only 27 are thought to be man-eaters. The most notorious of these are the tiger shark, the great white shark, and the whaler shark.

*Q. Why do sharks attack people?*
A. There is no single answer to this question. Some researchers think sharks attack people simply for food. Others think it is because the beast sees its human victim as an invader of its territory. Still others say the shark attacks merely because of its aggressive nature. One thing is certain, however: the animal will attack anything that moves—even a ship's propeller.

*Q. How common are shark attacks?*
A. Fortunately, they are very rare. For example, the National Oceanic and Atmospheric Administration reports that in the last quarter of a century, there has been a worldwide average of only 23 attacks a year. Of these, only 6 were fatal. In other words, a person has a one in a billion chance of being attacked by one of these so-called man-eaters. In fact, there are more deaths each year from lightning strikes and bee stings than from shark attacks.

*Q. How vicious is the shark when it attacks?*
A. Surprisingly enough, in most cases the shark bites its human victim only once or twice, then goes about its business. Rarely does it return for more. Rarer still are the cases in which the beast goes into a frenzy during an attack.

# Secrets of Loch Ness revealed at last?

## THE MONSTER HUNTERS

"A big beast, black, with a long thin neck and a small head. A huge bulky body which threw up a disturbance large enough to capsize a rowing boat." Such goes the typical description of the Loch Ness monster. Some have described the beast as "loathsome," others simply thought it "big." Someone said it had the head of a goat.

Has this fabled creature been dredged up from the depths of the human imagination—on a par with the abominable snowman, Bigfoot, and flying saucers? Or does it really exist? For hundreds of years, these questions have burned in the minds of men. Indeed, Nessie, as the behemoth is popularly called, has gained a larger reputation than many distinguished humans. She is the star of monsterdom, outtwinkling even the likes of Frankenstein and Dracula simply because of the possibility that she really exists. Now, that possibility appears to be approaching certainty. On the basis of recent photographic evidence, some think the mystery of Loch Ness has been penetrated once

and for all, and the legend of the beast has finally been laid to rest by Dr. Robert Rines, an American lawyer and professional monster hunter.

Rines, who heads up the Academy of Applied Science in Boston, has been on the trail of Nessie since 1970. In 1972, his underwater camera got a shot of what he said was Nessie's flipper, but the photo was very hazy. Scientists snorted or smiled politely at his achievement. Then, in the summer of 1975, Rines hit paydirt. Using a specially-designed 16-millimeter movie camera that included sonar and a strobe flash, he got clear photographs in living color. Taken in 35 feet of water, the photos show what look like the head, neck, and body of the great beast. For reasons of his own, Rines has refused to release these photos to the general media, hence they cannot be shown here. However, Nicholas Witchell, author of *The Loch Ness Story* and friend of Rines, has seen the actual color photos. He describes Nessie thus:

"The animal was facing almost head-on to the camera. Beneath the body were two clearly definable appendages. The skin looked rough and spotted and was red-brown in color. . . . A prominent bony ridge ran down the center of the face into a thin hard-looking upper lip. Two nostril-shaped marks were situated under the upper lip and two clearly defined stalks or tubes protruded from the top of the head. Parasites were seen clinging to and hanging off the belly.''

## Astounding photos

In an attempt to convince the scientific community of the validity of his find, Rines released his photos exclusively to the prestigious British science journal, *Nature* (issue of December 11, 1975). The photos, printed in black and white, are truly astounding. One in particular shows what appears to be a beast with a long, gracefully curved neck and a huge balloonlike body with a flipper sticking out of its side. According to Rines, the head and neck are about eight feet long, the body about twelve feet long.

Is science now convinced of Nessie's existence? Some distinguished researchers are. For example, Dr. George Zug, a zoologist at the Smithsonian Institution found the photos "exciting." "The pictures are good pictures this time," says Zug, "and they give us a good idea of what these things are. They are something that we are not familiar with." And Dr. John Prescott, Director of the New England Aquarium, cautiously notes, "Apparently, from the photos, he's got some sort of beast there."

Rines has gone a step further and baptized Nessie with a scientific name: *Nessiteras rhombopteryx* (Ness monster with diamond fins). The purpose of the naming is to assure that Nessie is protected under British laws that cover the conservation of wild plants and animals. Henceforth, anyone who tries to capture or kill the animal will be prosecuted.

## How many monsters are there?

Is there only one monster, or is the Loch full of others? Two marine biologists believe that the size of the lake and its fish population could support 10 to 20 giant beasts. The monsters are probably reptiles which have adapted to living at the murky bottom and sides of the lake. Witchell and Rines think the animal captured on film is undoubtedly a plesiosaur, which is a fish-eating dinosaur that stalked the earth about 80 million years ago. Nessie's ancestors probably entered the Loch some 10,000 years ago when it was linked to the sea. Later, either the land rose or the sea level fell, and the great beasts became

trapped in the Loch. Some scientists speculate that no bones or other remains have ever been found because like roaches, the monsters devour one another's corpses. According to another theory, the beasts are like crocodiles—they swallow stones to weight them down; they die on the bottom and become covered by drifting sediments.

The loch itself is part of the Scottish highlands. It is 24 miles long, 1.5 miles across at its widest point, and 970 feet deep in places. With its green-black waters and surrounding green-gray hills, it is just as gloomy and foreboding as the moors of the lowlands. A monster could not have chosen a more apt place to set up house.

Apparently, the animal has lived there for some time, since the days of Saint Columba in the sixth century. Legend has it that the holy man drove one luckless beast into the murky depths of its watery lair for killing a man. Since then, hundreds of sightings have been reported. The most recent wave of these began in the 1930s when Nessie was seen by all manner of people. Many of these were not your ordinary run-of-the-mill monster enthusiasts, who are often dismissed as being hysterical, insane, or out to gain publicity. The beast was spotted by such personages as the British Prime Minister's sister-in-law, a Nobel Prize winner, monks, lawyers, counts, naturalists, policemen, and military personnel trained in observation techniques. What they saw has generally been described as a large humped animal, black or gray in color, with a long curved neck—a description which partly fits the beast captured by Rines on film.

So what is the world to make of Rines's coup? One thing is certain at this point: If Nessie and her alleged companions turn out to be the real thing—bonafide flesh-and-blood dinosaurs—they will be one of the most important natural finds of our time.

**"There may be 10 or 20 Nessies in the Loch."**

**f**or astronauts in space, their craft forms a miniature ecosystem, supplying all they need to survive in the alien environment. Sheltered from the intense radiations of space and sealed off from its vacuum, they carry with them all the oxygen, water, and food that they will use on their journey. The sun will warm them, as it does on earth, and will provide energy through solar cells to run their craft. Looking back, the astronauts can see their planet, the earth, within whose ecosystems they evolved. The clouds reveal its atmosphere. They can pick out its oceans and land masses, distinguishing regions with vegetation from deserts and icecaps. There, turning below them, is our whole native ecosystem, the earth, on whose resources human beings are ultimately dependent.

Resources are all those things which contribute to the satisfaction of human needs and wants. We satisfy many of our basic needs directly through the natural resources that occur in our normal environments. Hold your breath for a moment and you will feel a growing desire for air, with its vital oxygen. Water of adequate purity diminishes our thirst. And various foods satisfy our hunger.

The earth provides for our basic needs. But our technological cultures have created many more. Now we need a vast new array of things—fire to warm our homes and cook our food; energy to give us light, power, and mobility; tools and utensils to equip our homes and our places of work. Under the favorable conditions that technology provides, human populations have increased exponentially. Standards of living have risen sharply, and with them, expectations for a better life. Add population growth to technology and rising expectations, and the total demand on our natural resources becomes enormous.

The question is, will the earth be able to satisfy our escalating demands? Citizens around the world are voicing concern about the limits of the material resources our planet can supply. Many of these resources are polluted. Other have shown signs of serious depletion.

## Resource depletion

We love our cars, but hate the smog with which they envelop our cities. We lure industries to our towns, but their wastes choke our air and poison our rivers and lakes. We prize the easy mobility of the jet age, but fret about what jet-engine emissions will do to the stratosphere and the ozone layer. When, we wonder, will the point be reached when all this pollution will affect our climate? The vastly increased use of resources to satisfy growing needs has produced many conflicts over the depletion of resources and the pollution which results from their use.

## Population

Population growth may be the most significant factor in the drain on natural resources. The "population explosion" on our earth raises the specter of a planet so overcrowded that our dwindling resources will soon be exhausted. This concern is not entirely justified. An analysis of world population growth distinguishes between the populations of developed and less-developed countries. With the industrial and medical advances in the developed countries over the last century, death rates plummeted. But birth rates remained at their old levels, dropping only gradually to stabilize with low death rates. The less-developed countries have felt the full effect of this revolution only during the last generation. Because of medical and public health programs in these countries, the death rate has declined sharply, but the birth rate is still high. However, with today's rapid technological progress, these countries might need only 30 to 50 years to reach a stable low birth and death rate, with zero population growth. This does not mean that most countries will not have serious population problems. But it does suggest that existing processes may help to resolve these problems.

| End uses | Percent of total use |
| --- | --- |
| Industrial uses | |
|   Process steam | 16.4 |
|   Direct heat | 11.0 |
|   Electric drive | 8.1 |
|   Fuels as raw materials | 5.6 |
|   Electrolysis | 1.2 |
|         Total | 42.3 |
| Commercial and residential uses | |
|   Space heating | 17.7 |
|   Water heating | 4.0 |
|   Air conditioning | 2.9 |
|   Refrigeration | 2.3 |
|   Cooking | 1.2 |
|   Lighting, small appliances | 4.9 |
|         Total | 33.0 |
| Transportation of people and freight | 24.7   24.7 |
|         Grand total | 100.0 |

26-1
A resource of which Americans have become abruptly, and rather painfully, conscious, is energy. This table shows what percentage of total energy use in the United States is accounted for by each of various main categories.

### Food and famines

Growing populations play their part in diminishing and polluting resources, but they are usually only one of many factors. Consider the complexities of one typical problem, famine. During 1973, famine struck six Sahelian countries (Senegal, Mauritania, Mali, Upper Volta, Niger, and Chad), along a belt just south of the Sahara Desert. In 1973, some 100,000 people died, and 7 million others survived on foreign food relief. In 1974, the famine struck again. Human population growth was one factor. These countries have a high rate of population increase, 2.5 percent a year. By 1970, they had a third more people and twice as many cattle as a generation earlier. Another factor

26-2
The new high yielding varieties of wheat and rice, grown on experimental plots such as this one, provide an important way for dealing with problems of overpopulation, malnutrition, and famine. The wheat in the photograph has short, stiff stems. These enable the plant to support the weight of heavier yields. There is hope that the earth will some day be able to feed all its people adequately. But fertilizer shortages and drought have cut down on the immediate impact of the so-called green revolution and move the achievement of its goals further into the future than originally expected. (See Food and famine)

was the drought that had begun in the late 1960s. Some observers blame this on a changing climate, as the Sahara expands southward at a rate of 30 miles a year. Others believe that this low-rainfall belt is not adequate to support the recent increase in cattle, and blame overgrazing. This theory was bolstered by the discovery of a green patch in the midst of the drought-stricken area. The owner had permitted grazing of only one-fifth of the land each year, thus keeping his pastures green. In turn, the overgrazing has been attributed to changes in the nomadic ways of tribesmen. New governments have prevented free movement, encouraged herders to settle down, and sought to develop cotton and peanut crops to profit from foreign exchange. Depletion of this vast marginal agricultural region was probably caused by a combination of all these factors, with the famine itself finally triggered by the long drought.

## Minerals and fossil fuels

Minerals can be found only in certain locations. They are mostly **nonrenewable**, dissipated after first use. While some can be recycled, this is usually expensive. In this, minerals differ from land, water, and air, **renewable** resources which can be reclaimed or purified. With proper treatment, these resources can be used time after time.

Industrial civilization has been based increasingly on the use of heavy metals. Such metals furnish the strength needed for construction of all sorts. As industry expands and its products become more numerous, more and more of these metals are being used up. Moreover, their processing consumes huge amounts of energy derived from the fossil fuels—coal, natural gas, and petroleum. These natural resources have begun to peter out all over the globe. At the current rate of consumption growth, half the known global reserves of industrial metals listed may well be depleted within 50 years. All of them are good for less than a century,

including aluminum, nickel, and iron. The precious metals are being depleted even faster, although the platinum group is in better shape.

A new "gold" rush is about to begin. Manganese nodules may be "mined" from the ocean floor. The value of these nodules lies in their rich metal content. They contain not only manganese but also iron, nickel, cobalt, and traces of many other metals. As land sources give out, the nodules may become our principal source for these substances. But nodules grow so slowly that they must be considered a nonrenewable resource.

| Natural resource | Known global reserves | Expected percentage rate of growth in consumption per year | Years to exhaustion at: | | |
|---|---|---|---|---|---|
| | | | Current rate of global consumption | Current rate of growth of consumption[1] | With five times known global reserves[1] |
| **Industrial metals** | | | | | |
| Tin | 4.3 million long tons | 1.1 | 17 | 15 | 61 |
| Zinc | 123 million tons | 2.9 | 23 | 18 | 50 |
| Lead | 91 million tons | 2.0 | 26 | 21 | 64 |
| Copper | 308 million tons | 4.6 | 36 | 21 | 48 |
| Tungsten | 1.5 million tons | 2.5 | 40 | 28 | 72 |
| Manganese | 0.8 million tons | 2.9 | 97 | 46 | 94 |
| Aluminum | 1.17 billion tons | 6.4 | 100 | 31 | 55 |
| Nickel | 0.07 billion tons | 3.4 | 150 | 53 | 96 |
| Iron | 100 billion tons | 1.8 | 240 | 93 | 173 |
| Chromium | 0.78 billion tons | 2.6 | 420 | 95 | 154 |
| **Precious metals** | | | | | |
| Gold | 0.353 billion troy oz. | 4.1 | 11 | 9 | 29 |
| Silver | 5.5 billion troy oz. | 2.7 | 16 | 13 | 42 |
| **Platinum group** | 0.429 billion troy oz. | 3.8 | 130 | 47 | 85 |
| **Fossil fuels** | | | | | |
| Petroleum | 455 billion barrels | 3.9 | 31 | 20 | 50 |
| Natural gas | $1.14 \times 10^{15}$ cu. ft. | 4.7 | 38 | 22 | 49 |
| Coal | 5000 billion tons | 4.1 | 2300 | 111 | 150 |

1. Data from D. H. Meadows, et al., The Limits to Growth, New York Universe Books, 1972, Data in other columns from U.S. Bureau of Mines, Mineral Facts and Problems, Washington, D.C., 1970.

26-3
Global reserves of nonrenewable natural resources, and their years to exhaustion at different rates of consumption, based on 1970 data.

26-4
As population grows, the farmland available for growing food shrinks. Often the best farmland is most attractive to developers. Above, an aerial photograph of land near Newport News, Virginia, in 1937. Below, the same area in 1953. Circles superimposed on the photographs identify the recognizable points of reference.

The known global reserves of petroleum and natural gas may last 15 to 20 years. If five times the known reserves can be discovered, this may be extended to 45 to 50 years. But in 1975, the U.S. Geological Survey halved its estimate of American petroleum reserves. The government now requires many power companies to use coal rather than gas, even though the poor grades of coal they use increase air pollution. Coal has become the only long-run fossil fuel, though still unrenewable and polluting. It is thus the long-run source of gas and of the many coal-tar and petroleum products that can be derived from it.

Known reserves of uranium ores, the source for fuel in nuclear fission plants, are enough to last at least until the year 2020. If nuclear fusion processes can be developed by the year 2000, as many scientists predict, sea water will supply enough fusion fuels—heavy hydrogen (deuterium and tritium)—for millions of years. But many questions have been raised about the safety of nuclear power plants. Until they are satisfactorily answered, nuclear energy remains a dubious solution to our energy problem.

## Land

It may come as a surprise to learn that in the 48 contiguous states (exclusive of Hawaii and Alaska) urban use takes only a little over 1 percent of the land. Recreational use takes only 2 to 3 percent. The greatest proportion is devoted to grazing (34 percent), farming (23 percent), and forestry (32 percent). The remaining 7 percent includes roads, airports, reservoirs, military reservations, deserts, marshes, and mountains.

So cities do not constitute the biggest land use problem in the United States. But there are other problems. Range lands can be overgrazed. The near extinction of the American bison may have been as much a result of overgrazing by ever-increasing herds as of overhunting by pioneer settlers. Again, unprotected soil is open to erosion by wind and water. This has been a serious land-use problem in America since the "dust-bowl" days of the 1930s. Wind sweeping across plowed prairies in a dry season can carry away tons of topsoil. When clear-cut logging or fires level forests, erosion sets in. Soil is carried off in the sediments of streams and rivers and finally deposited in the ocean. And while forests are renewable, the process requires many decades to approach complete recovery.

## Water

Water is the natural resource most directly important to us. It requires some degree of purity for each use that it serves, and there must be enough of it for each use. The water table has sunk in many areas of the United States. This shows that water is being used faster than it can be replaced. So much of the water of the Colorado River is now diverted for drinking or irrigation that the river has dried up and disappeared long before it reaches the sea.

It is true that water renews itself when it evaporates into the air. It generally comes back purified in rainfall, although "acid rains" fall when the air is polluted with sulfates. But our increasing demands for water require us to use it several times in each cycle. With each use it becomes more impure. Besides drinking, cooking, and washing, we use large amounts to carry off our sewage. The sewage can be purified in treatment plants. But these are costly, and we are having to build more and more of them to cope with the increasing waste load. Industrial uses drain far more water than do domestic needs, and often pollute the supply. Water used for cooling purposes may be heated so much that it kills the fish and aquatic plants when it is returned to its source. Phosphate detergents and the nitrates and phosphates in fertilizers cause eutrophication in rivers and lakes.

## Air

Except for minor losses, the atmosphere seems to remain constant, held to the earth by gravity. Meteors burning up in the upper

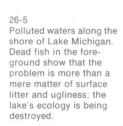

26-5
Polluted waters along the shore of Lake Michigan. Dead fish in the foreground show that the problem is more than a mere matter of surface litter and ugliness; the lake's ecology is being destroyed.

atmosphere contribute dust. More comes from volcanic eruptions, nuclear explosions, and winds carrying eroded particles aloft. Heavy gases, such as carbon dioxide and engine emissions, chemical substances, and dust from all sources stay in the lower atmospheric layers. This contamination depletes and pollutes air as a natural resource.

Many of us are rightfully concerned about the hydrocarbons emitted by jet planes and the chlorofluoromethanes used as aerosol propellants and refrigerants. They may reduce the earth's ozone layer, which protects all life from the sun's ultraviolet radiations. But this is a long-run possibility: pollution of the air at and near the surface of the earth confronts us now. Gases and particles from human activities, particularly from transportation and industry, produce heavy smogs, a serious threat to public health. If the worst of these pollutants are not reduced, smogs will probably take an increasing toll on human health.

## Climate

Climates are the long-term manifestations of weather, involving the average temperature and precipitation of regions over decades or centuries. Favorable, relatively unvarying climates are one of our basic natural resources. Recently, the question has been raised whether the waste products of technology may influence the atmosphere enough to change climates. For example, there is an increasing concentration of carbon dioxide in the atmosphere. On the other hand, scientists have detected a minor cooling of the atmosphere since a warm period that culminated in the 1930s. This could be caused by the increase in dust particles in the air. Whether this cooling will last, and how long, is unknown. But climatologists suggest that changes of less than a degree or two in average annual surface temperatures might trigger climatic changes that could last for centuries, perhaps even bringing on a new ice age. It remains to be determined whether or not

climatic changes can be caused by human activities.

## Resource destruction

In a broad sense, **pollution** is the buildup of any materials or forms of energy in an environment faster than they can be dispersed, broken down, stored, or recycled, so that they become detrimental to the lives of organisms in the environment. For example, sewage can be a good fertilizer in small amounts. But too much of it can spread infection and create epidemics. Pollution was not a serious problem until population grew dense, with industry producing large quantities of waste materials. When refuse heaps became obnoxious, ancient tribes or families could simply move to new locations. But cities cannot be moved around this way, and so pollution must be dealt with where it is.

### Pesticides and herbicides

We have learned that **biodegradable** substances can be broken down by organisms and dispersed. **Nonbiodegradable** materials, though, are virtually indestructible. Ingested in minute quantities, they move up the food chain, becoming more concentrated on the way. The most dangerous of these materials are the chlorinated hydrocarbon pesticides such as DDT, aldrin, and dieldrin, and the polychlorinated biphenyls (PCBs) used in many manufacturing processes. DDT is particularly serious because microorganisms in soil convert it into DDE, even more persistent and volatile. It has recently been discovered that these pesticides may also be converted into PCBs by ultraviolet light in the atmosphere.

DDT is poisonous to many pests. But it also poisons birds, fish, and a host of other creatures. Since it deteriorates very slowly, one application may produce toxic effects for 10 to 20 years. The use of DDT and many other nonbiodegradable materials has been restricted in recent years. Fortunately, there are other ways of attacking pests.

25-6
Pesticides: spraying a citrus orchard, and some of the unwanted consequences. The chemical control of pests attacking crops and livestock is of great importance to the human food supply, especially in view of the recent population explosion and the accompanying dangers of mass starvation. The harmful effect of pesticides on plant and animal life, though, remains of great concern to ecologists.

Quarantines, for example, can prevent their spread. Food species, such as wheat, can be genetically "tailored" to resist fungi. And insect pests can be attacked by releasing sexually sterile forms to prevent their reproduction.

## Industrial and transportation wastes

Coal- or oil-burning power plants cast huge volumes of dust and gases into the atmosphere, and release heated condensing water into lakes and streams. Smelting of ores contaminates the air and dots the landscape with piles of slag. Runoff from slag and from mines, particularly open-pit and strip mines, pollutes the waters. Manufacturing plants often use materials that add to the general pollution or pose specific dangers to human health. These include the asbestos fibers used in insulation, and vinyl chloride, a component of many plastics. Others are not toxic, but are also nonbiodegradable. Our coastal waters are laden with tiny plastic spheres, cylinders, styrofoam beads, and plastic sheets and fragments. These will accumulate indefinitely, clogging the seas and interfering with aquatic ecosystems.

A quarter of all our energy goes into the cars, trucks, trains, and planes that carry us and distribute our goods. Most of this energy is derived from petroleum products burned in internal combustion engines. Their emissions increasingly fill our air with toxic substances—carbon dioxide and monoxide, nitrogen oxides, hydrocarbons, and lead. The catalytic converter, which cuts down these emissions, is now controversial. Some believe the sulfuric acid it produces may be as polluting and as unhealthful as the emissions it was designed to prevent.

## Domestic wastes

Each week, every household in the United States produces at least one bag or barrel of garbage and rubbish, and gallons of liq-

26-7
This negative print of a photograph taken by satellite shows a barge in the act of dumping industrial acid wastes in the Atlantic Ocean outside New York harbor. The wriggly black trail at center is the acid wastes. Other dark splotches show differences in water temperature. Long Island appears at the top of the photo, and part of New Jersey is at lower left. (See Industrial and transportation wastes)

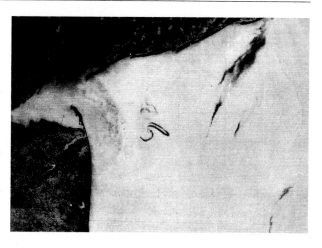

## Nuclear wastes

Disposal of wastes from nuclear plants presents a similar but more serious problem. Some of this spent fuel can be reprocessed. But much still remains, consisting of highly radioactive materials with half-lives ranging from 700 to over 25,000 years. It has been suggested that nuclear wastes might be rocketed far out into space, or into the sun itself, but this is far too expensive. It has also been proposed to dump them into the sea, in steel or cement containers. But this idea has been met with skepticism, since the containers are bound to spring leaks. Meanwhile, radioactive wastes are rapidly accumulating in thick-walled "mausoleums," where the inevitable leaks can be quickly repaired. To date, over 400,000 gallons of waste have leaked from these storage tanks.

## Approaches to solutions

We have seen how the rapid rise to dominance of *Homo sapiens* has affected the ecosystems of which he forms a part. This has caused continual and increasing depletion and pollution of the natural re-

26-8
Manmade salt marsh in Chesapeake Bay. Below, left: initial seeding of barren tidal flats. Right: the scene six months later. (See Land reclamation)

uid waste. The solid wastes can no longer be burnt in the back yard, since this pollutes the air. For health reasons, liquid wastes in highly populated areas must be collected in sewers and drained off. Carrying solid wastes out to sea harms the ocean life and may contaminate beaches. The main alternative has been to dump the wastes on land and cover them with earth. But available dump sites are being filled up, and the costs of disposal are rising. Some other solution must be found.

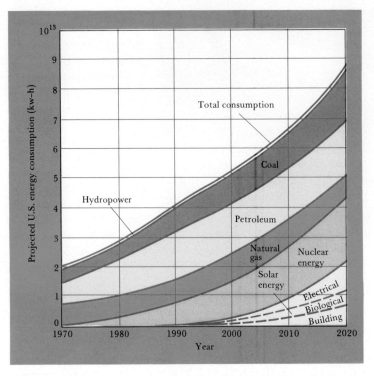

**26-9**
Projected energy sources for the United States in the next 50 years, showing the relative contribution of each to the total energy supply.

sources essential to human well-being. What steps can be taken to arrest this attrition?

## Recycling

One way to slow the depletion of natural resources is to treat the products of these resources so that they can be used again. Household refuse contains metals, glass, paper, food, wood, plastics, and other materials. The organic fraction of this trash can be separated. It can be used in part for fuel or generation of electricity and in part for wallboard, fibers, animal feed, and compost. The inert fraction can be separated into its various metals, glass, and other materials by magnetic and flotation processes, and put back into use. Old cars can be compacted and used in making steel. Paper can be recycled to make new paper products. Wood and sawdust can be treated to make wallboard, and many plastics can be reused. Factories are beginning to save materials by design changes and improved processing efficiency, thereby also saving energy.

## Land reclamation

More rational and productive methods are being worked out for recycling depleted land. Most federal lands now prohibit clear-cutting of forests and overgrazing of ranges. Eventually it will be required that landscapes destroyed by strip-mining be restored to their former conditions. Contour plowing, which helps to prevent erosion, is common. Earth-moving machinery can now assist in repairing eroded land. New techniques of planting and cultivating, crop rotation, fertilization, and harvesting help to prevent soil depletion. New irrigation techniques that apply water beneath the surface are being developed. These will prevent soil salinization and depletion and save precious water.

The wholesale destruction of estuaries and salt marshes appears to be on the wane. In one experiment, the Army Corps of Engineers covered tidewater areas with silt and sediments dredged from bays and seeded them with salt-water grasses. Within a year, salt marshes were created. They helped to prevent coastal erosion and provided a habitat for the creatures on which bay and coastal fish feed.

## New energy sources

Concern over fuel reserves has spurred efforts to find other sources of energy. Use of solar energy is not a new idea, but interest in its possibilities is at a new high. Intensive research is under way to produce cheap solar cells, the devices used in spacecraft to convert the sun's light directly into electricity. A system has been proposed for collecting such energy in huge stationary satellites and transmitting it to earth. Another proposal is the use of plant photosynthesis to produce sugars and other carbohydrates. These would then be fermented. yielding alcohols as a substitute or an additive for gasoline. Still another is the use of the enzyme systems of some plants to produce molecular hydrogen. This hydrogen could be burned to produce energy, yielding water as a valuable byproduct.

summary

Resources comprise whatever contributes to the satisfaction of human needs and wants. Natural resources are those occurring in our normal environments. Population growth, technology, and rising expectations have intensified the demands on our natural resources, some of which are becoming depleted and polluted.

Perhaps the most significant factor in the depletion of natural resources is population growth. In the developed countries over the last century, death rates fell. But birth rates have only recently begun to stabilize. Less developed countries still have high birth rates, but may reach zero population growth within 30 to 50 years. Population growth combined with such factors as natural disasters, overgrazing, and political and social changes can cause famines.

Most minerals are nonrenewable—dissipated after first use. Industrial expansion consumes minerals and also uses large quantities of energy derived from fossil fuels: coal, natural gas, and petroleum. At current rates, half the known global reserves of industrial metals may be depleted within 50 years. Manganese nodules "mined" from the ocean floor may become our principal source for that metal as well as iron, nickel, cobalt, and others. But they grow slowly and are thus nonrenewable. The use of nuclear energy as a power source is problematical.

Land can be overgrazed and eroded by wind. Forests can be leveled by fires and clear-cut logging. Improper irrigation and intensive agriculture can impoverish the soil. Nitrates and phosphates used in fertilizer are becoming expensive.

Water is a resource not only for us, but for organisms that are important to our existence. The sinking of the water table in many areas of the United States shows that water is being used faster than it can be replaced. Sewage, industrial pollutants, overheating of water used for cooling purposes, phosphate detergents, and nitrates and phosphates from fertilizers all cause water to become more impure with each cycle of use.

The upper atmosphere is contaminated by dust from meteors, volcanoes, nuclear explosions, and eroded particles. The lower atmosphere carries heavy gases such as carbon dioxide and engine emissions, chemical substances, and more dust. Hydrocarbons emitted by jet planes and chlorofluoromethanes from aerosol propellants and refrigerants may reduce the earth's ozone layer, which protects all life from ultraviolet radiations.

The long-term manifestations of weather, involving the average temperature and precipitation over decades or centuries, are called climate. Technological wastes may influence the atmosphere enough to change climates.

Pollution is the buildup of any materials or forms of energy in an environment faster than they can be dispersed, broken down, stored, or recycled, so that they become detrimental to the lives of organisms. Dense populations and industrialization have increased pollution. Biodegradable substances can be broken down by organisms and dispersed. Nonbiodegradable substances, such as DDT, are almost indestructible. Ingested in minute quantities, they move up the food chain, growing more concentrated.

The generation and use of energy are among the worst sources of pollution. Industry uses the greatest proportion of energy. It produces dust and gases, heated water, slag runoff, health-endangering materials like asbestos fibers and vinyl chloride, and nonbiodegradable plastics. Petroleum products burned in internal combustion engines fill the air with toxic substances. Household wastes also pollute, harming ocean life with solid wastes and filling the land dump sites. Highly radioactive waste from nuclear plants is rapidly accumulating. The disposal of such waste is particularly difficult, since it remains dangerous for so long.

Resource depletion can be slowed by recycling. Technologies are being developed for resource and energy recovery from solid wastes. Inert waste can be separated and put back into use. Land can be recycled by prohibiting overgrazing and clear-cutting of forests, by returning strip-mine sites to their former state, and by new techniques of agriculture to prevent soil depletion. Salt marshes can be created to prevent coastal erosion and provide a habitat for creatures on which bay and coastal fish feed.

Research efforts may yield inexpensive solar cells. These could convert the sun's rays to electricity. Plant photosynthesis may be used to produce carbohydrates that could be fermented to provide substitutes for gasoline. Plant enzyme systems could also be used as sources of energy and water, because of their capacity to produce molecular hydrogen.

taxonomy

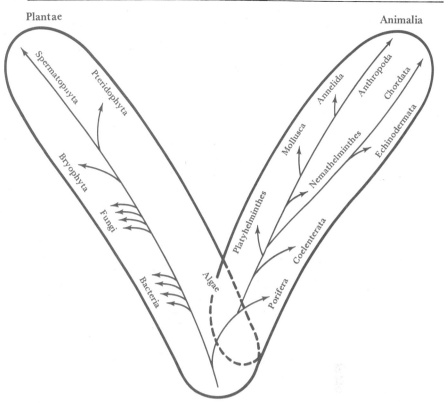

The number of known living things is enormous. It has been estimated that 1.5 million plants and animals have thus far been identified and studied. Some scientists predict that future discoveries of other organisms, particularly microorganisms, will double this figure. To facilitate communication among researchers, all of these plants and animals must be named and grouped in an intelligible manner. In other words, they must be ordered in some system of classification.

The first classificatory task, that of **nomenclature**, is done by giving each organism a Latin name. Why is it necessary to use a "dead" language to refer to a sparrow, a pocket gopher, or a weeping willow? Why not use everyday English or, where applicable, French, Spanish, or Russian? For one thing, Latin is a holdover from the times when scholars communicated in this tongue. Then, too, if the vernacular were used, some organisms would inevitably receive different names in different countries, or even in different parts of the same country. For example, an edible plant known most commonly as pigweed in the United States is also called lamb's-quarters, goosefoot, wild spinach, or amaranth in different parts of the country. But when a plant is referred to by its scientific classificatory name, *Chenopodium album*, a biologist in any part of the United States—or in any other country—immediately knows the organism being discussed. Thus, in order to differentiate each kind of organism in language that is precise, uniform, and understandable to investigators the world over, a formal system of Latin nomenclature is used.

But simply giving a Latin name to a living thing is not enough. The organism must be placed in a system which relates it to all other living things. Given such a system, a biologist, thinking he has come upon a new species of beetle, can compare it feature by feature to other known beetle species to determine if it deserves a new name. The discipline which helps scientists in such activities is known as **taxonomy.** It treats the nomenclature and classification of organisms according to their similarities and differences as revealed by structure, function, and evolution.

Man's first attempts to devise a taxonomy that would organize the many forms of life date back to the early Greeks. Aristotle attempted to classify living things according to their nature, by examining many specimens of similar organisms, determining which of their traits were common to all, and ignoring those traits which seemed to vary. Basically, Aristotle classified animals according to whether they lived on land, sea, or air. Plants were grouped by his student, Theophrastus, into four categories: trees, shrubs, undershrubs, and herbs.

Aristotle's schema was followed by Western scholars until the middle of the eighteenth century, when the Swedish biologist Carl Linnaeus developed the system of classification which, in modified form, is still used today. Linnaeus has been called the father of modern taxonomy, because he developed the binomial system of nomenclature in which every organism is given two Latin names, the first identifying its genus, the second its species. In this system, which was based upon that of Aristotle, Linnaeus attempted to group similar, related kinds of organisms into "natural" arrangements that indicated some degree of relationship among the organisms being treated. Attempts to group generally similar kinds of organisms ultimately led to the formulation of a hierarchy of abstract categories, or *taxa* (singular *taxon*). From most specific to most general, these are: species, genus, family, order, class, division or phylum, and kingdom. Species believed to be related to one another through the possession of a number of similar features were placed together in a genus. Genera that had an apparent relationship were grouped in a family; presumably related families formed an order, and so on. If necessary, each taxon can be expanded by prefixing modifiers such as super- or sub-, or by inserting intermediate taxa between those given above. Thus, there can be a subclass or a superorder, as well as a cohort (between class and order), tribe (between family and genus), and other intermediate levels.

For example, the classification of human beings according to the Linnaean system would be as follows: kingdom Animalia, phylum Chordata, subphylum Vertebrata, class Mammalia, suborder Anthropoidea, order Primates, superfamily Hominoidea, family Hominidae, genus *Homo,* species *Homo sapiens.*

Linnaeus' system first appeared in 1758, about 100 years before the publication of Darwin's *Origin of the Species*. Since the process of organic evolution was unknown and since every different kind of organism was thought to have been the result of a special act of creation by the Deity, no thought of relationship through time was expressed or implied in Linnaeus' system of classification. All taxa implied only present relationships based on varying degrees of morphological similarity.

Since 1859, classification systems have attempted to indicate, where possible, phylogenetic relationships. To do this, the taxonomists have, in the last half century, added genetics, physiology, biochemistry, cytology, and ecology to their morphological and anatomical studies to learn more about the phylogenetic

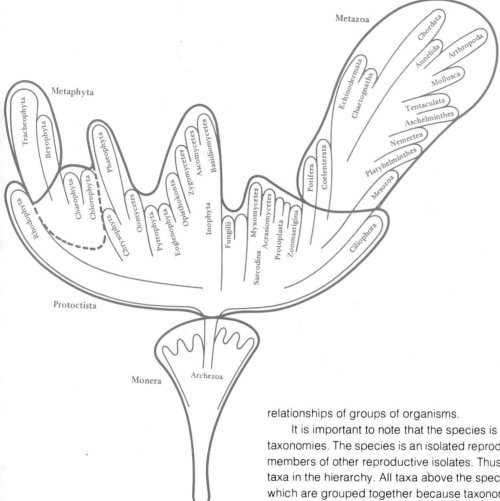

relationships of groups of organisms.

It is important to note that the species is the basic level of all modern taxonomies. The species is an isolated reproductive unit which does not mate with members of other reproductive isolates. Thus, it is the most unambiguous of all taxa in the hierarchy. All taxa above the species level are arbitrary constructs which are grouped together because taxonomists perceive certain common structural and functional resemblances.

It is also important to remember that evolution goes on at the population level and involves individual organisms. (A population is a group of individuals belonging to the same species and living in the same area.) Orders and families of organisms "evolve" only as their genera "evolve"; the genera "evolve" only as their species "evolve," and the species "evolve" only as the genes of their populations change through time. Thus, genera do not evolve from other genera at the genus level, nor families or orders at their respective levels, but all evolution must go on in populations of individuals.

As more and more is learned about the evolution of living things, taxonomic systems, attempting to be all-inclusive, change. This can be seen in the history of the highest division, the kingdom.

In the eyes of Aristotle and Linnaeus, the natural world contained two general classes of living things: animals and plants. Those organisms which moved about, gathering and ingesting food, were animals, whereas those that were rooted and made their own food were plants. Up to the early twentieth century, these two kingdoms were seen as the most logical and meaningful way to divide life.

## Kingdom Monera *(procaryotes)*

Phylum Schizophyta, or Schizomycetes   *(bacteria)*
Phylum Cyanophyta, or Myxophyta   *(blue-green algae)*

## Kingdom Protista *(protists)*

Phylum Euglenophyta   *(euglenophytes)*
Phylum Chrysophyta   *(golden algae and diatoms)*
Phylum Xanthophyta   *(yellow-green algae)*
Phylum Pyrrophyta   *(dinoflagellates and cryptomonads)*
Phylum Hyphochytridiomycota   *(hyphochytrids)*
Phylum Plasmodiophoromycota   *(plasmodiophores)*
Phylum Sporozoa   *(sporozoans)*
Phylum Cnidosporidia   *(cnidosporidians)*
Phylum Zoomastigina   *(animal flagellates)*
Phylum Sarcodina   *(rhizopods)*
Phylum Ciliophora   *(ciliates and suctorians)*

## Kingdom Plantae *(plants)*

Phylum Rhodophyta   *(red algae)*
Phylum Phaeophyta   *(brown algae)*
Phylum Chlorophyta   *(green algae)*
Phylum Charophyta   *(stoneworts)*
Phylum Bryophyta   *(liverworts, hornworts, and mosses)*
Phylum Psilophyta   *(psilophytes)*
Phylum Lycopsida   *(club mosses)*
Phylum Arthrophyta   *(horsetails)*
Phylum Pterophyta   *(ferns)*
Phylum Cycadophyta   *(cycads)*
Phylum Coniferophyta   *(conifers)*
Phylum Anthophyta   *(flowering plants)*

## Kingdom Fungi *(fungi)*

Phylum Myxomycophyta   *(slime molds)*
Phylum Eumycophyta   *(true fungi)*

## Kingdom Animalia *(animals)*

Phylum Mesozoa   *(mesozoans)*
Phylum Porifera   *(sponges)*
Phylum Archaeocyatha   *(extinct organisms)*
Phylum Coelenterata   *(coelenterates)*
Phylum Ctenophora   *(comb jellies)*
Phylum Platyhelminthes   *(flatworms)*
Phylum Nemertea   *(ribbon worms)*
Phylum Acanthocephala   *(spiny-headed worms)*
Phylum Aschelminthes   *(pseudocoelomate worms)*
Phylum Nematoda   *(round worms)*
Phylum Entoprocta   *(pseudocoelomate polyzoans)*
Phylum Bryozoa   *(sea mosses, or moss animals)*
Phylum Brachiopoda   *(brachiopods, or lampshells)*
Phylum Phoronida   *(phoronid worms)*
Phylum Mollusca   *(molluscs)*
Phylum Sipunculoidea   *(peanut worms)*
Phylum Echiuroidea   *(spoon worms)*
Phylum Annelida   *(segmented worms)*
Phylum Arthropoda   *(arthropods)*
Phylum Brachiata   *(beard worms)*
Phylum Chaetognatha   *(arrow worms)*
Phylum Echinodermata   *(echinoderms)*
Phylum Hemichordata   *(acorn worms)*
Phylum Chordata   *(chordates)*

Although the invention of the microscope in the seventeenth century revealed the existence of organisms which would not fit comfortably into either of these two categories, most scientists were inclined to shrug off these anomalies or to think of them as problems to be dealt with by future taxonomists. Among these organisms were the Protista, the single-celled "plants"' and "animals." As more was learned about Protista, biologists were forced to rethink their simple two-kingdom taxonomy and to develop a three-kingdom system that would provide the Protista with a kingdom of their own.

However, as techniques for examining microscopic life became more sophisticated, it became clear that even the three-kingdom approach was unsatisfactory. When bacteria were thoroughly studied, for example, it was learned that they did not have the same cell structure as the other organisms. They lacked a definite cell nucleus; hence, like blue-green algae, they are procaryotic organisms, organized quite differently from other known life forms. The discovery of the virus created another problem for taxonomists. Viruses appear in nature only as parasites. They reproduce by sending their genetic materials, which can be either DNA or RNA, into plant and animal cells. Since the hereditary materials are not held in any special structure, viruses are sometimes known as naked genes.

For these reasons, many biologists lean toward a four-kingdom system which includes Monera (bacteria and blue-green algae), Protista (protists and fungi), Plantae (higher plants), and Metazoa (higher animals).

But the position of the fungi raises a problem for this system. The fungi

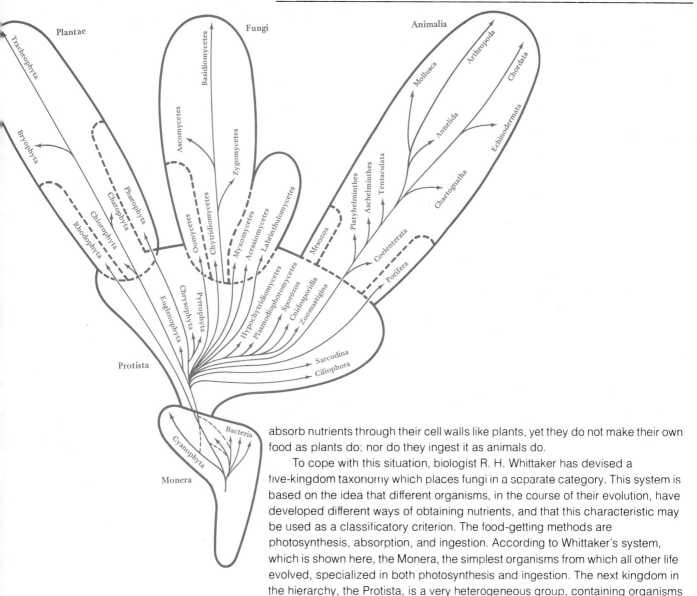

Plantae

Tracheophyta

Bryophyta

Phaeophyta

Charophyta

Chlorophyta

Rhodophyta

Fungi

Basidiomycetes

Ascomycetes

Zygomycetes

Oomycetes

Chytridiomycetes

Myxomycetes

Acrasiomycetes

Labrinthulomycetes

Animalia

Mollusca

Arthropoda

Chordata

Annelida

Echinodermata

Platyhelminthes

Aschelminthes

Tentaculata

Chaetognatha

Mesozoa

Coelenterata

Porifera

Euglenophyta

Chrysophyta

Pyrrophyta

Hypochytridiomycetes

Plasmodiophoromycetes

Sporozoa

Cnidosporidia

Zoomastigina

Sarcodina

Ciliophora

Protista

Bacteria

Cyanophyta

Monera

absorb nutrients through their cell walls like plants, yet they do not make their own food as plants do; nor do they ingest it as animals do.

To cope with this situation, biologist R. H. Whittaker has devised a five-kingdom taxonomy which places fungi in a separate category. This system is based on the idea that different organisms, in the course of their evolution, have developed different ways of obtaining nutrients, and that this characteristic may be used as a classificatory criterion. The food-getting methods are photosynthesis, absorption, and ingestion. According to Whittaker's system, which is shown here, the Monera, the simplest organisms from which all other life evolved, specialized in both photosynthesis and ingestion. The next kingdom in the hierarchy, the Protista, is a very heterogeneous group, containing organisms that engage in all three kinds of food-getting. From these organisms evolved the three higher kingdoms, Plantae, the Fungi, and the Animalia.

Although it is favored in this text, the five-kingdom system, like all other taxonomies, is a construct of the human mind, which attempts to impose upon nature boundaries that are largely arbitrary. Since nature is so diverse, precise and uniform classifications are difficult, if not impossible, and are subject to constant revision. Indeed, at present, there is no standard taxonomy because any classification is inherently subjective: its creator selects those characteristics which he or she perceives as being common to certain groups, and ignores others. A taxonomy that is acceptable to most investigators should serve as an index to what we know about life on earth. It should also prod scientists toward new thinking about the most meaningful ways to organize our knowledge of life.

credits

**Cover and title page**

Carl Moreus

**Introduction**

I-1, 2, 3   The Bettman Archive

I-4, 6, 7   NASA

I-8   E. S. Barghoorn

I-10   The Bettman Archive

**Chapter 1**

1-8   After James D. Watson, *Molecular Biology of the Gene,* 2nd Edition, W. A. Benjamin, Inc., 1970, p. 177

1-10   Courtesy of Daniel Branton

**Chapter 2**

2-2   Dr. J. F. Gennaro, NYU— Cellular Biology

2-5a   Dr. Alec N. Broers, IBM, Thomas J. Watson Research Center

2-5b   Dr. Alec N. Broers and Dr. Barbara J. Panessa, IBM, Thomas J. Watson Research Center

2-8   Dr. Richard R. Eger of The Rockefeller University

2-9   Don W. Fawcett, MD, Harvard Medical School

2-10   Courtesy of M. V. Parthasarathy

2-11   S. Hoffstein, NYU School of Medicine

2-14   D. E. Gennaro, NYU School of Medicine

2-15   Dr. J. F. Gennaro, NYU School of Medicine

2-17   Courtesy of H. W. Israel

2-23   Courtesy of Daniel Branton

2-24   Courtesy of Dr. James G. Hirsch, The Rockefeller University

**Chapter 3**

3-1   Dr. R. N. Goodman

3-13   Dr. Keith R. Porter

## Chapter 4

4-1   New York Botanical Garden

4-2   Professor William F. Sheridan

4-3a, b   Dr. J. F. Gennaro, NYU School of Medicine

4-3c   Dr. Myron C. Ledbetter of Brookhaven National Laboratory

4-6   Courtesy of Carolina Biological Supply Company

4-8, 9   Professor William F. Sheridan

4-10   Dr. Alec N. Broers, IBM, Thomas J. Watson Research Center

4-11   Andrew Skolnick

4-15   Courtesy Carolina Biological Supply Company

## Chapter 5

5-6   Dr. E. R. Degginger

5-10   Courtesy of Carolina Biology Supply Company

## Chapter 6

6-3   A. K. Kleinschmidt *et al.: Biochem. Biophys. Ac. 61: 857* (1962)

6-6   Professor M. H. F. Wilkins, King's College, London

6-9   David R. Wolstenholme, University of Utah

6-11   Oscar L. Miller, Jr., and Barbara R. Beatty, Biology Division, Oak Ridge National Laboratory

## Chapter 7

7-1a   W. A. Jensen and R. B. Park, *Cell Ultrastructure,* 1967. By permission of Wadsworth Publishing Co., Inc., Belmont, California

7-1b   R. W. Simpson and R. E. Hanson

7-1c   S. Dales, in *J. Cell. Biology, 13* (1962), p. 303. By permission of the Rockefeller University Press

7-2, 3   Dr. Alec N. Broers and Dr. Barbara J. Panessa, IBM, Thomas J. Watson Research Center

7-6a   J. F. Bennett and E. Canale-Parola, *Arch. f. Mikrobiol. 52* (1965), p. 197. By permission of Springer-Verlag, Berlin

7-6b   L. L. Campbell *et al., J. Bact. 92* (1966), p. 1122. By permission of the American Society for Microbiology

7-7a   Courtesy of W. L. Van Veen and E. G. Mulder

7-7b, c   Courtesy of M. P. and H. A. Lechevalier

7-8   From A. L. Houwink and W. van Iterson, *Biochem. et Biophys. Acta 5* (1950), p. 10. By permission of Elsevier Publishing Co.

7-9   Courtesy of H. Kuhlwein

7-12, 13, 14a   Eric Grave/Photo Researchers, Inc.

7-14b   Jerry Lesser/Bruce Coleman, Inc.

7-14c   G. Cox/Bruce Coleman, Inc.

7-15   Eric Grave/Photo Researchers, Inc.

## Chapter 8

8-1   Courtesy Carolina Biological Supply Company

8-2, 3, 5, 7, 12, 13, 15, 16, 17, 18, 19, 20, 22, 23, 25   Peter J. Davies

8-8, 10   Courtesy of D. J. Paolillo

8-26   Courtesy of M. V. Parthasarathy

## Chapter 9

9-1   R. Mendez/Animals Animals

9-3   William M. Stephens/Photo Researchers, Inc.

9-5   Eric Grave/Photo Researchers, Inc.

9-6   Russ Kinne/Photo Researchers, Inc.

9-7   Eric Grave, Russ Kinne/Photo Researchers, Inc.

9-8   Laurence Pringle/Photo Researchers, Inc.

9-9a   Dick Greene from National Audubon Society

9-9b   John Gerard from National Audubon Society

9-10a   Angermayer Munchen/Photo Researchers, Inc.

9-10b   Mary Thatcher/Photo Researchers, Inc.

9-11, 13   Russ Kinne/Photo Researchers, Inc.

9-14   Eric Grave/Photo Researchers, Inc.

## Chapter 10

10-1   D. Hardley/Bruce Coleman, Inc.

10-2   J. H. Carmichael/Bruce Coleman, Inc.

10-3   Jane Burton/Bruce Coleman, Inc.

10-4   S. C. Bisserot/Bruce Coleman, Inc.

10-6   Raymond Mendez/Animals Animals

10-7   S. C. Bisserot/Bruce Coleman, Inc.

10-10a   Oxford Scientific Films/Bruce Coleman, Inc.

10-10b    Allan Power/Bruce Coleman, Inc.

10-11    Ron Austing/Bruce Coleman, Inc.

10-12    Raymond Mendez/Animals, Animals

10-13    Carl Frank/Photo Researchers, Inc.

10-14    Leonard Lee Rue III/Bruce Coleman, Inc.

10-15a    S. C. Bisserot/Bruce Coleman, Inc.

10-15b, 16    Leonard Lee Rue III/Bruce Coleman, Inc.

10-17a    Marian Austerman/Animals, Animals

10-17b    George Roos/Animals Animals

10-17c    John Stevenson/Animals Animals

10-18    Marian Austerman/Animals Animals

**Chapter 11**

11-1    Courtesy of J. A. Millburn and J. I. Sprent

11-3    Peter J. Davies

11-4    Dr. Barbara J. Panessa, NYU—Cellular Biology

11-6, 7, 8    Peter J. Davies

11-9, 10    Dr. Barbara J. Panessa, NYU—Cellular Biology

11-16    M. H. Zimmerman

11-19    The Nitragin Company

**Chapter 12**

12-1    Russ Kinne/Photo Researchers, Inc.

12-2    Andrew Skolnick

12-11    Dr. J. F. Gennaro, NYU—Cellular Biology

12-13    Alfred M. Bailey from National Audubon Society

12-14    Leonard Lee Rue III/Bruce Coleman, Inc.

**Chapter 13**

13-4    Dr. J. F. Gennaro, NYU—Cellular Biology

13-11, 12    Dr. Lawrence Herman, State University of New York,
Downstate Medical Center

**Chapter 14**

14-3    H. Reinhard/Bruce Coleman, Inc.

14-7a    Russ Kinne/Photo Researchers, Inc.

14-7b    H. W. Kitchen from National Audubon Society

14-9    Fran Allen/Animals Animals

14-13    Thomas Eisner, Cornell University

14-17    A. W. Ambler from National Audubon Society

**Chapter 15**

15-4    Terence A. Milligan, Laboratory of Aquatic Biology, NYU

15-5, 8    D. T. Rutherford

15-9, 10    S. C. Bisserot/Bruce Coleman, Inc.

15-11    Terence A. Milligan, Laboratory of Aquatic Biology, NYU

15-12    Andrew Skolnick

15-13    S. C. Bisserot/Bruce Coleman, Inc.

15-14    Courtesy of Joseph L. Craft and Dr. Daniel Albert,
Department of Ophthalmology and Visual Science, Eye
Pathology and Tumor Research Section

15-16    Eric Hosking/Bruce Coleman, Inc.

15-18    S. C. Bisserot/Bruce Coleman, Inc.

15-28    Dr. Lawrence Herman, State University of New York,
Downstate Medical Center

15-29    Lennart Nielssen from *Behold Man*. By permission of
Little, Brown, and Company, Boston, Mass.

**Chapter 16**

16-1, 3    Andrew Skolnick

16-5, 8    Dr. Lawrence Herman, State University of New York,
Downstate Medical Center

**Chapter 17**

17-2-5    Peter J. Davies

17-10    Borthwick, *et al., Proceedings of National Academy
of Sciences US 38:* 662-666 (1952)

17-12    Peter J. Davies

17-13    Courtesy of F. C. Stewart and the Royal Society
of London

17-14    S. H. Wittwer, Michigan State University

17-15    Boyce Thompson Institute for Plant Research

## Chapter 18

18-1   Omikron

18-5   Courtesy Carolina Biological Supply Company

18-12a   Dr. E. R. Degginger

18-12b   Russ Kinne/Photo Researchers, Inc.

18-12c   Stephen Dalton/Photo Researchers, Inc.

18-14   Dr. J. F. Gennaro/NYU—Cellular Biology

18-16a   Leonard Lee Rue III from National Audubon Society

18-16b   Walter Dawn from National Audubon Society

## Chapter 19

19-3, 4, 5, 6, 7   Landrum Shettles

19-9   *O Medico Moderno,* August 1967

19-11a   Daniel Schiller

19-11b, c   Courtesy of Ortho Pharmaceutical Corp.

## Chapter 20

20-1   Culver Pictures, Inc.

20-2   Bettman Archive, Inc.

20-3   Culver Pictures, Inc.

20-4   Leonard Lee Rue III from National Audubon Society

20-6a   Ed Cesar from National Audubon Society

20-6b   A. W. Ambler from National Audubon Society

20-7   Carnegie Institution

20-11   Eiji Miyazawa/Black Star

20-12   M. W. F. Tweedie from National Audubon Society

20-13   A. W. Ambler from National Audubon Society

20-16   M. W. F. Tweedie from National Audubon Society

20-17   J. Stevenson/Animals Animals

## Chapter 21

21-1   A. A. Francesconi from National Audubon Society

21-3   Courtesy of Professor Dr. I. Eibl-Eibesfeldt

21-5   Courtesy of British Museum of Natural History

21-9a   John R. Brownlie/Bruce Coleman, Inc.

21-9b   L. R. Dawson/Bruce Coleman, Inc.

21-11   Gordon Smith from National Audubon Society

21-12   Jen and Des Bartlett/Bruce Coleman, Inc.

21-13   Courtesy of Australian News & Information Bureau

21-14   A. W. Ambler from National Audubon Society

## Chapter 22

22-2   The Smithsonian Institution

22-4   Peabody Museum of Natural History, Yale University

22-5   Courtesy of the American Museum of Natural History

22-6   Bob Campbell, National Geographic Society

22-8   From D. Pilbeam, *The Ascent of Man,* Macmillan, 1962

22-10, 11   Courtesy of the American Museum of Natural History

22-12   Peabody Museum of Natural History, Yale University

22-13, 14   Courtesy of the American Museum of Natural History

## Chapter 23

23-1   R. Peters/Animals Animals

23-3   Thomas D. McAvoy/Time-Life Picture Collection

23-5   S. C. Bisserot/Bruce Coleman, Inc.

23-6   Jen & Des Bartlett/Bruce Coleman, Inc.

23-9   Fred Bruemmer

23-10   Hugh Spencer from National Audubon Society

23-11   Gordon Smith from National Audubon Society

23-13   Raymond Mendez/Animals Animals

23-14   Andrew Skolnick

23-15   Jane Burton/Bruce Coleman, Inc.

23-16   Stephen J. Craig/Animals Animals

23-17   Terence O. Mathews/Photo Researchers, Inc.

23-18a   Allan Rose/Freelance Photo Guild

23-18b   Mary M. Thatcher/Photo Researchers, Inc.

23-19   Marian Austerman/Animals Animals

23-20   Fran Allen/Animals Animals

23-21   Mike Holmes/Animals Animals

23-22a   Courtesy of Professor Dr. I. Eibl-Eibesfeldt

23-22b   S. C. Bisserot/Bruce Coleman, Inc.

23-23   Bruce Coleman, Inc.

**Chapter 24**

24-1   Ylla/Rapho–Photo Researchers, Inc.
24-2   Shelley Grossman/Woodfin Camp
24-10   The Bettman Archive
24-11   Russ Kinne/Photo Researchers, Inc.
24-12   Animals Animals
24-13   Design Photographers International
24-14   Russ Kinne/Photo Researchers, Inc.
24-15   Karl H. Maslowski/Photo Researchers, Inc.
24-17   S. Collins/Photo Researchers, Inc.
24-18   Thomas Hopker/Woodfin Camp
24-19   Raymond A. Mendez/Animals Animals
24-20   Tom McHugh/Photo Researchers, Inc.
24-25   Ron Winch/Photo Researchers, Inc.
24-28   George Holton/Photo Researchers, Inc.

**Chapter 25**

25-2   Leo Touchet/Magnum Photos
25-3   Brett Wetson/Rapho–Photo Researchers, Inc.
25-4   Mark Stouffer/Animals Animals
25-5   Burt Glinn/Magnum Photos
25-6   Carlson Baldwin, Jr./Animals Animals
25-7   Crista Armstrong/Rapho–Photo Researchers, Inc.
25-8   Zig Leszczynski/Animals Animals
25-9   C. C. Cerastes/Animals Animals
25-12   Zig Leszczynski/Animals Animals
25-13   Shelley Grossman/Woodfin Camp
25-15   Darwin Van Campen/Design Photographers International

**Chapter 26**

26-2   Marc and Evelyne Bernheim/Woodfin Camp
26-4   Soil Conservation Service, USDA
26-5   Van Bucher/Photo Researchers, Inc.
26-6   Joe Munroe/Photo Researchers, Inc.
26-7   NASA
26-8   Environmental Concern

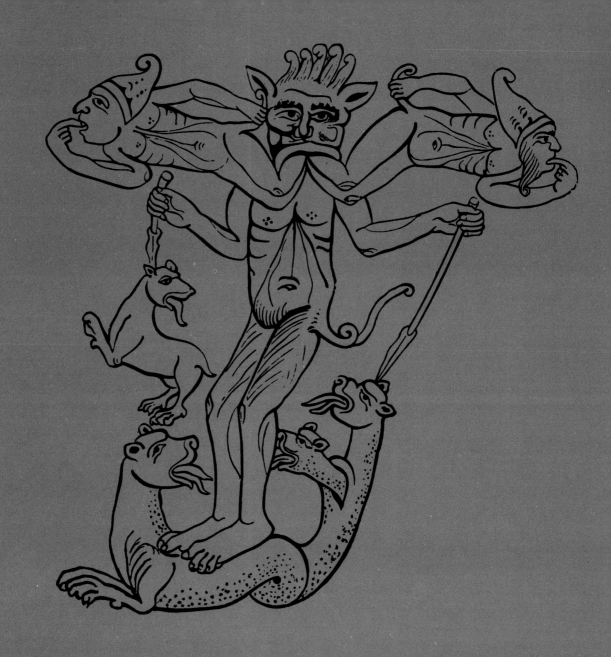

**glossary**

**acrosome**   a cap that partially covers the head of a sperm, containing enzymes needed for fusion of the sperm with the egg

**active transport**   an energy-requiring permease activity that transports molecules across cell membranes against the concentration gradient, from areas of low concentration to areas of high concentration

**adaptive radiation**   the formation of a large number of ecologically diverse species all descended from a common ancestor

**adenosine diphosphate (ADP)**   a compound associated in energy transfer in cells

**adenosine triphosphate (ATP)**   an energy-carrying molecule consisting of the sugar ribose linked to the nucleotide adenine, and three attached phosphate groups, the last two of which are linked by high-energy bonds

**adrenalin**   a hormone secreted by the adrenal medulla that prepares an animal for fight-or-flight situations

**adrenocorticotropic hormone (ACTH)**   a tropic hormone that stimulates the adrenal cortex

**aerobic**   an organism utilizing molecular oxygen

**agglutination**   the clumping of foreign cells due to the antibody–antigen reaction

**aggressive mimicry**   a form of mimicry in which a predator imitates a harmless animal in order to deceive and capture its prey

**agonistic**   a symbolic ritualized aggressive display which takes the place of fighting in a species

**albumin**   smallest of the plasma proteins; it maintains the osmotic potential of the blood

**alleles**   all of the different genes for any one character trait

**allopatric speciation**   a speciation process involving a population's division from others by a physical barrier

**$\alpha$ (alpha) helix**   a protein structure that is a right-handed corkscrew arrangement stabilized by hydrogen bonds

**alveolus**   a cell or other concavity such as milk-producing sacs in the breasts or air sacs in the lungs

**amino acid**   a compound containing a carboxyl group (−COOH), an amino group (NH$_2$) and an R group; 20 different amino acids occur naturally as protein constituents

**amniotic cavity**   a closed, fluid-filled sac that protects the developing embryo

**anaerobic**   an organism that can live without molecular oxygen

**anaphase**   the third stage of cell division, in which the two sets of daughter chromosomes migrate toward opposite poles of one spindle

**aneuploid**   a karyotype in which one or more chromosomes are represented more frequently than the others

**angiosperm**   flowering vascular plant, bearing seeds in an enclosed organ

**annulus**   part of the spore-bearing structure of some plants, consisting of a ring of cells around the edge of the sporangium which bursts open to release the ripened spores

**anther**   the part of a stamen that develops and contains pollen

**antheridium**   multicellular male reproductive organ on a plant

**antherozoid**   plant sperm cell

**antibody**   protein that combines with antigens and neutralizes toxic substances

**anticodon**   a sequence of three bases located on the transfer RNA molecule that complements the three bases, or codon, on the messenger RNA

**antigen**   molecule often located on the surface of foreign cells, with which an antibody combines to inactivate the foreign cell

**anus**   the posterior opening of the digestive canal through which wastes are eliminated from the body

**aorta**   the main artery of the body carrying blood from the left ventricle of the heart to all organs except the lungs

**aphotic layer**   the lightless bottom layer of the open sea

**appendix**   a small, fingerlike projection from the cecum, or blind pouch, in which the large intestine begins

**archegonium**   structure in seed plants that houses female reproductive cells

**archenteron**   primitive gut of an embryo

**arteriole**   small, terminal branch of an artery that ends in capillaries

**artery**   a muscular, highly elastic vessel that conducts blood away from the heart

**association**   where a secondary stimulus is repeatedly produced in close association with the sign stimulus until production of the secondary stimulus alone will produce the response originally produced by the sign stimulus

**assortive mating**   a type of nonrandom mating within a population, based on geographical and behavioral factors, that leads individuals to select mates with characteristics like their own

**atrio-ventricular (A-V) node**  node tissue located in the right atrium of the heart that receives the impulses of the S-A node and then generates impulses which spread to all parts of the ventricles, causing them to contract

**atrium**  upper chamber of the heart

**autosomes**  the chromosomes which determine traits other than sex

**autotroph**  an organism that can synthesize almost everything it requires for its metabolic processes from the simplest compounds in its environment, and that converts the energy of sunlight into the energy of chemical bonds

**auxin**  an organic substance which promotes elongation of plant shoots

**axil**  the angle between the upper side of the petiole and the stem from which it arises

**axon**  extension of a neuron which transmits impulses to nearby cells

**backcross**  the mating of an original parent with its offspring

**balanced polymorphism**  a stable proportion of homozygotes to heterozygotes for any one gene that preserves all the alleles in the gene pool

**basal body**  a structure formed by certain centrioles at the point where a cilium or flagellum attaches to a cell

**basal cells**  a single layer of cells in the epithelium located next to the basement membrane

**Batesian mimicry**  a sort of mimicry by which harmless animals imitate one or more aspects of a distasteful or poisonous species and thus avoid predation

**bile salts**  substances secreted by the liver and stored in the gall bladder serving to break down fat

**biomass**  the total weight or volume of the plant or animal oranisms in a biotic community

**biome**  the total of all biological communities interacting within a single life zone

**biota**  flora and fauna of an ecosystem

**blastocoel**  a liquid-filled cavity which forms in the center of the embryo and around which the cells become arranged in a single layer

**blastocyst**  a hollow ball of cells formed about four days after conception of an animal embryo

**blastopore**  the rim portion of a slight indentation that forms at the boundary between the gray crescent and the vegetal region of an animal embryo

**blastula**  early stage of animal development characterized by the formation of a hollow, liquid-filled cavity bounded by a single layer of cells

**Bowman's capsule**  a long microscopically thin tubule, one end of which is closed and folded into a cup-shaped receptacle in the renal cortex

**branchial heart**  an extra heart at the base of the gills that boosts the pressure as the blood passes through the constricted gill capillaries

**bronchiole**  small, thin-walled subdivision of the bronchus

**budding**  a form of asexual reproduction in which a new organism develops as an offshoot of the parent organism

**calorie**  a unit of energy; the amount of heat needed to raise the temperature of one gram of water from 14.5 to 15.5 degrees centigrade

**cambium**  a thin layer of small cells which appears brick-shaped when seen in cross section, separates the xylem and phloem of most vascular plants, gives rise to new cells, and is responsible for secondary growth

**capillaries**  an extensive network of microscopically thin tubes through whose walls nutrients, gases, and other substances are exchanged between blood and tissues

**carbohydrates**  a class of biomolecules including sugars and starches containing carbon in combination with hydrogen and oxygen in a 2-to-1 ratio

**carboxyhemoglobin**  a combination of carbon dioxide and hemoglobin

**carnivore**  meat-eating animal

**carotenoid**  yellow or red plant pigment

**carpel**  a highly modified plant megaspore

**carrying capacity**  the number of members of a population which can be supported by the environment

**Casparian strip**  a waterproof structure that bands each endodermal cell of a root

**cecum**  a blind sac loacted at the juncture of the small and large intestines

**cell cycle**  one cycle in which each newly formed cell grows, prepares for division, and then undergoes mitotic division

**cell totipotency**  retention by a mature cell of the ability to divide and give rise to other types of specialized cells

**centrioles**  hollow cylindrical structures found in animal cells generally near the nucleus and lying at right angles to one another

**centromere** a structure on each chromosome that holds the two strands, or chromatids, together

**cerebral cortex** the deeply convoluted outer covering of the forebrain; the center of logical thought, memory, and imagination

**cervix** a narrow channel plugged with mucus which permits selective passage in and out of the uterus from the vagina

**chalone** an internal secretion that inhibits growth and division in animal cells

**chelicera** anterior appendage often specialized as mouth part on arthropods

**chemosynthesis** a process as of bacteria in which the biomolecules are synthesized from inorganic constituents without using the energy of light

**chiasmata** the points of contact between chromatids during prophase I of meiosis; these are believed to be the result of crossing over

**chlorenchyma** plant cells found primarily in leaves and containing most of the chloroplasts

**chlorophyll** green photosynthetic pigment found in the chloroplasts of some bacteria and all photosynthetic plants which enables the capture of solar energy

**chorion** outer covering for the embryo of higher vertebrates

**chromatid** one of the two strands of DNA that make up the chromosome

**chromatin** thin dark threads of DNA in the cell nucleus

**chromosome** dense threadlike structure made of DNA in the cell nucleus that is the genetic information

**chyme** a semiliquid mass of partially digested food that is expelled by the stomach into the small intestine

**cilium** a short, densely packed hair-like structure that protrudes from the plasma membrane

**cisternae** large flattened bags or sacs formed by the rough endoplasmic reticulum and used to store newly synthesized proteins

**cistron** the genetic function unit, composed of sequences of codons on a DNA molecule

**cleavage** the series of mitotic divisions of the egg that change a single-celled zygote into a multicellular organism

**climax community** a biotic community that maintains long-term equilibrium with the environment and continues to reproduce itself for an indefinite length of time

**cline** a group of populations capable of interbreeding that vary in one or more traits in regular gradations from one locality to the next

**clitellum** an organ that secretes a cocoon in which the eggs of a segmented worm are laid

**cnidoblast** a cell on the tentacles of coelenterates that paralyzes prey or entangles it in a lasso-like entension

**coacervates** large molecules which may spontaneously organize themselves into structures that, though not alive, exhibit several of the properties of living systems

**codon** a nucleotide triplet in the genetic code; a different sequence of three bases on the DNA molecule represents each amino acid

**coelenteron** the central gastrovascular cavity of an organism

**coelom** an organ-containing body cavity formed of mesoderm and lined with epithelium

**coenzyme** small nonprotein molecule that acts in conjunction with the protein part of the enzyme system

**collagen** a type of thick durable connective tissue

**collenchyma** elongate thick-walled cells which lie just beneath the epidermis and furnish support to young plants

**colon** the large intestine, with the primary function of absorbing water and salts from undigested residues that pass into it from the small intestine

**colostrum** a yellow fluid secreted by the breasts for a few days after childbirth; it is rich in antibodies, proteins, minerals, and vitamin A

**columnar cell** epithelial cell, thicker than it is wide, found beneath the layer of squamous cells or in the lining of internal organs

**commensalism** a symbiotic relationship in which one species benefits, while the other is neither helped nor harmed

**condensation reaction** a reaction between two molecules that leads to bond formation; one molecule loses an H, the other an OH, so that water is a byproduct of the reaction

**cone** receptor cell in the eye which is sensitive to high intensities of light

**conjugation** the exchange of genetic material between two unicellular organisms that will later reproduce asexually

**cork cambium** a layer of cells developed in the cortex that pushes old cork cells outward as new ones are produced

**cornified layer**   a layer of cells produced by the upward flow of cells from the basal layer and made up of dead or dying cells that are continually sloughed off

**corpus luteum**   a yellowish body (once the egg-containing follicle) in the ovary that secretes estrogen and progesterone

**cortex**   in animals, the outermost portion of cytoplasm which takes the form of a viscous gell; in plants, a tissue composed of parenchyma cells and located outside the vascular bundles

**cortical reaction**   the disruption of the structural organization of the cortex, during which the cortical granules fuse with the egg plasma membrane, then rupture to release a portion of their content into the perivitelline space between the plasma membrane and the vitelline membrane which then forms a protective layer around the egg

**corticoids**   hormones secreted by the adrenal cortex; they are all steroids

**cotyledons**   seed leaves in a young plant

**coupling**   the process through which cells influence one another's differentation

**cristae**   the folds and pleats of the inner membrane of the mitochondrion

**crop**   an enlarged chamber of the gullet of an insect or bird for food storage

**cuticle**   a protective waxy surface, formed by the combination of cutin with cellulose, that covers plant epidermis and helps to relieve water loss

**cutin**   a waxy substance that accumulates on the surface wall of plant epidermal cells

**cyclic AMP (cAMP)**   compound produced in target cells as a result of hormone stimulation; the secondary messenger or mediator of hormonal function

**cytochrome**   respiratory pigment prominent in intracellular oxidations and bound to a ring very much like that found in chlorophyll but with an atom of iron replacing the magnesium atom

**cytokinesis**   the splitting of cell cytoplasm to form two new cells

**cytokinins**   the name for the group of adenine derivatives which regulate plant growth

**deletion**   a chromosomal aberration in which part of the chromosome is absent

**denaturation**   breaking the hydrogen bonds that hold a protein molecule in its characteristic three-dimensional configuration, changing the physical properties of the protein

**dendrite**   a branching cytoplasmic tendril of a neuron which receives impulses from a receptor cell or another neuron

**denitrifying bacteria**   organisms which return some of the nitrites to make nitrates

**deoxyribonucleic acid (DNA)**   nucleic acid found in cell nuclei that carries in its structure information that specifies the amino acid sequences of proteins; it is the storehouse of genetic information

**detritivore**   organism that feeds on dead plants and animal tissue

**diaphragm**   a dome-shaped muscular sheet that separates the chest and abdominal cavities

**diastema**   the gap between the incisors and the canines of the upper jaw, found in most of the primates, but not in humans

**diastole**   period of relaxation in the heartbeat cycle

**dicotyledon**   a plant with two cotyledons (seed leaves)

**differentiation**   the process by which cells and tissues of different types develop from common ancestors to perform a particular function

**diffusion**   the net movement of randomly moving particles away from areas of high concentration toward areas of low concentration

**dihybrid**   a genotype which is heterozygous for two sets of alleles

**dioecious**   type of plant that has male and female cones growing on different trees

**diploid**   having the 2n number of chromosomes, one of each pair inherited from each parent

**displacement activity**   behavior which occurs when a single stimulus provokes conflicting responses

**dorsal lip**   the animal portion of the blastopore, which marks the side of the embryo that will become the back

**duplication**   where a portion of the chromosome is repeated as a result of unequal crossing-over between two non-sister chromatids

**ecology**   the science which studies the totality of relationships between organisms and environment

**ecosystem**   an area smaller than the ecosphere which consists of organisms and the relatively self-contained environment in which they live and interact

**ectoderm**   the thick outer layer of embryonic cells that will become the nervous system, skin, and sensory organs

**elaters**   filamentous plant structure which twists about in the air with changing moisture and in so doing flicks spores into the wind

**embryogenesis**   the development of the embryo

**embryonic disc (blastoderm)**  mass of embryonic cells that group themselves to one side of the blastocoel and will become the embryo

**emigration**  the migration of individuals out of a population

**endergonic**  energy-requiring

**endocrine**  type of tissue or gland that secretes hormones that flow directly into the circulatory system

**endoderm**  the inner layer of embryonic cells that will develop into the lining of the digestive tract

**endodermis**  a cylinder of cells, one layer thick, which encloses the pericycle, forming the innermost tissue of the cortex in many roots and stems

**endoplasmic reticulum**  membranous system lined by ribosomes; serves as path of communication between interior and exterior of cell

**enzyme**  agent which enhances the rate of reactions without being altered in the process

**epidermis**  the outermost single layer of tightly-knit cells covering the entire surface of plant roots, stems, and leaves and preventing evaporation from the underlying cells

**epididymis**  a convoluted 20-foot passageway which collects spermatozoa from many smaller ducts and conducts them to the vas deferens

**epiphyte**  flowering plant that grows on other plants using them for support and often as a source of moisture and nutrients

**epistasis**  the interaction of gene pairs in which one pair completely mask the expression of genes at a different chromosomal locus

**epithelium**  tissue lining outer and inner surfaces of the body of an animal organism, composed of cells tightly packed together and interconnected by the matrix which they themselves secrete

**erythroblast**  a young red blood cell

**erythrocyte**  a mature red blood cell

**esophagus**  a long muscular tube that leads from the pharynx to the stomach

**estrogen**  female sex hormones secreted by the ovaries

**estrous cycle**  cyclic changes in the condition of the female reproductive tract and in the sexual responsiveness of the female, due to changes in the rate of secretion of gonadotropic hormones

**estuary**  place on the coastline where fresh and salt water meet and mix

**ethylene**  a hydrocarbon gas whose effect on plants is most prominent in fruit ripening

**eucaryotic**  having a fairly complex structure and defined nucleus, as the cells of unicellular organisms

**euphotic layer**  the uppermost layer of the open sea, extending downward from the surface to the limit of light, at about 650 feet

**eutrophication**  a condition of oxygen depletion, as in a lake, with the resultant buildup of undecomposed plants and the death of organisms whose survival depends on normal oxygen levels

**exergonic**  energy-yielding

**exocrine**  type of gland, such as the gall bladder, that secretes substances into tubes or ducts rather than directly into the bloodstream

**exoskeleton**  hard body covering of an arthropod that is composed of chitin and to which the muscles are attached

**facilitated diffusion**  biological process utilizing carrier molecules that transports substances across cell membranes in the direction of the concentration gradient

**fermentation**  a chemical process that proceeeds in the absence of oxygen and in which glucose is reduced to either lactic acid or ethyl alcohol

**fibrinogen**  a protein contained in plasma which is converted into fibrin when a capillary is ruptured or severed

**fibroblast**  immature connective tissue cell

**fibrous proteins**  structural protein, such as collagen, with extended polypeptide chains that do not fold back on themselves

**filtrate**  a combination of plasma and dissolved substances

**fission**  simple asexual cell division

**flagella**  relatively long and sparsely packed hair-like structures which project from the plasma membranes of a number of plant, animal, and bacterial cells

**flame-cells**  the tiny bulb-like structures in a tubular excretory system; clusters of cilia create a current that washes the tissue fluid along the branches into the main tubules and out through one of a number of excretory pores

**follicle**  a sphere of cells in which oogenesis take place in female animals

**foramen magnum**  the opening at the base of the skull through which the spinal cord is attached to the brain

**founder effect**   a form of genetic drift in which the presence of deleterious alleles in relatively high frequency is due to the nonrepresentative sample that founded an isolated population

**gametangium**   a multinucleate organ in which the haploid gametes of lower plants are developed

**gametes**   special diploid cells produced by meiosis; they fuse during sexual reproduction to form a zygote

**gametogenesis**   the formation of gametes, a process that involves meiotic division

**gametophyte**   the haploid plant that produces gametes which fuse to form a diploid zygote that will mature into a sporophyte

**gastrovascular cavity**   an interior digestive cavity with only one opening within which enzymes break down food

**gastrula**   the stage of development in which the embryo consists of a hollow cellular cup made up of two layers that meet along the line of the blastopore and enclose the gut

**gastrulation**   the developmental process during which the vegetal plate begins to invaginate, forming the archenteron, and the primary mesenchyme has formed a ring around the archenteron to produce the skeleton of the embryo

**gene**   the basic unit of heredity which produces the identifying characteristics of a species

**gene frequency**   the proportion of various alleles found in a population

**gene pool**   all of the genes of all of the gametes found in all of the individuals of a population

**genetic code**   the chemical code contained in nucleic acids that is responsible for sequencing amino acids during protein synthesis

**genetic drift**   random changes in the gene pool of a population resulting from accidents of sampling

**genotype**   the combination of expressed and unexpressed genes an individual inherits

**geotropism**   growth response of a plant to gravity

**gibberellic acid**   the compound that produces symptoms of hyperelongation in plants

**gland**   a localized aggregation of cells that secretes one or more hormones

**globular proteins**   water-soluble proteins with extensively folded polypeptide chains; enzymes and blood proteins are globular

**glomerulus**   a cluster of capillaries, enclosed in the Bowman's capsule of the kidney

**glucagon**   a hormone secreted by the pancreas that functions as an antagonist to insulin

**glycogen**   the form in which glucose is stored in the liver

**glycolysis**   the partial enzymatic breakdown of complex organic molecules without the use of oxygen, and the release of some of their free energy

**Golgi complex**   organelle that processes and repackages materials to be used in other parts of the cell or secreted extracellularly

**gonadotropic hormone**   tropic hormone that stimulates the gonads; there are two types: follicle-stimulating hormone (FSH) and luteinizing hormone (LH)

**gonads**   germ-cell producing organs

**gray crescent**   embryonic material which is crucial in determining the future pathway of development that cells will take

**guttation**   the secretion of drops of water at the ends of veins on the leaf margins

**gymnosperm**   seed plant bearing naked seeds

**habituation**   the simplest form of learning, which is a stimulus-specific waning of a response upon repeated or continuous presentation of that stimulus

**haploid**   having the 1n number of chromosomes, that is, only one chromosome of each pair

**Hardy-Weinberg principle**   hypothesis that in a large, randomly mating population, gene frequencies will remain constant generation after generation so long as no mutations occur and no phenotype has a selective advantage

**hemocoel**   large blood space in the main body cavity

**hemoglobin**   a blood protein that readily combines with oxygen; the principal component of mammalian blood cells

**herbivore**   animal that feeds on plants

**heterogametic**   having the ability to produce X chromosomes and Y chromosomes

**heterosis**   adaptive superiority of the heterozygotic form of a trait; an agent of evolutionary change

**heterothallic**   type of sexual reproduction in which the two sexes are produced on different plants

**heterotroph**   a living organism deriving its energy from the breakdown of large organic molecules which it is unable to synthesize and has to find ready-made in its environment, as from another organism

**heterozygous condition**   where an individual has two different genes for one character

**histamine**   a hormone secreted by damaged cells that causes muscles in the walls of the blood vessels to relax, promoting the flow of white cells and immunological agents to the site

**homeostasis**   the tendency of living things to maintain a constant internal environment despite outside environmental fluctuations

**homogametic**   having the ability to produce X or Y chromosomes, but not both

**homothallic**   type of sexual reproduction in which the two sexes are produced on the same plant

**homozygous condition**   where an individual has two identical genes for a character

**hormone**   an agent of intercellular chemical control

**hydrogen bond**   the attractive force between a hydrogen atom bonded to an electron-attracting atom and another atom that has unbonded electrons

**hydrolysis**   the breaking of chemical bonds by the addition of water molecules

**hyperosmotic**   a type of external medium with a higher osmotic pressure than the cell it surrounds; water flows out of the cell into the medium

**hypoglycemia**   low blood sugar, due to chronic overproduction of insulin

**hypoosmotic**   a type of external medium with a lower osmotic pressure than the cell it surrounds; water flows from the medium into the cell

**hypothalamus**   the part of the brain which controls temperature regulation

**immunity**   the ability of the body to prevent the development of a disease-causing organism, or counteract the effects of its products

**immunoglobulins**   antibodies within the plasma

**implantation**   a gradual process during which the blastocyst burrows deep into the lining of the uterus, rupturing blood vessels, and causing the mother's tissues to regroup protectively about it

**induction**   the process by which one tissue stimulates another, either near it or in contact with it, to differentiate

**inhibitors**   a variety of substances, many of which are proteins, that tend to reduce the activity of a particular enzyme

**insulin**   blood-sugar controlling hormone secreted by islets of Langerhans in the pancreas

**intercalated disc**   heavy crossband that separates individual cells of the cardiac muscle

**interphase**   the part of the cell cycle in which it is not dividing, characterized by $G_1$, S, and $G_2$ periods

**inversion**   a type of chromosomal recombination in which part of the chromosome becomes looped causing a reversal in gene sequence

**islets of Langerhans**   clusters of cells in the pancreas that secrete insulin

**isosmotic**   a type of external medium with an osmotic pressure equal to that of the cell it surrounds; there is no net movement of water into or out of the cell

**karyotype**   the set of chromosomes of a species or individual which is characteristic of its body cells

**kinetin**   the substance formed from autoclaved DNA which is highly active in promoting cell division

**lenticels**   pores on the surface of the stem which allow oxygen and carbon dioxide to penetrate through the impervious layers of the bark to the living plant cells beneath

**leucocyte**   white blood cell principally concerned with defense against harmful bacterial or viral agents

**lichen**   a fungus and an alga which can live together in symbiotic union on dry rocks, ground, and trees in a variety of improbable situations

**lignin**   a substance related to cellulose and forming a large part of the secondary layers of a cell

**limnetic region**   moderately deep region of a lake, where some light penetrates

**linked**   genes which are located on the same chromosome and which transmit their effects as a unit

**lipase**   a pancreatic enzyme that hydrolyzes fat

**lipid**   a class of biomolecules insoluble in water that do not form polymers

**littoral region**   the shallowest region in a lake, through which light penetrates all the way to the bottom

**locus**   the specific place of a gene on a specific chromosome

**loop of Henle**   U-shaped extension of the proximal tubule of the nephron

**lymphocyte**   a type of white cell within the lymph, important in the body's resistance to infection

**lysis**   the dissolving or rupturing of the cell membrane, with consequent loss of cytoplasm and cell death

**lysogeny**   viral infectious process that allows some infected cells to remain alive

**lysosome**   membranous sac within the cell which contains a large variety of hydrolytic enzymes

**madreporite**  a button-shaped sieve plate on the dorsal surface of the disc at the center of a starfish

**Malpighian tubules**  the excretory organs of insects and some other arthropods, consisting of a group of flexible tubular vessels attached to the intestinal tract

**mandibles**  mouth parts of insects, crustaceans, centipedes, and millipedes used to hold or bite food

**mantle**  a thin tissue surrounding the visceral mass in a mollusk

**matrix**  the liquid area in the mitochondrion encircled by the inner membrane and containing granules, certain enzymes used in energy-producing activities, DNA molecules, and ribosomes smaller than those found in the cytoplasm; in tissues, the intercellular substance secreted by cells

**medusa**  dispersal and feeding stage of a jellyfish

**megastrobili**  female reproductive cones

**meiosis**  a form of cell division in which a diploid parent cell produces four haploid daughter cells

**menarche**  the onset of menstruation

**menopause**  the cessation of menstruation, usually between the ages of 40 and 55

**meristematic cell**  growth cell in a plant

**mesenchyme**  embryonic connective tissue derived from mesoderm

**mesoderm**  the third and last layer of embryonic cells to develop and the one which forms the basis of many organs of the skeletal and muscular systems

**mesoglea**  an unstructured gelatinous area between the epidermis and the inner layer of the digestive cells surrounding a central sac

**metabolism**  the ability of living things to absorb, transform, and use material from their environment as a source of energy and as raw material necessary in building molecules

**metamorphosis**  a process during which the larva undergoes a major reorganization of its tissues and organs and becomes transformed into adult form

**metaphase**  the second stage of cell division, in which the chromosomes align in the equatorial plane; at the end of this stage, the centromeres divide and the chromatids separate

**micropyle**  a channel in the female plant gametophyte which reaches from the outer edge of the integument down to the nucellus

**microstrobili**  male reproductive cones

**microtubules**  long; hollow, fairly rigid tubes found in the cytoplasm of plant and animal cells

**microvilli**  microscopic projections from the layer of columnar epithelial cells that compose the surface of the villi

**migration**  the movement of individuals into or out of a population, thus altering the gene pool

**mitochondrion**  an organelle containing all the enzymes and structural components by which organic molecules can be oxidized

**mitosis**  cell division process that creates two new diploid cells, each of which has the same genetic information as the parent cell

**monocotyledon**  plant with one cotyledon (seed leaf)

**monohybrid**  an individual heterozygous for a single set of alleles

**monomer**  a small unit of molecules that can be linked together in long chains to form a polymer

**monosaccharide**  a simple sugar containing from two to seven carbon atoms in straight chains or rings

**morphogenesis**  the development of the form and structure of an organism

**morula**  a cluster of 16 to 32 proliferating embryonic cells which passes down the Fallopian tube into the more spacious uterus

**mosaic**  individuals having cells with different karyotypes

**motor neuron**  nerve cell that carries signals from the central nervous system to effectors

**mucosa**  an inner mucous membrane, found in the wall of the stomach, composed of epithelial tissue and containing many glands

**mutation**  sudden accidental changes in genetic material that produce new characteristics

**mutualism**  a symbiotic relationship in which both species benefit

**mycelium**  a mass of threadlike hyphae found in a fungus

**mycoplasma**  microorganism containing the smallest cells known which measure about 0.1 micron in diameter

**myofibril**  contractile protein fiber whose longitudinal light and dark pattern produces the striped appearance of the striated muscle cell

**natural selection**  Darwin's evolutionary theory which stated that organisms whose inherited characteristics best fit them to adapt to their environment will be most likely to produce offspring, so that eventually their characteristics will dominate the population

**nectary** a gland at the base of flower petals in which the sweet liquid nectar is secreted and stored

**nektonic** free-swimming

**nephridium** excretory organ found in many invertebrates, consisting of a tube which receives body fluids at the inner end and opens to the exterior of the body at the other end. Helps control salt and water balance

**nephron** the functional unit of the kidney

**nephrotomes** a row of pouches which are formed when the dorsal part of the mesoderm segments

**neural folds** folds of embryonic tissue which form at the edges of the neural plate, move toward one another, and meet

**neural tube** structure which is formed when the neural folds meet and fuse, and which eventually gives rise to the brain and spinal cord

**neurula stage** the period from 18 to 28 days after conception during which the critical development of the nervous system occurs

**neurulation** the period of formation of the basic structures of the animal nervous system

**niche** the place where an organism lives and the function it serves

**nicotinamide adenine dinucleotide (NAD)** coenzyme I; oxidizing–reducing coenzyme

**nicotinamide adenine dinucleotide phosphate (NADP)** coenzyme II; an oxidizing–reducing coenzyme

**node** the point on a plant where the leaf and the stem join

**nonseptate** without cross walls

**noradrenalin** a hormone secreted by the adrenal medulla that, along with adrenalin, functions in fight-or-flight situations

**notochord** a cartilage-like rod running parallel to the dorsal nerve cord, present at some stage of development in all members of phylum Chordata

**nucellus** a tissue which surrounds the multicellular female gametophyte and is equivalent to the megasporangium

**nucleic acid** an information macromolecule, a linear polymer of nucleotides

**nucleoid** in procaryotic cells (nuclear region) a region containing genetic material which has no membrane to separate it from the rest of the cellular contents, and is not organized into chromosomes

**nucleolus** spherical structure found within the nucleus which is not enclosed by a membrane and appears to be composed primarily of protein and nucleic acids

**nucleotide** a monomer consisting of a purine or pyrimidine base, a sugar, and a phosphate group linked together and that may form nucleic acids

**nurse cells** oocytes that never mature but instead surround each mature egg, apparently protecting it until it is released from the ovary

**omnivore** animal that eats both plants and meat

**oogonia** the primordial germ cells which differentiate into eggs

**ootid** the haploid product of meiotic division in female animals; will mature into an ovum

**operator site** a segment of DNA adjacent to one or more structural genes

**operculum** a flap of skin which develops to cover the gills

**operon** a unit composed of an operator site and the structural genes associated with it

**organ** a combination of tissues which may vary in type but work together as a functional unit

**organogenesis** the second phase of animal devleopment during which further growth and differentiation of already existent structures occur

**osmosis** diffusion of water molecules through a selectively permeable membrane

**osmotic potential** the potential amount of osmotic pressure that could build up on one side of a selectively permeable membrane

**osmotic pressure** the pressure exerted upon molecules in relatively high concentration on one side of a selectively permeable membrane that forces them across the membrane barrier

**ossicles** calcareous plates composing the internal skeleton of echinoderms and covered by a tough skin

**ostia** pores in an open circulatory system through which blood is returned from the coelom to the posterior end of the main blood vessel

**ovary** part of the female reproductive system; in plants, a highly modified megasporophyll folded over and sealed around the ovules; in many animals, the egg-producing organ

**ovulation** the process in which the Graafian follicle bursts, spewing the ovum and its nurse cells from the ovary

**ovule** female reproductive organ of a plant

**ovum** mature egg

**oxidation–reduction reaction** process in which electrons are transferred from one substance to another

**oxygen dissociation curve** the ability of hemoglobin to take up or release oxygen at different partial pressures, expressed in graph form

**oxyhemoglobin** a fully saturated molecule of hemoglobin carrying four oxygen molecules

**paddle stage** second phase of development of a tadpole into a frog during which the end of each limb bud flattens into a paddle-shaped structure

**palisade mesophyll** one or more layers of cylindrical cells below the upper epidermis and arranged at right angles to it

**panspermia** the theory that life arrived on earth at some early epoch in our planet's history from elsewhere in the cosmos

**parasitism** a relationship between members of two species in which one species benefits to the detriment of the other

**parathyroid** one of four pea-sized glands located on the surface of the thyroid but independent of it; it excretes the hormone parathormone, which regulates calcium–phosphate balance

**parenchyma** plant cells with thin primary walls which retain their ability to divide and in some cases to differentiate into specialized cells

**parthenogenesis** asexual reproductive process in which a new multicellular organism develops from an unfertilized egg

**pathogen** causative agent of disease

**pellicle** inner area of a unicellular organism's membranous surface coating

**pepsin** a group of enzymes that begin the digestion of protein in the stomach

**pepsinogen** an inactive secretion of the stomach that can be converted to pepsin

**peptide linkage** a form of chemical bond in which an $NH_2$ (amino) group is joined to a COOH (carboxyl) group; peptide linkages form proteins

**perichondrium** a layer of dense tissue covering the outer surface of cartilage where it is not superseded by bone

**pericycle** parenchyma cells outside the vascular tissue of a root

**perinuclear space** the space between the inner and outer membrane layers separating the nucleus from the cytoplasm

**peristalsis** contraction and relaxation of the alimentary canal

**permease** a membrane component that bonds with molecules of water-soluble substances and thus transports them across the membrane

**petal** a modified leaf covering which attracts insects to the flower after it opens

**petiole** leaf stalk

**phagocytosis** a means through which cells or one-celled organisms ingest particles of solid matter by engulfing the particle in a pseudopod, or cell extension

**pharynx** part of the upper respiratory and/or digestive tract in some invertebrates (e.g. earthworm, planarian), it is actively involved in food procurement; in other animals (e.g., humans) it serves mainly as a passageway associated with swallowing

**phenotype** the morphological characteristics, or appearance of inherited traits, in an individual

**pheromone** a chemical secreted by one individual that affects the behavior of other individuals of the same species

**phloem** vascular tissue that transports materials, particularly organic molecules, from the leaves where they were synthesized to other parts of the plant

**phospholipid** a class of lipids closely related to triglycerides in which one fatty acid is replaced by a phosphate-containing group, making the molecule highly polar

**photon** a discrete unit of energy

**photoperiodism** response of plants to the relative length of day and night

**photosynthesis** the process of converting water and carbon dioxide into sugars, starches, and oxygen, using energy from sunlight

**phototropism** growth response of a plant to light

**phyllotaxy** genetic programming that determines the pattern in which leaf primordia form

**phytoplankton** single-celled, photsynthetic marine organisms

**pineal gland** an endocrine gland located in the rear portion of the forebrain; it secretes melatonin, a hormone which stimulates changes in response to light

**pinocytosis** a transport process in which the cell membrane folds inward to form vesicles that enclose small volumes of extracellular solution; the vesicles then pinch off and move into the cell interior

**pith**   parenchyma cells inside the vascular bundles

**pituitary**   an endocrine gland (also called the hypophysis) located just below the hypothalamus; its two lobes are functionally separate

**placenta**   an organ formed within the uterus, and attached to the developing baby's body by an umbilical cord, which allows the mother's body to carry on digestive, excretory, circulatory, and respiratory functions for the immature embryo and fetus

**plasma**   the fluid element of blood, and a component of the fluid which surrounds all animal cells

**plasmodium**   a fan-shaped network of protoplasm that flows over the substrate on which it feeds, engulfing food particles

**plasmolysis**   separation of the protoplast from the cell wall and permanent wilting of the plant even after the addition of water

**plastid**   organelle in plant cells specialized as the site of synthesis

**platelet**   thrombocyte found in the mammalian blood stream that disintegrates in the neighborhood of a wound to cause clotting

**plumule**   the embryo plant shoot

**polar body**   the smaller of two cells produced during meiotic division of one primary oocyte

**polar molecule**   a molecule with a bonding arrangement that causes one end of the molecule to have a slight positive charge and the other end to have a slight negative charge

**polar nuclei**   two nuclei which move to the center of the embryo sac where they are suspended by cytoplasmic bridges at the center of a vacuole

**polymer**   a macromolecule made up of a chain of smaller molecular units (monomers) linked end to end

**polymorphic**   a type of population in which individuals differ strikingly from each other in one or more traits

**polypeptide**   a polymer consisting of amino acids joined together by peptide linkages

**polyploid**   having more than two of each type of chromosome

**polyribosome (also polysome)**   the combination of messenger RNA with more than one ribosome at a time

**polysaccharide**   a polymer consisting of linked monosaccharides; examples are starch, glycogen, and cellulose

**population**   a community of sexually interbreeding individuals in one locality

**precursor**   a type of molecule that can be rapidly changed into specific hormones when they are needed

**predation**   the feeding of one organism on another

**primary oocyte**   the germ cell in the female that undergoes meiotic division

**primary spermatocyte**   the innermost layer of cells in the testis, produced by the last division of the spermatogonia; primary spermatocytes divide again to form spermatids

**procambial strands**   lines of cells which form just below each leaf primordium and continue to differentiate as the apex grows further away from them, maturing into the vascular bundles of the stem

**procaryotic cell**   a simple cell, such as a bacterium or blue-green alga, with no distinct nucleus and no organelle

**proembryo**   a plant zygote which has gone through numerous cell divisions

**profundal region**   the deepest part of a lake to which no light penetrates

**promoter site**   the point on the DNA chain at which RNA can attach and begin transcription

**prophase**   the first stage of cell division, during which the chromosomes appear as distinct strands and the spindle begins to form

**prostaglandins**   compounds synthesized at cell membranes by the operation of hormones; they change the membrane's permeability characteristics

**protein**   a class of information-carrying biomolecules that are linear polymers of amino acids

**proximal tubule**   a tubule that extends from Bowman's capsule toward or into the medulla, and bends up again forming a loop-shaped section

**pseudocoelom**   a fluid-filled cavity that is not formed entirely out of mesoderm

**pulvinule**   an enlargement at the base of certain leaflets that functions in turgor movements

**pyloric sphincter**   a valve at the lower end of the stomach which controls the rate at which chyme enters the small intestine

**pyruvic acid**   a three-carbon compound formed during glycolysis

**radicle**   the embryo plant root

**receptacles**   stalked structures upon which the sex organs are carried in flowering plants and some others

**recombination**   the production of a new genotype when crossing over occurs during prophase in meiosis, forming new chromatids

**rectum**   the last section of the colon which serves as the final storage area for waste material

**reef**   ocean shallows which may be either the remains of islands that have been taken over and built upon by colonies of coral polyps; or sheer stretches of coral and similar organisms

**regeneration**   the process of restoring a whole limb or organ if it is lost or destroyed

**regulator gene**   a gene that produces a protein that represses, or switches off, the action of another gene

**releasers**   signals which produce a direct and immediate response in an organism

**releasing factor**   a neurosecretion that stimulates hormone production in the pituitary

**reticular fiber**   intricately woven protein that provides a durable joint between connective tissue and other types of specialized animal cell

**retinene**   the photosensitive chemical in rods and cones whose molecules are stimulated by the presence of light

**ribonucleic acid(RNA)**   a nucleic acid found primarily in the cytoplasm; it participates directly in protein synthesis

**ribosome**   spherical structure, small in size, which synthesizes enzymes and other protein used in digesting food, building and repairing the cell structure, and carrying out chemical processes through which energy is produced and made available to the cell

**rod**   receptor cell in the eye which is sensitive to low intensities of light

**rumen**   the largest of the four stomachs in the ruminant animals

**saprophytic**   feeding on dead or decaying organic matter

**sapwood**   the outer annual rings of a tree which serve for water transport

**scavenger**   animal which eats dead animal and plant remains

**Schwann cell**   specialized cell which, as it grows, wraps the nerve fiber in successive layers of myelin

**sclereids**   irregularly shaped sclerenchyma cells, granular in appearance

**sclerenchyma**   supportive cells which are dead at maturity and possess uniformly thick secondary walls strenthened by lignin

**scrotum**   sac containing the testes

**secondary oocyte**   the product of the first meiotic division of the primary oocyte

**semen**   a mixture of seminal plasma and spermatozoa, released during ejaculation

**seminal vesicles**   structure within which the millions of spermatozoa produced each day by the mature male will be stored just prior to ejaculation

**senescence**   the process of aging

**sensory neuron**   sensory nerve cell that carries signals from sensory receptors to the central nervous system

**sepal**   a modified leaf structure which forms a protective covering over the developing flower while it is in bud

**septum**   a partition or dividing membrane

**sere**   a stage in an ecological succession

**sessile**   incapable of movement

**seta**   stalk of the gametophyte in moss plants; a bristle-like appendage on the segments of annelids

**sieve tube**   series of phloem sieve cells connected by strands of cytoplasm, which serve as conducting pathways

**sign stimuli**   signals which produce a direct and immediate response in an organism

**sino-atrial (S-A) node**   node of tissue located in the right atrium of the heart that generates rhythmic electrical impulses which spread across the muscle fibers of both atria, inducing a wave of contractions

**sodium–potassium pump**   an active transport mechanism that moves sodium ions out of the cell and moves potassium ions into the cell

**somatic cells**   nonreproductive animal cells which make up all body tissues exclusive of germ cells

**somites**   segments which form near the upper part of the notochord and which later differentiate into muscle and cartilage

**sori**   group of stalked plant reproductive bodies on the lower side of the leaf

**speciation**   the process through which genetically isolated populations form new species

**species**   groups of potentially interbreeding populations that are reproductively isolated from other such groups

**spermatid**   the haploid product of meiotic division of spermatogonia; spermatids then mature into sperm

**spermatogonia**   the germ cells in the testis that undergo meiotic division

**spermatozoa**    male germ cells

**spindle fiber**    thread-like structure that guides the chromosomes through cell division

**spiracles**    rows of openings along each side of the insect's body from which the tracheae penetrate inward

**spleen**    lymphoid organ; important to disease resistance and in storage of red blood cells

**spontaneous generation**    the theory that life arises continually from nonlife

**sporangia**    structures in which spores are produced and contained

**sporophyte**    the diploid plant that produces haploid spores that will grow into the haploid plant generation

**sporulation**    form of asexual reproduction common in plants and fungi in which they form spores capable of producing new organisms without fertilization

**squamous cell**    flat, tile-like cell, found in the outer layer of the skin and in the lining of the mucous membrane

**stamen**    the male sex organ of a seed plant

**stereoisomers**    molecules that have the same molecular formula but may have one of two mirror-image structures

**steroid**    a class of lipids with molecules made up of carbon atoms interlocked into four rings to which various atomic groups may be attached

**stigma**    surface for the reception and germination of pollen at the tip of the style

**stomata**    pores which penetrate the lower epidermis on the underside of a leaf and are flanked by the guard cells

**strobili**    spore-bearing plant structures which are produced either at the tips of some of the leafy shoots, or on short side branches

**stroma**    the inner substance of the chloroplast which is analogous to the matrix of the mitochondrion and contains ribosomes and many enzymes

**style**    the extension of the ovary in the form of a column, bearing a stigma at its apex

**substrate**    the particular substance with which an enzyme is reactive

**succession**    the process in which biotic communities pass through transient stages in their evolutionary growth from simple to complex

**survivorship curve**    the number of each 1,000 born into a population that are still alive at every year between birth and the maximum life-span for the species

**symbiosis**    any close association between two or more members of different species

**sympatric speciation**    speciation that occurs in the absence of geographical barriers, due to assortive mating and selection pressure against intermediate phenotypes

**synapse**    the juncture between two neurons, or between a neuron and a muscle

**synapsis**    a pairing process of homologous chromosomes during prophase I of meiosis

**systole**    period of contraction in the heartbeat cycle

**taxis**    form of orientation in which the receptor system and the nature of the stimulus both enable the organism to receive specific directional information

**telophase**    the fourth stage of cell division, in which the daughter chromosomes arrive at opposite poles and begin to form new nuclei

**template**    the model or pattern for synthesis of acids and proteins

**teratogens**    destructive environmental prenatal influences

**test cross**    mating with one or more homozygous recessive mates to determine the genotype of the individual

**testa**    seed coat

**testis**    organ in male animals in which the gametes, or sperm, are produced

**tetrad**    a group of four chromatids that results from synapsis during prophase I of meiosis

**thorax**    central body segment of an arthropod, where wings or jointed appendages are attached

**thrombocyte**    a type of cell instrumental in blood clotting

**thyroid**    U-shaped endocrine gland in the neck that secretes the hormone thyroxin

**thyrotropic hormone (TSH)**    a tropic hormone that stimulates the thyroid gland

**thyroxin**    hormone secreted by thyroid gland that controls oxidation and energy-producing reactions

**tissue**    collection of specialized cells which are similar in both structure and function

**tonoplast**    a membrane which separates the cytoplasm of a cell

**trachea**    in vertebrates, a cartilaginous passage linking the upper respiratory tract to the bronchi and lungs; in insects, a system of respiratory ducts

**tracheids**    long xylem cells which occur in an overlapping pattern and contain tiny holes in their cell walls through which water passes

**transcription**    the formation of a molecule of messenger RNA using a strand of chromosomal DNA as a template

**transduction**   a beneficial result of lysogeny that makes possible the exchange of genetic information within bacterial populations

**transformer**   organism that converts simple compounds produced by decomposers into forms which can be used again by plants in the production of food

**translation**   the synthesis of an amino acid chain from information coded in a molecule of messenger RNA

**translocation**   a chromosomal aberration in which a major part of one chromosome has become attached to the nonhomologous chromosome

**transpiration**   the loss of water vapor from the leaf

**trichocysts**   bottle-shaped organelles in unicellular organisms that discharge a sticky toxic substance

**triglyceride**   a compound formed by a condensation reaction, linking a molecule of glycerol with three fatty acid molecules

**trophic level**   a group of organisms with similar patterns of nourishment that share the same position in the food chain

**tropic hormone**   a hormone that has no direct physiological action but instead stimulates the action of other endocrine glands

**tropism**   growth response of a plant to a unidirectional stimulus

**trypsin**   enzyme secreted by the pancreas that helps to complete protein digestion in the small intestine

**turgor pressure**   a force which builds up in plant cells when water enters the vacuoles and creates pressure against the relatively inelastic cell wall

**urea**   a nontoxic substance into which ammonia is converted by many terrestrial vertebrates for temporary storage, until it is excreted in the urine

**ureter**   organ in the excretory system that carries urine from the kidney to the bladder where it is stored

**urethra**   a passageway in the penis through which semen is ejaculated from the body

**uric acid**   a solid, crystalline nitrogen compound excreted by birds, insects, and most reptiles which is insoluble in water, and does not build up in the body

**uterus**   structure within the female body in which an embryo grows and develops

**vacuole**   a storage space in the cell which serves as a reservoir for water and other substances

**vagina**   flexible, tubular structure which serves as an opening to the inside of the female body

**vascular bundle**   part of the dicotyledonous stem containing xylem and phloem, which constitute the chief means of transport, and the vascular cambium, separating the xylem and phloem

**vas deferens**   a canal which leads to the seminal vesicles

**vasectomy**   a relatively simple sterilization procedure for males in which small incisions are made on either side of the scrotum, the vas deferens from each testicle is tied in two places, and the part in between is cut out

**vegetal hemisphere**   the half of an embryonic egg which contains most of the yolk

**vegetal plate**   an embryonic structure formed by the flattening of cells at the vegetal pole

**vegetal pole**   the point on the surface of the egg opposite from that nearest to the nucleus

**ventral lip**   the vegetal rim of the blastopore, inside which a second region of mesoderm forms

**ventricle**   lower chamber of the heart

**vesicles**   any small membranous cavity; in particular, a small pouch pinched off from extensions of the rough endoplasmic reticulum and containing the newly synthesized proteins

**villi**   finger-like projections

**virion**   a unit of viral nucleic acid wrapped in a protein coat

**vitamins**   organic compounds which are required in the diet in minute amounts and classed together on the basis of their similar physiological functions

**vitelline membrane**   a protective layer which forms around the egg, and later become the fertilization membrane

**xylem**   vascular tissue that transports water and minerals from the ground throught the plant

**yolk**   large reserves of lipids, carbohydrates, and proteins which the oocyte accumulates and stockpiles as it grows prior to fertilization

**zona pellucida**   the outer capsule of the ovum

**zoospores**   flagellated motile spores

**zygote**   product of the fusion of male and female gametes; a fertilized egg

bibliography

## Cellular level

Ardrey, R., *African Genesis*. New York: Atheneum, 1961.

Arey, L. B., *Human Histology,* 3rd ed. Philadelphia: Saunders, 1968.

Arnon, D. I., "The Role of Light in Photosynthesis." *Scientific American,* 1960.

Baker, J. J. W., and G. E. Allen, *Matter, Energy, and Life,* 2nd ed. Reading, Mass: Addison-Wesley, 1970.

Bassham, J. A., "The Path of Carbon in Photosynthesis." *Scientific American,* 1962.

Bloom, W., and D. W. Fawcett, *A Textbook of Histology,* 9th ed. Philadelphia: Saunders, 1968.

Brachet, J., and A. E. Mirsky, eds., *The Cell,* Vol. 2. New York: Academic Press, 1961.

Calvin, M., and J. A. Bassham, *The Photosynthesis of Carbon Compounds*. New York: Benjamin, 1962.

Changeux, J. P., "The Control of Biochemical Reactions." *Scientific American,* 1965.

*Cold Spring Harbor Symposia on Quantitative Biology, 26. Cellular Regulatory Mechanisms*. Cold Spring Harbor, L.I., New York, 1961

Darwin, C., *The Origin of Species*. Variorum ed. Philadelphia: University of Pennsylvania Press, 1959.

DeRobertis, E. D. P., W. W. Nowinski, and F. A. Saez, *Cell Biology,* 5th ed. Philadelphia: Saunders, 1970.

Dickerson, R. E., and I. Geis, *The Structure and Action of Proteins*. New York: Harper & Row, 1969.

Dobzhansky, T., *Genetics and the Origin of Species,* 3rd ed. New York: Columbia University Press, 1951.

Dose, K., S. W. Fox, G. A. Deborin, and T. E. Pavlovskaya, eds., *The Origin of Life and Evolutionary Biochemistry*. New York: Plenum Press, 1974.

Dulbecco, R., "The Induction of Cancer by Viruses." *Scientific American,* 1967.

Du Praw, E. J., *Cell and Molecular Biology*. New York: Academic Press, 1970.

Eames, A. J., and L. H. MacDaniels, *An Introduction to Plant Anatomy,* 2nd ed. New York: McGraw-Hill, 1947.

Ebert, J., *Interacting Systems in Development*. New York: Holt, Rinehart & Winston, 1965.

Eiseley, L., *Darwin's Century*. Garden City, N.Y.: Doubleday, 1961.

Esau, K., *Plant Anatomy,* 2nd ed. New York: Wiley, 1965.

Fox, S. W., ed., *The Origins of Prebiological Systems*. New York: Academic Press, 1965.

Fruton, J. S., *Molecules and Life*. New York: Wiley, 1972.

Greep, Roy O. and Leon Weiss, *Histology,* 3rd ed. New York: McGraw-Hill Book Company, 1973.

Haldane, J. B. S., "The Origin of Life," *The Rationalist Annual*. London: 1929.

Hokin, L. E., and M. R. Hokin, "The Chemistry of Cell Membranes." *Scientific American,* 1965.

Holter, H., "How Things Get into Cells." *Scientific American,* 1961.

Jensen, W. A., *The Plant Cell,* 2nd ed. Belmont, Calif.: Wadsworth, 1970.

Jensen, W. A., and R. B. Park, *Cell Ultrastructure*. Belmont, Calif.: Wadsworth, 1967.

Kendrew, J. C., "The Three-Dimensional Structure of a Protein Molecule." *Scientific American,* 1961.

Lack, D., "Darwin's Finches." *Scientific American,* 1953.

Lehninger, A. L., *Biochemistry*. New York: Worth, 1970.

Lehninger, A. L., *Bioenergetics,* 2nd ed. New York: Benjamin, 1971.

Lehninger, A. L., "How Cells Transform Energy." *Scientific American,* 1961.

Lehninger, A. L., *The Mitochondrion: Molecular Basis of Structure and Function*. New York: Benjamin, 1964.

Levine, R. P., "The Mechanism of Photosynthesis." *Scientific American,* 1969.

Loewy, A. G., and P. Siekevitz, *Cell Structure and Function,* 2nd ed. New York: Holt, Rinehart & Winston, 1969.

Oparin, A. I., "The Origin of Life." Moscow, 1924.

Rabinowitch, E. I., "Photosynthesis." *Scientific American,* 1948.

Rabinowitch, E. I., and Govindjee, "The Role of Chlorophyll in Photosynthesis." *Scientific American,* 1965.

Roberts, J. D., "Organic Chemical Reactions." *Scientific American,* 1957.

Robertson, J. D., "The Membrane of the Living Cell." *Scientific American, 1962.*

Romer, A. S., *Vertebrate Paleontology.* Chicago: University of Chicago Press, 1966.

Singer, S. J., and Garth L. Nicolson, "The Fluid Mosaic Model of the Structure of Cell Membranes." *Science* 175:720–730, 1972.

Solomon, A. K., "Pores in the Cell Membrane." *Scientific American,* 1960.

Stern, H., and D. L. Nanney, *The Biology of Cells.* New York: Wiley, 1965.

Swanson, C. P., *The Cell,* 3rd ed. Englewood Cliffs, N.J.: Prentice-Hall, 1969.

Waddington, C. H., *The Nature of Life.* London: Allen & Unwin, 1961.

Wald, G., "The Origin of Life," in *The Physics and Chemistry of Life*, eds. *Scientific American.* New York: Simon & Schuster, 1955.

Wald, George, "The Origins of Life," *The Scientific Endeavor.* New York: Rockefeller University Press, 1964.

## Continuity of Life

Beadle, G., and M., *The Language of Life.* New York, Doubleday, 1967.

Carlson, E. A., *The Gene: A Critical History.* Philadelphia: Saunders, 1966.

DeRobertis, E. D. P., W. W. Nowinski, and F. A. Saez, *Cell Biology,* 5th ed., Philadelphia: Saunders, 1970.

DuPraw, E. J., *Cell and Molecular Biology.* New York: Academic Press, 1968.

DuPraw, E. J., *DNA and Chromosomes.* New York: Holt, Rinehart & Winston, 1970.

Edgar, R. S., and R. H. Epstein, "The Genetics of a Bacterial Virus." *Scientific American,* 1965.

Jacob, F., and E. L. Wollman, "Viruses and Genes." *Scientific American,* 1961.

Kudo, R. R., *Protozoology,* 5th ed. Springfield, Ill.: Thomas, 1966.

Levine, R. P., *Genetics,* 2nd ed. New York: Holt, Rinehart & Winston, 1968.

Mazia, D., "Cell Division." *Scientific American,* 1953.

Mazia, D., "How Cells Divide." *Scientific American,* 1961.

Moody, P. A., *Genetics of Man.* New York: Norton, 1967.

Moore, J. A., *Heredity and Development.* New York: Oxford University Press, 1963.

Morowitz, H. J., and M. E. Tourtellotte, "The Smallest Living Cells." *Scientific American,* 1962.

Peters, J. A., ed., *Classic Papers in Genetics.* Englewood Cliffs, N.J.: Prentice-Hall, 1959.

Ptashne, M., and W. Gilbert, "Genetic Repressors." *Scientific American,* 1970.

Srb, A. M., R. D. Owen, and R. S. Edgar, *General Genetics.* San Francisco: Freeman, 1965.

Stent, G. S., *Molecular Genetics.* San Francisco: Freeman, 1971.

Stern, C., *Principles of Human Genetics.* 2nd ed. San Francisco: Freeman, 1960.

Strickberger, Monroe W., *Genetics.* New York: Macmillan, 1968.

Sturtevant, A. H., *A History of Genetics.* New York: Harper & Row, 1965.

Watson, J. D., *The Double Helix.* New York: Atheneum, 1968.

Watson, J. D., *Molecular Biology of the Gene,* 2nd ed. New York: Benjamin, 1970.

## Organismic Level

Alexopoulos, C. J., *Introductory Mycology.* New York: Wiley, 1962.

Andrews, H. N., *Ancient Plants and the World They Lived In.* Ithaca, N.Y.: Comstock, 1947.

Andrews, H. N., *Studies in Paleobotany.* New York: Wiley, 1961.

Barnes, R. D., *Invertebrate Zoology,* 2nd ed. Philadelphia: Saunders, 1968.

Bold, H. C., *Morphology of Plants,* 2nd ed. New York: Harper & Row, 1967.

Bold, H. C., *The Plant Kingdom,* 3rd ed. Englewood Cliffs, N.J.: Prentice-Hall, 1970.

Bonner, J. T., *The Cellular Slime Molds.* Princeton, N.J.: Princeton University Press, 1959.

Bonner, J. T., "Differentiation in Social Amoebae." *Scientific American,* 1959.

Bonner, J. T., "The Growth of Mushrooms." *Scientific American,* 1956.

Bonner, J. T., "Hormones in Social Amoebae and Mammals." *Scientific American,* 1969.

Bonner, J. T., "How Slime Molds Communicate." *Scientific American,* 1963.

Braude, A. I., "Bacterial Endotoxins," *Scientific American,* 1964.

Buchsbaum, R., *Animals Without Backbones,* 2nd ed. Chicago: University of Chicago Press, 1948.

Buchsbaum, R., and L. J. Milne, *The Lower Animals: Living Invertebrates of the World.* Garden City, N.Y.: Doubleday, 1960.

Chapman, V. J., *The Algae.* New York: St. Martin's Press, 1962.

Christensen, C. M., *The Molds and Man,* 3rd ed. Minneapolis: University of Minnesota Press, 1965.

Cochran, D. M., *Living Amphibians of the World.* Garden City, N.Y.: Doubleday, 1961.

DeKruif, P., *Microbe Hunters,* New York: Harcourt, Brace, 1926.

Delevoryas, T., *Morphology and Evolution of Fossil Plants.* New York: Holt, Rinehart & Winston, 1962.

Dulbecco, R., "The Induction of Cancer by Viruses." *Scientific American,* 1967.

Eames, A. J., *Morphology of the Angiosperms.* New York: McGraw-Hill, 1961.

Easton, W. H., *Invertebrate Paleontology.* New York: Harper & Row, 1960.

Emerson, R., "Molds and Men." *Scientific American,* 1952.

Esau, K., *Anatomy of Seed Plants,* 2nd ed. New York: Wiley, 1965.

Foster, A. F., and E. M. Gifford, *Comparative Morphology of Vascular Plants.* San Francisco: Freeman, 1959.

Fritsch, F. E., *The Structure and Reproduction of the Algae,* 2 Vols. New York: Cambridge University Press, 1945.

Gilliard, E. T., *Living Birds of the World.* Garden City, N.Y.: Doubleday, 1958.

Grant, V., "The Fertilization of Flowers." *Scientific American,* 1951.

Hanson, E. D., Animal Diversity, 2nd ed. Englewood Cliffs, N.J.: Prentice-Hall, 1964.

Herald, E. S., *Living Fishes of the World.* Garden City, N.Y.: Doubleday, 1961.

Hotchkiss, R. D., and E. Weiss, "Transformed Bacteria." *Scientific American,* 1956.

Hyman, L. H., *The Invertebrates,* Vols. 1–6. New York: McGraw-Hill, 1940–1967.

Imms, A.D., *A General Textbook of Entomology,* 9th ed. London: Methuen, 1957.

Klots, A. B., and E. B. Klots, *Living Insects of the World.* Garden City, N.Y.: Doubleday, 1959.

Lagler, K. F., J. E. Bardach, and R. R. Miller, *Ichthyology.* New York: Wiley, 1967.

Lamb, I. M., "Lichens." *Scientific American,* 1959.

Luria, S. E., and J. E. Darnell, *General Virology.* New York: Wiley, 1967.

Mendel, G., *Experiments in Plant Hybridisation.* Cambridge, Mass: Harvard University Press, 1948.

Romer, A.S., *The Vertebrate Body,* 4th ed. Philadelphia: Saunders, 1970.

Romer, A. S., *Vertebrate Paleontology,* 3rd ed. Chicago: University of Chicago Press, 1966.

Sanderson, I. T., *Living Mammals of the World.* Garden City, N.Y.: Doubleday, 1955.

Scagel, R. F., *et al.*, *An Evolutionary Survey of the Plant Kingdom.* Belmont, Calif.: Wadsworth, 1965.

Schmidt, K. P., and R. F. Inger, *Living Reptiles of the World.* Garden City, N.Y.: Doubleday, 1957.

Sistrom, W. R., *Microbial Life,* 2nd ed. New York: Holt, Rinehart & Winston, 1969.

Smith, G. M., *Cryptogamic Botany,* 2nd ed., Vols. 1 and 2. New York: McGraw-Hill, 1955.

Stanier, R. Y., M. Doudoroff, and E. A. Adelberg, *The Microbial World,* 3rd ed. Englewood Cliffs, N.J.: Prentice-Hall, 1970.

Storer, T. I., and R. L. Usinger, *General Zoology,* 4th ed. New York: McGraw-Hill, 1965.

Van Tyne, J., and A. J. Berger, *Fundamentals of Ornithology.* New York: Wiley, 1959.

Villee, C. A., W. F. Walker, and F. E. Smith, *General Zoology,* 3rd ed. Philadelphia: Saunders, 1968.

Weisz, P. B., *The Science of Zoology.* New York: McGraw-Hill, 1966.

Welty, J. C., The Life of Birds. Philadelphia: Saunders, 1962.

Young, J. Z., *The Life of Mammals.* New York: Oxford University Press, 1957.

Young, J. Z., *The Life of Vertebrates,* 2nd ed. New York: Oxford University Press, 1962.

Zinsser, H., *Rats, Lice and History.* Boston: Little, Brown, 1935.

## Life Functions

Amoore, J. E., *Molecular Basis of Odor.* Springfield, Ill.: Thomas, 1970.

Amoore, J. E., J. W. Johnston, and M. Rubin, "The Stereochemical Theory of Odor," *Scientific American,* 1964.

Baker, P. F., "The Nerve Axon." *Scientific American,* 1966.

Best, C. H., and N. B. Taylor, *The Human Body; Its Anatomy and Physiology,* 4th ed. New York: Holt, Rinehart & Winston, 1963.

Best, C.H., and N. B. Taylor, *The Physiological Basis of Medical Practice,* 8th ed. Baltimore: Williams & Wilkins, 1966.

Bloom, W., and D. W. Fawcett, *A Textbook of Histology,* 9th ed. Philadelphia: Saunders, 1968.

Bonner, J., and J. E. Varner, *Plant Biochemistry,* 2nd ed. New York: Academic Press, 1973.

Bower, T. G. R., "The Object in the World of the Infant." *Scientific American,* 1971.

Boycott, B. B., "Learning in the Octopus." *Scientific American,* 1965.

Buvat, R., *Plant Cells.* New York: McGraw-Hill, 1969.

Cannon, W. B., *Bodily Changes in Pain, Hunger, Fear, and Rage.* New York: Appleton-Century-Crofts, 1st ed. 1915, 2nd ed. 1929.

Chaffee, Ellen E., and Esther M. Greisheimer, *Basic Physiology and Anatomy,* 2nd ed. Philadelphia: J. B. Lippincott Company, 1969.

Clowes, F. A. L., and B. E. Juniper, *Plant Cells.* Blackwell, 1968.

Colligan, D., "That Helpless Feeling: The Dangers of Stress." *New York Magazine,* July 14, 1975.

Devlin, R. M., *Plant Physiology,* 2nd ed. New York: Van Nostrand Reinhold, 1969.

DiCara, L. V., "Learning in the Autonomic Nervous System." *Scientific American,* 1970.

Dohrenwend, B. S., and B. P. Dohrenwend, eds., *Stressful Life Events: Their Nature and Effects.* New York: Wiley Interscience, 1974.

Eastin, J. D., *et. al., Physiological Aspects of Crop Yield.* American Society of Agronomy, 1969.

Eccles, J. C., "The Physiology of Imagination." *Scientific American,* 1958.

Eccles, J. C., *The Physiology of Nerve Cells.* Baltimore: Johns Hopkins Press, 1957.

Eccles, J. C., *The Physiology of Synapses.* New York: Academic Press, 1963.

Eccles, J. C., "The Synapse." *Scientific American,* 1965.

Gazzaniga, M. S., "The Split Brain in Man." *Scientific American,* 1967.

Gunderson, E. K. E., and R. H. Rahe, eds., *Life Stress and Illness*. Springfield, Ill.: Thomas, 1974.

Guyton, A. C., *Function of the Human Body*. Philadelphia: Saunders, 1969.

Held, R., "Plasticity in Sensory-Motor Systems," *Scientific American,* 1965.

Hodgkin, A. L. "The Ionic Basis of Nervous Conduction." *Science,* 1964.

Hubel, D. H., "The Visual Cortex of the Brain." *Scientific American,* 1963.

Kandel, E. R., "Nerve Cells and Behavior." *Scientific American,* 1970.

Katz, B., "How Cells Communicate." *Scientific American,* 1961.

Katz, B., *Nerve, Muscle, and Synapse*. New York: McGraw-Hill, 1966.

Kennedy, D., "Inhibition in Visual Systems." *Scientific American,* 1963.

Kennedy, D., "Small Systems of Nerve Cells." *Scientific American,* 1967.

Keynes, R. D., "The Nerve Impulse and the Squid." *Scientific American,* 1958.

Kramer, P. J., *Plant and Soil Water Relationships: A Modern Synthesis*. New York: McGraw-Hill, 1969.

Levitt, J., *Introduction to Plant Physiology*. St. Louis: Mosby, 1969.

Loewenstein, W. R., "Biological Transducers." *Scientific American,* 1960.

Menaker, M., "Nonvisual Light Reception." *Scientific American,* 1972.

Miller, W. H., F. Ratliff, and H. K. Hartline, "How Cells Receive Stimuli." *Scientific American,* 1961.

Muntz, W. R. A., "Vision in Frogs." *Scientific American,* 1964.

Nobel, P. S., *Plant Cell Physiology*. San Francisco: Freeman, 1970.

Penfield, W., and T. Rasmussen, *The Cerebral Cortex of Man*. New York: Macmillan, 1950.

Pritchard, R. M., "Stabilized Images on the Retina." *Scientific American,* 1961.

Prosser, C. L., and F. A. Brown, *Comparative Animal Physiology,* 2nd ed. Philadelphia: Saunders, 1961.

Ruston, W. A. H., "Visual Pigments in Man." *Scientific American,* 1962.

Salisbury, F., and C. Ross, *Plant Physiology*. Belmont, Ca.: Wadsworth, 1969.

Seligman, M. E. P., *Helplessness: On Depression, Development, and Death*. San Francisco: Freeman, 1975.

Selye, H., *The Stress of Life*. New York: McGraw-Hill, 1956.

Sperry, R. W., "The Great Cerebral Commissure." *Scientific American,* 1964.

Sperry, R. W., "The Growth of Nerve Circuits." *Scientific American,* 1959.

Street, H. E., and H. Opik, *The Physiology of Flowering Plants*. New York: American Elsevier, 1970.

Weiss, J. M., "Effects of Coping Response on Stress." *Journal of Comparative and Physiological Psychology, 65,* 1968.

Witham, F. H., D. F. Blaydes, and R. M. Devlin, *Experiments in Plant Physiology*. New York: Van Nostrand Reinhold, 1971.

Woolbridge, D. E., *The Machinery of the Brain*. New York: McGraw-Hill, 1963.

## Development of organisms

Abler, R., J. S. Adams, and P. Gould, *Spatial Organization*. Englewood Cliffs, N.J.: Prentice-Hall, 1971.

Alston, R. E., and B. Turner, *Biochemical Systematics*. Englewood Cliffs, N.J.: Prentice-Hall, 1963.

Audus, L. J., *Plant Growth Substances,* 2nd ed. London: Leonard Hill, 1959.

Balinsky, B. P., *An Introduction to Embryology*. Philadelphia: Saunders, 1968.

Barth, L. G., *Embryology*. Philadelphia: Dryden Press, 1953.

Berrill, N. J., *Developmental Biology*. New York: McGraw-Hill, 1971.

Best, C. H., and N. B. Taylor, *The Physiological Basis of Medical Practice,* 8th ed. (See esp. Chapters 74–78.) Baltimore: Williams & Wilkins, 1966.

Blackwelder, R. E., *Classification of the Animal Kingdom.* Carbondale, Ill.: Southern Illinois University Press, 1963.

Blackwelder, R. E., *Taxonomy: A Text and Reference Book.* New York: Wiley, 1967.

Butler, W. L., and R. J. Downs, "Light and Plant Development." *Scientific American,* 1960.

Csapo, A., "Progesterone." *Scientific American,* 1968.

Cutter, E. G., *Plant Anatomy: Experiment and Interpretation—Part II, Organs.* Reading, Mass.: Addison-Wesley, 1971.

DeHaan, R. L., and H. Ursprung, *Organogenesis.* New York: Holt, Rinehart & Winston, 1965.

Galston, A. W., and P. J. Davies, *Control Mechanisms in Plant Development.* Englewood Cliffs, N.J.:Prentice-Hall, 1970.

Levey, R. H., "The Thymus Hormone." *Scientific American,* 1964.

Mayr, E., *Animal Species and Evolution.* Cambridge, Mass.: Harvard University Press (Belknap Press), 1963.

Mayr, E., *Principles of Systematic Zoology.* New York: McGraw-Hill, 1969.

Mayr, E., *Systematics and the Origin of Species.* New York: Dover, 1942.

Phillips, I. D. J., *Introduction to the Biochemistry and Physiology of Plant Growth Hormones.* New York: McGraw-Hill, 1971.

Pincus, G., and K. V. Thimann, eds., *The Hormones,* 4 Vols. New York: Academic Press, 1948–1964.

Rasmussen, H., "The Parathyroid Hormone." *Scientific American,* 1961.

Raven, D. P., *Oogenesis: The Storage of Developmental Information.* New York: Pergamon Press, 1961.

Raven, C. R., *An Outline of Developmental Physiology.* Oxford: Pergamon Press, 1959.

Salisbury, F. B., *The Flowering Process.* Oxford: Pergamon Press, 1963.

Salisbury, F. B., and R. V. Parke, *Vascular Plants: Form and Function.* (See esp. Chapters 8, 14–18.) Belmont, Calif.: Wadsworth, 1964.

Simpson, G. G., *Principles of Animal Taxonomy.* New York: Columbia University Press, 1961.

Steeves, T. A., and I. M. Sussex, *Patterns in Plant Development.* Englewood Cliffs, N.J.: Prentice-Hall, 1972.

Steward, F. C., "The Control of Growth in Plant Cells." *Scientific American,* 1963.

Steward, F. C., and A. D. Krikorian, *Plants,Chemicals and Growth.* New York: Academic Press, 1971.

Sussex, I. M., and J. D. Ebert, *Interacting Systems in Development.* New York: Holt, Rinehart & Winston, 1970.

Torrey, T. W., *Morphogenesis of the Vertebrates.* New York: Wiley, 1962.

Waddington, C. H., *Principles of Embryology.* New York: Macmillan, 1962.

Wareing, P. F., and I. D. J. Phillips, *The Control of Growth and Differentiation in Plants.* New York: Pergamon, 1970.

Weiss, P., *Principles of Development.* New York: Hafner, 1969.

Wilkins, M. B., *The Physiology of Plant Growth and Development.* New York: McGraw-Hill, 1969.

Williams, C. M., "The Metamorphosis of Insects." *Scientific American,* 1950.

Wolff, E., *Tissue Interactions during Organogenesis.* New York: Gordon and Breach, 1970.

Wurtman, R. J., and J. Axelrod, "The Pineal Gland." *Scientific American,* 1965.

## Evolution and survival

Andrewartha, H. G., *Introduction to the Study of Animal Populations.* Chicago: University of Chicago Press, 1970.

Andrewartha, H. G., and L. C. Birch, *The Distribution and Abundance of Animals.* Chicago: University of Chicago Press, 1954.

Ardrey, R., *The Social Contract.* New York: Atheneum, 1970.

Ardrey, R., *The Territorial Imperative*. New York: Atheneum, 1966.

Armstrong, E. A., *Bird Display and Behaviour*. New York: Dover, 1965.

Aschoff, J., ed., *Circadian Clocks*. Amsterdam: North Holland Publishing Co., 1965.

Barghoorn, E. S., and J. W. Schopf, "Microorganisms Three Billion Years Old From the Precambrian of South Africa." *Science 152*, 1966.

Bullock, T. H., "Physiological Bases of Behavior," in J. A. Moore; ed., *Ideas in Evolution and Behavior*. Garden City, N.Y.: Natural History Press, 1970.

Campbell, B., *Human Evolution: An Introduction to Man's Adaptations*. Chicago: Aldine, 1966.

Cavalli-Sforza, Luigi Luca, "Genetic Drift in an Italian Population." *Scientific American*, 1969.

Clark, W. E. LeGros, *History of the Primates*, Chicago: University of Chicago Press (Phoenix Books edition), 1963.

*Cold Spring Harbor Symposia on Quantitative Biology: Biological Clocks*. Cold Spring Harbor, N.Y.: The Biological Laboratory, 1960.

*Cold Spring Harbor Symposia on Quantitative Biology No. 20, Population Genetics: The Nature and Causes of Genetic Variability in Populations*. Cold Spring Harbor, N.Y.: The Biological Laboratory, 1955.

Darling, F. F., *A Herd of Red Deer*. New York: Oxford University Press, 1937.

Darwin, C., *The Origin of Species and the Descent of Man*. New York: Modern Library, 1948.

Dethier, V. G., and E. Stellar, *Animal Behavior*, 3rd ed. Englewood Cliffs, N.J.: Prentice-Hall, 1970.;

Dilger, W. C., "The Behavior of Lovebirds." *Scientific American*, 1962.

Dobzhansky, T., *Genetics and the Origin of Species*, 3rd ed. New York: Columbia University Press, 1951.

Dobzhansky, T., *et al.*, *Evolutionary Biology*. New York: Appleton-Century-Crofts, 1968.

Dodson, E. O., *Evolution, Process and Product*. New York: Reinhold, 1960.

Eckhardt, Robert B., "Population Genetics and Human Origins." *Scientific American*, 1972.

Ehrlich, P. R., and R. W. Holm, *The Process of Evolution*. New York: McGraw-Hill, 1963.

Eibl-Eibesfeldt, I., *Ethology: The Biology of Behavior*. New York: Holt, Rinehart & Winston, 1970.

Eibl-Eibesfeldt, I., "The Fighting Behavior of Animals." *Scientific American*, 1961.

Eiseley, L. C., "Charles Darwin." *Scientific American*, 1956.

Etkin, W., ed., *Social Behavior and Organization Among Vertebrates*. Chicago: University of Chicago Press, 1964.

Ford, E. B., *Ecological Genetics*, 3rd ed. New York: Barnes & Noble, 1970.

Fraenkel, Gottfried S., and Donald L. Gunn, *The Orientation of Animals*, New York: Dover Publications, Inc., 1961.

Frisch, K. von, *Bees: Their Vision, Chemical Senses, and Language*, rev.ed. Ithaca, N.Y.: Cornell University Press, 1971.

Goldsby, R. A. *Race and Races*. New York: Macmillan, 1971.

Grant, V., "The Fertilization of Flowers." *Scientific American*, 1951.

Grant, V., *The Origin of Adaptations*. New York: Columbia University Press, 1963.

Grant, V., *Plant Speciation*. New York: Columbia University Press, 1971.

Griffin, D. R., *Bird Migration*. Garden City, N.Y.: Natural History Press, 1964.

Hinde, R. A., *Animal Behavior*, 2nd ed. New York: McGraw-Hill, 1970.

Holst, E. von, and U. von Saint Paul, "Ele ctrically Controlled Behavior," *Scientific American*, 1962.

Jacobson, M., and M. Beroza, "Insect Attractants." *Scientific American*, 1964.

Jolly, Clifford J., "The Seed-Eaters: A New Model of Hominid Differentiation Based on a Baboon Analogy," *Man*, Vol. 5, No 1, p 5–26, 1970.

Kettlewell, H. B. D. "Darwin's Missing Evidence." *Scientific American*, 1959.

Kikkawa, Jiro, and Malcolm J. Thorne, *The Behavior of Animals*. New York: New American Library, Plume Books, 1971.

Klopfer, P. H., *Behavioral Aspects of Ecology,* 2nd ed. Englewood Cliffs, N. J.: Prentice-Hall, 1973.

Klopfer, P.H., and J. P. Hailman, *An Introduction to Animal Behavior; Ethology's First Half Century.* Englewood Cliffs, N. J.: Prentice-Hall, 1967.

Lack, D., *Darwin's Finches.* New York: Cambridge University Press, 1947.

Lack, D., "Darwin's Finches." *Scientific American,* 1953.

Lasker, Gabriel Ward, *Physical Anthropology.* New York: Holt, Rinehart & Winston, 1961.

Lehrman, D. S., "The Reproductive Behavior of Ring Doves." *Scientific American,* 1964.

Lehrman, D. S., R. A. Hinde, and E. Shaw, *Advances in the Study of Behavior,* 3 Vols. New York: Academic Press, 1970.

Leibowitz, "Perspectives on the Evolution of Sex Differences," in *Toward an Anthropology of Women,* Rayna Reiter, ed. New York: Monthly Review Press, 1975.

Lindauer, M., *Communication Among Social Bees,* 3rd printing. Cambridge, Mass.: Harvard University Press, 1971.

Lorenz, K., *Evolution and Modification of Behavior.* Chicago: University of Chicago Press, 1967.

Lorenz, K. Z., "The Evolution of Behavior." *Scientific American,* 1958.

Lorenz, K. Z., *King Solomon's Ring.* New York: Crowell, 1952.

Lorenz, K. Z., *On Aggression.* New York: Harcourt, Brace & World, 1966.

Luce, G.G., and J. Segal, *Sleep.* New York: Coward-McCann, 1966.

Maier, R. A., and B. M. Maier, *Comparative Animal Behavior.* Monterey, Calif.: Brooks/Cole, 1970.

Maier, N. R. F., and T. C. Schneirla, *Principles of Animal Psychology.* New York: Dover, 1964.

Manning, A., *An Introduction to Animal Behavior,* Reading, Mass.: Addison-Wesley, 1967.

Marler, P. R., and W. J. Hamilton III, *Mechanisms of Animal Behavior.* New York: Wiley, 1966.

Mayr, E., *Animal Species and Evolution.* Cambridge, Mass.: Harvard University Press, 1963.

Mayr, E., *Populations, Species and Evolution.* Cambridge, Mass.: Harvard University Press, 1970.

Mayr, E., *Principles of Systematic Zoology.* New York: McGraw-Hill, 1969.

Mayr, E., ed., *The Species Problem.* Washington, D. C.,: American Association for the Advancement of Science, 1957.

Mayr, E., *Systematics and the Origin of Species.* New York: Columbia University Press, 1942.

McGill, T. E., *Readings in Animal Behavior.* New York: Holt, Rinehart & Winston, 1965.

McMahan, Pamela, "The Victorious Coyote," *Natural History,* 84, no.1, pp. 42–51, Jan. 1975.

Mettler, Lawrence E., and Thomas G. Gregg, *Population Genetics and Evolution.* Englewood Cliffs, N.J.: Prentice-Hall, 1969.

Moody, P. A., *Introduction to Evolution,* 3rd ed. New York: Harper & Row, 1970.

Morris, D., *The Naked Ape.* New York: McGraw-Hill, 1967.

Pilbeam, David, *Ascent of Man.* New York: Macmillan, 1972.

Roe, A., and G. G. Simpson, *Behavior and Evolution.* New Haven, Conn.: Yale University Press, 1958.

Roeder, K. D., "Moths and Ultrasound." *Scientific American,* 1965.

Ross, H. H., *A Synthesis of Evolutionary Theory.* Englewood Cliffs, N.J.: Prentice-Hall, 1962.

Savory, T., *Naming the Living World.* New York: Wiley, 1963.

Scott, J. P., *Animal Behavior.* Chicago: University of Chicago Press, 1958.

Simpson, G. G., *The Major Features of Evolution.* New York: Columbia University Press, 1953.

Simpson, G. G., *The Meaning of Evolution,* 2nd ed. New Haven, Conn.: Yale University Press, 1967.

Smith, N. G., "Visual Isolation in Gulls." *Scientific American,* 1967.

Stebbins, G. L., *Chromosomal Evolution in Higher Plants.* Reading, Mass.: Addison-Wesley, 1971.

Stebbins, G. L., *Processes of Organic Evolution*. Englewood Cliffs, N.J.: Prentice-Hall, 1971.

Thorpe, W. H., *Bird-Song: The Biology of Vocal Communication and Expression in Birds*. New York: Cambridge University Press, 1961.

Tinbergen, N., "Behavior and Natural Selection" in J. A. Moore, ed., *Ideas in Evolution and Behavior*. Garden City, N.Y.: Natural History Press, 1970.

Tinbergen, N., "The Curious Behavior of the Stickleback." Scientific American, 1952.

Tinbergen, N., *Curious Naturalists*. New York: Basic Books, 1958.

Tinbergen, N., "The Evolution of Behavior in Gulls." *Scientific American,* 1960.

Tinbergen, N., *The Herring Gull's World*. London: Collins, 1953.

Tinbergen, N., *Social Behaviour in Animals*. New York: Wiley, 1953.

Tinbergen, N., *The Study of Instinct*. New York: Oxford University Press, 1951.

Van Lawick-Goodall, J., *In the Shadow of Man*. Boston, Mass.: Houghton-Mifflin, 1971.

Wallace, B., *Genetic Load*. Englewood Cliffs, N.J.: Prentice-Hall, 1970.

Wallace, B. and A. M., *Adaptation,* 2nd ed. Englewood Cliffs, N.J.: Prentice-Hall, 1964.

Williams, B.J., *Evolution and Human Origins*. New York: Harper & Row, 1973.

Wills, Christopher, "Genetic Load." *Scientific American,* 1970.

Wilson, E. O., "Pheromones." *Scientific American,* 1963.

Young, W. C., ed., *Sex and Internal Secretions,* 3rd ed., Vol. 2. Baltimore, Md.: Williams & Wilkins, 1961.

## Aspects of the biosphere

Andrewartha, H. G., *Introduction to the Study of Animal Populations*. Chicago: University of Chicago Press, 1961.

Andrewartha, H. G., and L. C. Birch, *The Distribution and Abundance of Animals*. Chicago: University of Chicago Press, 1954.

Bates, M., *The Forest and the Sea*. New York: Vintage Books, 1960.

Billings, W. D., *Plants, Man, and the Ecosystem,* 2nd ed. Belmont, Calif.: Wadsworth, 1969.

Bresler, J. B., ed., *Environments of Man*. Reading, Mass.: Addison-Wesley, 1968.

Cole, L. C., "The Ecosphere." *Scientific American,* 1958.

Cooper, C. F.,"The Ecology of Fire." *Scientific American,* 1961.

Dubos, R., *Man Adapting*. New Haven, Conn.: Yale University Press, 1965.

Ehrenfield, D. W., *Biological Conservation*. New York: Holt, Rinehart & Winston, 1970.

Ehrlich, P. R., *The Population Bomb*. New York: Ballantine Books, 1968.

Ehrlich, P. R., and A. H., *Population, Resources, Environment*. San Francisco: Freeman, 1970.

Elton, C. S., *The Ecology of Invasions by Animals and Plants*. London: Methuen, 1958.

Farb, P., and the Editors of *Life, Ecology*. New York: Time, 1963.

Hardin, G., ed., *Population, Evolution, and Birth Control,* 2nd ed. San Francisco: Freeman, 1969.

Hazen, W. E., ed., *Readings in Population and Community Ecology,* 2nd ed. Philadelphia: Saunders, 1970.

Hutchinson, G. E., "The Biosphere." *Scientific American,* 1970.

Irving, L., "Adaptations to Cold." *Scientific American,* 1966.

Kormondy, E.J., *Concepts of Ecology*. Englewood Cliffs, N.J.: Prentice-Hall, 1969.

Kormondy, E. J., *Readings in Ecology*. Englewood Cliffs, N.J.: Prentice-Hall, 1965.

Leopold, A., *A Sand County Almanac*. New York: Ballantine, 1949.

McVay, S., "The Last of the Great Whales." *Scientific American,* 1966.

Odum, E.P., *Fundamentals of Ecology*, 3rd ed. Philadelphia: Saunders, 1971.

Paine, R. T., "Food Web Complexity and Species Diversity." *American Naturalist,* Vol. 100, 1966.

Plass, G. N., "Carbon Dioxide and Climate." *Scientific American,* 1959.

Slobodkin, L. B., *Growth and Regulation of Animal Populations*. New York: Holt, Rinehart & Winston, 1961.

Smith, R. L., *Ecology and Field Biology*. New York: Harper & Row, 1966.

Wecker, S. C., "Habitat Selection." *Scientific American,* 1964.

Whittaker, R. H., *Communities and Ecosystems*. New York: Macmillan, 1970.

Woodwell, G. M., "The Ecological Effects of Radiation." *Scientific American,* 1963.

Woodwell, G. M., "Toxic Substances and Ecological Cycles." *Scientific American,* 1967.

Wynne-Edwards, V. C., "Population Control in Animals." *Scientific American, 1964.*

Young, L. B., ed., *Population in Perspective*. New York: Oxford University Press, 1968.

# Biology and human affairs

Abell, P. I., *et al.,* "Survey of Lunar Carbon Compounds, I, The Presence of Indigenous Gases and Hydrolyzable Carbon Compounds in Apollo 11 and Apollo 12 Samples," *Proc. Second Lunar Sci. Conf. Geochim. Cosmochim. Acta.* Cambridge: M.I.T.Press, 1971.

Avduevskii, V. S., *et al.,* "Soft Landing on the Venus Surface and Preliminary Results of Investigation of the Venus Atmosphere." *Proc. Second Lunar Sci. Cònf. Geochim. Cosmochim. Acta.* Cambridge: M.I.T. Press, 1971.

Avduevskii, V. S., *et al.* "A Tentative Model of the Venus Atmosphere Based on the Measurements of Veneras 5 and 6," *J. Atmos. Sci. 27,* 1970.

Beaton, G. H., and E. W. McHenry, *Nutrition: A Comprehensive Treatise,* Vols. 1–3. New York: Academic Press, 1964–66.

Berelson, B., "Beyond Family Planning." *Science,* 1969.

Brown, F. A., *et al., Biological Clocks, Two Views.* New York: Academic Press, 1970.

Carr, M. H., *et al.,* "Imaging Experiment—The Viking Mars Orbiter." *Icarus, 16,* 1972.

Chang, S., and R. S. Young, Report of a Conference on "The Organic Analysis and Carbon Chemistry of Lunar Samples," Oct. 26–28, 1971, College Park, Maryland, *Icarus 16,* 1972.

Chase, S. C., Jr., *et al.,* "Infrared Radiometry Experiment on Mariner 9." *Science 175,* 1972.

Fox, S. W., *et al.,* "Simulation of Organismic Morphology and Behavior by Synthetic Poly-Alpha-Amino Acids" in *Life Sciences and Space Research IV,* eds., A. H. Brown and M. Florkin. Washington, D. C.: Spartan, 1966.

Glasstone, S., *The Book of Mars, NASA SP-179.* Washington, D.C.: Govt. Printing Office, 1968.

Halpern, S. L., ed., *The Medical Clinics of North America, Recent Advances in Applied Nutrition,* Vol. 48, No.5. Philadelphia: Saunders, 1964.

Harada, K. *et.al.,* "Evidence for Compounds Hydrolyzable to Amino Acids in Aqueous Extracts of Apollo 11 and Apollo 12 Lunar Fines." *Science,* 173,1971.

Hayes, J. M., "Extralunar Sources for Carbon on the Moon." *Space Life Sciences,* Vol. 3, 1971.

Hinners, N. W., "The New Moon—A View." *Reviews of Geophysics and Space Physics, 9,* 1971.

Hodgson, G. W., *et al.,* "Lunar Pigments: Porphyrin-like Compounds from Apollo 12 Sample." *Proc. Second Lunar Sci. Conf. Geochim Cosmochim. Acta.,* Suppl. 2, Vol. 2, 1971.

*Icarus:* Vol. 12, No. 1. New York: Academic Press, 1970.

*Icarus:* Vol. 17, No.2, Special Issue. New York: Academic Press, 1972.

Kaplan, I. R., and C. Petrowski, "Carbon and Sulfur Isotope Studies on Apollo 12 Lunar Samples." *Proc. Second Lunar Sci. Conf. Geochim. Cosmochim. Acta,* Cambridge: M.I.T. Press, 1971.

Kvenvolden, K. A., *et al.,* "Non-protein Amino Acids in the Murchison Meteorite." *Proc. Nat'l. Acad. Sci., 68,* 1971.

Lawless, J. G., *et al.,* "Amino Acids Indigenous to the Murray Meteorite." *Science, 173,* 1971.

Lewis, J. S., "Satellites of the Outer Planets —Thermal Models." *Science, 172,* 1971: pp. 1127, 1128, "Satellites of the Outer Planets—Their Physical and Chemical Nature." *Icarus 15,* 1971.

Libby, W. F., "Ice Caps on Venus?" *Science, 159,* 1968: pp. 1097,1098.

Lyttleton, R. A., *The Comets and Their Origins.* Cambridge, England: Cambridge University Press, 1953.

McCollum, E. V., *A History of Nutrition.* Boston, Mass.: Houghton Mifflin Co., 1957.

Meyer, J. *Overweight.* Englewood Cliffs, N.J.: Prentice-Hall, 1968.

Morowitz, H. J., and C. E. Sagan, "Life in the Clouds of Venus?" *Nature, 215,* 1967.

Munro, H. N., and J. B. Allison, eds., *Mammalian Protein Metabolism,* Vols. 1–4. New York: Academic Press, 1964–1970.

Nagy, B., *et al.,* "Carbon Compounds in Apollo 12 Lunar Samples." *Nature 232.*

NASA (JPL) Technical Report, 32-1550, Vol. V. Mariner Mars 1971 Project Final Report. Science Experiment Reports.

National Research Council, Food and Nutrition Board, *Recommended Dietary Allowances,* 7th rev. ed. Washington, D. C.: National Academy of Sciences, 1968.

Oró, J., *et al.,* eds., *Cosmochemical Evolution and the Origins of Life.* Dordrecht, Holland: D. Reidel, 1974.

Oyama, V. I., E. L. Merek, M. P. Silverman, and C. W. Boylen, "Search for Viable Organisms in Lunar Samples: Further Biological Studies on Apollo 11 Core, Apollo 12 Bulk, and Apollo 12 Core Samples." *Proc. Second Lunar Sci. Conf. Geochim. Cosmochim. Acta.* Cambridge: M.I.T. Press, 1971.

Pike, R. L., and M. L. Brown, *Nutrition, An Integrated Approach.* New York: John Wiley amd Sons, 1967.

Pimentel, G. C., *et al.,* "Exotic Biochemistry in Exobiology," in C. S. Pittendrigh, W. Vishniac, and J. P. T. Pearman, eds. *Biology and the Exploration of Mars.* Washington, D. C.: National Academy of Sciences (NRC), 1966.

Ponnamperuma, C., ed., *Exobiology —A Series of Collected Papers.* Amsterdam: North Holland, 1972.

Ponnamperuma, C., and H. P. Klein, "The Coming Search for Life on Mars." *Quart. Rev. of Biology, 45,* 1970.

Robinson, C. H., *Normal and Therapeutic Nutrition,* 14th ed. New York: Macmillan, 1972.

Sagan, C. E., "The Long Winter Model of Martian Biology." *Icarus, 15,* 1971.

Sagan, C. E., "The Solar System Beyond Mars: An Exobiological Survey." *Space Science Reviews, 11,* 1971.

Sagan, C. E., J. Veverka, and P. Gierasch, "Observational Consequences of Martian Wind Regimes." *Icarus 15,* 1971.

Schwartz, Alan W., ed., *Theory and Experiment in Exobiology,* Vol. 1. Groningen, The Netherlands: Wolters-Noordhoff Publishing.

Shklovskii, I. S., and C. E. Sagan, *Intelligent Life in the Universe.* San Francisco: Holden-Day, Inc., 1966.

Snyder, L. E., and D. Buhl, "Molecules in the Interstellar Medium I and II." *Sky and Telescope 40,* 1970.

Sollberger, A., *Biological Rhythm Research.* Amsterdam: Elsevier, 1965.

Urey, H. C.,*The Planets, Their Origin and Development.* New Haven: University Press, 1962.

Walkinshaw, C. H., *et al.,* "Results of Apollo 11 and 12 Quarantine Studies on Planets." *Bioscience 20,* 1970.

Watt, B. K., and A. L. Merrill, *Composition of Foods.* Washington: U.S.D.A. Agriculture Handbook No. 8, 1963.

Woeller, F., and C. Ponnamperuma, "Organic Synthesis in a Simulated Jovian Atmosphere." *Icarus 10,* 1969.

Young, R. S., "Space Exploration and the Origin of Life." in D. L. Rohlfing and A. I. Oparin, eds., *Molecular Evolution: Prebiological and Biological.* New York: Plenum Press, 1972.